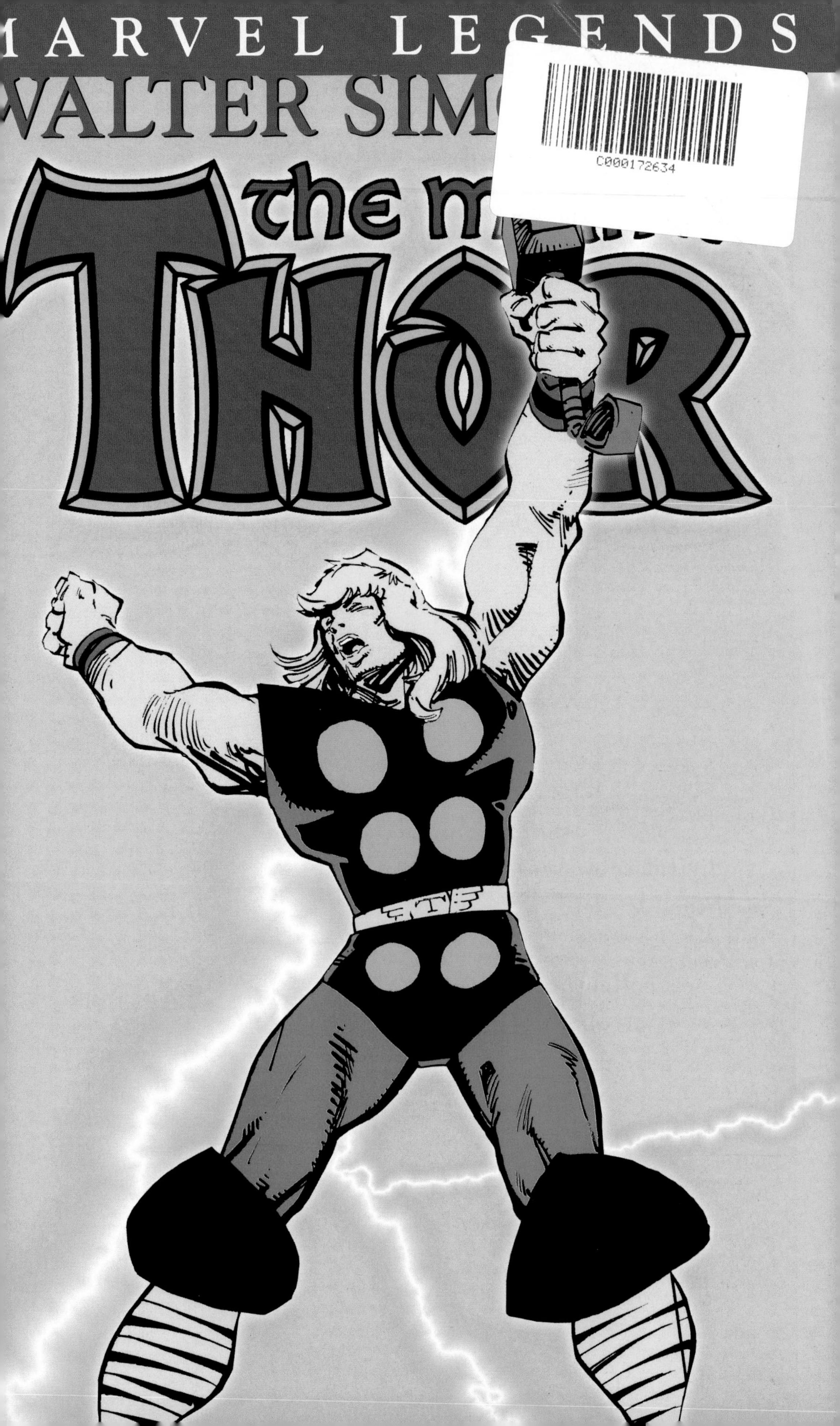
ARVEL LEGENDS
WALTER SIM
the m
THOR

the mighty THOR

art & story
WALTER SIMONSON
with *SAL BUSCEMA*

letters JOHN WORKMAN JR.
colors CHRISTIE SCHEELE
digital color retouch JERRON QUALITY COLOR
editors MARK GRUENWALD & RALPH MACCHIO

collections editor JEFF YOUNGQUIST
associate editor CORY SEDLMEIER
assistant editor JENNIFER GRÜNWALD
book designer JEOF VITA

editor in chief JOE QUESADA
president BILL JEMAS

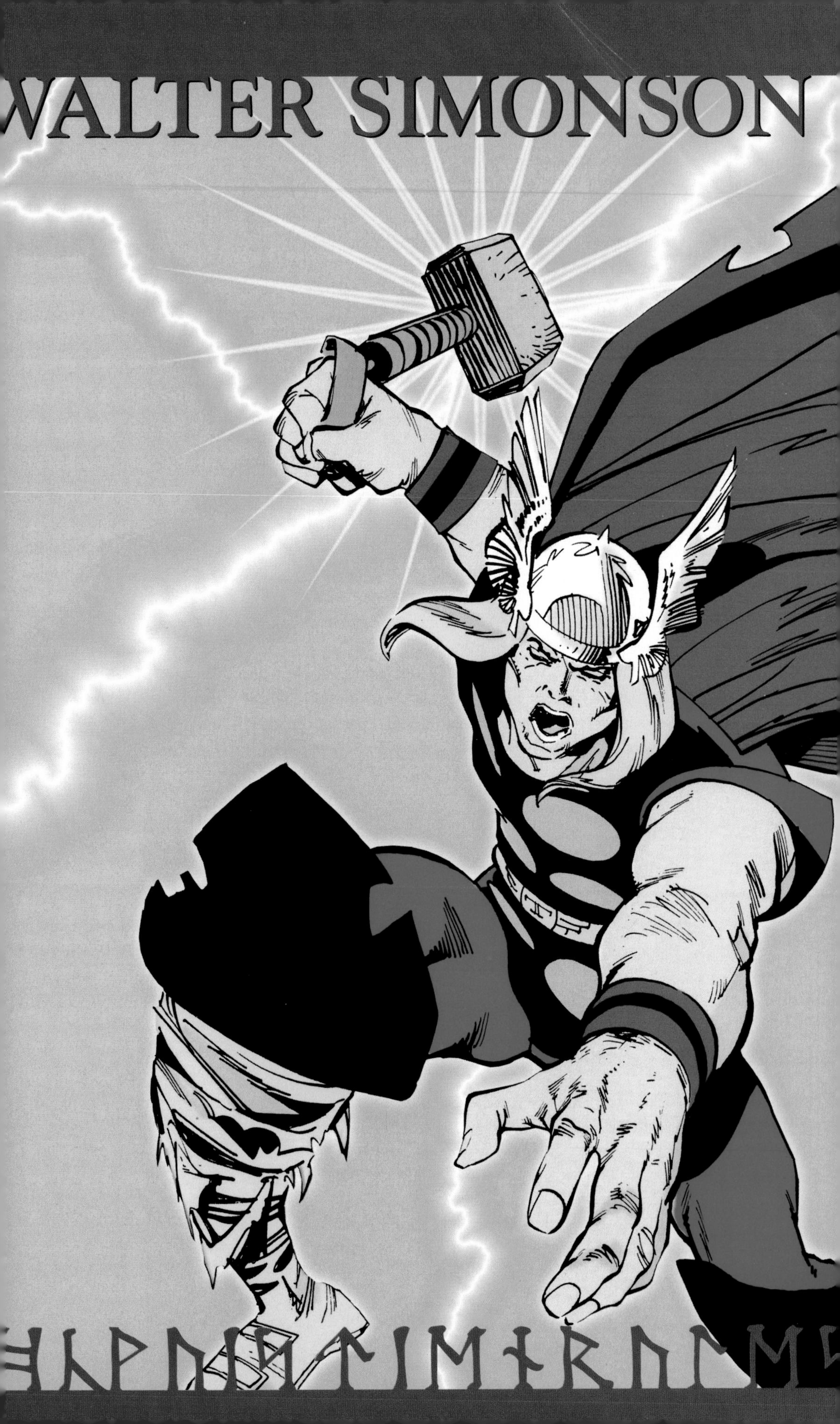
WALTER SIMONSON

INTRODUCTION

First off, I'd love to take credit for the brilliant move of placing Walter Simonson on *The Mighty Thor*. But I can't. That honor goes to my late, great friend, editor Mark Gruenwald, whose sudden loss several years ago is still being felt in our industry. Still, midway through Walt's run on *Thor*, I was asked to take the editorial reigns from Mark. Naturally, prior to that, I'd followed Walt's work here with great enthusiasm.

If there was ever a title someone was born to write and draw, for Simonson, it was *Thor*. Walt told me that Thor was his favorite Marvel character, bar none. And the magnificent "Surtur Saga" that concluded in issue #353 actually was conceived by Walter way back in high school! I can just see him daydreaming his Viking epics in geometry class as he sketched those first, fledgling panels that, decades later, became one of the finest *Thor* epics ever.

Thor is an intimidating assignment for even the most accomplished creator. This was one of the seminal Marvel comics of the '60s. Stan Lee and Jack Kirby were at the absolute peak of their powers when they collaborated on the Thunder God. In my opinion, Walter Simonson, more than any other talent in this field, has been able to build upon the cosmic Lee/Kirby concepts and make them his own. And on *Thor*, it didn't hurt that Simonson was extremely well-versed in Norse mythology. One of the real triumphs of Walt's run was the seamless melding of genuine Norse myths with the established *Thor* continuity. Done as only a master craftsman could do it.

In addition to his first-rate writing, Walt's rendering of Thor and company bears mentioning. Simonson is an original, graphically. His art style is unique. Significantly, every element from the balloon shape to sound-effects lettering is an integral part of the visual composition of each page. He was able to fully create the many mythological environs peopled by the Asgardians in a soaring style that combined stark simplicity with lush detail.

I think it's a sincere tribute that after some 40 years of *Thor's* continual publication, the Walt Simonson period is considered by many to be second only to the initial Lee/Kirby era.

A brief anecdote or two: Walt requested artist Sal Buscema to pinch-hit pencil and ink issue #355. Walt and I were so pleased with the results we asked Sal on later as regular penciler during the final third of Walt's run. Finally, I'll never forget being contacted by an agent of the Federal Reserve system after issue #358 appeared. Seems the Fed was curious as to how we came by that information on how to pull off a successful heist of the gold in New York's Federal Reserve Bank. Who alerted them to our little fable I'll never know.

What I do know is that you're in for a rare treat as you savor these Simonson-style Asgardian epics. This is what *Thor* was meant to be! This is what Asgard is all about! So whirl that magic hammer, Froggy, and prepare to journey to the farthest reaches of the greatest fantasy realm of all—the Marvel universe! Don't plan on coming back the same.

Ralph Macchio

Editor
May 2003

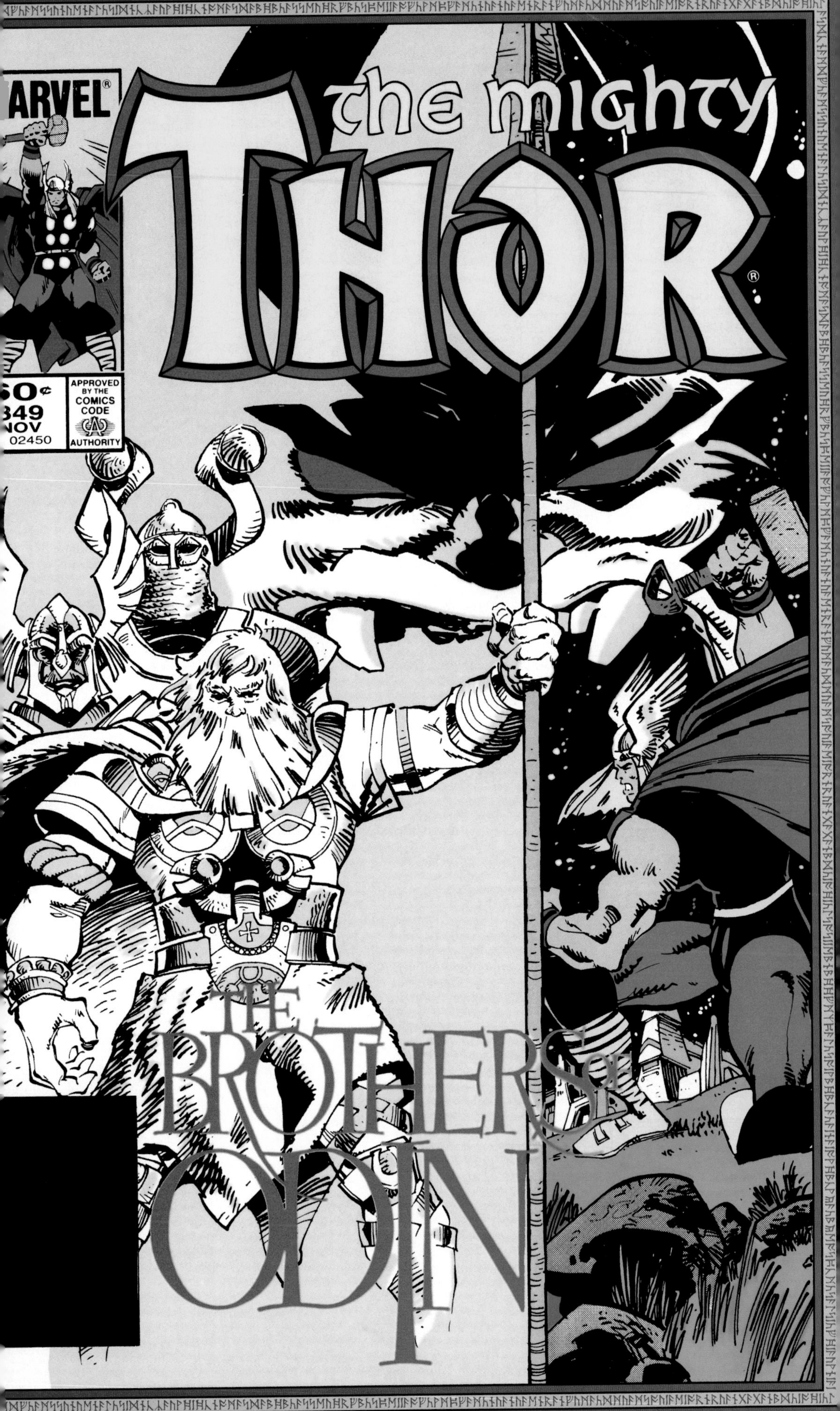
MARVEL
the mighty
THOR
349
NOV
02450
APPROVED BY THE COMICS CODE AUTHORITY
THE BROTHERS OF ODIN

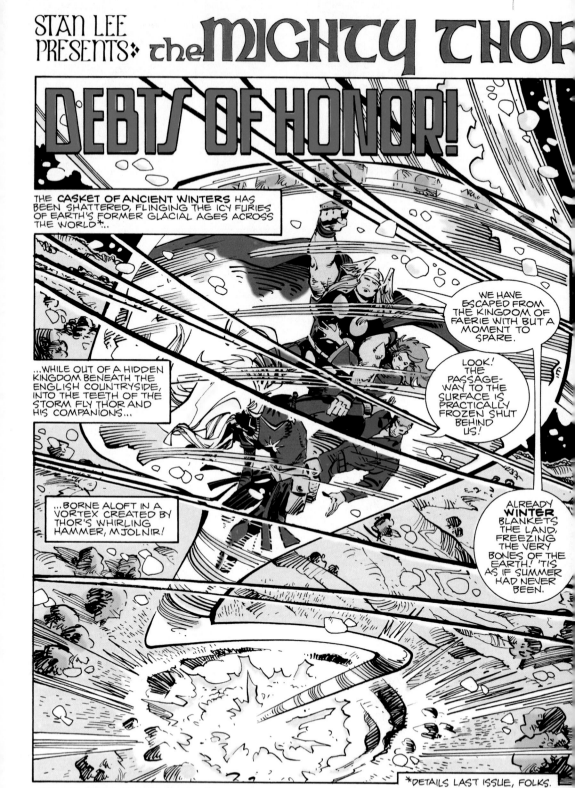

STAN LEE PRESENTS: the MIGHTY THOR

DEBTS OF HONOR!

THE **CASKET OF ANCIENT WINTERS** HAS BEEN SHATTERED, FLINGING THE ICY FURIES OF EARTH'S FORMER GLACIAL AGES ACROSS THE WORLD*...

...WHILE OUT OF A HIDDEN KINGDOM BENEATH THE ENGLISH COUNTRYSIDE, INTO THE TEETH OF THE STORM FLY THOR AND HIS COMPANIONS...

...BORNE ALOFT IN A VORTEX CREATED BY THOR'S WHIRLING HAMMER, MJOLNIR!

WE HAVE ESCAPED FROM THE KINGDOM OF FAERIE WITH BUT A MOMENT TO SPARE.

LOOK! THE PASSAGE-WAY TO THE SURFACE IS PRACTICALLY FROZEN SHUT BEHIND US!

ALREADY **WINTER** BLANKETS THE LAND, FREEZING THE VERY BONES OF THE EARTH! 'TIS AS IF SUMMER HAD NEVER BEEN.

*DETAILS LAST ISSUE, FOLKS.

ART AND STORY: WALTER SIMONSON · LETTERING: JOHN WORKMAN, JR. · COLORS: CHRISTIE SCHEEL
EDITING: MARK GRUENWALD · EDITOR-IN-CHIEF: JIM SHOOTER

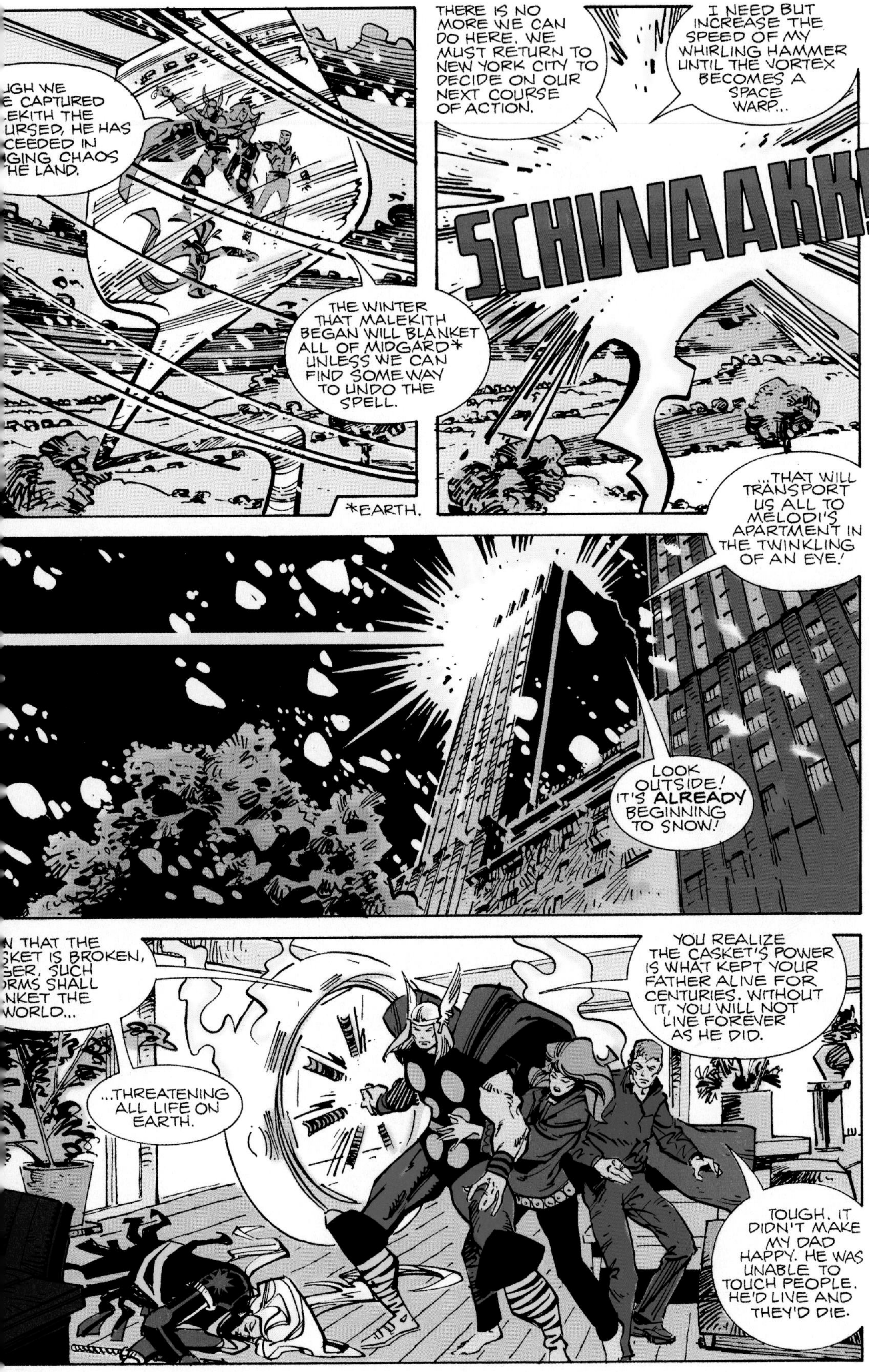

UGH WE
E CAPTURED
LEKITH THE
URSED, HE HAS
CEEDED IN
IGING CHAOS
HE LAND.
THE WINTER THAT MALEKITH BEGAN WILL BLANKET ALL OF MIDGARD* UNLESS WE CAN FIND SOME WAY TO UNDO THE SPELL.
*EARTH.
THERE IS NO MORE WE CAN DO HERE. WE MUST RETURN TO NEW YORK CITY TO DECIDE ON OUR NEXT COURSE OF ACTION.
I NEED BUT INCREASE THE SPEED OF MY WHIRLING HAMMER UNTIL THE VORTEX BECOMES A SPACE WARP...
SCHVVAAKK!
...THAT WILL TRANSPORT US ALL TO MELODI'S APARTMENT IN THE TWINKLING OF AN EYE!
LOOK OUTSIDE! IT'S ALREADY BEGINNING TO SNOW!
N THAT THE
SKET IS BROKEN,
GER, SUCH
ORMS SHALL
NKET THE
WORLD...
...THREATENING ALL LIFE ON EARTH.
YOU REALIZE THE CASKET'S POWER IS WHAT KEPT YOUR FATHER ALIVE FOR CENTURIES. WITHOUT IT, YOU WILL NOT LIVE FOREVER AS HE DID.
TOUGH. IT DIDN'T MAKE MY DAD HAPPY. HE WAS UNABLE TO TOUCH PEOPLE. HE'D LIVE AND THEY'D DIE.

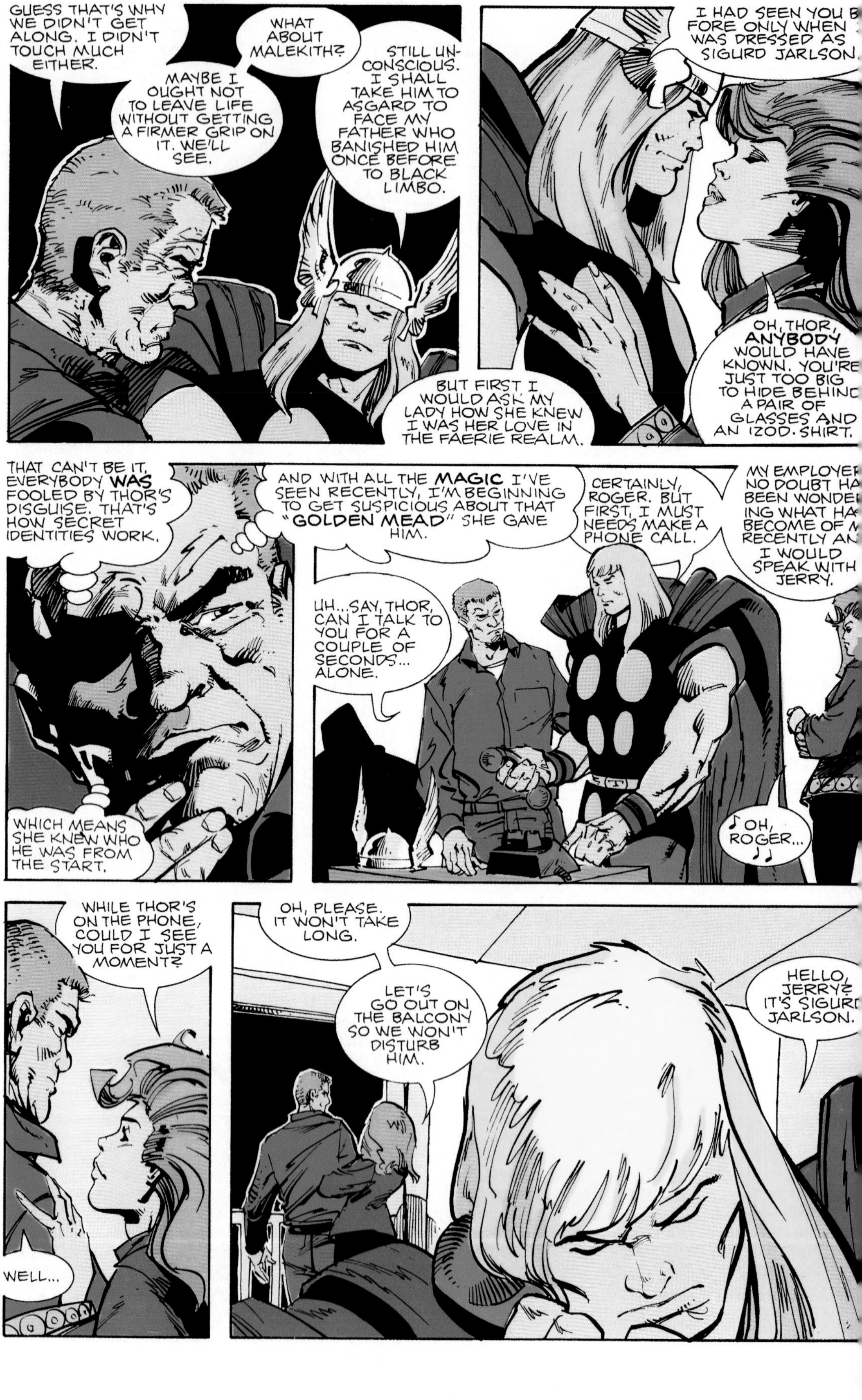
GUESS THAT'S WHY WE DIDN'T GET ALONG. I DIDN'T TOUCH MUCH EITHER.
MAYBE I OUGHT NOT TO LEAVE LIFE WITHOUT GETTING A FIRMER GRIP ON IT. WE'LL SEE.
WHAT ABOUT MALEKITH?
STILL UNCONSCIOUS. I SHALL TAKE HIM TO ASGARD TO FACE MY FATHER WHO BANISHED HIM ONCE BEFORE TO BLACK LIMBO.
BUT FIRST I WOULD ASK MY LADY HOW SHE KNEW I WAS HER LOVE IN THE FAERIE REALM.
I HAD SEEN YOU BE- FORE ONLY WHEN I WAS DRESSED AS SIGURD JARLSON.
OH, THOR, ANYBODY WOULD HAVE KNOWN. YOU'RE JUST TOO BIG TO HIDE BEHIND A PAIR OF GLASSES AND AN IZOD SHIRT.
THAT CAN'T BE IT. EVERYBODY WAS FOOLED BY THOR'S DISGUISE. THAT'S HOW SECRET IDENTITIES WORK.
WHICH MEANS SHE KNEW WHO HE WAS FROM THE START.
AND WITH ALL THE MAGIC I'VE SEEN RECENTLY, I'M BEGINNING TO GET SUSPICIOUS ABOUT THAT "GOLDEN MEAD" SHE GAVE HIM.
UH...SAY, THOR, CAN I TALK TO YOU FOR A COUPLE OF SECONDS... ALONE.
CERTAINLY, ROGER. BUT FIRST, I MUST NEEDS MAKE A PHONE CALL.
MY EMPLOYER NO DOUBT HA BEEN WONDER ING WHAT HA BECOME OF M RECENTLY AN I WOULD SPEAK WITH JERRY.
♪OH, ROGER...♪♪
WHILE THOR'S ON THE PHONE, COULD I SEE YOU FOR JUST A MOMENT?
WELL...
OH, PLEASE. IT WON'T TAKE LONG.
LET'S GO OUT ON THE BALCONY SO WE WON'T DISTURB HIM.
HELLO, JERRY? IT'S SIGURD JARLSON.

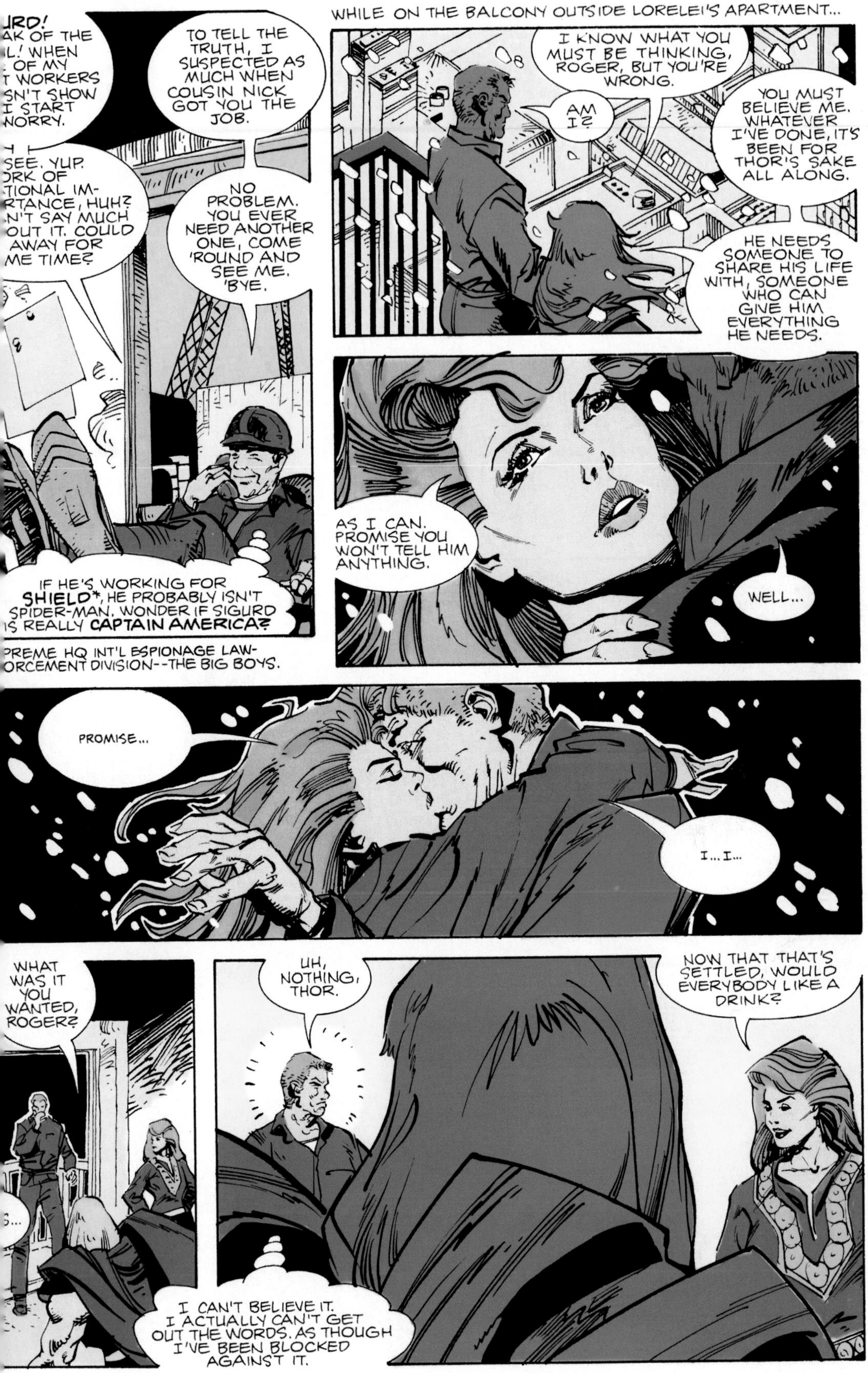

...URD! ...AK OF THE ...L! WHEN ... OF MY ...T WORKERS ...SN'T SHOW ...I START ...WORRY.
TO TELL THE TRUTH, I SUSPECTED AS MUCH WHEN COUSIN NICK GOT YOU THE JOB.
...SEE. YUP. ...ORK OF ...TIONAL IM- ...RTANCE, HUH? ...N'T SAY MUCH ...OUT IT. COULD ...AWAY FOR ...ME TIME?
NO PROBLEM. YOU EVER NEED ANOTHER ONE, COME 'ROUND AND SEE ME. 'BYE.
IF HE'S WORKING FOR SHIELD*, HE PROBABLY ISN'T SPIDER-MAN. WONDER IF SIGURD IS REALLY CAPTAIN AMERICA?
...PREME HQ INT'L ESPIONAGE LAW- ...ORCEMENT DIVISION--THE BIG BOYS.
WHILE ON THE BALCONY OUTSIDE LORELEI'S APARTMENT...
I KNOW WHAT YOU MUST BE THINKING, ROGER, BUT YOU'RE WRONG.
AM I?
YOU MUST BELIEVE ME. WHATEVER I'VE DONE, IT'S BEEN FOR THOR'S SAKE ALL ALONG.
HE NEEDS SOMEONE TO SHARE HIS LIFE WITH, SOMEONE WHO CAN GIVE HIM EVERYTHING HE NEEDS.
AS I CAN. PROMISE YOU WON'T TELL HIM ANYTHING.
WELL...
PROMISE...
I... I...
WHAT WAS IT YOU WANTED, ROGER?
UH, NOTHING, THOR.
NOW THAT THAT'S SETTLED, WOULD EVERYBODY LIKE A DRINK?
I CAN'T BELIEVE IT. I ACTUALLY CAN'T GET OUT THE WORDS. AS THOUGH I'VE BEEN BLOCKED AGAINST IT.

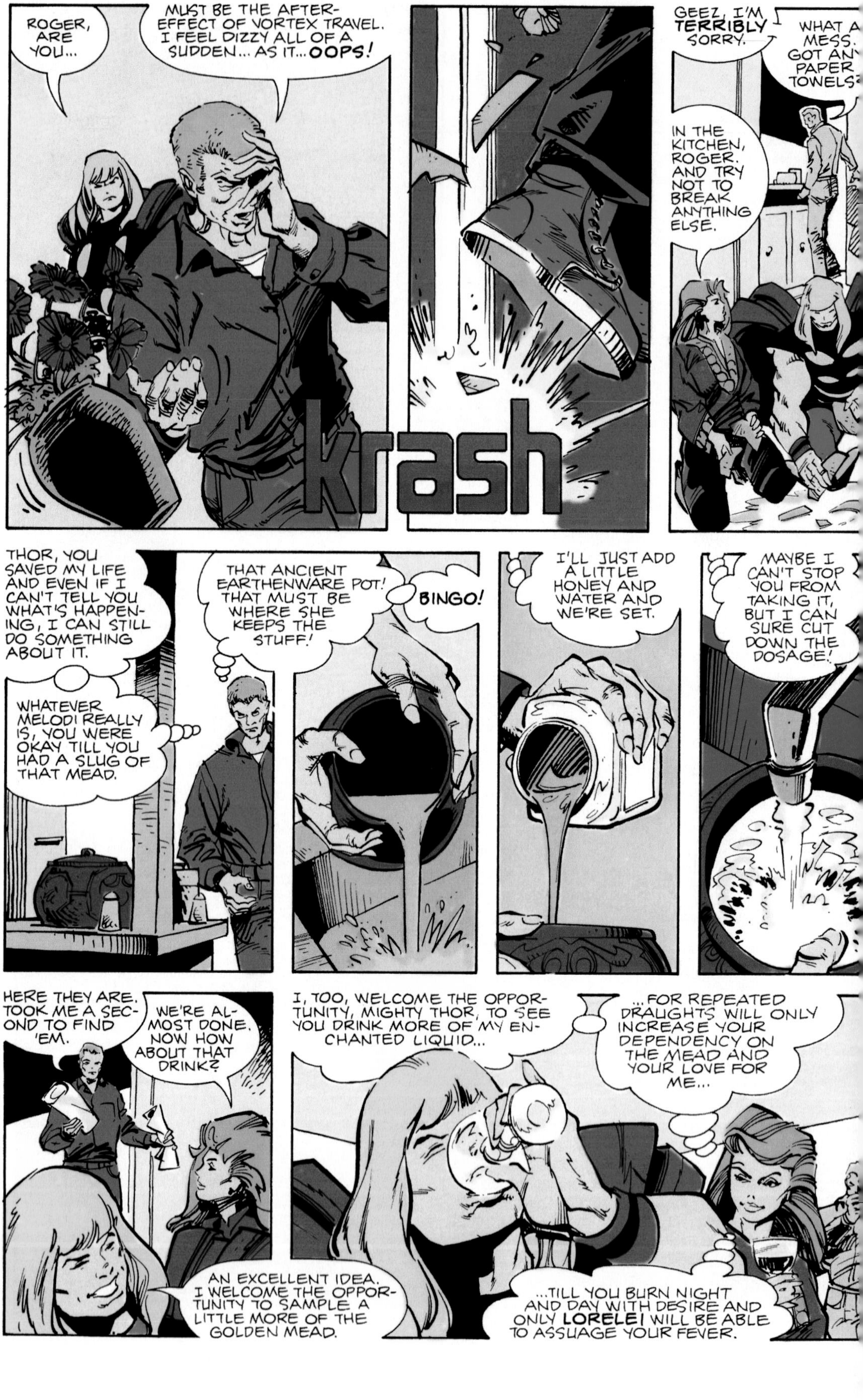
ROGER, ARE YOU...
MUST BE THE AFTER-EFFECT OF VORTEX TRAVEL. I FEEL DIZZY ALL OF A SUDDEN... AS IT... **OOPS!**
krash
GEEZ, I'M **TERRIBLY** SORRY.
WHAT A MESS. GOT ANY PAPER TOWELS?
IN THE KITCHEN, ROGER. AND TRY NOT TO BREAK ANYTHING ELSE.
THOR, YOU SAVED MY LIFE AND EVEN IF I CAN'T TELL YOU WHAT'S HAPPENING, I CAN STILL DO SOMETHING ABOUT IT.
WHATEVER MELODI REALLY IS, YOU WERE OKAY TILL YOU HAD A SLUG OF THAT MEAD.
THAT ANCIENT EARTHENWARE POT! THAT MUST BE WHERE SHE KEEPS THE STUFF!
BINGO!
I'LL JUST ADD A LITTLE HONEY AND WATER AND WE'RE SET.
MAYBE I CAN'T STOP YOU FROM TAKING IT, BUT I CAN SURE CUT DOWN THE DOSAGE!
HERE THEY ARE. TOOK ME A SECOND TO FIND 'EM.
WE'RE ALMOST DONE. NOW HOW ABOUT THAT DRINK?
AN EXCELLENT IDEA. I WELCOME THE OPPORTUNITY TO SAMPLE A LITTLE MORE OF THE GOLDEN MEAD.
I, TOO, WELCOME THE OPPORTUNITY, MIGHTY THOR, TO SEE YOU DRINK MORE OF MY ENCHANTED LIQUID...
...FOR REPEATED DRAUGHTS WILL ONLY INCREASE YOUR DEPENDENCY ON THE MEAD AND YOUR LOVE FOR ME...
...TILL YOU BURN NIGHT AND DAY WITH DESIRE AND ONLY **LORELEI** WILL BE ABLE TO ASSUAGE YOUR FEVER.

...NWHILE, OUTSIDE THE GATES OF ASGARD, HOME [OF] THE NORSE GODS, THE STEED SILVERHOOF [CAR]RYING **BALDER THE BRAVE** AND **AGNAR [OF] VANAHEIM** THUNDERS TOWARDS THE [SHIN]ING CITY...

THE END OF OUR WILD RIDE IS IN SIGHT, MY FRIEND.

BUT WE MUST PAUSE NOT A MOMENT, FOR IF MY DREAM SPOKE TRULY, ALL OUR LIVES MAY BE IN DANGER.

[HE] THUNDERS [THR]OUGH THE [GA]TES AT FULL [TILT] AND THE [GU]ARDS MAKE [WAY] BEFORE HIS [GRI]M VISAGE.

WHAT A FOOL I WAS TO EVER TRY TO ENGAGE HIM IN SINGLE COMBAT.

...AS I KNOW NOW HE MIGHT HAVE DONE WITHOUT THE SLIGHTEST EFFORT *...

...SO MATCHLESS A MAN AT ARMS IS HE.

GOOD AGNAR, TIME IS OF THE ESSENCE NOW.

[AND] YET, HE [NEI]THER SLEW ME, [NOR] HUMILIATED [ME] BEFORE [HEIM]STAGG...

*BACK AROUND THOR 338.

WOULD YOU SEE THAT SILVERHOOF IS STABLED PROPERLY WHILE I AWAY TO LORD ODIN?

I KNOW I CAN DEPEND UPON YOU.

WE SHALL MEET AGAIN.

HE KNEW! HE KNEW WHO I WAS ALL THE TIME!

AND RODE WITH HIS BACK UNDEFENDED AGAINST ME THOUGH I HAD TRIED TO SLAY HIM.

GODSPEED, WARRIOR. I OWE YOU MORE THAN I CAN SAY. YES, WE SHALL MEET AGAIN!

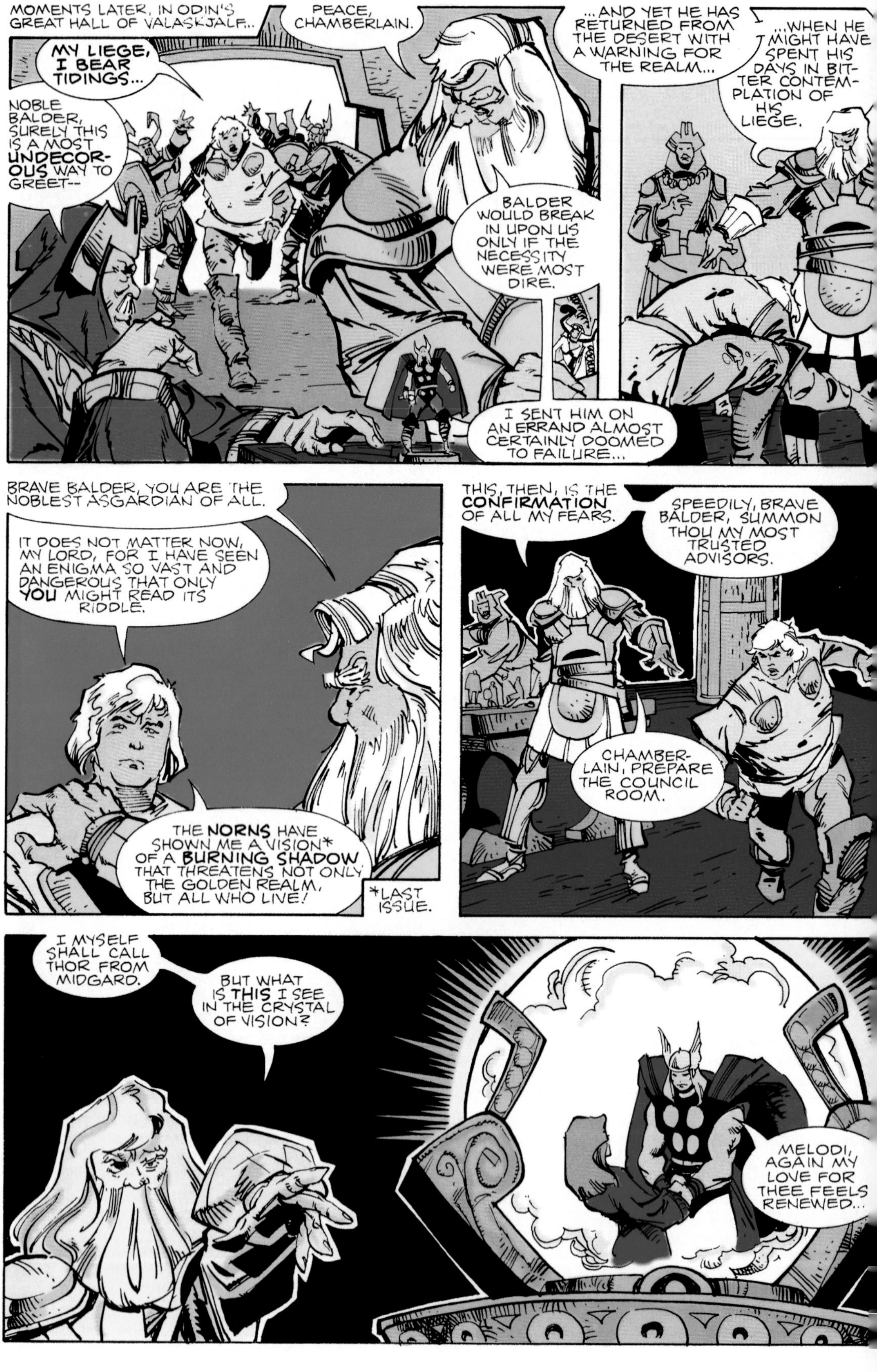

MOMENTS LATER, IN ODIN'S GREAT HALL OF VALASKJALF...
MY LIEGE, I BEAR TIDINGS...
NOBLE BALDER, SURELY THIS IS A MOST UNDECOROUS WAY TO GREET--
PEACE, CHAMBERLAIN.
BALDER WOULD BREAK IN UPON US ONLY IF THE NECESSITY WERE MOST DIRE.
I SENT HIM ON AN ERRAND ALMOST CERTAINLY DOOMED TO FAILURE...
...AND YET HE HAS RETURNED FROM THE DESERT WITH A WARNING FOR THE REALM...
...WHEN HE MIGHT HAVE SPENT HIS DAYS IN BITTER CONTEMPLATION OF HIS LIEGE.
BRAVE BALDER, YOU ARE THE NOBLEST ASGARDIAN OF ALL.
IT DOES NOT MATTER NOW, MY LORD, FOR I HAVE SEEN AN ENIGMA SO VAST AND DANGEROUS THAT ONLY YOU MIGHT READ ITS RIDDLE.
THE NORNS HAVE SHOWN ME A VISION* OF A BURNING SHADOW THAT THREATENS NOT ONLY THE GOLDEN REALM, BUT ALL WHO LIVE!
*LAST ISSUE.
THIS, THEN, IS THE CONFIRMATION OF ALL MY FEARS.
SPEEDILY, BRAVE BALDER, SUMMON THOU MY MOST TRUSTED ADVISORS.
CHAMBERLAIN, PREPARE THE COUNCIL ROOM.
I MYSELF SHALL CALL THOR FROM MIDGARD.
BUT WHAT IS THIS I SEE IN THE CRYSTAL OF VISION?
MELODI, AGAIN MY LOVE FOR THEE FEELS RENEWED...

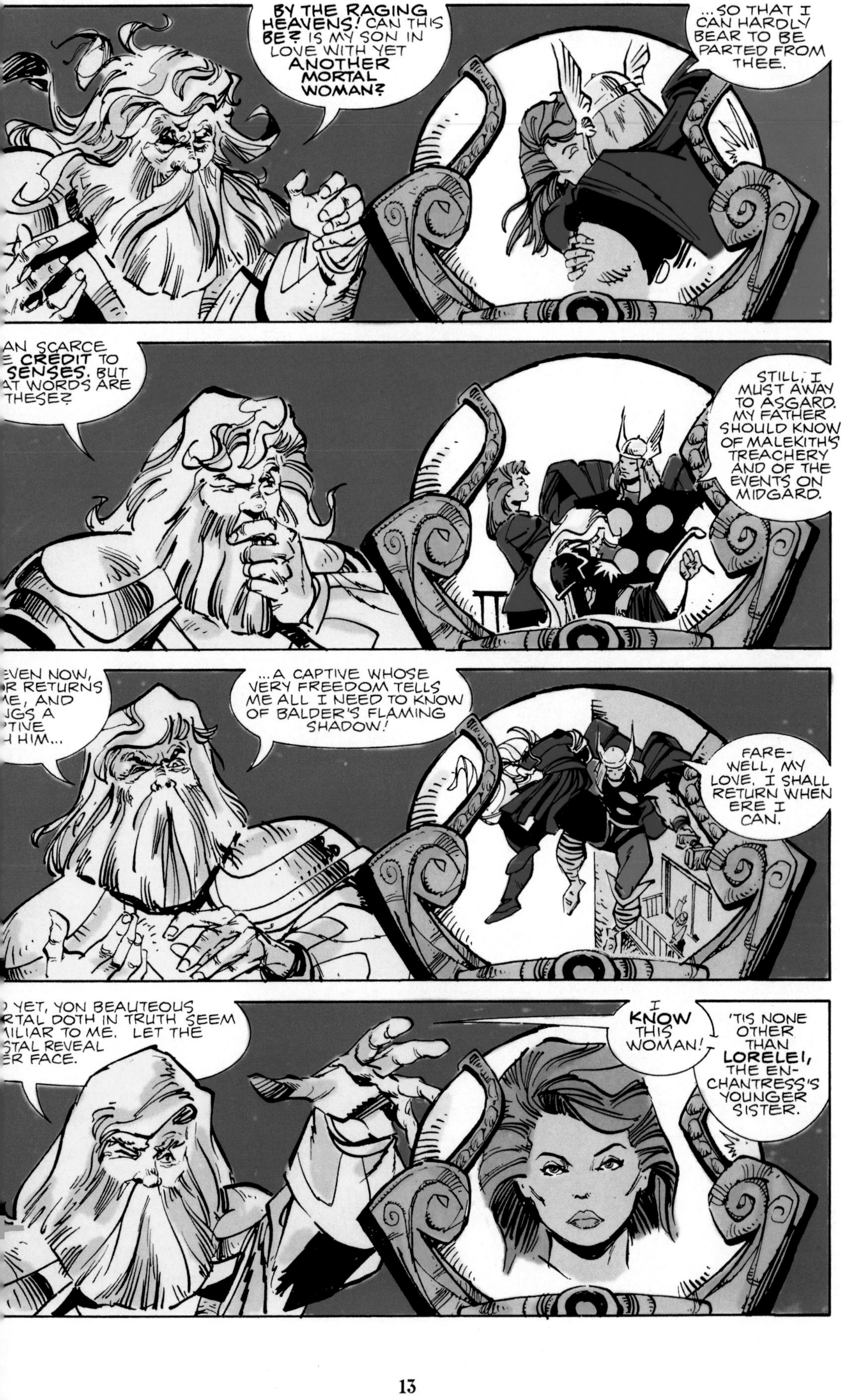
BY THE RAGING HEAVENS! CAN THIS BE? IS MY SON IN LOVE WITH YET ANOTHER MORTAL WOMAN?
...SO THAT I CAN HARDLY BEAR TO BE PARTED FROM THEE.
AN SCARCE E CREDIT TO SENSES. BUT AT WORDS ARE THESE?
STILL, I MUST AWAY TO ASGARD. MY FATHER SHOULD KNOW OF MALEKITH'S TREACHERY AND OF THE EVENTS ON MIDGARD.
EVEN NOW, R RETURNS ME, AND NGS A PTIVE H HIM...
...A CAPTIVE WHOSE VERY FREEDOM TELLS ME ALL I NEED TO KNOW OF BALDER'S FLAMING SHADOW!
FARE-WELL, MY LOVE. I SHALL RETURN WHEN ERE I CAN.
YET, YON BEAUTEOUS RTAL DOTH IN TRUTH SEEM MILIAR TO ME. LET THE STAL REVEAL ER FACE.
I KNOW THIS WOMAN!
'TIS NONE OTHER THAN LORELEI, THE EN-CHANTRESS'S YOUNGER SISTER.

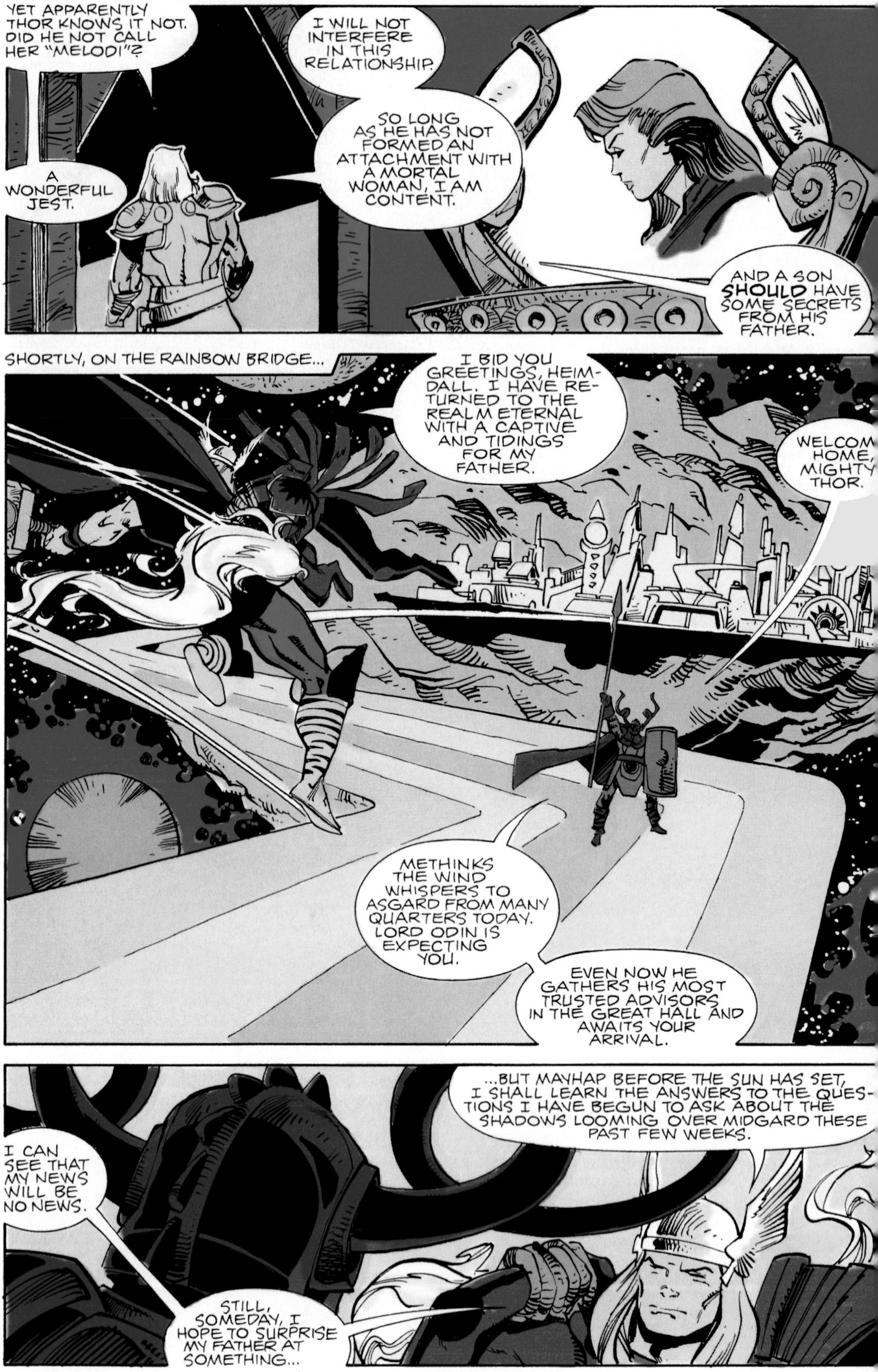
YET APPARENTLY THOR KNOWS IT NOT. DID HE NOT CALL HER "MELODI"?
I WILL NOT INTERFERE IN THIS RELATIONSHIP.
A WONDERFUL JEST.
SO LONG AS HE HAS NOT FORMED AN ATTACHMENT WITH A MORTAL WOMAN, I AM CONTENT.
AND A SON SHOULD HAVE SOME SECRETS FROM HIS FATHER.
SHORTLY, ON THE RAINBOW BRIDGE...
I BID YOU GREETINGS, HEIMDALL. I HAVE RETURNED TO THE REALM ETERNAL WITH A CAPTIVE AND TIDINGS FOR MY FATHER.
WELCOM HOME, MIGHTY THOR.
METHINKS THE WIND WHISPERS TO ASGARD FROM MANY QUARTERS TODAY. LORD ODIN IS EXPECTING YOU.
EVEN NOW HE GATHERS HIS MOST TRUSTED ADVISORS IN THE GREAT HALL AND AWAITS YOUR ARRIVAL.
I CAN SEE THAT MY NEWS WILL BE NO NEWS.
STILL, SOMEDAY, I HOPE TO SURPRISE MY FATHER AT SOMETHING...
...BUT MAYHAP BEFORE THE SUN HAS SET, I SHALL LEARN THE ANSWERS TO THE QUESTIONS I HAVE BEGUN TO ASK ABOUT THE SHADOWS LOOMING OVER MIDGARD THESE PAST FEW WEEKS.

SHORTLY, IN THE GREAT HALL...

WELL MET, MY FATHER.

WELCOME HOME, MY SON. THY STEPMOTHER FRIGGA, BRAVE BALDER, THE WARRIORS THREE, AND THE CHAMBERLAIN ARE HERE ALREADY.

NOW OUR NUMBERS ARE COMPLETE. WE HAVE MUCH TO DISCUSS AND LITTLE TIME FOR IT.

VERY GOOD, MY SIRE. YET I HAVE SOME UNFINISHED BUSINESS I PRESENT TO YOU AT ONCE.

I HAVE BROUGHT MALEKITH THE ACCURSED BACK TO ASGARD. HE RETURNED FROM THE BANISHMENT INTO WHICH YOU SENT HIM...

...AND DESTROYED THE CASKET OF ANCIENT WINTERS, RE- LEASING ITS FATAL SPELL OF COLD UPON MIDGARD.

I FEARED AS MUCH, THOR.

FOOL THAT YOU ARE, MALEKITH. THINK YOU THAT YOUR MASTER WILL SPARE YOU WHEN HE IS SET- TING THE WORLD TO THE TORCH?

LET THE GUARDS BE SUMMONED AND REMOVE THIS EVIL DOER TO THE DUNGEON OF NO-ESCAPE TO AWAIT OUR FURTHER PLEASURE.

I HAVE BEFORE ME MY IMME- DIATE MATTERS TO PONDER BEFORE...

BALDER, MY BOSOM COMPANION.

I HAVE HEARD SOMETHING OF YOUR TRAVAILS.* HOW FARE YOU?

BETTER THAN I HAVE IN A LONG TIME, THOR. I THINK PERHAPS THE DESERT AGREED WITH ME.

*CHRONICLED AT SOME LENGTH THROUGH PREVIOUS ISSUES OF THOR.

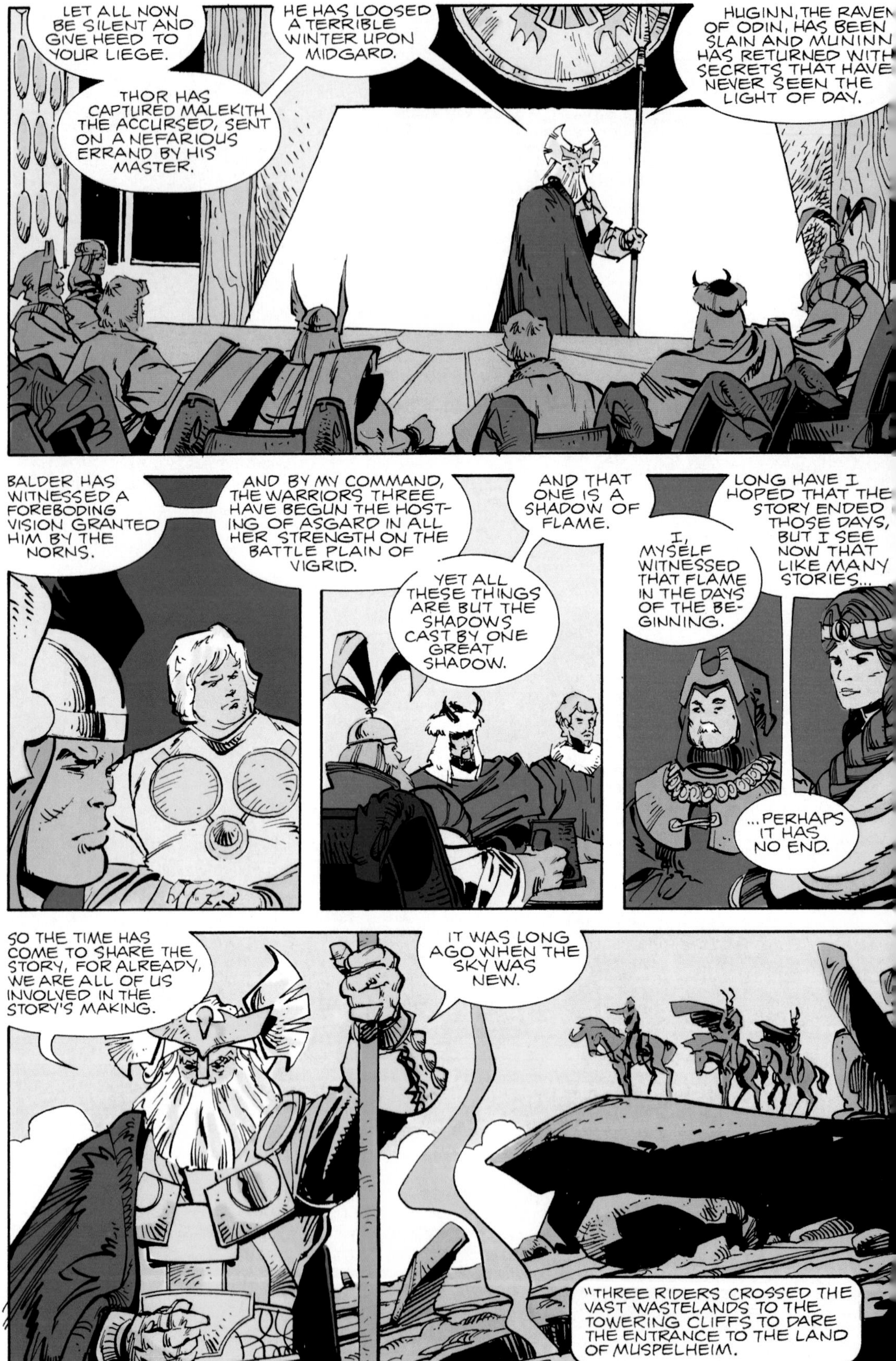
LET ALL NOW BE SILENT AND GIVE HEED TO YOUR LIEGE.
THOR HAS CAPTURED MALEKITH THE ACCURSED, SENT ON A NEFARIOUS ERRAND BY HIS MASTER.
HE HAS LOOSED A TERRIBLE WINTER UPON MIDGARD.
HUGINN, THE RAVEN OF ODIN, HAS BEEN SLAIN AND MUNINN HAS RETURNED WITH SECRETS THAT HAVE NEVER SEEN THE LIGHT OF DAY.
BALDER HAS WITNESSED A FOREBODING VISION GRANTED HIM BY THE NORNS.
AND BY MY COMMAND, THE WARRIORS THREE HAVE BEGUN THE HOSTING OF ASGARD IN ALL HER STRENGTH ON THE BATTLE PLAIN OF VIGRID.
YET ALL THESE THINGS ARE BUT THE SHADOWS CAST BY ONE GREAT SHADOW.
AND THAT ONE IS A SHADOW OF FLAME.
I, MYSELF WITNESSED THAT FLAME IN THE DAYS OF THE BEGINNING.
LONG HAVE I HOPED THAT THE STORY ENDED THOSE DAYS, BUT I SEE NOW THAT LIKE MANY STORIES...
...PERHAPS IT HAS NO END.
SO THE TIME HAS COME TO SHARE THE STORY, FOR ALREADY, WE ARE ALL OF US INVOLVED IN THE STORY'S MAKING.
IT WAS LONG AGO WHEN THE SKY WAS NEW.
"THREE RIDERS CROSSED THE VAST WASTELANDS TO THE TOWERING CLIFFS TO DARE THE ENTRANCE TO THE LAND OF MUSPELHEIM.

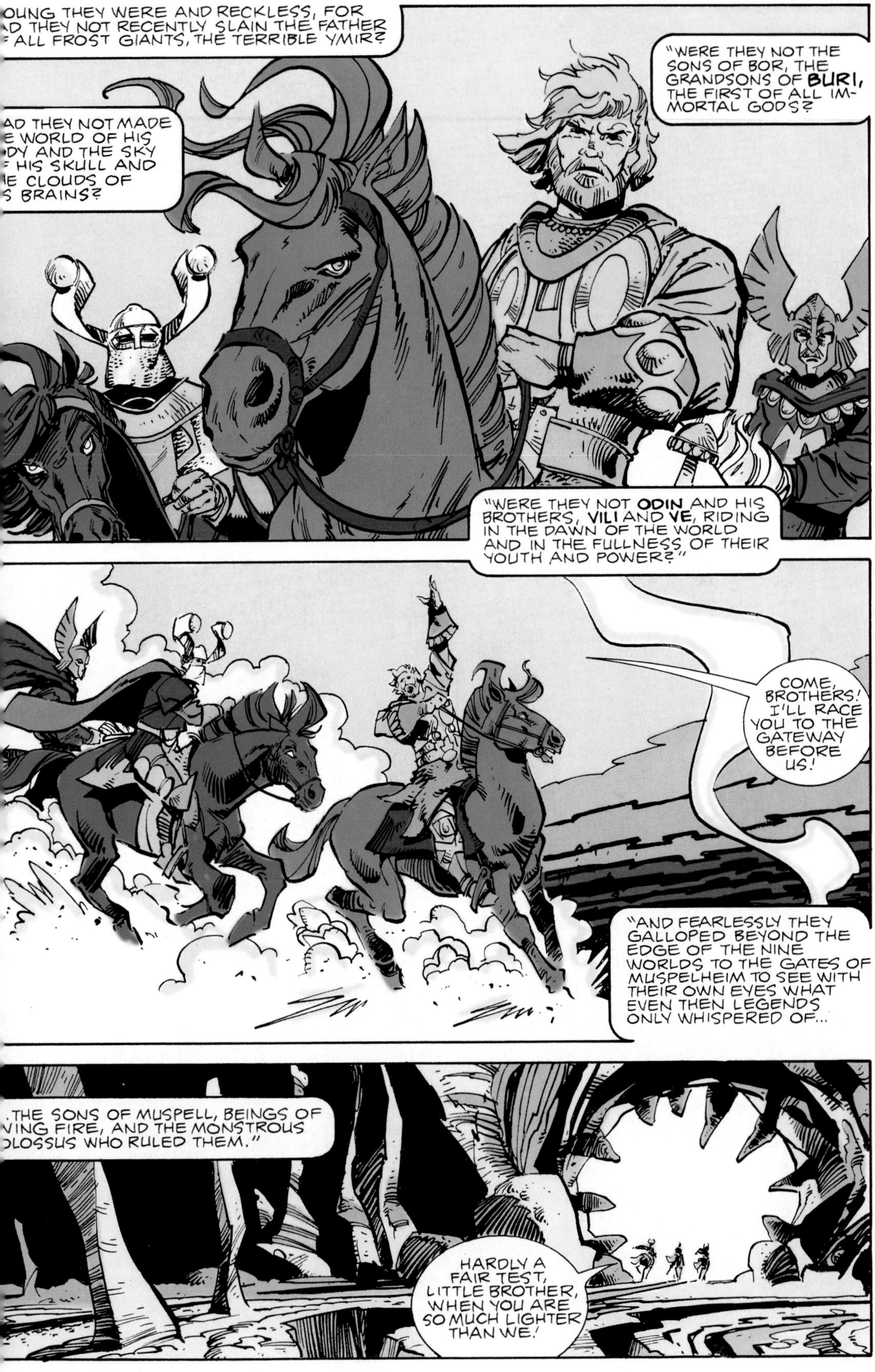
OUNG THEY WERE AND RECKLESS, FOR AD THEY NOT RECENTLY SLAIN THE FATHER F ALL FROST GIANTS, THE TERRIBLE YMIR?
"WERE THEY NOT THE SONS OF BOR, THE GRANDSONS OF **BURI**, THE FIRST OF ALL IM-MORTAL GODS?
AD THEY NOT MADE E WORLD OF HIS DY AND THE SKY F HIS SKULL AND E CLOUDS OF S BRAINS?
"WERE THEY NOT **ODIN** AND HIS BROTHERS, **VILI** AND **VE**, RIDING IN THE DAWN OF THE WORLD AND IN THE FULLNESS OF THEIR YOUTH AND POWER?"
COME, BROTHERS! I'LL RACE YOU TO THE GATEWAY BEFORE US!
"AND FEARLESSLY THEY GALLOPED BEYOND THE EDGE OF THE NINE WORLDS TO THE GATES OF MUSPELHEIM TO SEE WITH THEIR OWN EYES WHAT EVEN THEN LEGENDS ONLY WHISPERED OF...
.THE SONS OF MUSPELL, BEINGS OF VING FIRE, AND THE MONSTROUS OLOSSUS WHO RULED THEM."
HARDLY A FAIR TEST, LITTLE BROTHER, WHEN YOU ARE SO MUCH LIGHTER THAN WE!

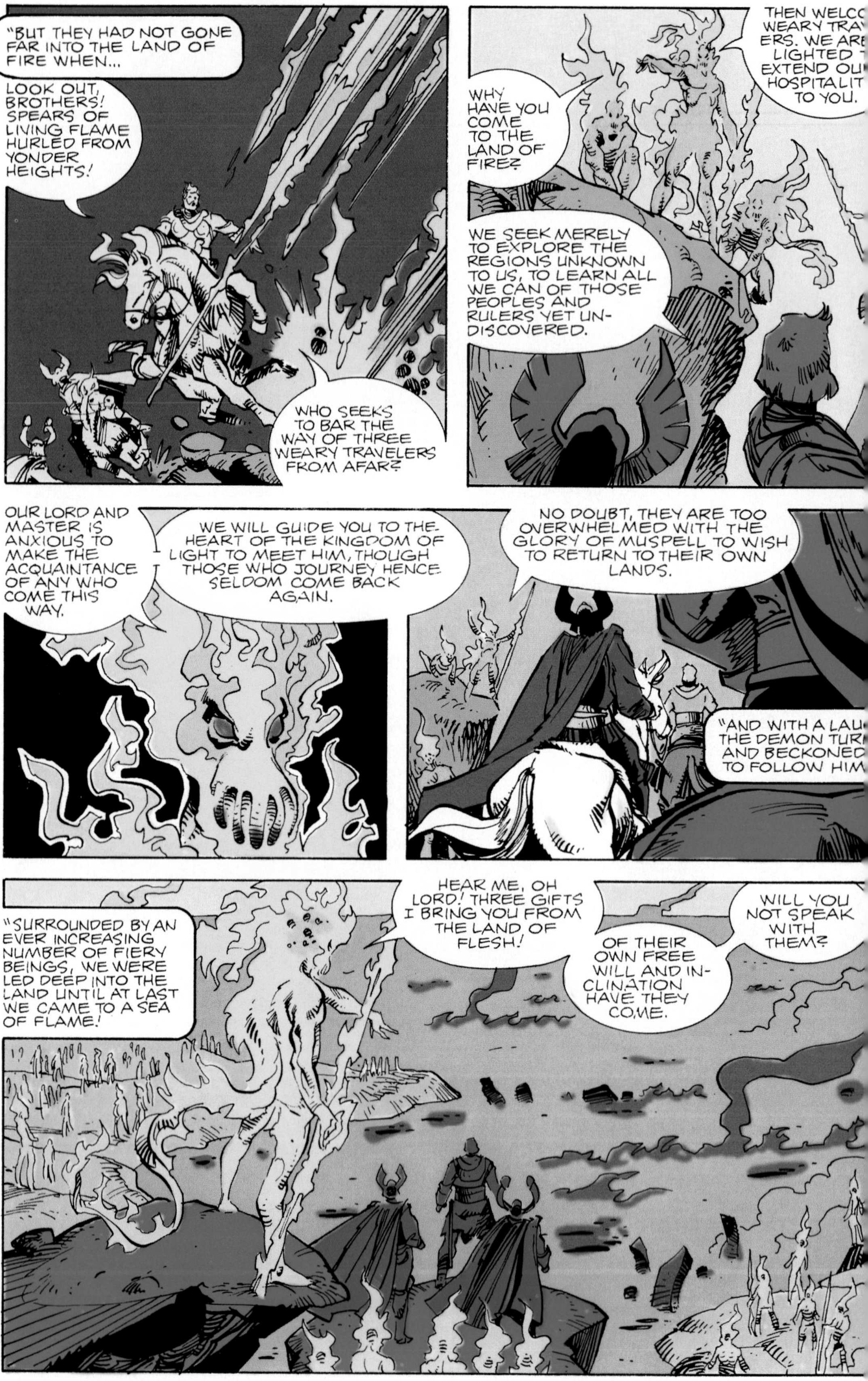
"BUT THEY HAD NOT GONE FAR INTO THE LAND OF FIRE WHEN...
LOOK OUT, BROTHERS! SPEARS OF LIVING FLAME HURLED FROM YONDER HEIGHTS!
WHO SEEKS TO BAR THE WAY OF THREE WEARY TRAVELERS FROM AFAR?
WHY HAVE YOU COME TO THE LAND OF FIRE?
WE SEEK MERELY TO EXPLORE THE REGIONS UNKNOWN TO US, TO LEARN ALL WE CAN OF THOSE PEOPLES AND RULERS YET UNDISCOVERED.
THEN WELC WEARY TRA ERS. WE AR LIGHTED EXTEND OU HOSPITALIT TO YOU.
OUR LORD AND MASTER IS ANXIOUS TO MAKE THE ACQUAINTANCE OF ANY WHO COME THIS WAY.
WE WILL GUIDE YOU TO THE HEART OF THE KINGDOM OF LIGHT TO MEET HIM, THOUGH THOSE WHO JOURNEY HENCE SELDOM COME BACK AGAIN.
NO DOUBT, THEY ARE TOO OVERWHELMED WITH THE GLORY OF MUSPELL TO WISH TO RETURN TO THEIR OWN LANDS.
"AND WITH A LAU THE DEMON TUR AND BECKONED TO FOLLOW HIM
"SURROUNDED BY AN EVER INCREASING NUMBER OF FIERY BEINGS, WE WERE LED DEEP INTO THE LAND UNTIL AT LAST WE CAME TO A SEA OF FLAME!
HEAR ME, OH LORD! THREE GIFTS I BRING YOU FROM THE LAND OF FLESH!
OF THEIR OWN FREE WILL AND INCLINATION HAVE THEY COME.
WILL YOU NOT SPEAK WITH THEM?

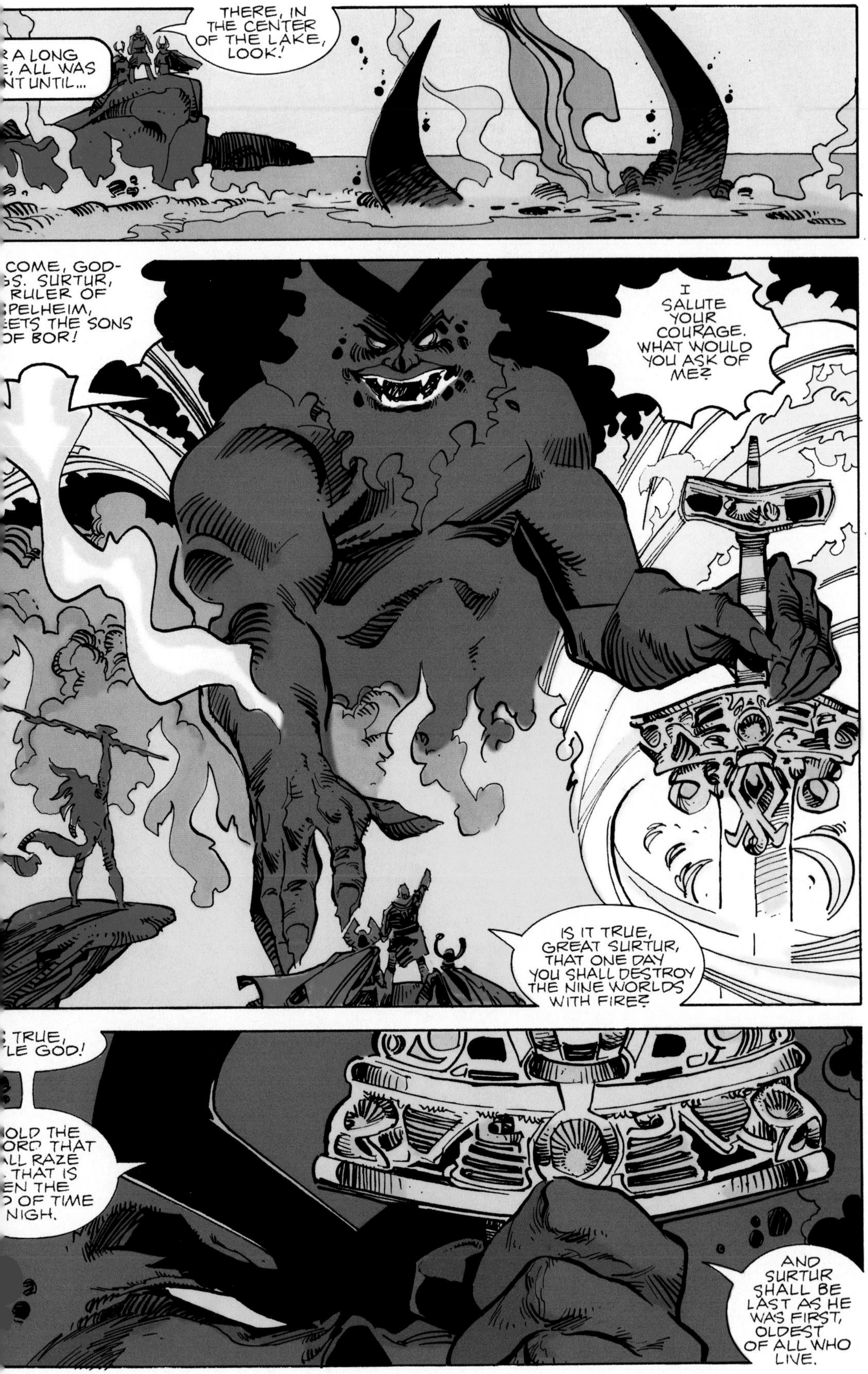

R A LONG
E, ALL WAS
NT UNTIL...
THERE, IN THE CENTER OF THE LAKE, LOOK!
COME, GOD-
GS. SURTUR,
RULER OF
PELHEIM,
EETS THE SONS
OF BOR!
I SALUTE YOUR COURAGE. WHAT WOULD YOU ASK OF ME?
IS IT TRUE, GREAT SURTUR, THAT ONE DAY YOU SHALL DESTROY THE NINE WORLDS WITH FIRE?
TRUE,
LE GOD!
OLD THE
ORD THAT
LL RAZE
THAT IS
EN THE
OF TIME
NIGH.
AND SURTUR SHALL BE LAST AS HE WAS FIRST, OLDEST OF ALL WHO LIVE.

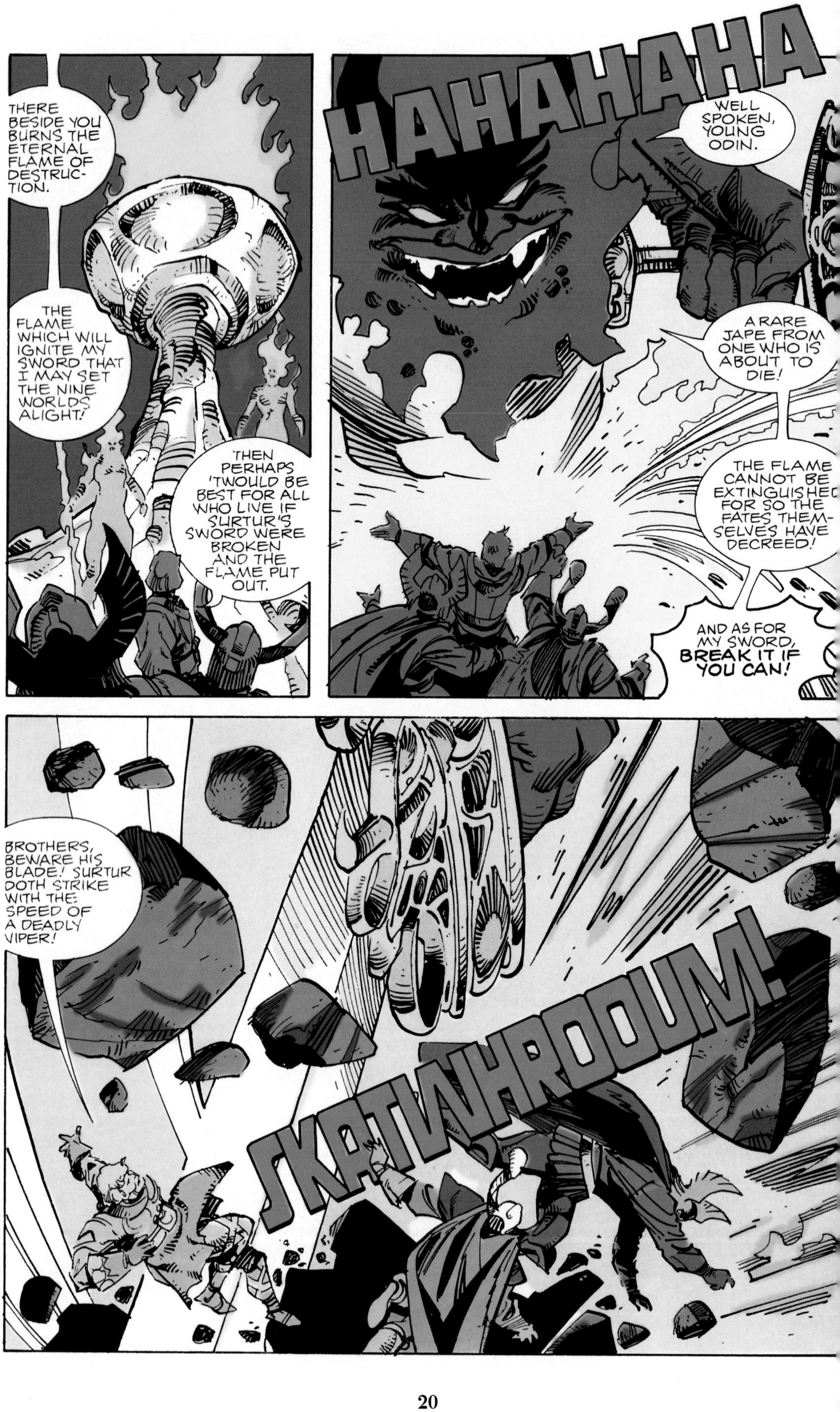
THERE BESIDE YOU BURNS THE ETERNAL FLAME OF DESTRUC-TION.
THE FLAME WHICH WILL IGNITE MY SWORD THAT I MAY SET THE NINE WORLDS ALIGHT!
THEN PERHAPS 'TWOULD BE BEST FOR ALL WHO LIVE IF SURTUR'S SWORD WERE BROKEN AND THE FLAME PUT OUT.
HAHAHAHAHA
WELL SPOKEN, YOUNG ODIN.
A RARE JAPE FROM ONE WHO IS ABOUT TO DIE!
THE FLAME CANNOT BE EXTINGUISHED FOR SO THE FATES THEM-SELVES HAVE DECREED!
AND AS FOR MY SWORD, **BREAK IT IF YOU CAN!**
BROTHERS, BEWARE HIS BLADE! SURTUR DOTH STRIKE WITH THE SPEED OF A DEADLY VIPER!
SKATWHROOM!

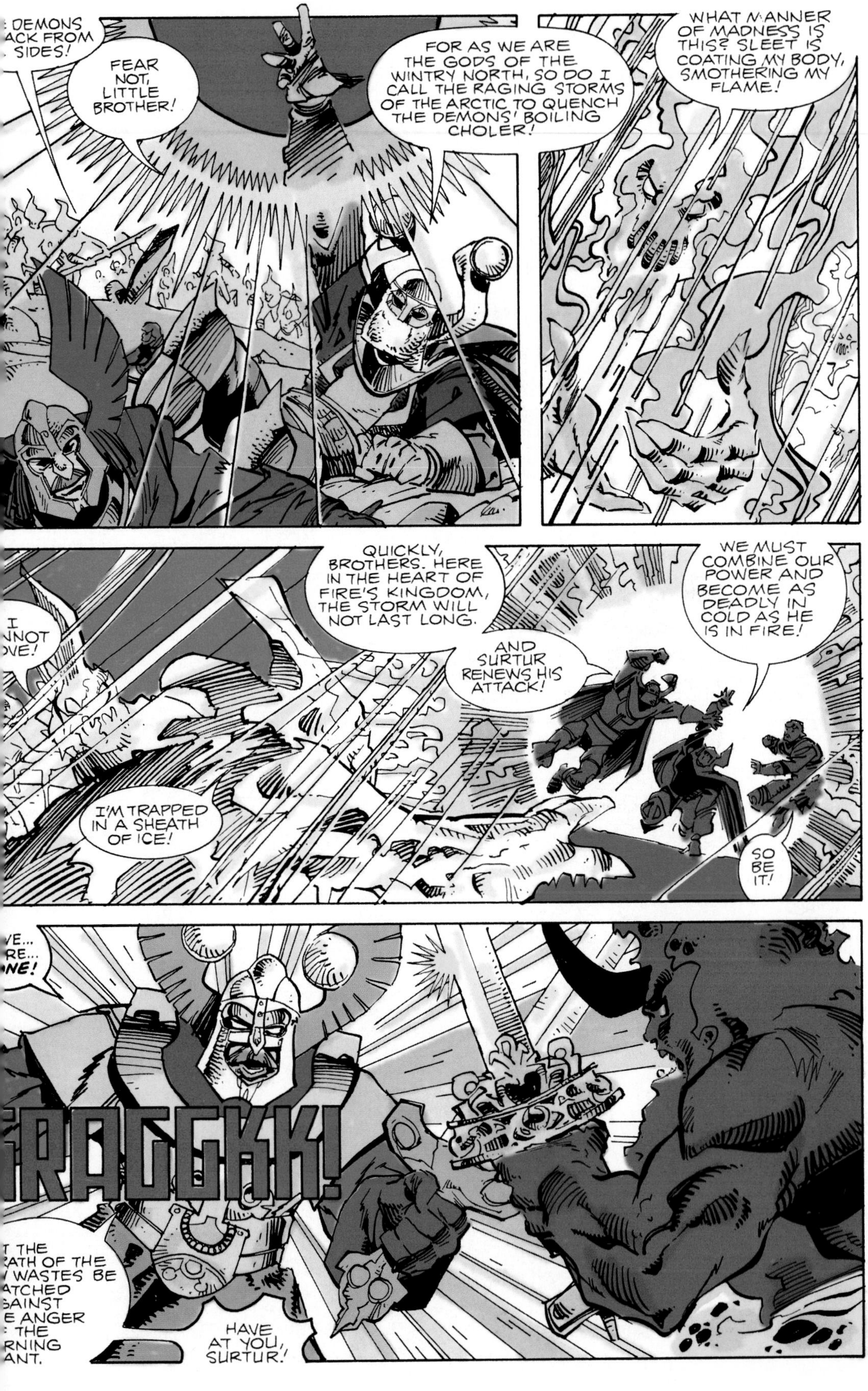
E DEMONS ACK FROM SIDES!
FEAR NOT, LITTLE BROTHER!
FOR AS WE ARE THE GODS OF THE WINTRY NORTH, SO DO I CALL THE RAGING STORMS OF THE ARCTIC TO QUENCH THE DEMONS' BOILING CHOLER!
WHAT MANNER OF MADNESS IS THIS? SLEET IS COATING MY BODY, SMOTHERING MY FLAME!
I NNOT OVE!
QUICKLY, BROTHERS. HERE IN THE HEART OF FIRE'S KINGDOM, THE STORM WILL NOT LAST LONG.
WE MUST COMBINE OUR POWER AND BECOME AS DEADLY IN COLD AS HE IS IN FIRE!
AND SURTUR RENEWS HIS ATTACK!
I'M TRAPPED IN A SHEATH OF ICE!
SO BE IT!
VE... RE... NE!
RAGGKK!
T THE RATH OF THE WASTES BE ATCHED GAINST E ANGER THE RNING ANT.
HAVE AT YOU, SURTUR!

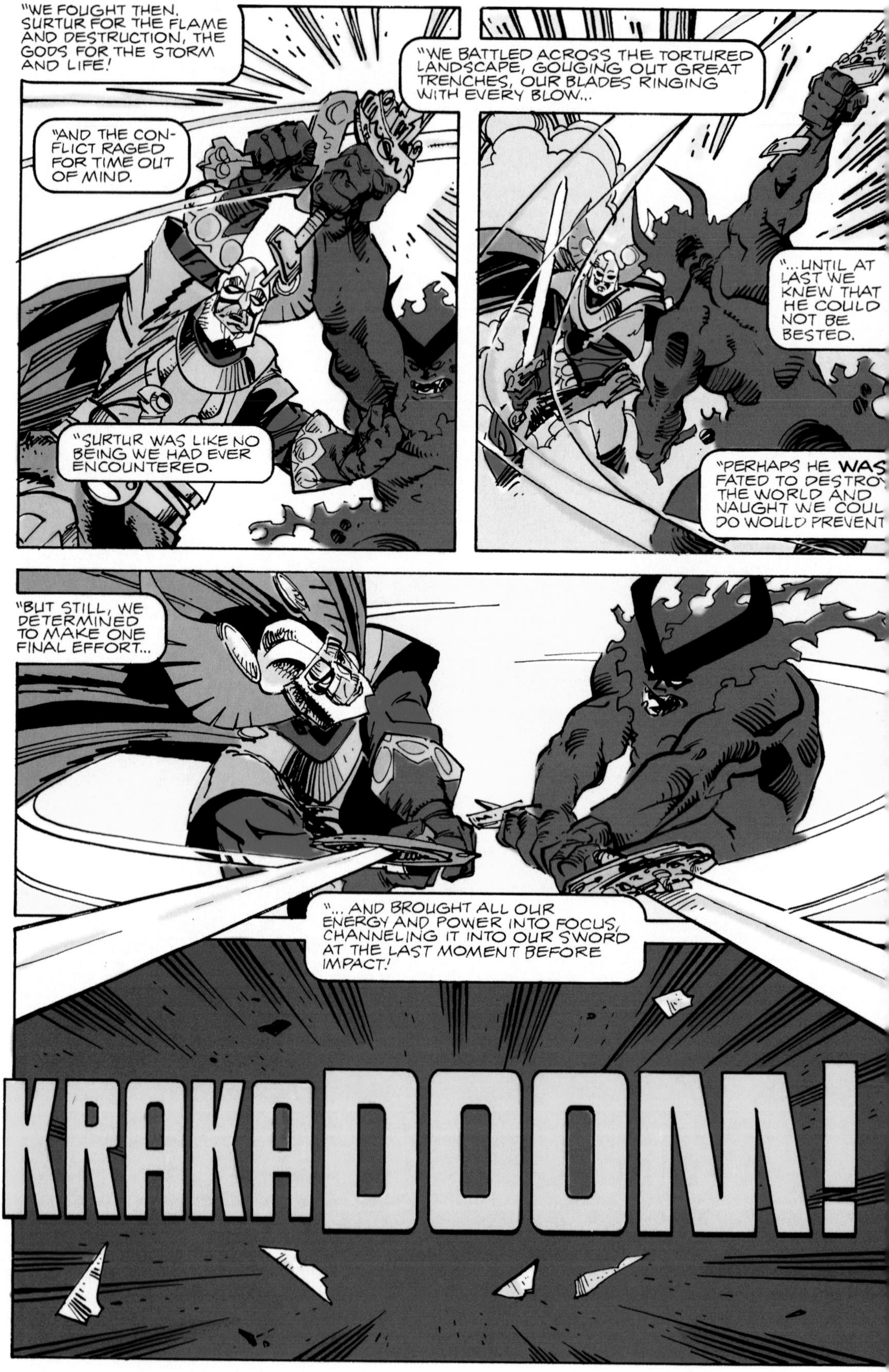
"WE FOUGHT THEN. SURTUR FOR THE FLAME AND DESTRUCTION, THE GODS FOR THE STORM AND LIFE!
"AND THE CONFLICT RAGED FOR TIME OUT OF MIND.
"SURTUR WAS LIKE NO BEING WE HAD EVER ENCOUNTERED.
"WE BATTLED ACROSS THE TORTURED LANDSCAPE, GOUGING OUT GREAT TRENCHES, OUR BLADES RINGING WITH EVERY BLOW...
"...UNTIL AT LAST WE KNEW THAT HE COULD NOT BE BESTED.
"PERHAPS HE **WAS** FATED TO DESTRO THE WORLD AND NAUGHT WE COUL DO WOULD PREVENT
"BUT STILL, WE DETERMINED TO MAKE ONE FINAL EFFORT...
"... AND BROUGHT ALL OUR ENERGY AND POWER INTO FOCUS, CHANNELING IT INTO OUR SWORD AT THE LAST MOMENT BEFORE IMPACT!
KRAKADOOM!

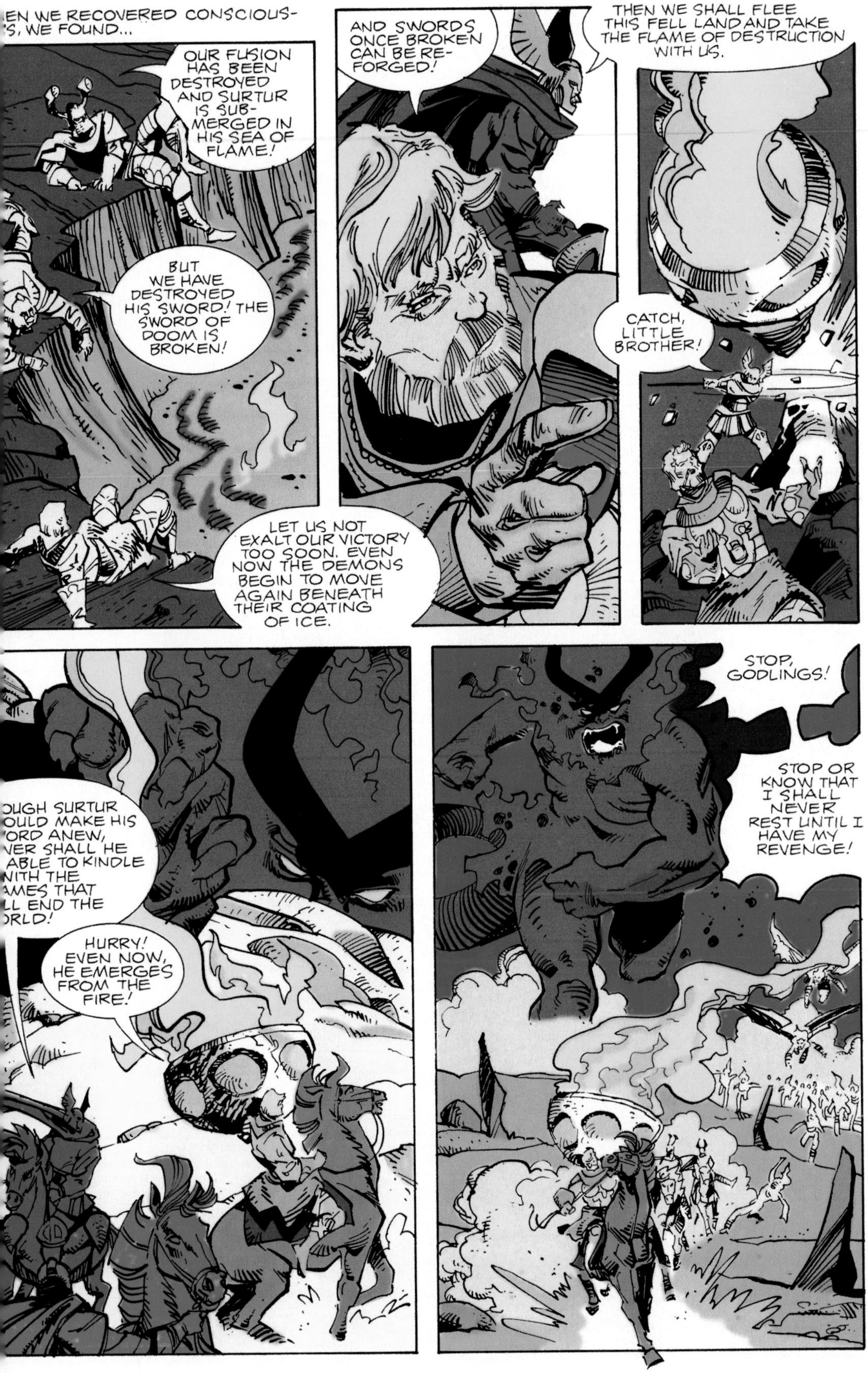
EN WE RECOVERED CONSCIOUS-
'S, WE FOUND...
OUR FUSION HAS BEEN DESTROYED AND SURTUR IS SUBMERGED IN HIS SEA OF FLAME!
BUT WE HAVE DESTROYED HIS SWORD! THE SWORD OF DOOM IS BROKEN!
AND SWORDS ONCE BROKEN CAN BE RE-FORGED!
LET US NOT EXALT OUR VICTORY TOO SOON. EVEN NOW THE DEMONS BEGIN TO MOVE AGAIN BENEATH THEIR COATING OF ICE.
THEN WE SHALL FLEE THIS FELL LAND AND TAKE THE FLAME OF DESTRUCTION WITH US.
CATCH, LITTLE BROTHER!
OUGH SURTUR OULD MAKE HIS ORD ANEW, VER SHALL HE ABLE TO KINDLE WITH THE AMES THAT LL END THE ORLD!
HURRY! EVEN NOW, HE EMERGES FROM THE FIRE!
STOP, GODLINGS!
STOP OR KNOW THAT I SHALL NEVER REST UNTIL I HAVE MY REVENGE!

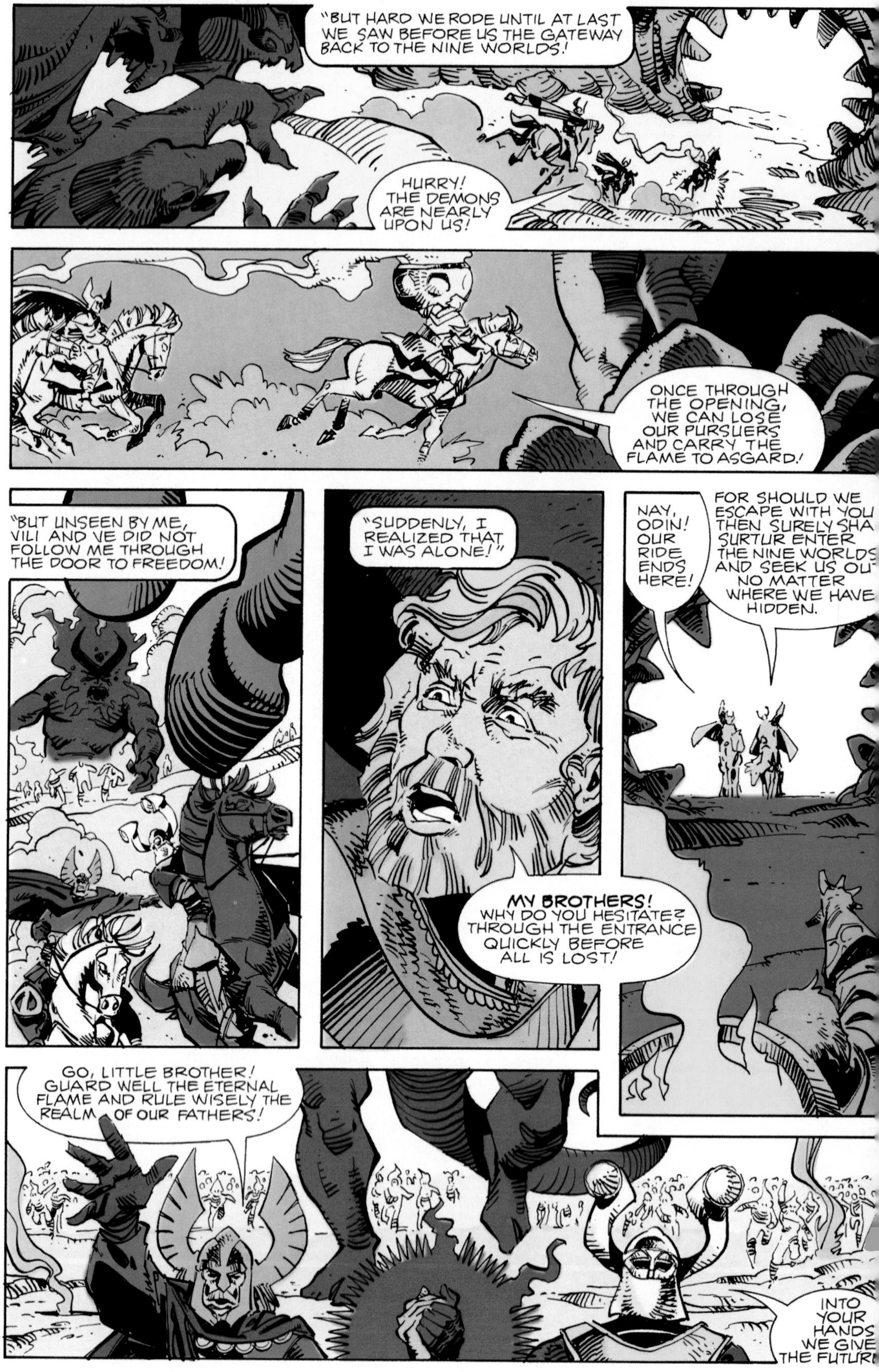
"BUT HARD WE RODE UNTIL AT LAST WE SAW BEFORE US THE GATEWAY BACK TO THE NINE WORLDS!
HURRY! THE DEMONS ARE NEARLY UPON US!
ONCE THROUGH THE OPENING, WE CAN LOSE OUR PURSUERS AND CARRY THE FLAME TO ASGARD!
"BUT UNSEEN BY ME, VILI AND VE DID NOT FOLLOW ME THROUGH THE DOOR TO FREEDOM!
"SUDDENLY, I REALIZED THAT I WAS ALONE!"
MY BROTHERS! WHY DO YOU HESITATE? THROUGH THE ENTRANCE QUICKLY BEFORE ALL IS LOST!
NAY, ODIN! OUR RIDE ENDS HERE!
FOR SHOULD WE ESCAPE WITH YOU THEN SURELY SHA SURTUR ENTER THE NINE WORLDS AND SEEK US OU NO MATTER WHERE WE HAVE HIDDEN.
GO, LITTLE BROTHER! GUARD WELL THE ETERNAL FLAME AND RULE WISELY THE REALM OF OUR FATHERS!
INTO YOUR HANDS WE GIVE THE FUTUR

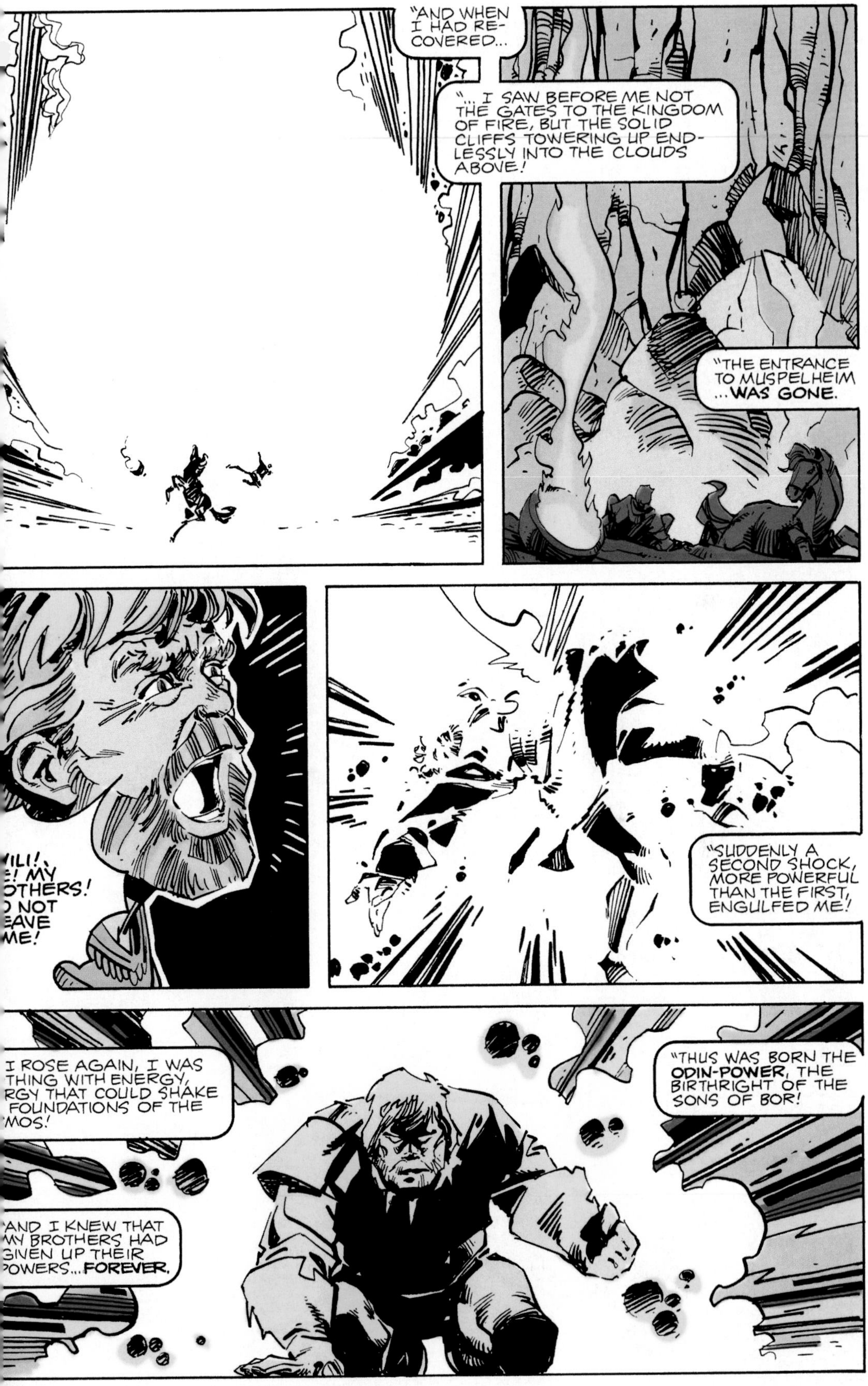
"AND WHEN I HAD RE- COVERED...
"... I SAW BEFORE ME NOT THE GATES TO THE KINGDOM OF FIRE, BUT THE SOLID CLIFFS TOWERING UP END- LESSLY INTO THE CLOUDS ABOVE!
"THE ENTRANCE TO MUSPELHEIM ...WAS GONE.
ILI! E! MY OTHERS! O NOT EAVE ME!
"SUDDENLY A SECOND SHOCK, MORE POWERFUL THAN THE FIRST, ENGULFED ME!
I ROSE AGAIN, I WAS THING WITH ENERGY, RGY THAT COULD SHAKE FOUNDATIONS OF THE MOS!
AND I KNEW THAT MY BROTHERS HAD GIVEN UP THEIR POWERS... FOREVER.
"THUS WAS BORN THE ODIN-POWER, THE BIRTHRIGHT OF THE SONS OF BOR!

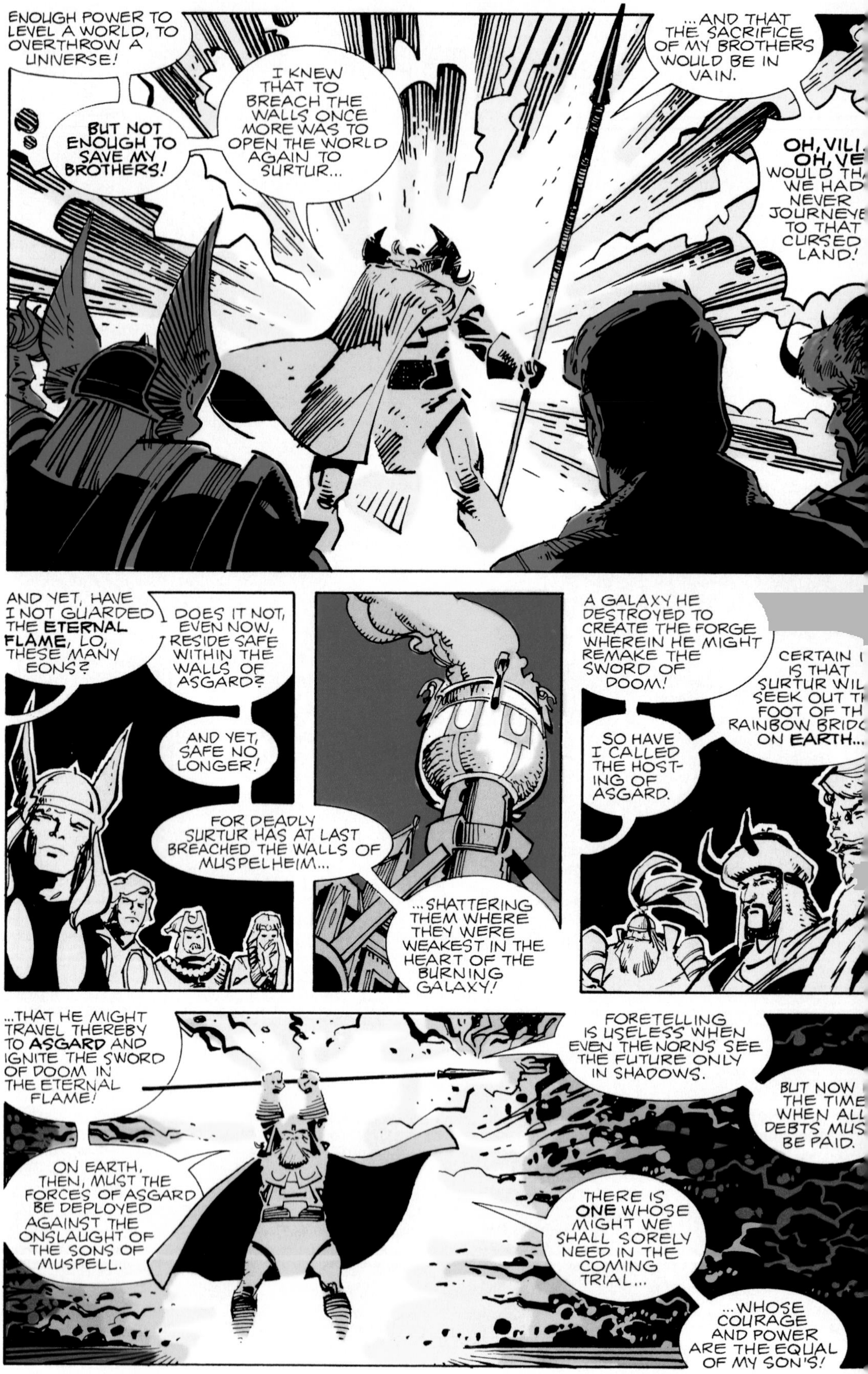

ENOUGH POWER TO LEVEL A WORLD, TO OVERTHROW A UNIVERSE!
BUT NOT ENOUGH TO SAVE MY BROTHERS!
I KNEW THAT TO BREACH THE WALLS ONCE MORE WAS TO OPEN THE WORLD AGAIN TO SURTUR...
...AND THAT THE SACRIFICE OF MY BROTHERS WOULD BE IN VAIN.
OH, VILI. OH, VE
WOULD TH WE HAD NEVER JOURNEYE TO THAT CURSED LAND!
AND YET, HAVE I NOT GUARDED THE ETERNAL FLAME, LO, THESE MANY EONS?
DOES IT NOT, EVEN NOW, RESIDE SAFE WITHIN THE WALLS OF ASGARD?
AND YET, SAFE NO LONGER!
FOR DEADLY SURTUR HAS AT LAST BREACHED THE WALLS OF MUSPELHEIM...
...SHATTERING THEM WHERE THEY WERE WEAKEST IN THE HEART OF THE BURNING GALAXY!
A GALAXY HE DESTROYED TO CREATE THE FORGE WHEREIN HE MIGHT REMAKE THE SWORD OF DOOM!
CERTAIN IS THAT SURTUR WIL SEEK OUT T FOOT OF TH RAINBOW BRID ON EARTH...
SO HAVE I CALLED THE HOSTING OF ASGARD.
...THAT HE MIGHT TRAVEL THEREBY TO ASGARD AND IGNITE THE SWORD OF DOOM IN THE ETERNAL FLAME!
ON EARTH, THEN, MUST THE FORCES OF ASGARD BE DEPLOYED AGAINST THE ONSLAUGHT OF THE SONS OF MUSPELL.
FORETELLING IS USELESS WHEN EVEN THE NORNS SEE THE FUTURE ONLY IN SHADOWS.
BUT NOW THE TIME WHEN ALL DEBTS MUS BE PAID.
THERE IS ONE WHOSE MIGHT WE SHALL SORELY NEED IN THE COMING TRIAL...
...WHOSE COURAGE AND POWER ARE THE EQUAL OF MY SON'S!

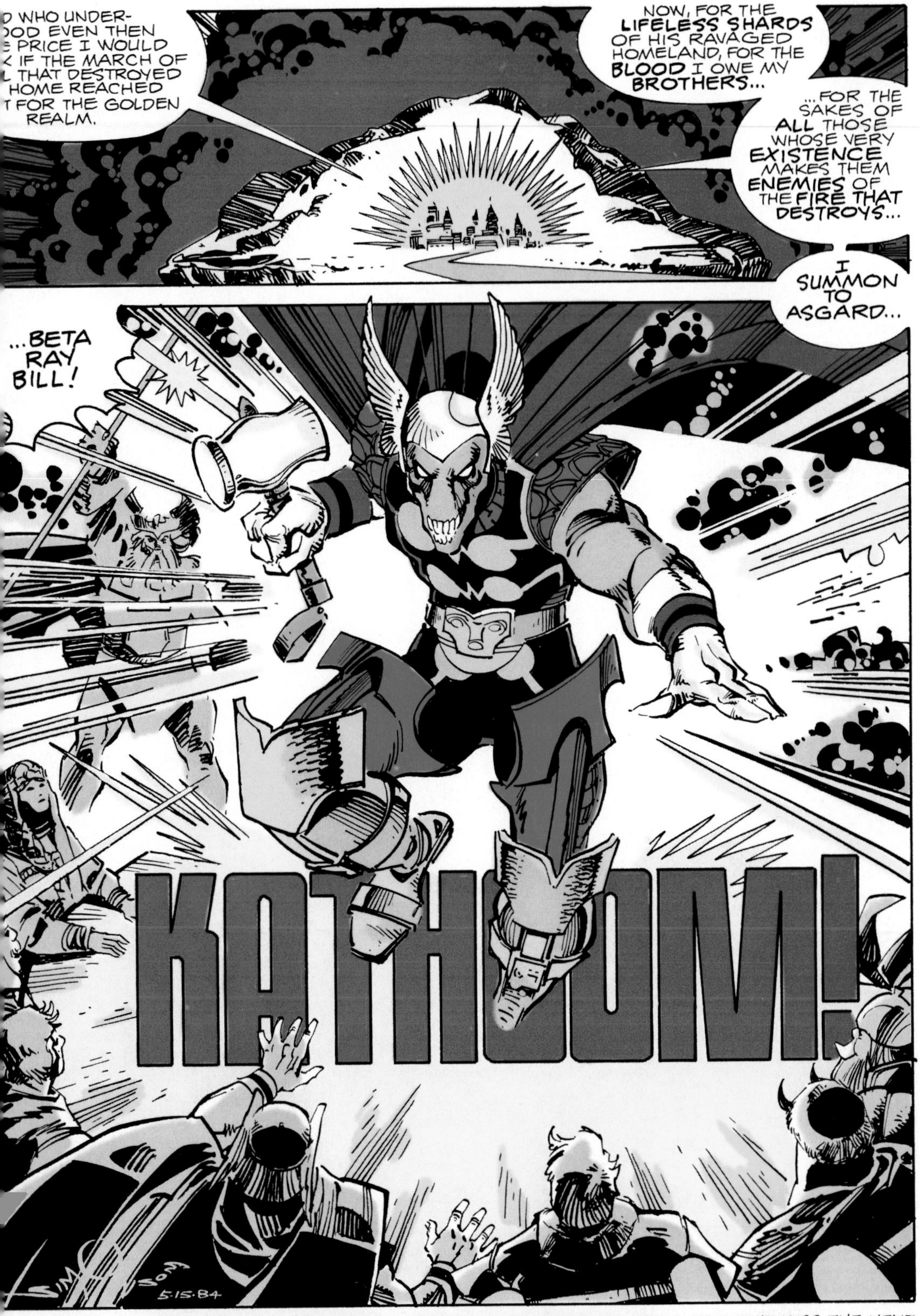
D WHO UNDER-
OOD EVEN THEN
E PRICE I WOULD
K IF THE MARCH OF
L THAT DESTROYED
HOME REACHED
T FOR THE GOLDEN
REALM.
NOW, FOR THE LIFELESS SHARDS OF HIS RAVAGED HOMELAND, FOR THE BLOOD I OWE MY BROTHERS...
...FOR THE SAKES OF ALL THOSE WHOSE VERY EXISTENCE MAKES THEM ENEMIES OF THE FIRE THAT DESTROYS...
I SUMMON TO ASGARD...
...BETA RAY BILL!
KATHOOM!
SIMONSON 5.15.84

NEXT: RAGNAROK AND ROLL!

I WOULDN'T MISS THE NEXT ISSUE IF I WERE YOU, KIDS. YOU JUST MIGHT REGRET IT FOR THE REST OF YOUR LIFE. 'NUFF SAID!

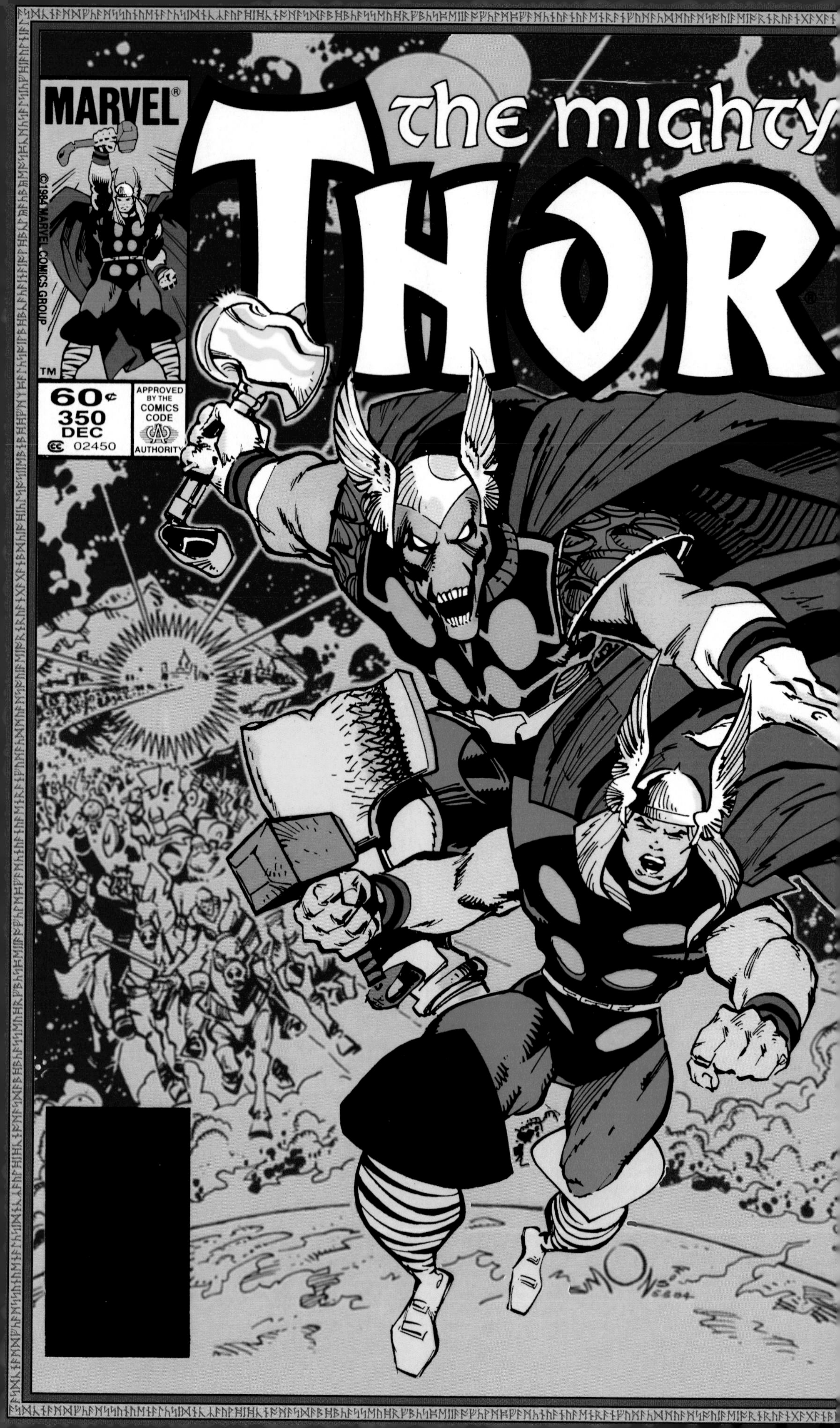
MARVEL®
the mighty
THOR®
©1984 MARVEL COMICS GROUP
TM
60¢
350
DEC
02450
APPROVED BY THE COMICS CODE AUTHORITY

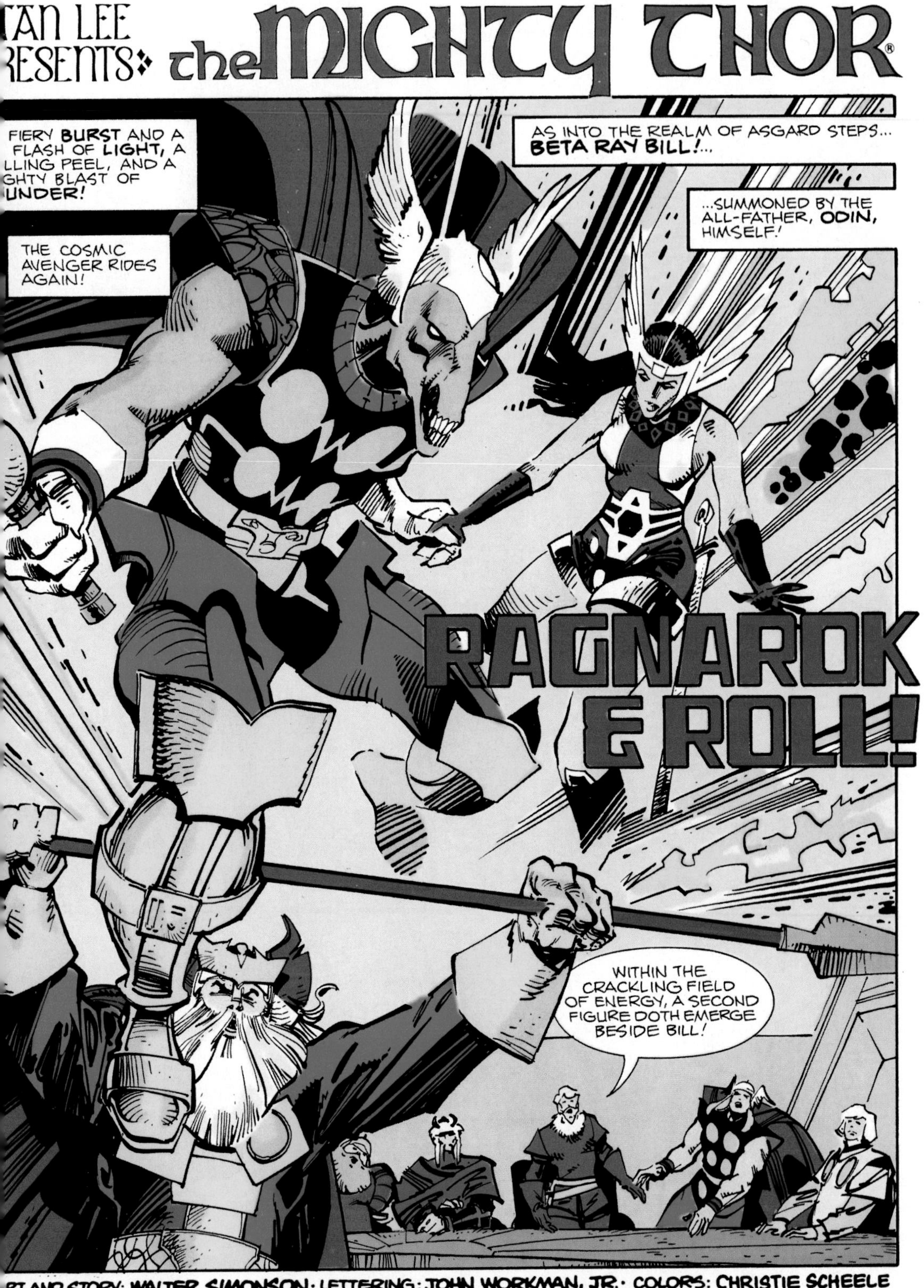
TAN LEE
RESENTS: the MIGHTY THOR®
FIERY BURST AND A FLASH OF LIGHT, A LLING PEEL, AND A GHTY BLAST OF UNDER!
THE COSMIC AVENGER RIDES AGAIN!
AS INTO THE REALM OF ASGARD STEPS... BETA RAY BILL!...
...SUMMONED BY THE ALL-FATHER, ODIN, HIMSELF!
RAGNAROK E ROLL!
WITHIN THE CRACKLING FIELD OF ENERGY, A SECOND FIGURE DOTH EMERGE BESIDE BILL!

RT AND STORY: WALTER SIMONSON · LETTERING: JOHN WORKMAN, JR. · COLORS: CHRISTIE SCHEELE
EDITING: MARK GRUENWALD · EDITOR-IN-CHIEF: JIM SHOOTER

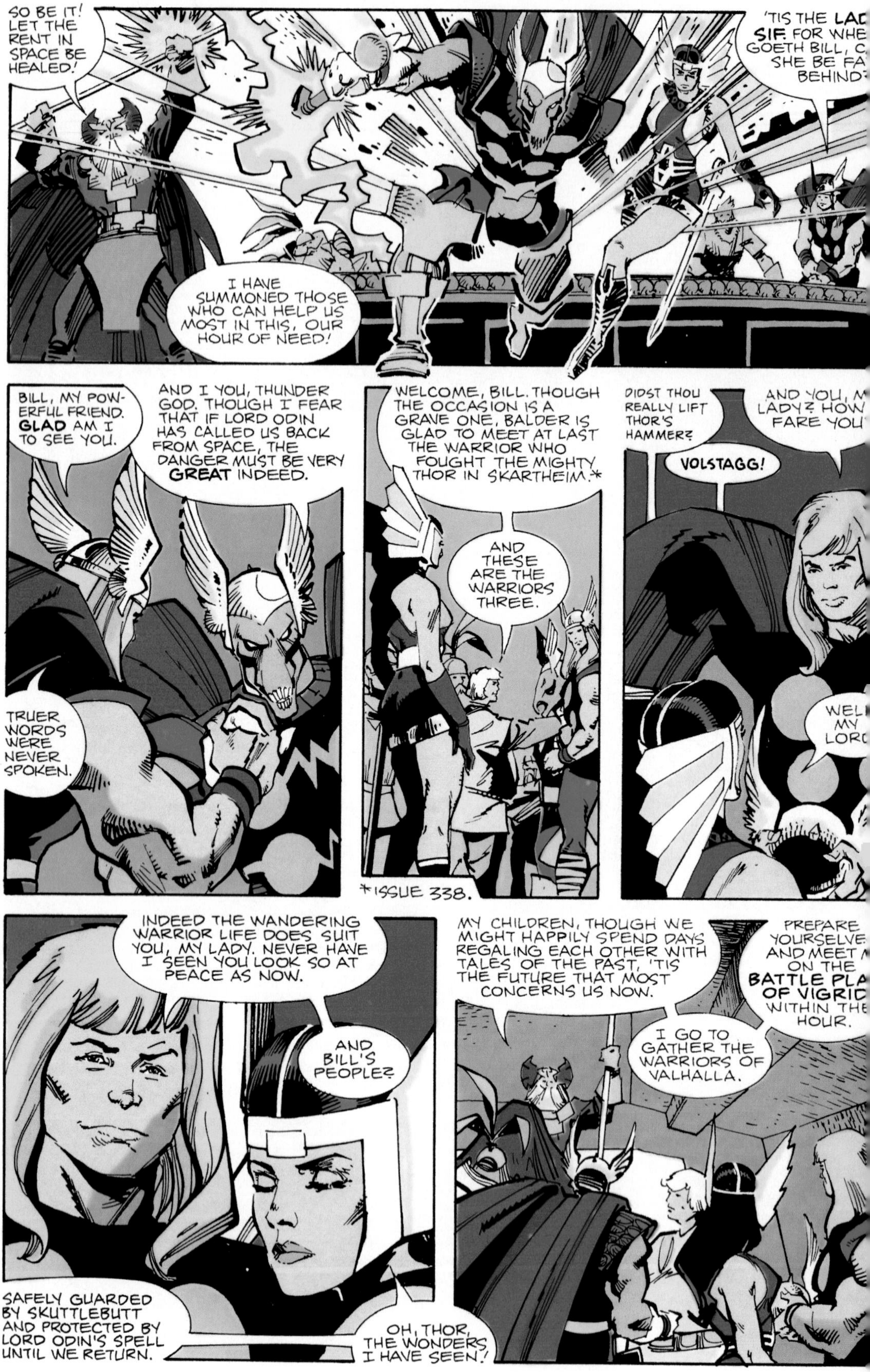
SO BE IT! LET THE RENT IN SPACE BE HEALED!
I HAVE SUMMONED THOSE WHO CAN HELP US MOST IN THIS, OUR HOUR OF NEED!
'TIS THE LAD SIF. FOR WHE GOETH BILL, C SHE BE FA BEHIND?
BILL, MY POWERFUL FRIEND. GLAD AM I TO SEE YOU.
AND I YOU, THUNDER GOD. THOUGH I FEAR THAT IF LORD ODIN HAS CALLED US BACK FROM SPACE, THE DANGER MUST BE VERY GREAT INDEED.
TRUER WORDS WERE NEVER SPOKEN.
WELCOME, BILL. THOUGH THE OCCASION IS A GRAVE ONE, BALDER IS GLAD TO MEET AT LAST THE WARRIOR WHO FOUGHT THE MIGHTY THOR IN SKARTHEIM.*
AND THESE ARE THE WARRIORS THREE.
*ISSUE 338.
DIDST THOU REALLY LIFT THOR'S HAMMER?
VOLSTAGG!
AND YOU, M LADY? HOW FARE YOU
WEL MY LORD
INDEED THE WANDERING WARRIOR LIFE DOES SUIT YOU, MY LADY. NEVER HAVE I SEEN YOU LOOK SO AT PEACE AS NOW.
AND BILL'S PEOPLE?
SAFELY GUARDED BY SKUTTLEBUTT AND PROTECTED BY LORD ODIN'S SPELL UNTIL WE RETURN.
OH, THOR, THE WONDERS I HAVE SEEN!
MY CHILDREN, THOUGH WE MIGHT HAPPILY SPEND DAYS REGALING EACH OTHER WITH TALES OF THE PAST, 'TIS THE FUTURE THAT MOST CONCERNS US NOW.
PREPARE YOURSELVE AND MEET M ON THE BATTLE PLA OF VIGRID WITHIN THE HOUR.
I GO TO GATHER THE WARRIORS OF VALHALLA.

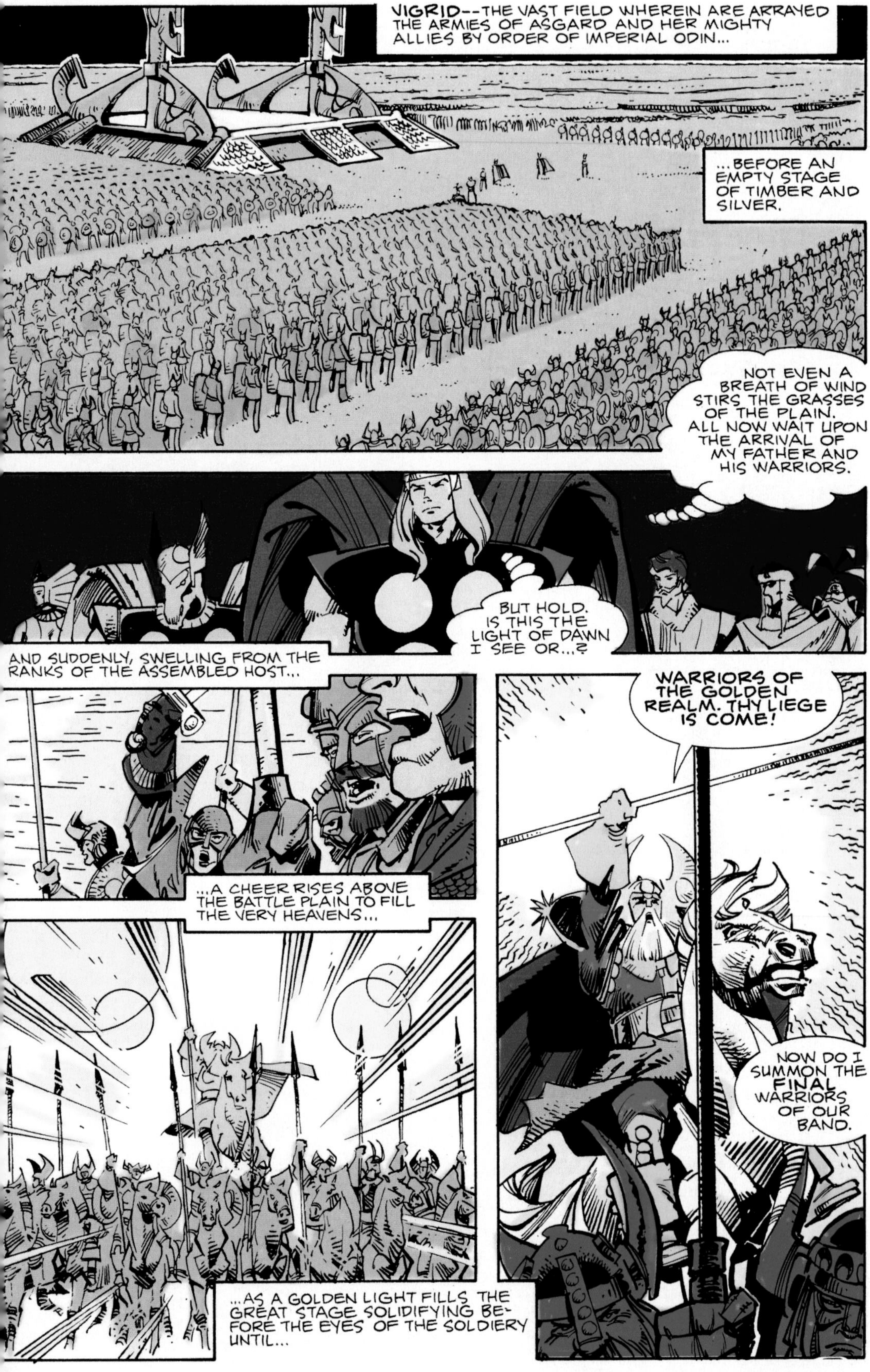
VIGRID--THE VAST FIELD WHEREIN ARE ARRAYED THE ARMIES OF ASGARD AND HER MIGHTY ALLIES BY ORDER OF IMPERIAL ODIN...
...BEFORE AN EMPTY STAGE OF TIMBER AND SILVER.
NOT EVEN A BREATH OF WIND STIRS THE GRASSES OF THE PLAIN. ALL NOW WAIT UPON THE ARRIVAL OF MY FATHER AND HIS WARRIORS.
BUT HOLD. IS THIS THE LIGHT OF DAWN I SEE OR...?
AND SUDDENLY, SWELLING FROM THE RANKS OF THE ASSEMBLED HOST...
...A CHEER RISES ABOVE THE BATTLE PLAIN TO FILL THE VERY HEAVENS...
WARRIORS OF THE GOLDEN REALM. THY LIEGE IS COME!
NOW DO I SUMMON THE FINAL WARRIORS OF OUR BAND.
...AS A GOLDEN LIGHT FILLS THE GREAT STAGE SOLIDIFYING BEFORE THE EYES OF THE SOLDIERY UNTIL...

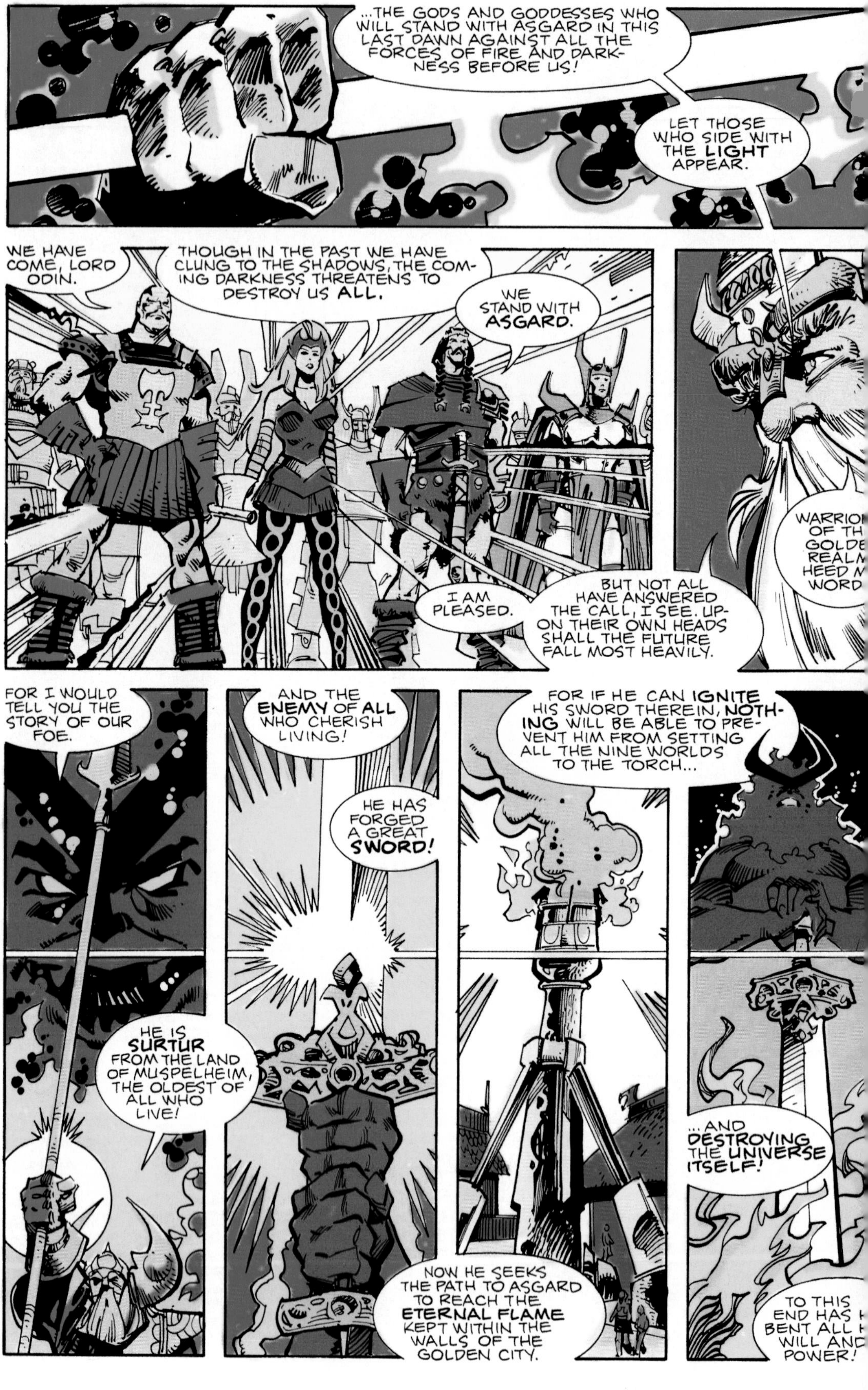
...THE GODS AND GODDESSES WHO WILL STAND WITH ASGARD IN THIS LAST DAWN AGAINST ALL THE FORCES OF FIRE AND DARKNESS BEFORE US!
LET THOSE WHO SIDE WITH THE LIGHT APPEAR.
WE HAVE COME, LORD ODIN.
THOUGH IN THE PAST WE HAVE CLUNG TO THE SHADOWS, THE COMING DARKNESS THREATENS TO DESTROY US ALL.
WE STAND WITH ASGARD.
I AM PLEASED.
BUT NOT ALL HAVE ANSWERED THE CALL, I SEE. UPON THEIR OWN HEADS SHALL THE FUTURE FALL MOST HEAVILY.
FOR I WOULD TELL YOU THE STORY OF OUR FOE.
HE IS SURTUR FROM THE LAND OF MUSPELHEIM, THE OLDEST OF ALL WHO LIVE!
AND THE ENEMY OF ALL WHO CHERISH LIVING!
HE HAS FORGED A GREAT SWORD!
NOW HE SEEKS THE PATH TO ASGARD TO REACH THE ETERNAL FLAME KEPT WITHIN THE WALLS OF THE GOLDEN CITY.
FOR IF HE CAN IGNITE HIS SWORD THEREIN, NOTHING WILL BE ABLE TO PREVENT HIM FROM SETTING ALL THE NINE WORLDS TO THE TORCH...
...AND DESTROYING THE UNIVERSE ITSELF!

S SERVANT, MALEKITH, RELEASED E SPELL OF ANCIENT WINTERS, NGING CHAOS TO MANKIND...

FREEZING THE ATEWAY BETWEEN REALM AND EIRS...

"...PERMITTING HIM TO SHATTER THE GREAT PORTAL AND RELEASE HIS NUMBERLESS HORDES ACROSS THE MORTAL LANDS. *

*THOR 348/349.

"EVEN NOW IN THE DESERT KNOWN AS THE SAHARA, HIS FORCES MUSTER AND PREPARE TO ATTACK...

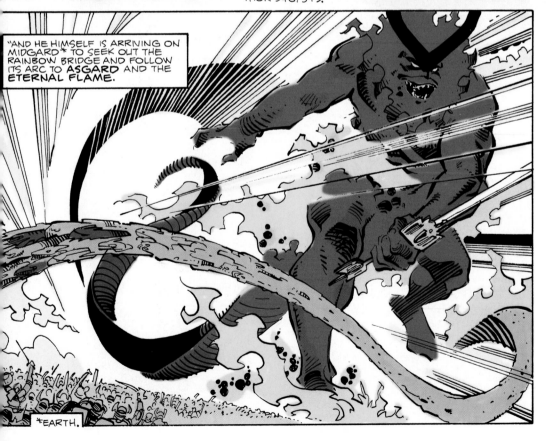

"AND HE HIMSELF IS ARRIVING ON MIDGARD* TO SEEK OUT THE RAINBOW BRIDGE AND FOLLOW ITS ARC TO ASGARD AND THE ETERNAL FLAME.

*EARTH.

33

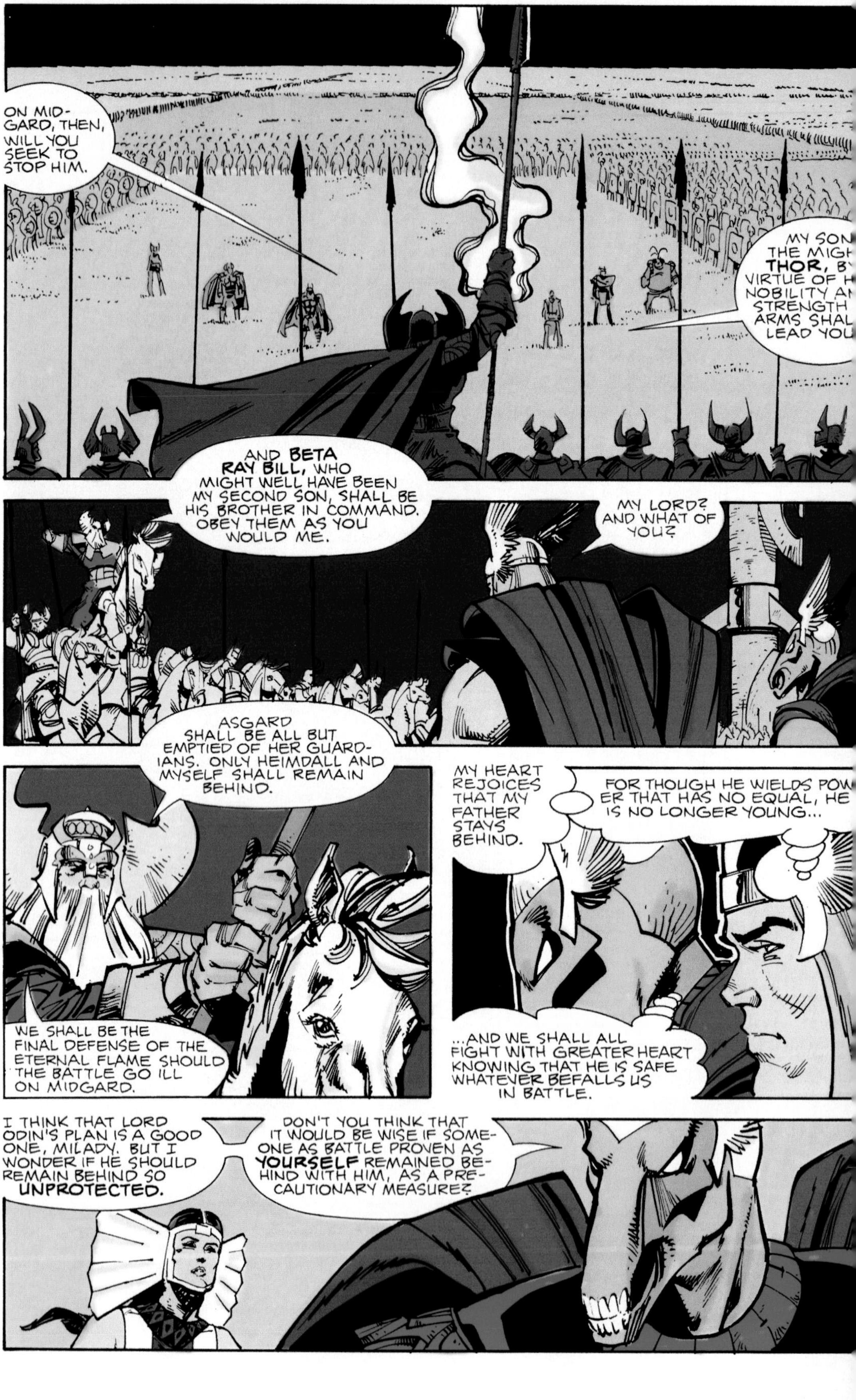
ON MID-GARD, THEN, WILL YOU SEEK TO STOP HIM.
MY SON THE MIGH THOR, BY VIRTUE OF H NOBILITY AN STRENGTH ARMS SHAL LEAD YOU
AND BETA RAY BILL, WHO MIGHT WELL HAVE BEEN MY SECOND SON, SHALL BE HIS BROTHER IN COMMAND. OBEY THEM AS YOU WOULD ME.
MY LORD? AND WHAT OF YOU?
ASGARD SHALL BE ALL BUT EMPTIED OF HER GUARD-IANS. ONLY HEIMDALL AND MYSELF SHALL REMAIN BEHIND.
WE SHALL BE THE FINAL DEFENSE OF THE ETERNAL FLAME SHOULD THE BATTLE GO ILL ON MIDGARD.
MY HEART REJOICES THAT MY FATHER STAYS BEHIND.
FOR THOUGH HE WIELDS POW ER THAT HAS NO EQUAL, HE IS NO LONGER YOUNG...
...AND WE SHALL ALL FIGHT WITH GREATER HEART KNOWING THAT HE IS SAFE WHATEVER BEFALLS US IN BATTLE.
I THINK THAT LORD ODIN'S PLAN IS A GOOD ONE, MILADY. BUT I WONDER IF HE SHOULD REMAIN BEHIND SO UNPROTECTED.
DON'T YOU THINK THAT IT WOULD BE WISE IF SOME-ONE AS BATTLE PROVEN AS YOURSELF REMAINED BE-HIND WITH HIM, AS A PRE-CAUTIONARY MEASURE?

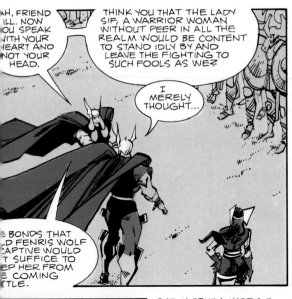

AH, FRIEND ILL. NOW OU SPEAK ITH YOUR HEART AND NOT YOUR HEAD.

THINK YOU THAT THE LADY SIF, A WARRIOR WOMAN WITHOUT PEER IN ALL THE REALM WOULD BE CONTENT TO STAND IDLY BY AND LEAVE THE FIGHTING TO SUCH FOOLS AS WE?

I MERELY THOUGHT...

E BONDS THAT D FENRIS WOLF CAPTIVE WOULD T SUFFICE TO EP HER FROM E COMING TLE.

THOR HAS KNOWN ME SINCE I WORE PIGTAILS, WHEN HE SOUGHT TO KEEP ME FROM FOLLOW-ING HIM INTO BATTLE AGAINST THE FROST GIANTS.

LED.

T I KNOW LL THE HEART U SPEAK WITH, L, AND I ERISH YOU R IT.

BUT IN TRUTH, WERE I TO REMAIN BEHIND, LORD ODIN WOULD SPEND THE TIME TELLING ME ENDLESS STORIES OF THE WORLD AS IT WAS WHEN HE WAS YOUNG TILL I COULD STAND NO MORE.

I WOULD RATHER GO TO WAR.

IF MY COMMAND-ERS HAVE QUITE FINISHED THEIR DELIBERA-TIONS AS TO THE ORDER OF BATTLE...

WE ARE READY, MY LORD.

THE DAWN BREAKS AND THE DAY BECKONS.

UNT UP, WARRIORS! D IN GLORY!

FOR ASGARD AND ODIN! FORWARD TO VICTORY!

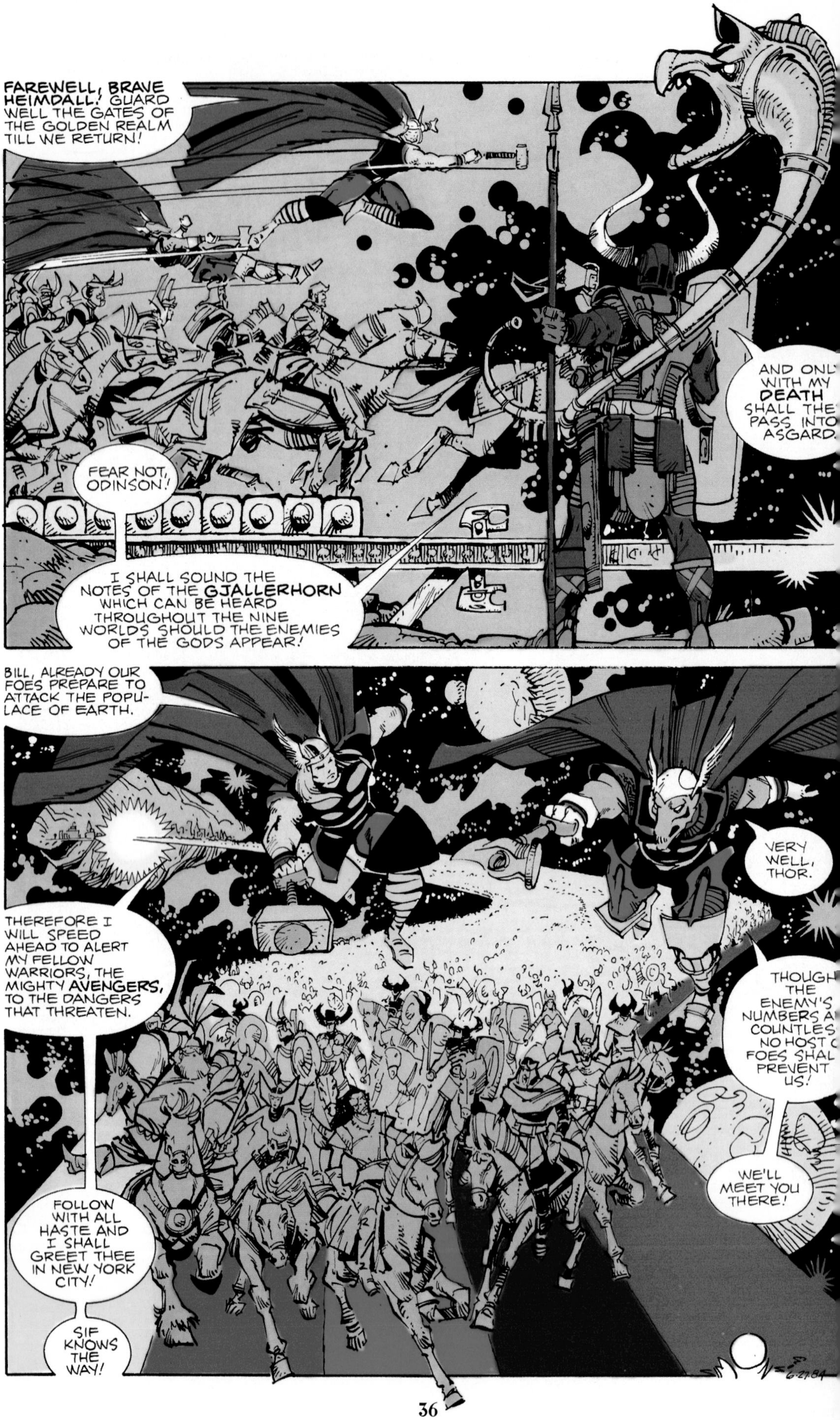
FAREWELL, BRAVE HEIMDALL! GUARD WELL THE GATES OF THE GOLDEN REALM TILL WE RETURN!
AND ONL WITH MY DEATH SHALL THE PASS INTO ASGARD.
FEAR NOT, ODINSON!
I SHALL SOUND THE NOTES OF THE GJALLERHORN WHICH CAN BE HEARD THROUGHOUT THE NINE WORLDS SHOULD THE ENEMIES OF THE GODS APPEAR!
BILL, ALREADY OUR FOES PREPARE TO ATTACK THE POPULACE OF EARTH.
THEREFORE I WILL SPEED AHEAD TO ALERT MY FELLOW WARRIORS, THE MIGHTY AVENGERS, TO THE DANGERS THAT THREATEN.
VERY WELL, THOR.
THOUGH THE ENEMY'S NUMBERS A COUNTLES NO HOST FOES SHAL PREVENT US!
FOLLOW WITH ALL HASTE AND I SHALL GREET THEE IN NEW YORK CITY!
WE'LL MEET YOU THERE!
SIF KNOWS THE WAY!

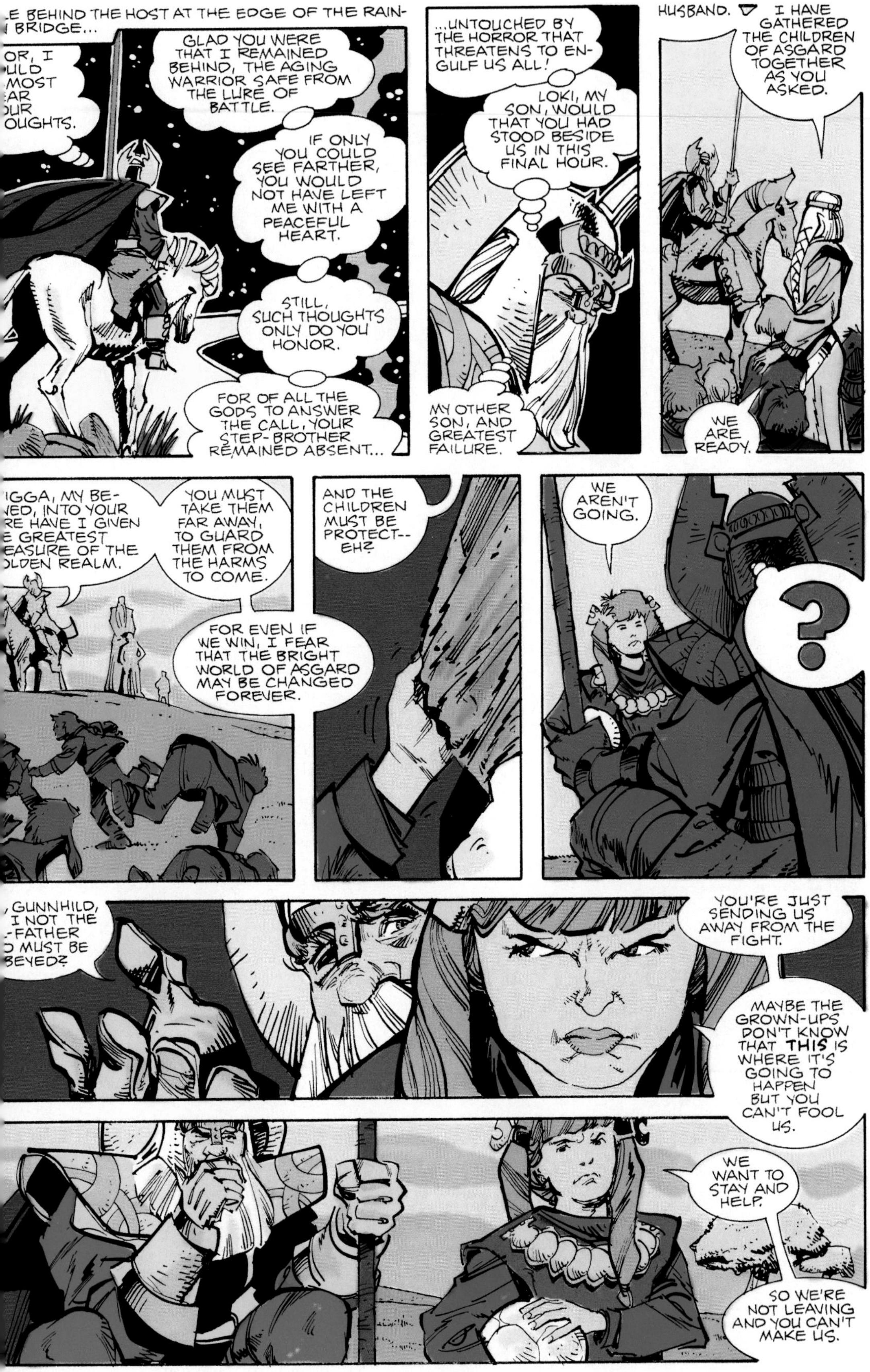

...E BEHIND THE HOST AT THE EDGE OF THE RAIN-
... BRIDGE...
...OR, I
...ULD
...MOST
...EAR
...OUR
...OUGHTS.
GLAD YOU WERE THAT I REMAINED BEHIND, THE AGING WARRIOR SAFE FROM THE LURE OF BATTLE.
IF ONLY YOU COULD SEE FARTHER, YOU WOULD NOT HAVE LEFT ME WITH A PEACEFUL HEART.
STILL, SUCH THOUGHTS ONLY DO YOU HONOR.
FOR OF ALL THE GODS TO ANSWER THE CALL, YOUR STEP-BROTHER REMAINED ABSENT...
...UNTOUCHED BY THE HORROR THAT THREATENS TO ENGULF US ALL!
LOKI, MY SON, WOULD THAT YOU HAD STOOD BESIDE US IN THIS FINAL HOUR.
MY OTHER SON, AND GREATEST FAILURE.
HUSBAND.
I HAVE GATHERED THE CHILDREN OF ASGARD TOGETHER AS YOU ASKED.
WE ARE READY.
...IGGA, MY BE-
...VED, INTO YOUR
...RE HAVE I GIVEN
...E GREATEST
...EASURE OF THE
...OLDEN REALM.
YOU MUST TAKE THEM FAR AWAY, TO GUARD THEM FROM THE HARMS TO COME.
FOR EVEN IF WE WIN, I FEAR THAT THE BRIGHT WORLD OF ASGARD MAY BE CHANGED FOREVER.
AND THE CHILDREN MUST BE PROTECT-- EH?
WE AREN'T GOING.
?
..., GUNNHILD,
... I NOT THE
...-FATHER
...O MUST BE
...BEYED?
YOU'RE JUST SENDING US AWAY FROM THE FIGHT.
MAYBE THE GROWN-UPS DON'T KNOW THAT **THIS** IS WHERE IT'S GOING TO HAPPEN BUT YOU CAN'T FOOL US.
WE WANT TO STAY AND HELP.
SO WE'RE NOT LEAVING AND YOU CAN'T MAKE US.

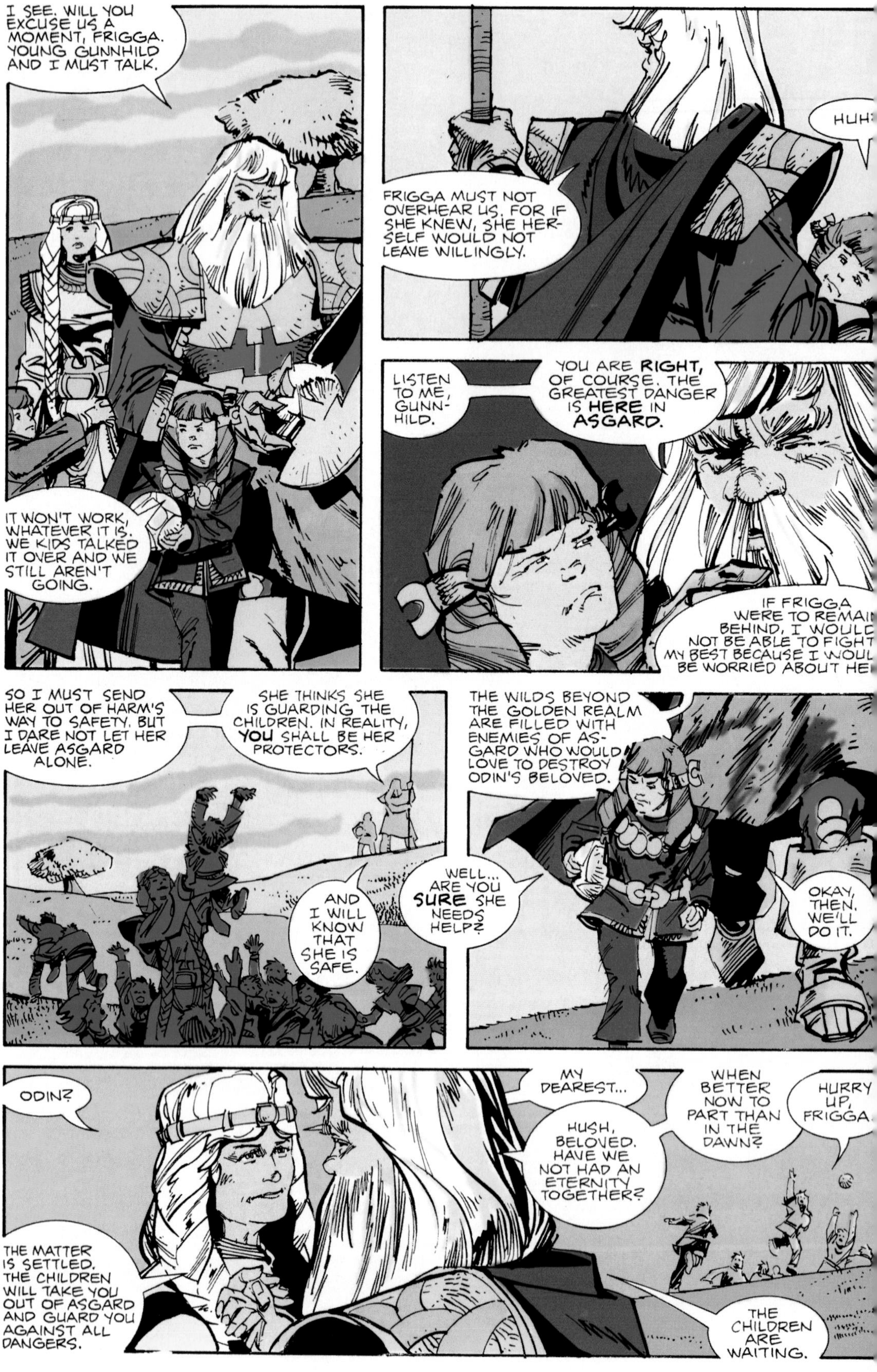
I SEE. WILL YOU EXCUSE US A MOMENT, FRIGGA. YOUNG GUNNHILD AND I MUST TALK.
IT WON'T WORK, WHATEVER IT IS. WE KIDS TALKED IT OVER AND WE STILL AREN'T GOING.
HUH
FRIGGA MUST NOT OVERHEAR US. FOR IF SHE KNEW, SHE HER-SELF WOULD NOT LEAVE WILLINGLY.
LISTEN TO ME, GUNN-HILD.
YOU ARE **RIGHT,** OF COURSE. THE GREATEST DANGER IS **HERE** IN **ASGARD.**
IF FRIGGA WERE TO REMAI BEHIND, I WOULD NOT BE ABLE TO FIGHT MY BEST BECAUSE I WOUL BE WORRIED ABOUT HE
SO I MUST SEND HER OUT OF HARM'S WAY TO SAFETY. BUT I DARE NOT LET HER LEAVE ASGARD ALONE.
SHE THINKS SHE IS GUARDING THE CHILDREN. IN REALITY, **YOU** SHALL BE HER PROTECTORS.
AND I WILL KNOW THAT SHE IS SAFE.
WELL... ARE YOU **SURE** SHE NEEDS HELP?
THE WILDS BEYOND THE GOLDEN REALM ARE FILLED WITH ENEMIES OF AS-GARD WHO WOULD LOVE TO DESTROY ODIN'S BELOVED.
OKAY, THEN. WE'LL DO IT.
ODIN?
MY DEAREST...
WHEN BETTER NOW TO PART THAN IN THE DAWN?
HUSH, BELOVED. HAVE WE NOT HAD AN ETERNITY TOGETHER?
HURRY UP, FRIGGA
THE MATTER IS SETTLED. THE CHILDREN WILL TAKE YOU OUT OF ASGARD AND GUARD YOU AGAINST ALL DANGERS.
THE CHILDREN ARE WAITING.

...THINKS YOU ...KE MORE ...TH WITH YOUNG ...NHILD THAN ...GGA MIGHT ...E GUESSED, ...O ODIN.

YET I AM STILL PUZZLED AS TO WHY YOU ASKED ME TO REMAIN BEHIND THE DEPARTING HOSTS WITH YOU.

BECAUSE, BRAVE BALDER, I HAVE ANOTHER MISSION FOR YOU.

...OULD ASK YOU TO ...RNEY TO SEEK KAR- ...A AND PERSUADE ...TO JOIN WITH US IN ...FIGHT AGAINST THE ...S OF MUSPELL.

...LORD! SURELY ...RESULTS OF MY ...MISSION FOR ...WOULD PERSUADE ...ONE NOT TO SEND ...ON SUCH ERRANDS ...AGAIN*!

DO NOT UNDERESTIMATE YOURSELF, BALDER.

*THOR 344.

THE GOD KARNILLA KNEW IS NOT THE GOD TO WHOM THE NORNS HAVE SHOWN THE TAPESTRY OF LIFE.

AND THE FINAL RESULTS OF YOUR FIRST MISSIONS ARE NOT YET IN.

BESIDES, WAS THERE NOT A CERTAIN SATISFACTION IN REMOVING LOKI'S HEAD...

...HOWEVER IMPERMANENT THE OUTCOME?

I LEAVE AT ONCE, MY LORD.

...ANWHILE, IN NEW YORK CITY, WHERE THE DAWN'S SUMMER LIGHT IS PRACTICALLY OBLITERATED BY THE ...TER STORM THAT SWEEPS ACROSS THE GLOBE FROM POLE TO POLE...

...E EARLY RISERS OF THE ...SLOGGING THROUGH ...SLUSH AND PELTING ...OF THE MORNING RUSH ...R LOOK UP TO SEE...

...A CLOUD SWEEPING LOW ACROSS THE SKY FROM OUT OF THE EAST.

THE SONS OF MUSPELL HAVE COME A-CALLING.

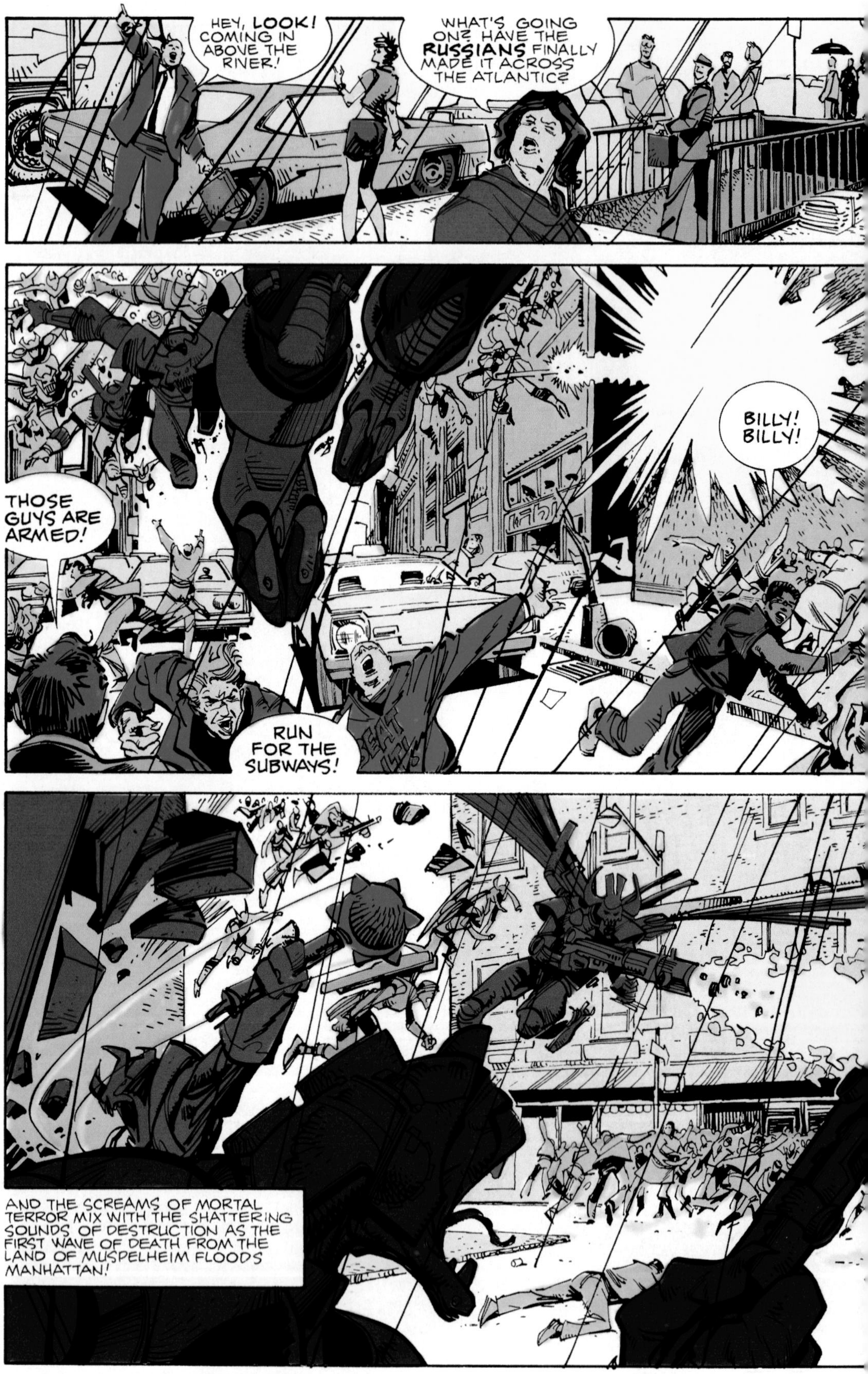
HEY, LOOK! COMING IN ABOVE THE RIVER!
WHAT'S GOING ON? HAVE THE RUSSIANS FINALLY MADE IT ACROSS THE ATLANTIC?
BILLY! BILLY!
THOSE GUYS ARE ARMED!
RUN FOR THE SUBWAYS!
AND THE SCREAMS OF MORTAL TERROR MIX WITH THE SHATTERING SOUNDS OF DESTRUCTION AS THE FIRST WAVE OF DEATH FROM THE LAND OF MUSPELHEIM FLOODS MANHATTAN!

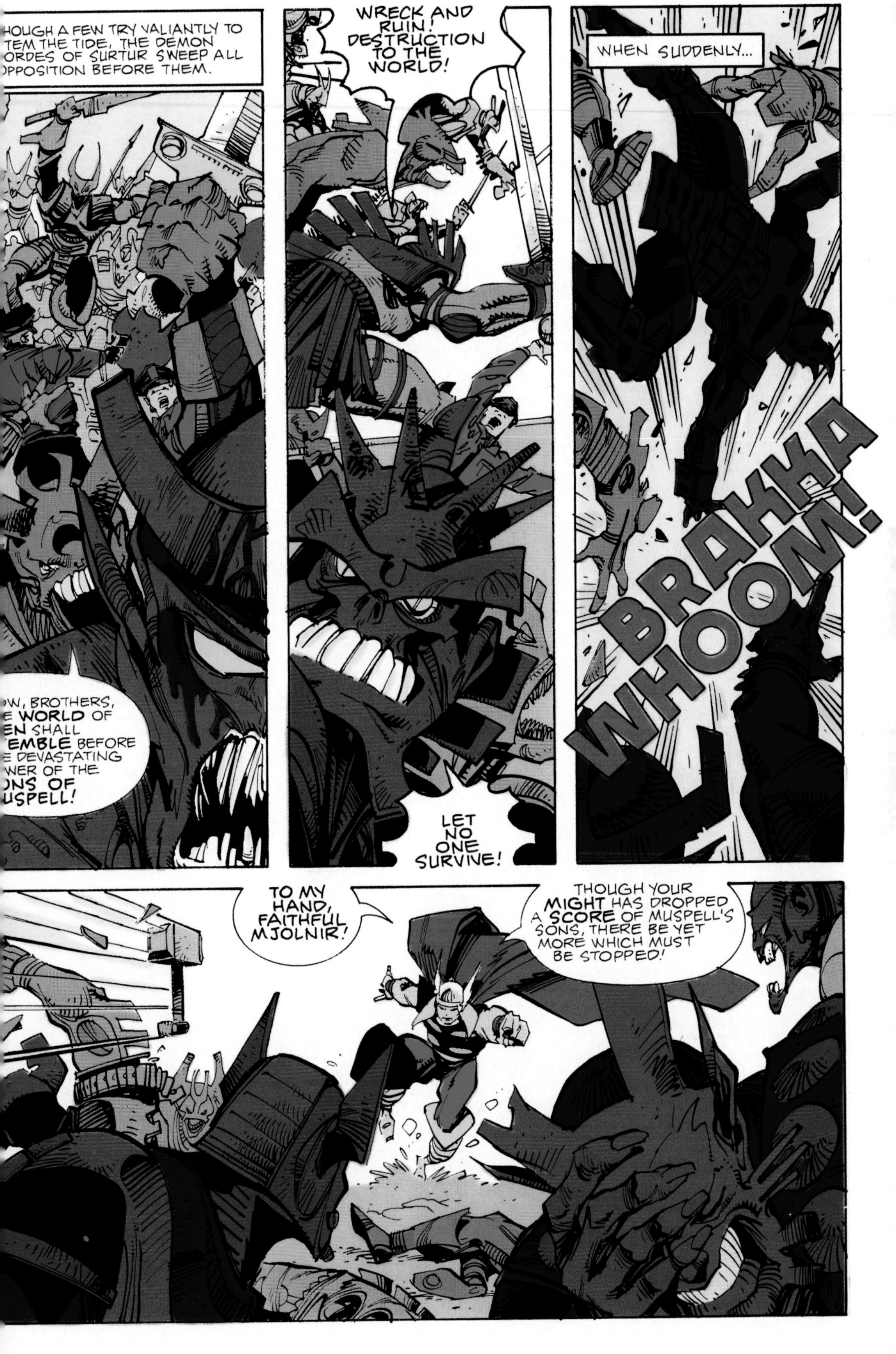
HOUGH A FEW TRY VALIANTLY TO
TEM THE TIDE, THE DEMON
ORDES OF SURTUR SWEEP ALL
OPPOSITION BEFORE THEM.
W, BROTHERS,
E WORLD OF
EN SHALL
TREMBLE BEFORE
E DEVASTATING
WER OF THE
ONS OF
USPELL!
WRECK AND RUIN! DESTRUCTION TO THE WORLD!
LET NO ONE SURVIVE!
WHEN SUDDENLY...
BRAKKA WHOOM!
TO MY HAND, FAITHFUL MJOLNIR!
THOUGH YOUR MIGHT HAS DROPPED A SCORE OF MUSPELL'S SONS, THERE BE YET MORE WHICH MUST BE STOPPED!

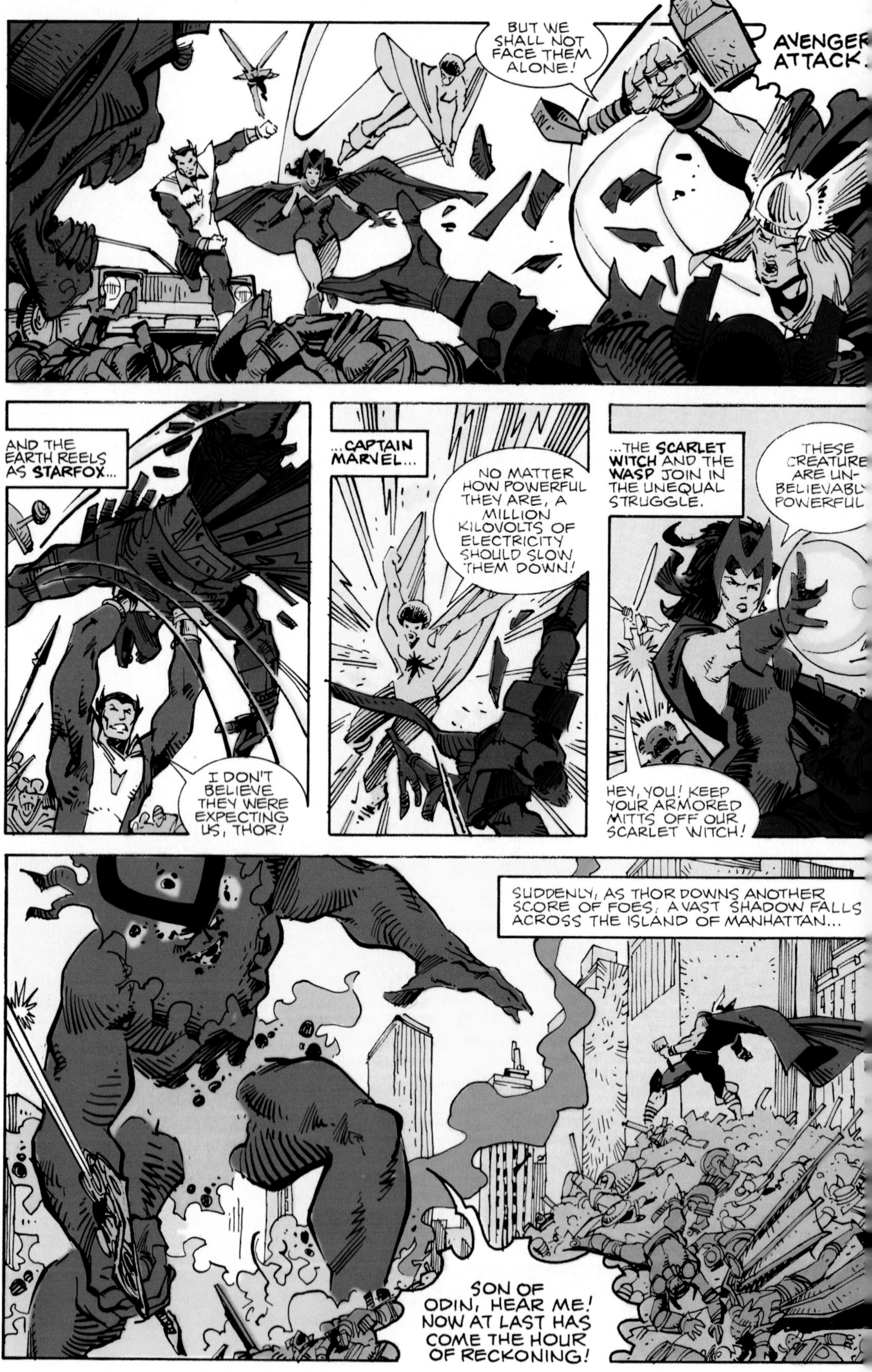

BUT WE SHALL NOT FACE THEM ALONE!
AVENGER ATTACK
AND THE EARTH REELS AS STARFOX...
I DON'T BELIEVE THEY WERE EXPECTING US, THOR!
...CAPTAIN MARVEL...
NO MATTER HOW POWERFUL THEY ARE, A MILLION KILOVOLTS OF ELECTRICITY SHOULD SLOW THEM DOWN!
...THE SCARLET WITCH AND THE WASP JOIN IN THE UNEQUAL STRUGGLE.
THESE CREATURE ARE UN-BELIEVABLY POWERFUL
HEY, YOU! KEEP YOUR ARMORED MITTS OFF OUR SCARLET WITCH!
SUDDENLY, AS THOR DOWNS ANOTHER SCORE OF FOES, A VAST SHADOW FALLS ACROSS THE ISLAND OF MANHATTAN...
SON OF ODIN, HEAR ME! NOW AT LAST HAS COME THE HOUR OF RECKONING!

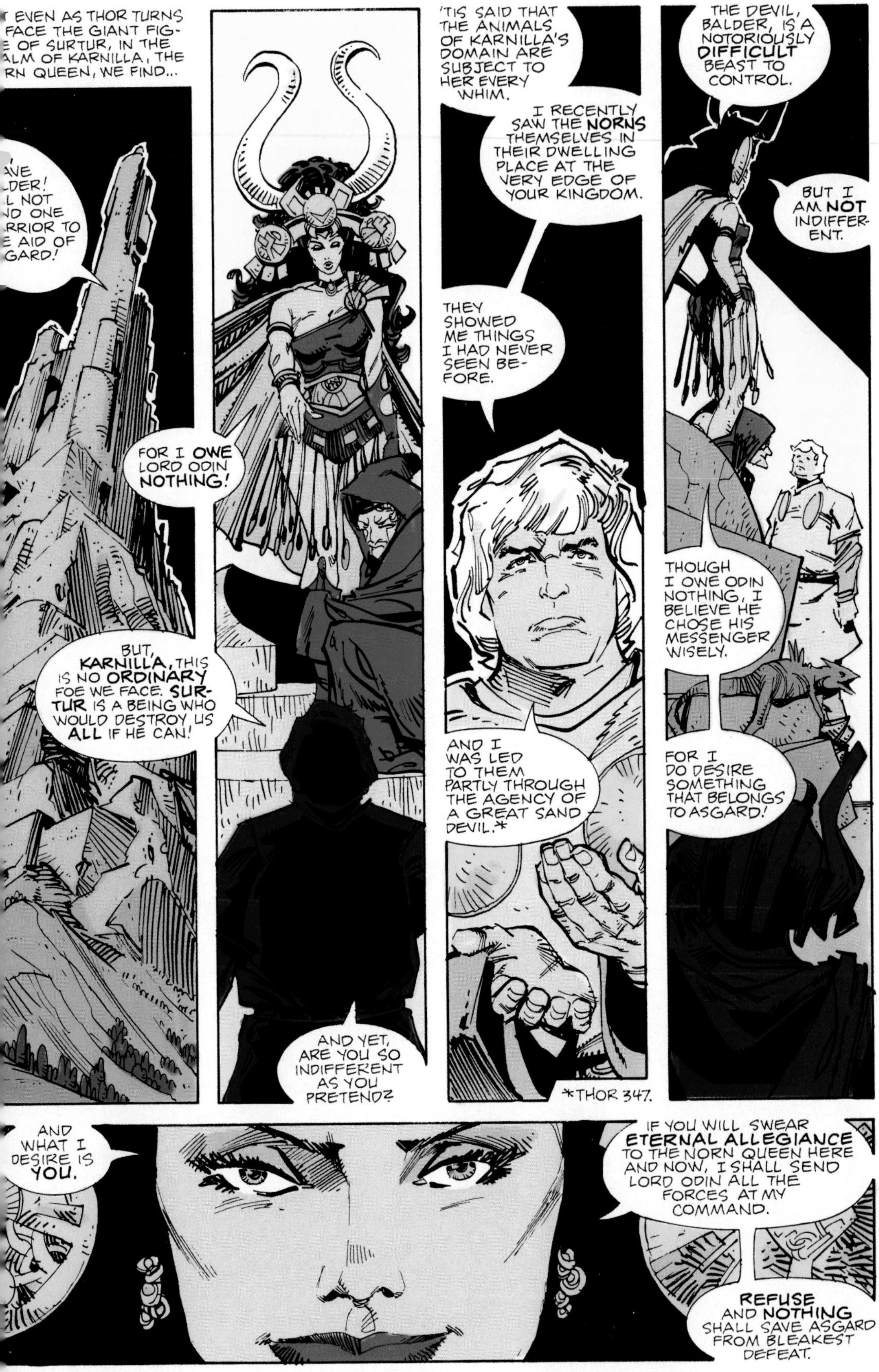

...EVEN AS THOR TURNS ...FACE THE GIANT FIG... ...OF SURTUR, IN THE ...ALM OF KARNILLA, THE ...RN QUEEN, WE FIND...
...AVE ...LDER! ...L NOT ...ND ONE ...RRIOR TO ...E AID OF ...GARD!
FOR I OWE LORD ODIN NOTHING!
BUT, KARNILLA, THIS IS NO ORDINARY FOE WE FACE. SURTUR IS A BEING WHO WOULD DESTROY US ALL IF HE CAN!
AND YET, ARE YOU SO INDIFFERENT AS YOU PRETEND?
'TIS SAID THAT THE ANIMALS OF KARNILLA'S DOMAIN ARE SUBJECT TO HER EVERY WHIM.
I RECENTLY SAW THE NORNS THEMSELVES IN THEIR DWELLING PLACE AT THE VERY EDGE OF YOUR KINGDOM.
THEY SHOWED ME THINGS I HAD NEVER SEEN BEFORE.
AND I WAS LED TO THEM PARTLY THROUGH THE AGENCY OF A GREAT SAND DEVIL.*
*THOR 347.
THE DEVIL, BALDER, IS A NOTORIOUSLY DIFFICULT BEAST TO CONTROL.
BUT I AM NOT INDIFFERENT.
THOUGH I OWE ODIN NOTHING, I BELIEVE HE CHOSE HIS MESSENGER WISELY.
FOR I DO DESIRE SOMETHING THAT BELONGS TO ASGARD!
AND WHAT I DESIRE IS YOU.
IF YOU WILL SWEAR ETERNAL ALLEGIANCE TO THE NORN QUEEN HERE AND NOW, I SHALL SEND LORD ODIN ALL THE FORCES AT MY COMMAND.
REFUSE AND NOTHING SHALL SAVE ASGARD FROM BLEAKEST DEFEAT.

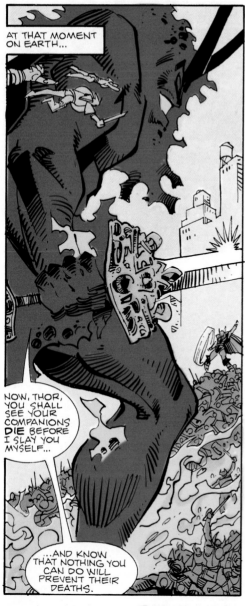

AT THAT MOMENT ON EARTH...

NOW, THOR, YOU SHALL SEE YOUR COMPANIONS *DIE* BEFORE I SLAY YOU MYSELF...

...AND KNOW THAT NOTHING YOU CAN DO WILL PREVENT THEIR DEATHS.

SLAY THEM, MY MINIONS!

WE'RE PINNED DOWN AND MY HANDS ARE CAUGHT!

I'LL NEVER BE ABLE TO FREE THEM IN TIME TO WARD OFF THE BLOW!

KLA THASSH

WHA- I'M *FREE* BUT THA NOT THO HAMME

AND THUNDERING ACROSS THE FROZEN HUDSON RIVER INTO THE REALM OF MIDGARD...

FOR ODIN!

DEATH TO THE SONS OF FLAME!

THE FORCES OF ASGARD!

WELL MET, THOR!

IT SEEMS WE HAVE COME JUST IN TIME!

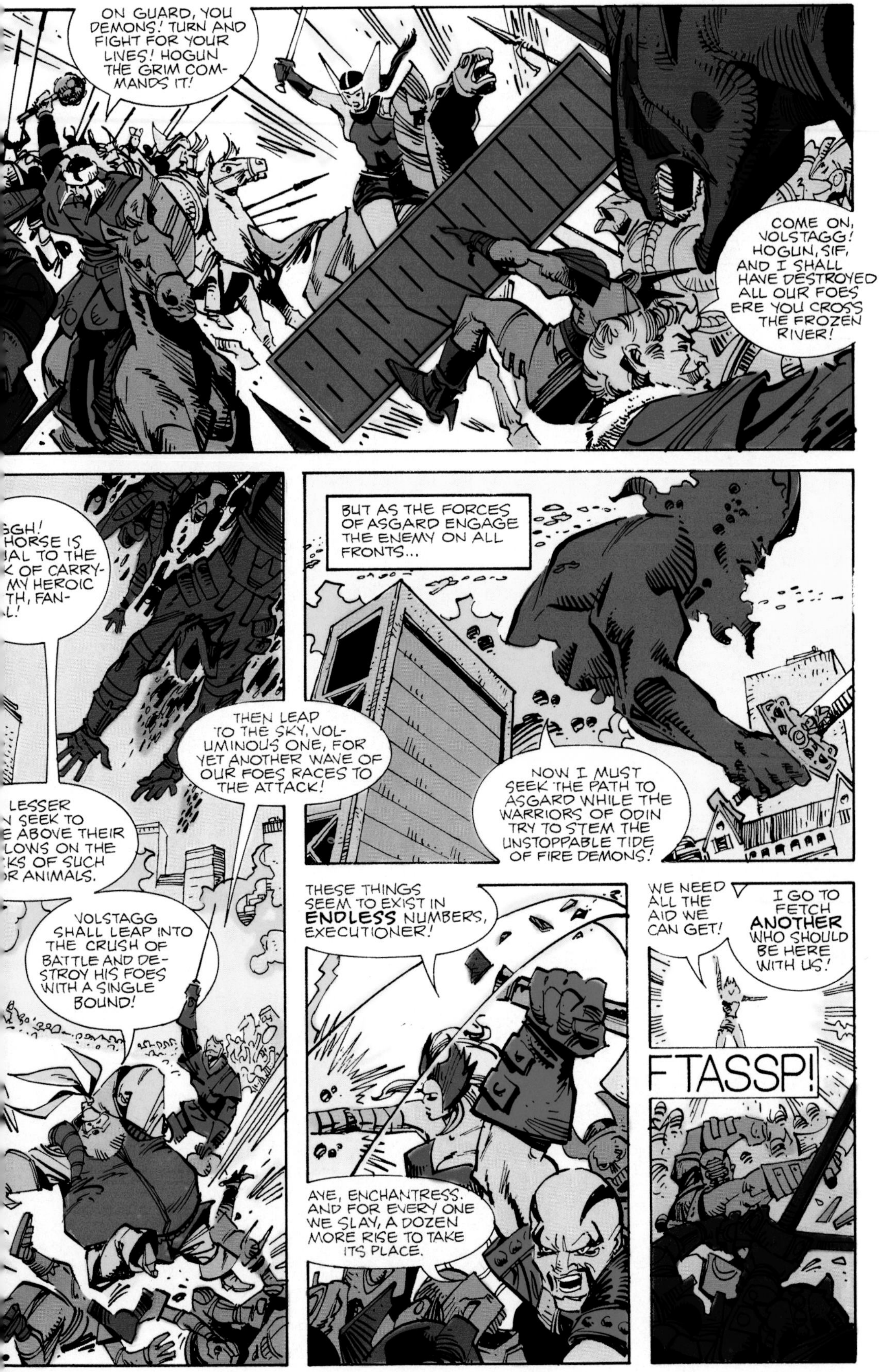
ON GUARD, YOU DEMONS! TURN AND FIGHT FOR YOUR LIVES! HOGUN THE GRIM COMMANDS IT!
COME ON, VOLSTAGG! HOGUN, SIF, AND I SHALL HAVE DESTROYED ALL OUR FOES ERE YOU CROSS THE FROZEN RIVER!
GGH! HORSE IS JAL TO THE K OF CARRY- MY HEROIC TH, FAN- L!
THEN LEAP TO THE SKY, VOLUMINOUS ONE, FOR YET ANOTHER WAVE OF OUR FOES RACES TO THE ATTACK!
LESSER N SEEK TO E ABOVE THEIR LOWS ON THE KS OF SUCH OR ANIMALS.
VOLSTAGG SHALL LEAP INTO THE CRUSH OF BATTLE AND DESTROY HIS FOES WITH A SINGLE BOUND!
BUT AS THE FORCES OF ASGARD ENGAGE THE ENEMY ON ALL FRONTS...
NOW I MUST SEEK THE PATH TO ASGARD WHILE THE WARRIORS OF ODIN TRY TO STEM THE UNSTOPPABLE TIDE OF FIRE DEMONS!
THESE THINGS SEEM TO EXIST IN ENDLESS NUMBERS, EXECUTIONER!
AYE, ENCHANTRESS. AND FOR EVERY ONE WE SLAY, A DOZEN MORE RISE TO TAKE ITS PLACE.
WE NEED ALL THE AID WE CAN GET!
I GO TO FETCH ANOTHER WHO SHOULD BE HERE WITH US!
FTASSP!

CENTRAL PARK, COVERED WITH ICE AND SNOW BUT NORTH OF THE IMMEDIATE LINE OF BATTLE...

...AND IN A PENTHOUSE OVERLOOKING THE FROZEN LAKE...

THAT FLASH OF LIGHT! AN ASGARDIAN HAS ENTERED THIS PLACE!

IT'S...

YES, DEAR SISTER! THE ENCHANTRESS! COME TO CALL YOU TO BATTLE!

THOUGH WE HAVE NO LOVE LOST BETWEEN US, LORELEI, THE VERY EXISTENCE OF THE NINE WORLDS IS THREATENED BY THE FORCES OF FIRE AND EVERY HELP IS NEEDED!

I HAVE CO... TO ASK YOU TO PUT ASID... OUR FEUD... AND JOIN WITH US...

DON'T BE SILLY, AMORA.

WHAT?

DO YOU THINK THAT I DO NOT KNOW WHAT YOU ARE ABOUT?

LONG HAVE YOU SOUGHT TO WIN THE HANDSOME THOR...

...AND NOW THAT I HAVE MADE HIM MINE FOREVER WITH THE ENCHANTED MEAD, YOU SEEK TO HAVE ME SLAIN AND TAKE FOR YOURSELF WHAT YOU COULD NEVER WIN.

GO, AND LEAVE ME TO MY VICTORY. THOR IS MINE.

HOW SIMPLE YOU ARE, LOR... LEI. TO BA... ANCE A M... INFATUATI... AGAINST TH... DESTRUCTI... OF ALL THA... IS.

BUT MARK M... WORDS. SHOULD... WIN THE BATTLE, I... SEE TO IT THAT AL... YOUR CONTRIVAN... ARE UNDONE...

AND COUNT YOURSELF LUCKY THAT I CAN SPARE NO ENERGY TO DEAL WITH YOU AS YOU DESERVE!

FTAASSP!

I WONDER IF THAT WAS WISE.

BUT NO, THE GOLDEN MEAD HAS MADE THOR MINE FOREVER. THE MORE HE TASTES, THE TIGHTER HE WILL BE BOUND TO ME.

AND NOTHING MY SISTER CAN DO WILL CHANGE THAT!

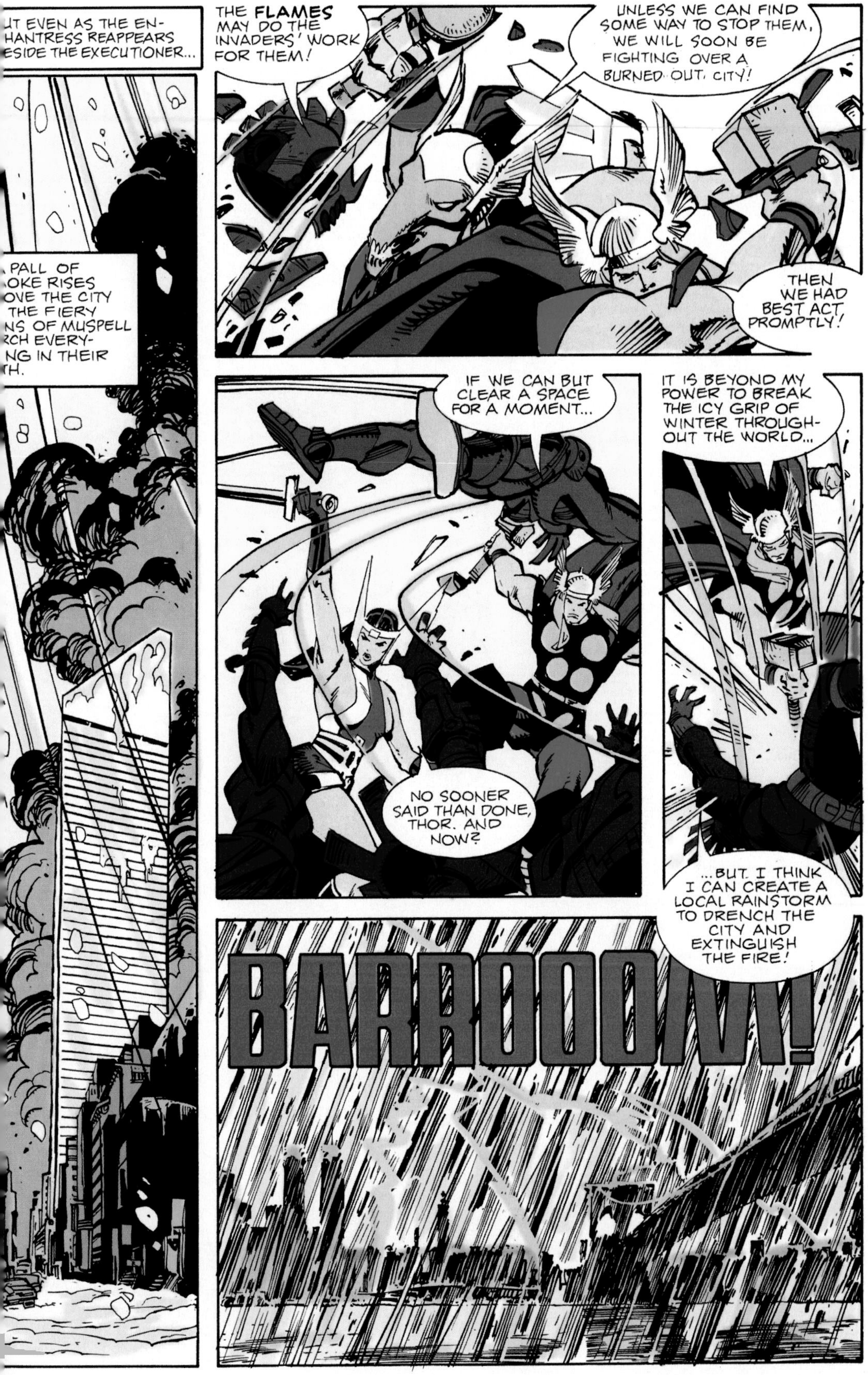
UT EVEN AS THE EN-HANTRESS REAPPEARS ESIDE THE EXECUTIONER...
THE FLAMES MAY DO THE INVADERS' WORK FOR THEM!
UNLESS WE CAN FIND SOME WAY TO STOP THEM, WE WILL SOON BE FIGHTING OVER A BURNED-OUT CITY!
THEN WE HAD BEST ACT PROMPTLY!
PALL OF OKE RISES OVE THE CITY THE FIERY NS OF MUSPELL RCH EVERY-NG IN THEIR TH.
IF WE CAN BUT CLEAR A SPACE FOR A MOMENT...
NO SOONER SAID THAN DONE, THOR. AND NOW?
IT IS BEYOND MY POWER TO BREAK THE ICY GRIP OF WINTER THROUGH-OUT THE WORLD...
...BUT I THINK I CAN CREATE A LOCAL RAINSTORM TO DRENCH THE CITY AND EXTINGUISH THE FIRE!
BARROOOM!

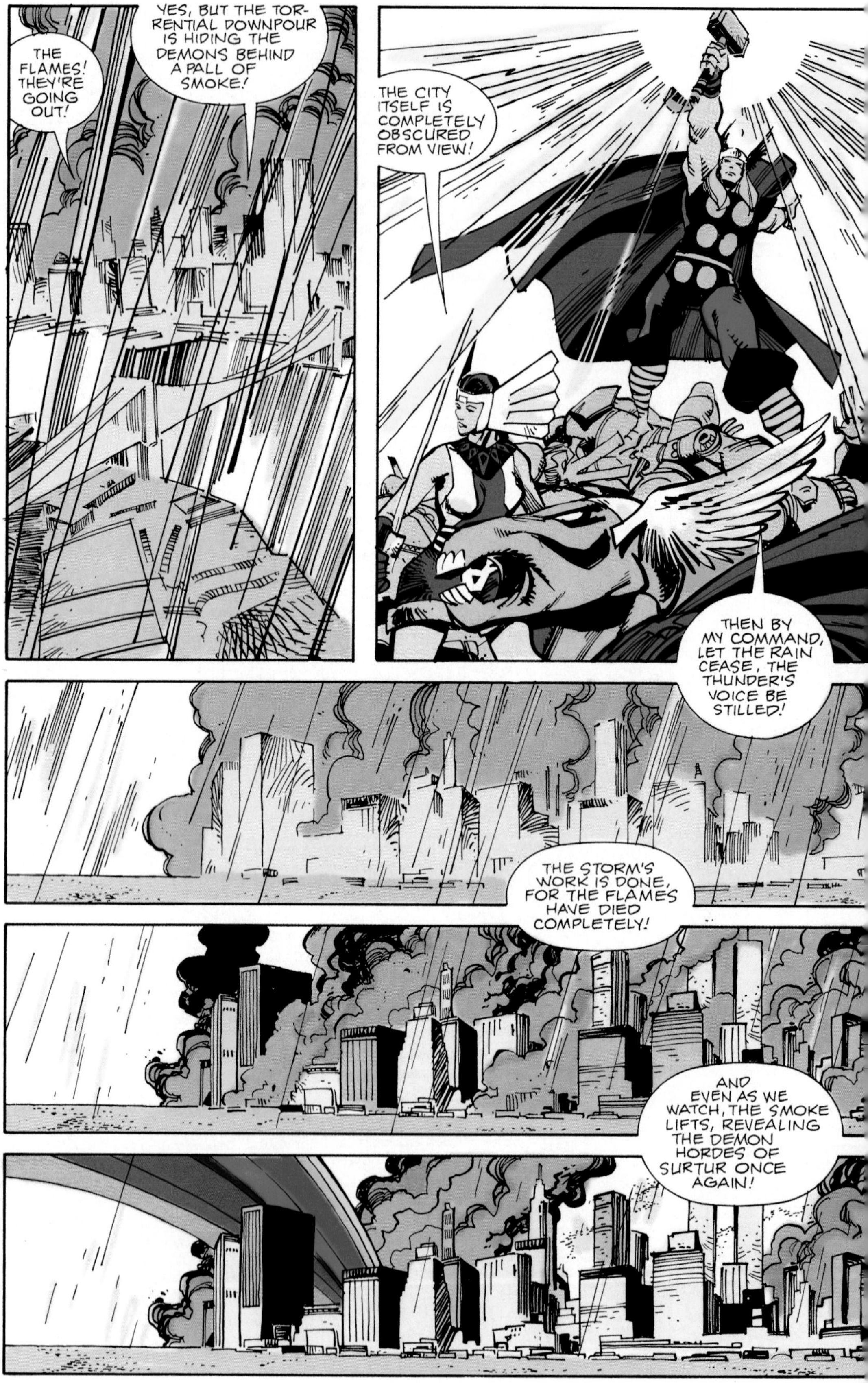
THE FLAMES! THEY'RE GOING OUT!
YES, BUT THE TOR-RENTIAL DOWNPOUR IS HIDING THE DEMONS BEHIND A PALL OF SMOKE!
THE CITY ITSELF IS COMPLETELY OBSCURED FROM VIEW!
THEN BY MY COMMAND, LET THE RAIN CEASE, THE THUNDER'S VOICE BE STILLED!
THE STORM'S WORK IS DONE, FOR THE FLAMES HAVE DIED COMPLETELY!
AND EVEN AS WE WATCH, THE SMOKE LIFTS, REVEALING THE DEMON HORDES OF SURTUR ONCE AGAIN!

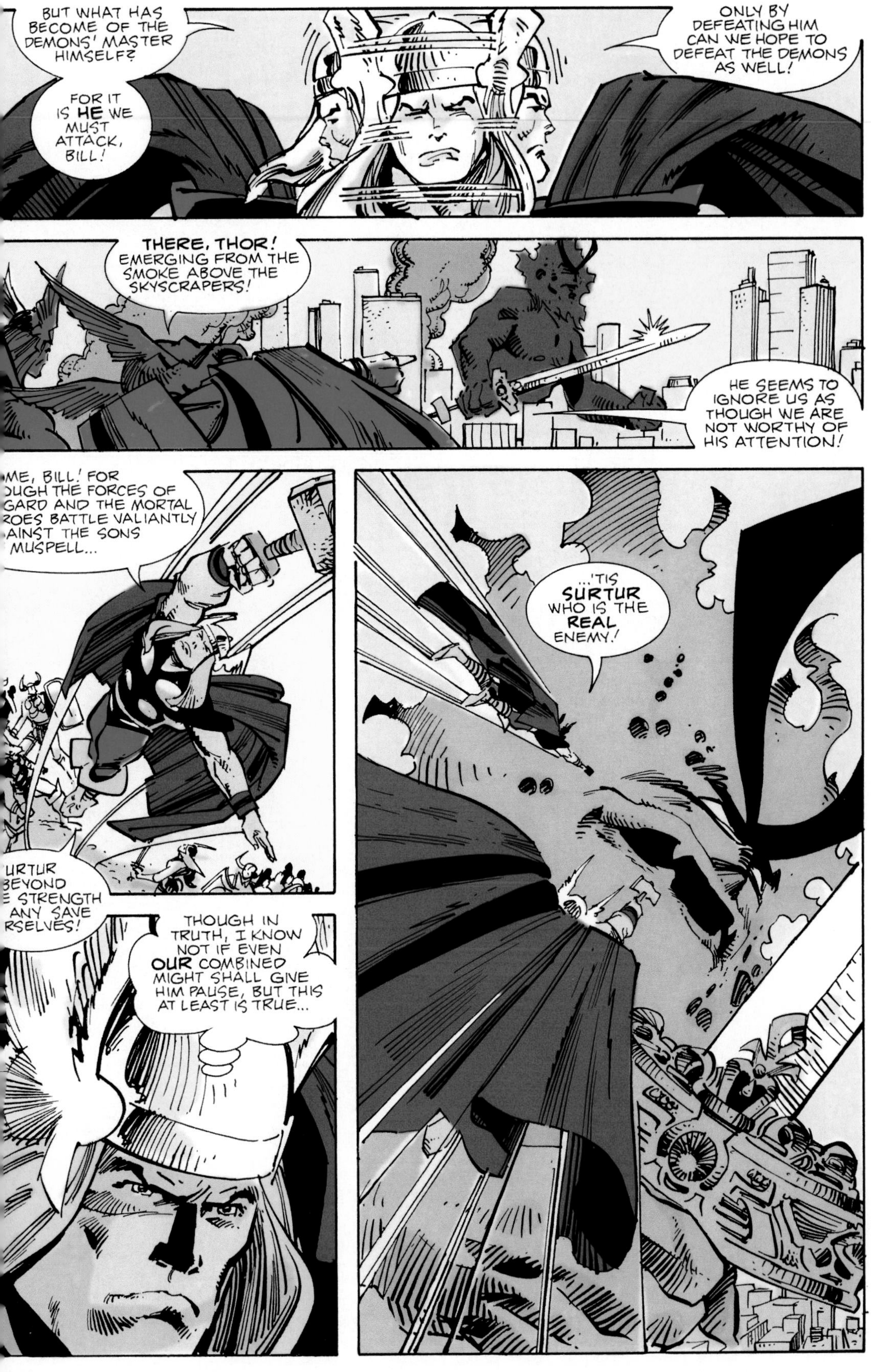
BUT WHAT HAS BECOME OF THE DEMONS' MASTER HIMSELF?
FOR IT IS HE WE MUST ATTACK, BILL!
ONLY BY DEFEATING HIM CAN WE HOPE TO DEFEAT THE DEMONS AS WELL!
THERE, THOR! EMERGING FROM THE SMOKE ABOVE THE SKYSCRAPERS!
HE SEEMS TO IGNORE US AS THOUGH WE ARE NOT WORTHY OF HIS ATTENTION!
ME, BILL! FOR OUGH THE FORCES OF GARD AND THE MORTAL ROES BATTLE VALIANTLY AINST THE SONS MUSPELL...
...'TIS SURTUR WHO IS THE REAL ENEMY!
URTUR BEYOND STRENGTH ANY SAVE RSELVES!
THOUGH IN TRUTH, I KNOW NOT IF EVEN OUR COMBINED MIGHT SHALL GIVE HIM PAUSE, BUT THIS AT LEAST IS TRUE...

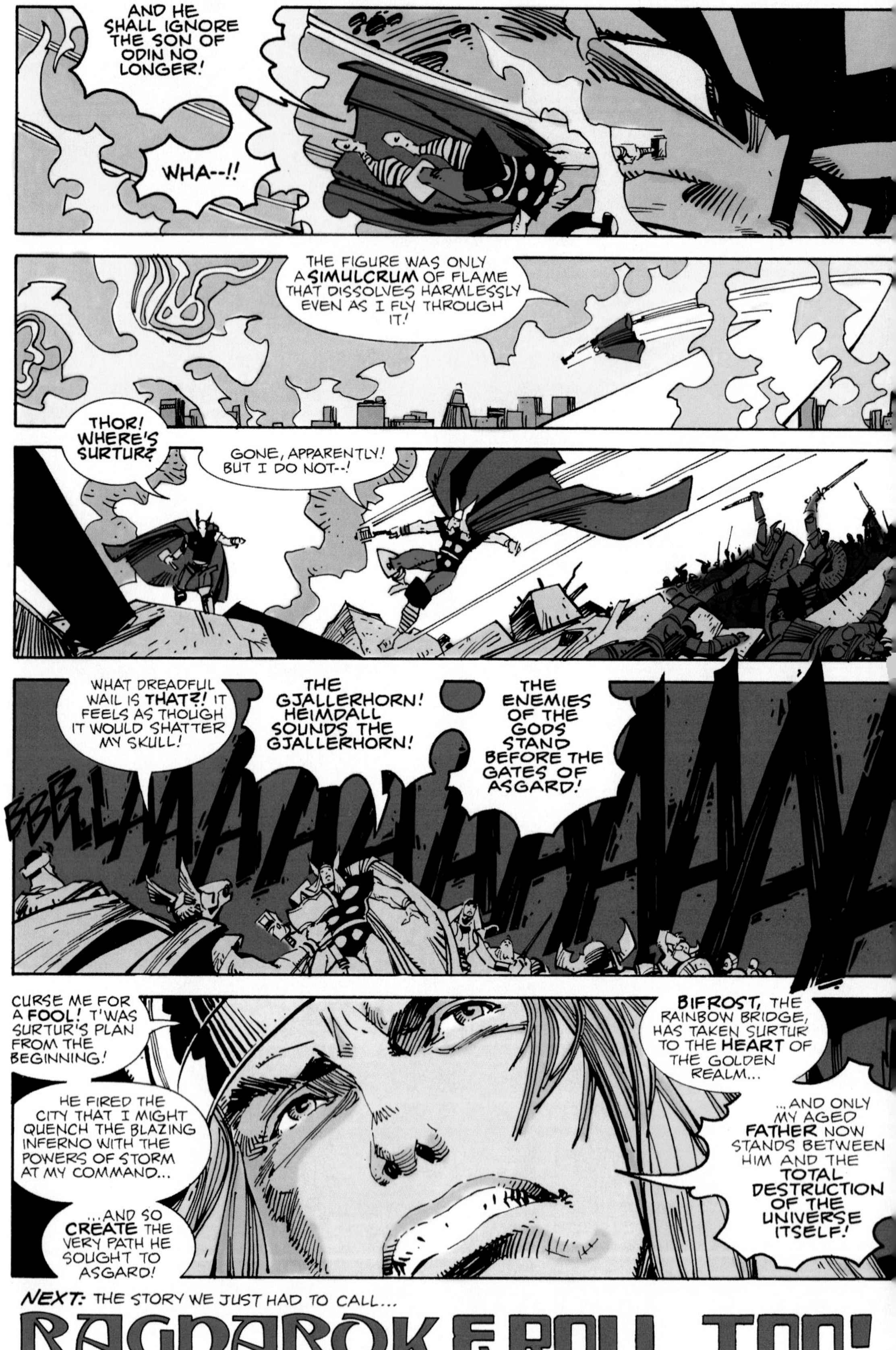
AND HE SHALL IGNORE THE SON OF ODIN NO LONGER!
WHA--!!
THE FIGURE WAS ONLY A SIMULCRUM OF FLAME THAT DISSOLVES HARMLESSLY EVEN AS I FLY THROUGH IT!
THOR! WHERE'S SURTUR?
GONE, APPARENTLY! BUT I DO NOT--!
WHAT DREADFUL WAIL IS THAT?! IT FEELS AS THOUGH IT WOULD SHATTER MY SKULL!
THE GJALLERHORN! HEIMDALL SOUNDS THE GJALLERHORN!
THE ENEMIES OF THE GODS STAND BEFORE THE GATES OF ASGARD!
BBBRLAAAHHHHHHAAAAAAAAAAA
CURSE ME FOR A FOOL! T'WAS SURTUR'S PLAN FROM THE BEGINNING!
HE FIRED THE CITY THAT I MIGHT QUENCH THE BLAZING INFERNO WITH THE POWERS OF STORM AT MY COMMAND...
...AND SO CREATE THE VERY PATH HE SOUGHT TO ASGARD!
BIFROST, THE RAINBOW BRIDGE, HAS TAKEN SURTUR TO THE HEART OF THE GOLDEN REALM...
...AND ONLY MY AGED FATHER NOW STANDS BETWEEN HIM AND THE TOTAL DESTRUCTION OF THE UNIVERSE ITSELF!

NEXT: THE STORY WE JUST HAD TO CALL...

RAGNAROK & ROLL, TOO!

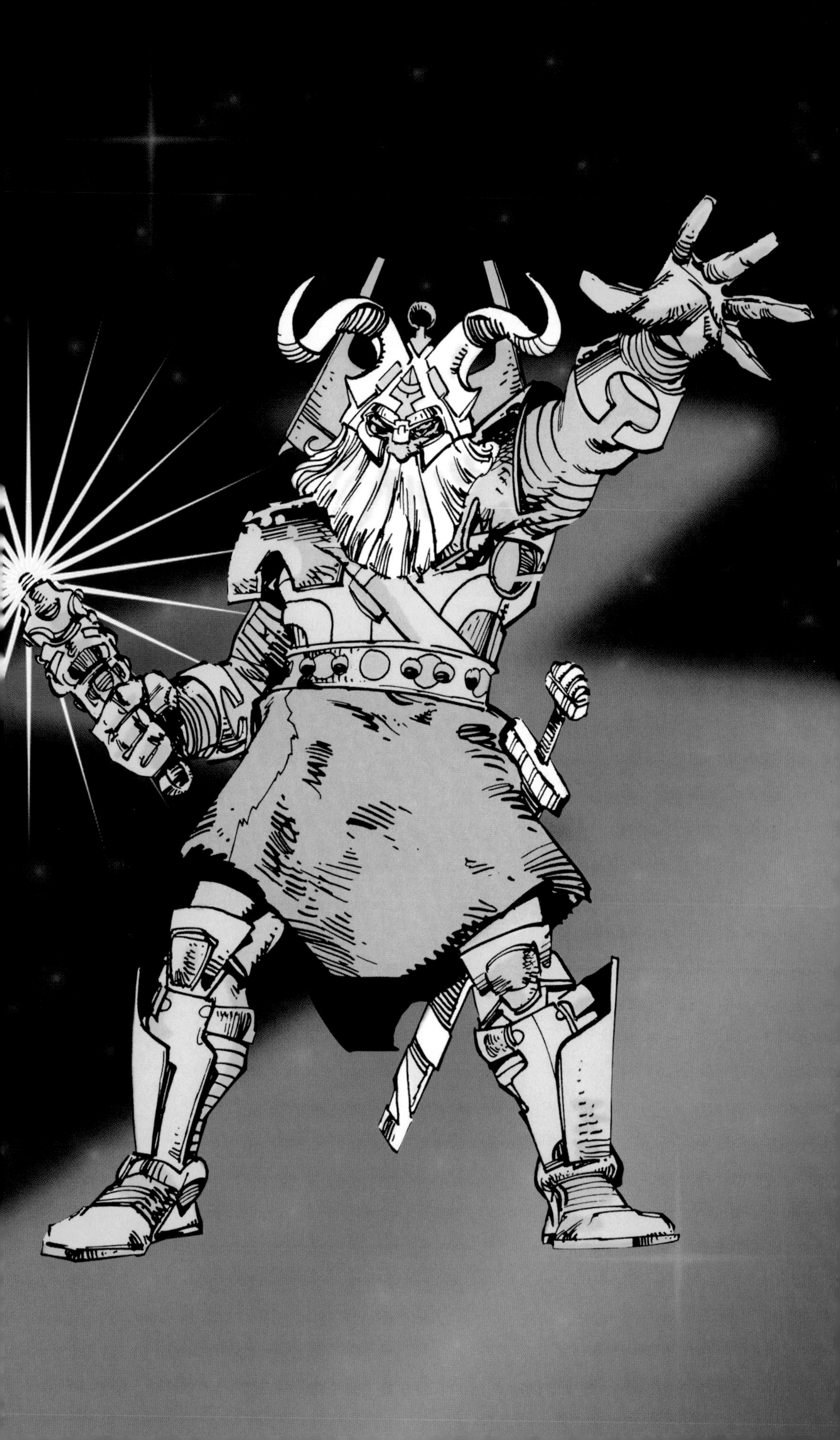

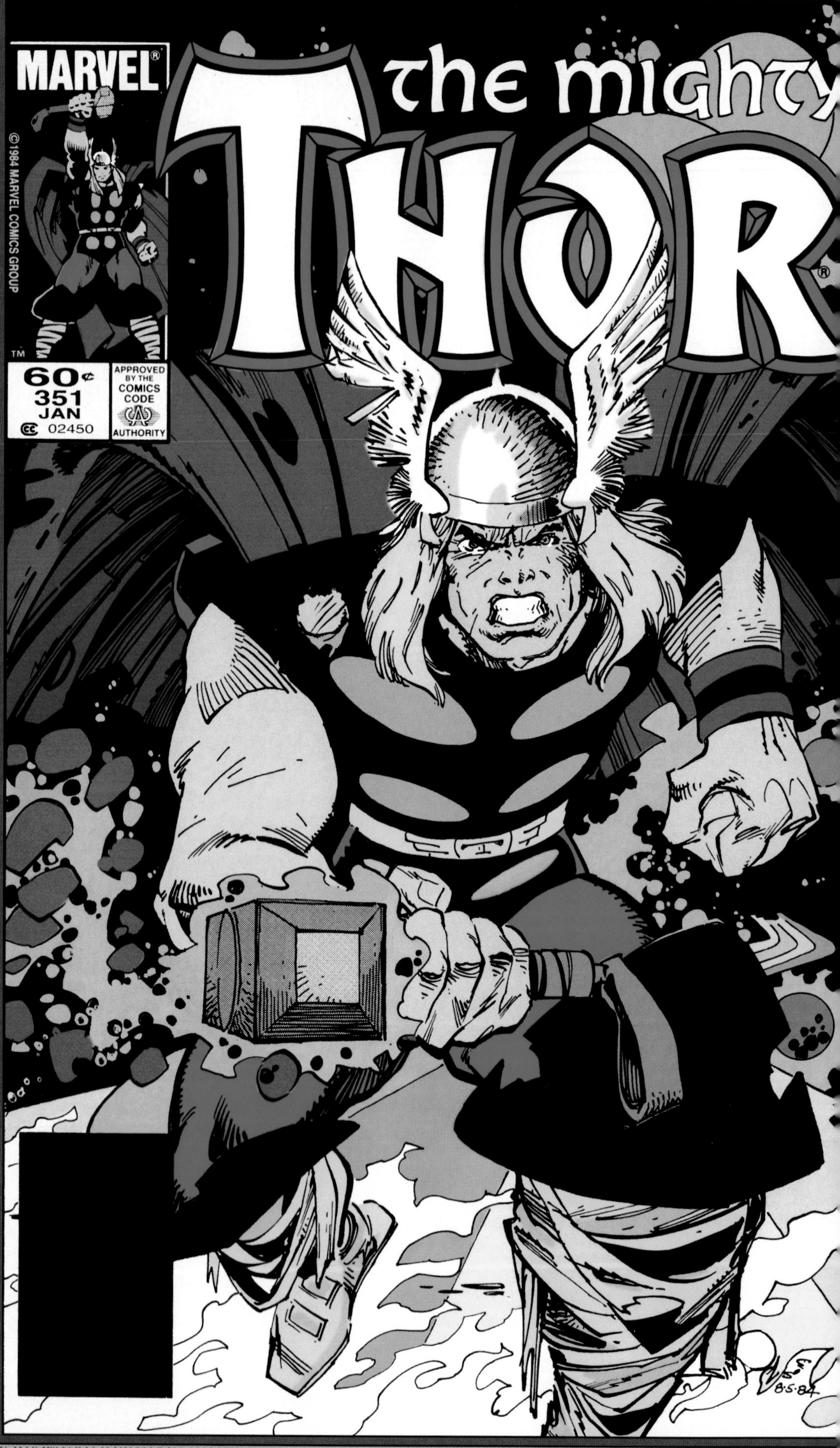
MARVEL®
©1984 MARVEL COMICS GROUP
TM
the mighty
THOR®
60¢
351
JAN
02450
APPROVED BY THE COMICS CODE AUTHORITY
8·5·84

AN LEE RESENTS: RAGNAROK & ROLL, TOO!

ANCIENT AND POWERFUL FIRE DEMON, SURTUR, HAS GONE TO ASGARD TO CONFRONT ODIN HIMSELF
MASTERY OF THE FABLED ETERNAL FLAME!

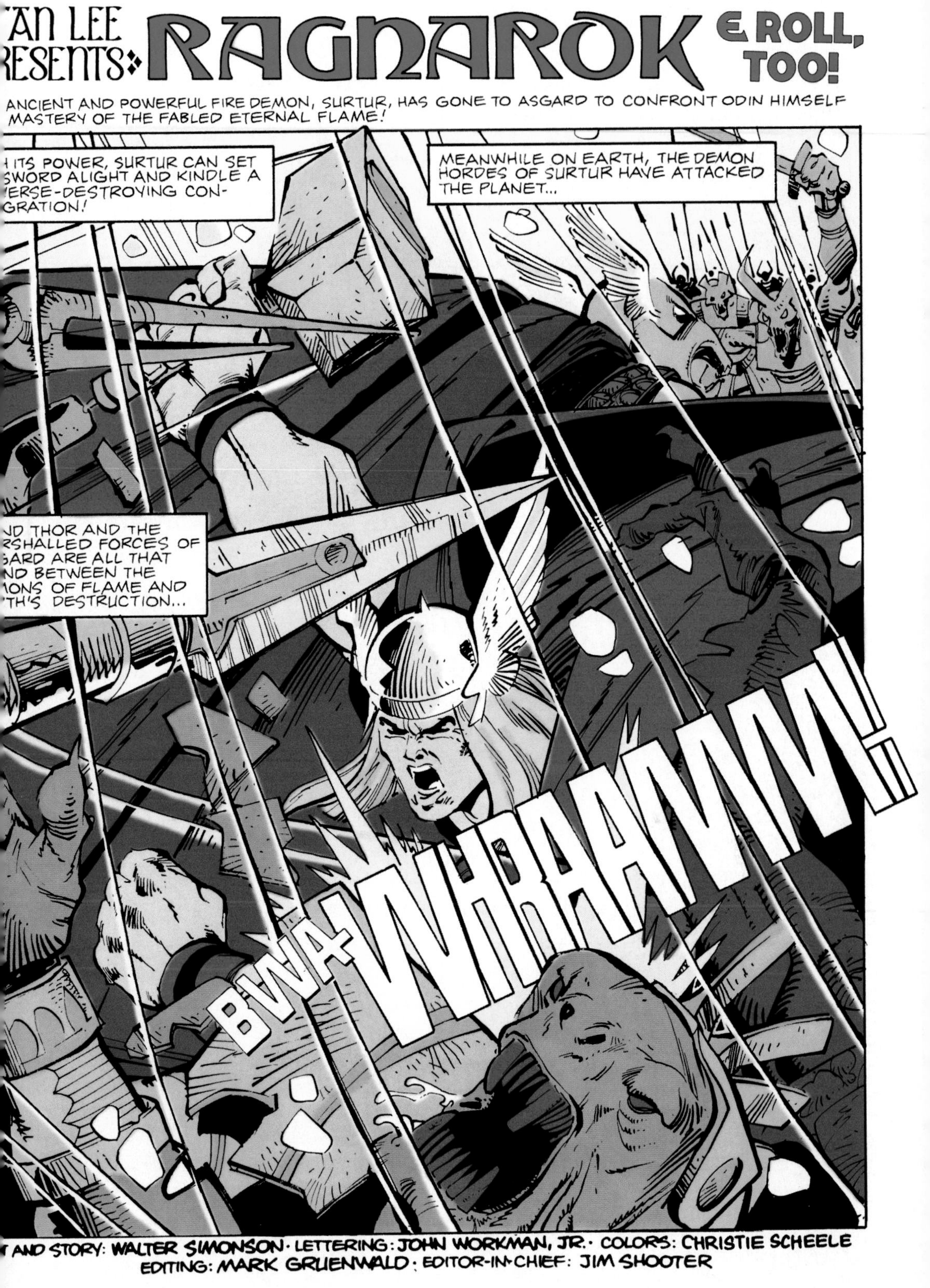
H ITS POWER, SURTUR CAN SET SWORD ALIGHT AND KINDLE A 'ERSE-DESTROYING CON- GRATION!
MEANWHILE ON EARTH, THE DEMON HORDES OF SURTUR HAVE ATTACKED THE PLANET...
ND THOR AND THE RSHALLED FORCES OF GARD ARE ALL THAT ND BETWEEN THE MONS OF FLAME AND 'TH'S DESTRUCTION...
BWA
WHRAAMM!!

T AND STORY: WALTER SIMONSON · LETTERING: JOHN WORKMAN, JR. · COLORS: CHRISTIE SCHEELE
EDITING: MARK GRUENWALD · EDITOR-IN-CHIEF: JIM SHOOTER

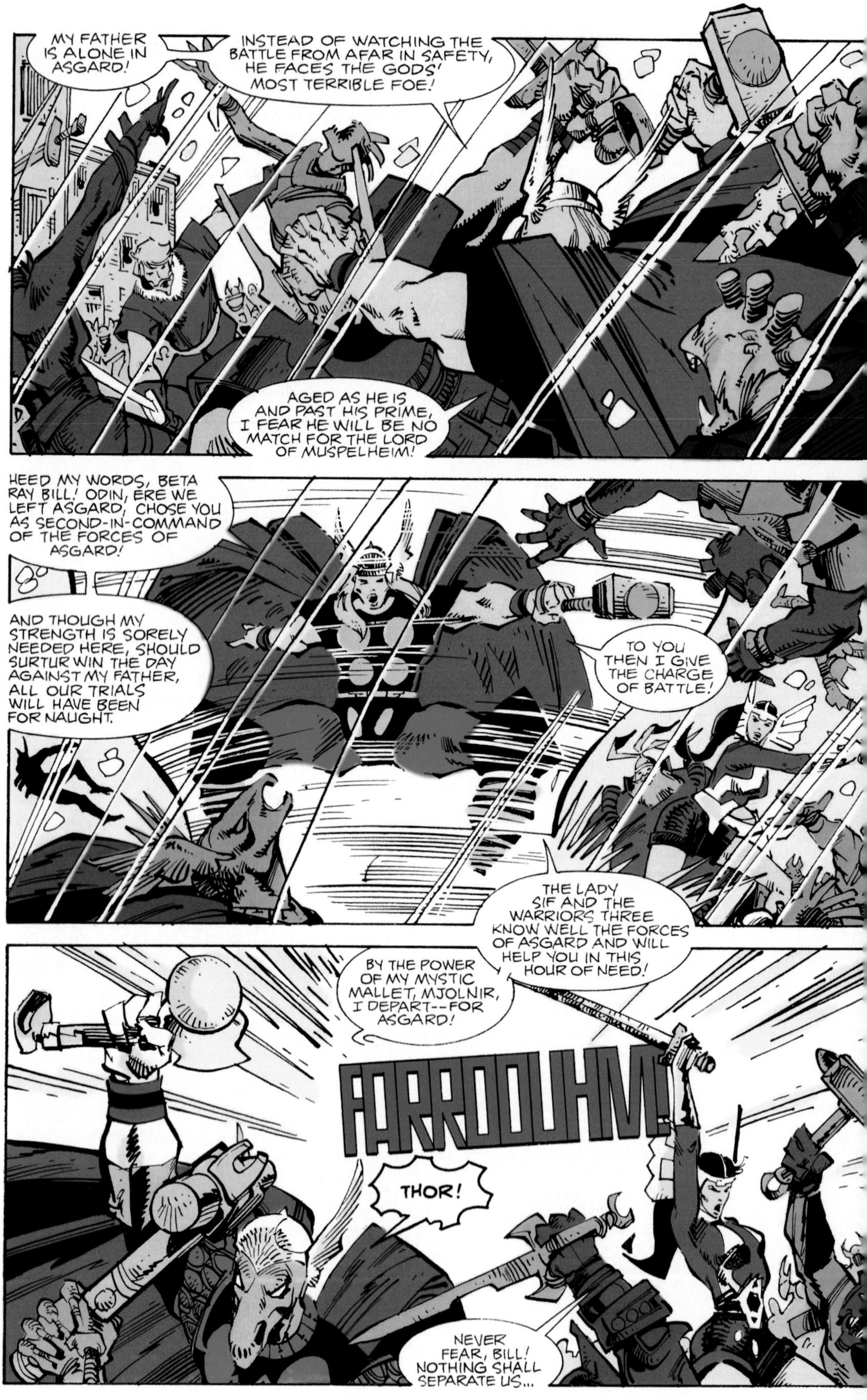
MY FATHER IS ALONE IN ASGARD!
INSTEAD OF WATCHING THE BATTLE FROM AFAR IN SAFETY, HE FACES THE GODS' MOST TERRIBLE FOE!
AGED AS HE IS AND PAST HIS PRIME, I FEAR HE WILL BE NO MATCH FOR THE LORD OF MUSPELHEIM!
HEED MY WORDS, BETA RAY BILL! ODIN, ERE WE LEFT ASGARD, CHOSE YOU AS SECOND-IN-COMMAND OF THE FORCES OF ASGARD!
AND THOUGH MY STRENGTH IS SORELY NEEDED HERE, SHOULD SURTUR WIN THE DAY AGAINST MY FATHER, ALL OUR TRIALS WILL HAVE BEEN FOR NAUGHT.
TO YOU THEN I GIVE THE CHARGE OF BATTLE!
THE LADY SIF AND THE WARRIORS THREE KNOW WELL THE FORCES OF ASGARD AND WILL HELP YOU IN THIS HOUR OF NEED!
BY THE POWER OF MY MYSTIC MALLET, MJOLNIR, I DEPART--FOR ASGARD!
FARROOUHM!
THOR!
NEVER FEAR, BILL! NOTHING SHALL SEPARATE US...

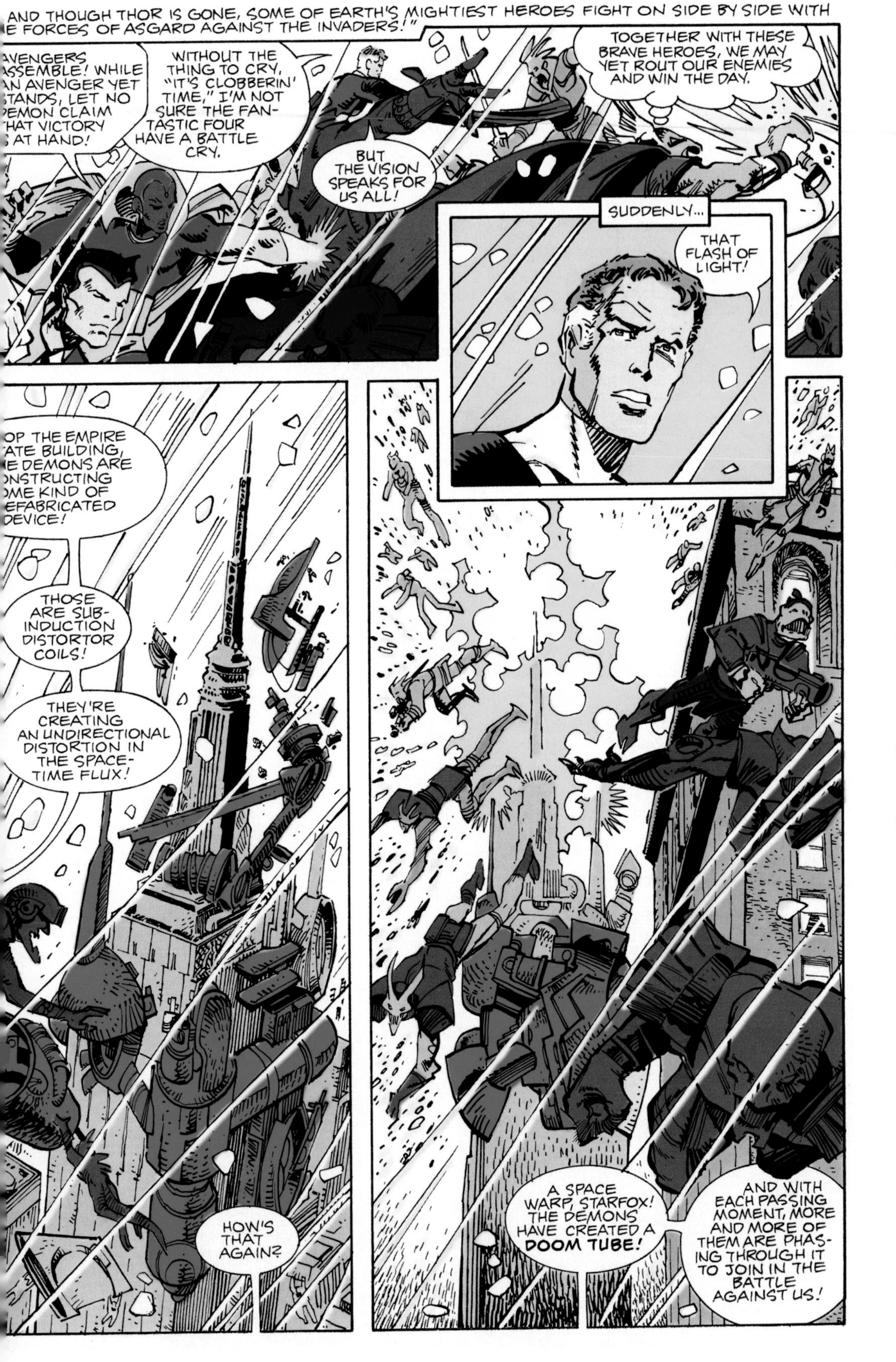
AND THOUGH THOR IS GONE, SOME OF EARTH'S MIGHTIEST HEROES FIGHT ON SIDE BY SIDE WITH E FORCES OF ASGARD AGAINST THE INVADERS!"
AVENGERS ASSEMBLE! WHILE AN AVENGER YET STANDS, LET NO DEMON CLAIM THAT VICTORY IS AT HAND!
WITHOUT THE THING TO CRY, "IT'S CLOBBERIN' TIME," I'M NOT SURE THE FANTASTIC FOUR HAVE A BATTLE CRY.
BUT THE VISION SPEAKS FOR US ALL!
TOGETHER WITH THESE BRAVE HEROES, WE MAY YET ROUT OUR ENEMIES AND WIN THE DAY.
SUDDENLY...
THAT FLASH OF LIGHT!
OP THE EMPIRE TATE BUILDING, E DEMONS ARE ONSTRUCTING OME KIND OF EFABRICATED DEVICE!
THOSE ARE SUB-INDUCTION DISTORTOR COILS!
THEY'RE CREATING AN UNDIRECTIONAL DISTORTION IN THE SPACE-TIME FLUX!
HOW'S THAT AGAIN?
A SPACE WARP, STARFOX! THE DEMONS HAVE CREATED A DOOM TUBE!
AND WITH EACH PASSING MOMENT, MORE AND MORE OF THEM ARE PHASING THROUGH IT TO JOIN IN THE BATTLE AGAINST US!

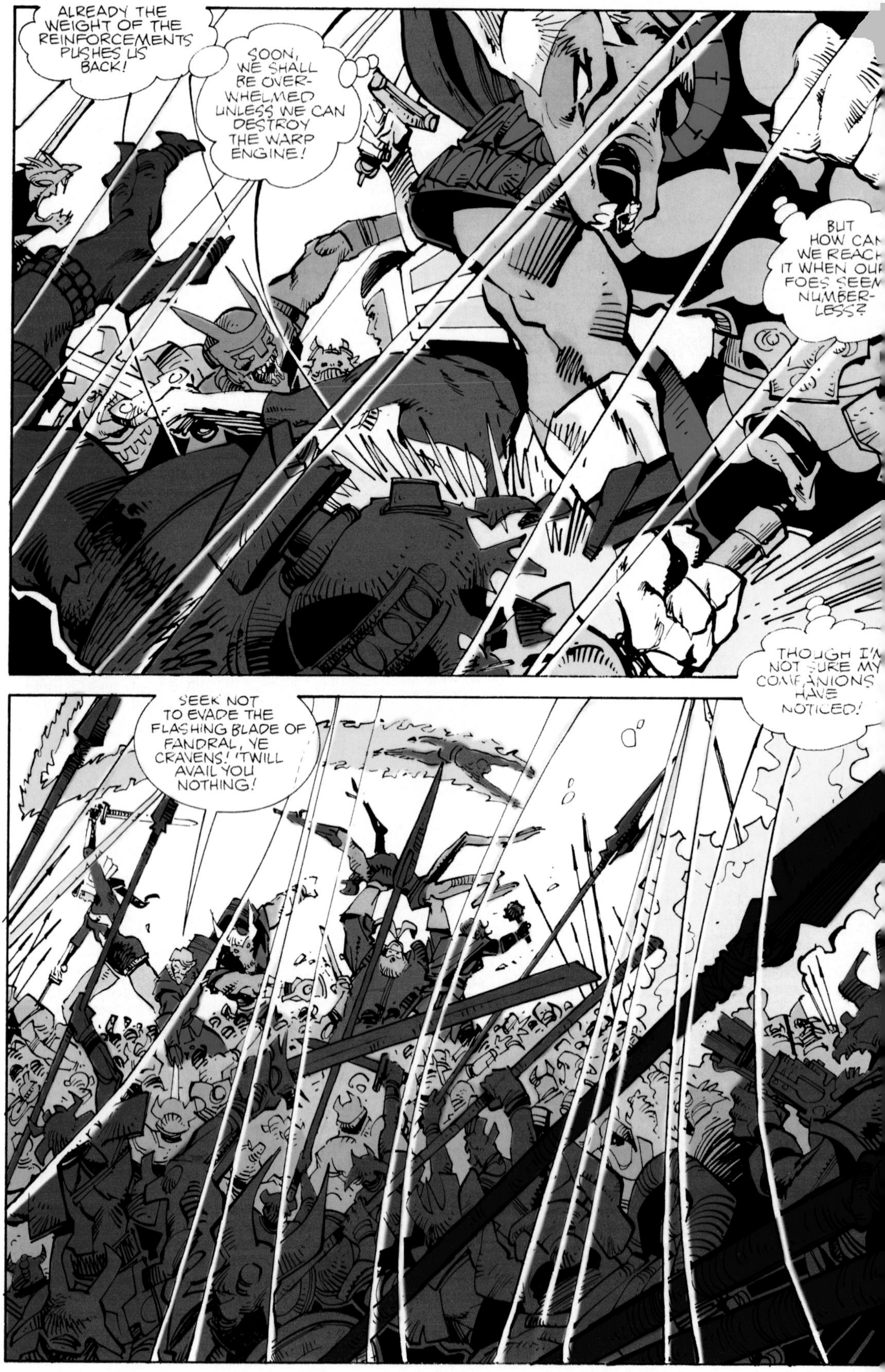
ALREADY THE WEIGHT OF THE REINFORCEMENTS PUSHES US BACK!
SOON, WE SHALL BE OVER-WHELMED UNLESS WE CAN DESTROY THE WARP ENGINE!
BUT HOW CAN WE REACH IT WHEN OUR FOES SEEM NUMBER-LESS?
THOUGH I'M NOT SURE MY COMPANIONS HAVE NOTICED!
SEEK NOT TO EVADE THE FLASHING BLADE OF FANDRAL, YE CRAVENS! 'TWILL AVAIL YOU NOTHING!

MEANWHILE, IN THE LAND OF THE NORN QUEEN...

ODIN HAS CHOSEN HIS AMBASSADOR WELL, NOBLE BALDER.

SWEAR TO BE MINE FOREVER AND I WILL SEND ALL THE AID AT MY COMMAND TO HELP THE HOSTS OF ASGARD.

REFUSE, AND ASGARD WILL SURELY FALL BEFORE THE FORCES OF SURTUR.

HAHAHA
HAHAHA
HA
HO

OH, KARNILLA, WILL YOU NEVER TIRE OF SUCH GAMES?

THE VERY UNIVERSE TEETERS ON THE BRINK OF DISASTER...

...AND YET YOU PRETEND THAT ONCE AGAIN 'TIS TIME TO TRY TO COLLAR BALDER AS THOUGH HE WERE A LAPDOG!

FIE!

I AM NO GAMES-PLAYER THAT I SHOULD MATCH MY LIFE AGAINST THE LIVES OF BILLIONS.

NOR ARE YOU.

THE WOMAN I KNOW YOU TO BE.

BUT THOU THE WOMAN THAT YOU ARE, NOT THE SPOILED CHILD THAT YOU PRETEND.

THE BALDER BEFORE YOU IS NO LONGER THE GOD YOU ONCE KNEW.

BUT YOU SHALL KNOW ME, MADAM.

INDEED YOU SHALL.

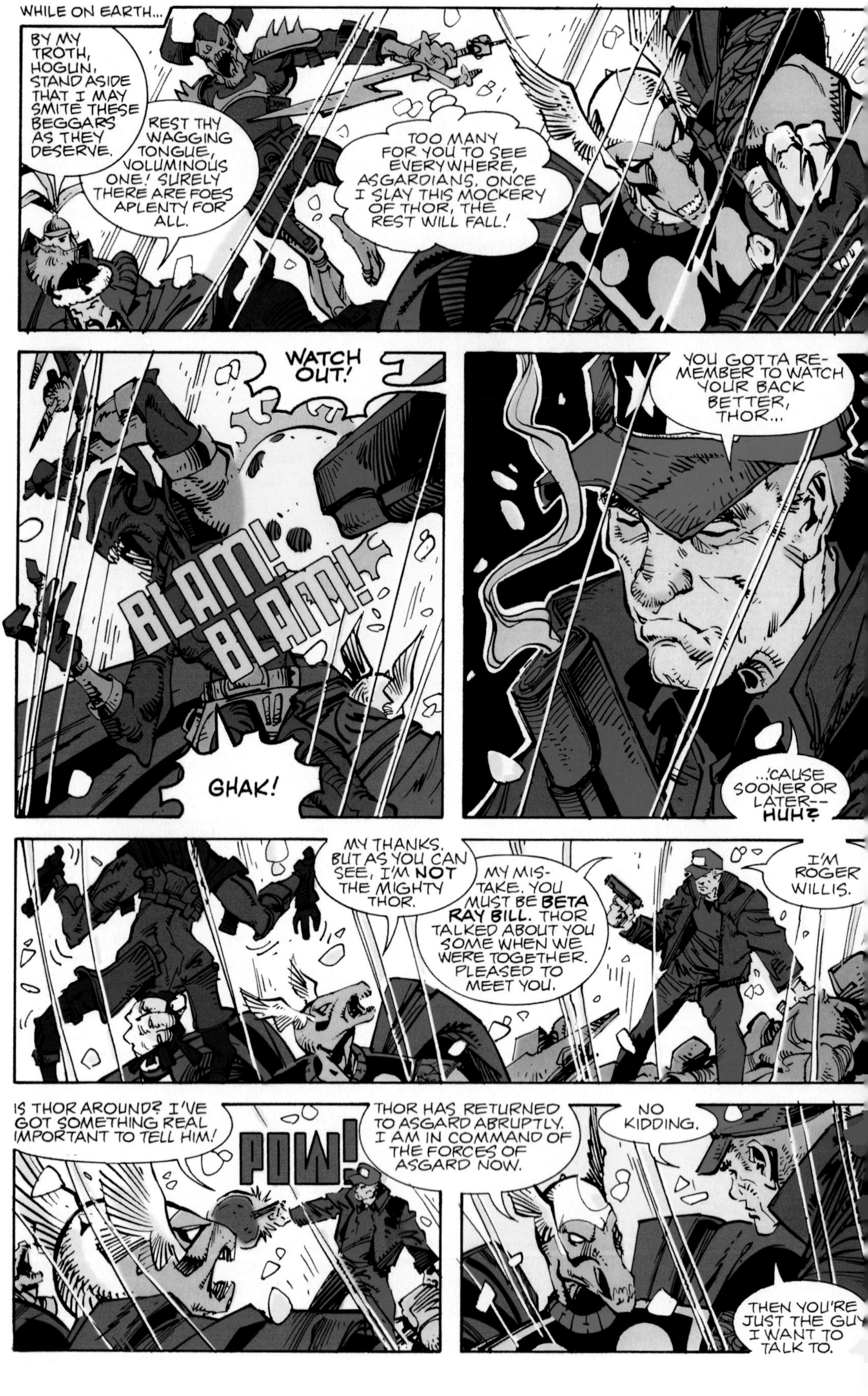
WHILE ON EARTH...
BY MY TROTH, HOGUN, STAND ASIDE THAT I MAY SMITE THESE BEGGARS AS THEY DESERVE.
REST THY WAGGING TONGUE, VOLUMINOUS ONE! SURELY THERE ARE FOES APLENTY FOR ALL.
TOO MANY FOR YOU TO SEE EVERYWHERE, ASGARDIANS. ONCE I SLAY THIS MOCKERY OF THOR, THE REST WILL FALL!
WATCH OUT!
BLAM! BLAM!
GHAK!
YOU GOTTA REMEMBER TO WATCH YOUR BACK BETTER, THOR...
...'CAUSE SOONER OR LATER-- HUH?
MY THANKS. BUT AS YOU CAN SEE, I'M NOT THE MIGHTY THOR.
MY MISTAKE. YOU MUST BE BETA RAY BILL. THOR TALKED ABOUT YOU SOME WHEN WE WERE TOGETHER. PLEASED TO MEET YOU.
I'M ROGER WILLIS.
IS THOR AROUND? I'VE GOT SOMETHING REAL IMPORTANT TO TELL HIM!
POW!
THOR HAS RETURNED TO ASGARD ABRUPTLY. I AM IN COMMAND OF THE FORCES OF ASGARD NOW.
NO KIDDING.
THEN YOU'RE JUST THE GUY I WANT TO TALK TO.

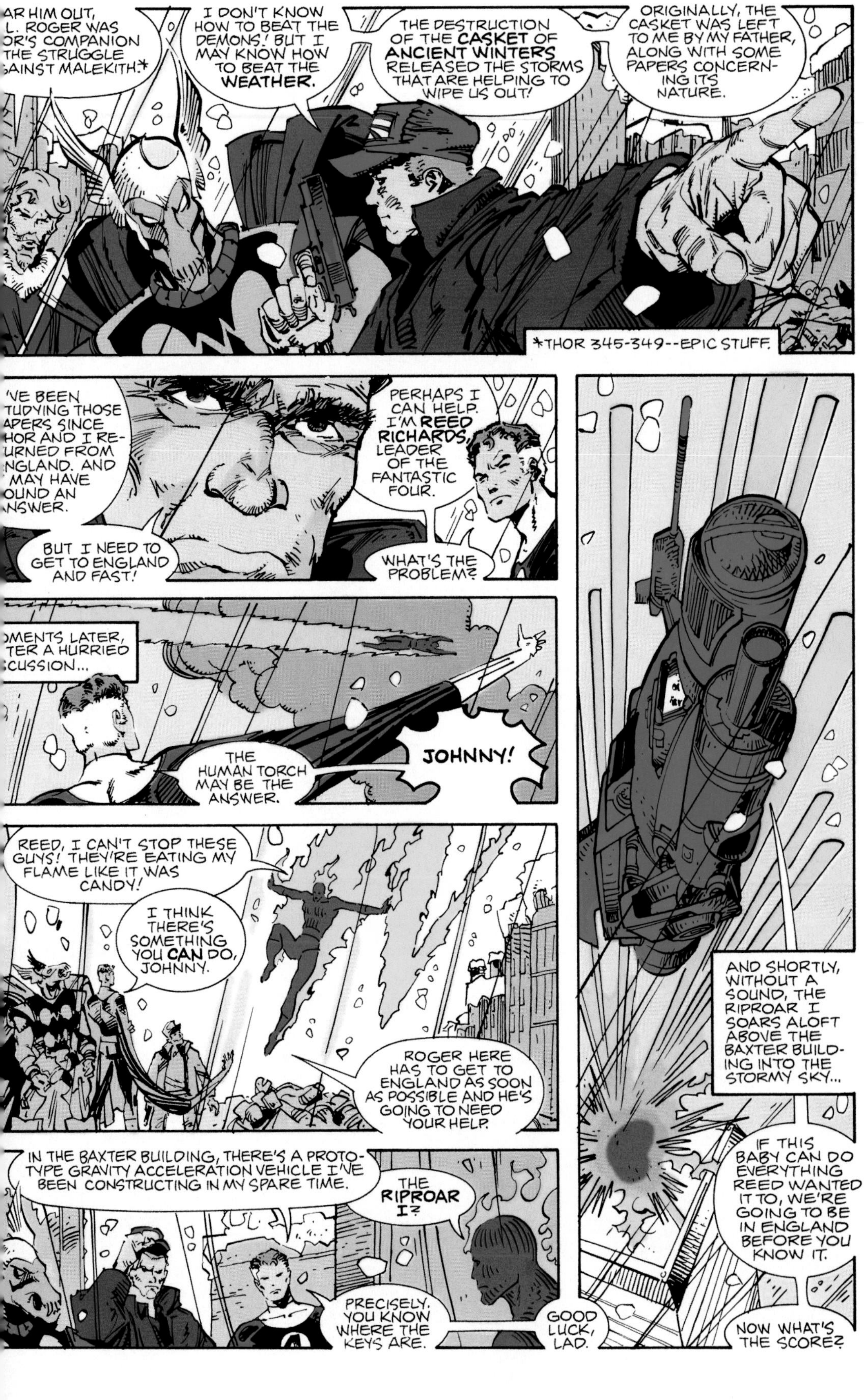
AR HIM OUT, L. ROGER WAS OR'S COMPANION THE STRUGGLE AINST MALEKITH.*
I DON'T KNOW HOW TO BEAT THE DEMONS! BUT I MAY KNOW HOW TO BEAT THE WEATHER.
THE DESTRUCTION OF THE CASKET OF ANCIENT WINTERS RELEASED THE STORMS THAT ARE HELPING TO WIPE US OUT!
ORIGINALLY, THE CASKET WAS LEFT TO ME BY MY FATHER, ALONG WITH SOME PAPERS CONCERNING ITS NATURE.
*THOR 345-349--EPIC STUFF.
'VE BEEN TUDYING THOSE APERS SINCE HOR AND I RE-URNED FROM NGLAND. AND MAY HAVE OUND AN NSWER.
BUT I NEED TO GET TO ENGLAND AND FAST!
PERHAPS I CAN HELP. I'M REED RICHARDS, LEADER OF THE FANTASTIC FOUR.
WHAT'S THE PROBLEM?
OMENTS LATER, TER A HURRIED CUSSION...
THE HUMAN TORCH MAY BE THE ANSWER.
JOHNNY!
REED, I CAN'T STOP THESE GUYS! THEY'RE EATING MY FLAME LIKE IT WAS CANDY!
I THINK THERE'S SOMETHING YOU CAN DO, JOHNNY.
ROGER HERE HAS TO GET TO ENGLAND AS SOON AS POSSIBLE AND HE'S GOING TO NEED YOUR HELP.
IN THE BAXTER BUILDING, THERE'S A PROTOTYPE GRAVITY ACCELERATION VEHICLE I'VE BEEN CONSTRUCTING IN MY SPARE TIME.
THE RIPROAR I?
PRECISELY. YOU KNOW WHERE THE KEYS ARE.
GOOD LUCK, LAD.
AND SHORTLY, WITHOUT A SOUND, THE RIPROAR I SOARS ALOFT ABOVE THE BAXTER BUILDING INTO THE STORMY SKY...
IF THIS BABY CAN DO EVERYTHING REED WANTED IT TO, WE'RE GOING TO BE IN ENGLAND BEFORE YOU KNOW IT.
NOW WHAT'S THE SCORE?

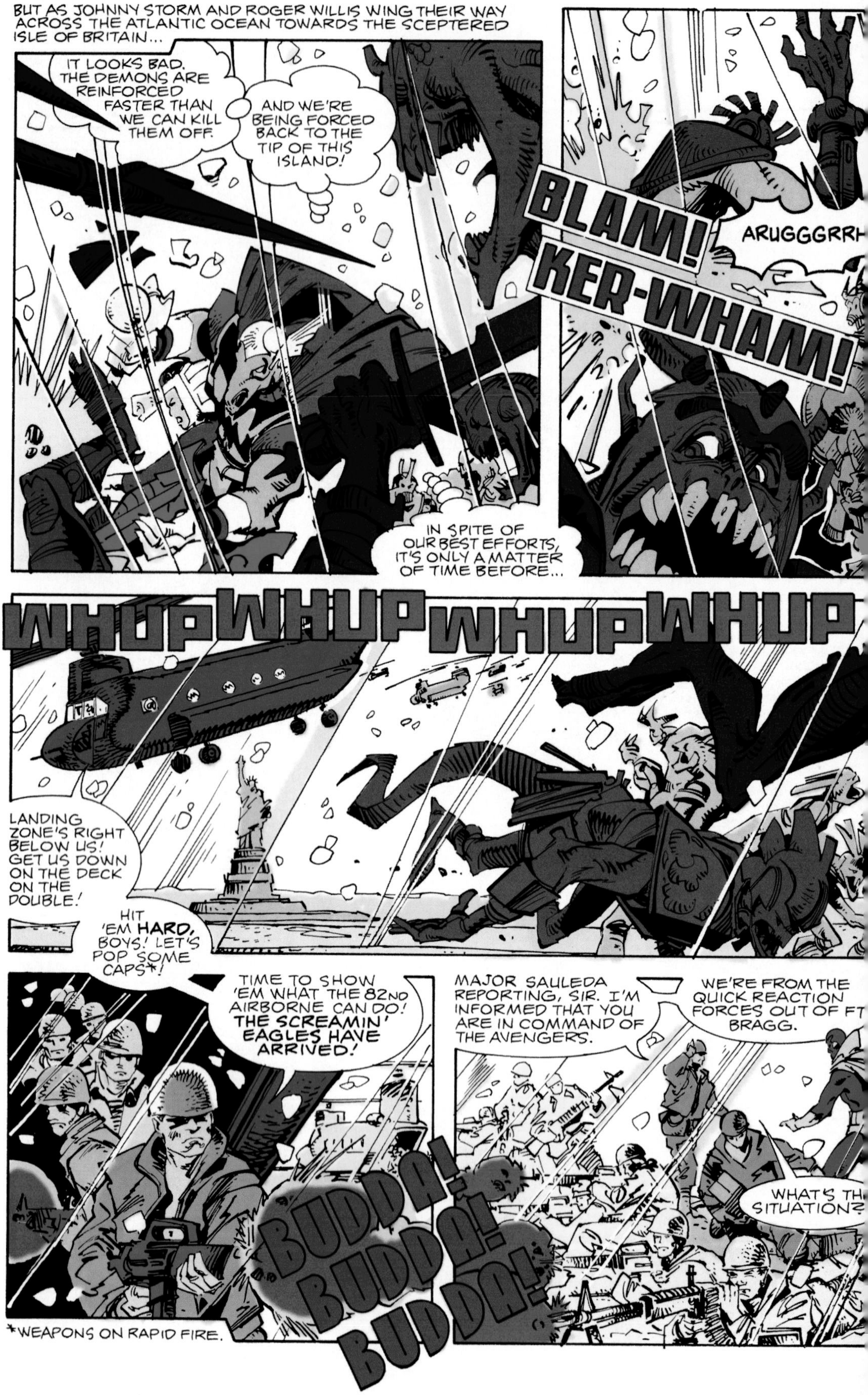
BUT AS JOHNNY STORM AND ROGER WILLIS WING THEIR WAY ACROSS THE ATLANTIC OCEAN TOWARDS THE SCEPTERED ISLE OF BRITAIN...
IT LOOKS BAD. THE DEMONS ARE REINFORCED FASTER THAN WE CAN KILL THEM OFF.
AND WE'RE BEING FORCED BACK TO THE TIP OF THIS ISLAND!
BLAM!
KER-WHAM!
ARUGGGRRH
IN SPITE OF OUR BEST EFFORTS, IT'S ONLY A MATTER OF TIME BEFORE...
WHUP WHUP WHUP WHUP
LANDING ZONE'S RIGHT BELOW US! GET US DOWN ON THE DECK ON THE DOUBLE!
HIT 'EM HARD, BOYS! LET'S POP SOME CAPS*!
TIME TO SHOW 'EM WHAT THE 82ND AIRBORNE CAN DO! THE SCREAMIN' EAGLES HAVE ARRIVED!
BUDDA! BUDDA! BUDDA!
*WEAPONS ON RAPID FIRE.
MAJOR SAULEDA REPORTING, SIR. I'M INFORMED THAT YOU ARE IN COMMAND OF THE AVENGERS.
WE'RE FROM THE QUICK REACTION FORCES OUT OF FT BRAGG.
WHAT'S TH SITUATION?

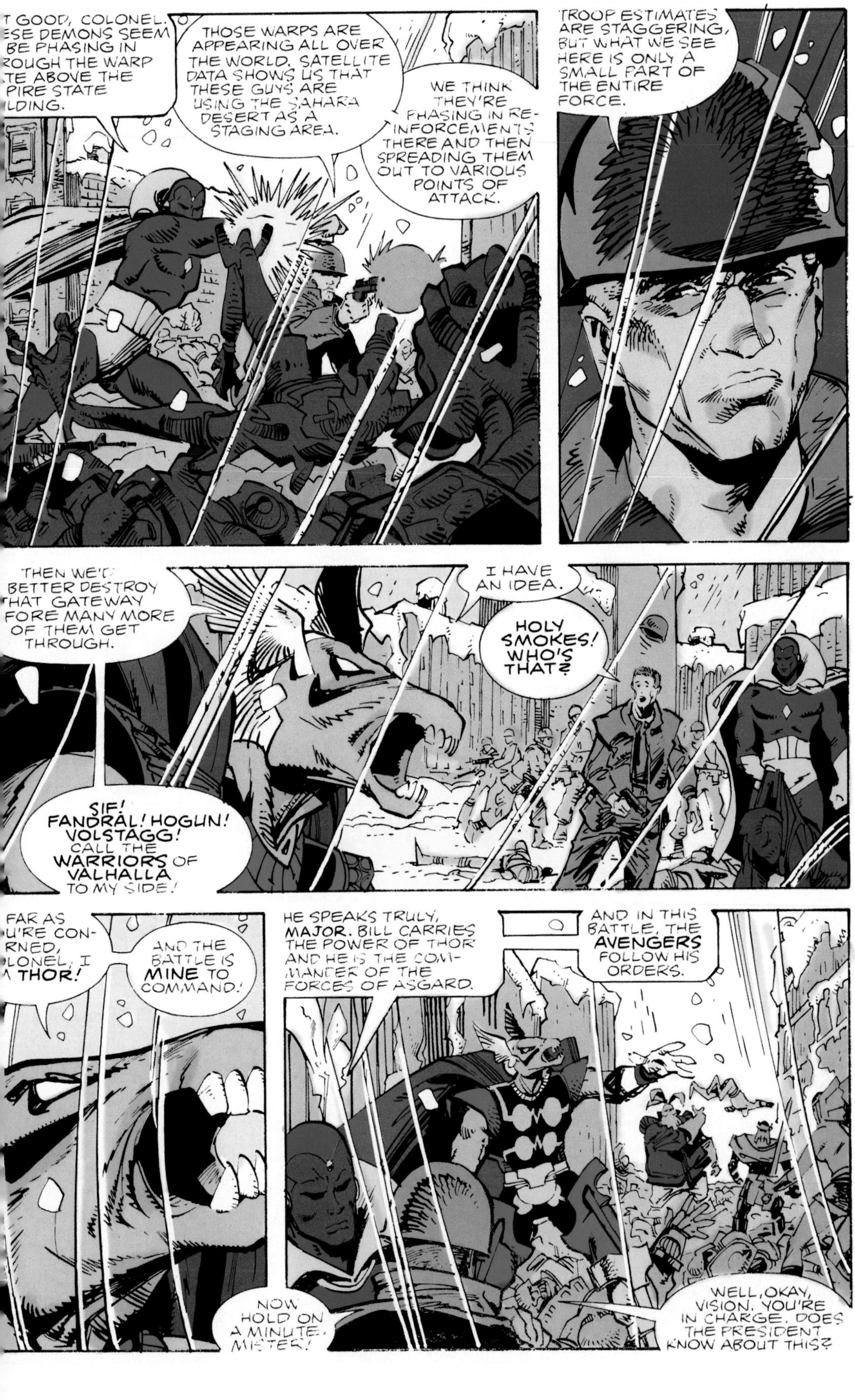

T GOOD, COLONEL. ESE DEMONS SEEM BE PHASING IN ROUGH THE WARP TE ABOVE THE PIRE STATE LDING.
THOSE WARPS ARE APPEARING ALL OVER THE WORLD. SATELLITE DATA SHOWS US THAT THESE GUYS ARE USING THE SAHARA DESERT AS A STAGING AREA.
WE THINK THEY'RE PHASING IN RE-INFORCEMENTS THERE AND THEN SPREADING THEM OUT TO VARIOUS POINTS OF ATTACK.
TROOP ESTIMATES ARE STAGGERING, BUT WHAT WE SEE HERE IS ONLY A SMALL PART OF THE ENTIRE FORCE.
THEN WE'D BETTER DESTROY THAT GATEWAY FORE MANY MORE OF THEM GET THROUGH.
I HAVE AN IDEA.
HOLY SMOKES! WHO'S THAT?
SIF! FANDRAL! HOGUN! VOLSTAGG! CALL THE WARRIORS OF VALHALLA TO MY SIDE!
FAR AS U'RE CON-RNED, OLONEL, I A THOR!
AND THE BATTLE IS MINE TO COMMAND!
HE SPEAKS TRULY, MAJOR. BILL CARRIES THE POWER OF THOR AND HE IS THE COM-MANDER OF THE FORCES OF ASGARD.
AND IN THIS BATTLE, THE AVENGERS FOLLOW HIS ORDERS.
NOW HOLD ON A MINUTE, MISTER!
WELL, OKAY, VISION. YOU'RE IN CHARGE. DOES THE PRESIDENT KNOW ABOUT THIS?

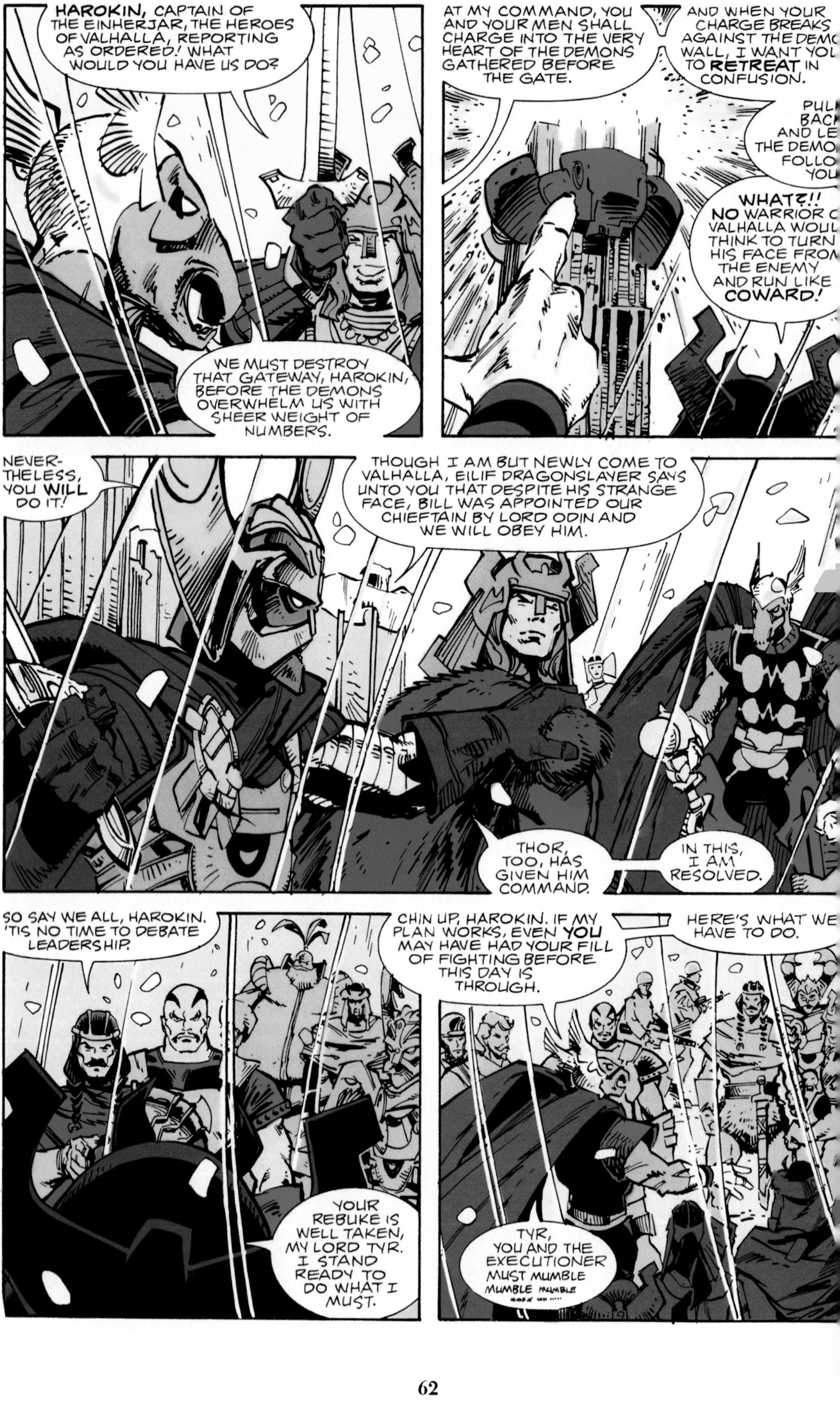
HAROKIN, CAPTAIN OF THE EINHERJAR, THE HEROES OF VALHALLA, REPORTING AS ORDERED! WHAT WOULD YOU HAVE US DO?
WE MUST DESTROY THAT GATEWAY, HAROKIN, BEFORE THE DEMONS OVERWHELM US WITH SHEER WEIGHT OF NUMBERS.
AT MY COMMAND, YOU AND YOUR MEN SHALL CHARGE INTO THE VERY HEART OF THE DEMONS GATHERED BEFORE THE GATE.
AND WHEN YOUR CHARGE BREAKS AGAINST THE DEMO WALL, I WANT YOU TO RETREAT IN CONFUSION.
PUL BAC AND LE THE DEMO FOLLO YOU
WHAT?!! NO WARRIOR O VALHALLA WOUL THINK TO TURN HIS FACE FROM THE ENEMY AND RUN LIKE COWARD!
NEVER-THELESS, YOU WILL DO IT!
THOUGH I AM BUT NEWLY COME TO VALHALLA, EILIF DRAGONSLAYER SAYS UNTO YOU THAT DESPITE HIS STRANGE FACE, BILL WAS APPOINTED OUR CHIEFTAIN BY LORD ODIN AND WE WILL OBEY HIM.
THOR, TOO, HAS GIVEN HIM COMMAND.
IN THIS, I AM RESOLVED.
SO SAY WE ALL, HAROKIN. 'TIS NO TIME TO DEBATE LEADERSHIP.
YOUR REBUKE IS WELL TAKEN, MY LORD TYR. I STAND READY TO DO WHAT I MUST.
CHIN UP, HAROKIN. IF MY PLAN WORKS, EVEN YOU MAY HAVE HAD YOUR FILL OF FIGHTING BEFORE THIS DAY IS THROUGH.
HERE'S WHAT WE HAVE TO DO.
TYR, YOU AND THE EXECUTIONER MUST MUMBLE
MUMBLE MUMBLE

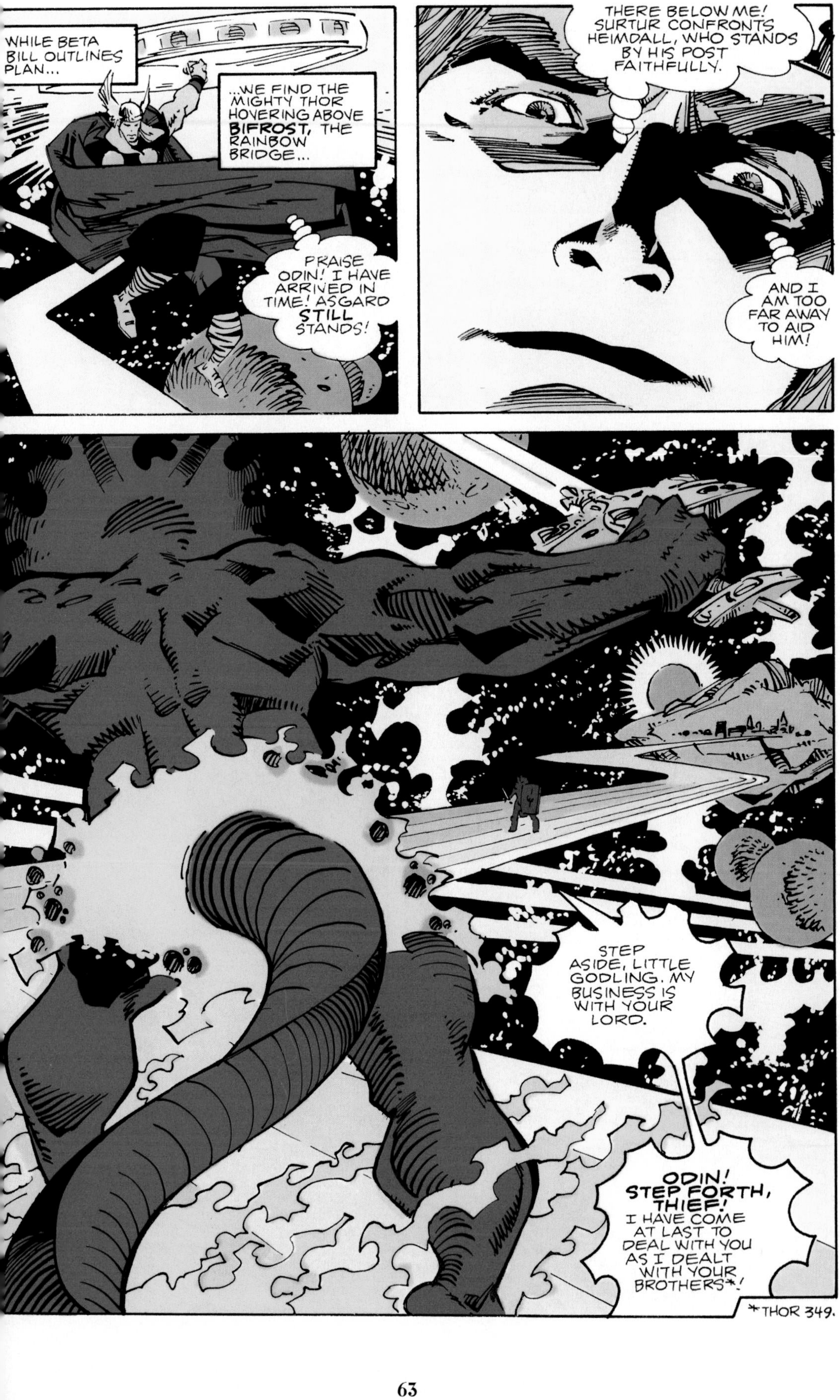
WHILE BETA BILL OUTLINES PLAN...
...WE FIND THE MIGHTY THOR HOVERING ABOVE BIFROST, THE RAINBOW BRIDGE...
PRAISE ODIN! I HAVE ARRIVED IN TIME! ASGARD STILL STANDS!
THERE BELOW ME! SURTUR CONFRONTS HEIMDALL, WHO STANDS BY HIS POST FAITHFULLY.
AND I AM TOO FAR AWAY TO AID HIM!
STEP ASIDE, LITTLE GODLING. MY BUSINESS IS WITH YOUR LORD.
ODIN! STEP FORTH, THIEF! I HAVE COME AT LAST TO DEAL WITH YOU AS I DEALT WITH YOUR BROTHERS*!
*THOR 349.

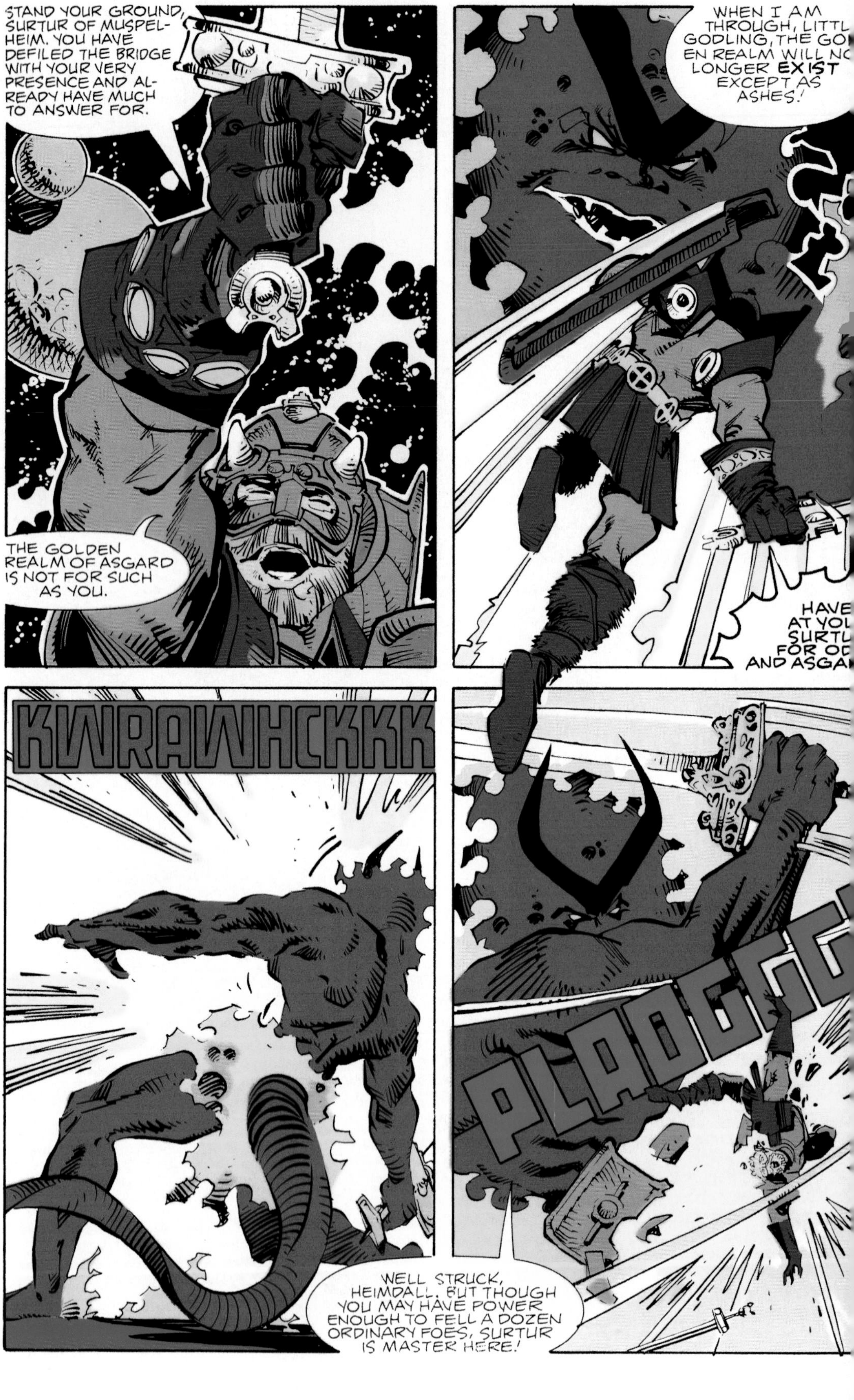
STAND YOUR GROUND, SURTUR OF MUSPELHEIM. YOU HAVE DEFILED THE BRIDGE WITH YOUR VERY PRESENCE AND ALREADY HAVE MUCH TO ANSWER FOR.
THE GOLDEN REALM OF ASGARD IS NOT FOR SUCH AS YOU.
WHEN I AM THROUGH, LITTL GODLING, THE GO EN REALM WILL NO LONGER EXIST EXCEPT AS ASHES!
HAVE AT YOU SURTU FOR OD AND ASGA
KWRAWHCKKK
PLADNG
WELL STRUCK, HEIMDALL. BUT THOUGH YOU MAY HAVE POWER ENOUGH TO FELL A DOZEN ORDINARY FOES, SURTUR IS MASTER HERE!

FASTER, MJOLNIR, FASTER! MAY WE NOT BE TOO LATE WHEN WE ARE SO CLOSE! HEIMDALL MOVES NOT!

HEIMDALL!

SO THE WHELP OF ODIN HAS ABANDONED MIDGARD!*

*EARTH.

AND ASGARD IS EMPTY OF GUARDIANS, SAVE YOU AND YOUR FATHER!

THEN LET THE FIGHT BE- TWEEN US BE WITH- OUT INTER- FERENCE!

LL SUNDER RAINBOW BRIDGE DESTROY THE BETWEEN THE RTAL REALM ASGARD!

NOW SHALL THE LORD OF ASGARD TRULY BE BEYOND ALL HELP!

KRRAKADOOOM

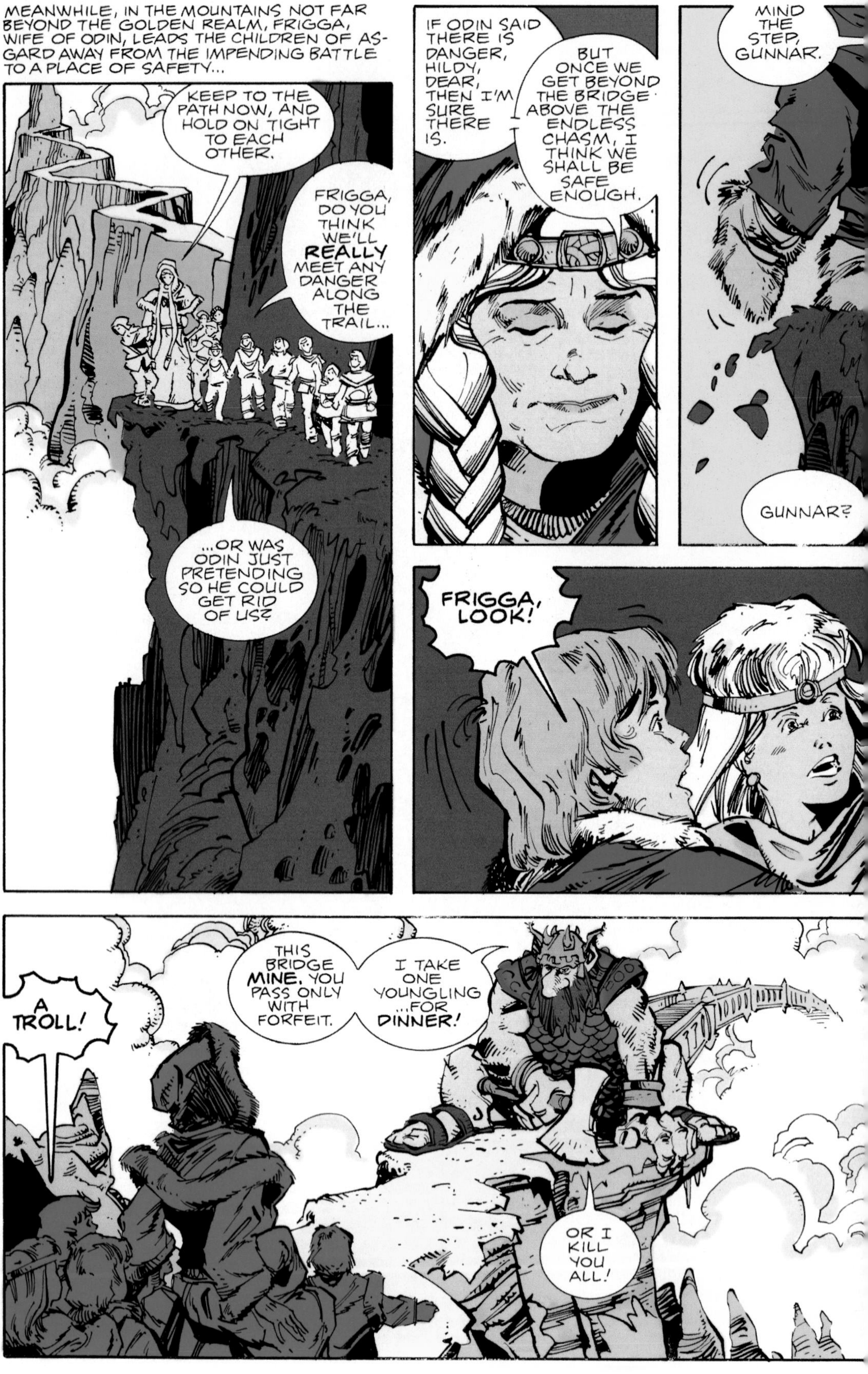
MEANWHILE, IN THE MOUNTAINS NOT FAR BEYOND THE GOLDEN REALM, FRIGGA, WIFE OF ODIN, LEADS THE CHILDREN OF ASGARD AWAY FROM THE IMPENDING BATTLE TO A PLACE OF SAFETY...
KEEP TO THE PATH NOW, AND HOLD ON TIGHT TO EACH OTHER.
FRIGGA, DO YOU THINK WE'LL **REALLY** MEET ANY DANGER ALONG THE TRAIL...
...OR WAS ODIN JUST PRETENDING SO HE COULD GET RID OF US?
IF ODIN SAID THERE IS DANGER, HILDY, DEAR, THEN I'M SURE THERE IS.
BUT ONCE WE GET BEYOND THE BRIDGE ABOVE THE ENDLESS CHASM, I THINK WE SHALL BE SAFE ENOUGH.
MIND THE STEP, GUNNAR.
GUNNAR?
FRIGGA, LOOK!
A TROLL!
THIS BRIDGE **MINE**. YOU PASS ONLY WITH FORFEIT.
I TAKE ONE YOUNGLING ...FOR **DINNER**!
OR I KILL YOU ALL!

MEANWHILE, ON MANHATTAN ISLAND...

...AND THE EXECUTIONER HAVE TAKEN THEIR FORCES AND BEGUN TO PREPARE, SIF.

AND THE MORTAL ARMY IS HOLDING ITS OWN FOR NOW. BUT THE SKY BEGINS TO BLACKEN WITH THE FORCES OF THE DEMONS! I WONDER IF-- SIF?

BILL! THE AIR!

...LED WITH HORDES OF COLOR!

WHAT ARE THEY?

DON'T YOU SEE? IT'S FROM THE BRIDGE! THE RAINBOW BRIDGE HAS BEEN BROKEN!

SOMETHING TERRIBLE IS HAPPENING IN ASGARD!

THOR AND ODIN MAY EVEN NOW BE DYING!

AND I AM NOT THERE!

BUT BY THE GODDESS-BORN POWERS OF SPACE AND TIME I POSSESS, I SHALL BE!

NO!

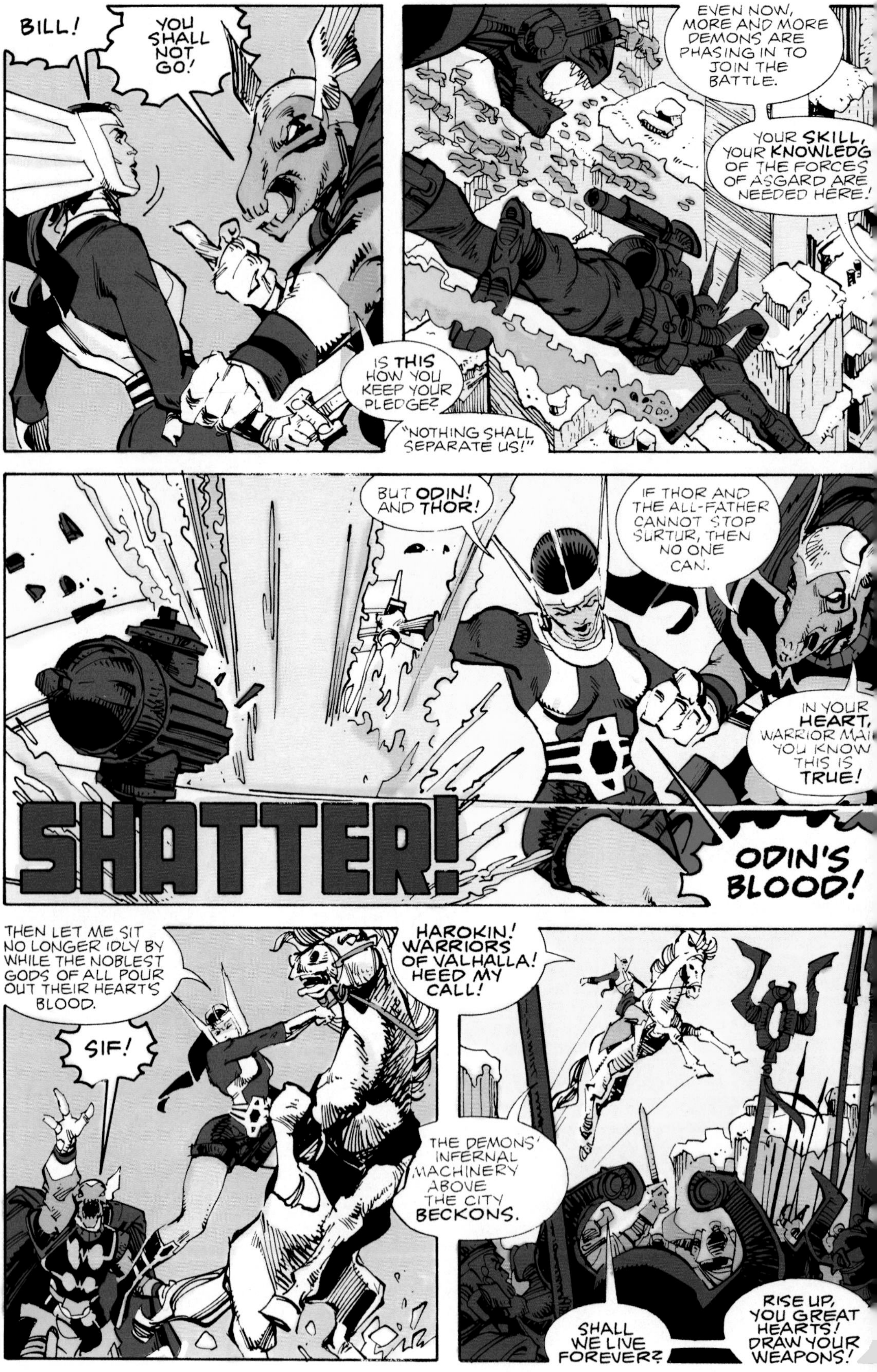
BILL!
YOU SHALL NOT GO!
IS THIS HOW YOU KEEP YOUR PLEDGE?
"NOTHING SHALL SEPARATE US!"
EVEN NOW, MORE AND MORE DEMONS ARE PHASING IN TO JOIN THE BATTLE.
YOUR SKILL, YOUR KNOWLEDG OF THE FORCES OF ASGARD ARE NEEDED HERE!
BUT ODIN! AND THOR!
IF THOR AND THE ALL-FATHER CANNOT STOP SURTUR, THEN NO ONE CAN.
IN YOUR HEART, WARRIOR MAI YOU KNOW THIS IS TRUE!
SHATTER!
ODIN'S BLOOD!
THEN LET ME SIT NO LONGER IDLY BY WHILE THE NOBLEST GODS OF ALL POUR OUT THEIR HEART'S BLOOD.
HAROKIN! WARRIORS OF VALHALLA! HEED MY CALL!
SIF!
THE DEMONS' INFERNAL MACHINERY ABOVE THE CITY BECKONS.
SHALL WE LIVE FOREVER?
RISE UP, YOU GREAT HEARTS! DRAW YOUR WEAPONS!

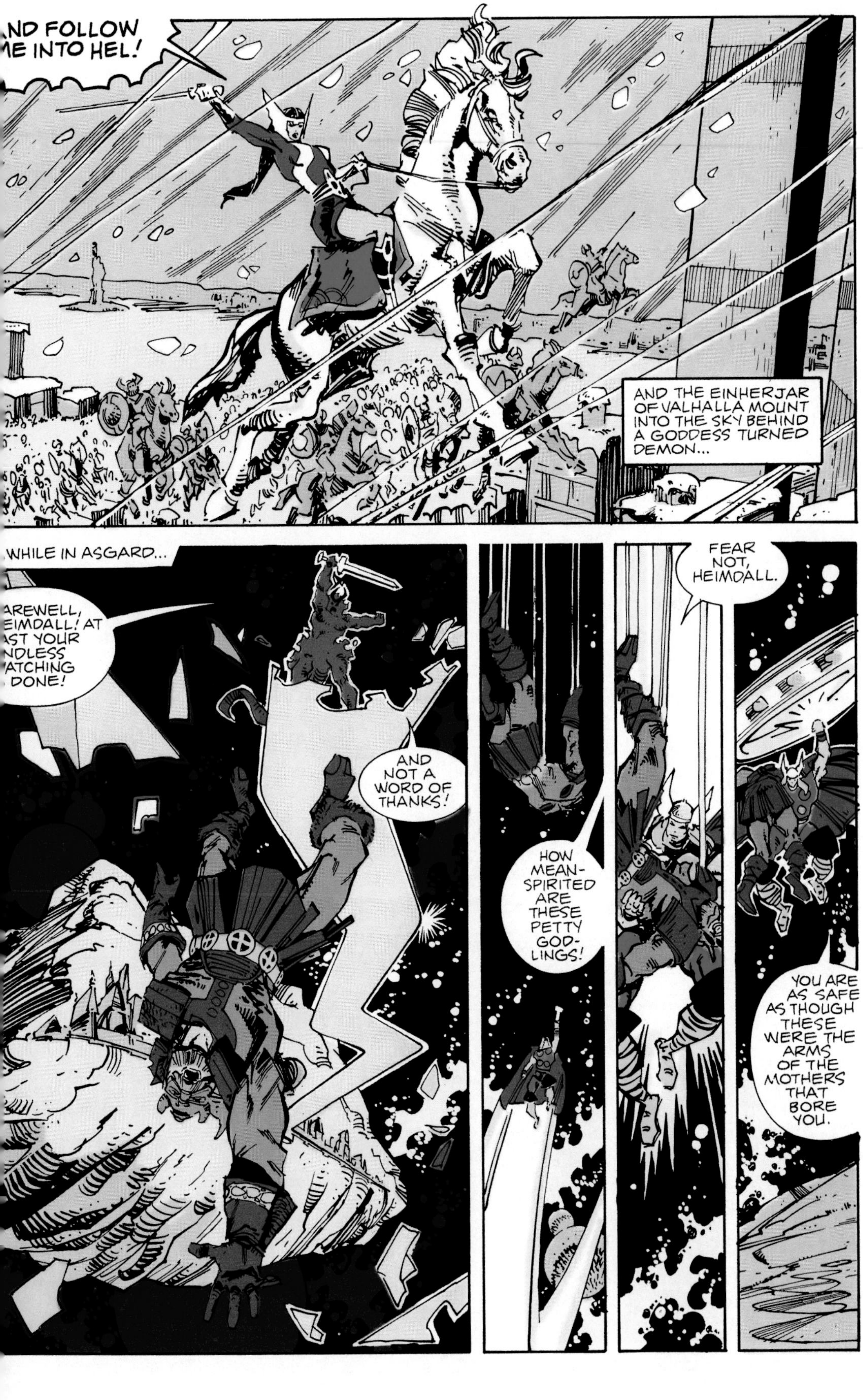
ND FOLLOW E INTO HEL!
AND THE EINHERJAR OF VALHALLA MOUNT INTO THE SKY BEHIND A GODDESS TURNED DEMON...
WHILE IN ASGARD...
AREWELL, EIMDALL! AT AST YOUR NDLESS ATCHING DONE!
AND NOT A WORD OF THANKS!
HOW MEAN-SPIRITED ARE THESE PETTY GOD-LINGS!
FEAR NOT, HEIMDALL.
YOU ARE AS SAFE AS THOUGH THESE WERE THE ARMS OF THE MOTHERS THAT BORE YOU.

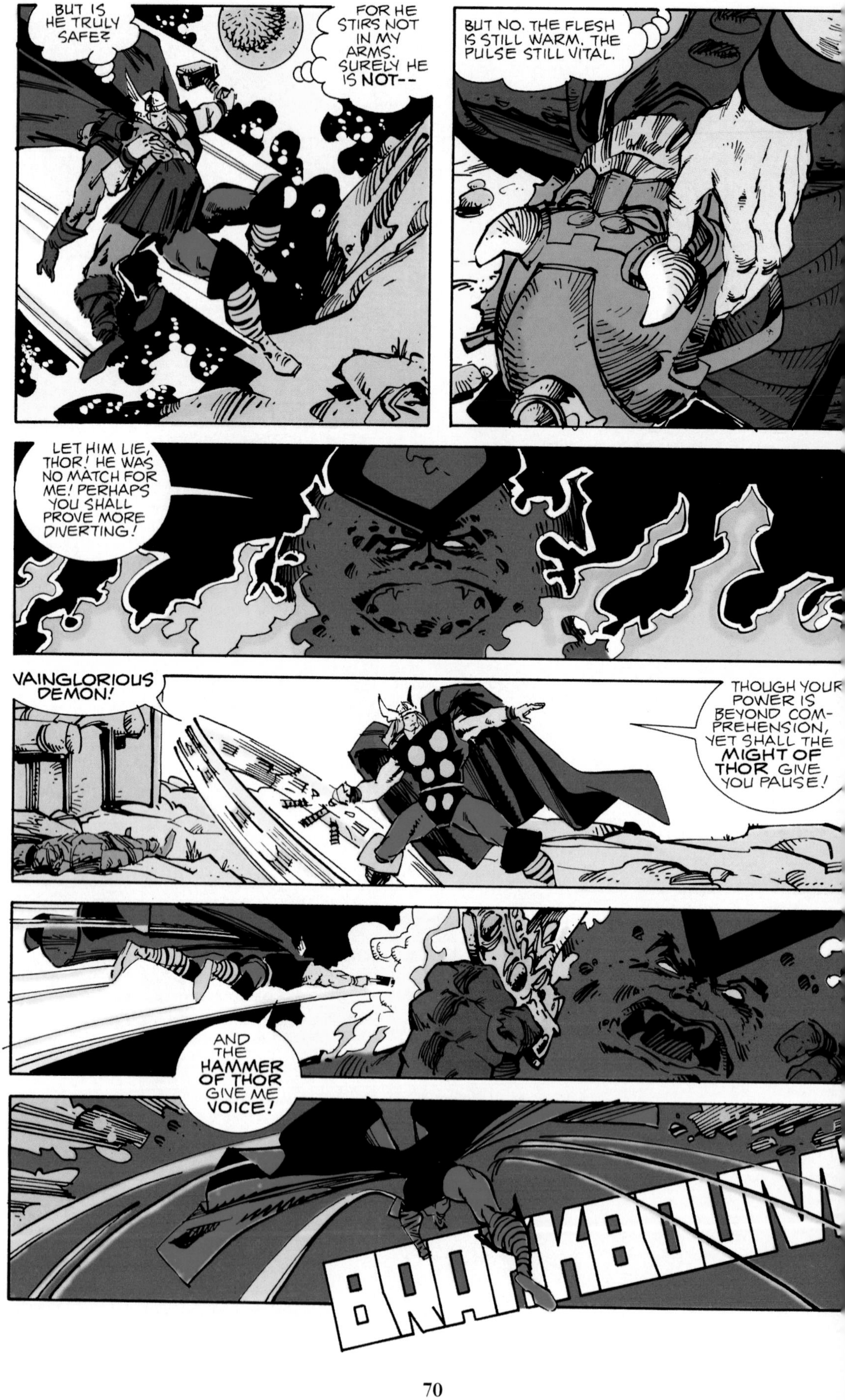
BUT IS HE TRULY SAFE?
FOR HE STIRS NOT IN MY ARMS. SURELY HE IS NOT--
BUT NO. THE FLESH IS STILL WARM. THE PULSE STILL VITAL.
LET HIM LIE, THOR! HE WAS NO MATCH FOR ME! PERHAPS YOU SHALL PROVE MORE DIVERTING!
VAINGLORIOUS DEMON!
THOUGH YOUR POWER IS BEYOND COMPREHENSION, YET SHALL THE MIGHT OF THOR GIVE YOU PAUSE!
AND THE HAMMER OF THOR GIVE ME VOICE!
BRAKKBOOM

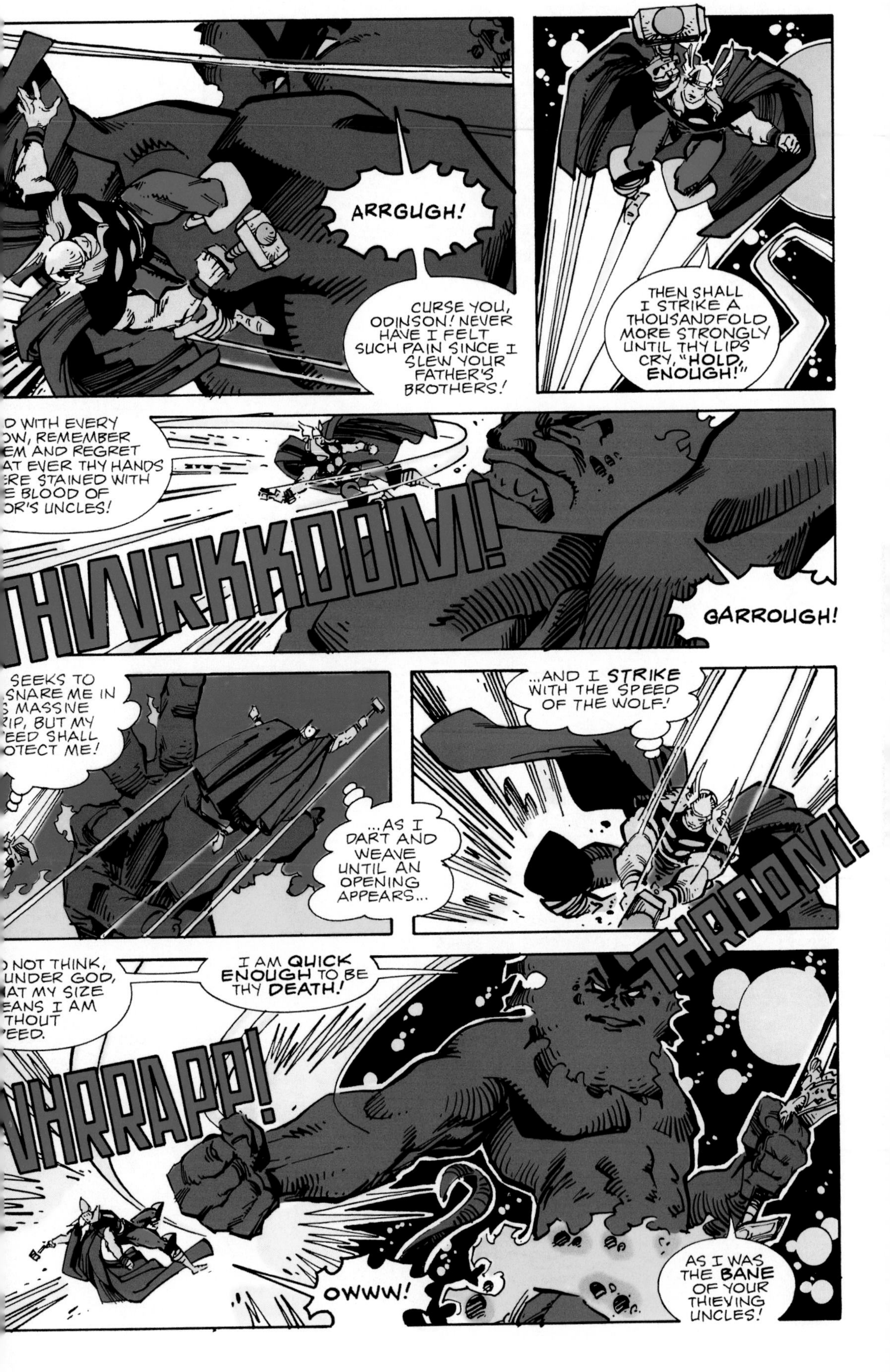
ARRGUGH!
CURSE YOU, ODINSON! NEVER HAVE I FELT SUCH PAIN SINCE I SLEW YOUR FATHER'S BROTHERS!
THEN SHALL I STRIKE A THOUSANDFOLD MORE STRONGLY UNTIL THY LIPS CRY, "HOLD, ENOUGH!"
D WITH EVERY OW, REMEMBER EM AND REGRET AT EVER THY HANDS ERE STAINED WITH E BLOOD OF OR'S UNCLES!
THWRKKOOM!
GARROUGH!
SEEKS TO SNARE ME IN S MASSIVE RIP, BUT MY EED SHALL OTECT ME!
...AS I DART AND WEAVE UNTIL AN OPENING APPEARS...
...AND I STRIKE WITH THE SPEED OF THE WOLF!
THROOM!
D NOT THINK, UNDER GOD, AT MY SIZE EANS I AM THOUT EED.
I AM QUICK ENOUGH TO BE THY DEATH!
WHRRAPP!
OWWW!
AS I WAS THE BANE OF YOUR THIEVING UNCLES!

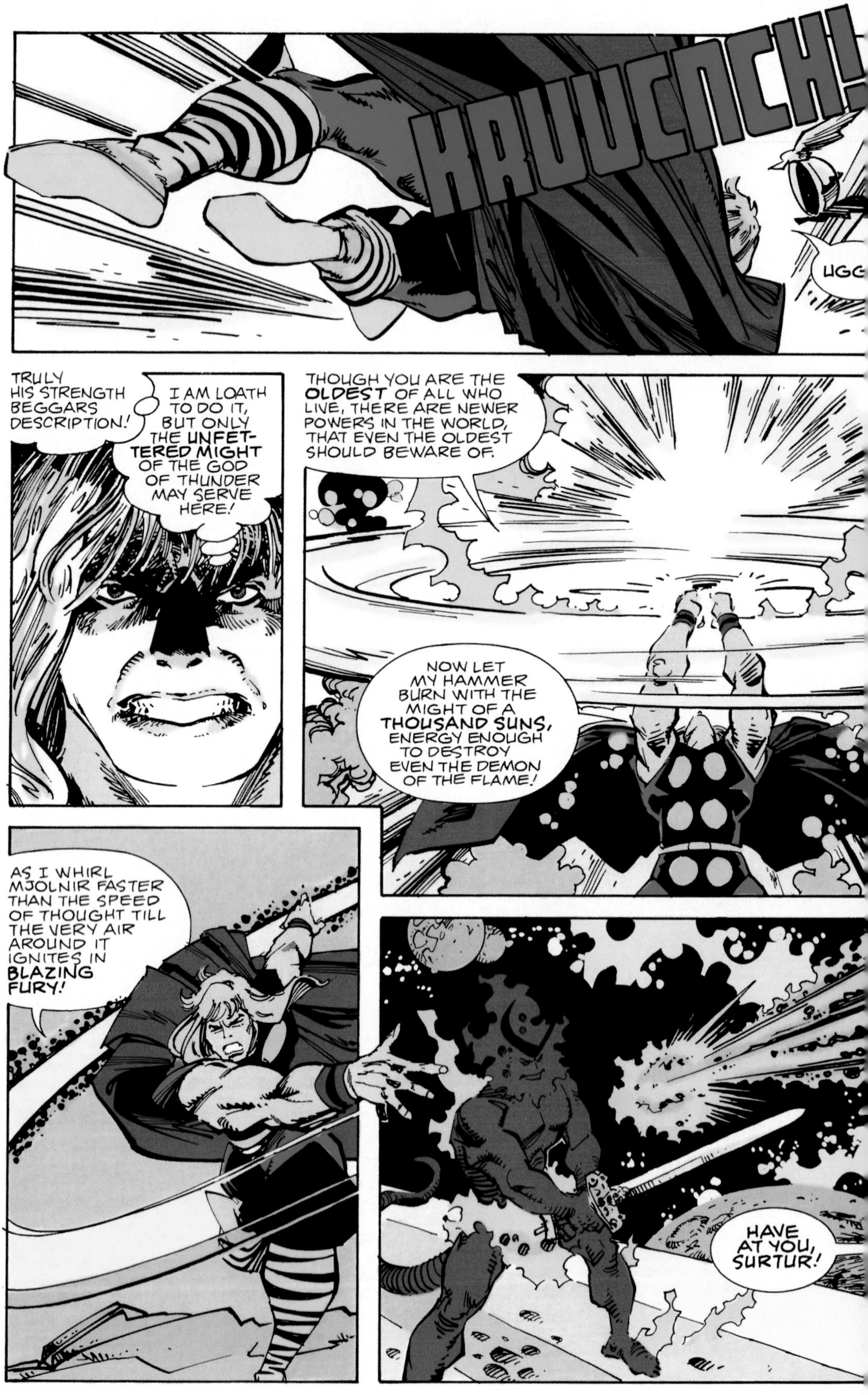
KRUUCNCH!
UGG
TRULY HIS STRENGTH BEGGARS DESCRIPTION!
I AM LOATH TO DO IT, BUT ONLY THE UNFETTERED MIGHT OF THE GOD OF THUNDER MAY SERVE HERE!
THOUGH YOU ARE THE OLDEST OF ALL WHO LIVE, THERE ARE NEWER POWERS IN THE WORLD, THAT EVEN THE OLDEST SHOULD BEWARE OF.
NOW LET MY HAMMER BURN WITH THE MIGHT OF A THOUSAND SUNS, ENERGY ENOUGH TO DESTROY EVEN THE DEMON OF THE FLAME!
AS I WHIRL MJOLNIR FASTER THAN THE SPEED OF THOUGHT TILL THE VERY AIR AROUND IT IGNITES IN BLAZING FURY!
HAVE AT YOU, SURTUR!

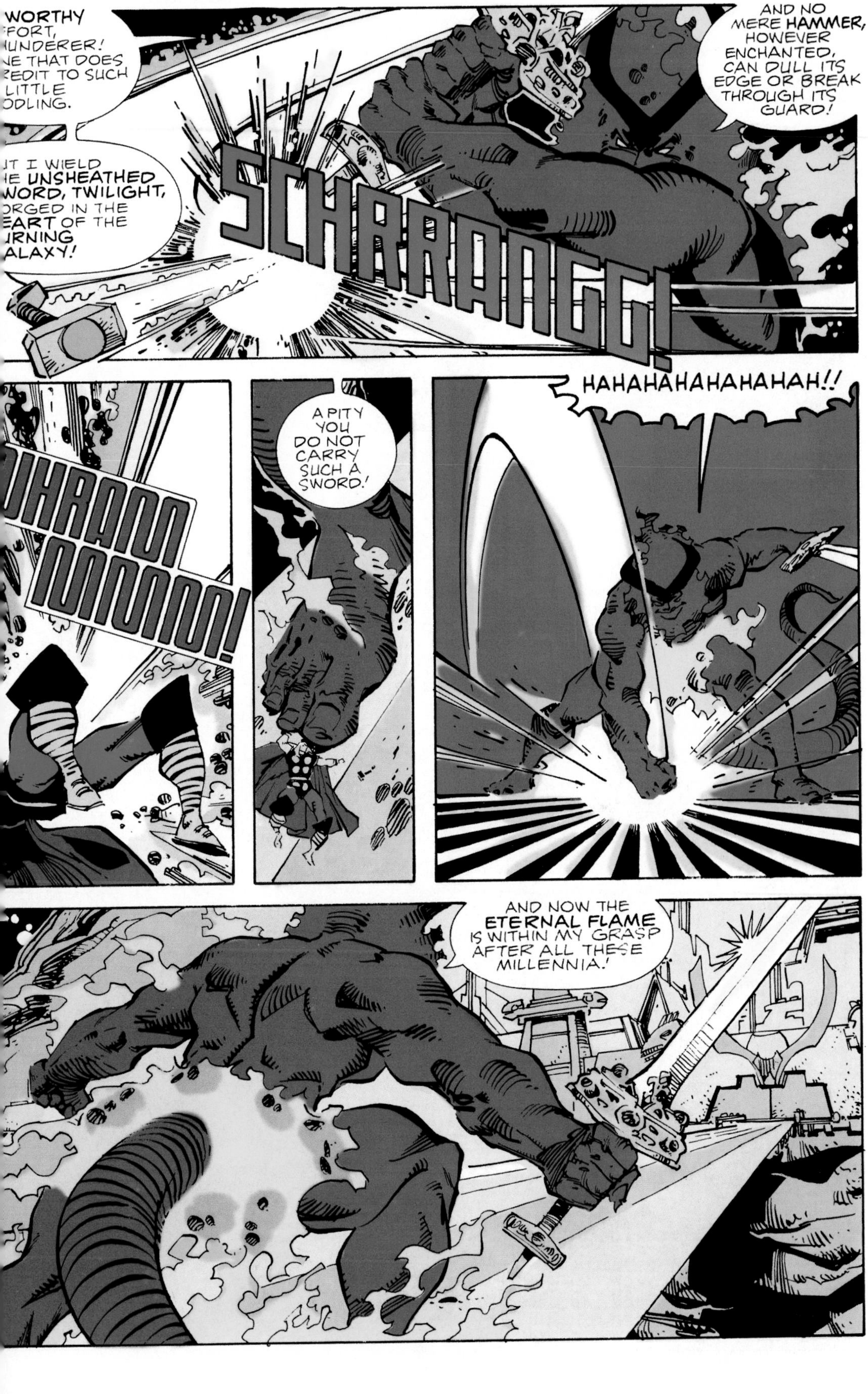
WORTHY FORT, UNDERER! NE THAT DOES REDIT TO SUCH LITTLE ODLING.
IT I WIELD HE UNSHEATHED WORD, TWILIGHT, ORGED IN THE EART OF THE IRNING ALAXY!
SCHRRANGG!
AND NO MERE HAMMER, HOWEVER ENCHANTED, CAN DULL ITS EDGE OR BREAK THROUGH ITS GUARD!
A PITY YOU DO NOT CARRY SUCH A SWORD!
HAHAHAHAHAHAHAH!!
AND NOW THE ETERNAL FLAME IS WITHIN MY GRASP AFTER ALL THESE MILLENNIA!

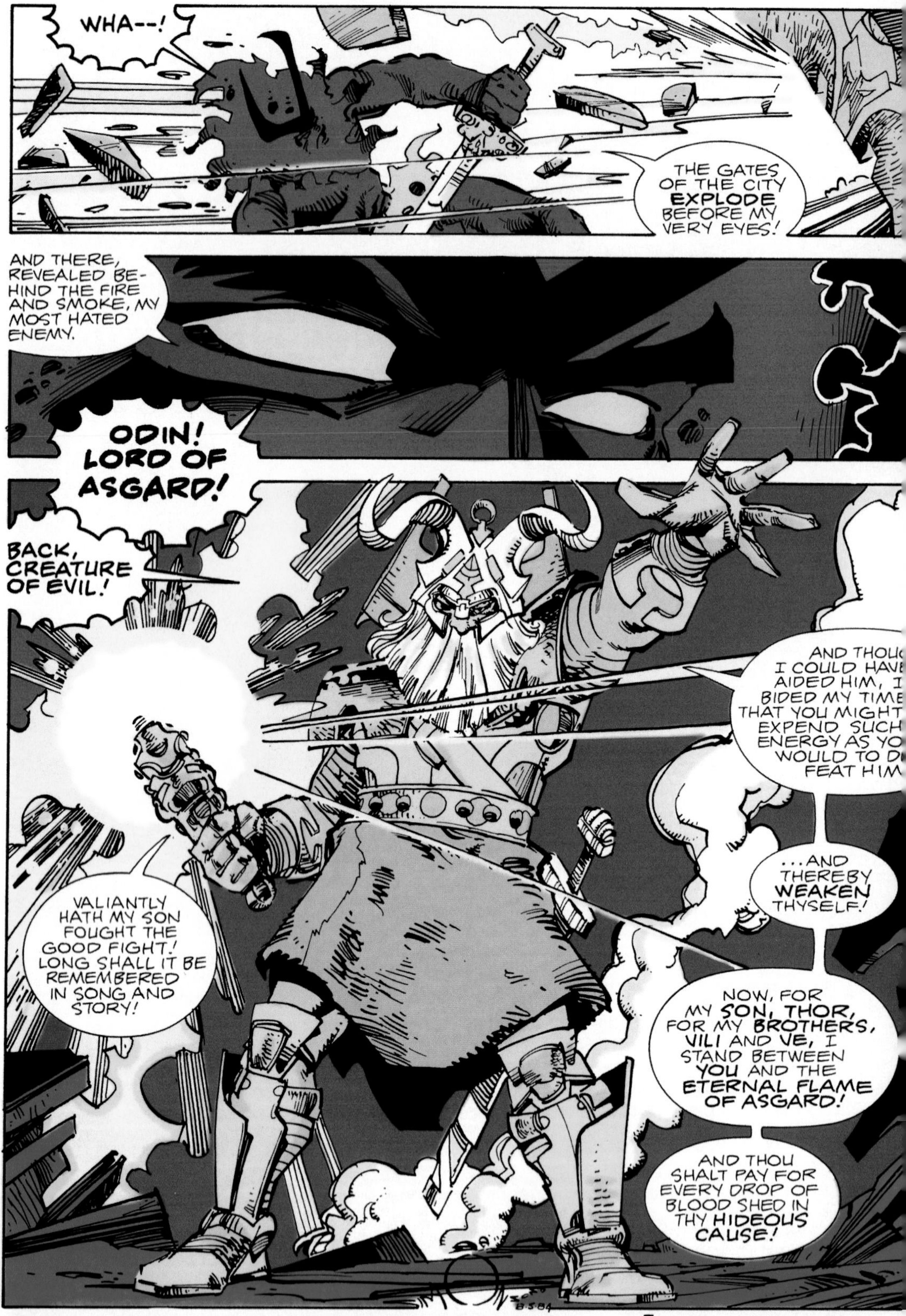
WHA--!
THE GATES OF THE CITY EXPLODE BEFORE MY VERY EYES!
AND THERE, REVEALED BEHIND THE FIRE AND SMOKE, MY MOST HATED ENEMY.
ODIN! LORD OF ASGARD!
BACK, CREATURE OF EVIL!
AND THOU I COULD HAVE AIDED HIM, I BIDED MY TIME THAT YOU MIGHT EXPEND SUCH ENERGY AS YO WOULD TO D FEAT HIM
...AND THEREBY WEAKEN THYSELF!
VALIANTLY HATH MY SON FOUGHT THE GOOD FIGHT! LONG SHALL IT BE REMEMBERED IN SONG AND STORY!
NOW, FOR MY SON, THOR, FOR MY BROTHERS, VILI AND VE, I STAND BETWEEN YOU AND THE ETERNAL FLAME OF ASGARD!
AND THOU SHALT PAY FOR EVERY DROP OF BLOOD SHED IN THY HIDEOUS CAUSE!

NEXT RAGNAROK & RUIN!

'NUFF SAID!

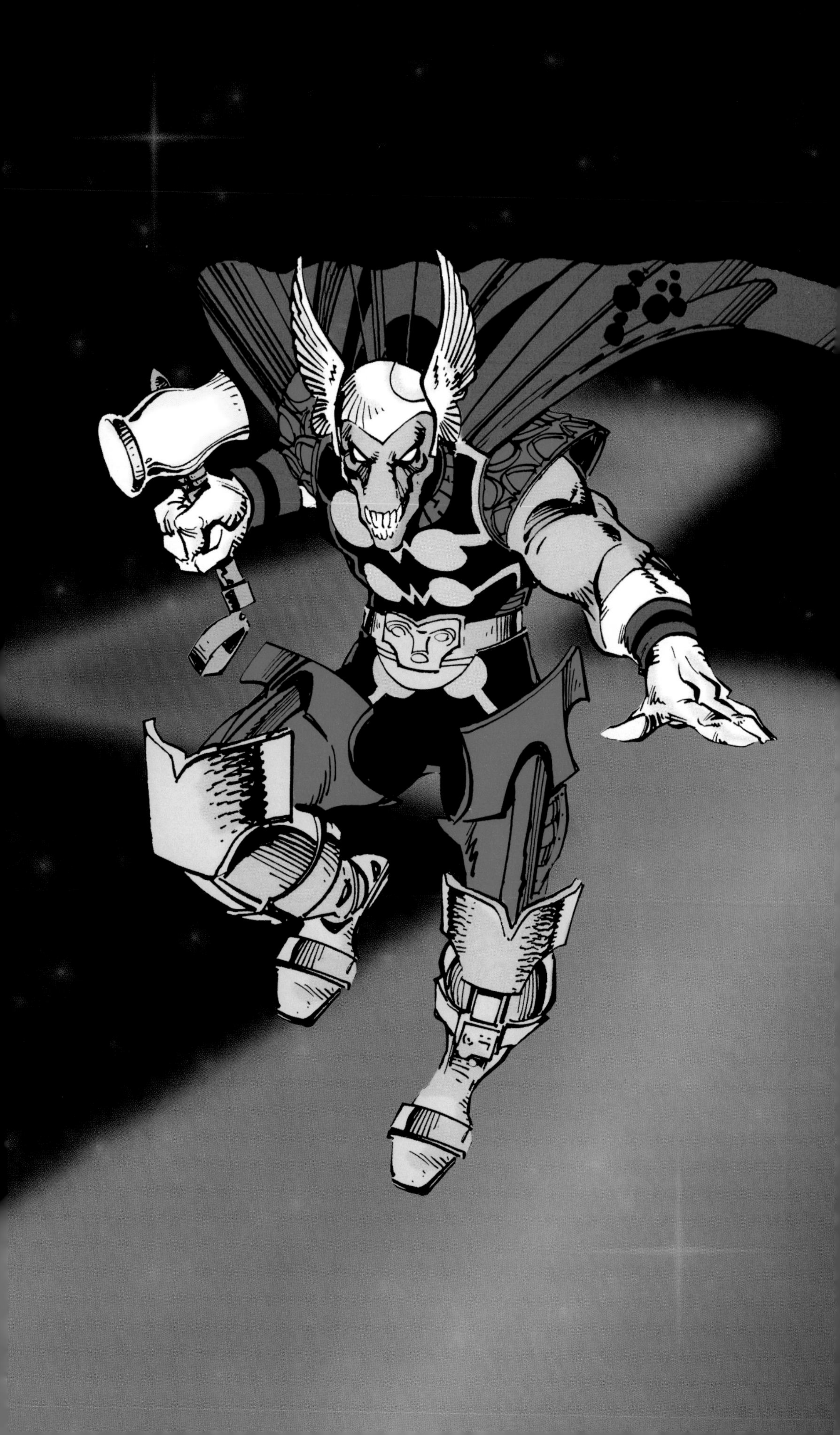

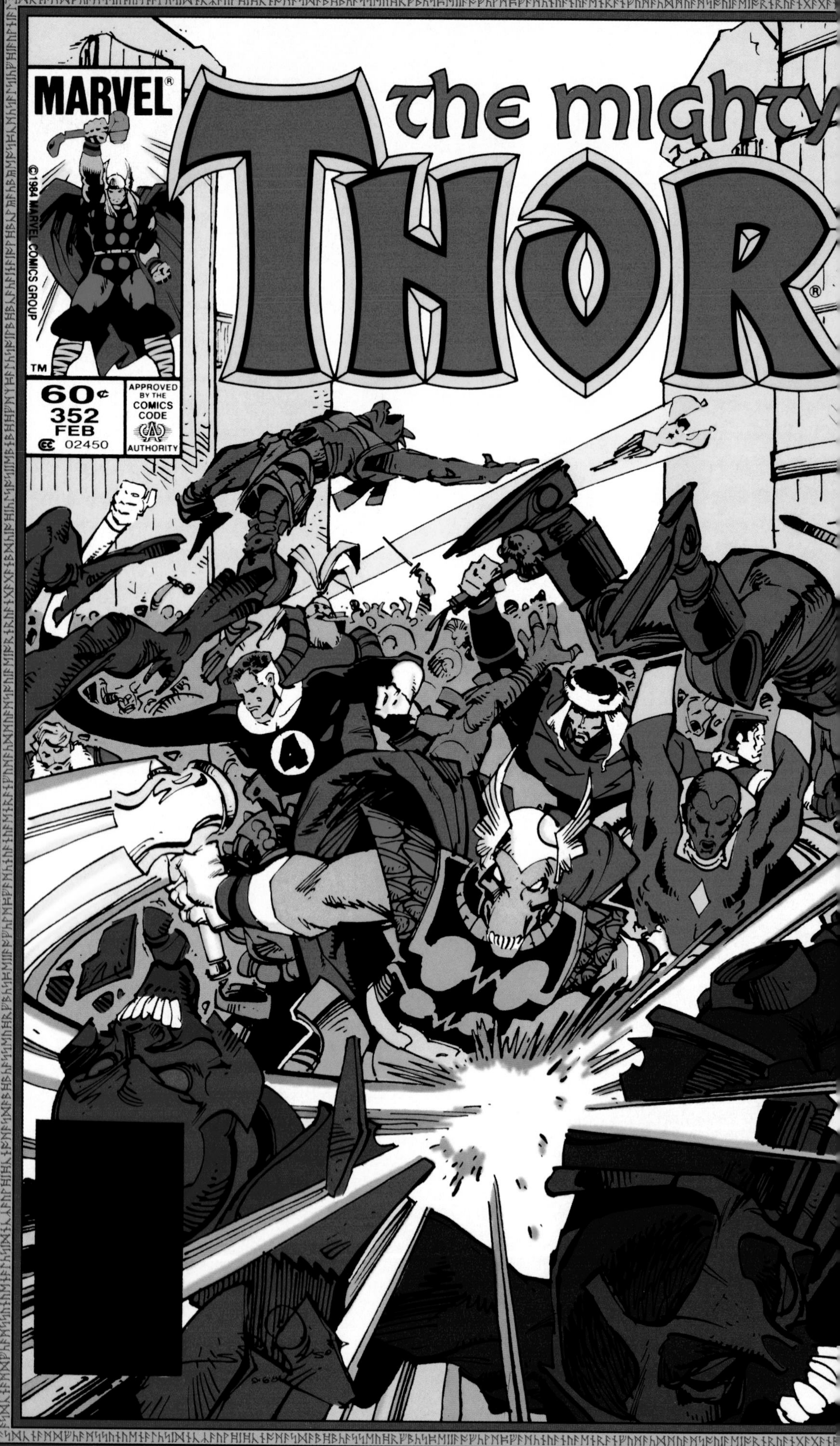
MARVEL®
the mighty THOR®
©1984 MARVEL COMICS GROUP
TM
60¢
352
FEB
02450
APPROVED BY THE COMICS CODE AUTHORITY

STAN LEE PRESENTS: **RAGNAROK AND RUIN!**

...GARD, HOME OF THE FABLED NORSE GODS!

AND BEFORE ITS GATES STANDS **SURTUR**, FIERY RULER OF THE LAND OF MUSPELHEIM...

EVEN AS HIS HORDES RAVAGE THE EARTH, SURTUR CONFRONTS **ODIN**, LORD OF ASGARD...

...AND THE STARS SHIVER IN THEIR ETERNAL COURSES.

STAND ASIDE, ALL-FATHER. I HAVE BROKEN THE RAINBOW BRIDGE, CRUSHED ITS GUARDIAN, HEIMDALL, AND DEFEATED THE MIGHTY THOR!*

I HAVE COME FOR THE **ETERNAL FLAME** YOU STOLE FROM ME IN THE BEGINNING OF TIME...

...AND I WILL NOT BE DENIED!

*LAST ISSUE.

ART AND STORY: WALTER SIMONSON · LETTERS: JOHN WORKMAN, JR.· COLORS: CHRISTIE SCHEELE
EDITING: MARK GRUENWALD · EDITOR-IN-CHIEF: JIM SHOOTER

I KNEW YOU WERE COMING, SURTUR, WHEN THE LAST SEAT IN THE HEROES HALL OF VALHALLA WAS FILLED*...

*THOR #345.

...JUST AS I KNOW THAT YOU SEEK THE **DESTRUCTION** OF ALL THINGS.

BUT THE TIME IS NOT YET RIPE. THE **NORNS**, DESTINY'S WEAVERS, HAVE NOT YET CUT THE THREAD OF LIFE.

WHAT CARE I FOR THE NORNS, OLD FOOL?

WHEN I FINISHE THERE WI BE NO DESTIN FOR THE TO WEAV

YONDER STANDS THE ETERNAL FLAME AND ONCE I HAVE PLUNGED MY SWORD INTO ITS FIERY EMBRACE...

...I WILL SET THE UNIVERSE ALIGHT!

I SHALL DO WHAT I WAS BORN TO DO FROM THE BEGINNING OF TIME.

THIS WAY IS BARRED TO YOU, DENIZEN OF THE FLAME!

RETURN TO YOUR ETERNAL LAKE OF LAVA. LEAVE THE GOLDEN REALM FOREVER AND I WILL BE MERCIFUL.

ADVANCE... AND FACE MY AWESOME WRATH!

STAND ASIDE, LITTLE GODLING. I DO BUT TAKE WHAT WAS ONCE MINE!

NOW, SO NEAR THE FLAME, MY FIRE BURNS **BRIGHTER** AND **HOTTER** WITH EVERY PASSING MOMENT!

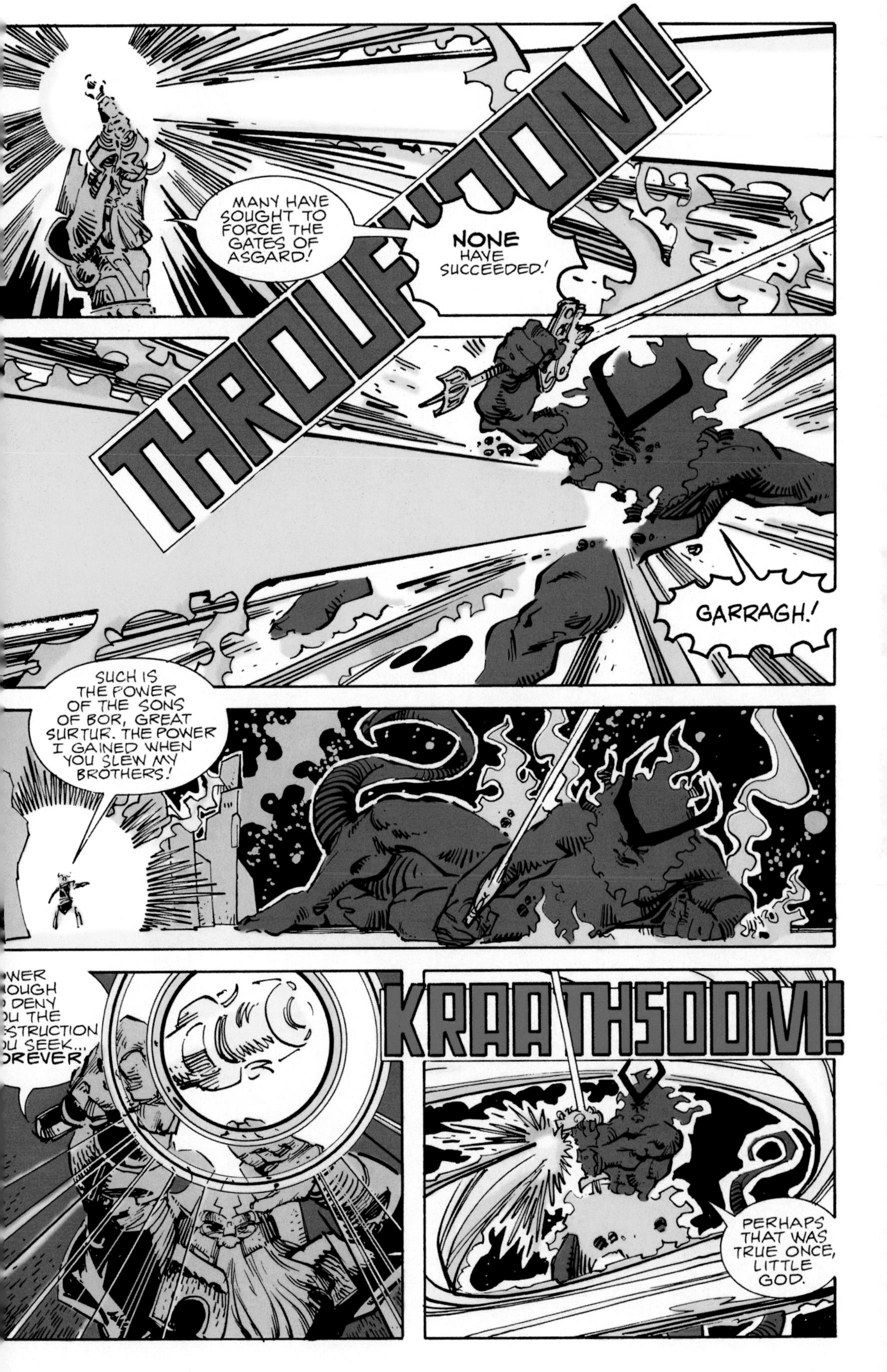
THROOFWOOM!
MANY HAVE SOUGHT TO FORCE THE GATES OF ASGARD!
NONE HAVE SUCCEEDED!
GARRAGH!
SUCH IS THE POWER OF THE SONS OF BOR, GREAT SURTUR. THE POWER I GAINED WHEN YOU SLEW MY BROTHERS!
KRAATHSOOM!
OREVER
PERHAPS THAT WAS TRUE ONCE, LITTLE GOD.

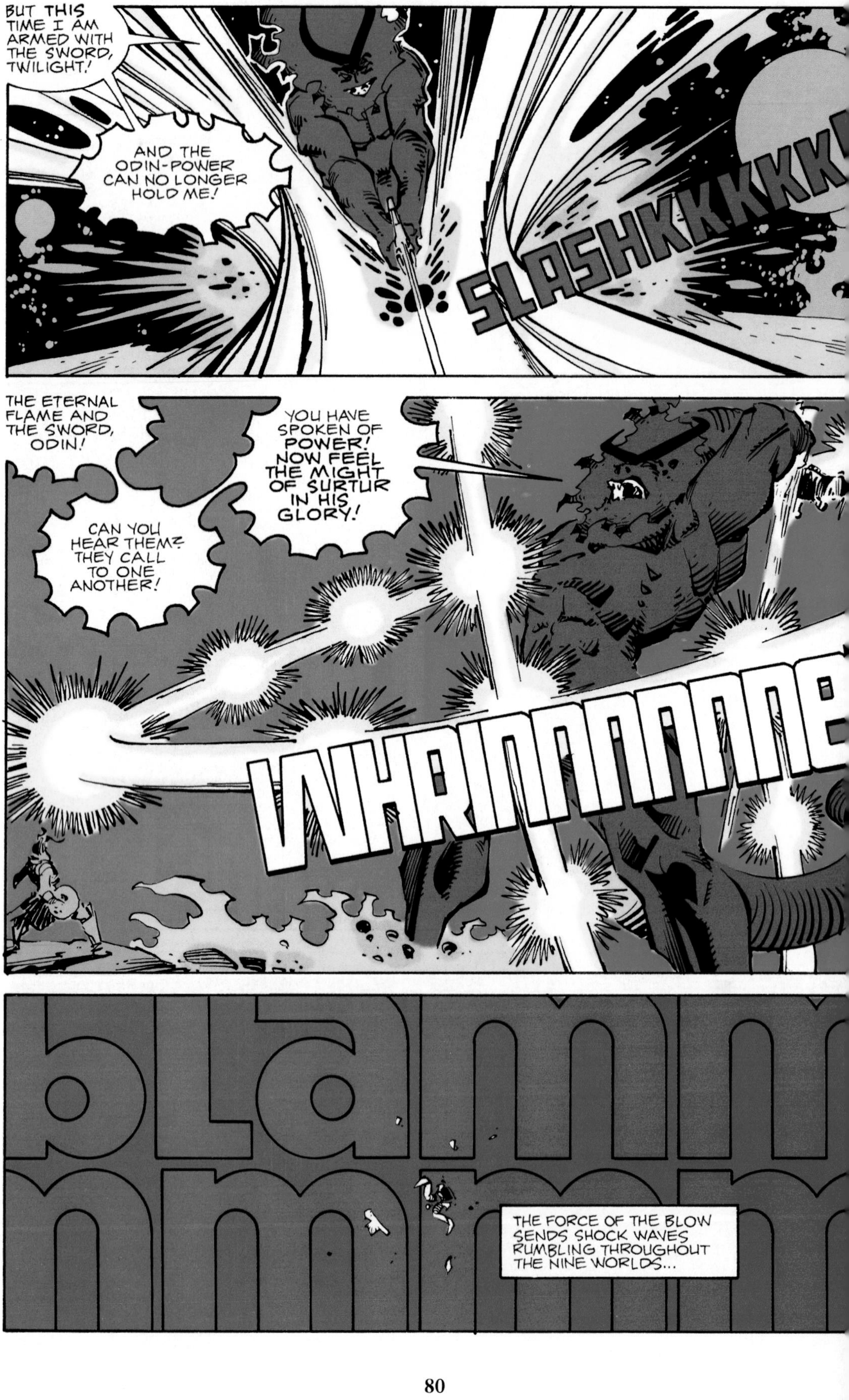
BUT THIS TIME I AM ARMED WITH THE SWORD, TWILIGHT!
AND THE ODIN-POWER CAN NO LONGER HOLD ME!
SLASHKKKKKK
THE ETERNAL FLAME AND THE SWORD, ODIN!
YOU HAVE SPOKEN OF POWER! NOW FEEL THE MIGHT OF SURTUR IN HIS GLORY!
CAN YOU HEAR THEM? THEY CALL TO ONE ANOTHER!
WHRINNNNNNE
blammm
THE FORCE OF THE BLOW SENDS SHOCK WAVES RUMBLING THROUGHOUT THE NINE WORLDS...

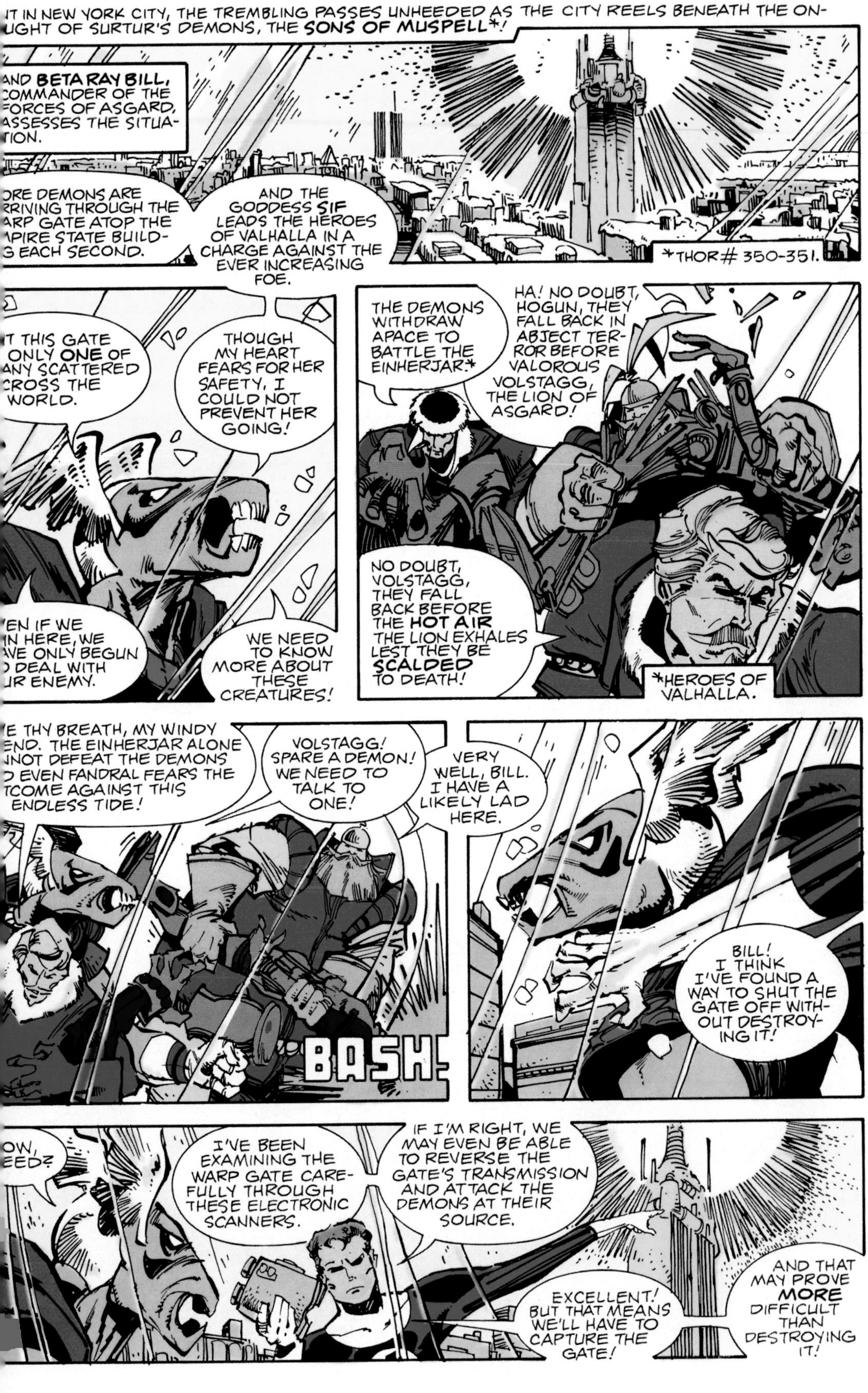
IT IN NEW YORK CITY, THE TREMBLING PASSES UNHEEDED AS THE CITY REELS BENEATH THE ON-UGHT OF SURTUR'S DEMONS, THE SONS OF MUSPELL*!
AND BETA RAY BILL, COMMANDER OF THE FORCES OF ASGARD, ASSESSES THE SITUATION.
ORE DEMONS ARE RRIVING THROUGH THE ARP GATE ATOP THE PIRE STATE BUILD-G EACH SECOND.
AND THE GODDESS SIF LEADS THE HEROES OF VALHALLA IN A CHARGE AGAINST THE EVER INCREASING FOE.
*THOR # 350-351.
T THIS GATE ONLY ONE OF ANY SCATTERED CROSS THE WORLD.
THOUGH MY HEART FEARS FOR HER SAFETY, I COULD NOT PREVENT HER GOING!
EN IF WE N HERE, WE AVE ONLY BEGUN DEAL WITH IR ENEMY.
WE NEED TO KNOW MORE ABOUT THESE CREATURES!
THE DEMONS WITHDRAW APACE TO BATTLE THE EINHERJAR.*
HA! NO DOUBT, HOGUN, THEY FALL BACK IN ABJECT TERROR BEFORE VALOROUS VOLSTAGG, THE LION OF ASGARD!
NO DOUBT, VOLSTAGG, THEY FALL BACK BEFORE THE HOT AIR THE LION EXHALES LEST THEY BE SCALDED TO DEATH!
*HEROES OF VALHALLA.
E THY BREATH, MY WINDY END. THE EINHERJAR ALONE NNOT DEFEAT THE DEMONS D EVEN FANDRAL FEARS THE TCOME AGAINST THIS ENDLESS TIDE!
VOLSTAGG! SPARE A DEMON! WE NEED TO TALK TO ONE!
VERY WELL, BILL. I HAVE A LIKELY LAD HERE.
BASH
BILL! I THINK I'VE FOUND A WAY TO SHUT THE GATE OFF WITHOUT DESTROYING IT!
OW, EED?
I'VE BEEN EXAMINING THE WARP GATE CAREFULLY THROUGH THESE ELECTRONIC SCANNERS.
IF I'M RIGHT, WE MAY EVEN BE ABLE TO REVERSE THE GATE'S TRANSMISSION AND ATTACK THE DEMONS AT THEIR SOURCE.
EXCELLENT! BUT THAT MEANS WE'LL HAVE TO CAPTURE THE GATE!
AND THAT MAY PROVE MORE DIFFICULT THAN DESTROYING IT!

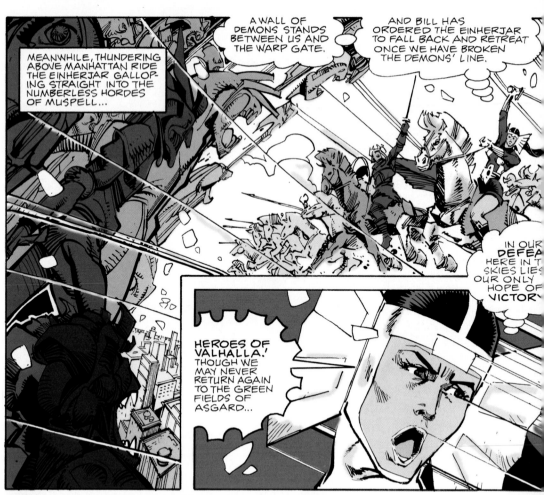

MEANWHILE, THUNDERING ABOVE MANHATTAN RIDE THE EINHERJAR GALLOPING STRAIGHT INTO THE NUMBERLESS HORDES OF MUSPELL...

A WALL OF DEMONS STANDS BETWEEN US AND THE WARP GATE.

AND BILL HAS ORDERED THE EINHERJAR TO FALL BACK AND RETREAT ONCE WE HAVE BROKEN THE DEMONS' LINE.

IN OUR DEFEAT HERE IN T SKIES LIES OUR ONLY HOPE OF VICTORY

HEROES OF VALHALLA! THOUGH WE MAY NEVER RETURN AGAIN TO THE GREEN FIELDS OF ASGARD...

...LET US SHOW THESE DEMONS THAT THE WARRIORS OF THE GOLDEN REALM ARE DEADLIER THAN ALL THE FIENDS OF HEL!

KRRRNHOUNN

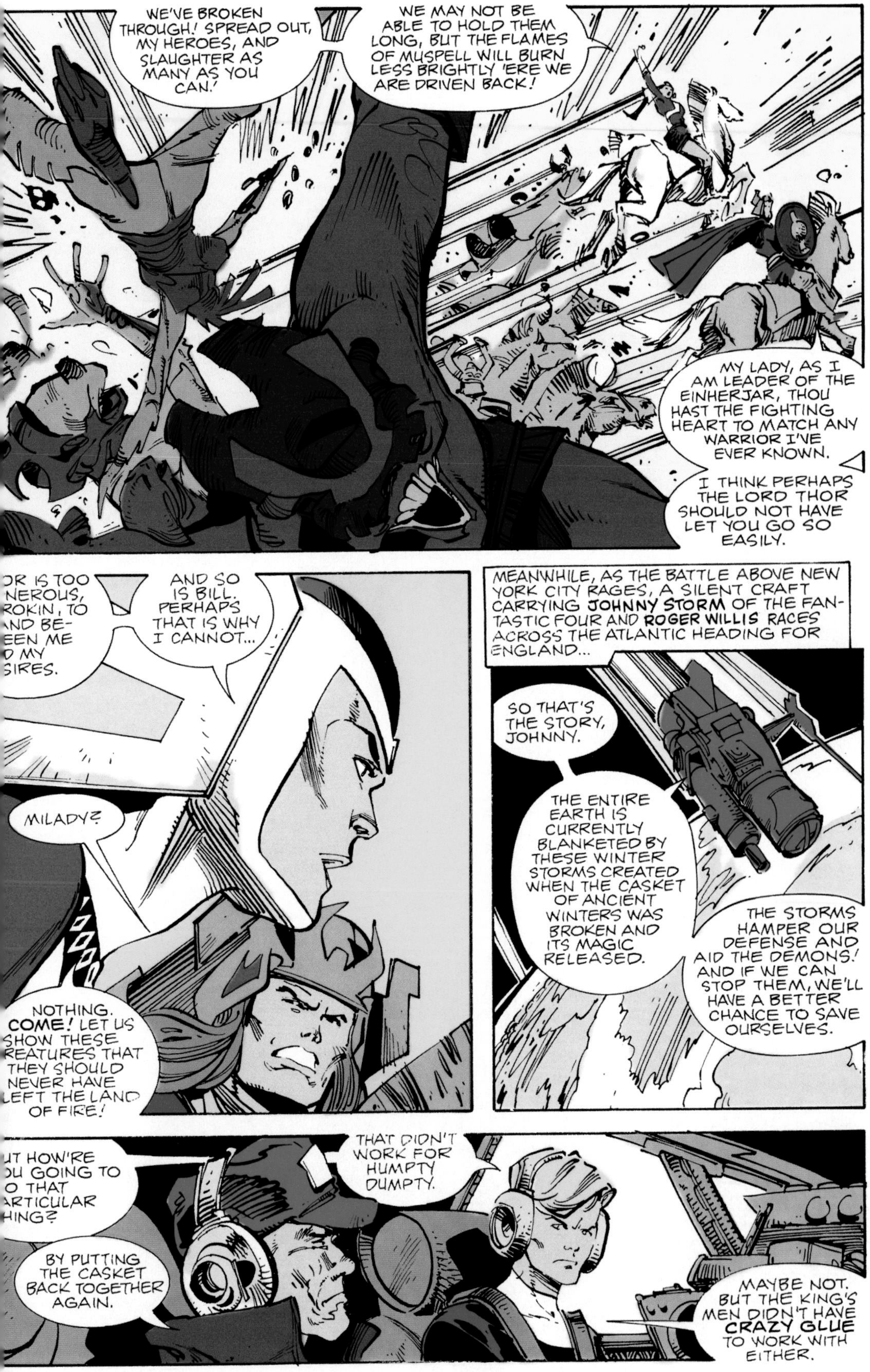

WE'VE BROKEN THROUGH! SPREAD OUT, MY HEROES, AND SLAUGHTER AS MANY AS YOU CAN.'
WE MAY NOT BE ABLE TO HOLD THEM LONG, BUT THE FLAMES OF MUSPELL WILL BURN LESS BRIGHTLY 'ERE WE ARE DRIVEN BACK!
MY LADY, AS I AM LEADER OF THE EINHERJAR, THOU HAST THE FIGHTING HEART TO MATCH ANY WARRIOR I'VE EVER KNOWN.
I THINK PERHAPS THE LORD THOR SHOULD NOT HAVE LET YOU GO SO EASILY.
OR IS TOO NEROUS, ROKIN, TO AND BE- EEN ME D MY SIRES.
AND SO IS BILL. PERHAPS THAT IS WHY I CANNOT...
MILADY?
NOTHING. COME! LET US SHOW THESE REATURES THAT THEY SHOULD NEVER HAVE LEFT THE LAND OF FIRE!
MEANWHILE, AS THE BATTLE ABOVE NEW YORK CITY RAGES, A SILENT CRAFT CARRYING JOHNNY STORM OF THE FANTASTIC FOUR AND ROGER WILLIS RACES ACROSS THE ATLANTIC HEADING FOR ENGLAND...
SO THAT'S THE STORY, JOHNNY.
THE ENTIRE EARTH IS CURRENTLY BLANKETED BY THESE WINTER STORMS CREATED WHEN THE CASKET OF ANCIENT WINTERS WAS BROKEN AND ITS MAGIC RELEASED.
THE STORMS HAMPER OUR DEFENSE AND AID THE DEMONS! AND IF WE CAN STOP THEM, WE'LL HAVE A BETTER CHANCE TO SAVE OURSELVES.
UT HOW'RE OU GOING TO O THAT ARTICULAR HING?
BY PUTTING THE CASKET BACK TOGETHER AGAIN.
THAT DIDN'T WORK FOR HUMPTY DUMPTY.
MAYBE NOT. BUT THE KING'S MEN DIDN'T HAVE CRAZY GLUE TO WORK WITH EITHER.

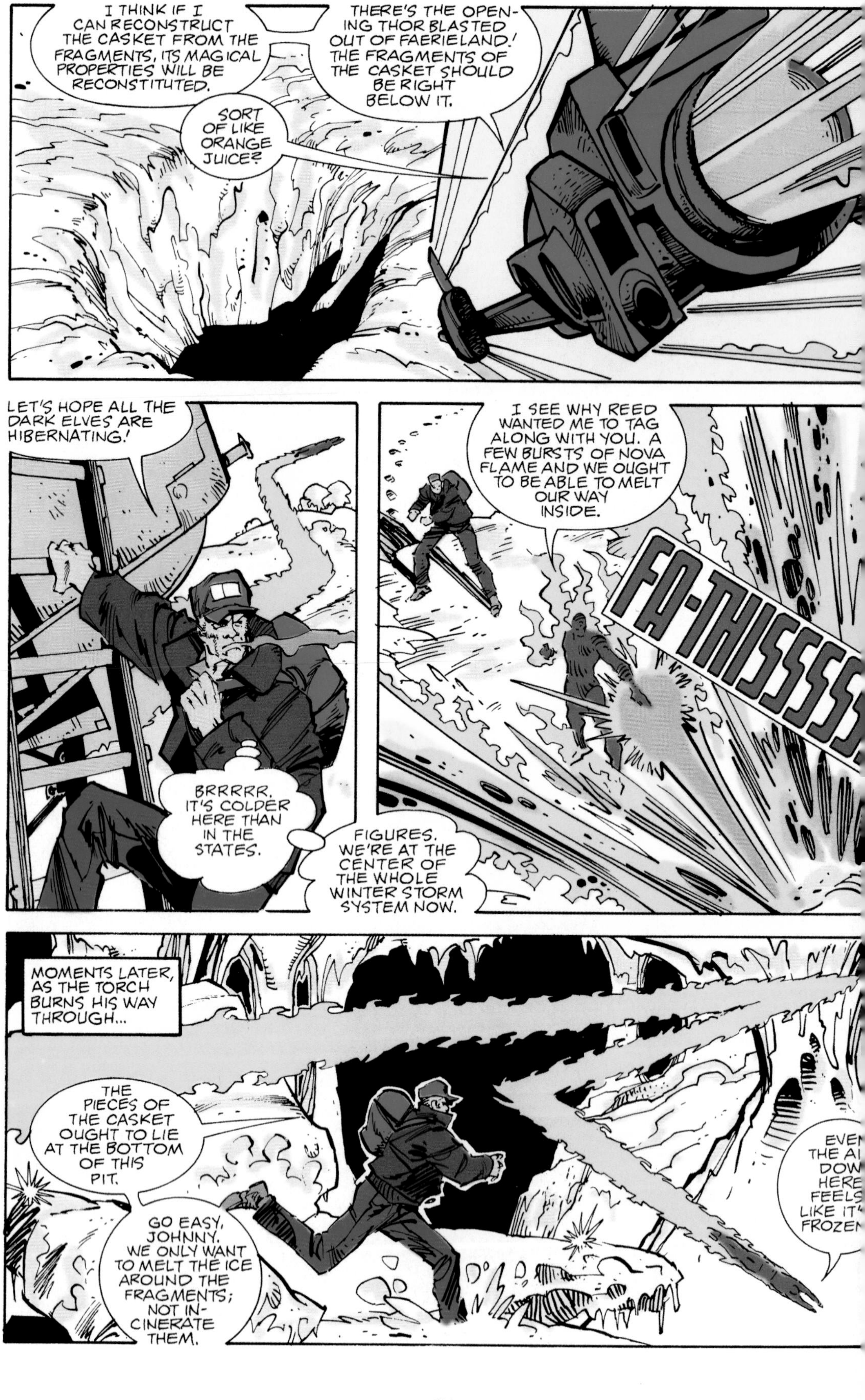
I THINK IF I CAN RECONSTRUCT THE CASKET FROM THE FRAGMENTS, ITS MAGICAL PROPERTIES WILL BE RECONSTITUTED.
THERE'S THE OPENING THOR BLASTED OUT OF FAERIELAND! THE FRAGMENTS OF THE CASKET SHOULD BE RIGHT BELOW IT.
SORT OF LIKE ORANGE JUICE?
LET'S HOPE ALL THE DARK ELVES ARE HIBERNATING!
BRRRRR. IT'S COLDER HERE THAN IN THE STATES.
I SEE WHY REED WANTED ME TO TAG ALONG WITH YOU. A FEW BURSTS OF NOVA FLAME AND WE OUGHT TO BE ABLE TO MELT OUR WAY INSIDE.
FA-THISSSSS
FIGURES. WE'RE AT THE CENTER OF THE WHOLE WINTER STORM SYSTEM NOW.
MOMENTS LATER, AS THE TORCH BURNS HIS WAY THROUGH...
THE PIECES OF THE CASKET OUGHT TO LIE AT THE BOTTOM OF THIS PIT.
GO EASY, JOHNNY. WE ONLY WANT TO MELT THE ICE AROUND THE FRAGMENTS; NOT INCINERATE THEM.

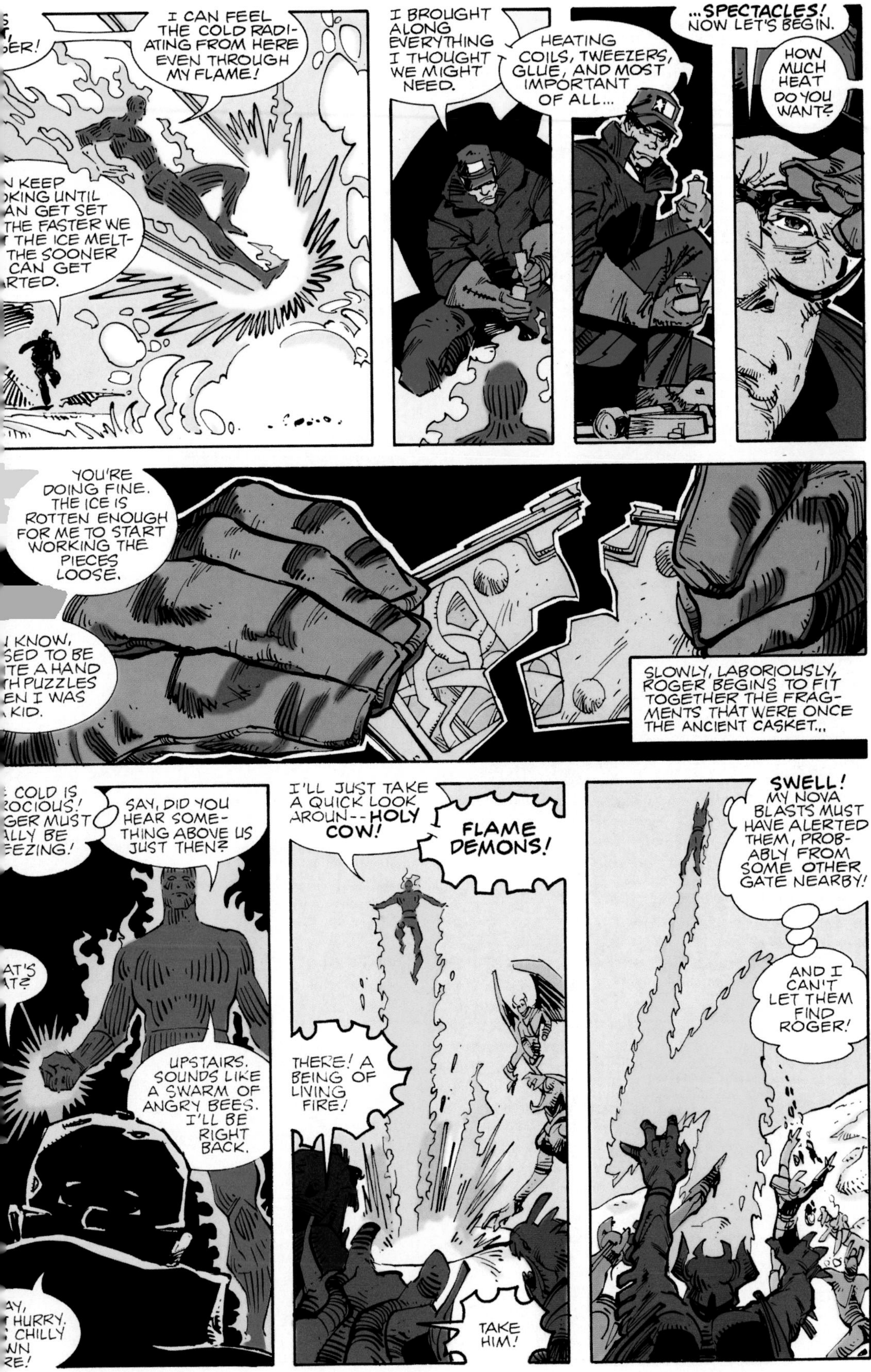

I CAN FEEL THE COLD RADI-ATING FROM HERE EVEN THROUGH MY FLAME!
N KEEP OKING UNTIL AN GET SET THE FASTER WE T THE ICE MELT-THE SOONER CAN GET RTED.
I BROUGHT ALONG EVERYTHING I THOUGHT WE MIGHT NEED.
HEATING COILS, TWEEZERS, GLUE, AND MOST IMPORTANT OF ALL...
...SPECTACLES! NOW LET'S BEGIN.
HOW MUCH HEAT DO YOU WANT?
YOU'RE DOING FINE. THE ICE IS ROTTEN ENOUGH FOR ME TO START WORKING THE PIECES LOOSE.
I KNOW, SED TO BE TE A HAND TH PUZZLES EN I WAS KID.
SLOWLY, LABORIOUSLY, ROGER BEGINS TO FIT TOGETHER THE FRAG-MENTS THAT WERE ONCE THE ANCIENT CASKET...
COLD IS ROCIOUS! GER MUST ALLY BE EEZING!
SAY, DID YOU HEAR SOME-THING ABOVE US JUST THEN?
AT'S AT?
UPSTAIRS. SOUNDS LIKE A SWARM OF ANGRY BEES. I'LL BE RIGHT BACK.
AY, T HURRY. CHILLY WN RE!
I'LL JUST TAKE A QUICK LOOK AROUN--HOLY COW!
FLAME DEMONS!
THERE! A BEING OF LIVING FIRE!
TAKE HIM!
SWELL! MY NOVA BLASTS MUST HAVE ALERTED THEM, PROB-ABLY FROM SOME OTHER GATE NEARBY!
AND I CAN'T LET THEM FIND ROGER!

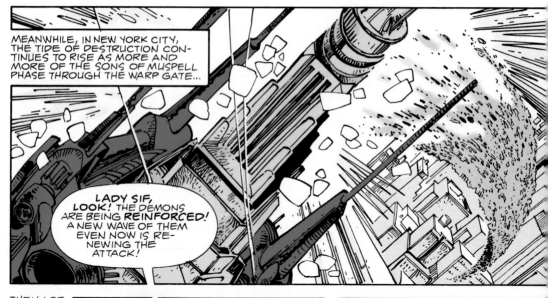

MEANWHILE, IN NEW YORK CITY, THE TIDE OF DESTRUCTION CONTINUES TO RISE AS MORE AND MORE OF THE SONS OF MUSPELL PHASE THROUGH THE WARP GATE...

LADY SIF, **LOOK!** THE DEMONS ARE BEING **REINFORCED!** A NEW WAVE OF THEM EVEN NOW IS RENEWING THE ATTACK!

THEN LET US WITHDRAW ACCORDING TO PLAN!

GATHER THE HEROES AND RIDE FOR THE WORLD TRADE CENTER! I SHALL COVER OUR RETREAT!

BUT MILADY...!

HURRY, HAROKIN, BEFORE ALL ESCAPE IS CUT OFF! I'LL REJOIN YOU ON THE GROUND!

TELL BILL I SHALL BE TRUE TO MY WORD. **NOTHING** SHALL SEPARATE US!

SO SAYING, THE LADY SIF SPURS HER MOUNT AND TURNS TO MEET THE ONCOMING HORDE...

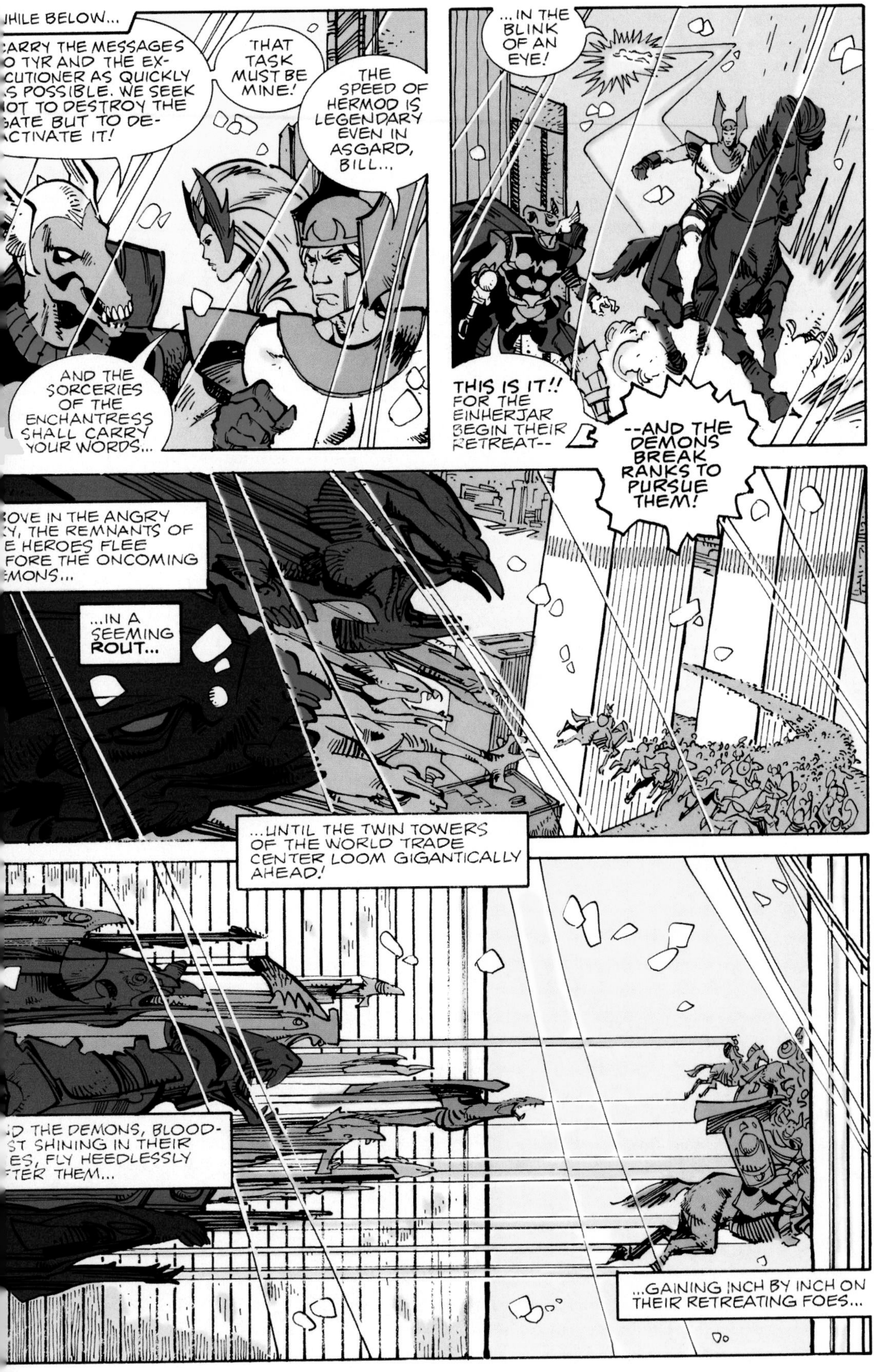

WHILE BELOW...
CARRY THE MESSAGES TO TYR AND THE EXECUTIONER AS QUICKLY AS POSSIBLE. WE SEEK NOT TO DESTROY THE GATE BUT TO DEACTIVATE IT!
THAT TASK MUST BE MINE!
THE SPEED OF HERMOD IS LEGENDARY EVEN IN ASGARD, BILL...
AND THE SORCERIES OF THE ENCHANTRESS SHALL CARRY YOUR WORDS...
...IN THE BLINK OF AN EYE!
THIS IS IT!! FOR THE EINHERJAR BEGIN THEIR RETREAT--
--AND THE DEMONS BREAK RANKS TO PURSUE THEM!
ABOVE IN THE ANGRY SKY, THE REMNANTS OF THE HEROES FLEE BEFORE THE ONCOMING DEMONS...
...IN A SEEMING ROUT...
...UNTIL THE TWIN TOWERS OF THE WORLD TRADE CENTER LOOM GIGANTICALLY AHEAD!
AND THE DEMONS, BLOODLUST SHINING IN THEIR EYES, FLY HEEDLESSLY AFTER THEM...
...GAINING INCH BY INCH ON THEIR RETREATING FOES...

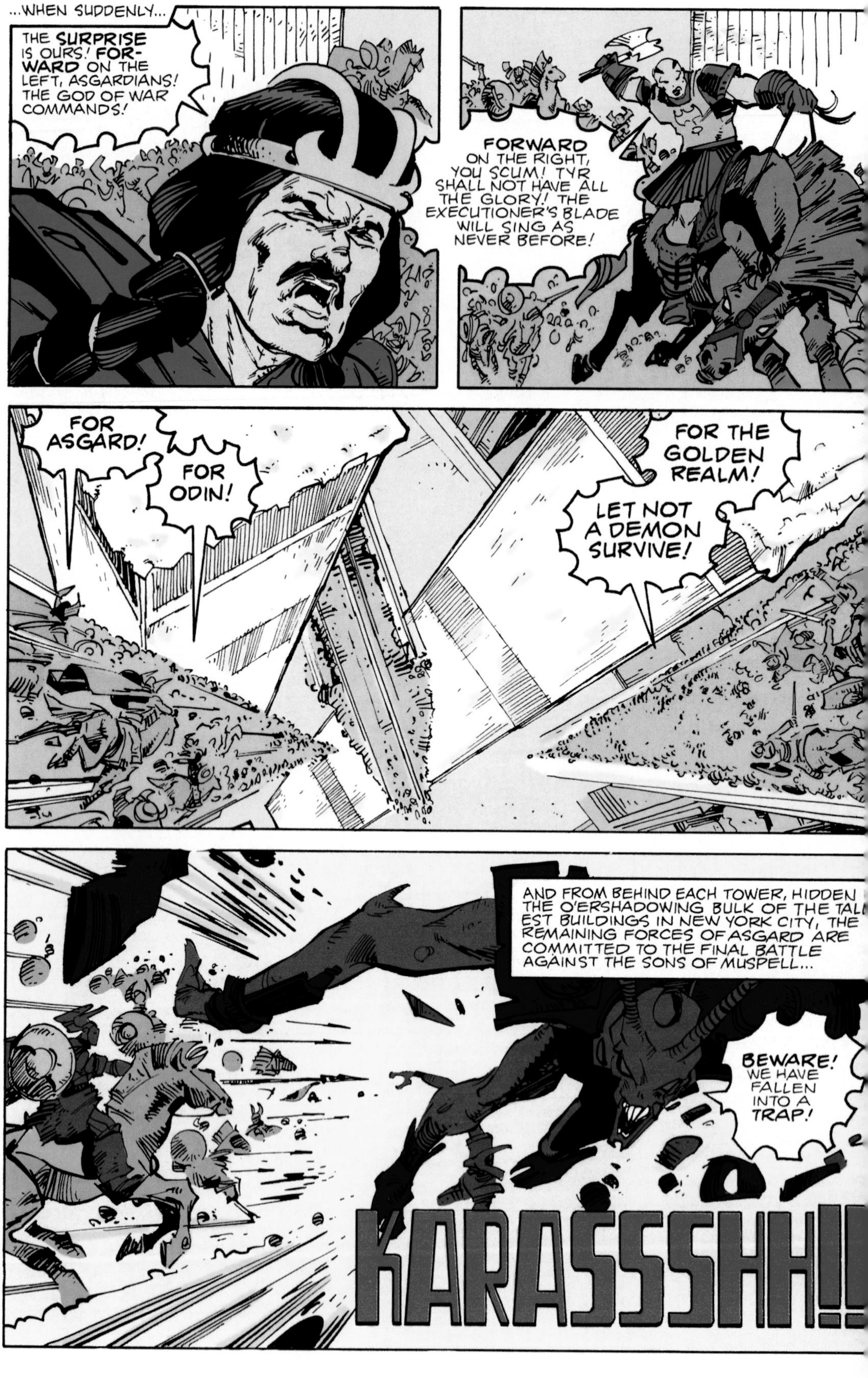
...WHEN SUDDENLY...
THE SURPRISE IS OURS! FORWARD ON THE LEFT, ASGARDIANS! THE GOD OF WAR COMMANDS!
FORWARD ON THE RIGHT, YOU SCUM! TYR SHALL NOT HAVE ALL THE GLORY! THE EXECUTIONER'S BLADE WILL SING AS NEVER BEFORE!
FOR ASGARD!
FOR ODIN!
FOR THE GOLDEN REALM!
LET NOT A DEMON SURVIVE!
AND FROM BEHIND EACH TOWER, HIDDEN THE O'ERSHADOWING BULK OF THE TALL EST BUILDINGS IN NEW YORK CITY, THE REMAINING FORCES OF ASGARD ARE COMMITTED TO THE FINAL BATTLE AGAINST THE SONS OF MUSPELL...
BEWARE! WE HAVE FALLEN INTO A TRAP!
KARASSSHH!!

...WHILE THE EINHERJAR REGROUP AND...

TURN, YOU HEROES! TURN AGAIN! WE SHALL DRIVE THE FOE BACK TO MUSPELHEIM!

FOR SEEMINGLY ENDLESS MINUTES, THE BATTLE HANGS IN THE BALANCE...

...BUT THE DEMORALIZED CREATURES OF THE FLAME ARE NO MATCH FOR THE FIGHTING FURY OF THE SONS OF ASGARD!

ARE YOU READY, REED?

MY CALCULATIONS ARE FINISHED, BILL. LET'S GO!

THE TIME IS NOW, YOU WARRIORS! RISE IN YOUR WRATH AND FOLLOW ME!

WE RIDE TO TAKE THE GATE ITSELF!

AND THE VANGUARD OF THE ASGARDIAN FORCES SOARS INTO THE SKY...

...PIERCING THE WEAKENED GUARD OF THE DEMON LEGIONS...

...DRIVING UP AND THROUGH UNTIL...

THAT'S THE LAST DEMON BETWEEN US AND THE GATE, REED! CAN YOU MAKE IT?

IF MY DEDUCTIONS ABOUT THE MACHINE'S OPERATIONS ARE CORRECT...

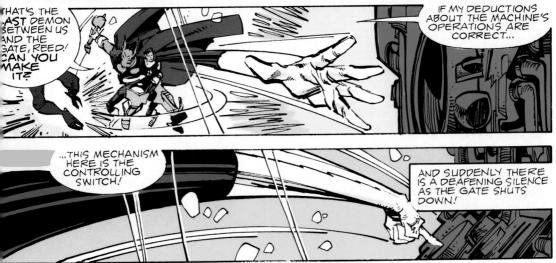

...THIS MECHANISM HERE IS THE CONTROLLING SWITCH!

AND SUDDENLY THERE IS A DEAFENING SILENCE AS THE GATE SHUTS DOWN!

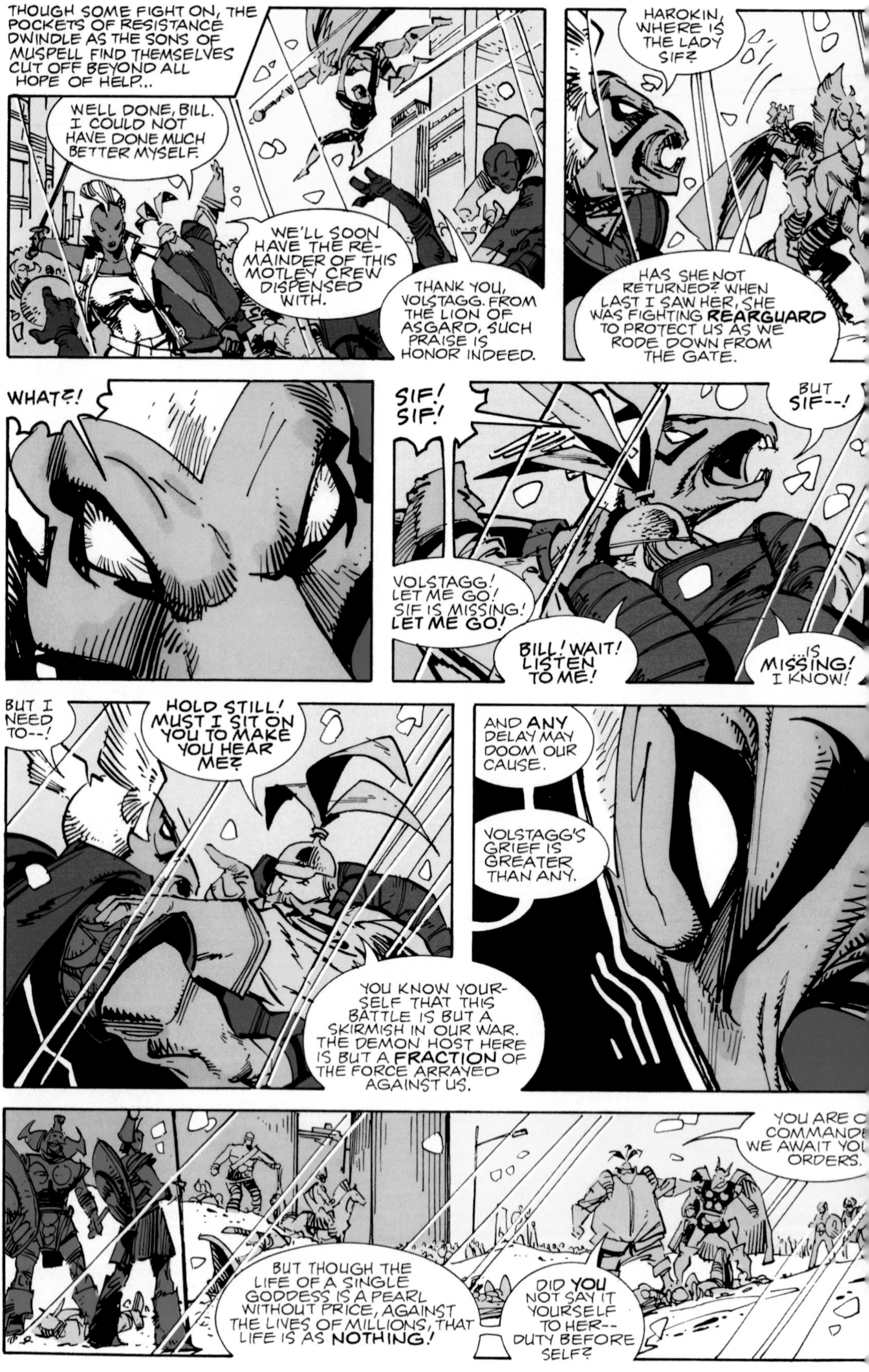
THOUGH SOME FIGHT ON, THE POCKETS OF RESISTANCE DWINDLE AS THE SONS OF MUSPELL FIND THEMSELVES CUT OFF BEYOND ALL HOPE OF HELP...
WELL DONE, BILL. I COULD NOT HAVE DONE MUCH BETTER MYSELF.
WE'LL SOON HAVE THE RE-MAINDER OF THIS MOTLEY CREW DISPENSED WITH.
THANK YOU, VOLSTAGG. FROM THE LION OF ASGARD, SUCH PRAISE IS HONOR INDEED.
HAROKIN, WHERE IS THE LADY SIF?
HAS SHE NOT RETURNED? WHEN LAST I SAW HER, SHE WAS FIGHTING REARGUARD TO PROTECT US AS WE RODE DOWN FROM THE GATE.
WHAT?!
SIF! SIF!
BUT SIF--!
VOLSTAGG! LET ME GO! SIF IS MISSING! LET ME GO!
BILL! WAIT! LISTEN TO ME!
...IS MISSING! I KNOW!
BUT I NEED TO--!
HOLD STILL! MUST I SIT ON YOU TO MAKE YOU HEAR ME?
YOU KNOW YOUR-SELF THAT THIS BATTLE IS BUT A SKIRMISH IN OUR WAR. THE DEMON HOST HERE IS BUT A FRACTION OF THE FORCE ARRAYED AGAINST US.
AND ANY DELAY MAY DOOM OUR CAUSE.
VOLSTAGG'S GRIEF IS GREATER THAN ANY.
BUT THOUGH THE LIFE OF A SINGLE GODDESS IS A PEARL WITHOUT PRICE, AGAINST THE LIVES OF MILLIONS, THAT LIFE IS AS NOTHING!
DID YOU NOT SAY IT YOURSELF TO HER-- DUTY BEFORE SELF?
YOU ARE O COMMANDE WE AWAIT YOU ORDERS.

BUT EVEN AS BETA RAY BILL STANDS WITH HEAD BOWED, LET US TURN TO ASGARD WHERE THE AWESOME ENERGIES UNLEASHED BY THE COMBATANTS ILLUMINATE THE SURROUNDING HEAVENS...

YOUR POWER HAS INDEED GROWN LARGE, SURTUR.

IT PREVENTS ME FROM ASSUMING THE GUISE OF THE GREAT WARRIOR WITH WHICH MY BROTHERS AND I ONCE DEFEATED YOU AGES AGONE.*

IN MY HAND, I HOLD A WEAPON OF INCALCULABLE POWER, THE SCEPTER SUPREME...

BUT I STAND IN THE VERY HEART OF MY OWN KINGDOM AND NOT ALL THE POWER OF MUSPELL SHALL MOVE ME FROM THE GATES OF MY REALM!

*THOR #349.

...AND WITH IT, I WILL CHANNEL THE COSMIC ENERGY OF THE ODIN POWER INTO A BOLT OF IRRESISTIBLE FORCE THAT CAN CAST DOWN EVEN THE UNMOVABLE!

YOU ONLY DELAY THE INEVITABLE, ODIN!

SO CLOSE TO THE ETERNAL FLAME, MY SWORD DRAWS UPON ITS LIMITLESS POWER AND REPLENISHES MY STRENGTH!

YOU CANNOT INJURE ME! YOU CANNOT STOP ME!

SOONER OR LATER, YOUR POWER WILL BE EXHAUSTED WHILE MINE ONLY INCREASES!

THOU HAST SAID ENOUGH!

THEN SHALL I HURL IT WITH ALL THE MIGHT AT MY COMMAND!

LET ALL MY POWER ENTER INTO THE SCEPTER UNTIL IT DOTH GLOW WITH AN INCANDESCENCE RIVALING THAT OF THE ETERNAL FLAME ITSELF!

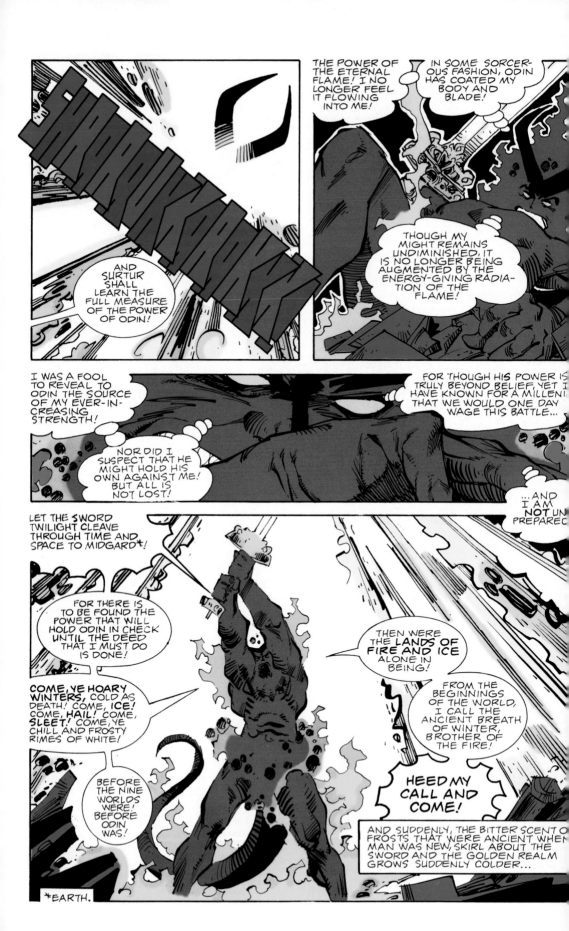

FHRAADDKRAAKK!

AND SURTUR SHALL LEARN THE FULL MEASURE OF THE POWER OF ODIN!

THE POWER OF THE ETERNAL FLAME! I NO LONGER FEEL IT FLOWING INTO ME!

IN SOME SORCEROUS FASHION, ODIN HAS COATED MY BODY AND BLADE!

THOUGH MY MIGHT REMAINS UNDIMINISHED, IT IS NO LONGER BEING AUGMENTED BY THE ENERGY-GIVING RADIATION OF THE FLAME!

I WAS A FOOL TO REVEAL TO ODIN THE SOURCE OF MY EVER-INCREASING STRENGTH!

NOR DID I SUSPECT THAT HE MIGHT HOLD HIS OWN AGAINST ME! BUT ALL IS NOT LOST!

FOR THOUGH HIS POWER IS TRULY BEYOND BELIEF, YET I HAVE KNOWN FOR A MILLENI THAT WE WOULD ONE DAY WAGE THIS BATTLE...

...AND I AM NOT UN PREPAREC

LET THE SWORD TWILIGHT CLEAVE THROUGH TIME AND SPACE TO MIDGARD*!

FOR THERE IS TO BE FOUND THE POWER THAT WILL HOLD ODIN IN CHECK UNTIL THE DEED THAT I MUST DO IS DONE!

THEN WERE THE LANDS OF FIRE AND ICE ALONE IN BEING!

FROM THE BEGINNINGS OF THE WORLD, I CALL THE ANCIENT BREATH OF WINTER, BROTHER OF THE FIRE!

COME, YE HOARY WINTERS, COLD AS DEATH! COME, ICE! COME, HAIL! COME, SLEET! COME, YE CHILL AND FROSTY RIMES OF WHITE!

HEED MY CALL AND COME!

BEFORE THE NINE WORLDS WERE! BEFORE ODIN WAS!

AND SUDDENLY, THE BITTER SCENT O FROSTS THAT WERE ANCIENT WHEN MAN WAS NEW, SKIRL ABOUT THE SWORD AND THE GOLDEN REALM GROWS SUDDENLY COLDER...

*EARTH.

...WHERE ODIN'S WIFE **FRIGGA** AND THE CHILDREN OF THE GODS CONFRONT A DEADLY TROLL BEFORE THE BRIDGE ABOVE THE ENDLESS CHASM.

A CHILL FELT EVEN IN [DI]STANT CORNER OF [A]SGARD...

FEED ME A YOUNGLING AND I LET YOU PASS!

OR YOU ALL **DIE** NOW!

[YO]U GUYS [KE]EP HIM [OCC]UPIED, [L]EIF!

GUNNHILD! WAIT! WHERE DO YOU--!

HROLF! ARNGRIM! BOOST ME UP! I'VE GOT AN IDEA!

WHAT'S SHE DOING?

I DON'T KNOW, BUT WE BETTER DISTRACT THE TROLL FAST!

HUH?

[H]EY, **UGLY!** [W]HERE WERE [YO]U WHEN ODIN [HAN]DED OUT [TH]E BRAINS?

WHAT?

IS THAT A NOSE OR ARE YOU TROLLS GROWING TOMATOES OUT OF SEASON?

WHY YOU--!

WHY DOES IT TAKE **FOUR** TROLLS TO LOSE WEIGHT?

[T]hukk!

ARRGH!

WRONG! TWO TO HOLD HIM DOWN AND ONE TO CUT OFF HIS HEAD!

PERFECT, GUYS! HE'S FORGOTTEN ALL ABOUT ME!

SCRITHH!

BUT NOT FOR LONG!

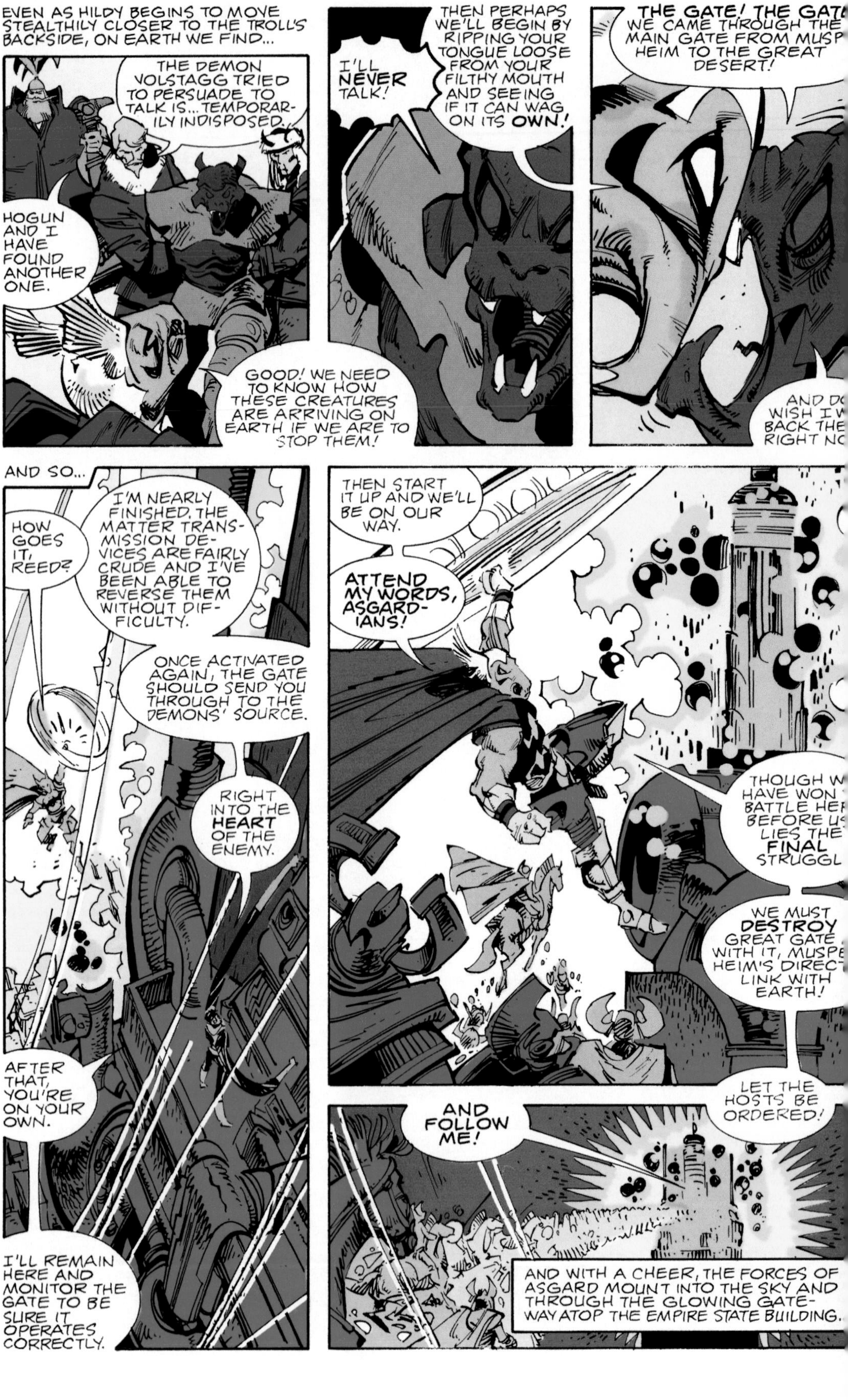
EVEN AS HILDY BEGINS TO MOVE STEALTHILY CLOSER TO THE TROLL'S BACKSIDE, ON EARTH WE FIND...
THE DEMON VOLSTAGG TRIED TO PERSUADE TO TALK IS... TEMPORARILY INDISPOSED.
HOGUN AND I HAVE FOUND ANOTHER ONE.
GOOD! WE NEED TO KNOW HOW THESE CREATURES ARE ARRIVING ON EARTH IF WE ARE TO STOP THEM!
I'LL NEVER TALK!
THEN PERHAPS WE'LL BEGIN BY RIPPING YOUR TONGUE LOOSE FROM YOUR FILTHY MOUTH AND SEEING IF IT CAN WAG ON ITS OWN!
THE GATE! THE GAT
WE CAME THROUGH THE MAIN GATE FROM MUSP HEIM TO THE GREAT DESERT!
AND DO WISH I W BACK THE RIGHT NO
AND SO...
HOW GOES IT, REED?
I'M NEARLY FINISHED. THE MATTER TRANSMISSION DEVICES ARE FAIRLY CRUDE AND I'VE BEEN ABLE TO REVERSE THEM WITHOUT DIFFICULTY.
ONCE ACTIVATED AGAIN, THE GATE SHOULD SEND YOU THROUGH TO THE DEMONS' SOURCE.
RIGHT INTO THE HEART OF THE ENEMY.
AFTER THAT, YOU'RE ON YOUR OWN.
I'LL REMAIN HERE AND MONITOR THE GATE TO BE SURE IT OPERATES CORRECTLY.
THEN START IT UP AND WE'LL BE ON OUR WAY.
ATTEND MY WORDS, ASGARDIANS!
THOUGH W HAVE WON BATTLE HE BEFORE US LIES THE FINAL STRUGGL
WE MUST DESTROY GREAT GATE WITH IT, MUSPE HEIM'S DIRECT LINK WITH EARTH!
LET THE HOSTS BE ORDERED!
AND FOLLOW ME!
AND WITH A CHEER, THE FORCES OF ASGARD MOUNT INTO THE SKY AND THROUGH THE GLOWING GATEWAY ATOP THE EMPIRE STATE BUILDING.

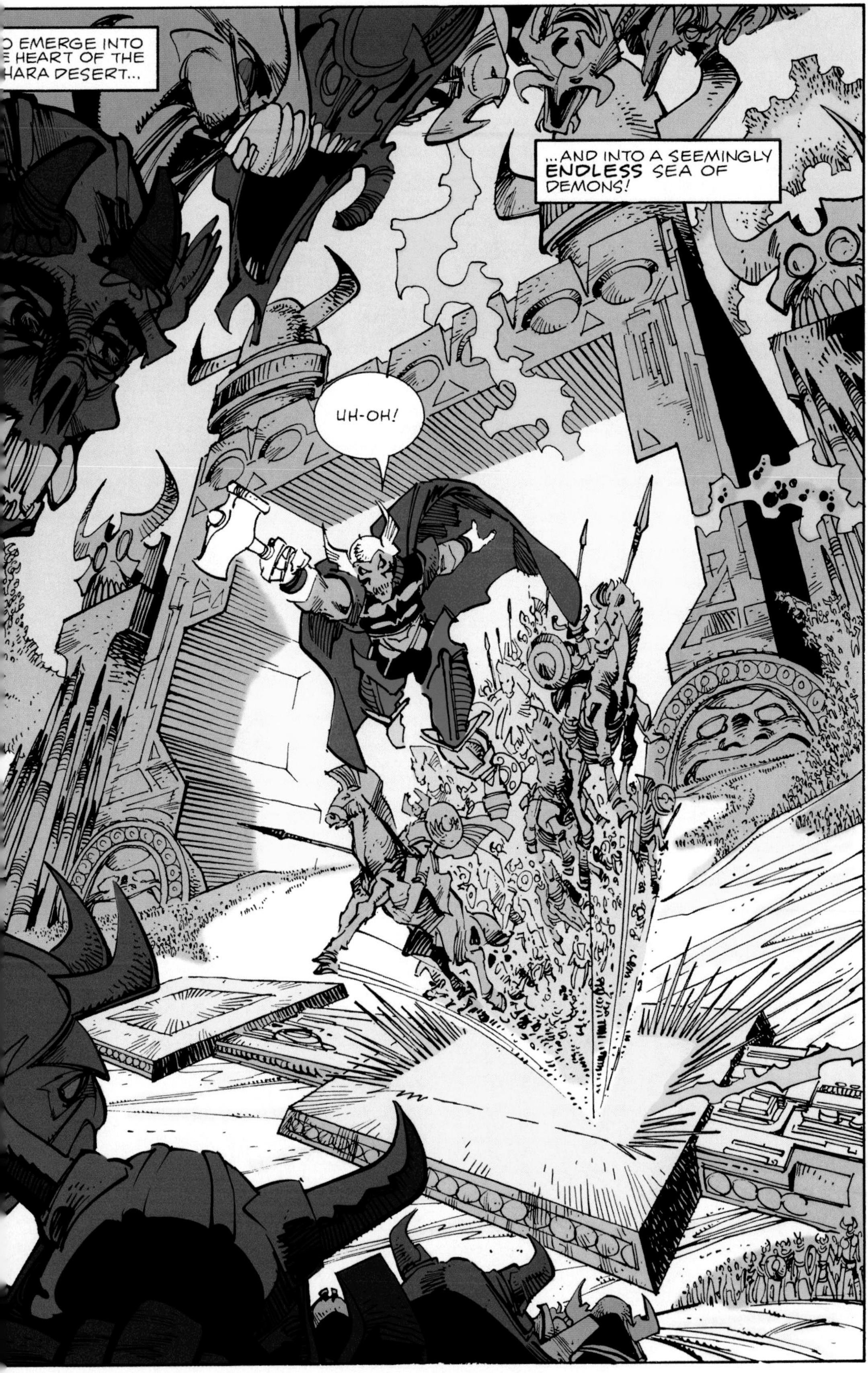
O EMERGE INTO
E HEART OF THE
HARA DESERT...
...AND INTO A SEEMINGLY ENDLESS SEA OF DEMONS!
UH-OH!

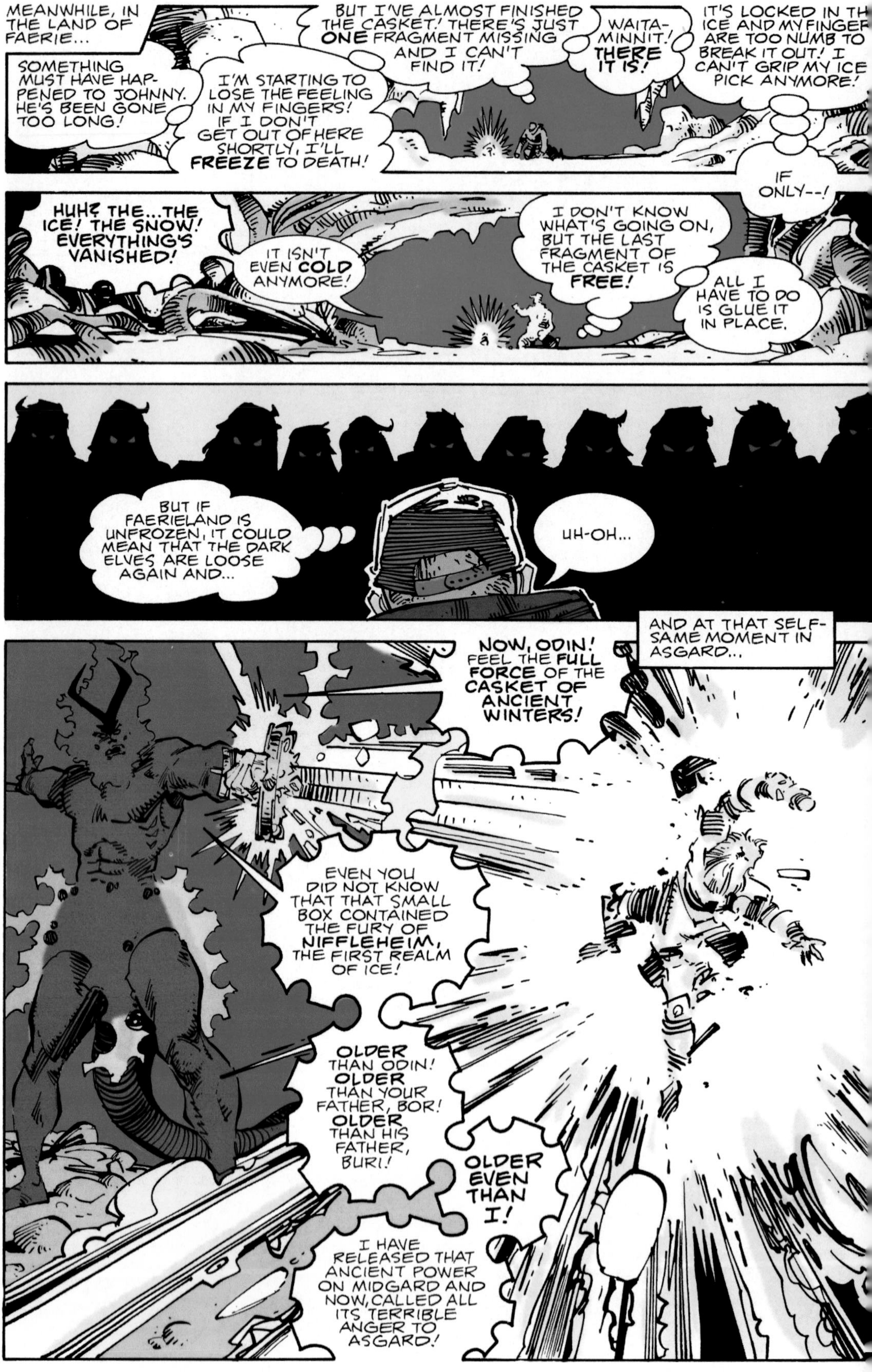

MEANWHILE, IN THE LAND OF FAERIE...
SOMETHING MUST HAVE HAPPENED TO JOHNNY. HE'S BEEN GONE TOO LONG!
I'M STARTING TO LOSE THE FEELING IN MY FINGERS! IF I DON'T GET OUT OF HERE SHORTLY, I'LL **FREEZE** TO DEATH!
BUT I'VE ALMOST FINISHED THE CASKET! THERE'S JUST **ONE** FRAGMENT MISSING AND I CAN'T FIND IT!
WAITA-MINNIT! **THERE IT IS!**
IT'S LOCKED IN TH ICE AND MY FINGER ARE TOO NUMB TO BREAK IT OUT! I CAN'T GRIP MY ICE PICK ANYMORE!
IF ONLY--!
HUH? THE...THE ICE! THE SNOW! EVERYTHING'S VANISHED!
IT ISN'T EVEN **COLD** ANYMORE!
I DON'T KNOW WHAT'S GOING ON, BUT THE LAST FRAGMENT OF THE CASKET IS **FREE!**
ALL I HAVE TO DO IS GLUE IT IN PLACE.
BUT IF FAERIELAND IS UNFROZEN, IT COULD MEAN THAT THE DARK ELVES ARE LOOSE AGAIN AND...
UH-OH...
AND AT THAT SELF-SAME MOMENT IN ASGARD...
NOW, ODIN! FEEL THE **FULL FORCE** OF THE **CASKET OF ANCIENT WINTERS!**
EVEN YOU DID NOT KNOW THAT THAT SMALL BOX CONTAINED THE FURY OF **NIFFLEHEIM,** THE FIRST REALM OF ICE!
OLDER THAN ODIN! **OLDER** THAN YOUR FATHER, BOR! **OLDER** THAN HIS FATHER, BURI!
OLDER EVEN THAN I!
I HAVE RELEASED THAT ANCIENT POWER ON MIDGARD AND NOW, CALLED ALL ITS TERRIBLE ANGER TO ASGARD!

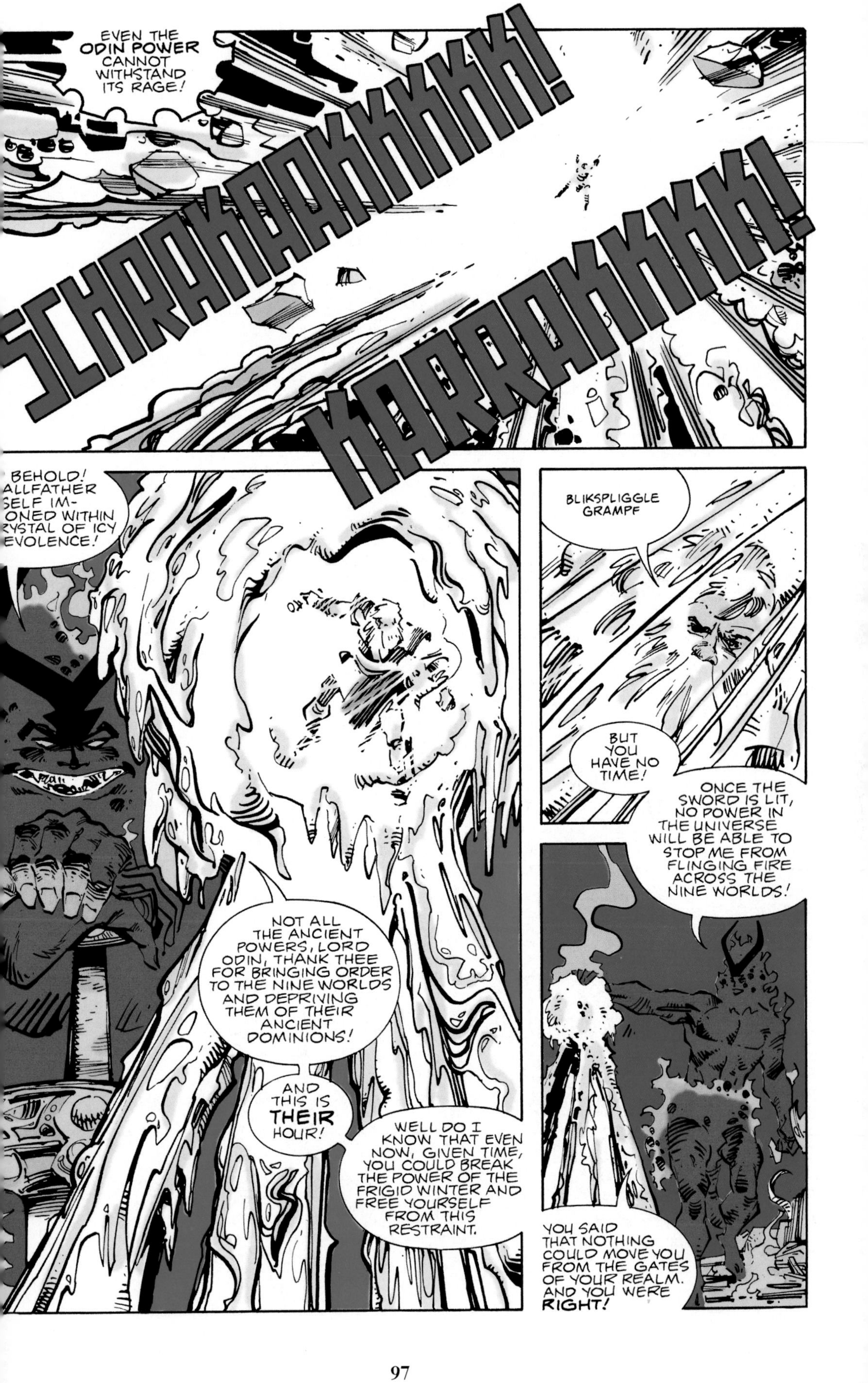

EVEN THE ODIN POWER CANNOT WITHSTAND ITS RAGE!
SCHRAKRAKKKKKKK!
KARRAKKKKK!
BEHOLD! ALLFATHER SELF IM- ONED WITHIN RYSTAL OF ICY EVOLENCE!
NOT ALL THE ANCIENT POWERS, LORD ODIN, THANK THEE FOR BRINGING ORDER TO THE NINE WORLDS AND DEPRIVING THEM OF THEIR ANCIENT DOMINIONS!
AND THIS IS THEIR HOUR!
WELL DO I KNOW THAT EVEN NOW, GIVEN TIME, YOU COULD BREAK THE POWER OF THE FRIGID WINTER AND FREE YOURSELF FROM THIS RESTRAINT.
BLIKSPLIGGLE GRAMPF
BUT YOU HAVE NO TIME!
ONCE THE SWORD IS LIT, NO POWER IN THE UNIVERSE WILL BE ABLE TO STOP ME FROM FLINGING FIRE ACROSS THE NINE WORLDS!
YOU SAID THAT NOTHING COULD MOVE YOU FROM THE GATES OF YOUR REALM. AND YOU WERE RIGHT!

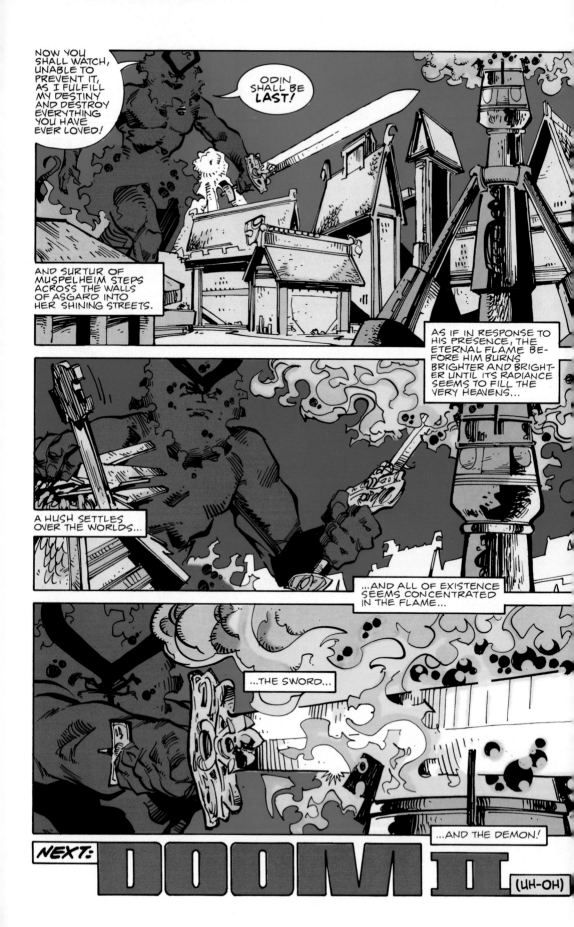

NOW YOU SHALL WATCH, UNABLE TO PREVENT IT, AS I FULFILL MY DESTINY AND DESTROY EVERYTHING YOU HAVE EVER LOVED!

ODIN SHALL BE LAST!

AND SURTUR OF MUSPELHEIM STEPS ACROSS THE WALLS OF ASGARD INTO HER SHINING STREETS.

AS IF IN RESPONSE TO HIS PRESENCE, THE ETERNAL FLAME BEFORE HIM BURNS BRIGHTER AND BRIGHTER UNTIL ITS RADIANCE SEEMS TO FILL THE VERY HEAVENS...

A HUSH SETTLES OVER THE WORLDS...

...AND ALL OF EXISTENCE SEEMS CONCENTRATED IN THE FLAME...

...THE SWORD...

...AND THE DEMON!

NEXT: DOOM II (UH-OH)

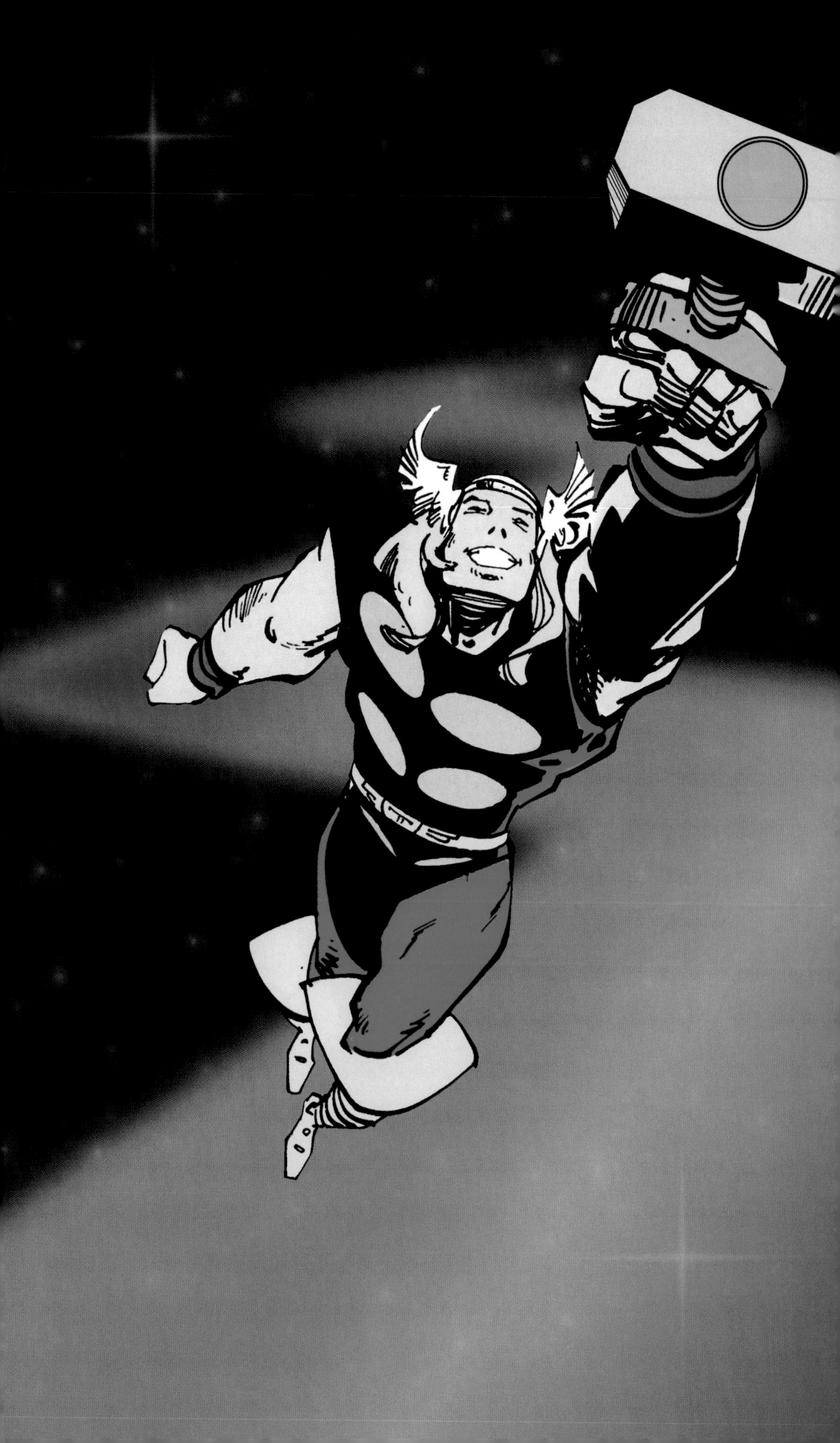

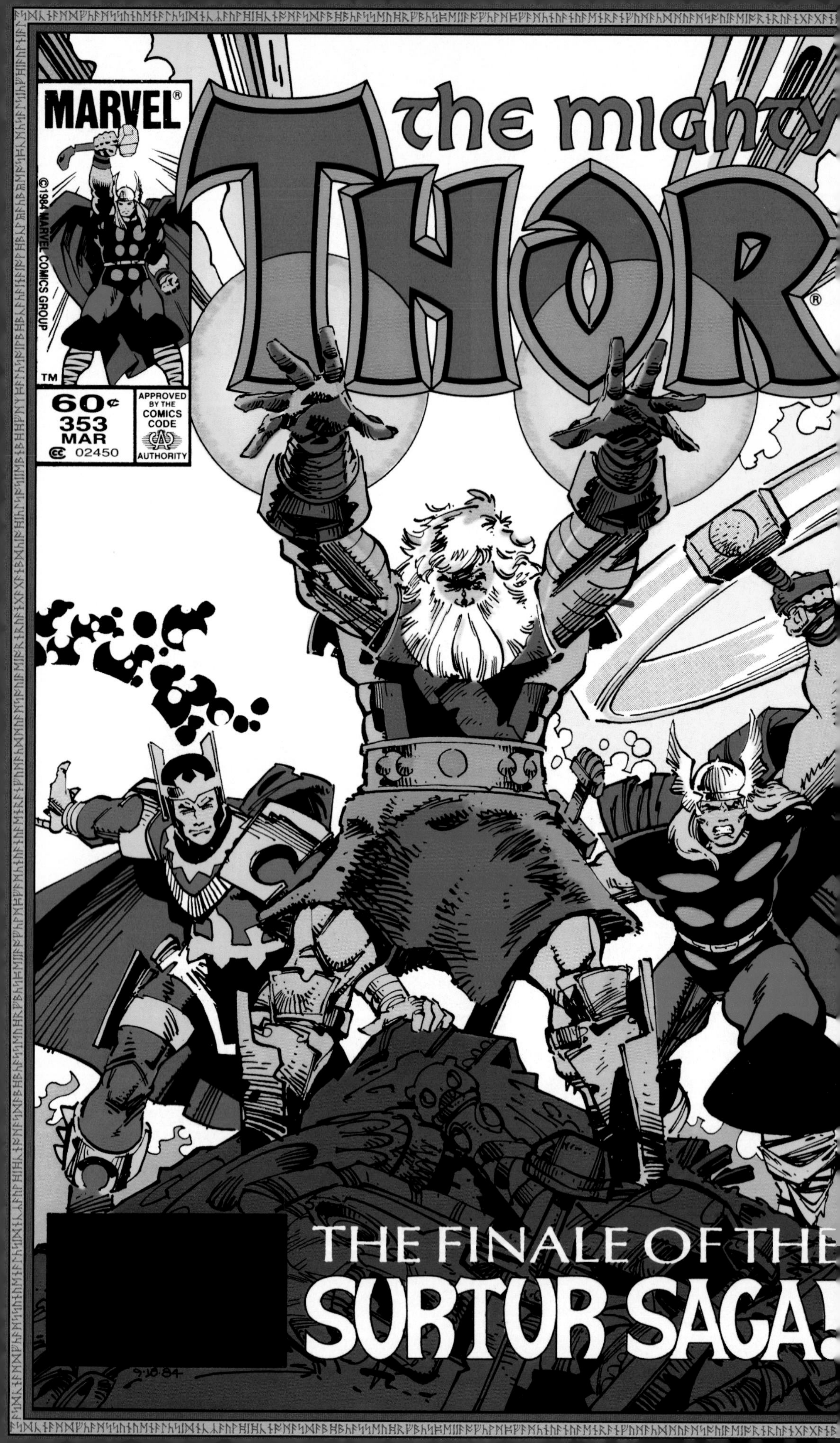
MARVEL®
the mighty
THOR®
©1984 MARVEL COMICS GROUP
TM
60¢
353
MAR
02450
APPROVED BY THE COMICS CODE AUTHORITY
THE FINALE OF THE
SURTUR SAGA!

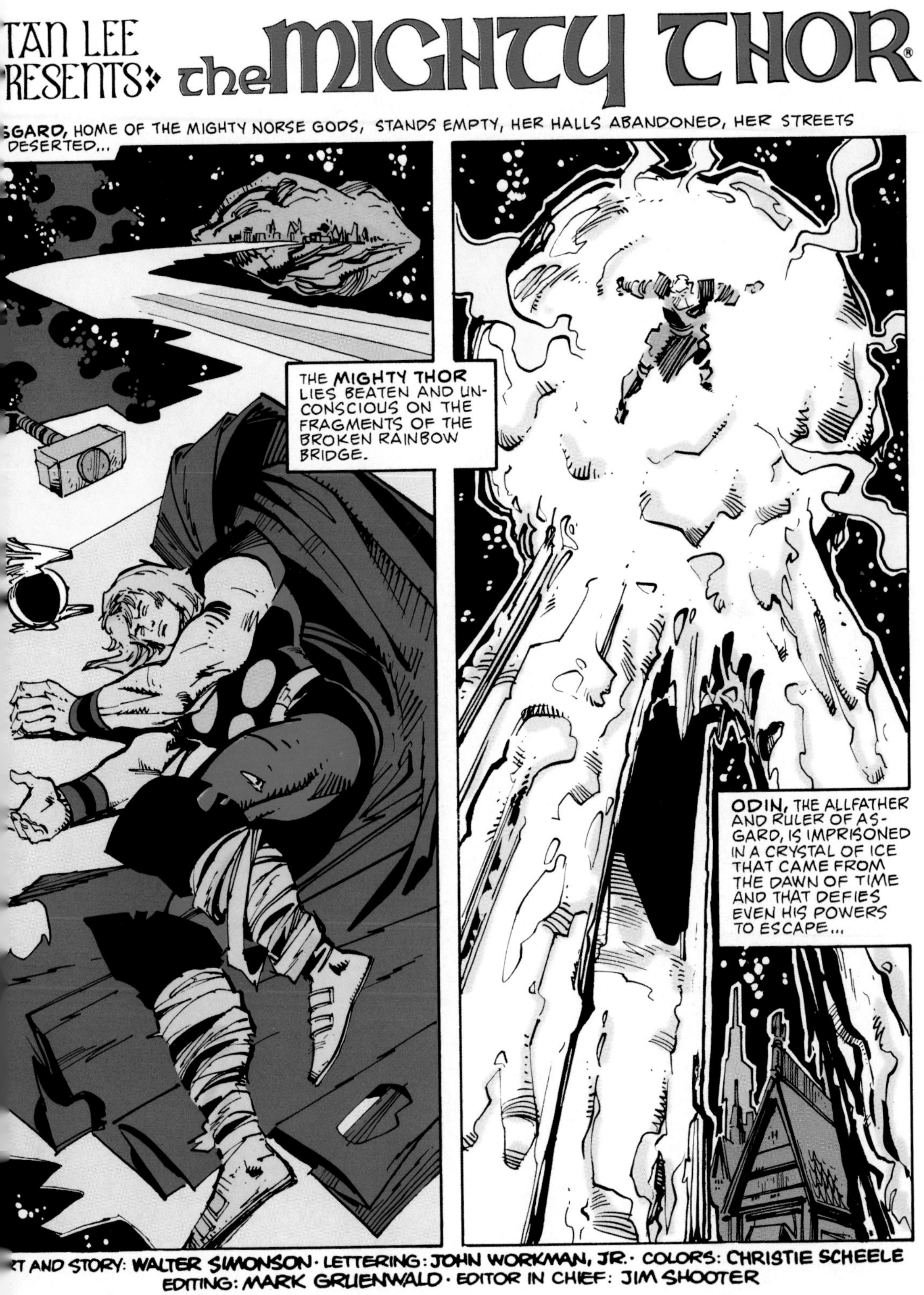
TAN LEE
RESENTS: the MIGHTY THOR®
GARD, HOME OF THE MIGHTY NORSE GODS, STANDS EMPTY, HER HALLS ABANDONED, HER STREETS DESERTED...
THE MIGHTY THOR LIES BEATEN AND UNCONSCIOUS ON THE FRAGMENTS OF THE BROKEN RAINBOW BRIDGE.
ODIN, THE ALLFATHER AND RULER OF ASGARD, IS IMPRISONED IN A CRYSTAL OF ICE THAT CAME FROM THE DAWN OF TIME AND THAT DEFIES EVEN HIS POWERS TO ESCAPE...
RT AND STORY: WALTER SIMONSON · LETTERING: JOHN WORKMAN, JR. · COLORS: CHRISTIE SCHEELE
EDITING: MARK GRUENWALD · EDITOR IN CHIEF: JIM SHOOTER

...AND IN THE CENTER OF THE FORSAKEN REALM STANDS THE AUTHOR OF THESE EVENTS-- **SURTUR OF MUSPELHEIM,** LORD OF FLAME, ANCIENT OF DAYS, AND DEMON OF PROPHECY.

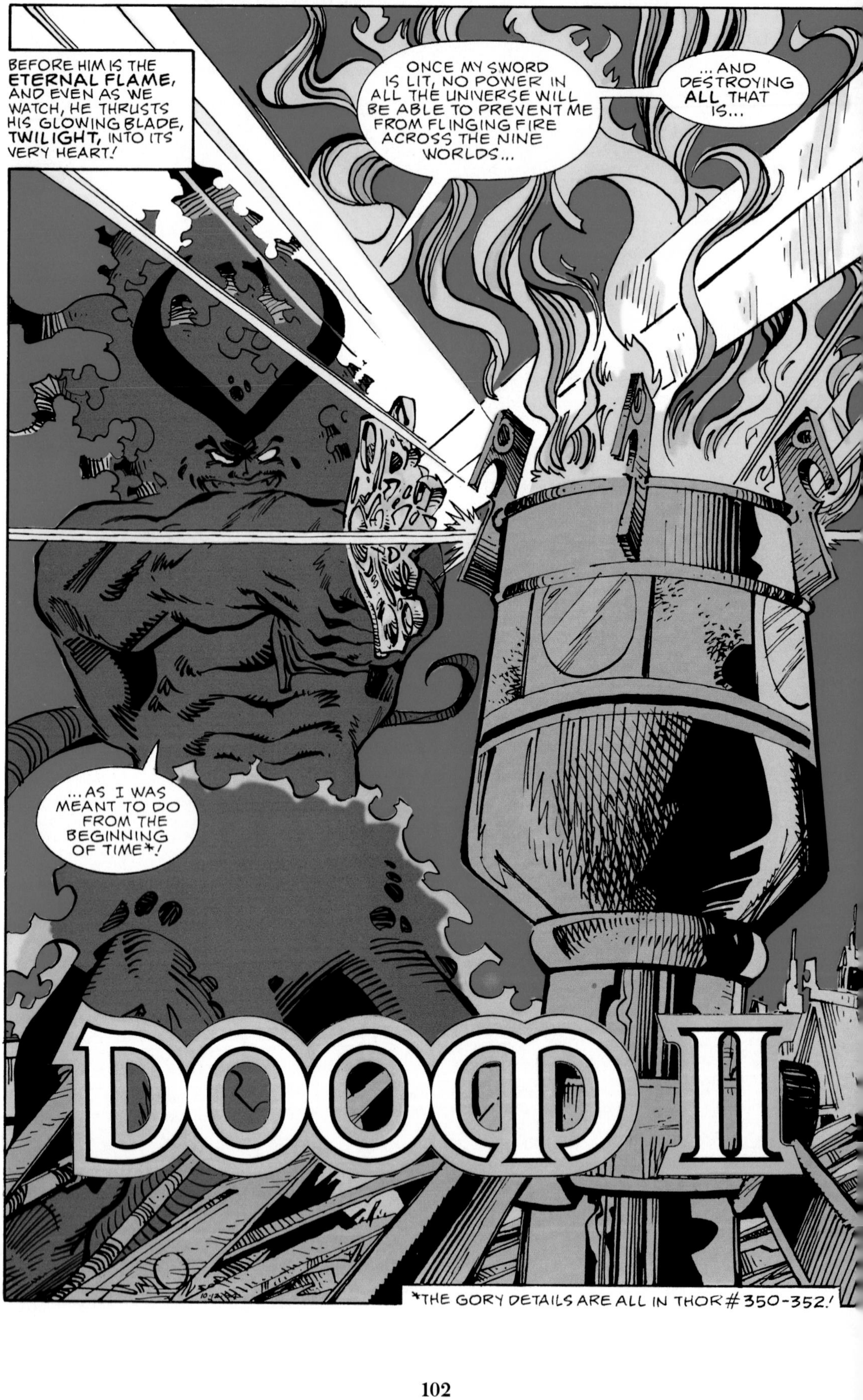

BEFORE HIM IS THE **ETERNAL FLAME,** AND EVEN AS WE WATCH, HE THRUSTS HIS GLOWING BLADE, **TWILIGHT,** INTO ITS VERY HEART!
ONCE MY SWORD IS LIT, NO POWER IN ALL THE UNIVERSE WILL BE ABLE TO PREVENT ME FROM FLINGING FIRE ACROSS THE NINE WORLDS...
...AND DESTROYING **ALL** THAT IS...
...AS I WAS MEANT TO DO FROM THE BEGINNING OF TIME*!
DOOM II

*THE GORY DETAILS ARE ALL IN THOR # 350-352!

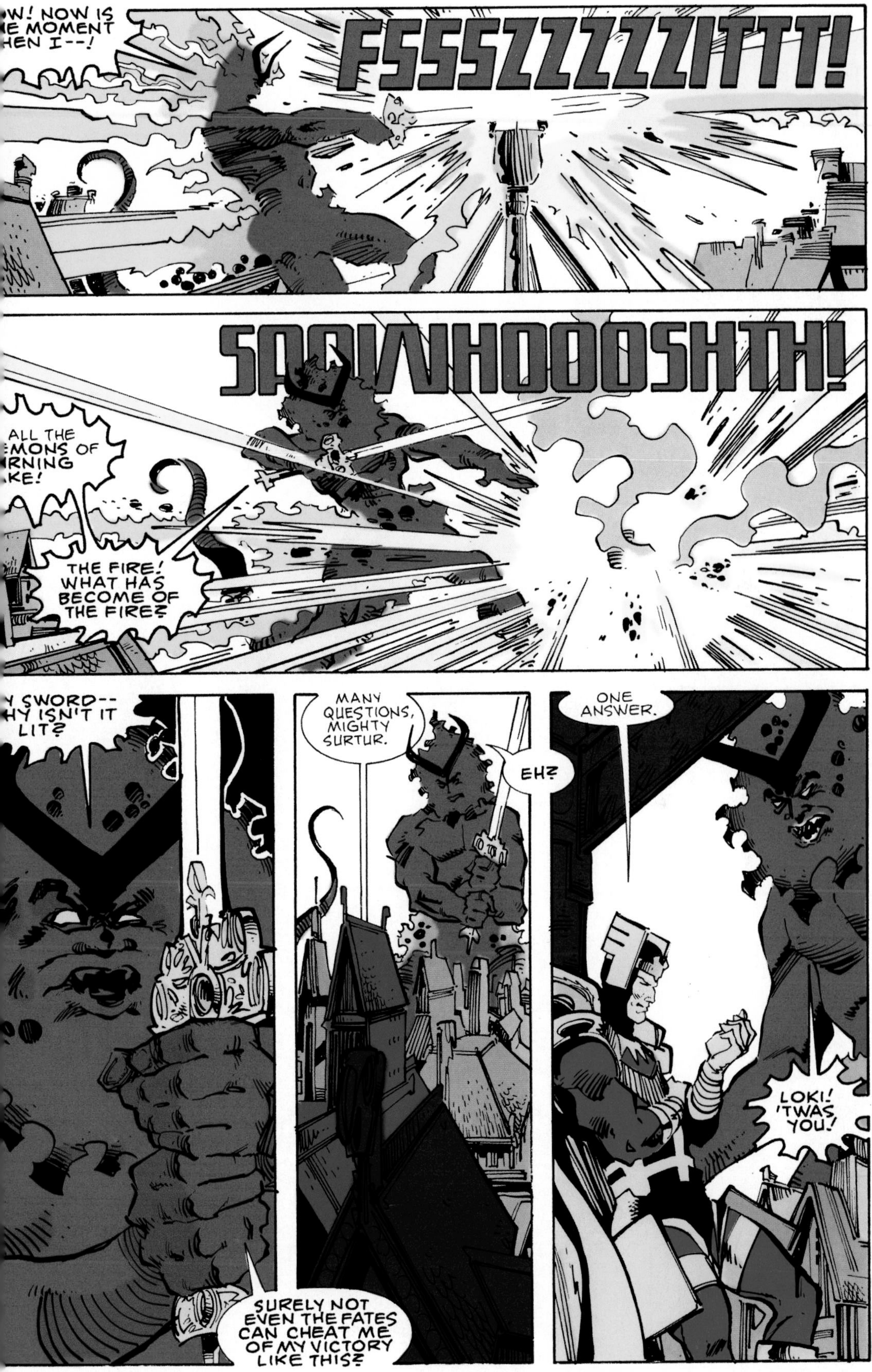
W! NOW IS E MOMENT HEN I--!
FSSSZZZZZITTT!
SPPWHOOOSHTH!
ALL THE EMONS OF RNING KE!
THE FIRE! WHAT HAS BECOME OF THE FIRE?
SWORD-- HY ISN'T IT LIT?
SURELY NOT EVEN THE FATES CAN CHEAT ME OF MY VICTORY LIKE THIS?
MANY QUESTIONS, MIGHTY SURTUR.
EH?
ONE ANSWER.
LOKI! 'TWAS YOU!

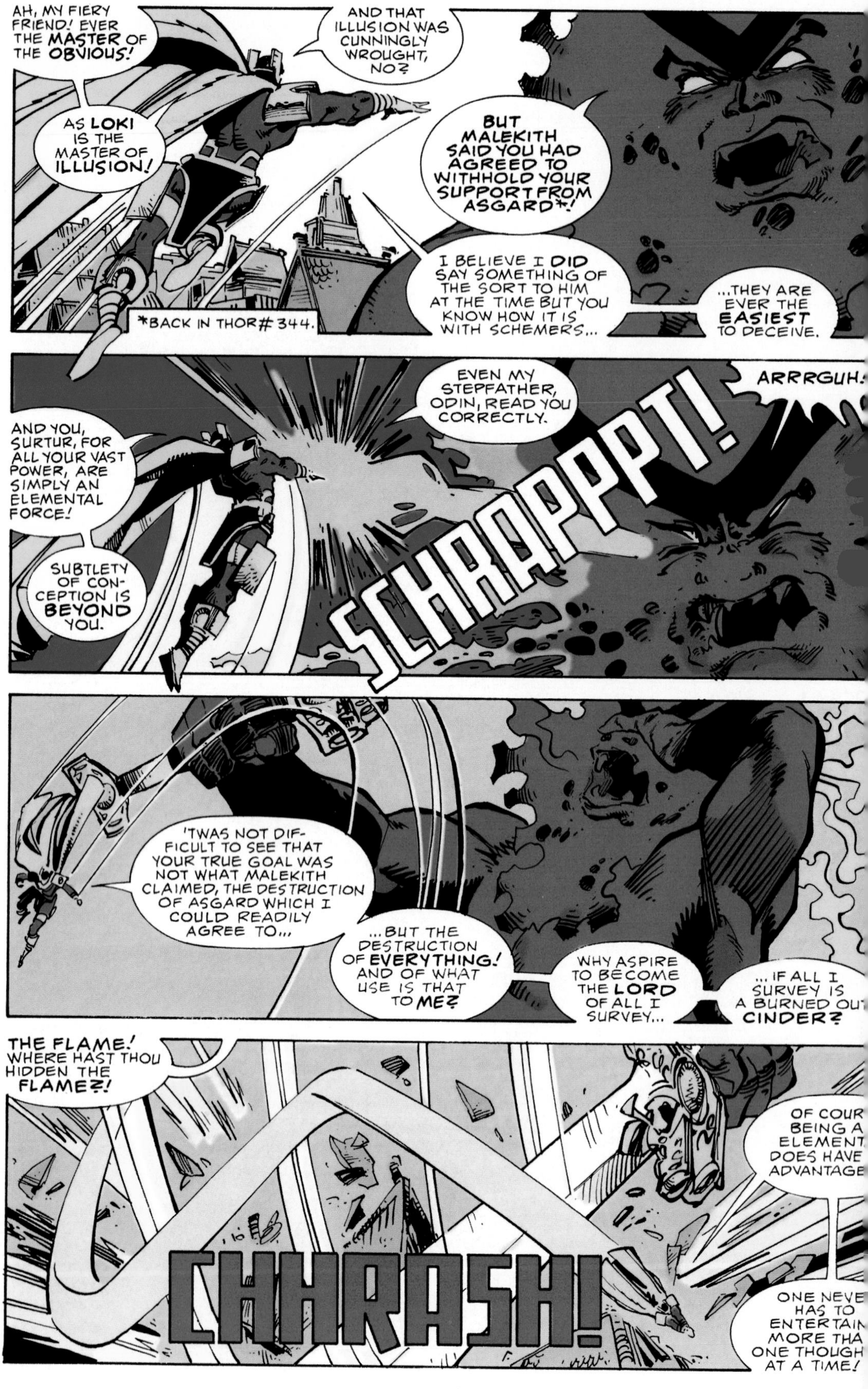

AH, MY FIERY FRIEND! EVER THE MASTER OF THE OBVIOUS!
AS LOKI IS THE MASTER OF ILLUSION!
AND THAT ILLUSION WAS CUNNINGLY WROUGHT, NO?
BUT MALEKITH SAID YOU HAD AGREED TO WITHHOLD YOUR SUPPORT FROM ASGARD*!
I BELIEVE I DID SAY SOMETHING OF THE SORT TO HIM AT THE TIME BUT YOU KNOW HOW IT IS WITH SCHEMERS...
...THEY ARE EVER THE EASIEST TO DECEIVE.
*BACK IN THOR #344.
AND YOU, SURTUR, FOR ALL YOUR VAST POWER, ARE SIMPLY AN ELEMENTAL FORCE!
SUBTLETY OF CON-CEPTION IS BEYOND YOU.
EVEN MY STEPFATHER, ODIN, READ YOU CORRECTLY.
SCHRAPPPT!
ARRRGUH!
'TWAS NOT DIF-FICULT TO SEE THAT YOUR TRUE GOAL WAS NOT WHAT MALEKITH CLAIMED, THE DESTRUCTION OF ASGARD WHICH I COULD READILY AGREE TO...
...BUT THE DESTRUCTION OF EVERYTHING! AND OF WHAT USE IS THAT TO ME?
WHY ASPIRE TO BECOME THE LORD OF ALL I SURVEY...
...IF ALL I SURVEY IS A BURNED OUT CINDER?
THE FLAME! WHERE HAST THOU HIDDEN THE FLAME?!
OF COUR
BEING A
ELEMENT
DOES HAVE
ADVANTAGE
CHHRASH!
ONE NEVE
HAS TO
ENTERTAIN
MORE THA
ONE THOUGH
AT A TIME!

EVEN A SIMPLE MIND, [GR]ANTED A BODY OF GREAT [POW]ER, MAY ACCOMPLISH [M]UCH IF ONE IS NOT CAREFUL.

MY STEP-BROTHER **THOR** IS THE LIVING PROOF OF THAT!

SO WE WILL TRY TO MAKE THE PURSUIT MORE INTERESTING!

ALL OF US!

FWAUKKTH!

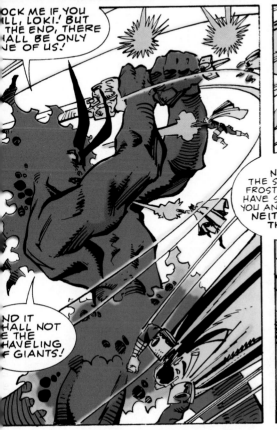

[M]OCK ME IF YOU [WI]LL, LOKI! BUT [IN] THE END, THERE [SH]ALL BE ONLY [O]NE OF US!

[A]ND IT [SH]ALL NOT [B]E THE [S]HAVELING [O]F GIANTS!

PERHAPS NONE BUT I, THE SCION OF THE FROST GIANTS, COULD HAVE STOOD BETWEEN YOU AND THE FLAME AS NEITHER ODIN NOR THOR COULD!

FZAPPT!

105

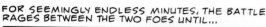

FOR SEEMINGLY ENDLESS MINUTES, THE BATTLE RAGES BETWEEN THE TWO FOES UNTIL...

ALL OF MY DUPLICATES HAVE BEEN DESTROYED!

I'D BEST RETREAT TILL I CAN SUMMON UP ANOTHER HOST OF GHOSTLY IMAGES!

MY STRENGTH BEGINS TO WANE AND SURTUR PRESSES ME HARD!

TOO LONG HAVE YOU LINGERED THIS TIME IN MY SIGHT, FARBAUTI'S SON!

AND THOUGH MY SWORD IS NOT YET ABLAZE WITH THE FIRE OF THE ETERNAL FLAME...

SKAGGERRAC

...THE FIERY ENERGY OF MUSPELHEIM IS STILL MINE TO COMMAND!

WHERE NOW, BOLD LOKI, IS ALL YOUR CRAFT AND GUILE?

AND WHERE IS THE FLAME I HAVE COME SO FAR TO FIND?

SOMEWHERE HERE IN ASGARD, IT MUST BE HIDDEN, BUT I SHALL UN-COVER IT!

AND WHEN I HAVE, THE FATES SHALL NO LONGER DENY ME MY DESTINY!

I SHALL TAKE WHAT WAS MINE IN THE BEGINNING AND LO, THERE SHALL BE AN ENDING!

THAT ANCIENT HALL! IT SHIMMERS BEFORE MY EYES! 'TIS AN ENCHANT-MENT OF LOKI'S WHICH FADES AND REVEALS--

--THE ETERNAL FLAME! IT IS MINE AT LAST!

EVEN AS SURTUR TURNS TOWARD THE SEETHING
[CAU]LDRON OF FIRE, WE FIND BENEATH THE ISLE [OF]
[OF] GREAT BRITAIN IN THE REALM OF FAERIE...

...ROGER WILLIS IN
A RACE FOR LIFE!

[AF]TER THE
[PO]RTAL! LET
[HIM] SEE US AND
[KNO]W THE FEAR
[OF] THE [DAM]NED!

FOR HE IS
THE ONE WHO
[H]ELPED CAPTURE
MALEKITH AND
WE SHALL
PAY HIM OUT IN
BLOOD*!

*THOR #348.

SOMETHING
MUST HAVE HAP-
PENED TO THE HUMAN
TORCH! HE NEVER
CAME BACK--

--AND THOUGH
I'VE GOT THE
CASKET OF ANCIENT
WINTERS NEARLY
PUT TOGETHER, IT
LOOKS AS THOUGH
I MAY NOT LIVE
LONG ENOUGH
TO ENJOY IT!

FASTER,
MY BROTHERS! A
MOMENT MORE
AND HE IS OURS!

[TH]EN WE'LL JUST
[HA]VE TO SKIP THAT
[MO]MENT, BOYS!
[BE]SIDES, ROGER
[AN]D I ARE FIN-
[ISH]ED HERE
[ANY]WAY!

RIGHT,
ROGER?

[JO]HNNY!

I'VE
NEVER BEEN
SO GLAD
TO SEE ANY-
ONE IN ALL
MY LIFE!

WHAT
HAP-
PENED
TO
YOU?

I RAN
INTO A FEW
FIRE DEMONS UP
ABOVE! MANAGED
TO SHAKE 'EM,
BUT IT KEPT ME
FROM GETTING
BACK TO YOU!

DON'T LOOK
NOW BUT I
THINK THOSE
DEMONS HAVE
COME BACK FOR
A RETURN
MATCH!

LOOKS
LIKE THE NEXT
ROUND IS ABOUT
TO START ANY
SECOND!

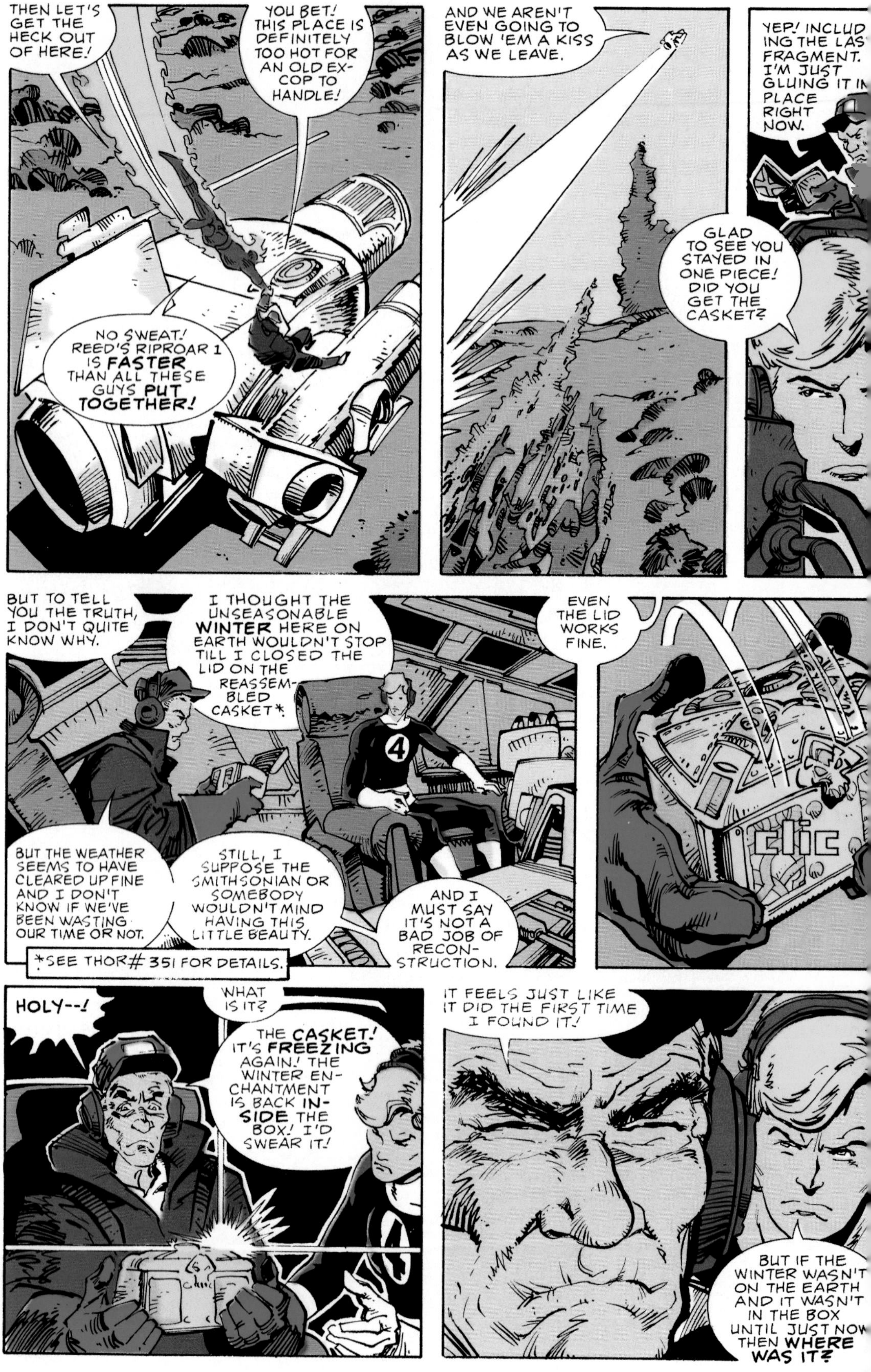
THEN LET'S GET THE HECK OUT OF HERE!
YOU BET! THIS PLACE IS DEFINITELY TOO HOT FOR AN OLD EX-COP TO HANDLE!
NO SWEAT! REED'S RIPROAR 1 IS FASTER THAN ALL THESE GUYS PUT TOGETHER!
AND WE AREN'T EVEN GOING TO BLOW 'EM A KISS AS WE LEAVE.
GLAD TO SEE YOU STAYED IN ONE PIECE! DID YOU GET THE CASKET?
YEP! INCLUD ING THE LAS FRAGMENT. I'M JUST GLUING IT IN PLACE RIGHT NOW.
BUT TO TELL YOU THE TRUTH, I DON'T QUITE KNOW WHY.
I THOUGHT THE UNSEASONABLE WINTER HERE ON EARTH WOULDN'T STOP TILL I CLOSED THE LID ON THE REASSEMBLED CASKET*.
BUT THE WEATHER SEEMS TO HAVE CLEARED UP FINE AND I DON'T KNOW IF WE'VE BEEN WASTING OUR TIME OR NOT.
STILL, I SUPPOSE THE SMITHSONIAN OR SOMEBODY WOULDN'T MIND HAVING THIS LITTLE BEAUTY.
AND I MUST SAY IT'S NOT A BAD JOB OF RECONSTRUCTION.
*SEE THOR# 351 FOR DETAILS.
EVEN THE LID WORKS FINE.
CLIC
HOLY--!
WHAT IS IT?
THE CASKET! IT'S FREEZING AGAIN! THE WINTER ENCHANTMENT IS BACK INSIDE THE BOX! I'D SWEAR IT!
IT FEELS JUST LIKE IT DID THE FIRST TIME I FOUND IT!
BUT IF THE WINTER WASN'T ON THE EARTH AND IT WASN'T IN THE BOX UNTIL JUST NOW THEN WHERE WAS IT?

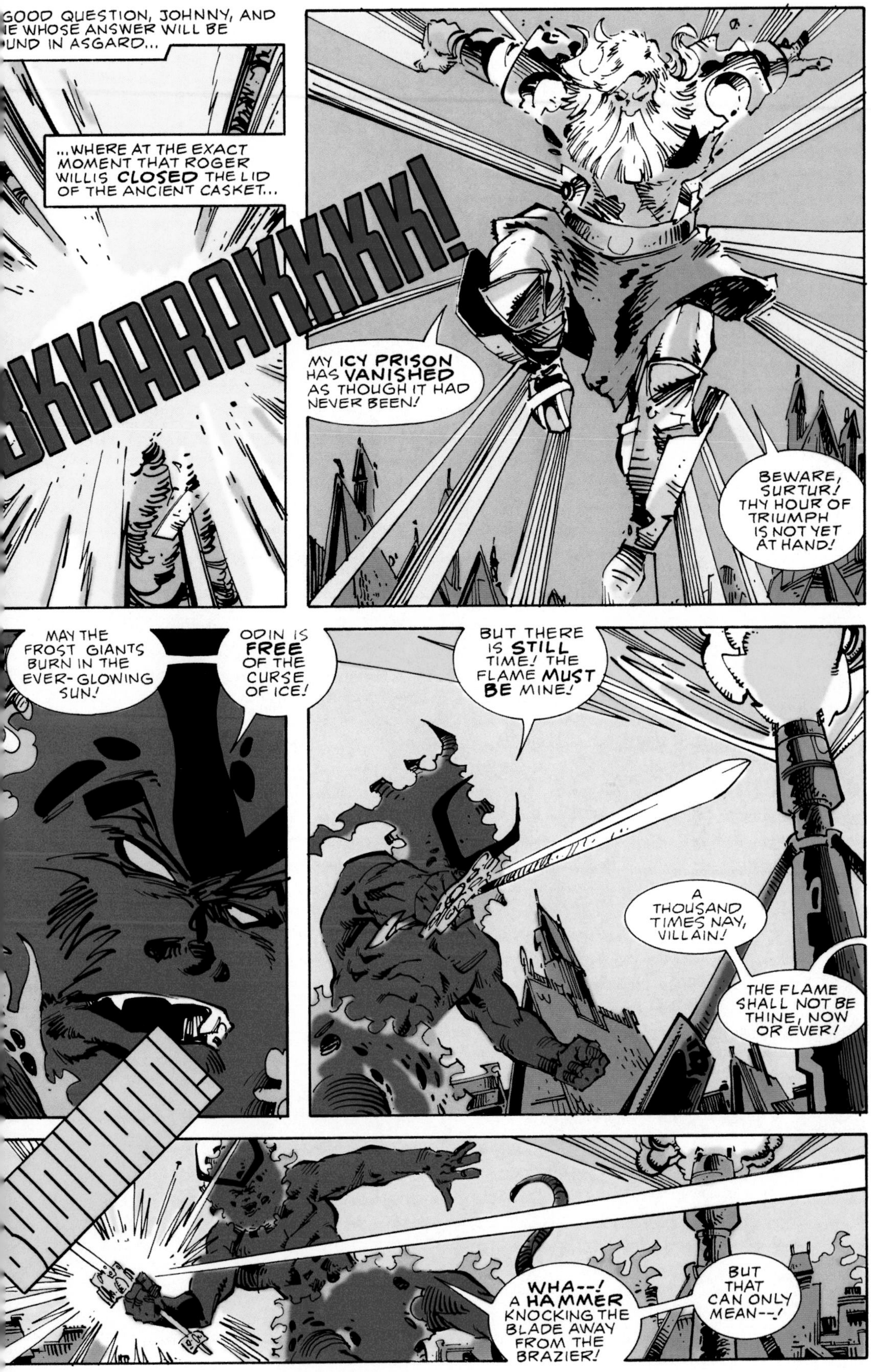
GOOD QUESTION, JOHNNY, AND
IE WHOSE ANSWER WILL BE
UND IN ASGARD...
...WHERE AT THE EXACT MOMENT THAT ROGER WILLIS CLOSED THE LID OF THE ANCIENT CASKET...
BKKARAKKKK!
MY ICY PRISON HAS VANISHED AS THOUGH IT HAD NEVER BEEN!
BEWARE, SURTUR! THY HOUR OF TRIUMPH IS NOT YET AT HAND!
MAY THE FROST GIANTS BURN IN THE EVER-GLOWING SUN!
ODIN IS FREE OF THE CURSE OF ICE!
BUT THERE IS STILL TIME! THE FLAME MUST BE MINE!
A THOUSAND TIMES NAY, VILLAIN!
THE FLAME SHALL NOT BE THINE, NOW OR EVER!
WHA--! A HAMMER KNOCKING THE BLADE AWAY FROM THE BRAZIER!
BUT THAT CAN ONLY MEAN--!

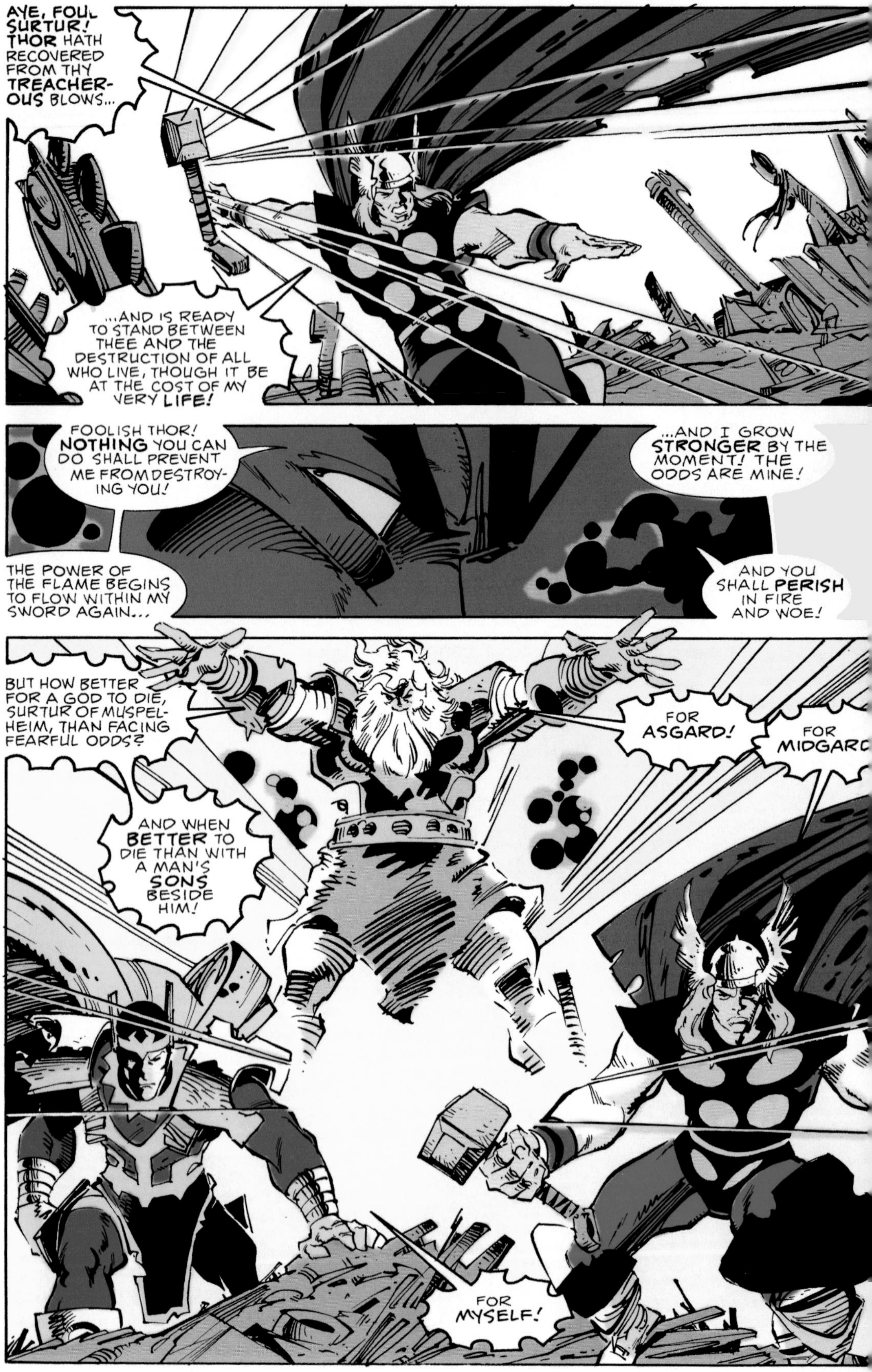
AYE, FOUL SURTUR! THOR HATH RECOVERED FROM THY TREACHER-OUS BLOWS...
...AND IS READY TO STAND BETWEEN THEE AND THE DESTRUCTION OF ALL WHO LIVE, THOUGH IT BE AT THE COST OF MY VERY LIFE!
FOOLISH THOR! NOTHING YOU CAN DO SHALL PREVENT ME FROM DESTROY-ING YOU!
...AND I GROW STRONGER BY THE MOMENT! THE ODDS ARE MINE!
THE POWER OF THE FLAME BEGINS TO FLOW WITHIN MY SWORD AGAIN...
AND YOU SHALL PERISH IN FIRE AND WOE!
BUT HOW BETTER FOR A GOD TO DIE, SURTUR OF MUSPEL-HEIM, THAN FACING FEARFUL ODDS?
AND WHEN BETTER TO DIE THAN WITH A MAN'S SONS BESIDE HIM!
FOR ASGARD!
FOR MIDGARD
FOR MYSELF!

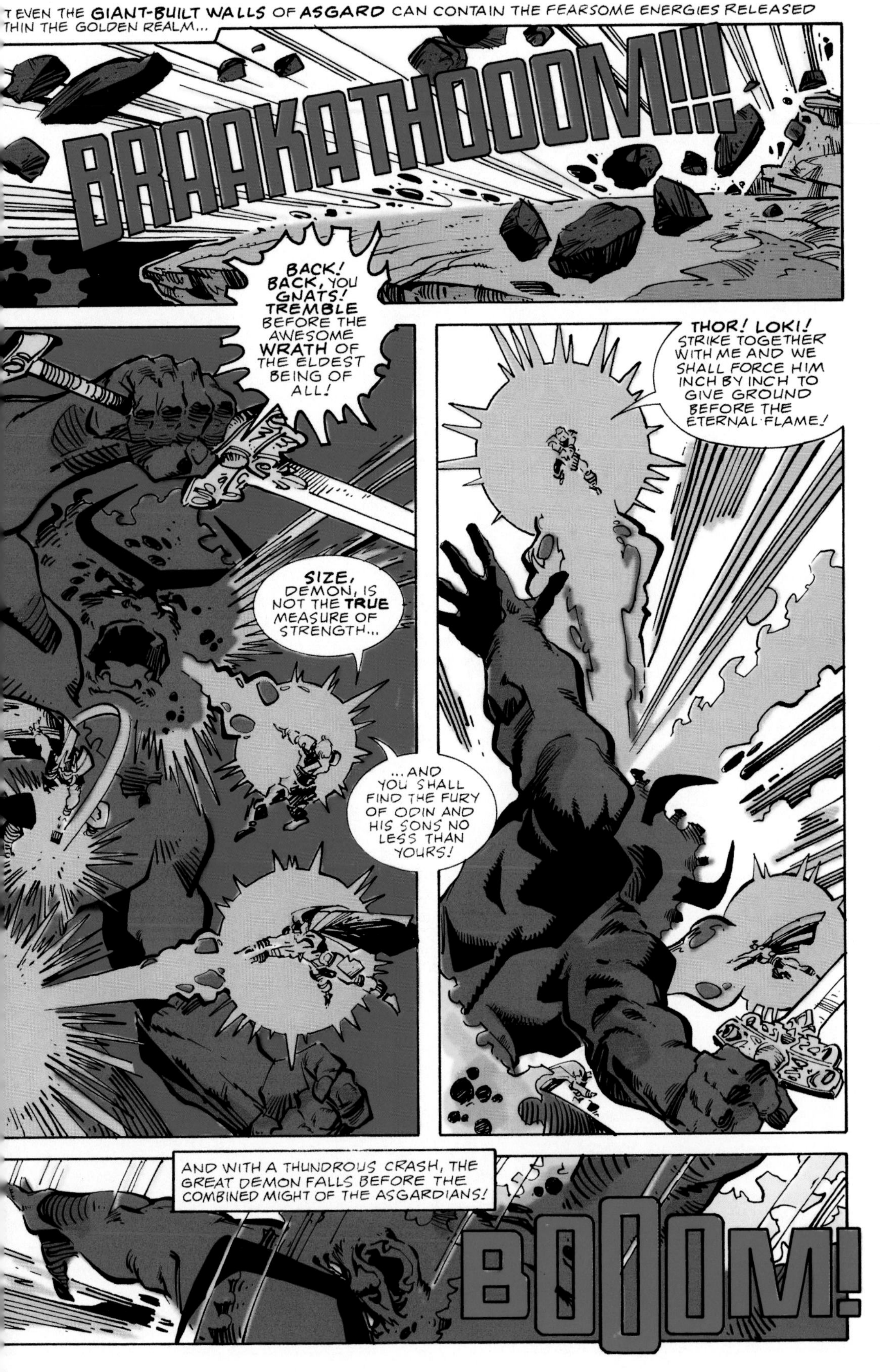
T EVEN THE GIANT-BUILT WALLS OF ASGARD CAN CONTAIN THE FEARSOME ENERGIES RELEASED THIN THE GOLDEN REALM...
BRAAKATHOOOM!!!
BACK! BACK, YOU GNATS! TREMBLE BEFORE THE AWESOME WRATH OF THE ELDEST BEING OF ALL!
SIZE, DEMON, IS NOT THE TRUE MEASURE OF STRENGTH...
...AND YOU SHALL FIND THE FURY OF ODIN AND HIS SONS NO LESS THAN YOURS!
THOR! LOKI! STRIKE TOGETHER WITH ME AND WE SHALL FORCE HIM INCH BY INCH TO GIVE GROUND BEFORE THE ETERNAL FLAME!
AND WITH A THUNDROUS CRASH, THE GREAT DEMON FALLS BEFORE THE COMBINED MIGHT OF THE ASGARDIANS!
BOOOM!

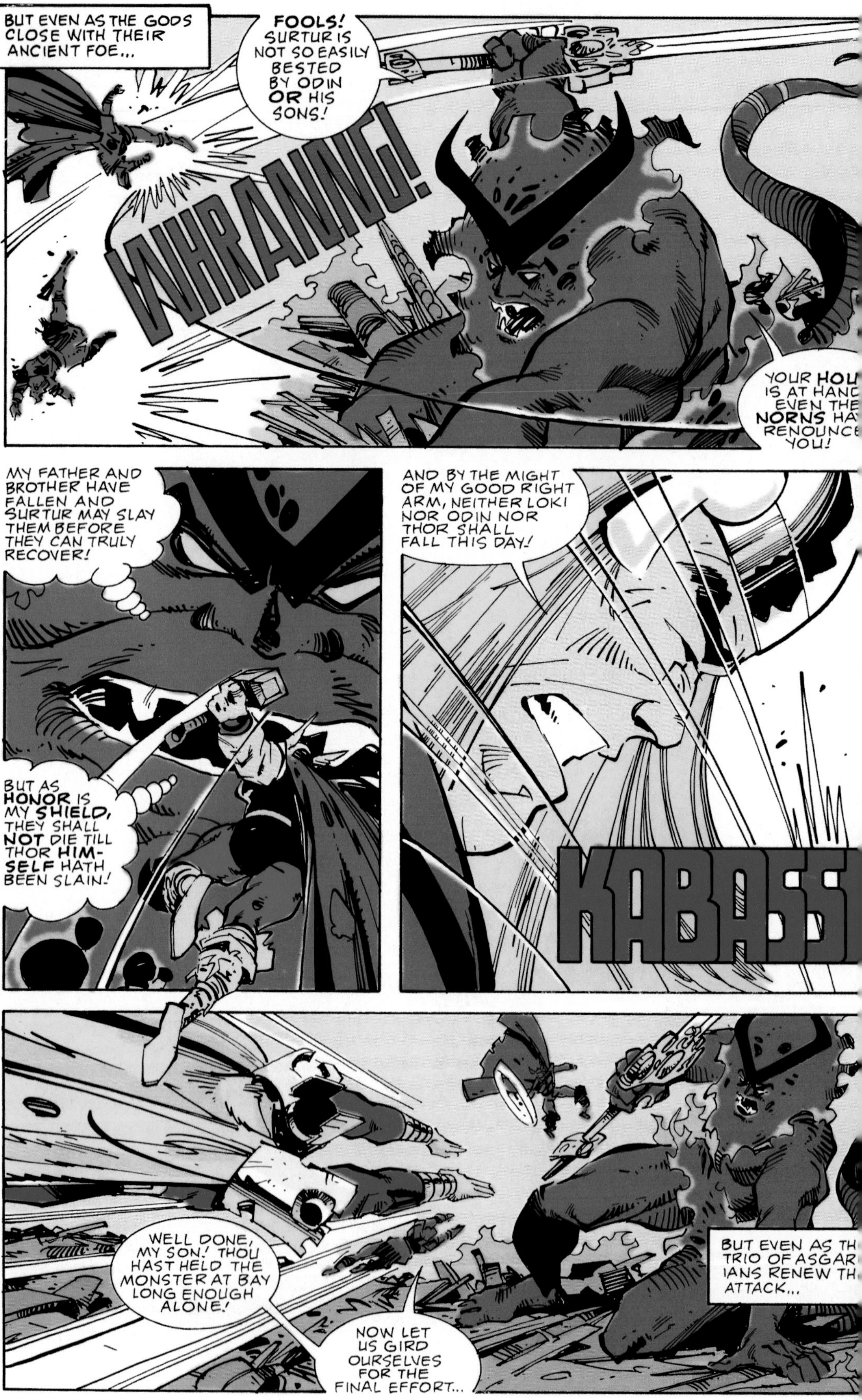
BUT EVEN AS THE GODS CLOSE WITH THEIR ANCIENT FOE...
FOOLS! SURTUR IS NOT SO EASILY BESTED BY ODIN OR HIS SONS!
WHRANNG!
YOUR HOU IS AT HAND EVEN THE NORNS HA RENOUNCE YOU!
MY FATHER AND BROTHER HAVE FALLEN AND SURTUR MAY SLAY THEM BEFORE THEY CAN TRULY RECOVER!
BUT AS HONOR IS MY SHIELD, THEY SHALL NOT DIE TILL THOR HIMSELF HATH BEEN SLAIN!
AND BY THE MIGHT OF MY GOOD RIGHT ARM, NEITHER LOKI NOR ODIN NOR THOR SHALL FALL THIS DAY!
KABASS
WELL DONE, MY SON! THOU HAST HELD THE MONSTER AT BAY LONG ENOUGH ALONE!
NOW LET US GIRD OURSELVES FOR THE FINAL EFFORT...
BUT EVEN AS TH TRIO OF ASGAR IANS RENEW TH ATTACK...

IN THE FURTHEST REACHES OF THE GOLDEN REALM, AT THE BRIDGE ABOVE THE BOTTOMLESS CHASM...

ENOUGH TIME! I TAKE YOUNGLING FOR DINNER **NOW!**

A LARGE TROLL CONFRONTS ODIN'S WIFE, FRIGGA, AND HER CHARGES, THE CHILDREN OF ASGARD...

FORGET IT, **FISHFACE!** WE'VE ALREADY EATEN!

NICE GOING, ARNGRIM!

HE'S COMPLETELY FORGOTTEN THAT I GOT BEHIND HIM* AND MY PREPARATIONS ARE FINISHED!

NOW TO REMIND HIM THAT I'M HERE!

*LAST ISSUE.

RAUUGH!

THAT DID IT! I HOPE THE ROPE I'VE GOT TIED AROUND MY WAIST HOLDS! **HERE** HE COMES!

AND HERE COMES THE **AXE!** RIGHT IN THE MIDDLE OF THE **BRIDGE!**

CRACCLAKK!

AAEEIIEE!

JUST LIKE EVERY TROLL! A DUMMY!

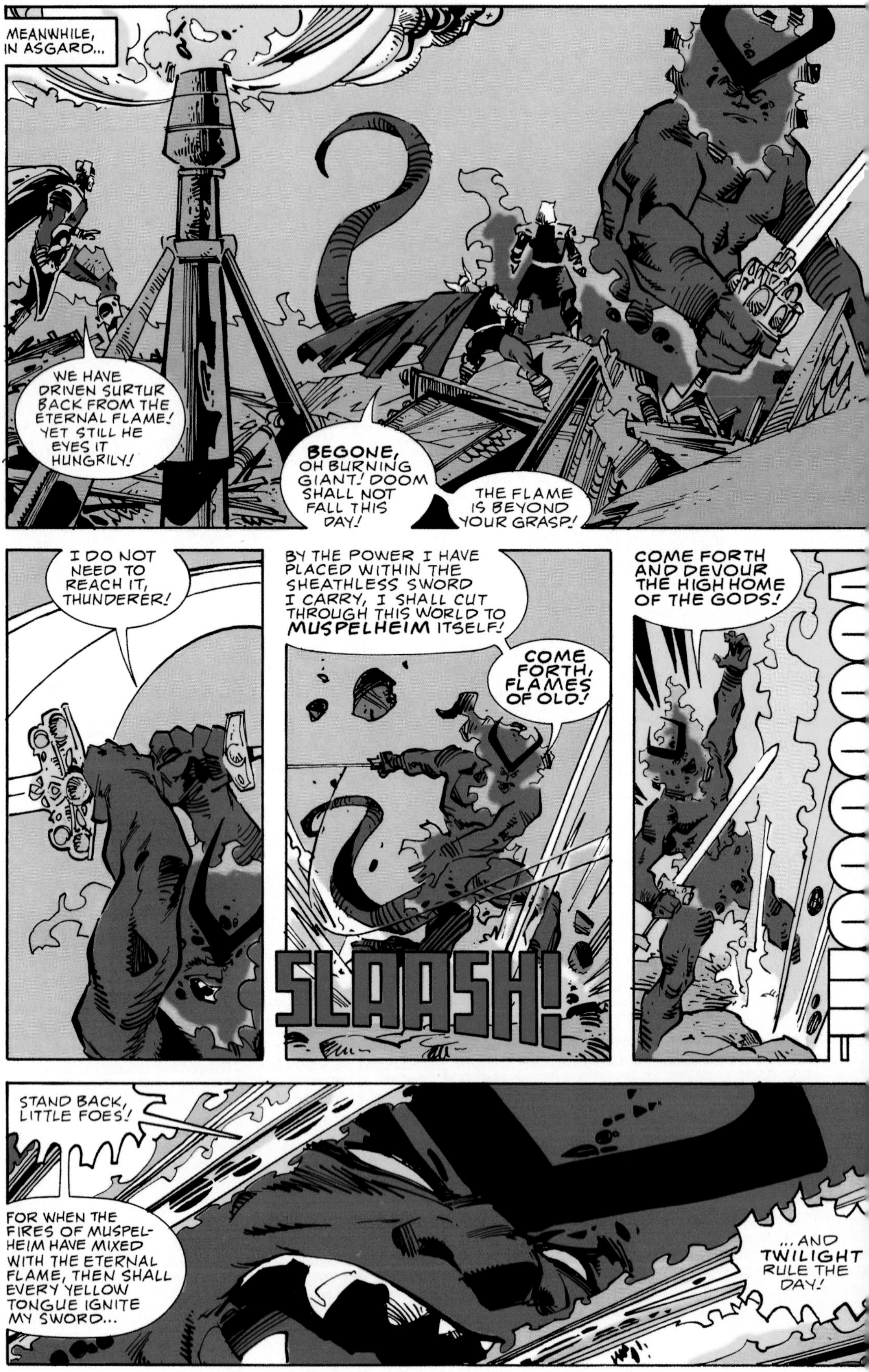
MEANWHILE, IN ASGARD...
WE HAVE DRIVEN SURTUR BACK FROM THE ETERNAL FLAME! YET STILL HE EYES IT HUNGRILY!
BEGONE, OH BURNING GIANT! DOOM SHALL NOT FALL THIS DAY!
THE FLAME IS BEYOND YOUR GRASP!
I DO NOT NEED TO REACH IT, THUNDERER!
BY THE POWER I HAVE PLACED WITHIN THE SHEATHLESS SWORD I CARRY, I SHALL CUT THROUGH THIS WORLD TO MUSPELHEIM ITSELF!
COME FORTH, FLAMES OF OLD!
SLAASH!
COME FORTH AND DEVOUR THE HIGH HOME OF THE GODS!
STAND BACK, LITTLE FOES!
FOR WHEN THE FIRES OF MUSPELHEIM HAVE MIXED WITH THE ETERNAL FLAME, THEN SHALL EVERY YELLOW TONGUE IGNITE MY SWORD...
...AND TWILIGHT RULE THE DAY!

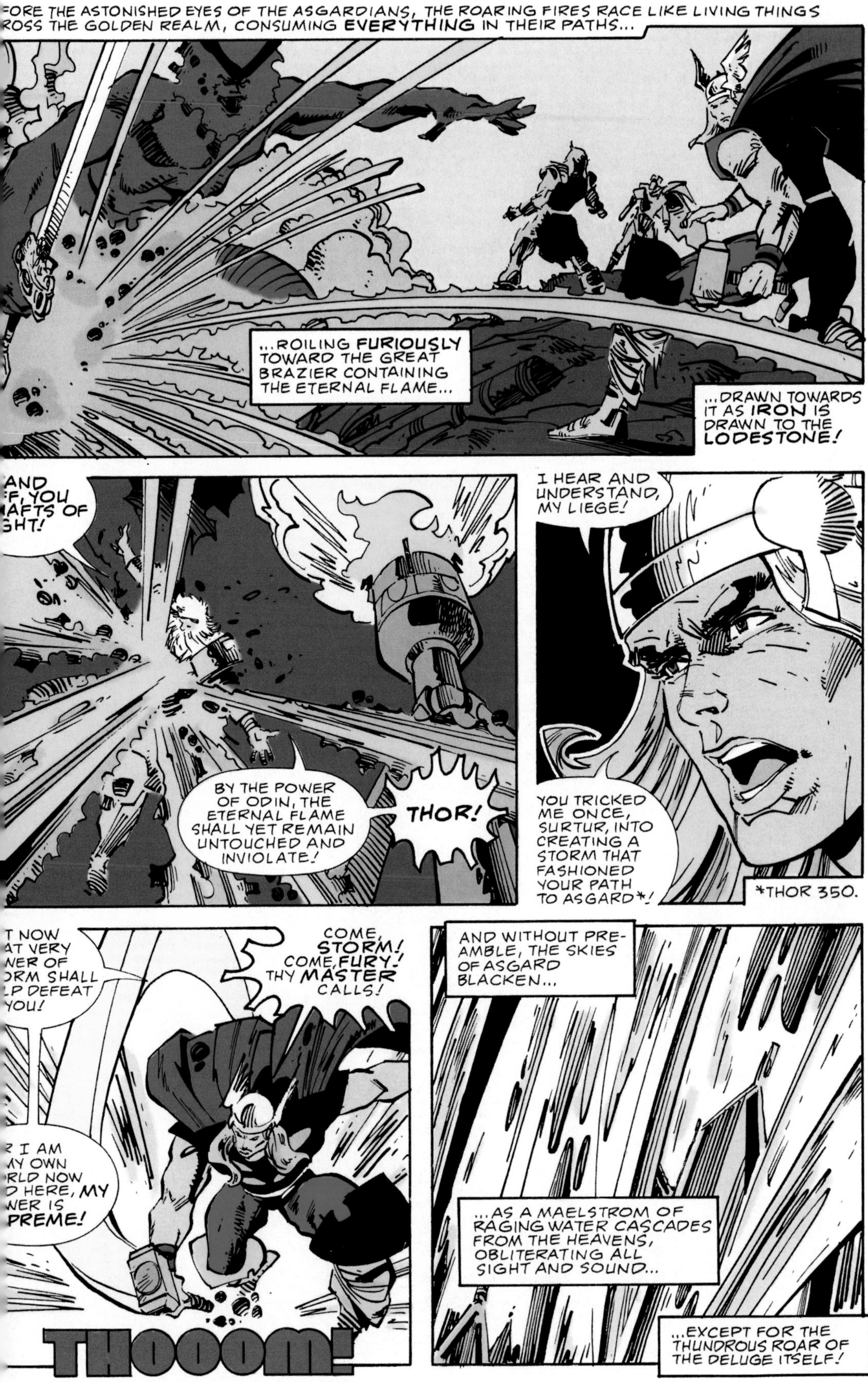
FORE THE ASTONISHED EYES OF THE ASGARDIANS, THE ROARING FIRES RACE LIKE LIVING THINGS ROSS THE GOLDEN REALM, CONSUMING EVERYTHING IN THEIR PATHS...
...ROILING FURIOUSLY TOWARD THE GREAT BRAZIER CONTAINING THE ETERNAL FLAME...
...DRAWN TOWARDS IT AS IRON IS DRAWN TO THE LODESTONE!
AND F, YOU AFTS OF GHT!
BY THE POWER OF ODIN, THE ETERNAL FLAME SHALL YET REMAIN UNTOUCHED AND INVIOLATE!
THOR!
I HEAR AND UNDERSTAND, MY LIEGE!
YOU TRICKED ME ONCE, SURTUR, INTO CREATING A STORM THAT FASHIONED YOUR PATH TO ASGARD*!
*THOR 350.
T NOW AT VERY NER OF ORM SHALL LP DEFEAT YOU!
COME, STORM! COME, FURY! THY MASTER CALLS!
R I AM MY OWN RLD NOW D HERE, MY NER IS PREME!
THOOOM!
AND WITHOUT PREAMBLE, THE SKIES OF ASGARD BLACKEN...
...AS A MAELSTROM OF RAGING WATER CASCADES FROM THE HEAVENS, OBLITERATING ALL SIGHT AND SOUND...
...EXCEPT FOR THE THUNDROUS ROAR OF THE DELUGE ITSELF!

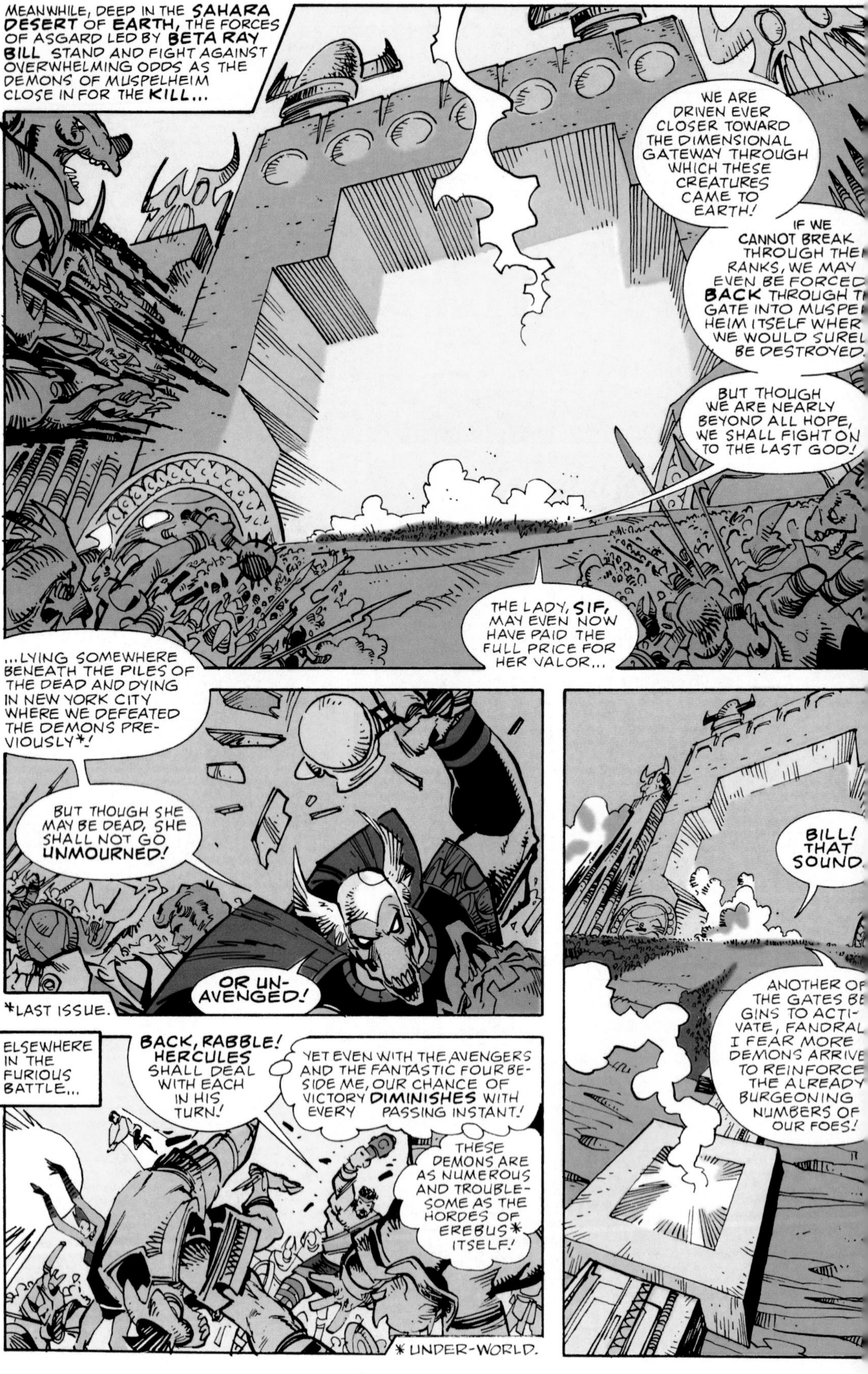

MEANWHILE, DEEP IN THE SAHARA DESERT OF EARTH, THE FORCES OF ASGARD LED BY BETA RAY BILL STAND AND FIGHT AGAINST OVERWHELMING ODDS AS THE DEMONS OF MUSPELHEIM CLOSE IN FOR THE KILL...
WE ARE DRIVEN EVER CLOSER TOWARD THE DIMENSIONAL GATEWAY THROUGH WHICH THESE CREATURES CAME TO EARTH!
IF WE CANNOT BREAK THROUGH THE RANKS, WE MAY EVEN BE FORCED BACK THROUGH THE GATE INTO MUSPELHEIM ITSELF WHERE WE WOULD SURELY BE DESTROYED.
BUT THOUGH WE ARE NEARLY BEYOND ALL HOPE, WE SHALL FIGHT ON TO THE LAST GOD!
THE LADY, SIF, MAY EVEN NOW HAVE PAID THE FULL PRICE FOR HER VALOR...
...LYING SOMEWHERE BENEATH THE PILES OF THE DEAD AND DYING IN NEW YORK CITY WHERE WE DEFEATED THE DEMONS PREVIOUSLY*!
BUT THOUGH SHE MAY BE DEAD, SHE SHALL NOT GO UNMOURNED!
OR UN-AVENGED!
*LAST ISSUE.
BILL! THAT SOUND
ANOTHER OF THE GATES BEGINS TO ACTIVATE, FANDRAL! I FEAR MORE DEMONS ARRIVE TO REINFORCE THE ALREADY BURGEONING NUMBERS OF OUR FOES!
ELSEWHERE IN THE FURIOUS BATTLE...
BACK, RABBLE! HERCULES SHALL DEAL WITH EACH IN HIS TURN!
YET EVEN WITH THE AVENGERS AND THE FANTASTIC FOUR BESIDE ME, OUR CHANCE OF VICTORY DIMINISHES WITH EVERY PASSING INSTANT!
THESE DEMONS ARE AS NUMEROUS AND TROUBLESOME AS THE HORDES OF EREBUS* ITSELF!
*UNDER-WORLD.

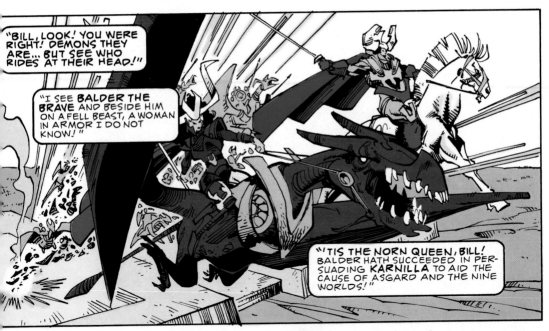

"BILL, LOOK! YOU WERE RIGHT! DEMONS THEY ARE... BUT SEE WHO RIDES AT THEIR HEAD!"

"I SEE BALDER THE BRAVE AND BESIDE HIM ON A FELL BEAST, A WOMAN IN ARMOR I DO NOT KNOW!"

"'TIS THE NORN QUEEN, BILL! BALDER HATH SUCCEEDED IN PERSUADING KARNILLA TO AID THE CAUSE OF ASGARD AND THE NINE WORLDS!"

UR FORCES CUT ROUGH THE DEMONS THE SCYTHE ROUGH THE WHEAT!

YOUR SORCERIES HAVE BROUGHT US TO THE BATTLE IN TIME, MILADY!

FOR ODIN AND THE QUEEN! LET NOT A FOE ESCAPE!

NCHANTRESS! UICKLY! USE YOUR AGIC AND CALL THE TRONGEST OF THE EROES TO MY SIDE HIS INSTANT!

MOMENTS LATER, AS HERCULES, VISION, AND SHE-HULK RESPOND...

WE HAVE EACH HEARD THE MENTAL SUMMONS, BILL! WHY HAVE YOU CALLED US?

LET OUR WARRIORS HOLD THE DEMONS AT BAY FOR A MOMENT LONGER AND VICTORY MAY YET BE OURS!

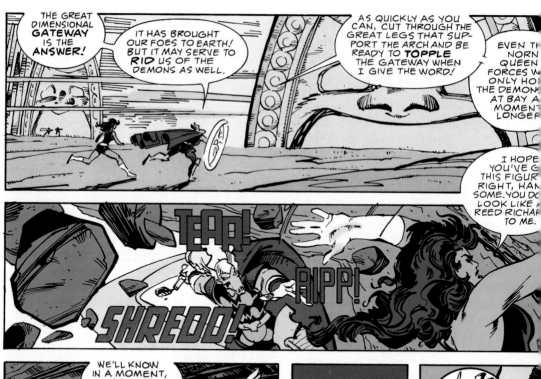

THE GREAT DIMENSIONAL **GATEWAY** IS THE **ANSWER!**

IT HAS BROUGHT OUR FOES TO EARTH! BUT IT MAY SERVE TO **RID** US OF THE DEMONS AS WELL.

AS QUICKLY AS YOU CAN, CUT THROUGH THE GREAT LEGS THAT SUPPORT THE ARCH AND BE READY TO **TOPPLE** THE GATEWAY WHEN I GIVE THE WORD!

EVEN TH NORN QUEEN FORCES W ONLY HO THE DEMON AT BAY A MOMENT LONGER

I HOPE YOU'VE G THIS FIGUR RIGHT, HAN SOME. YOU DO LOOK LIKE A REED RICHAR TO ME.

TEAR!

RIPP!

SHREDD!

WE'LL KNOW IN A MOMENT, MISS! THE PILLARS BEGIN TO TREMBLE!

ENCHANTRESS, TELL KARNILLA TO SWING HER FORCES AROUND AND DRIVE THE DEMONS TOWARD THE GATEWAY...

"...AND CALL THE ASGARDIANS TO FALL BACK BEYOND THE FEET OF THE GREAT PILLARS, DRAWING THE DEMONS AFTER THEM!"

HERCULES, DO YOU HEAR IT? THE ENCHANTRESS' MENTAL COMMAND! THE **MOMENT IS AT HAND!**

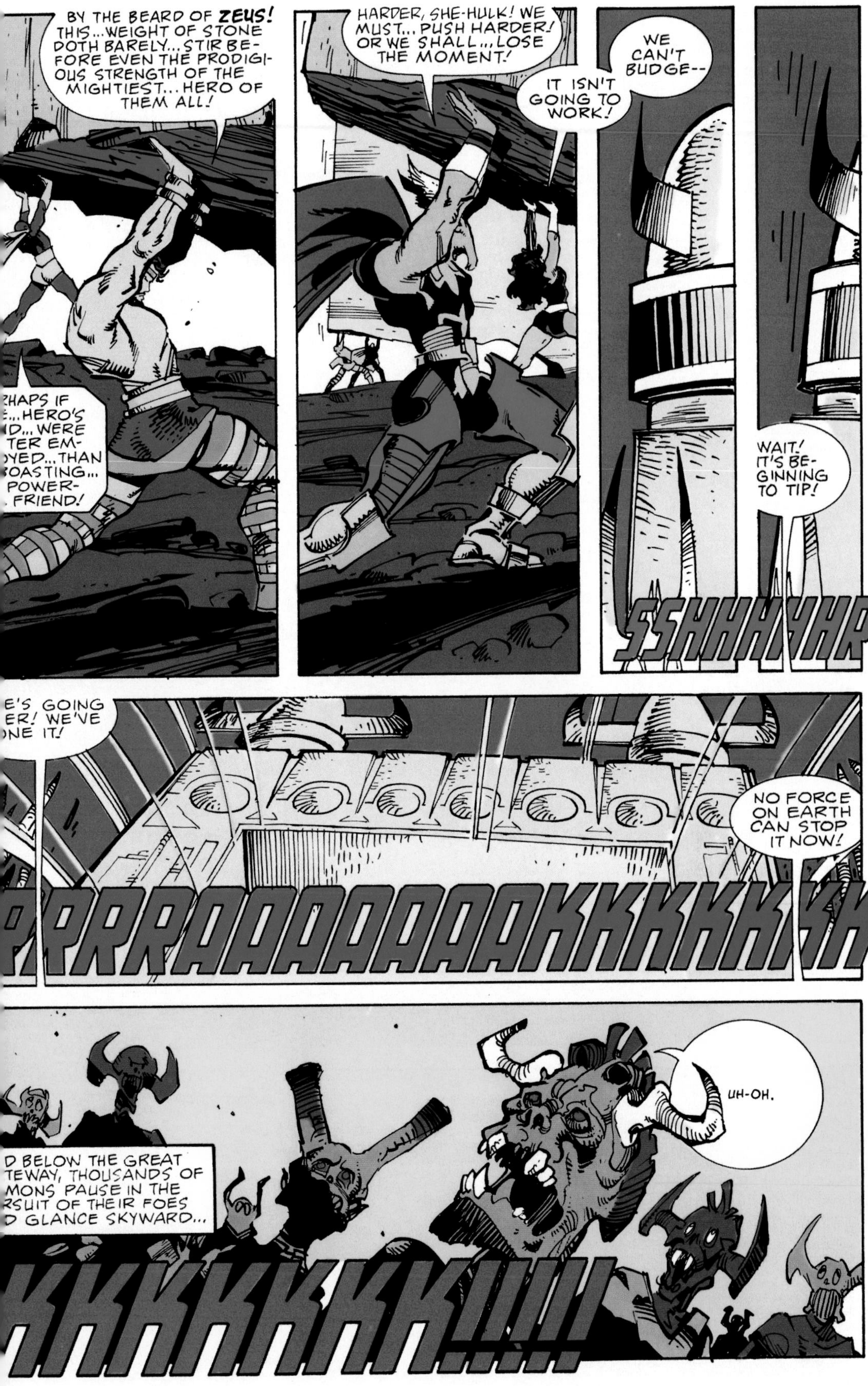
BY THE BEARD OF ZEUS! THIS... WEIGHT OF STONE DOTH BARELY... STIR BEFORE EVEN THE PRODIGIOUS STRENGTH OF THE MIGHTIEST... HERO OF THEM ALL!
ZHAPS IF E... HERO'S ID... WERE TER EMOYED... THAN OASTING... POWER- FRIEND!
HARDER, SHE-HULK! WE MUST... PUSH HARDER! OR WE SHALL... LOSE THE MOMENT!
WE CAN'T BUDGE--
IT ISN'T GOING TO WORK!
WAIT! IT'S BEGINNING TO TIP!
SSHHHYHR
E'S GOING ER! WE'VE NE IT!
NO FORCE ON EARTH CAN STOP IT NOW!
RRRAAAAAAAAKKKKKKK
UH-OH.
D BELOW THE GREAT TEWAY, THOUSANDS OF MONS PAUSE IN THE RSUIT OF THEIR FOES D GLANCE SKYWARD...
KKKKKKK!!!!!

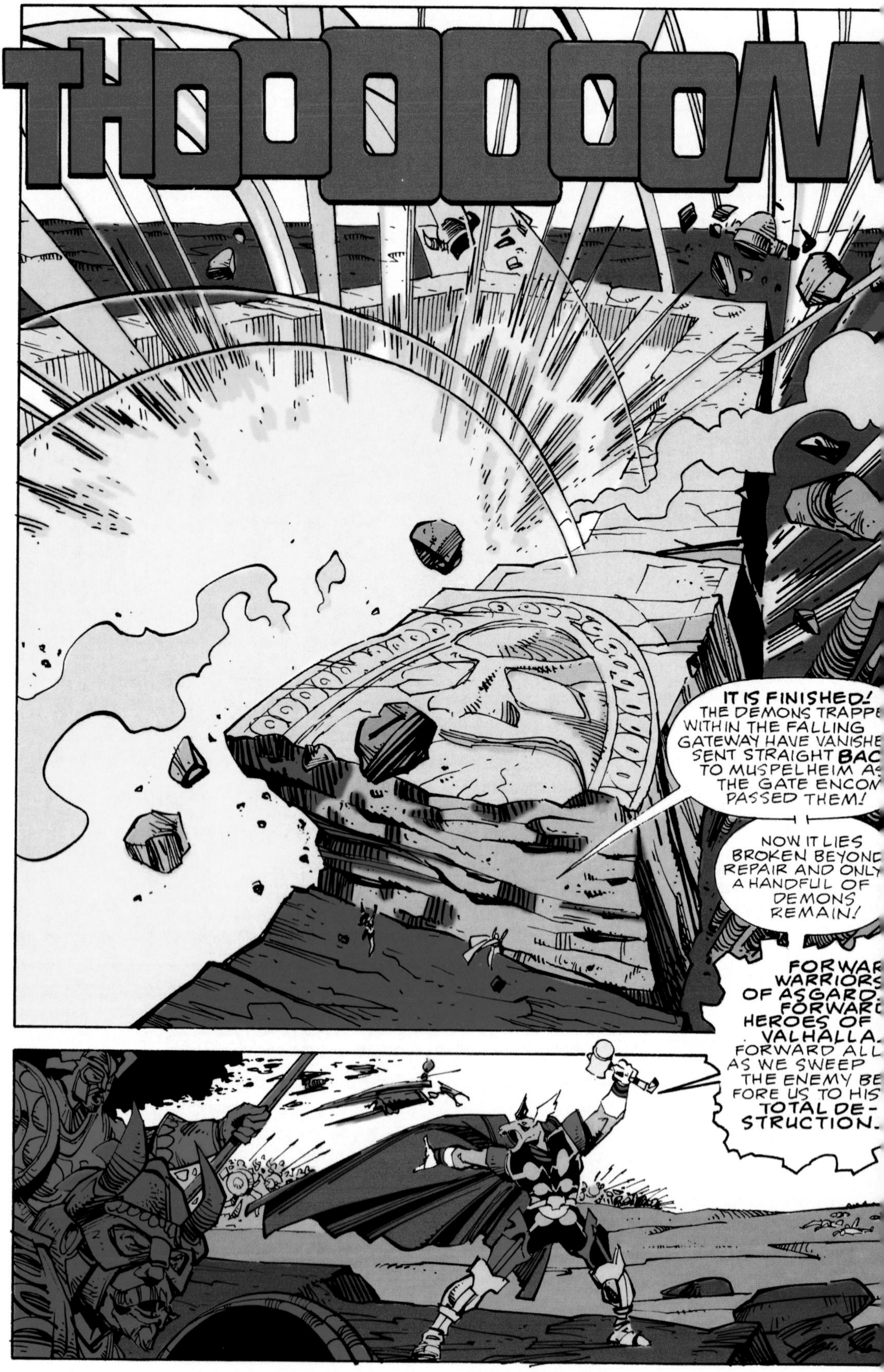
THOOOOOM
IT IS FINISHED! THE DEMONS TRAPPE WITHIN THE FALLING GATEWAY HAVE VANISHE SENT STRAIGHT BAC TO MUSPELHEIM A THE GATE ENCOM PASSED THEM!
NOW IT LIES BROKEN BEYOND REPAIR AND ONLY A HANDFUL OF DEMONS REMAIN!
FORWAR WARRIORS OF ASGARD! FORWARD HEROES OF VALHALLA. FORWARD ALL AS WE SWEEP THE ENEMY BE FORE US TO HIS TOTAL DE- STRUCTION.

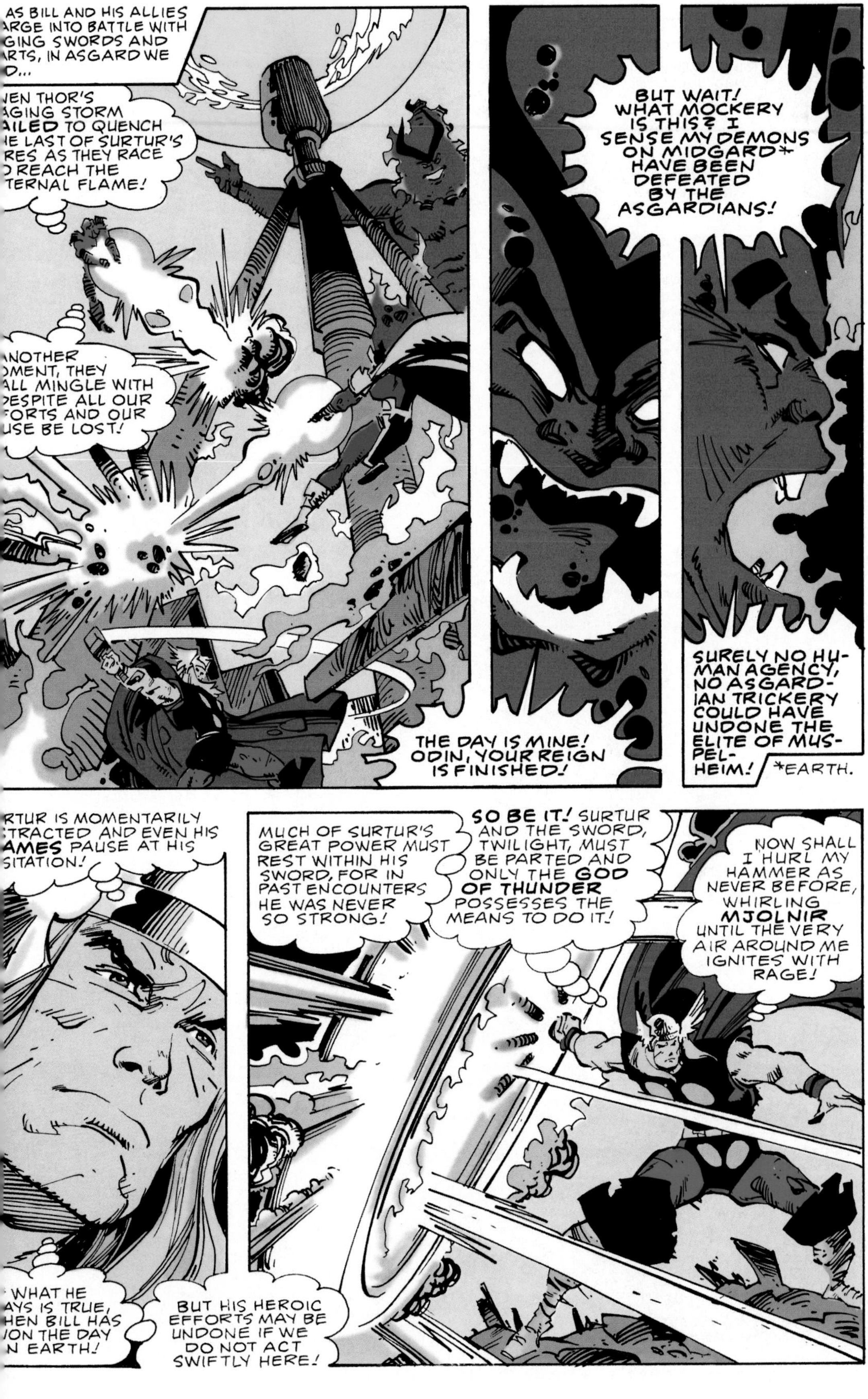
AS BILL AND HIS ALLIES
ARGE INTO BATTLE WITH
GING SWORDS AND
RTS, IN ASGARD WE
D...
EN THOR'S
AGING STORM
AILED TO QUENCH
E LAST OF SURTUR'S
RES AS THEY RACE
REACH THE
TERNAL FLAME!
NOTHER
OMENT, THEY
ALL MINGLE WITH
ESPITE ALL OUR
FORTS AND OUR
USE BE LOST!
BUT WAIT! WHAT MOCKERY IS THIS? I SENSE MY DEMONS ON MIDGARD* HAVE BEEN DEFEATED BY THE ASGARDIANS!
SURELY NO HUMAN AGENCY, NO ASGARDIAN TRICKERY COULD HAVE UNDONE THE ELITE OF MUSPELHEIM!
THE DAY IS MINE! ODIN, YOUR REIGN IS FINISHED!
*EARTH.
RTUR IS MOMENTARILY
STRACTED AND EVEN HIS
AMES PAUSE AT HIS
SITATION!
WHAT HE
AYS IS TRUE,
HEN BILL HAS
ON THE DAY
N EARTH!
MUCH OF SURTUR'S GREAT POWER MUST REST WITHIN HIS SWORD, FOR IN PAST ENCOUNTERS HE WAS NEVER SO STRONG!
SO BE IT! SURTUR AND THE SWORD, TWILIGHT, MUST BE PARTED AND ONLY THE GOD OF THUNDER POSSESSES THE MEANS TO DO IT!
NOW SHALL I HURL MY HAMMER AS NEVER BEFORE, WHIRLING MJOLNIR UNTIL THE VERY AIR AROUND ME IGNITES WITH RAGE!
BUT HIS HEROIC EFFORTS MAY BE UNDONE IF WE DO NOT ACT SWIFTLY HERE!

THOUGH MY HANDS DO BLISTER AND BURN WITH PAIN, ONLY THUS CAN I STRIKE WITH SUFFICIENT FORCE TO ACCOMPLISH WHAT MUST BE DONE!

ODIN GRANT THAT MY AIM IS TRUE!

SCHRAANG!

THE SHEATHLESS SWORD! I MUST RECOVER MY GRIP ERE--!

TOO LATE, SURTUR! YOUR CONNECTION WITH THE ETERNAL FLAME HAS BEEN SEVERED.

AND WITHOUT IT, YOU CAN NO LONGER SUPPRESS MY ABILITY TO ASSUME THE GUISE OF THE GREAT WARRIOR WHOM YOU FOUGHT IN MUSPELHEIM SO LONG AGO!*

NOW, DEMON, WE ARE EVENLY MATCHED!

AND THIS IS THE HOUR OF YOUR DEFEAT!

*THOR #349 TOLD THE TALE.

122

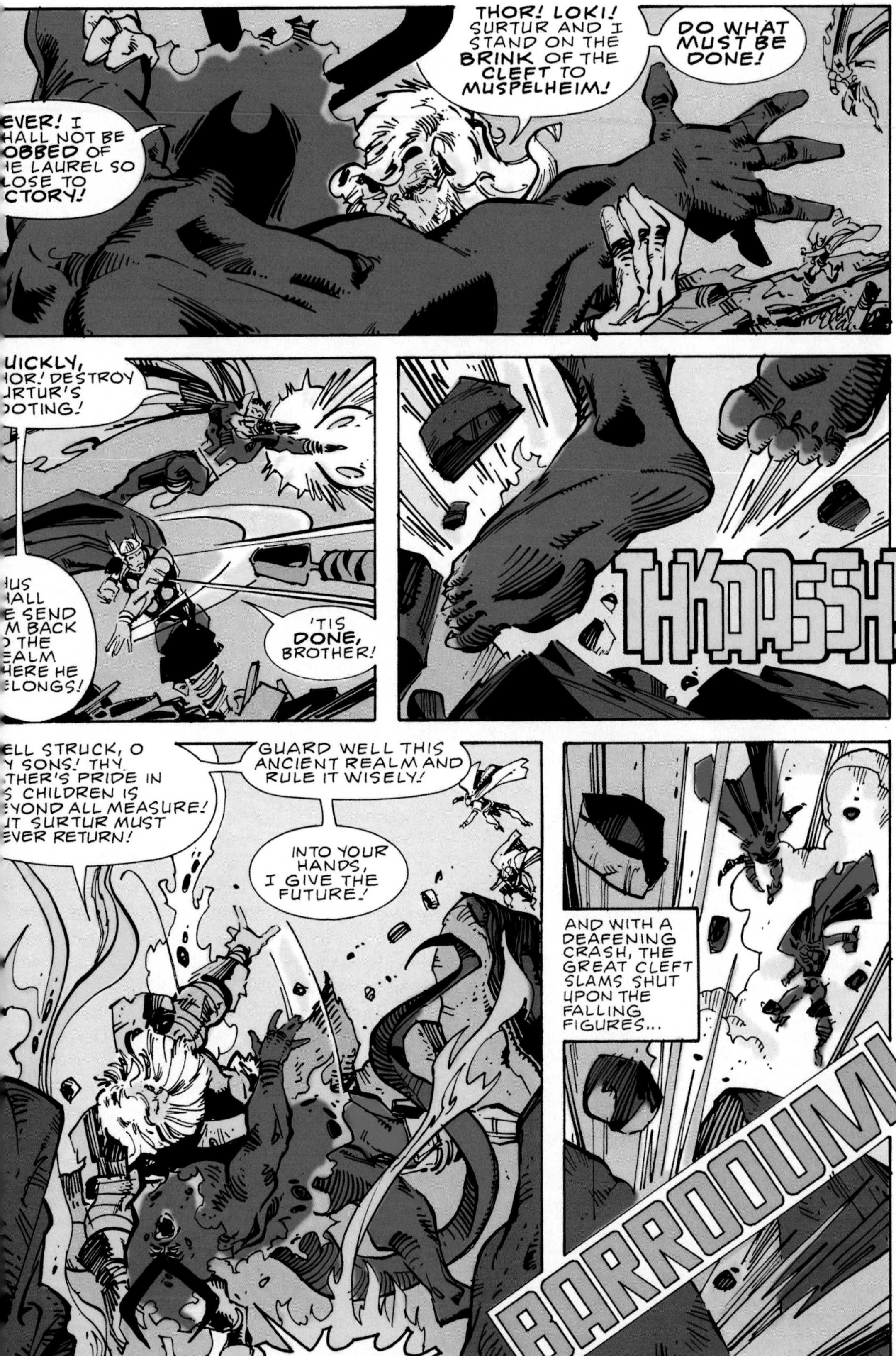
EVER! I HALL NOT BE OBBED OF HE LAUREL SO LOSE TO CTORY!
THOR! LOKI! SURTUR AND I STAND ON THE BRINK OF THE CLEFT TO MUSPELHEIM!
DO WHAT MUST BE DONE!
UICKLY, HOR! DESTROY URTUR'S OOTING!
HUS HALL E SEND M BACK D THE EALM HERE HE ELONGS!
'TIS DONE, BROTHER!
THKRASSH!
ELL STRUCK, O Y SONS! THY ATHER'S PRIDE IN S CHILDREN IS EYOND ALL MEASURE! UT SURTUR MUST EVER RETURN!
GUARD WELL THIS ANCIENT REALM AND RULE IT WISELY!
INTO YOUR HANDS, I GIVE THE FUTURE!
NOOOOOo!!
AND WITH A DEAFENING CRASH, THE GREAT CLEFT SLAMS SHUT UPON THE FALLING FIGURES...
BARROOUM!
...LEAVING ONLY SILENCE.

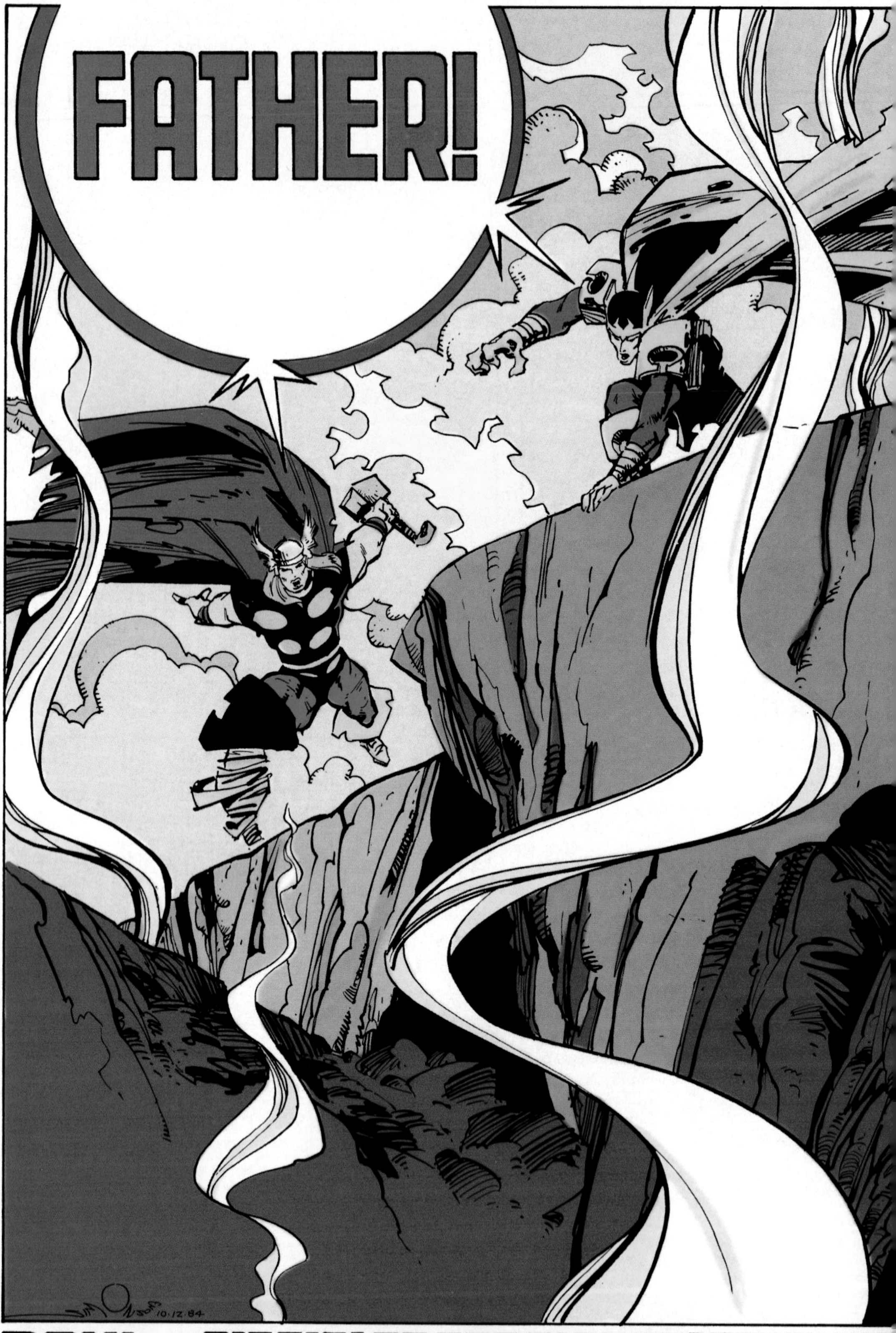
FATHER!
next: PICKIN' UP THE PIECES!
WHAT ELSE IS THERE TO SAY?
THIS ISSUE ESPECIALLY IS FOR STAN, JACK, VINNIE, ARTIE, AND SAM.

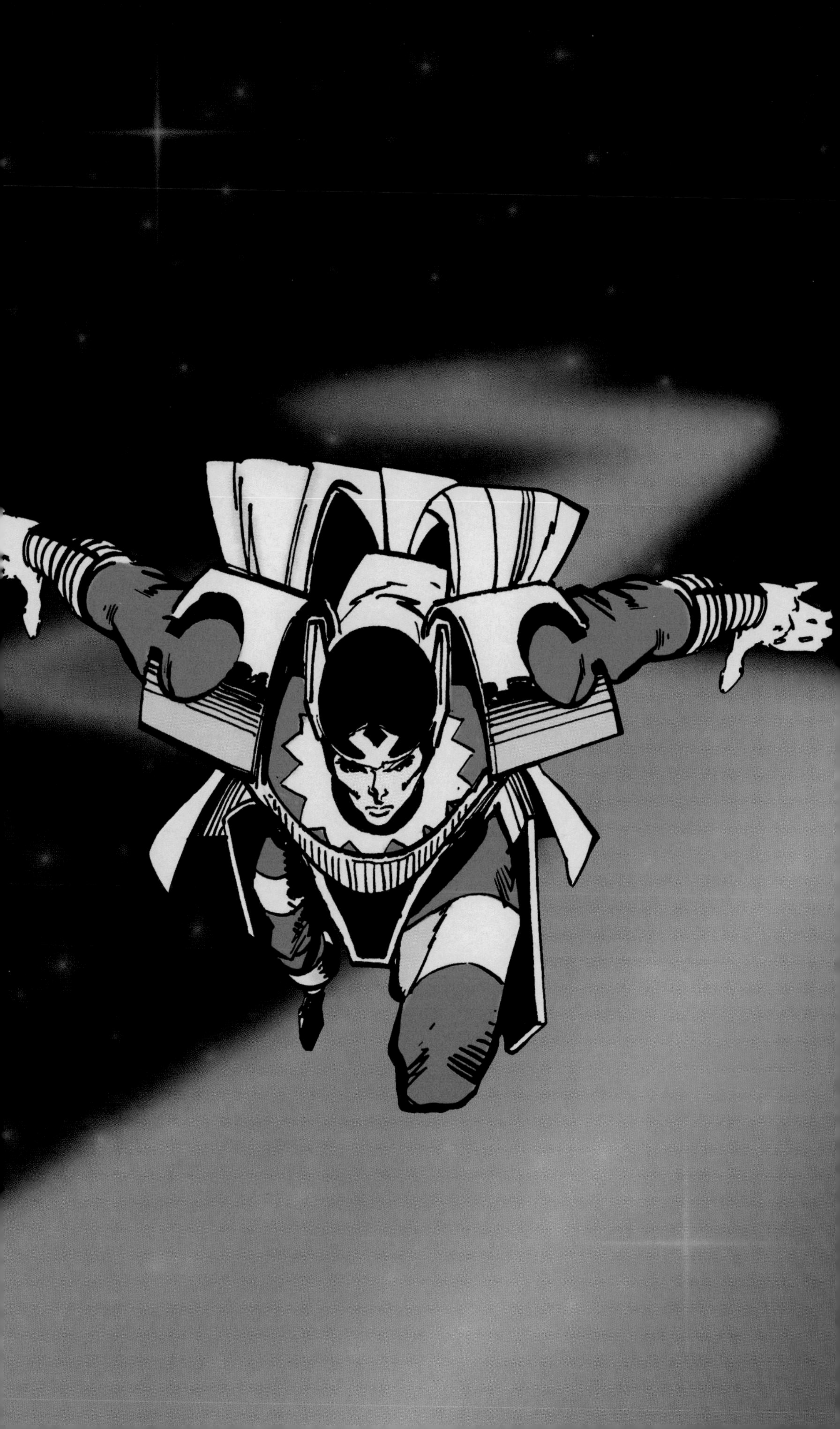

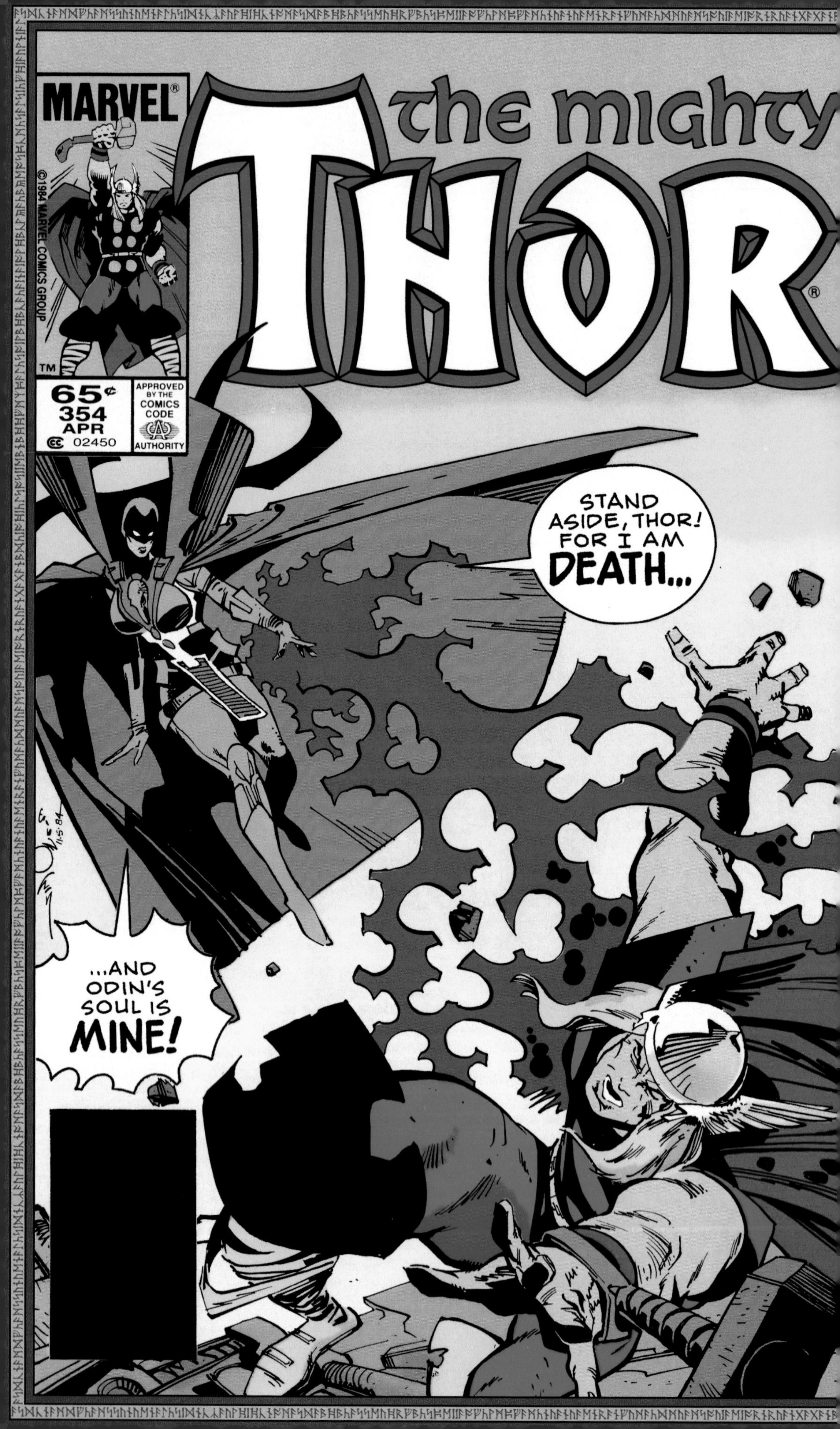
MARVEL®
the mighty
THOR®
© 1984 MARVEL COMICS GROUP
TM
65¢
354
APR
02450
APPROVED BY THE COMICS CODE AUTHORITY
STAND ASIDE, THOR! FOR I AM DEATH...
...AND ODIN'S SOUL IS MINE!

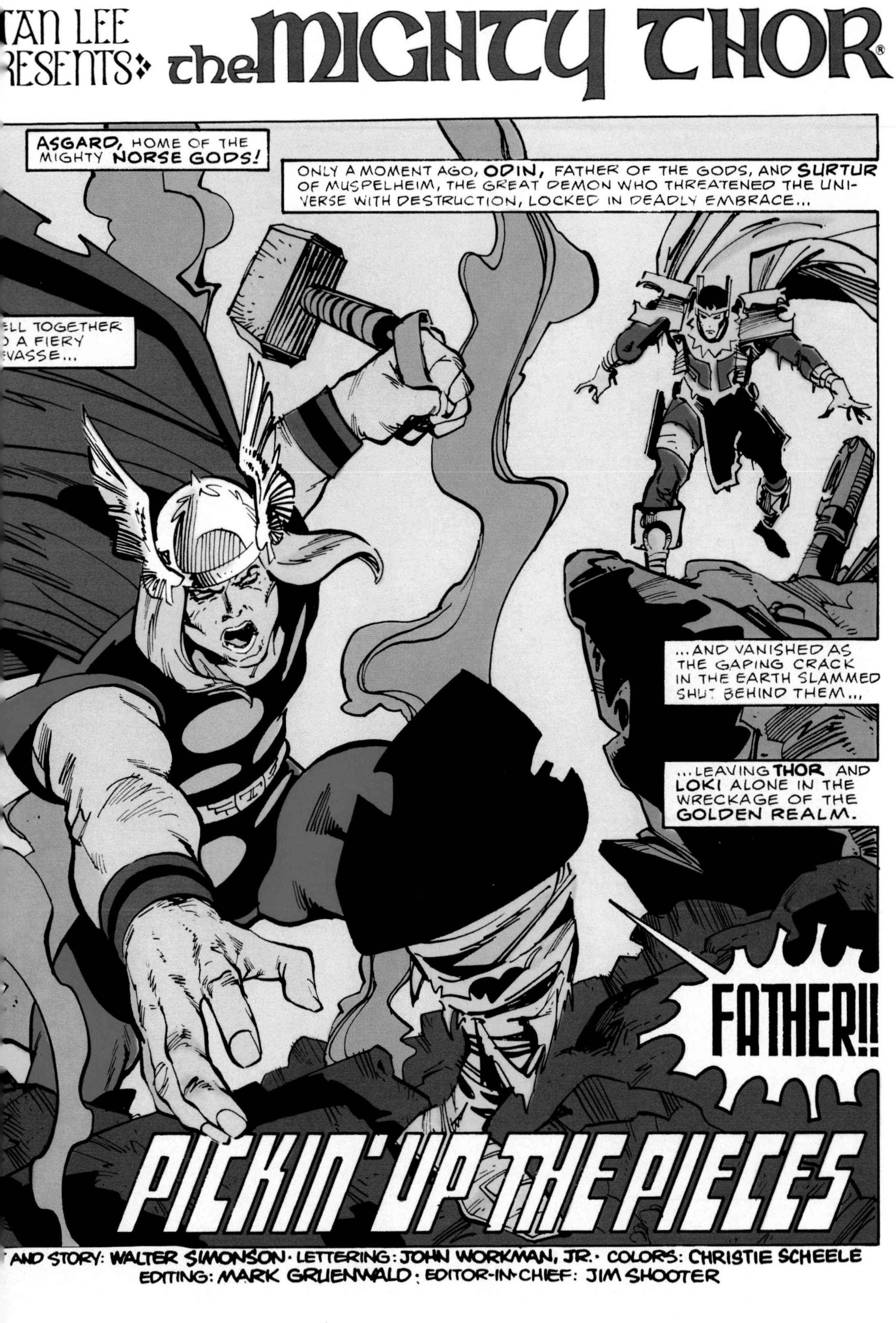

STAN LEE PRESENTS: the MIGHTY THOR
ASGARD, HOME OF THE MIGHTY NORSE GODS!
ONLY A MOMENT AGO, ODIN, FATHER OF THE GODS, AND SURTUR OF MUSPELHEIM, THE GREAT DEMON WHO THREATENED THE UNIVERSE WITH DESTRUCTION, LOCKED IN DEADLY EMBRACE...
ELL TOGETHER A FIERY EVASSE...
...AND VANISHED AS THE GAPING CRACK IN THE EARTH SLAMMED SHUT BEHIND THEM...
...LEAVING THOR AND LOKI ALONE IN THE WRECKAGE OF THE GOLDEN REALM.
FATHER!!
PICKIN' UP THE PIECES
AND STORY: WALTER SIMONSON · LETTERING: JOHN WORKMAN, JR. · COLORS: CHRISTIE SCHEELE
EDITING: MARK GRUENWALD · EDITOR-IN-CHIEF: JIM SHOOTER

HE'S GONE!

LORD ODIN IS GONE!

UNBELIEVABLE BUT THOR IS RIGHT! EVEN MY MAGIC CAN SENSE NO TRACE OF THEM!

ODIN AND SURTUR NO LONGER EXIST ANYWHERE IN THE NINE WORLDS!

NOW LAST, TIME H COME T WHAT

FEAR NOT, FATHER!

THOUGH I MAY SPLIT ASGARD ASUNDER, BY THE POWER OF MY ENCHANTED HAMMER, I SHALL REOPEN THE FIERY PATH TO MUSPELHEIM...

NO!

...AND FIND THEE!

THRWAAHM!

THOR! THOR! CEASE THIS FRUITLESS EFFORT ERE IT IS TOO LATE! YOU CANNOT HELP OUR FATHER NOW!

UNHAND ME, TRAITOR!

ODIN LIES SOME-WHERE WITH HIS FOE IN THE DEPTHS OF MUSPELHEIM AND NOTHING SHALL PREVENT ME FROM SEEKING HIM OUT!

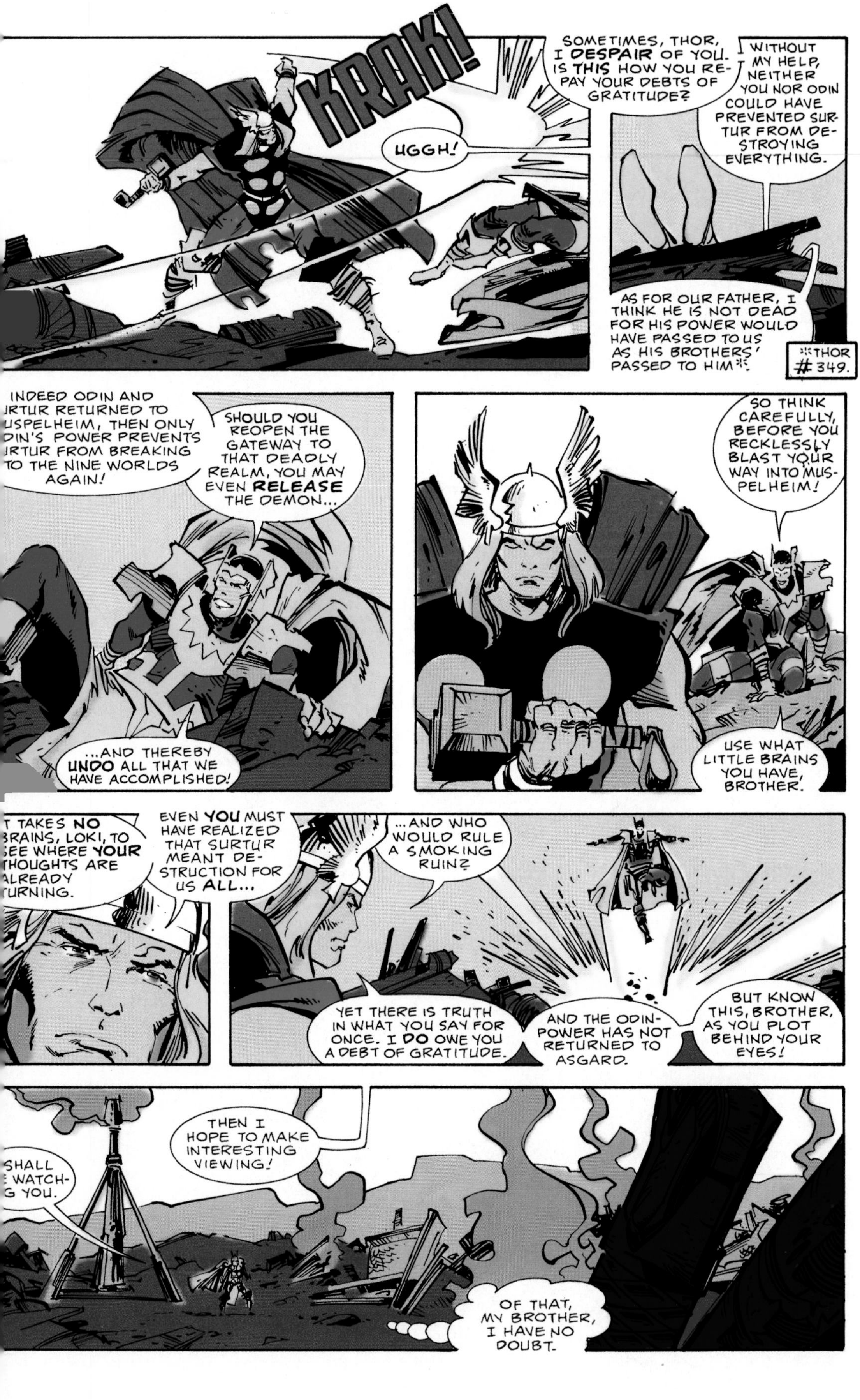
KRAK!
UGGH!
SOMETIMES, THOR, I DESPAIR OF YOU. IS THIS HOW YOU RE-PAY YOUR DEBTS OF GRATITUDE?
WITHOUT MY HELP, NEITHER YOU NOR ODIN COULD HAVE PREVENTED SUR-TUR FROM DE-STROYING EVERYTHING.
AS FOR OUR FATHER, I THINK HE IS NOT DEAD FOR HIS POWER WOULD HAVE PASSED TO US AS HIS BROTHERS' PASSED TO HIM*.
*THOR #349.
INDEED ODIN AND URTUR RETURNED TO USPELHEIM, THEN ONLY DIN'S POWER PREVENTS URTUR FROM BREAKING TO THE NINE WORLDS AGAIN!
SHOULD YOU REOPEN THE GATEWAY TO THAT DEADLY REALM, YOU MAY EVEN RELEASE THE DEMON...
...AND THEREBY UNDO ALL THAT WE HAVE ACCOMPLISHED!
SO THINK CAREFULLY, BEFORE YOU RECKLESSLY BLAST YOUR WAY INTO MUS-PELHEIM!
USE WHAT LITTLE BRAINS YOU HAVE, BROTHER.
T TAKES NO BRAINS, LOKI, TO EE WHERE YOUR THOUGHTS ARE LREADY TURNING.
EVEN YOU MUST HAVE REALIZED THAT SURTUR MEANT DE-STRUCTION FOR US ALL...
...AND WHO WOULD RULE A SMOKING RUIN?
YET THERE IS TRUTH IN WHAT YOU SAY FOR ONCE. I DO OWE YOU A DEBT OF GRATITUDE.
AND THE ODIN-POWER HAS NOT RETURNED TO ASGARD.
BUT KNOW THIS, BROTHER, AS YOU PLOT BEHIND YOUR EYES!
SHALL E WATCH-G YOU.
THEN I HOPE TO MAKE INTERESTING VIEWING!
OF THAT, MY BROTHER, I HAVE NO DOUBT.

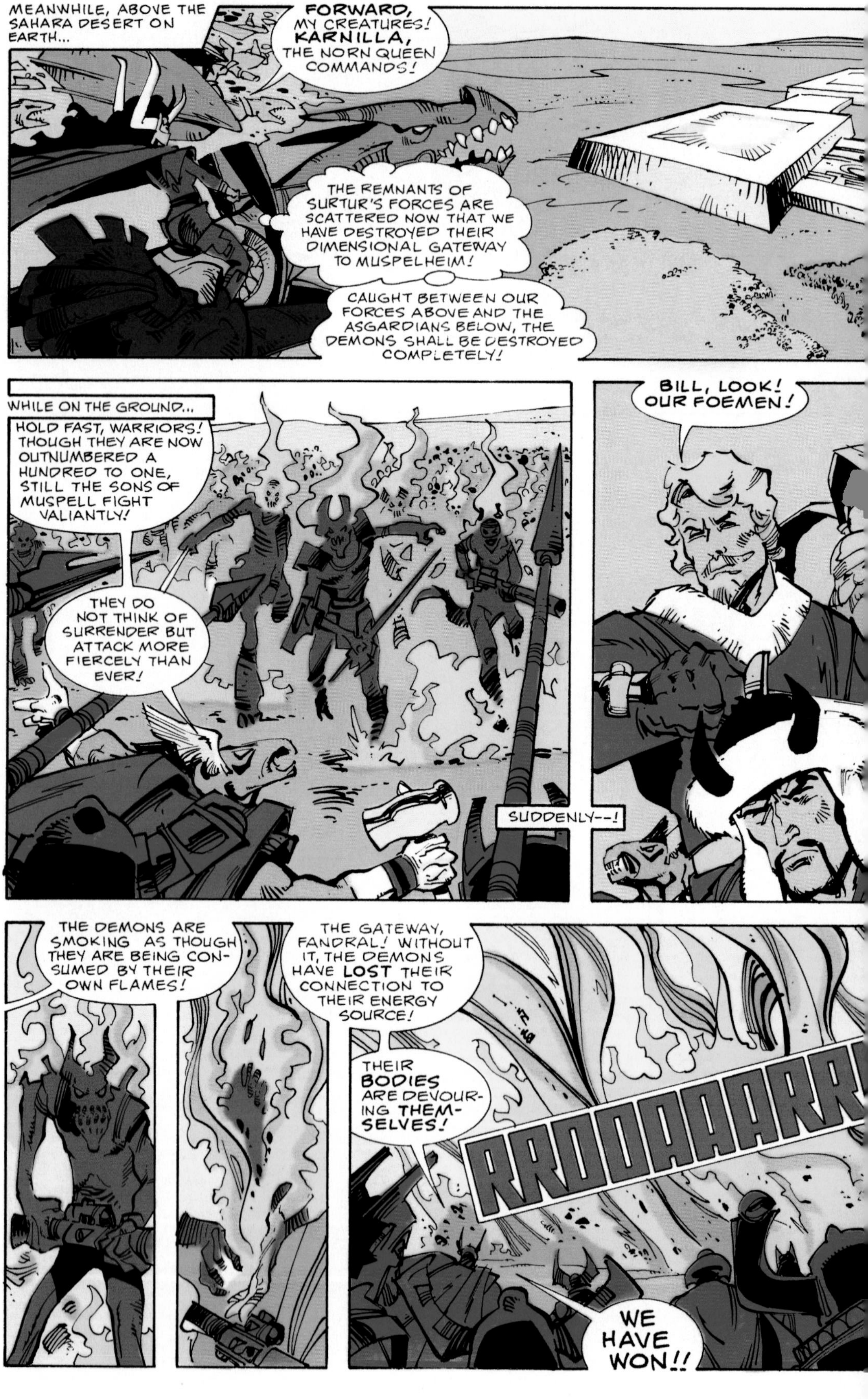

MEANWHILE, ABOVE THE SAHARA DESERT ON EARTH...
FORWARD, MY CREATURES! KARNILLA, THE NORN QUEEN COMMANDS!
THE REMNANTS OF SURTUR'S FORCES ARE SCATTERED NOW THAT WE HAVE DESTROYED THEIR DIMENSIONAL GATEWAY TO MUSPELHEIM!
CAUGHT BETWEEN OUR FORCES ABOVE AND THE ASGARDIANS BELOW, THE DEMONS SHALL BE DESTROYED COMPLETELY!
WHILE ON THE GROUND...
HOLD FAST, WARRIORS! THOUGH THEY ARE NOW OUTNUMBERED A HUNDRED TO ONE, STILL THE SONS OF MUSPELL FIGHT VALIANTLY!
THEY DO NOT THINK OF SURRENDER BUT ATTACK MORE FIERCELY THAN EVER!
SUDDENLY--!
BILL, LOOK! OUR FOEMEN!
THE DEMONS ARE SMOKING AS THOUGH THEY ARE BEING CONSUMED BY THEIR OWN FLAMES!
THE GATEWAY, FANDRAL! WITHOUT IT, THE DEMONS HAVE LOST THEIR CONNECTION TO THEIR ENERGY SOURCE!
THEIR BODIES ARE DEVOURING THEMSELVES!
RROOAAARR
WE HAVE WON!!

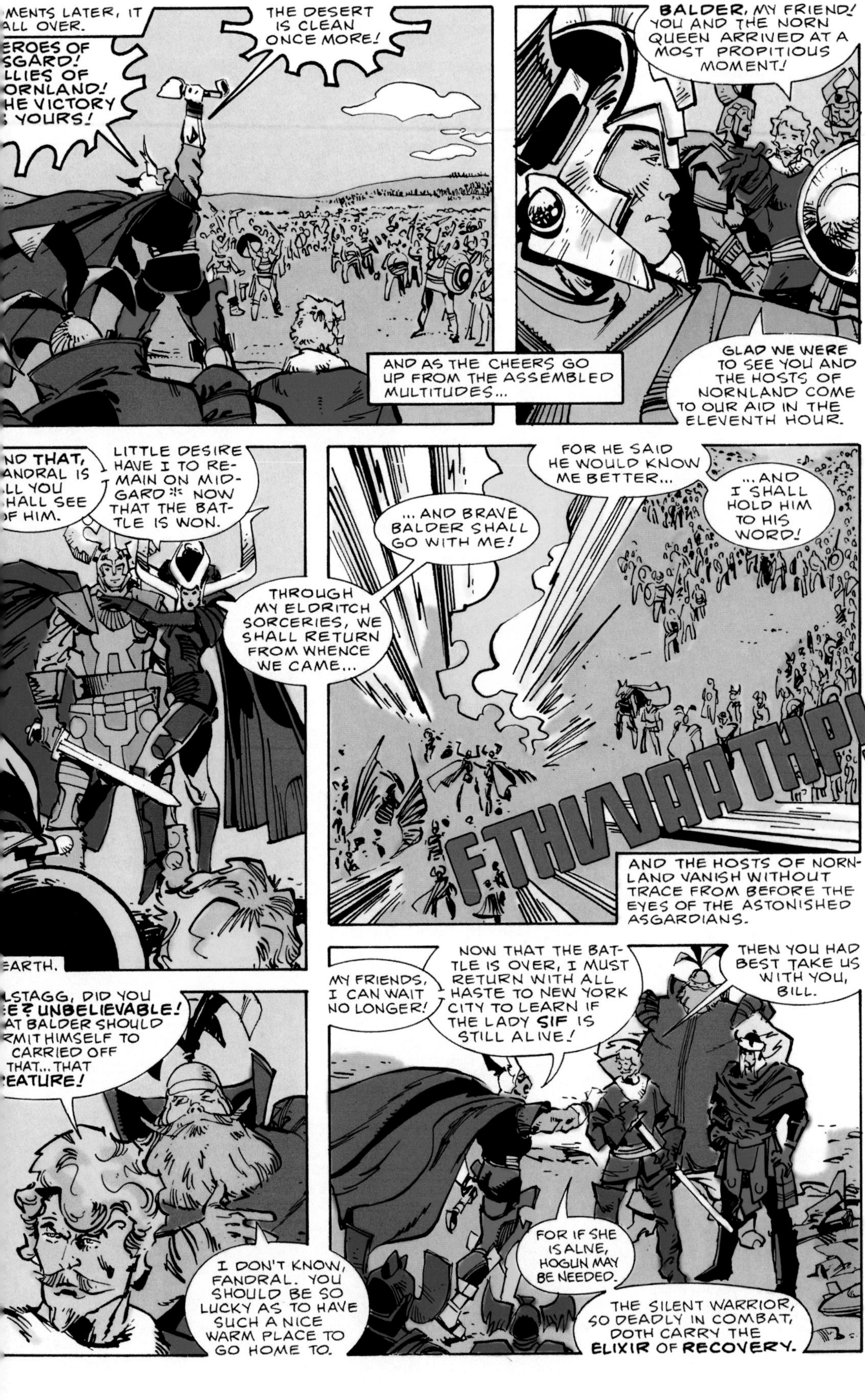

MENTS LATER, IT
ALL OVER.
EROES OF
SGARD!
LLIES OF
ORNLAND!
HE VICTORY
YOURS!
THE DESERT IS CLEAN ONCE MORE!
BALDER, MY FRIEND! YOU AND THE NORN QUEEN ARRIVED AT A MOST PROPITIOUS MOMENT!
AND AS THE CHEERS GO UP FROM THE ASSEMBLED MULTITUDES...
GLAD WE WERE TO SEE YOU AND THE HOSTS OF NORNLAND COME TO OUR AID IN THE ELEVENTH HOUR.
ND THAT, ANDRAL IS LL YOU HALL SEE F HIM.
LITTLE DESIRE HAVE I TO RE-MAIN ON MID-GARD* NOW THAT THE BAT-TLE IS WON.
THROUGH MY ELDRITCH SORCERIES, WE SHALL RETURN FROM WHENCE WE CAME...
...AND BRAVE BALDER SHALL GO WITH ME!
FOR HE SAID HE WOULD KNOW ME BETTER...
...AND I SHALL HOLD HIM TO HIS WORD!
FTHWAATHP!
AND THE HOSTS OF NORN-LAND VANISH WITHOUT TRACE FROM BEFORE THE EYES OF THE ASTONISHED ASGARDIANS.
EARTH.
LSTAGG, DID YOU E? UNBELIEVABLE! AT BALDER SHOULD RMIT HIMSELF TO CARRIED OFF THAT...THAT EATURE!
I DON'T KNOW, FANDRAL. YOU SHOULD BE SO LUCKY AS TO HAVE SUCH A NICE WARM PLACE TO GO HOME TO.
MY FRIENDS, I CAN WAIT NO LONGER!
NOW THAT THE BAT-TLE IS OVER, I MUST RETURN WITH ALL HASTE TO NEW YORK CITY TO LEARN IF THE LADY SIF IS STILL ALIVE!
THEN YOU HAD BEST TAKE US WITH YOU, BILL.
FOR IF SHE IS ALIVE, HOGUN MAY BE NEEDED.
THE SILENT WARRIOR, SO DEADLY IN COMBAT, DOTH CARRY THE ELIXIR OF RECOVERY.

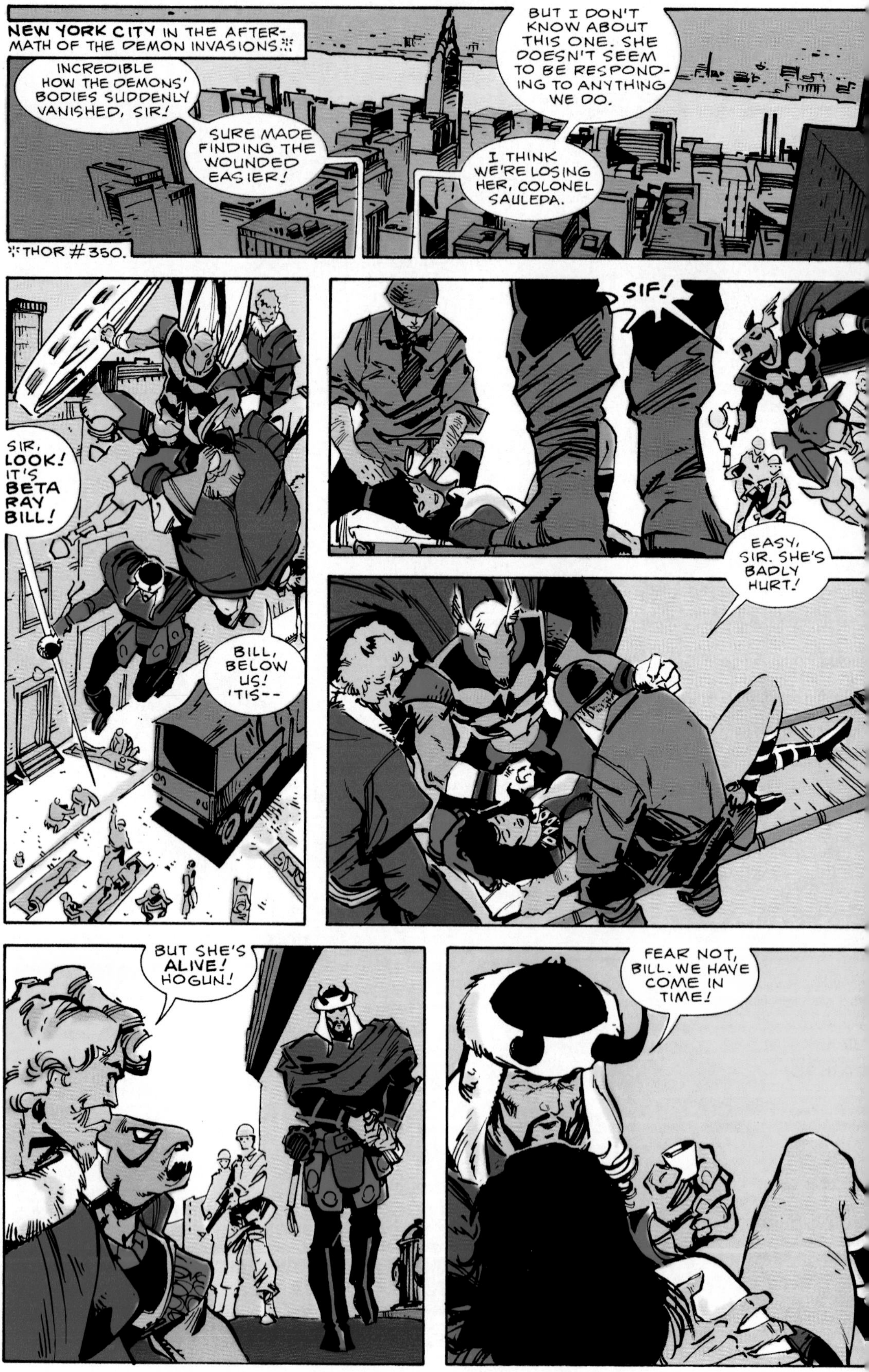
NEW YORK CITY IN THE AFTERMATH OF THE DEMON INVASIONS.*
INCREDIBLE HOW THE DEMONS' BODIES SUDDENLY VANISHED, SIR!
SURE MADE FINDING THE WOUNDED EASIER!
BUT I DON'T KNOW ABOUT THIS ONE. SHE DOESN'T SEEM TO BE RESPONDING TO ANYTHING WE DO.
I THINK WE'RE LOSING HER, COLONEL SAULEDA.
*THOR #350.
SIR, LOOK! IT'S BETA RAY BILL!
BILL, BELOW US! 'TIS--
SIF!
EASY, SIR. SHE'S BADLY HURT!
BUT SHE'S ALIVE! HOGUN!
FEAR NOT, BILL. WE HAVE COME IN TIME!

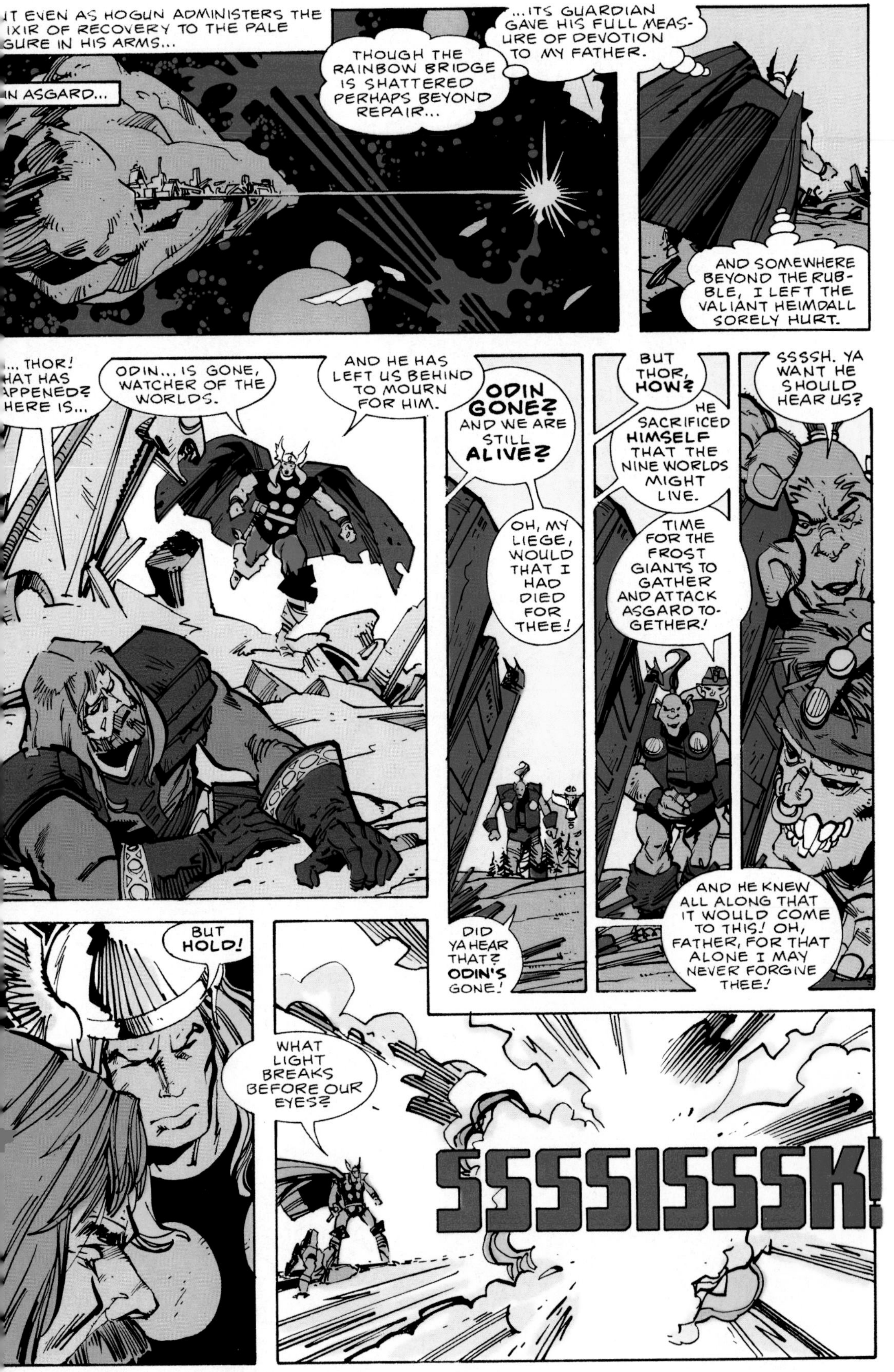

...T EVEN AS HOGUN ADMINISTERS THE ...IXIR OF RECOVERY TO THE PALE ...GURE IN HIS ARMS...
...N ASGARD...
THOUGH THE RAINBOW BRIDGE IS SHATTERED PERHAPS BEYOND REPAIR...
...ITS GUARDIAN GAVE HIS FULL MEASURE OF DEVOTION TO MY FATHER.
AND SOMEWHERE BEYOND THE RUBBLE, I LEFT THE VALIANT HEIMDALL SORELY HURT.
..., THOR! ...HAT HAS ...APPENED? ...HERE IS...
ODIN... IS GONE, WATCHER OF THE WORLDS.
AND HE HAS LEFT US BEHIND TO MOURN FOR HIM.
ODIN GONE? AND WE ARE STILL ALIVE?
OH, MY LIEGE, WOULD THAT I HAD DIED FOR THEE!
DID YA HEAR THAT? ODIN'S GONE!
BUT THOR, HOW?
HE SACRIFICED HIMSELF THAT THE NINE WORLDS MIGHT LIVE.
TIME FOR THE FROST GIANTS TO GATHER AND ATTACK ASGARD TOGETHER!
SSSSH. YA WANT HE SHOULD HEAR US?
AND HE KNEW ALL ALONG THAT IT WOULD COME TO THIS! OH, FATHER, FOR THAT ALONE I MAY NEVER FORGIVE THEE!
BUT HOLD!
WHAT LIGHT BREAKS BEFORE OUR EYES?
SSSSISSSSK!

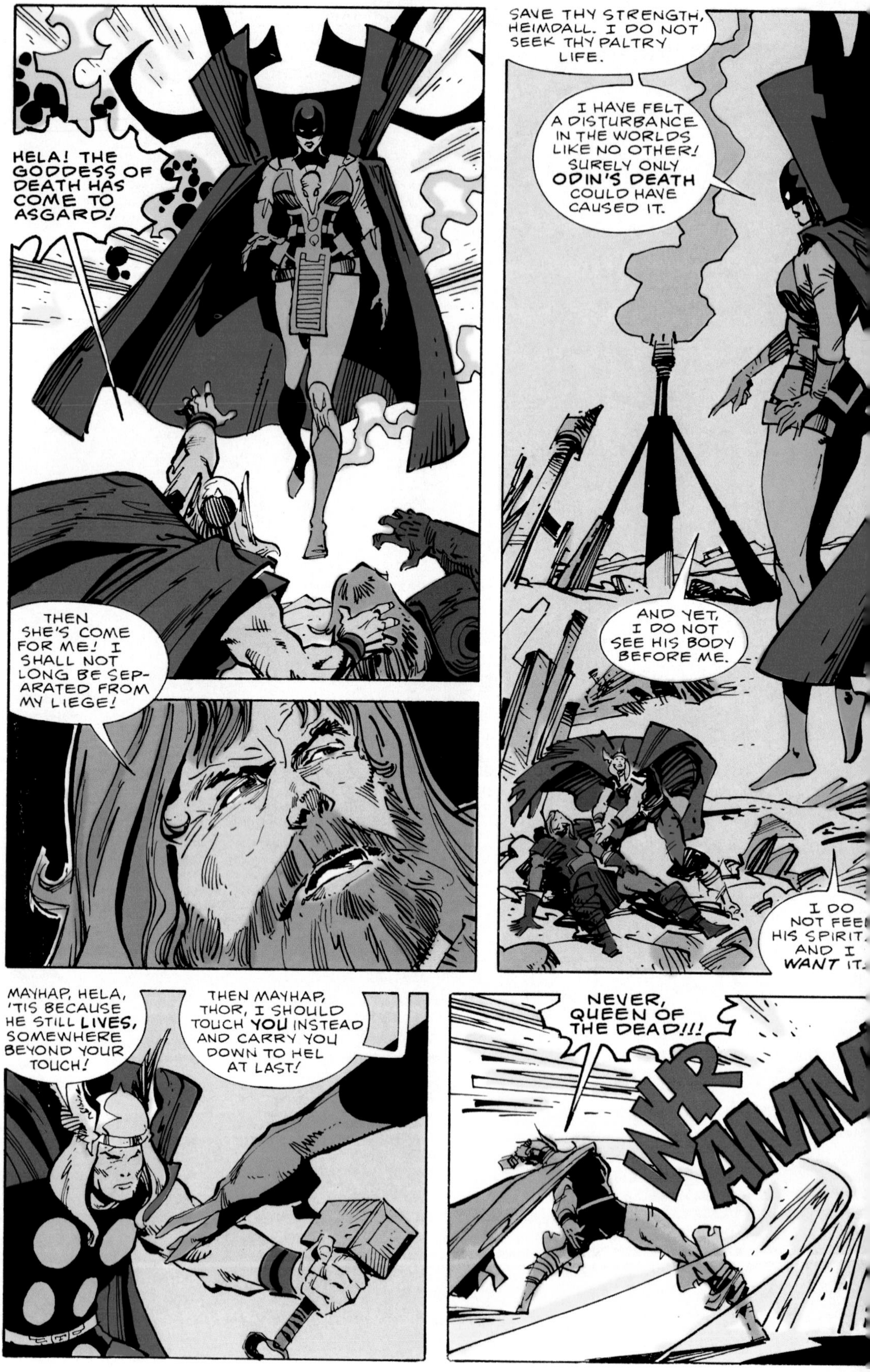
HELA! THE GODDESS OF DEATH HAS COME TO ASGARD!
SAVE THY STRENGTH, HEIMDALL. I DO NOT SEEK THY PALTRY LIFE.
I HAVE FELT A DISTURBANCE IN THE WORLDS LIKE NO OTHER! SURELY ONLY ODIN'S DEATH COULD HAVE CAUSED IT.
THEN SHE'S COME FOR ME! I SHALL NOT LONG BE SEP-ARATED FROM MY LIEGE!
AND YET, I DO NOT SEE HIS BODY BEFORE ME.
I DO NOT FEE HIS SPIRIT. AND I WANT IT.
MAYHAP, HELA, 'TIS BECAUSE HE STILL LIVES, SOMEWHERE BEYOND YOUR TOUCH!
THEN MAYHAP, THOR, I SHOULD TOUCH YOU INSTEAD AND CARRY YOU DOWN TO HEL AT LAST!
NEVER, QUEEN OF THE DEAD!!!
WHRAMM

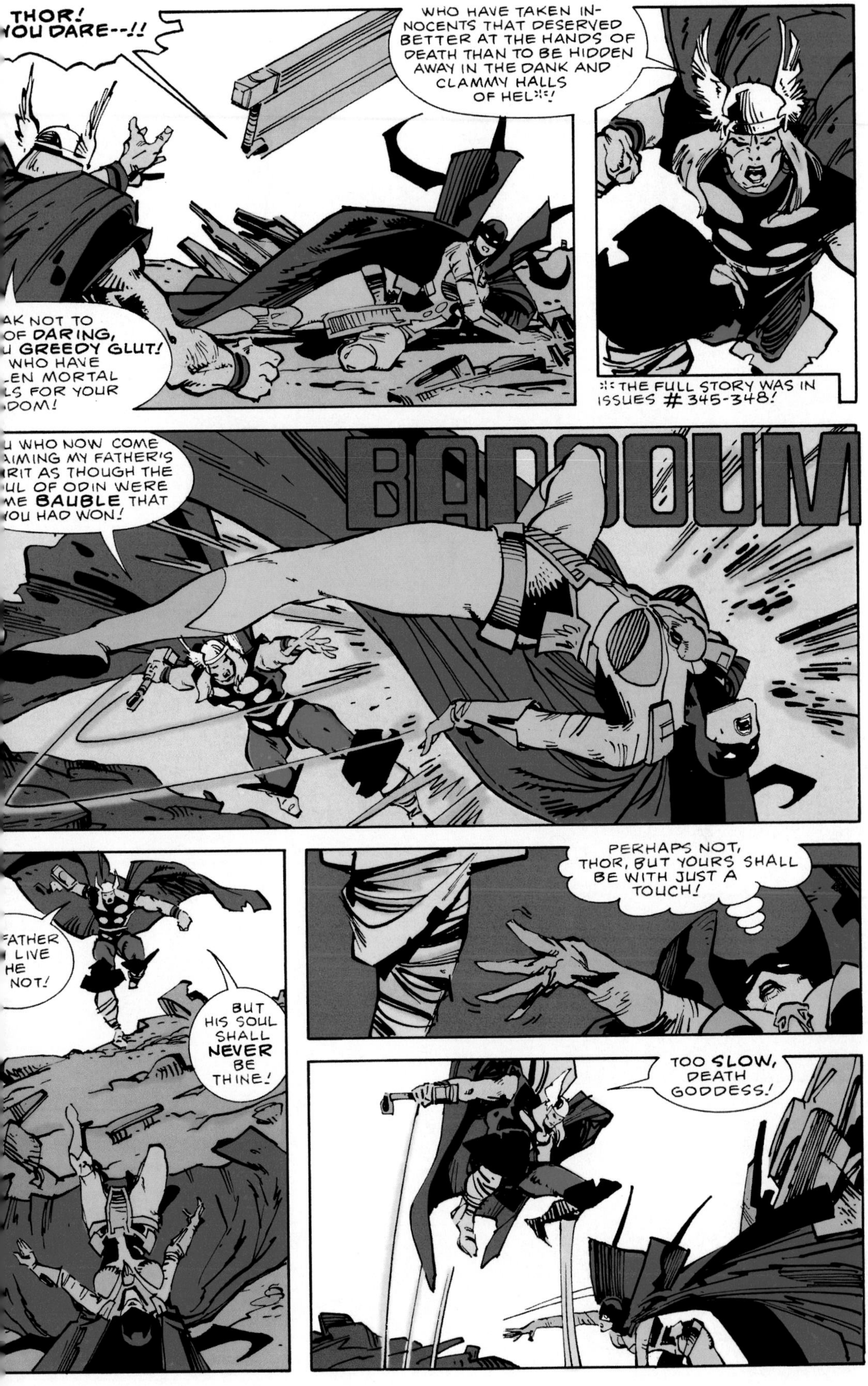

THOR! YOU DARE--!!
WHO HAVE TAKEN INNOCENTS THAT DESERVED BETTER AT THE HANDS OF DEATH THAN TO BE HIDDEN AWAY IN THE DANK AND CLAMMY HALLS OF HEL*!
AK NOT TO OF DARING, U GREEDY GLUT! WHO HAVE LEN MORTAL LS FOR YOUR DOM!
*THE FULL STORY WAS IN ISSUES #345-348!
U WHO NOW COME AIMING MY FATHER'S IRIT AS THOUGH THE UL OF ODIN WERE ME BAUBLE THAT YOU HAD WON!
BADOOUM
FATHER LIVE HE NOT!
BUT HIS SOUL SHALL NEVER BE THINE!
PERHAPS NOT, THOR, BUT YOURS SHALL BE WITH JUST A TOUCH!
TOO SLOW, DEATH GODDESS!

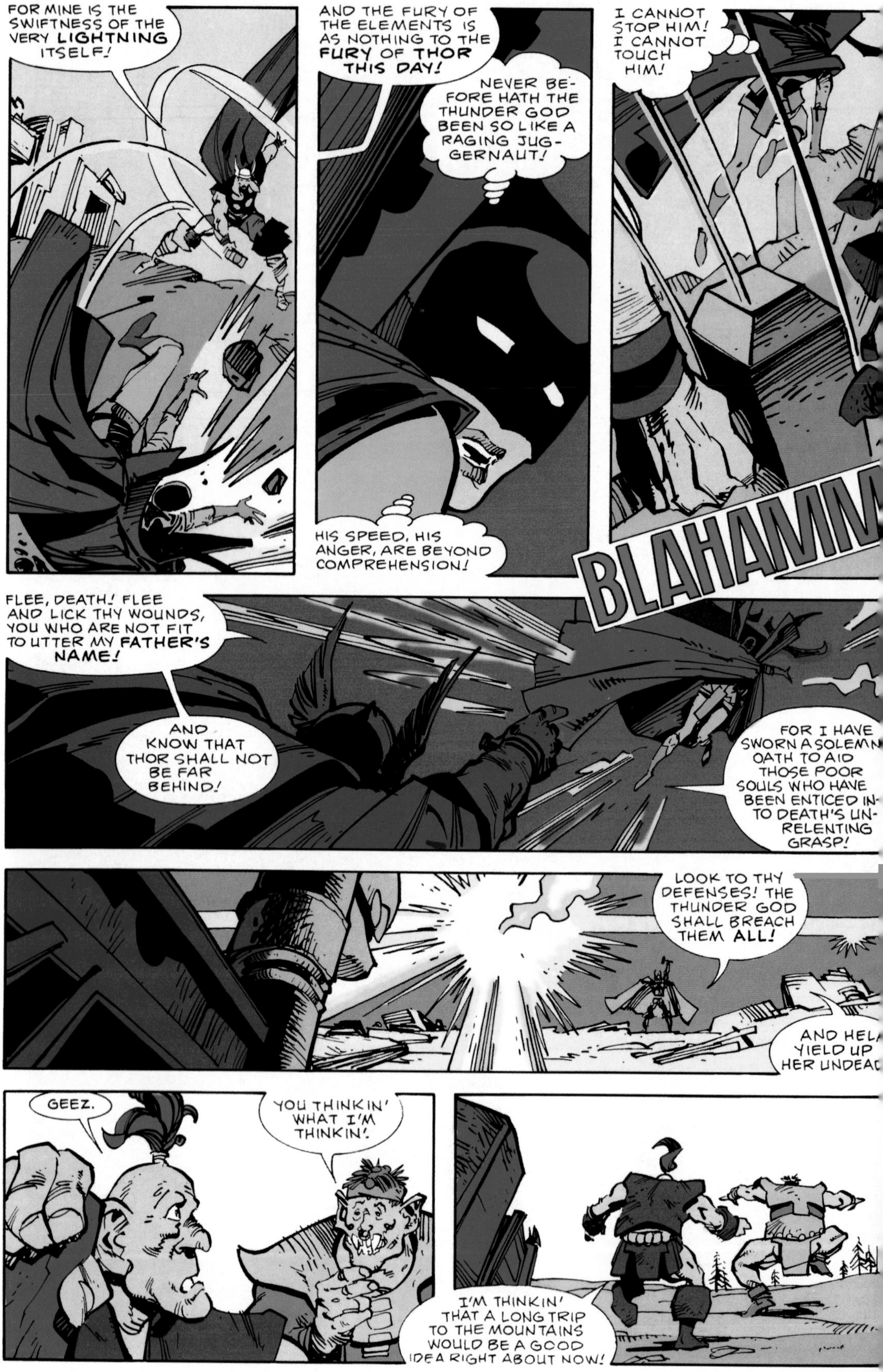
FOR MINE IS THE SWIFTNESS OF THE VERY LIGHTNING ITSELF!
AND THE FURY OF THE ELEMENTS IS AS NOTHING TO THE FURY OF THOR THIS DAY!
NEVER BEFORE HATH THE THUNDER GOD BEEN SO LIKE A RAGING JUGGERNAUT!
HIS SPEED, HIS ANGER, ARE BEYOND COMPREHENSION!
I CANNOT STOP HIM! I CANNOT TOUCH HIM!
BLAHAMM
FLEE, DEATH! FLEE AND LICK THY WOUNDS, YOU WHO ARE NOT FIT TO UTTER MY FATHER'S NAME!
AND KNOW THAT THOR SHALL NOT BE FAR BEHIND!
FOR I HAVE SWORN A SOLEMN OATH TO AID THOSE POOR SOULS WHO HAVE BEEN ENTICED INTO DEATH'S UNRELENTING GRASP!
LOOK TO THY DEFENSES! THE THUNDER GOD SHALL BREACH THEM ALL!
AND HEL YIELD UP HER UNDEAD
GEEZ.
YOU THINKIN' WHAT I'M THINKIN'.
I'M THINKIN' THAT A LONG TRIP TO THE MOUNTAINS WOULD BE A GOOD IDEA RIGHT ABOUT NOW!

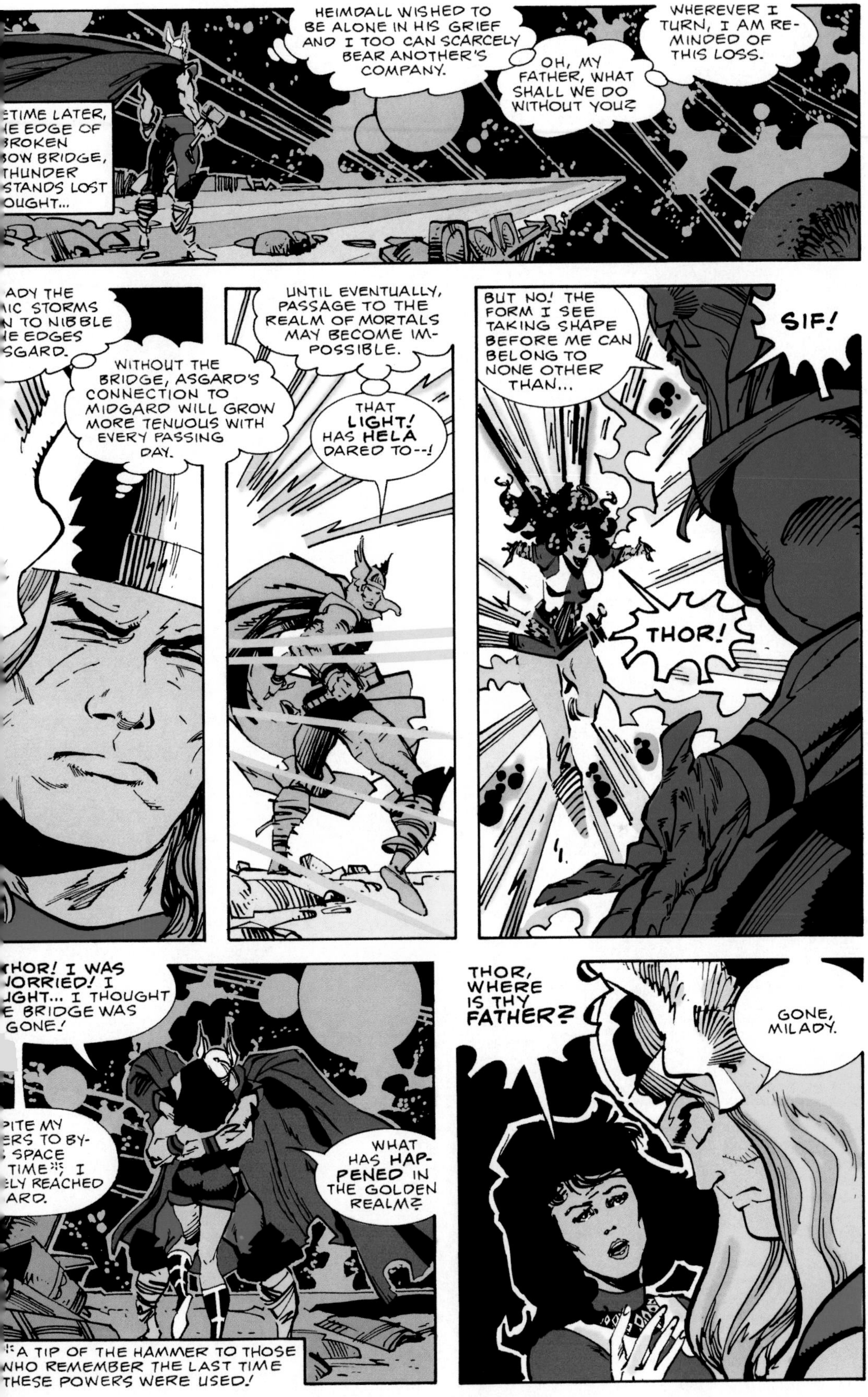

ETIME LATER, HE EDGE OF BROKEN BOW BRIDGE, THUNDER STANDS LOST OUGHT...
HEIMDALL WISHED TO BE ALONE IN HIS GRIEF AND I TOO CAN SCARCELY BEAR ANOTHER'S COMPANY.
OH, MY FATHER, WHAT SHALL WE DO WITHOUT YOU?
WHEREVER I TURN, I AM RE-MINDED OF THIS LOSS.
ADY THE IC STORMS N TO NIBBLE HE EDGES SGARD.
WITHOUT THE BRIDGE, ASGARD'S CONNECTION TO MIDGARD WILL GROW MORE TENUOUS WITH EVERY PASSING DAY.
UNTIL EVENTUALLY, PASSAGE TO THE REALM OF MORTALS MAY BECOME IM-POSSIBLE.
THAT LIGHT! HAS HELA DARED TO--!
BUT NO! THE FORM I SEE TAKING SHAPE BEFORE ME CAN BELONG TO NONE OTHER THAN...
SIF!
THOR!
THOR! I WAS ORRIED! I UGHT... I THOUGHT E BRIDGE WAS GONE!
PITE MY ERS TO BY- SPACE TIME*, I ELY REACHED ARD.
WHAT HAS HAP-PENED IN THE GOLDEN REALM?
*A TIP OF THE HAMMER TO THOSE WHO REMEMBER THE LAST TIME THESE POWERS WERE USED!
THOR, WHERE IS THY FATHER?
GONE, MILADY.

ODIN GONE!! BUT... WHERE?

LOKI THINKS THAT HE AND SURTUR NOW CONTEND ENDLESSLY IN MUSPELHEIM...

...WHILE HELA THINKS HIM DEAD AND SEEKS HIS SOUL.

ALL I KNOW IS THAT MY FATHER IS GONE AND ALL MY POWER COULD NOT SAVE HIM.

SIF, I HAVE FAILED HIM.

THOR, MY HEART, WHEREVER HE IS, YOUR FATHER KNOWS HIS SON FOUGHT UNAFRAID WITH THE COURAGE AND GALLANTRY AS BEFITS THE GOD OF THUNDER.

AS WOU HAV WISHE YOU

AND THE CONTINUED EXISTENCE OF THE NIN WORLDS IS THE TRUE MEASURE OF THAT ENDEAVOR.

NO MATTER WHAT THE COST, SURTUR HAS FAILED!

DO NOT PUNISH THYSELF FOR DEEDS NO MAN OR GOD COULD DO.

IN THIS, SIF, MY HEAD IS NOT THE MASTER OF MY HEART.

I WOULD LEAVE ASGARD FOR A TIME. I MUST NEEDS WEEP AND HERE MY TEARS REMAIN UNSHED.

THINK YOU THA BILL WOULD REMA ON EARTH AWHIL AND GUARD TH MORTALS AS I HAVE DONE?

BILL... WOULD STAY... IF I WISHED IT.

AS I THOUGHT. HE LOVES YOU AS WHO COULD NOT

I WOULD BID YOU TWO REMAIN ON EARTH TO GUIDE OUR PEOPLE.

WITHOUT THE RAINBOW BRIDGE, RETURNING OUR WARRIORS HOME WILL BE NO EASY TASK.

THEY MUST REMAIN ON EARTH A LITTLE WHILE...

...BUT WITHOUT THE KNOWLEDGE OF ODIN'S PASSING.

YET THIS VICTORY TODAY HAS TAUGHT ME SOMETHING OF THE SORROWS OF MORTALS WHO MUST ENDURE SUCH LOSSES THROUGHOUT THEIR LIVES.

FOR IN THEIR AWESOME GRIEF, THEY MIGHT DO MORE DAMAGE THAN SURTUR'S LEGIONS.

THEREFORE, THERE IS A FAVOR I WOULD HAVE Y ASK OF FANDRA FOR ME UPON YOUR RETURN

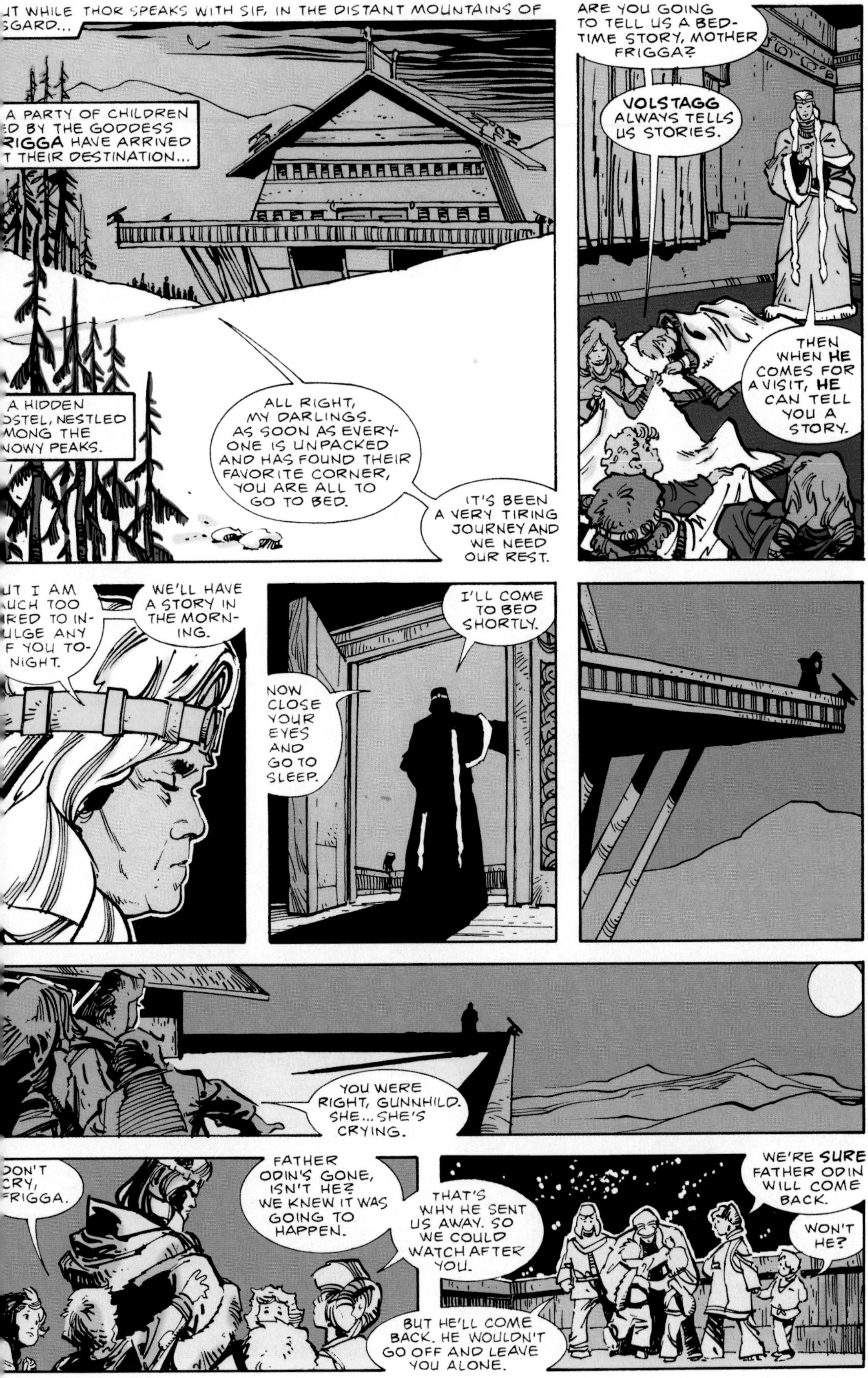
UT WHILE THOR SPEAKS WITH SIF, IN THE DISTANT MOUNTAINS OF SGARD...
A PARTY OF CHILDREN ED BY THE GODDESS RIGGA HAVE ARRIVED T THEIR DESTINATION...
A HIDDEN OSTEL, NESTLED MONG THE NOWY PEAKS.
ALL RIGHT, MY DARLINGS. AS SOON AS EVERYONE IS UNPACKED AND HAS FOUND THEIR FAVORITE CORNER, YOU ARE ALL TO GO TO BED.
IT'S BEEN A VERY TIRING JOURNEY AND WE NEED OUR REST.
ARE YOU GOING TO TELL US A BEDTIME STORY, MOTHER FRIGGA?
VOLSTAGG ALWAYS TELLS US STORIES.
THEN WHEN HE COMES FOR A VISIT, HE CAN TELL YOU A STORY.
UT I AM UCH TOO IRED TO INULGE ANY F YOU TONIGHT.
WE'LL HAVE A STORY IN THE MORNING.
I'LL COME TO BED SHORTLY.
NOW CLOSE YOUR EYES AND GO TO SLEEP.
YOU WERE RIGHT, GUNNHILD. SHE... SHE'S CRYING.
DON'T CRY, FRIGGA.
FATHER ODIN'S GONE, ISN'T HE? WE KNEW IT WAS GOING TO HAPPEN.
THAT'S WHY HE SENT US AWAY. SO WE COULD WATCH AFTER YOU.
BUT HE'LL COME BACK. HE WOULDN'T GO OFF AND LEAVE YOU ALONE.
WE'RE SURE FATHER ODIN WILL COME BACK.
WON'T HE?

CENTRAL PARK, MANHATTAN, HAS SEEN MARATHONS, VOLLEYBALL GAMES, AND ROLLER SKATERS...

...BUT NEVER BEFORE HAS IT BEEN THE SITE OF AN ARMORED HOST OF ASGARDIANS AS THEY BEGIN TO UNWIND AFTER A HARD DAY'S BATTLE.

BROTHER, 'TIS GOOD TO REMOVE THESE BOOTS. MY FEET...

YOU SHOULD HAVE SEEN TH WAY I CAUGHT HIM JUST UND THE...

IF IT HADN'T BEEN FOR THE RUNES IN SCRIBED ON MY SWORD...

LOOK! SIF HAS RE-TURNED!

HOW FARES ASGARD, MILADY?

THE REALM ETERNAL STILL STANDS, BILL. SURTUR HAS INDEED BEEN DEFEATED.

AND YOU THOUGH I HAVE BEEN GONE BUT FEW HOUR YOU LOOK STRANGELY TIRED.

I ASSISTED THE AVENGERS IN A SKIRMISH WITH SOME CREATURES KNOWN AS DIRE WRAITHS.* IT WAS NOTHING.

AND YOUR OWN PEOPLE?

MY INTERNAL MONITORS HAVE BEEN IN TOUCH WITH MY SHIP VIA SUBSPACE TRANSMISSION. ALL SEEMS WELL.

* FULL DETAILS IN ROM #65!

THEN YOU WOULD NOT MIND STAYING ON EARTH FOR A TIME?

BUT WHY? THE DANGER IS OVER.

I AM ABOUT TO EX-PLAIN.

HEROES OF ASGARD! I BRING A MESSAGE FROM THOR, YOUR COMMANDER!

THOUGH WE HA WON THE BATTL IT HAS NOT BEE WITHOUT COST.

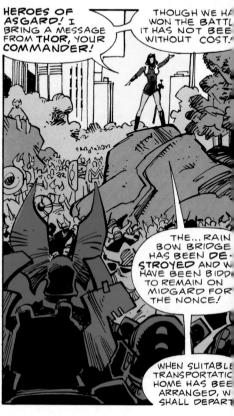

THE... RAIN BOW BRIDGE HAS BEEN DE-STROYED AND W HAVE BEEN BIDD TO REMAIN ON MIDGARD FOR THE NONCE!

WHEN SUITABLE TRANSPORTATIC HOME HAS BEE ARRANGED, W SHALL DEPART

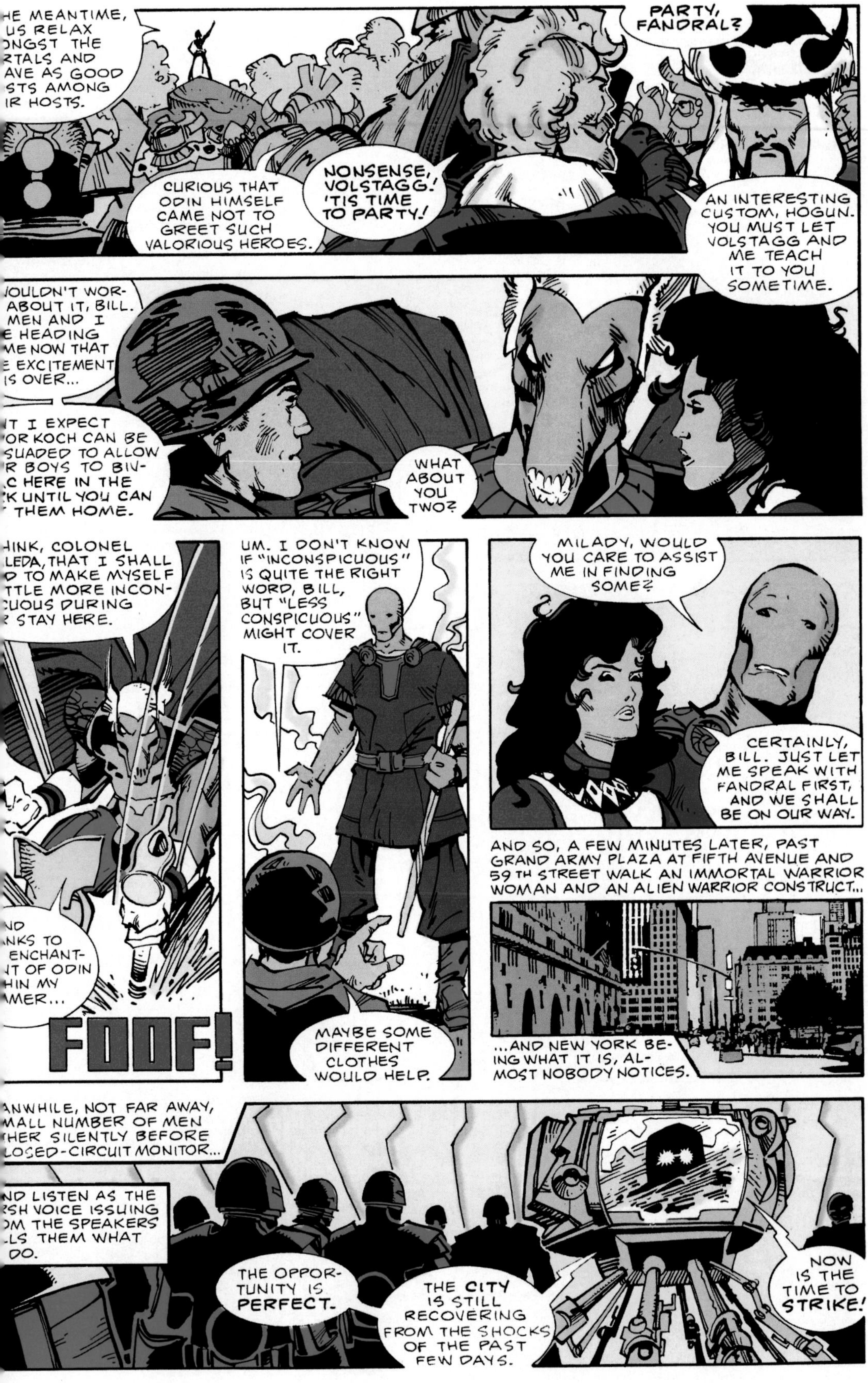

HE MEANTIME, US RELAX ONGST THE RTALS AND AVE AS GOOD STS AMONG IR HOSTS.
PARTY, FANDRAL?
CURIOUS THAT ODIN HIMSELF CAME NOT TO GREET SUCH VALORIOUS HEROES.
NONSENSE, VOLSTAGG! 'TIS TIME TO PARTY!
AN INTERESTING CUSTOM, HOGUN. YOU MUST LET VOLSTAGG AND ME TEACH IT TO YOU SOMETIME.
OULDN'T WOR- ABOUT IT, BILL. MEN AND I E HEADING ME NOW THAT E EXCITEMENT IS OVER...
T I EXPECT OR KOCH CAN BE SUADED TO ALLOW R BOYS TO BIV- C HERE IN THE K UNTIL YOU CAN THEM HOME.
WHAT ABOUT YOU TWO?
HINK, COLONEL LEDA, THAT I SHALL D TO MAKE MYSELF TTLE MORE INCON- CUOUS DURING STAY HERE.
ND NKS TO ENCHANT- NT OF ODIN HIN MY MER...
FOOF!
UM. I DON'T KNOW IF "INCONSPICUOUS" IS QUITE THE RIGHT WORD, BILL, BUT "LESS CONSPICUOUS" MIGHT COVER IT.
MAYBE SOME DIFFERENT CLOTHES WOULD HELP.
MILADY, WOULD YOU CARE TO ASSIST ME IN FINDING SOME?
CERTAINLY, BILL. JUST LET ME SPEAK WITH FANDRAL FIRST, AND WE SHALL BE ON OUR WAY.
AND SO, A FEW MINUTES LATER, PAST GRAND ARMY PLAZA AT FIFTH AVENUE AND 59 TH STREET WALK AN IMMORTAL WARRIOR WOMAN AND AN ALIEN WARRIOR CONSTRUCT...
...AND NEW YORK BE- ING WHAT IT IS, AL- MOST NOBODY NOTICES.
ANWHILE, NOT FAR AWAY, MALL NUMBER OF MEN HER SILENTLY BEFORE LOSED-CIRCUIT MONITOR...
ND LISTEN AS THE RSH VOICE ISSUING OM THE SPEAKERS LS THEM WHAT DO.
THE OPPOR- TUNITY IS PERFECT.
THE CITY IS STILL RECOVERING FROM THE SHOCKS OF THE PAST FEW DAYS.
NOW IS THE TIME TO STRIKE!

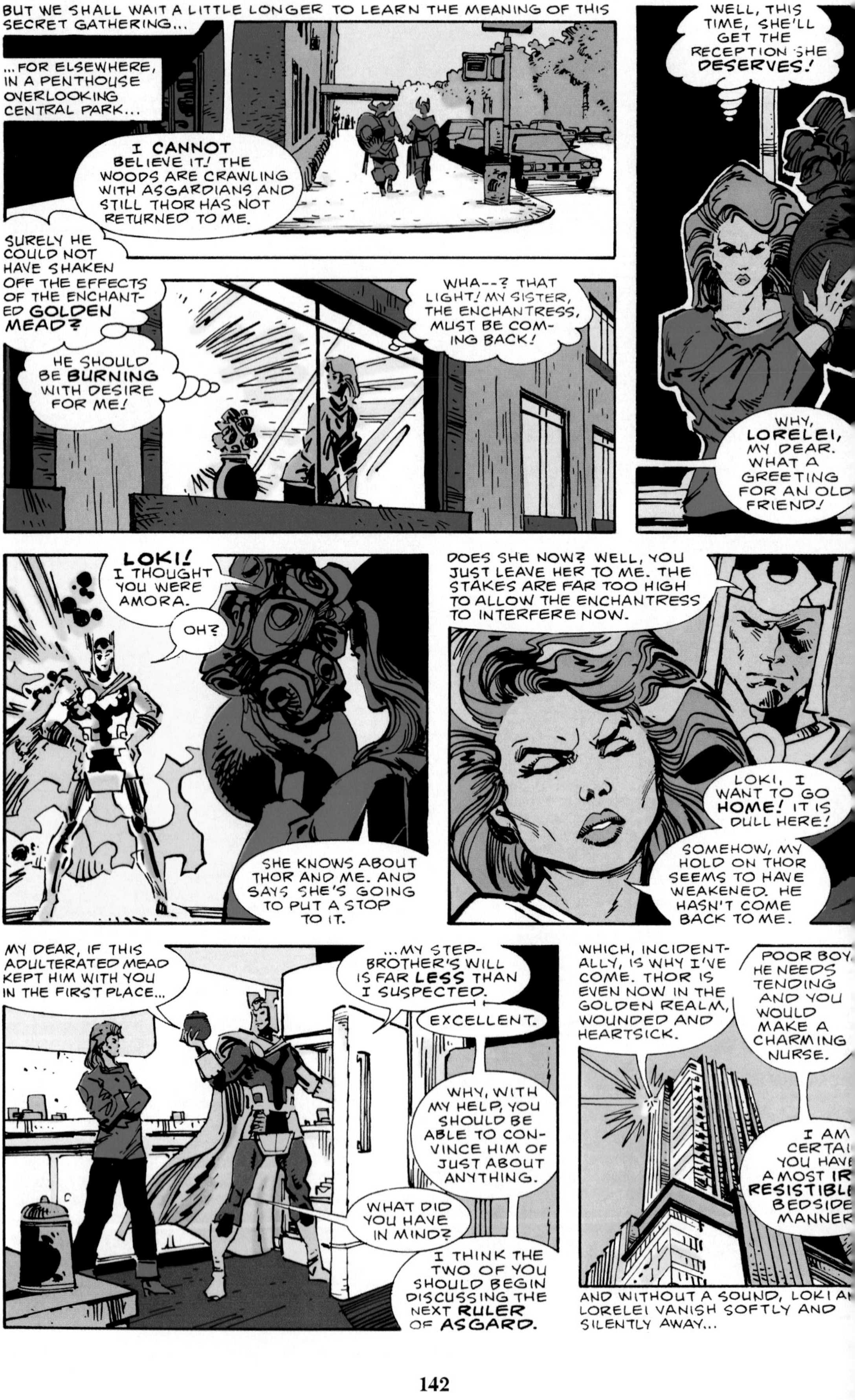

BUT WE SHALL WAIT A LITTLE LONGER TO LEARN THE MEANING OF THIS SECRET GATHERING...
...FOR ELSEWHERE, IN A PENTHOUSE OVERLOOKING CENTRAL PARK...
I CANNOT BELIEVE IT! THE WOODS ARE CRAWLING WITH ASGARDIANS AND STILL THOR HAS NOT RETURNED TO ME.
SURELY HE COULD NOT HAVE SHAKEN OFF THE EFFECTS OF THE ENCHANTED GOLDEN MEAD?
HE SHOULD BE BURNING WITH DESIRE FOR ME!
WHA--? THAT LIGHT! MY SISTER, THE ENCHANTRESS, MUST BE COMING BACK!
WELL, THIS TIME, SHE'LL GET THE RECEPTION SHE DESERVES!
WHY, LORELEI, MY DEAR. WHAT A GREETING FOR AN OLD FRIEND!
LOKI! I THOUGHT YOU WERE AMORA.
OH?
SHE KNOWS ABOUT THOR AND ME. AND SAYS SHE'S GOING TO PUT A STOP TO IT.
DOES SHE NOW? WELL, YOU JUST LEAVE HER TO ME. THE STAKES ARE FAR TOO HIGH TO ALLOW THE ENCHANTRESS TO INTERFERE NOW.
LOKI, I WANT TO GO HOME! IT IS DULL HERE!
SOMEHOW, MY HOLD ON THOR SEEMS TO HAVE WEAKENED. HE HASN'T COME BACK TO ME.
MY DEAR, IF THIS ADULTERATED MEAD KEPT HIM WITH YOU IN THE FIRST PLACE...
...MY STEP-BROTHER'S WILL IS FAR LESS THAN I SUSPECTED.
EXCELLENT.
WHY, WITH MY HELP, YOU SHOULD BE ABLE TO CONVINCE HIM OF JUST ABOUT ANYTHING.
WHAT DID YOU HAVE IN MIND?
I THINK THE TWO OF YOU SHOULD BEGIN DISCUSSING THE NEXT RULER OF ASGARD.
WHICH, INCIDENTALLY, IS WHY I'VE COME. THOR IS EVEN NOW IN THE GOLDEN REALM, WOUNDED AND HEARTSICK.
POOR BOY. HE NEEDS TENDING AND YOU WOULD MAKE A CHARMING NURSE.
I AM CERTAI YOU HAVE A MOST IRRESISTIBLE BEDSIDE MANNER
AND WITHOUT A SOUND, LOKI AN LORELEI VANISH SOFTLY AND SILENTLY AWAY...

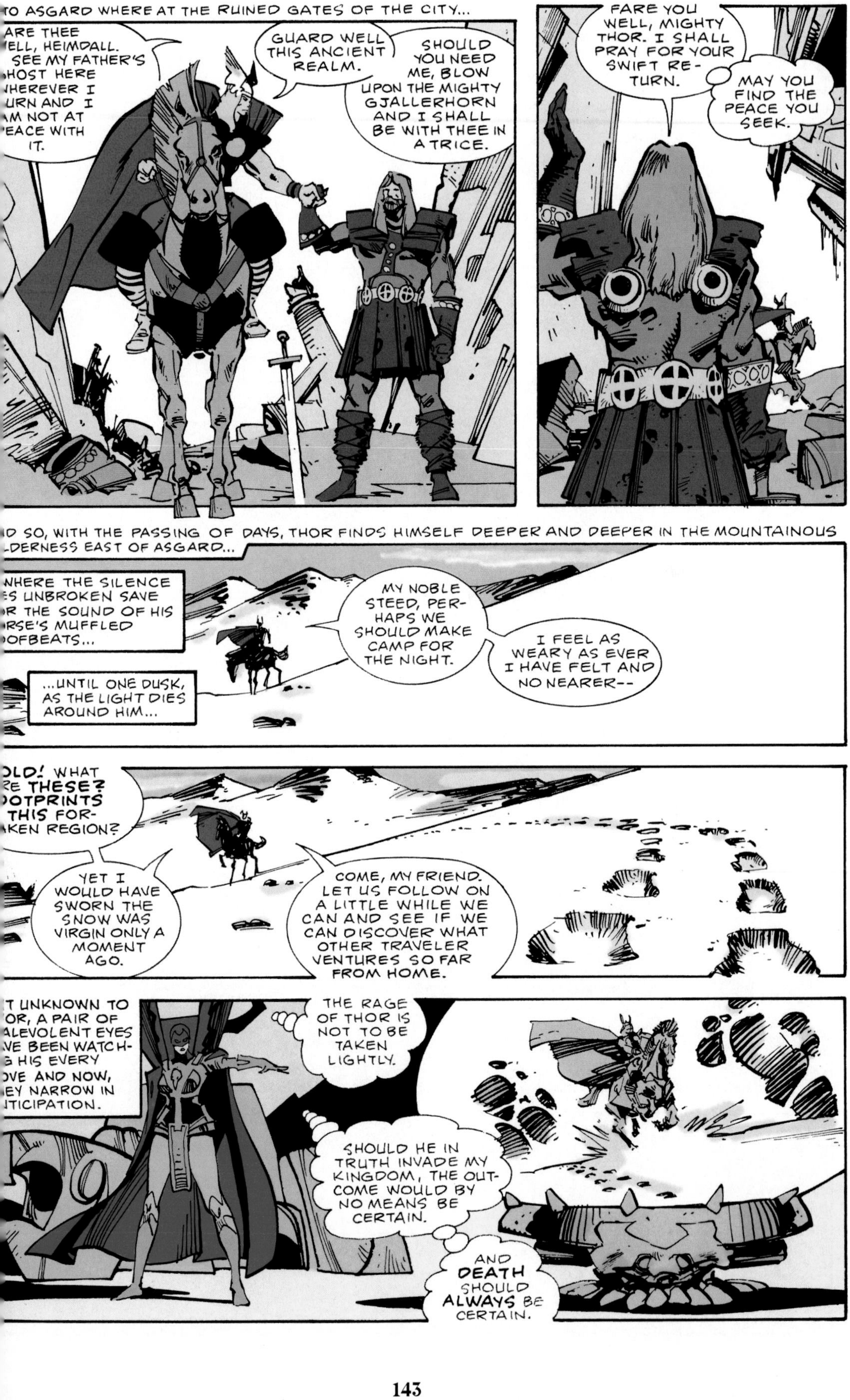
TO ASGARD WHERE AT THE RUINED GATES OF THE CITY...
ARE THEE ELL, HEIMDALL. SEE MY FATHER'S HOST HERE HEREVER I URN AND I M NOT AT EACE WITH IT.
GUARD WELL THIS ANCIENT REALM.
SHOULD YOU NEED ME, BLOW UPON THE MIGHTY GJALLERHORN AND I SHALL BE WITH THEE IN A TRICE.
FARE YOU WELL, MIGHTY THOR. I SHALL PRAY FOR YOUR SWIFT RE- TURN.
MAY YOU FIND THE PEACE YOU SEEK.
D SO, WITH THE PASSING OF DAYS, THOR FINDS HIMSELF DEEPER AND DEEPER IN THE MOUNTAINOUS LDERNESS EAST OF ASGARD...
WHERE THE SILENCE ES UNBROKEN SAVE R THE SOUND OF HIS RSE'S MUFFLED OFBEATS...
...UNTIL ONE DUSK, AS THE LIGHT DIES AROUND HIM...
MY NOBLE STEED, PER- HAPS WE SHOULD MAKE CAMP FOR THE NIGHT.
I FEEL AS WEARY AS EVER I HAVE FELT AND NO NEARER--
OLD! WHAT RE THESE? OTPRINTS THIS FOR- KEN REGION?
YET I WOULD HAVE SWORN THE SNOW WAS VIRGIN ONLY A MOMENT AGO.
COME, MY FRIEND. LET US FOLLOW ON A LITTLE WHILE WE CAN AND SEE IF WE CAN DISCOVER WHAT OTHER TRAVELER VENTURES SO FAR FROM HOME.
T UNKNOWN TO OR, A PAIR OF ALEVOLENT EYES VE BEEN WATCH- G HIS EVERY OVE AND NOW, EY NARROW IN TICIPATION.
THE RAGE OF THOR IS NOT TO BE TAKEN LIGHTLY.
SHOULD HE IN TRUTH INVADE MY KINGDOM, THE OUT- COME WOULD BY NO MEANS BE CERTAIN.
AND DEATH SHOULD ALWAYS BE CERTAIN.

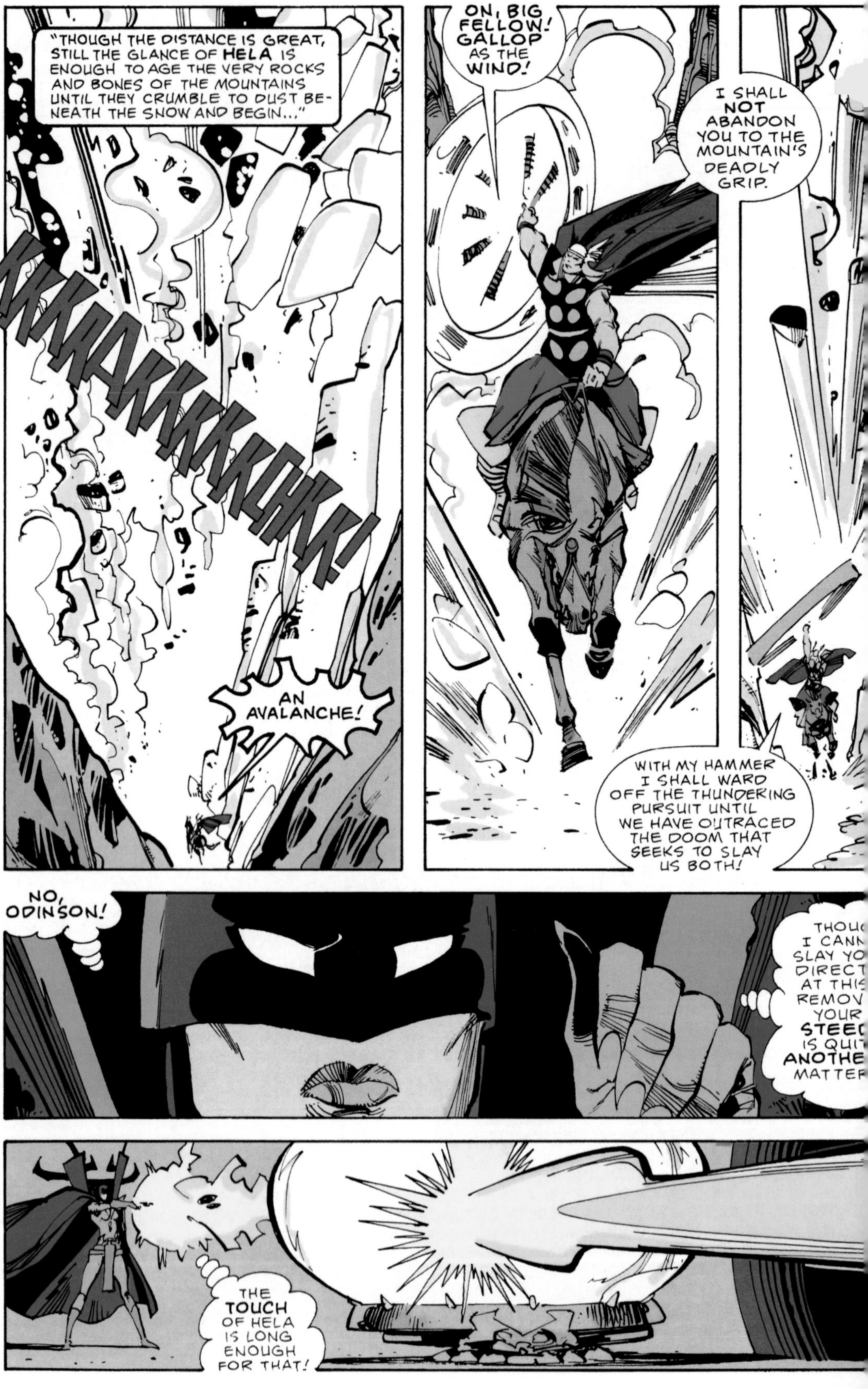
"THOUGH THE DISTANCE IS GREAT, STILL THE GLANCE OF HELA IS ENOUGH TO AGE THE VERY ROCKS AND BONES OF THE MOUNTAINS UNTIL THEY CRUMBLE TO DUST BENEATH THE SNOW AND BEGIN..."
KKKRAKKKKKKKCHKK!
AN AVALANCHE!
ON, BIG FELLOW! GALLOP AS THE WIND!
I SHALL NOT ABANDON YOU TO THE MOUNTAIN'S DEADLY GRIP.
WITH MY HAMMER I SHALL WARD OFF THE THUNDERING PURSUIT UNTIL WE HAVE OUTRACED THE DOOM THAT SEEKS TO SLAY US BOTH!
NO, ODINSON!
THOU
I CANN
SLAY YO
DIRECT
AT THIS
REMOV
YOUR
STEED
IS QUIT
ANOTHE
MATTER
THE TOUCH OF HELA IS LONG ENOUGH FOR THAT!

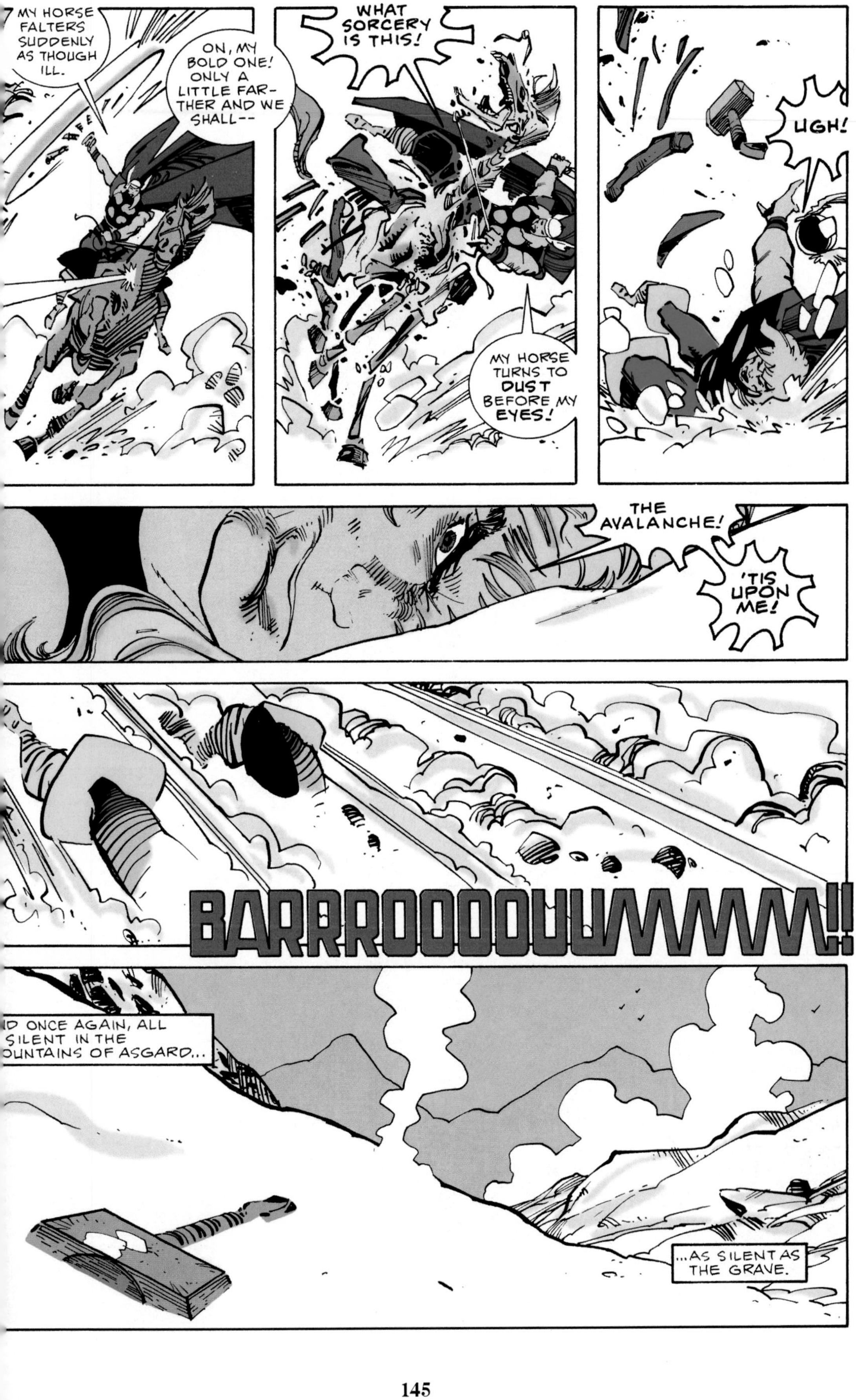

MY HORSE FALTERS SUDDENLY AS THOUGH ILL.
ON, MY BOLD ONE! ONLY A LITTLE FARTHER AND WE SHALL--
WHAT SORCERY IS THIS!
MY HORSE TURNS TO DUST BEFORE MY EYES!
UGH!
THE AVALANCHE!
'TIS UPON ME!
BARRROOOOUUMMMM!!
D ONCE AGAIN, ALL SILENT IN THE OUNTAINS OF ASGARD...
...AS SILENT AS THE GRAVE.

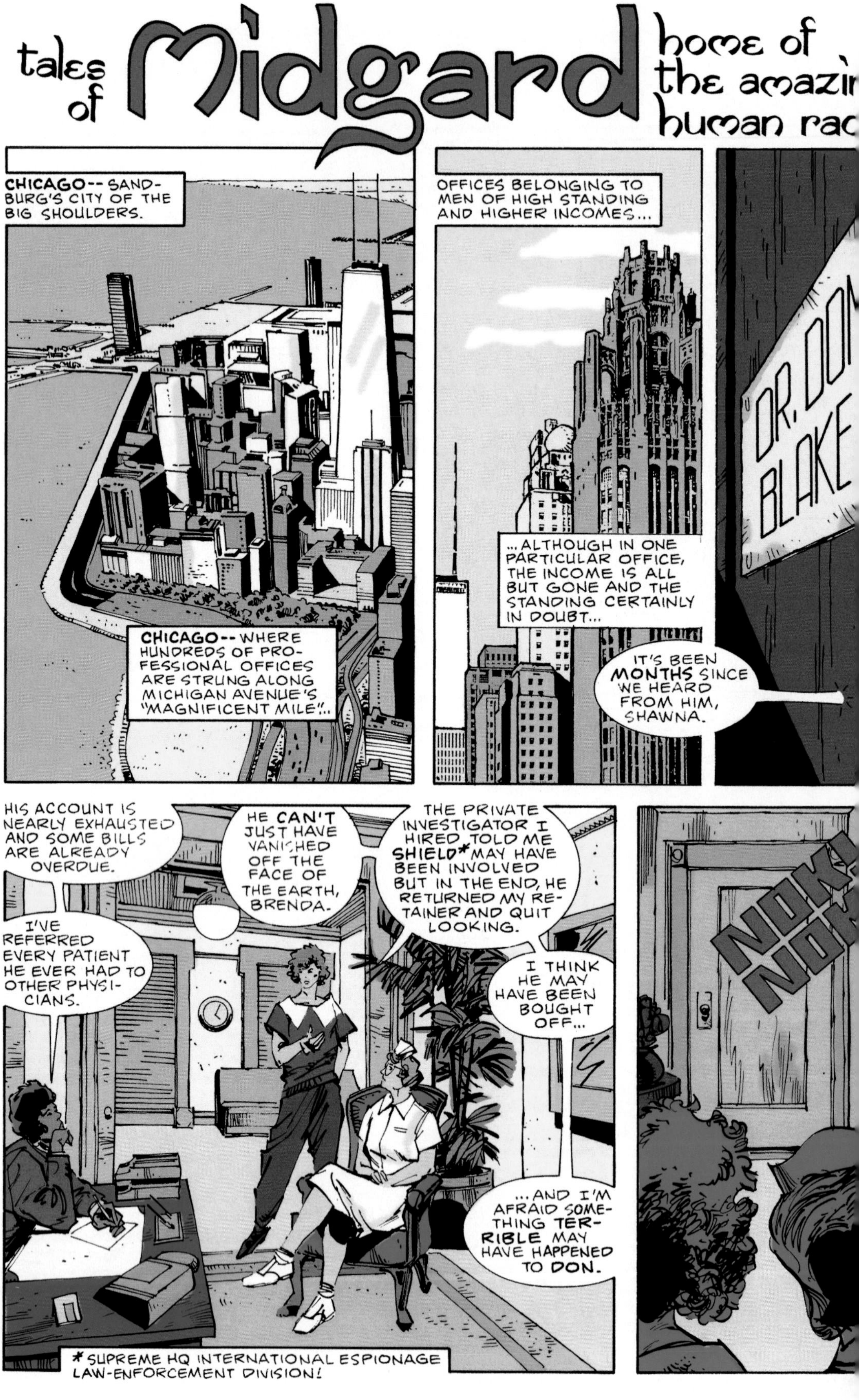
tales of Midgard home of the amazin human rac
CHICAGO-- SANDBURG'S CITY OF THE BIG SHOULDERS.
CHICAGO-- WHERE HUNDREDS OF PROFESSIONAL OFFICES ARE STRUNG ALONG MICHIGAN AVENUE'S "MAGNIFICENT MILE"...
OFFICES BELONGING TO MEN OF HIGH STANDING AND HIGHER INCOMES...
...ALTHOUGH IN ONE PARTICULAR OFFICE, THE INCOME IS ALL BUT GONE AND THE STANDING CERTAINLY IN DOUBT...
IT'S BEEN MONTHS SINCE WE HEARD FROM HIM, SHAWNA.
DR. DO
BLAKE
HIS ACCOUNT IS NEARLY EXHAUSTED AND SOME BILLS ARE ALREADY OVERDUE.
I'VE REFERRED EVERY PATIENT HE EVER HAD TO OTHER PHYSICIANS.
HE CAN'T JUST HAVE VANISHED OFF THE FACE OF THE EARTH, BRENDA.
THE PRIVATE INVESTIGATOR I HIRED TOLD ME SHIELD* MAY HAVE BEEN INVOLVED BUT IN THE END, HE RETURNED MY RETAINER AND QUIT LOOKING.
I THINK HE MAY HAVE BEEN BOUGHT OFF...
...AND I'M AFRAID SOMETHING TERRIBLE MAY HAVE HAPPENED TO DON.
*SUPREME HQ INTERNATIONAL ESPIONAGE LAW-ENFORCEMENT DIVISION!

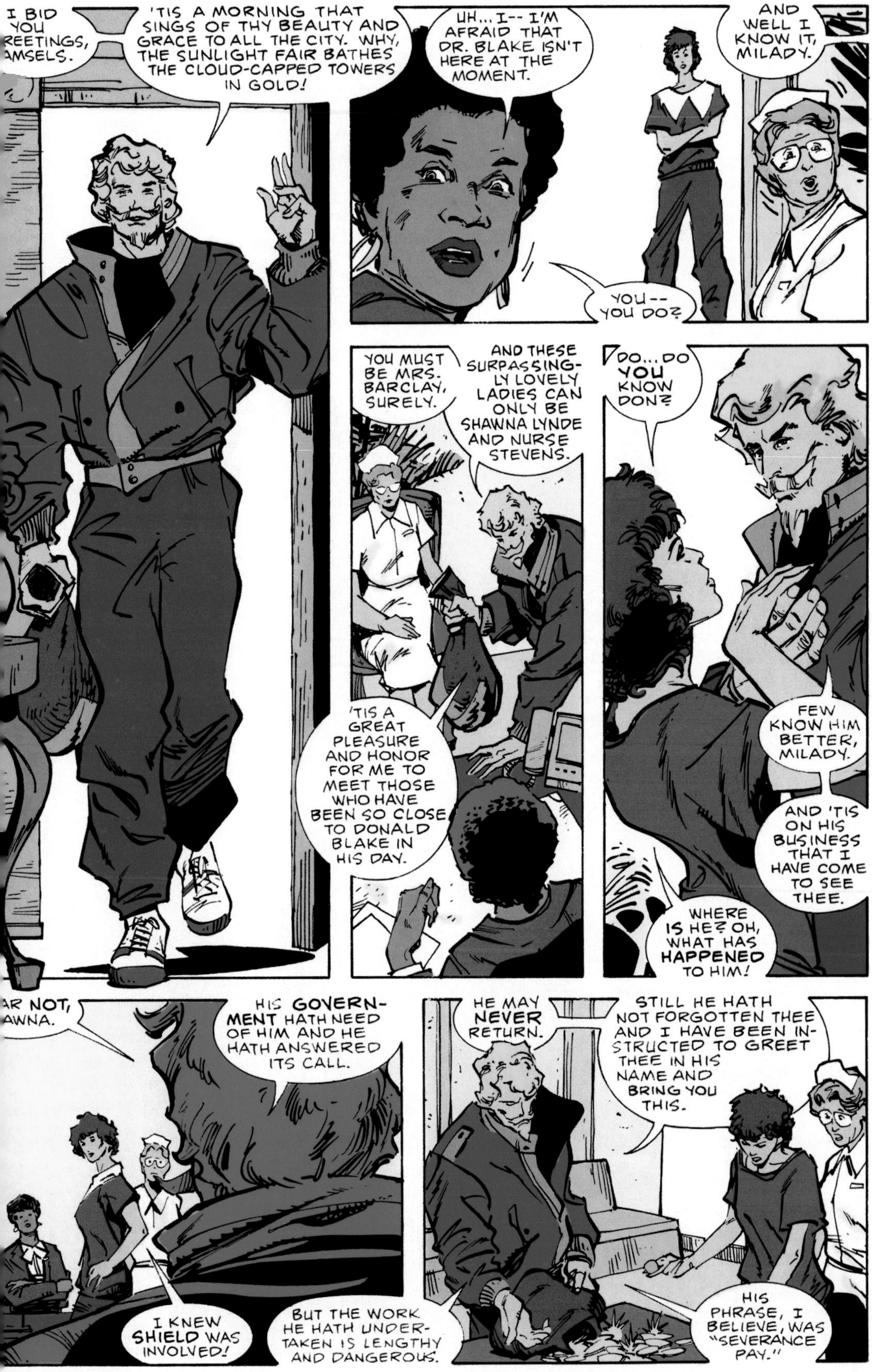
I BID YOU REETINGS, AMSELS.
'TIS A MORNING THAT SINGS OF THY BEAUTY AND GRACE TO ALL THE CITY. WHY, THE SUNLIGHT FAIR BATHES THE CLOUD-CAPPED TOWERS IN GOLD!
UH... I-- I'M AFRAID THAT DR. BLAKE ISN'T HERE AT THE MOMENT.
AND WELL I KNOW IT, MILADY.
YOU -- YOU DO?
YOU MUST BE MRS. BARCLAY, SURELY.
AND THESE SURPASSING-LY LOVELY LADIES CAN ONLY BE SHAWNA LYNDE AND NURSE STEVENS.
'TIS A GREAT PLEASURE AND HONOR FOR ME TO MEET THOSE WHO HAVE BEEN SO CLOSE TO DONALD BLAKE IN HIS DAY.
DO... DO YOU KNOW DON?
FEW KNOW HIM BETTER, MILADY.
AND 'TIS ON HIS BUSINESS THAT I HAVE COME TO SEE THEE.
WHERE IS HE? OH, WHAT HAS HAPPENED TO HIM!
AR NOT, AWNA.
HIS GOVERNMENT HATH NEED OF HIM AND HE HATH ANSWERED ITS CALL.
I KNEW SHIELD WAS INVOLVED!
BUT THE WORK HE HATH UNDERTAKEN IS LENGTHY AND DANGEROUS.
HE MAY NEVER RETURN.
STILL HE HATH NOT FORGOTTEN THEE AND I HAVE BEEN INSTRUCTED TO GREET THEE IN HIS NAME AND BRING YOU THIS.
HIS PHRASE, I BELIEVE, WAS "SEVERANCE PAY."

WAIT A MINUTE. THIS ISN'T AMERICAN CURRENCY.

IN SOOTH, FAIR LADY, 'TIS NOT.

BUT THE GOLD CONTAINED WITHIN THESE COINS IS OF A FINER GRADE THAN ANY TO BE FOUND IN THE MINES OF EARTH.

AND THESE CHARMS HATH BLAKE ALSO SENT AS TOKEN OF HIS ESTEEM.

SO COME. LOOK NOT TO THE PAST...

...BUT AHEAD TO THE FUTURE.

YOUR SERVICE TO DR. BLAKE IS AT AN END.

YOU HAVE KNOWN ONE OF THE NOBLEST BEINGS TO WALK THE VALES OF MIDGARD...

...AND THOUGH YOU SHALL NOT HENCEFORTH REMEMBER HIM IN YOUR WAKING LIVES...

...STILL YOUR DREAMS WILL ALWAYS BE COLORED BY THE RADIANCE OF HIS PRESENCE...

...AND YOUR HEARTS SHALL BE GLAD THOUGH THEY KNOW NOT WHY.

I SAY, GO IN PEACE.

AND SO, 'TIS DONE. IN MOMENTS, THEY WILL HAVE FORGOTTEN ALL THEY KNEW OF DONALD BLAKE.

AND BE NONE THE WORSE FOR IT.

DR. DONALD BLAKE, M.D.

RIPP!

BUT I THINK I SHOULD CARRY THIS PLACARD WITH ME

THOR MIGHT WELL DELIGHT IN SOUVENIR OF THE TIME HE SPENT AS MORTAL AMONGST SUCH BEAUTY.

NEXT! THE ICY HEARTS

IN WHICH WE MEET GENTLEMEN FROM LONG AGO AND FAR AWAY

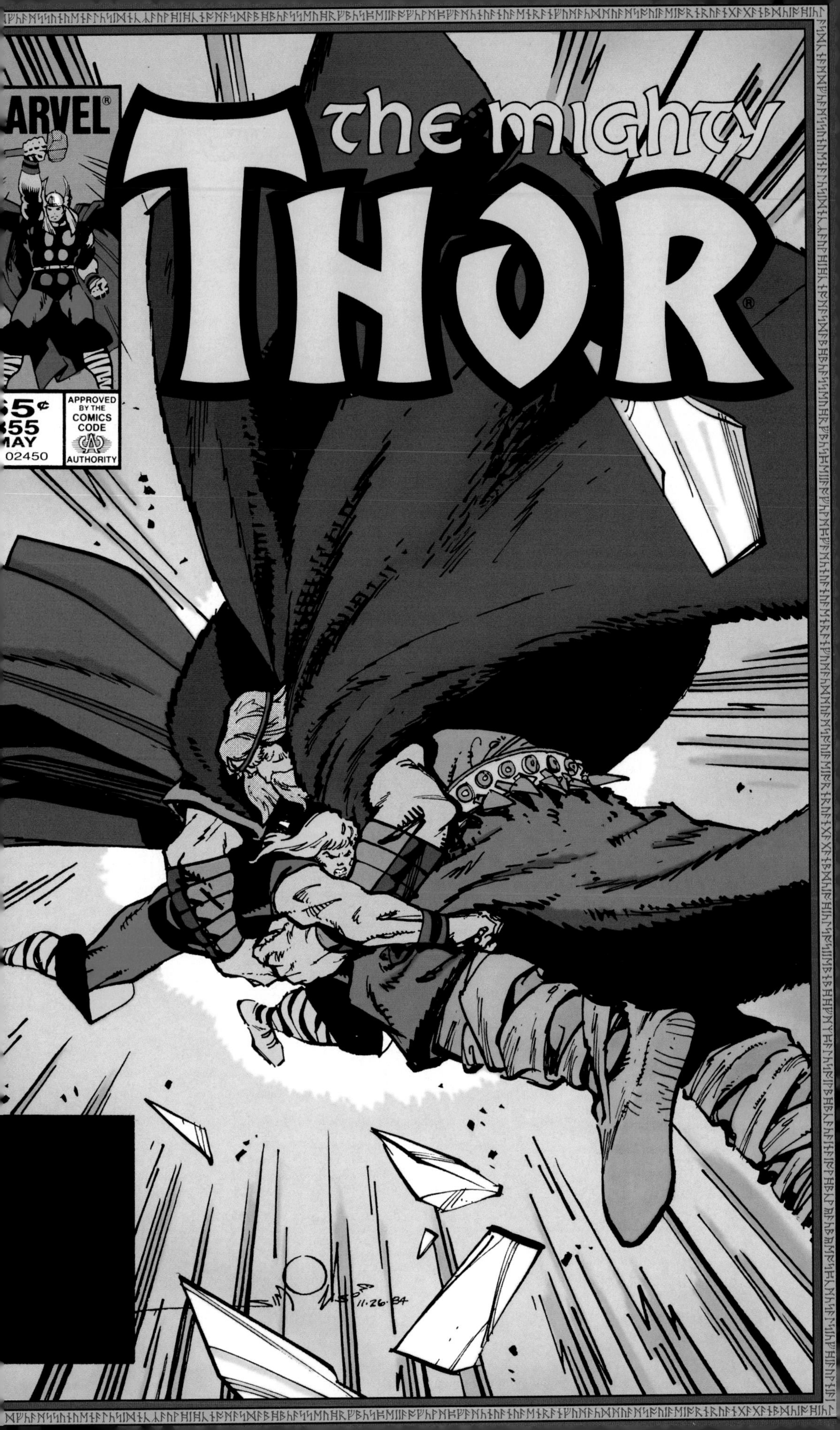

ARVEL
the mighty
THOR
5¢
355
MAY
02450
APPROVED BY THE COMICS CODE AUTHORITY

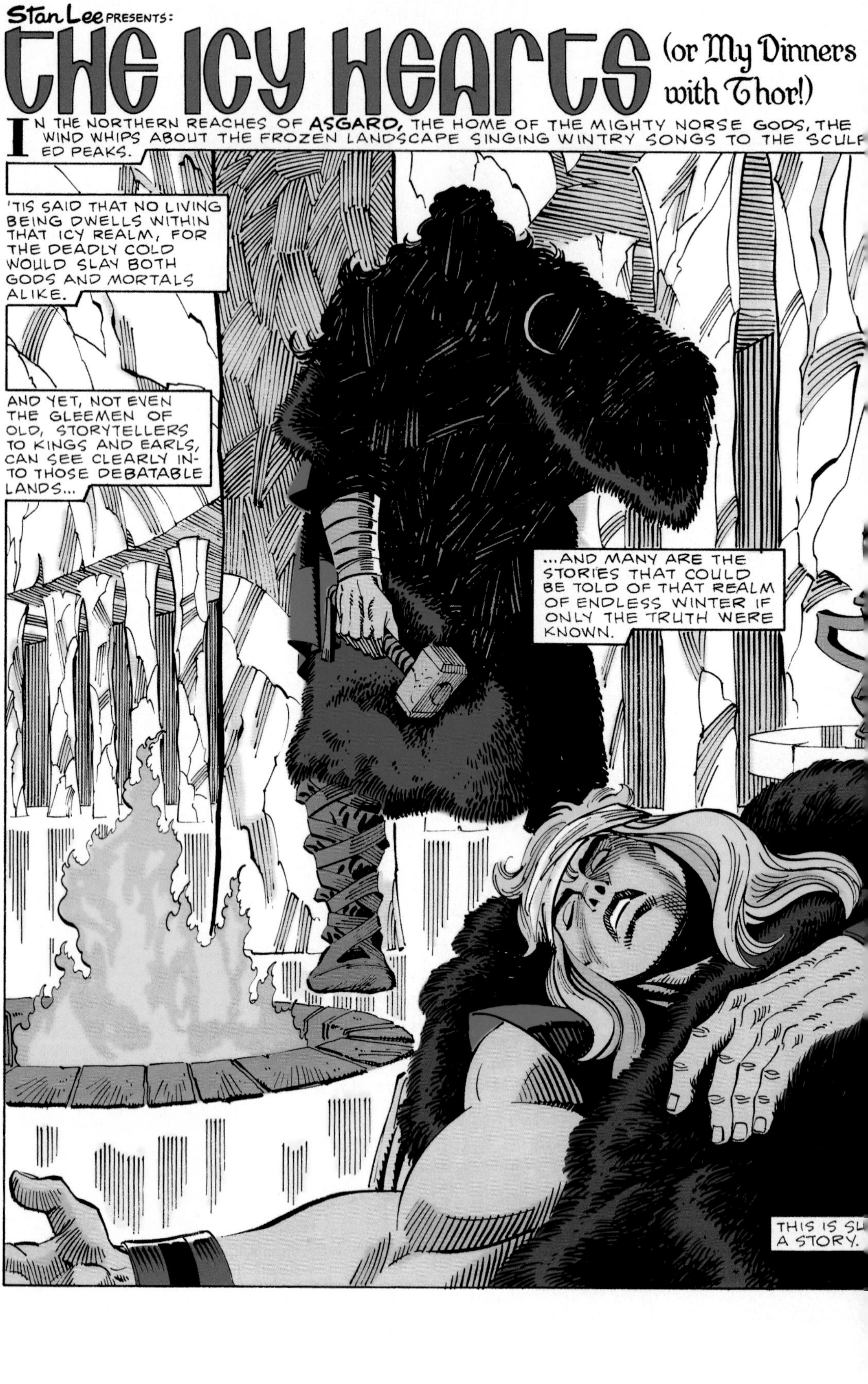
Stan Lee PRESENTS:
THE ICY HEARTS (or My Dinners with Thor!)
IN THE NORTHERN REACHES OF ASGARD, THE HOME OF THE MIGHTY NORSE GODS, THE WIND WHIPS ABOUT THE FROZEN LANDSCAPE SINGING WINTRY SONGS TO THE SCULP ED PEAKS.
'TIS SAID THAT NO LIVING BEING DWELLS WITHIN THAT ICY REALM, FOR THE DEADLY COLD WOULD SLAY BOTH GODS AND MORTALS ALIKE.
AND YET, NOT EVEN THE GLEEMEN OF OLD, STORYTELLERS TO KINGS AND EARLS, CAN SEE CLEARLY INTO THOSE DEBATABLE LANDS...
...AND MANY ARE THE STORIES THAT COULD BE TOLD OF THAT REALM OF ENDLESS WINTER IF ONLY THE TRUTH WERE KNOWN.
THIS IS SU A STORY.

'TIS A GOODLY MALLET, MJOLNIR.

THE DWARFS MADE WELL THIS MAGIC HAMMER.

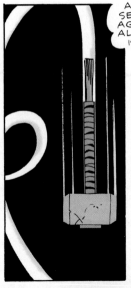

A TRUE SERVANT AGAINST ALL THAT IS EVIL.

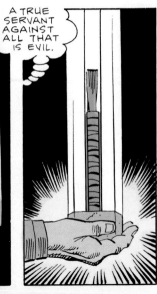

UHHH.

MY GUEST AWAKENS.

HH. THE ALANCHE!

THER, I'M OMING! I'M OMING!

I--I--!

I RE-MEMBER!

I FELL BEFORE THE ROARING AVALANCHE AND SHOULD HAVE DIED!

BUT WHO ARE YOU?!!

AM I TRULY DEAD AND THIS SOME CORNER OF VALHALLA?

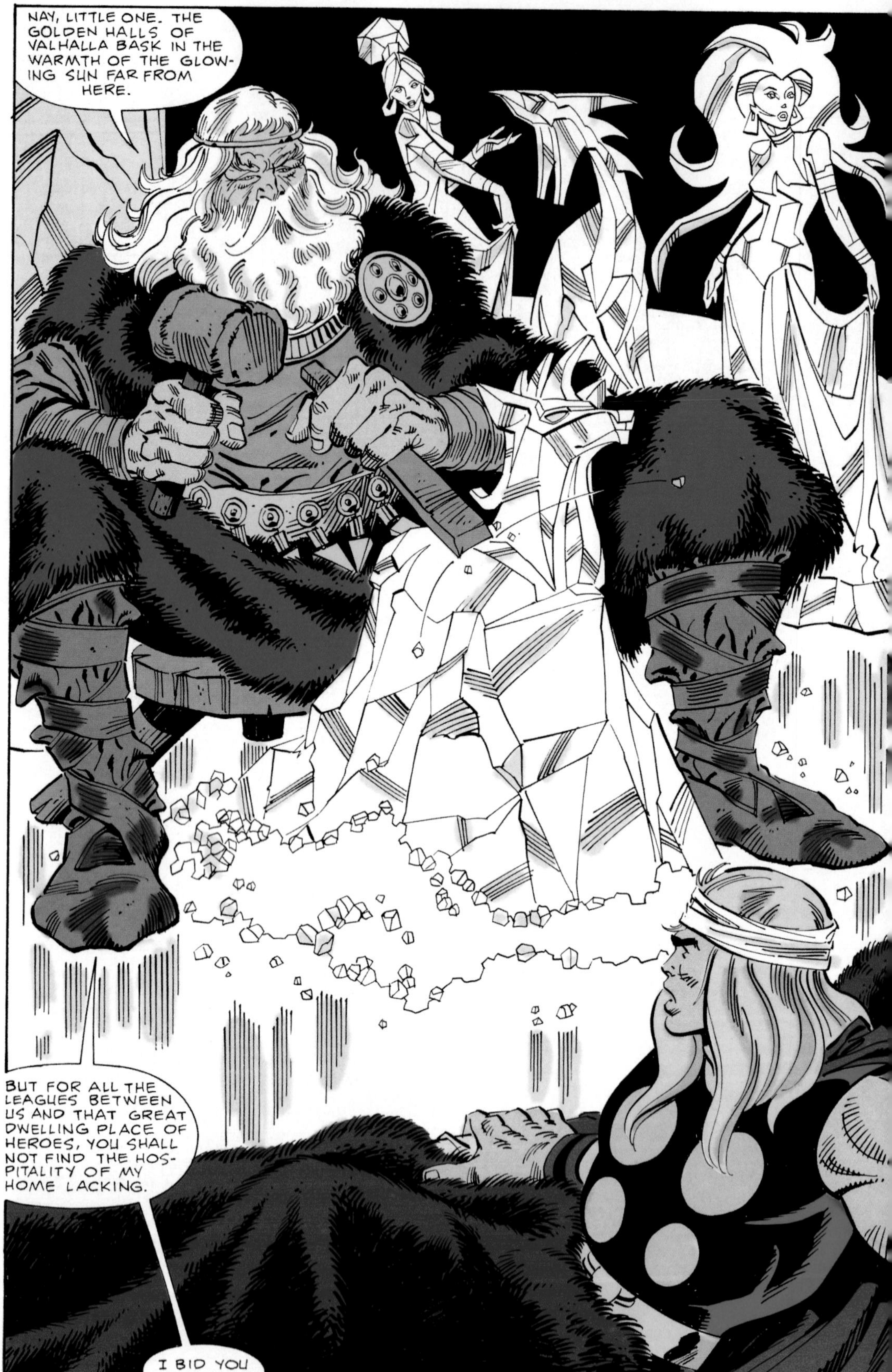
NAY, LITTLE ONE. THE GOLDEN HALLS OF VALHALLA BASK IN THE WARMTH OF THE GLOWING SUN FAR FROM HERE.
BUT FOR ALL THE LEAGUES BETWEEN US AND THAT GREAT DWELLING PLACE OF HEROES, YOU SHALL NOT FIND THE HOSPITALITY OF MY HOME LACKING.
I BID YOU WELCOME.

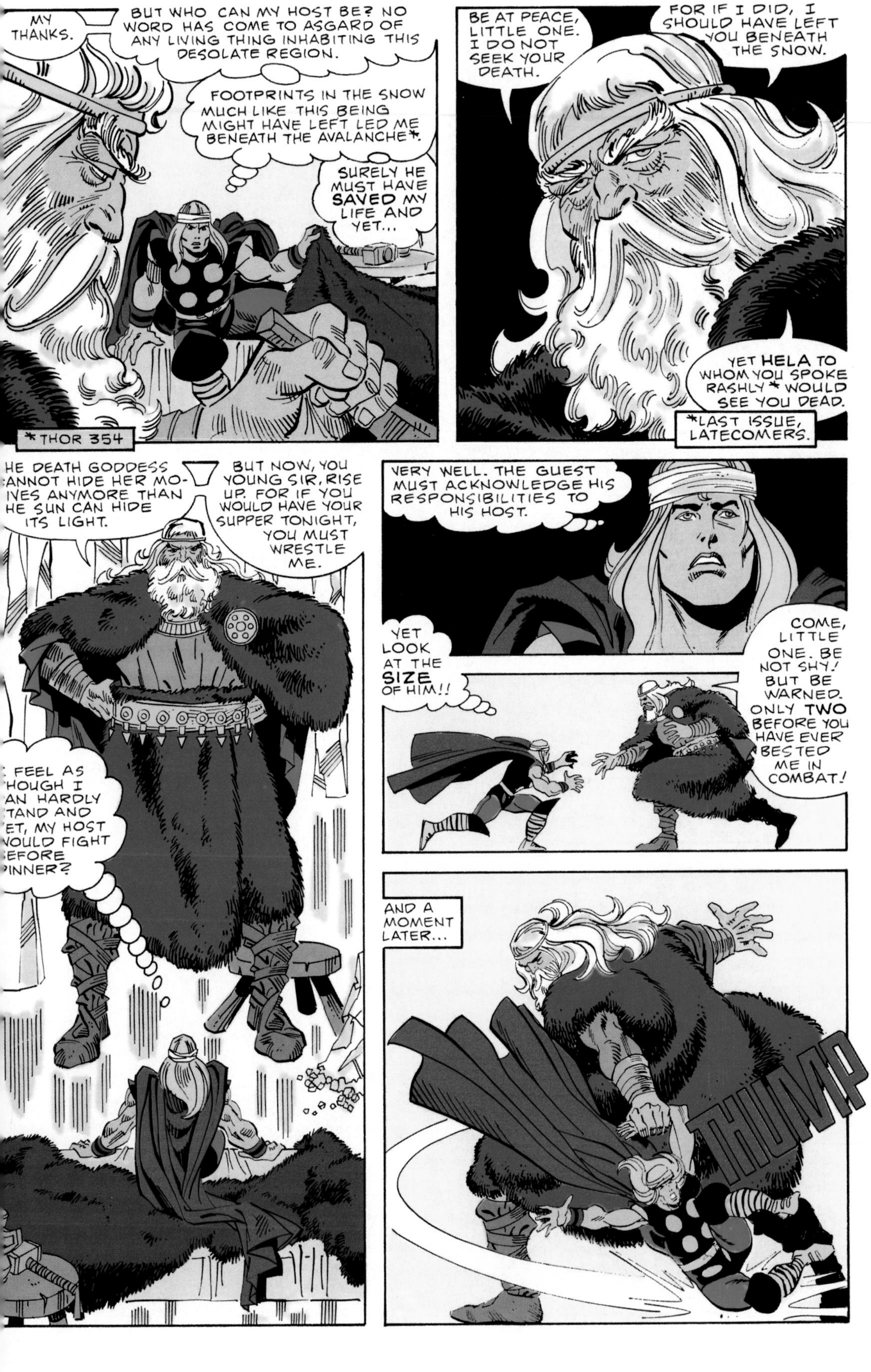
MY THANKS.
BUT WHO CAN MY HOST BE? NO WORD HAS COME TO ASGARD OF ANY LIVING THING INHABITING THIS DESOLATE REGION.
FOOTPRINTS IN THE SNOW MUCH LIKE THIS BEING MIGHT HAVE LEFT LED ME BENEATH THE AVALANCHE*.
SURELY HE MUST HAVE SAVED MY LIFE AND YET...
*THOR 354
BE AT PEACE, LITTLE ONE. I DO NOT SEEK YOUR DEATH.
FOR IF I DID, I SHOULD HAVE LEFT YOU BENEATH THE SNOW.
YET HELA TO WHOM YOU SPOKE RASHLY* WOULD SEE YOU DEAD.
*LAST ISSUE, LATECOMERS.
HE DEATH GODDESS CANNOT HIDE HER MO- IVES ANYMORE THAN HE SUN CAN HIDE ITS LIGHT.
BUT NOW, YOU YOUNG SIR, RISE UP. FOR IF YOU WOULD HAVE YOUR SUPPER TONIGHT, YOU MUST WRESTLE ME.
FEEL AS HOUGH I AN HARDLY TAND AND ET, MY HOST WOULD FIGHT EFORE INNER?
VERY WELL. THE GUEST MUST ACKNOWLEDGE HIS RESPONSIBILITIES TO HIS HOST.
YET LOOK AT THE SIZE OF HIM!!
COME, LITTLE ONE. BE NOT SHY! BUT BE WARNED. ONLY TWO BEFORE YOU HAVE EVER BESTED ME IN COMBAT!
AND A MOMENT LATER...
THUMP

WE MUST BUILD YOUR STRENGTH UP AGAIN, MY YOUNG DRAKE!

YOUR HEART IS VALIANT BUT YOUR FLESH HAS BEEN WEAKENED BY THE ORDEAL OF THE PAST FEW DAYS.*

*DETAILS CAN BE FOUND ALL THROUGH THOR 350-354.

COME, MY FRIENDS. BRING OUR GUEST SUCH NOURISHING BROTH AND BREAD AS CAN BE FOUND IN OUR ABODE.

YOU WERE FORTUNATE, LITTLE ONE.

HAD YOU NOT BEE[N] FOUND BENEATH TH[E] ICE AND SNOW, HE[?] WOULD EVEN NOW [?] GREETING YOU WIT[H] OPEN ARMS.

PERHAPS IT WOULD HAVE BEEN BETTER SO.

THE NINE WORLD[S] HAVE BEEN MADE SAFE FROM SURT[?] AND HIS DEMONS AT A TERRIBLE C[OST?]

"MY FATHER, ODIN, FELL WITH HIM INTO THE FIERY CREVASSE AND DID NOT RETURN. WHAT SHALL WE DO WITHOUT HIM?"

IS THIS THE NOBLE SON OF ODIN, THOR THE THUNDERER, WHO SHARES MY BREAD AND WHINES AT MY TABLE?

YOUR FATHER WOULD NEVER HAVE BE-LIEVED IT OF YOU.

SURELY YOU CAN HONOR HIS MEMORY IN SOME MORE GRACEFUL FASHION.

WHAT DO YOU KNOW O[F] MY FATHER AND HIS FA[SH]ION! HE WAS THE SON O[F] BOR, SON OF BURI AND [?] A GREATER WARRIOR [?] THESE WORLDS HAVE NE[V]ER SEEN!

AND NOW H[E'S] GONE. EVE[RY] LIVING THI[NG] SHOULD WE[EP] FOR SHAME[!]

154

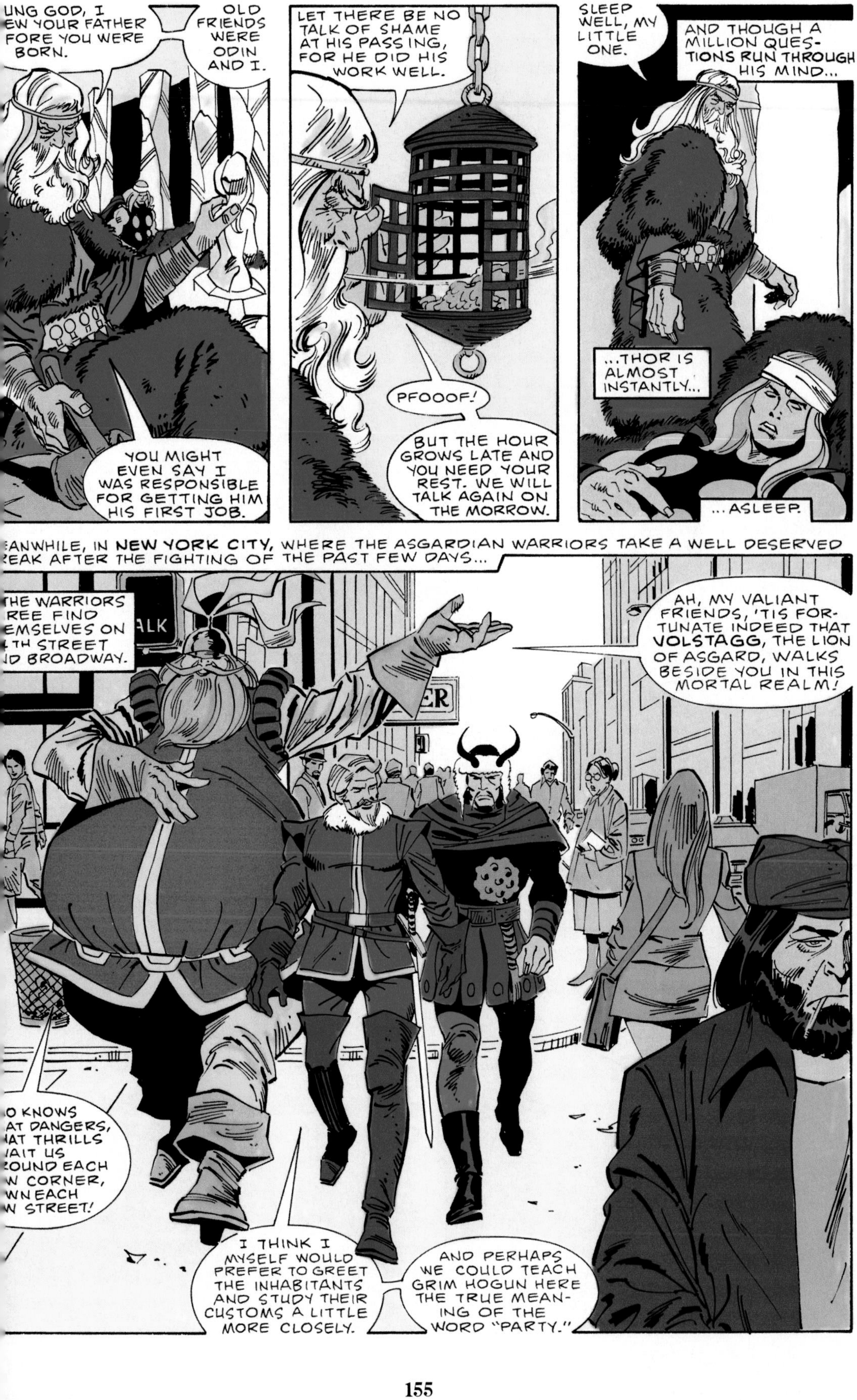
UNG GOD, I
EW YOUR FATHER
FORE YOU WERE
BORN.
OLD FRIENDS WERE ODIN AND I.
YOU MIGHT EVEN SAY I WAS RESPONSIBLE FOR GETTING HIM HIS FIRST JOB.
LET THERE BE NO TALK OF SHAME AT HIS PASSING, FOR HE DID HIS WORK WELL.
PFOOOF!
BUT THE HOUR GROWS LATE AND YOU NEED YOUR REST. WE WILL TALK AGAIN ON THE MORROW.
SLEEP WELL, MY LITTLE ONE.
AND THOUGH A MILLION QUESTIONS RUN THROUGH HIS MIND...
...THOR IS ALMOST INSTANTLY...
...ASLEEP.
EANWHILE, IN NEW YORK CITY, WHERE THE ASGARDIAN WARRIORS TAKE A WELL DESERVED
EAK AFTER THE FIGHTING OF THE PAST FEW DAYS...
HE WARRIORS
REE FIND
EMSELVES ON
TH STREET
D BROADWAY.
AH, MY VALIANT FRIENDS, 'TIS FORTUNATE INDEED THAT VOLSTAGG, THE LION OF ASGARD, WALKS BESIDE YOU IN THIS MORTAL REALM!
O KNOWS
AT DANGERS,
AT THRILLS
AIT US
OUND EACH
W CORNER,
WN EACH
N STREET!
I THINK I MYSELF WOULD PREFER TO GREET THE INHABITANTS AND STUDY THEIR CUSTOMS A LITTLE MORE CLOSELY.
AND PERHAPS WE COULD TEACH GRIM HOGUN HERE THE TRUE MEANING OF THE WORD "PARTY."

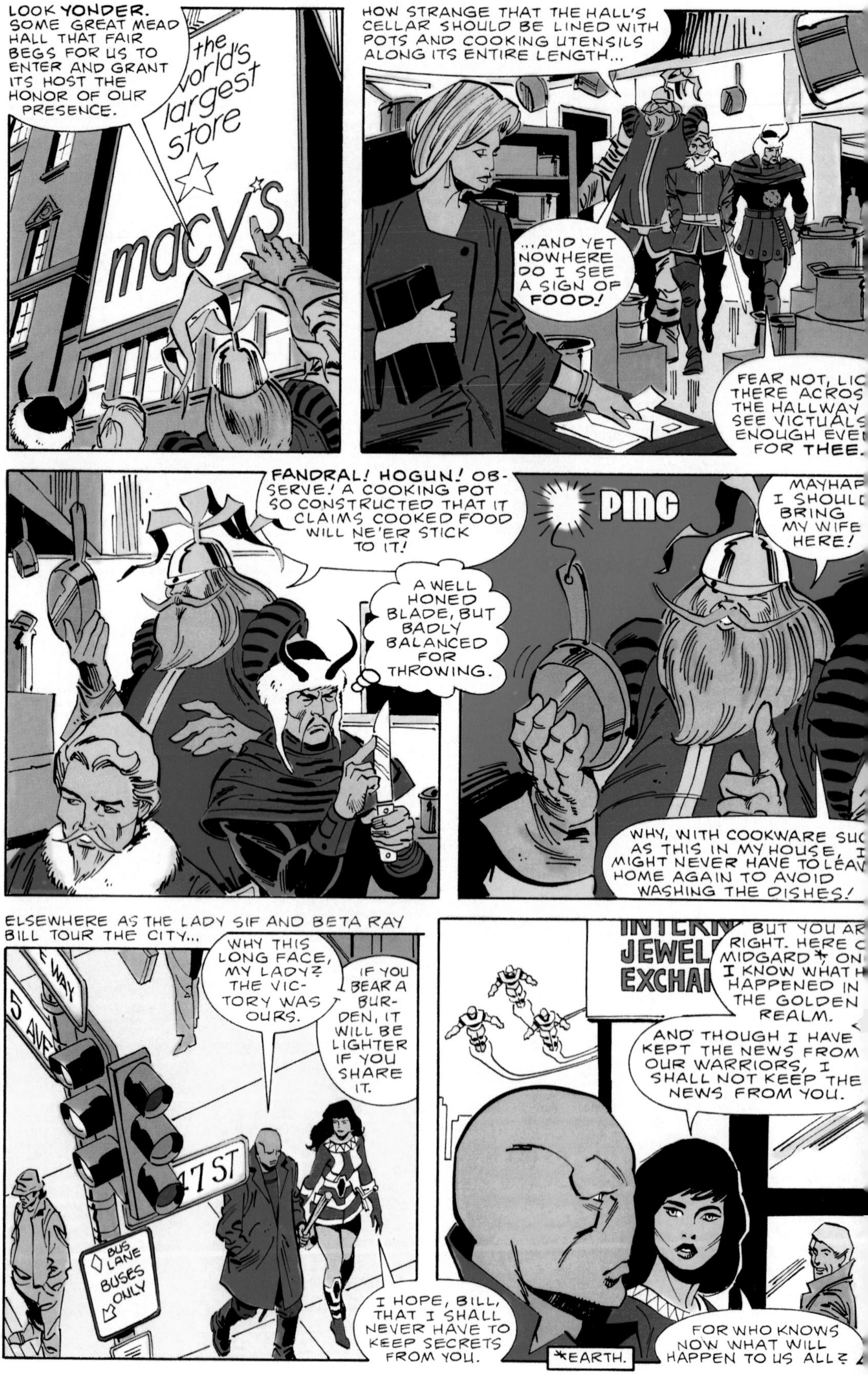

LOOK YONDER. SOME GREAT MEAD HALL THAT FAIR BEGS FOR US TO ENTER AND GRANT ITS HOST THE HONOR OF OUR PRESENCE.
the world's largest store
macy's
HOW STRANGE THAT THE HALL'S CELLAR SHOULD BE LINED WITH POTS AND COOKING UTENSILS ALONG ITS ENTIRE LENGTH...
...AND YET NOWHERE DO I SEE A SIGN OF FOOD!
FEAR NOT, LIO THERE ACROSS THE HALLWAY SEE VICTUALS ENOUGH EVEN FOR THEE.
FANDRAL! HOGUN! OBSERVE! A COOKING POT SO CONSTRUCTED THAT IT CLAIMS COOKED FOOD WILL NE'ER STICK TO IT!
A WELL HONED BLADE, BUT BADLY BALANCED FOR THROWING.
PING
MAYHAP I SHOULD BRING MY WIFE HERE!
WHY, WITH COOKWARE SUC AS THIS IN MY HOUSE, I MIGHT NEVER HAVE TO LEAV HOME AGAIN TO AVOID WASHING THE DISHES!
ELSEWHERE AS THE LADY SIF AND BETA RAY BILL TOUR THE CITY...
WHY THIS LONG FACE, MY LADY? THE VICTORY WAS OURS.
IF YOU BEAR A BURDEN, IT WILL BE LIGHTER IF YOU SHARE IT.
5 AVE
47 ST
BUS LANE BUSES ONLY
I HOPE, BILL, THAT I SHALL NEVER HAVE TO KEEP SECRETS FROM YOU.
JEWEL EXCHA
BUT YOU AR RIGHT. HERE O MIDGARD* ON I KNOW WHAT H HAPPENED IN THE GOLDEN REALM.
AND THOUGH I HAVE KEPT THE NEWS FROM OUR WARRIORS, I SHALL NOT KEEP THE NEWS FROM YOU.
FOR WHO KNOWS NOW WHAT WILL HAPPEN TO US ALL?
*EARTH.

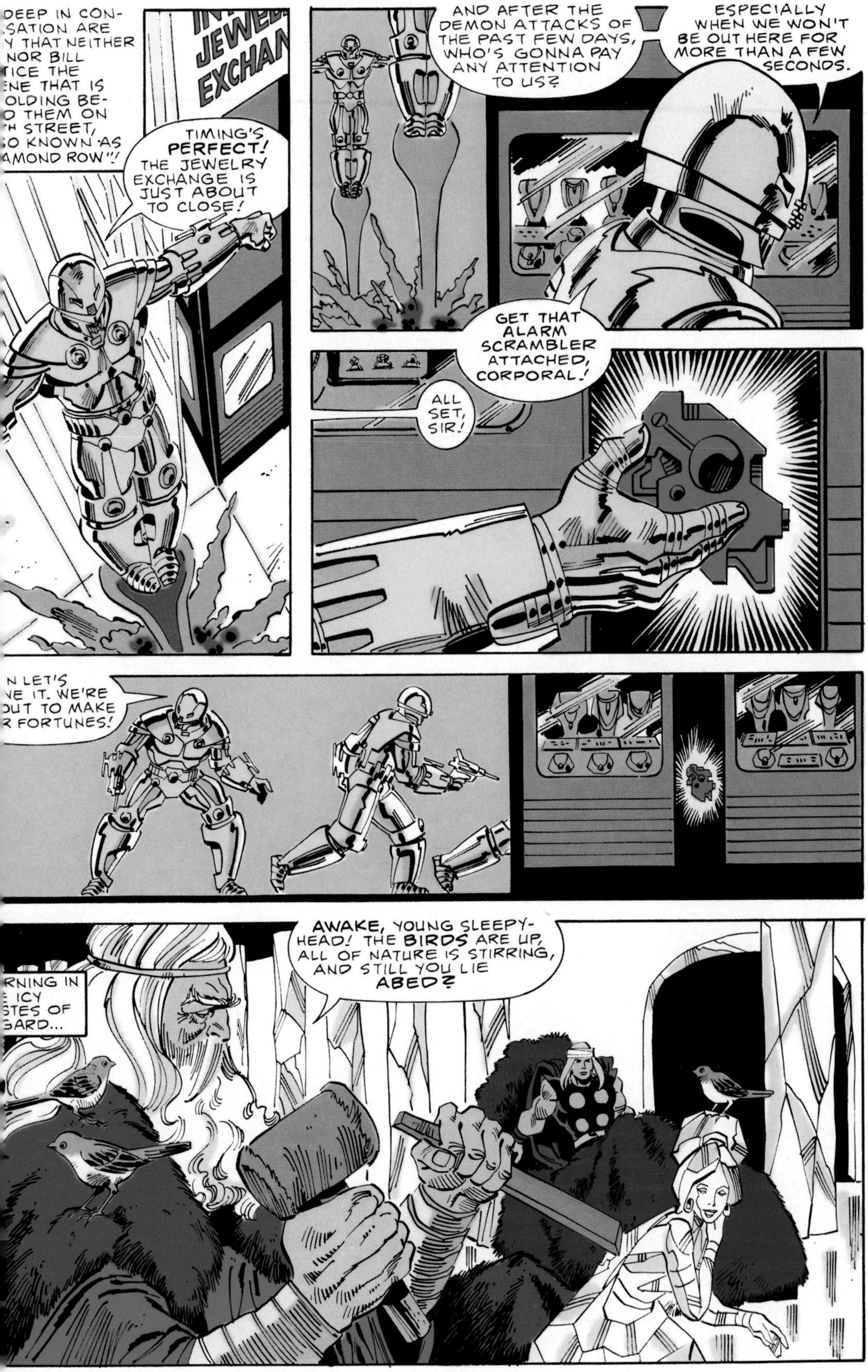
DEEP IN CON-
SATION ARE
Y THAT NEITHER
NOR BILL
TICE THE
ENE THAT IS
OLDING BE-
D THEM ON
TH STREET,
SO KNOWN AS
AMOND ROW"!
JEWEL
EXCHAN
TIMING'S PERFECT! THE JEWELRY EXCHANGE IS JUST ABOUT TO CLOSE!
AND AFTER THE DEMON ATTACKS OF THE PAST FEW DAYS, WHO'S GONNA PAY ANY ATTENTION TO US?
ESPECIALLY WHEN WE WON'T BE OUT HERE FOR MORE THAN A FEW SECONDS.
GET THAT ALARM SCRAMBLER ATTACHED, CORPORAL!
ALL SET, SIR!
N LET'S
VE IT. WE'RE
OUT TO MAKE
R FORTUNES!
RNING IN
E ICY
STES OF
GARD...
AWAKE, YOUNG SLEEPY-HEAD! THE BIRDS ARE UP, ALL OF NATURE IS STIRRING, AND STILL YOU LIE ABED?

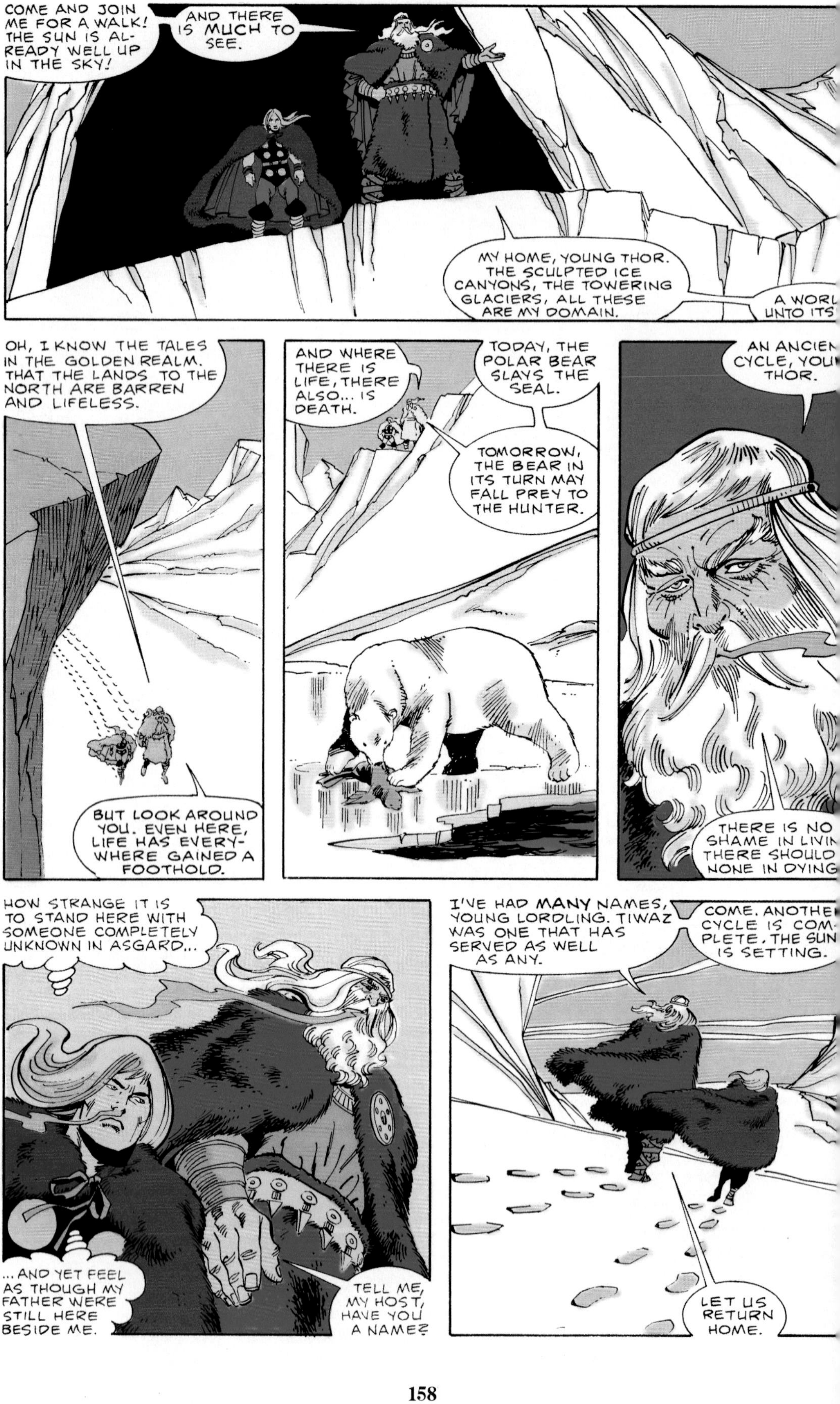
COME AND JOIN ME FOR A WALK! THE SUN IS ALREADY WELL UP IN THE SKY!
AND THERE IS MUCH TO SEE.
MY HOME, YOUNG THOR. THE SCULPTED ICE CANYONS, THE TOWERING GLACIERS, ALL THESE ARE MY DOMAIN.
A WORL UNTO ITS
OH, I KNOW THE TALES IN THE GOLDEN REALM. THAT THE LANDS TO THE NORTH ARE BARREN AND LIFELESS.
BUT LOOK AROUND YOU. EVEN HERE, LIFE HAS EVERYWHERE GAINED A FOOTHOLD.
AND WHERE THERE IS LIFE, THERE ALSO... IS DEATH.
TODAY, THE POLAR BEAR SLAYS THE SEAL.
TOMORROW, THE BEAR IN ITS TURN MAY FALL PREY TO THE HUNTER.
AN ANCIEN CYCLE, YOU THOR.
THERE IS NO SHAME IN LIVIN THERE SHOULD NONE IN DYING
HOW STRANGE IT IS TO STAND HERE WITH SOMEONE COMPLETELY UNKNOWN IN ASGARD...
...AND YET FEEL AS THOUGH MY FATHER WERE STILL HERE BESIDE ME.
TELL ME, MY HOST, HAVE YOU A NAME?
I'VE HAD MANY NAMES, YOUNG LORDLING. TIWAZ WAS ONE THAT HAS SERVED AS WELL AS ANY.
COME. ANOTHE CYCLE IS COMPLETE. THE SUN IS SETTING.
LET US RETURN HOME.

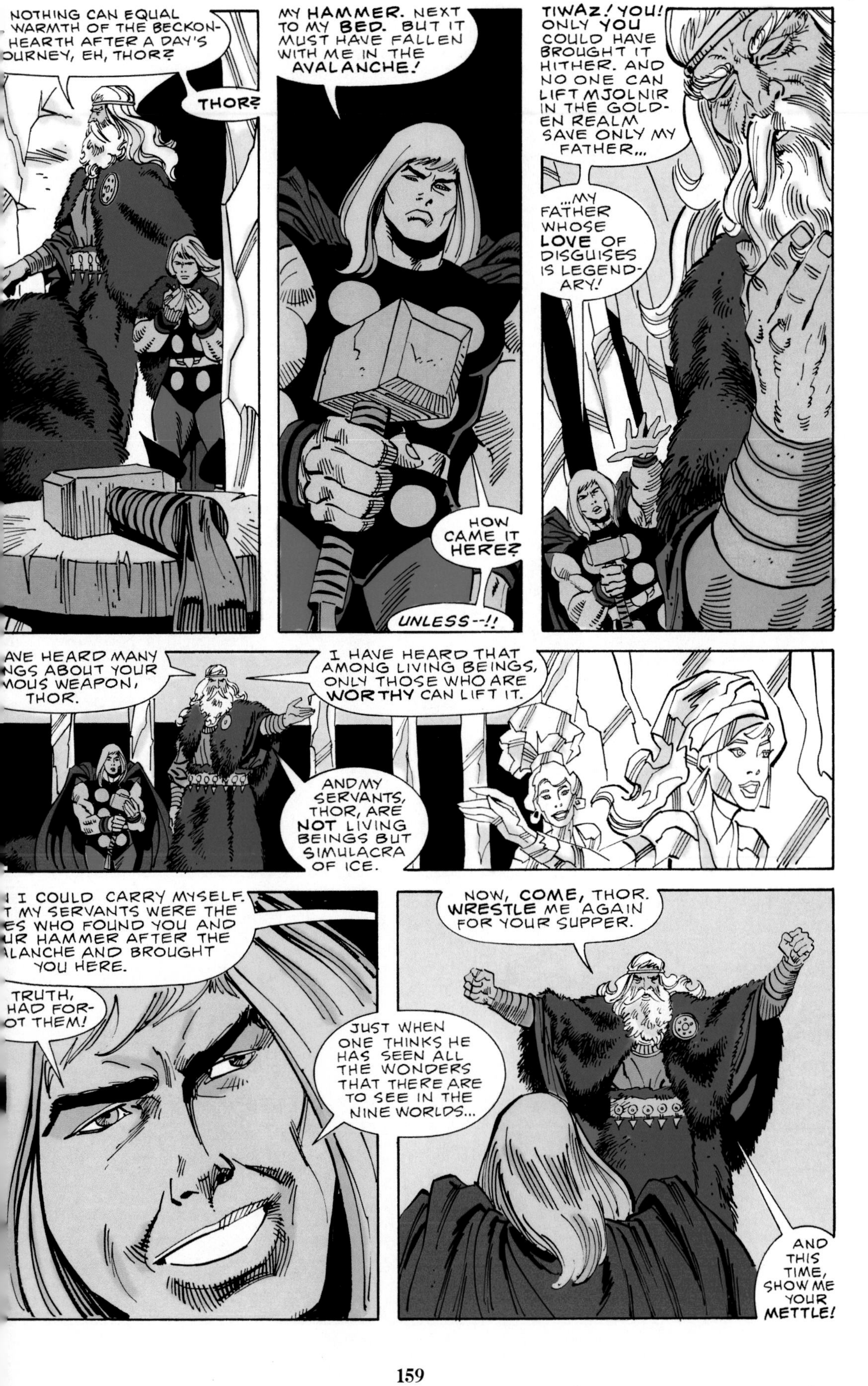
NOTHING CAN EQUAL WARMTH OF THE BECKON- HEARTH AFTER A DAY'S OURNEY, EH, THOR?
THOR?
MY HAMMER. NEXT TO MY BED. BUT IT MUST HAVE FALLEN WITH ME IN THE AVALANCHE!
HOW CAME IT HERE?
UNLESS--!!
TIWAZ! YOU! ONLY YOU COULD HAVE BROUGHT IT HITHER. AND NO ONE CAN LIFT MJOLNIR IN THE GOLD- EN REALM SAVE ONLY MY FATHER...
...MY FATHER WHOSE LOVE OF DISGUISES IS LEGEND- ARY!
AVE HEARD MANY NGS ABOUT YOUR MOUS WEAPON, THOR.
I HAVE HEARD THAT AMONG LIVING BEINGS, ONLY THOSE WHO ARE WORTHY CAN LIFT IT.
AND MY SERVANTS, THOR, ARE NOT LIVING BEINGS BUT SIMULACRA OF ICE.
I COULD CARRY MYSELF. T MY SERVANTS WERE THE ES WHO FOUND YOU AND UR HAMMER AFTER THE LANCHE AND BROUGHT YOU HERE.
TRUTH, HAD FOR- OT THEM!
JUST WHEN ONE THINKS HE HAS SEEN ALL THE WONDERS THAT THERE ARE TO SEE IN THE NINE WORLDS...
NOW, COME, THOR. WRESTLE ME AGAIN FOR YOUR SUPPER.
AND THIS TIME, SHOW ME YOUR METTLE!

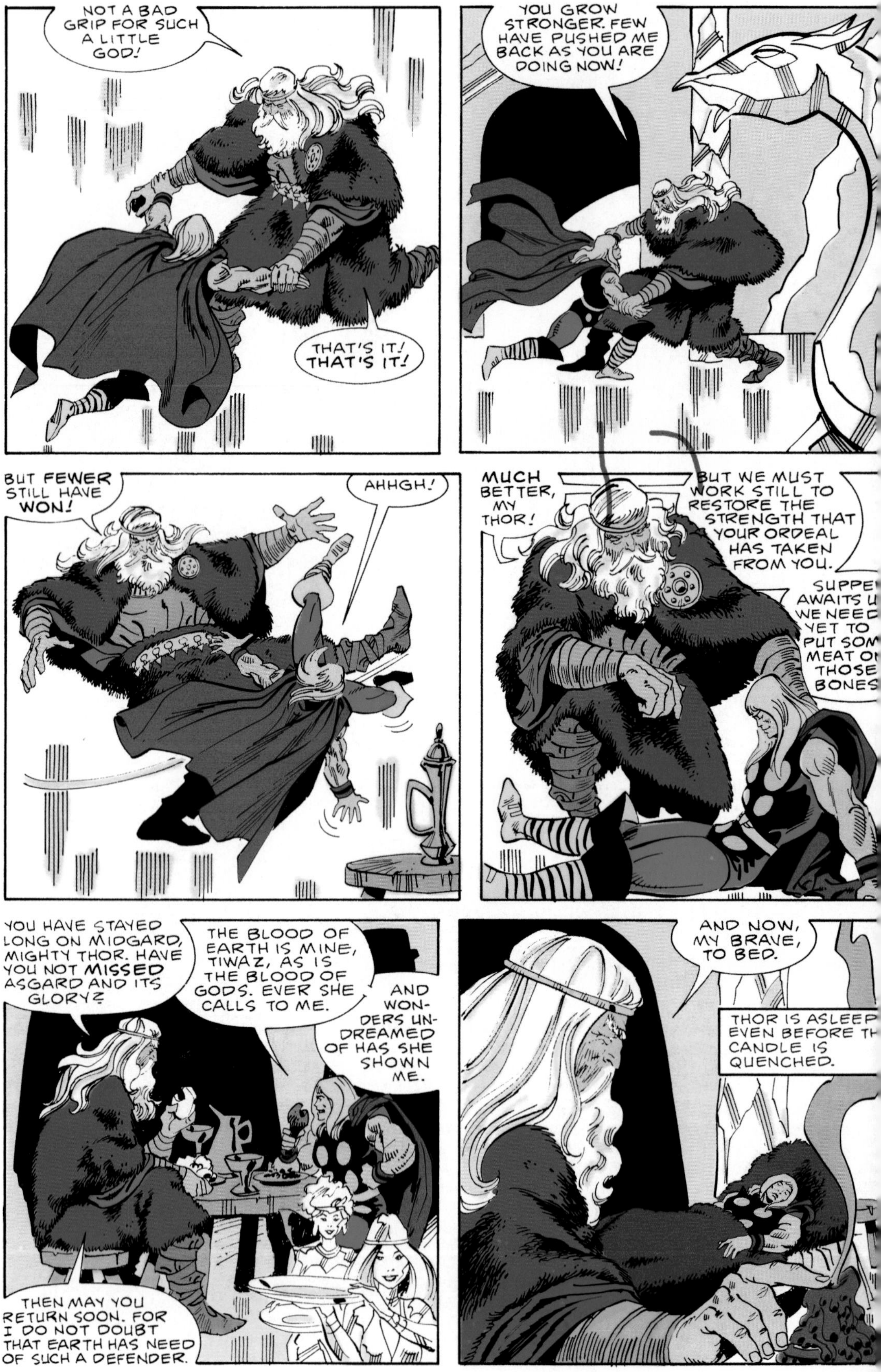
NOT A BAD GRIP FOR SUCH A LITTLE GOD!
THAT'S IT! THAT'S IT!
YOU GROW STRONGER. FEW HAVE PUSHED ME BACK AS YOU ARE DOING NOW!
BUT FEWER STILL HAVE WON!
AHHGH!
MUCH BETTER, MY THOR!
BUT WE MUST WORK STILL TO RESTORE THE STRENGTH THAT YOUR ORDEAL HAS TAKEN FROM YOU.
SUPPE AWAITS U WE NEED YET TO PUT SOM MEAT O THOSE BONES
YOU HAVE STAYED LONG ON MIDGARD, MIGHTY THOR. HAVE YOU NOT MISSED ASGARD AND ITS GLORY?
THE BLOOD OF EARTH IS MINE, TIWAZ, AS IS THE BLOOD OF GODS. EVER SHE CALLS TO ME.
AND WONDERS UNDREAMED OF HAS SHE SHOWN ME.
THEN MAY YOU RETURN SOON. FOR I DO NOT DOUBT THAT EARTH HAS NEED OF SUCH A DEFENDER.
AND NOW, MY BRAVE, TO BED.
THOR IS ASLEEP EVEN BEFORE TH CANDLE IS QUENCHED.

MEANWHILE, FAR AWAY ON THE EDGE OF ASGARD IN THE FORTRESS OF LOKI...

HAVE ARRIVED, LORELEI!

IT IS TRUE THEN? **ODIN** REALLY IS **GONE**?

YES, AND AT LAST THE WAY IS CLEAR TO THE THRONE OF ASGARD!

NO DOUBT, MY FELLOW ASGARDIANS WOULD PREFER A DULL AND PREDICTABLE FELLOW SUCH AS MY STEP-BROTHER TO RULE THEM.

BUT AM **I** NOT THE GOD WHO STOOD BETWEEN SURTUR AND THE FLAME WHEN ALL OTHERS HAD FALLEN?

IF **THOR** WERE TO SUPPORT MY EFFORT, WHY WHO THEN COULD SAY ME NAY?

AND IN THIS ENTERPRISE, LORELEI, I THINK **YOU** MAY BE A MOST PERSUASIVE ALLY.

MORNING IN THE COUNTRY WASTES...

ANOTHER FIGURE IS COMPLETE.

AND NOW, MY FINE LADY, 'TIS TIME FOR YOU TO DANCE, IS IT NOT?

WOOOOOFF

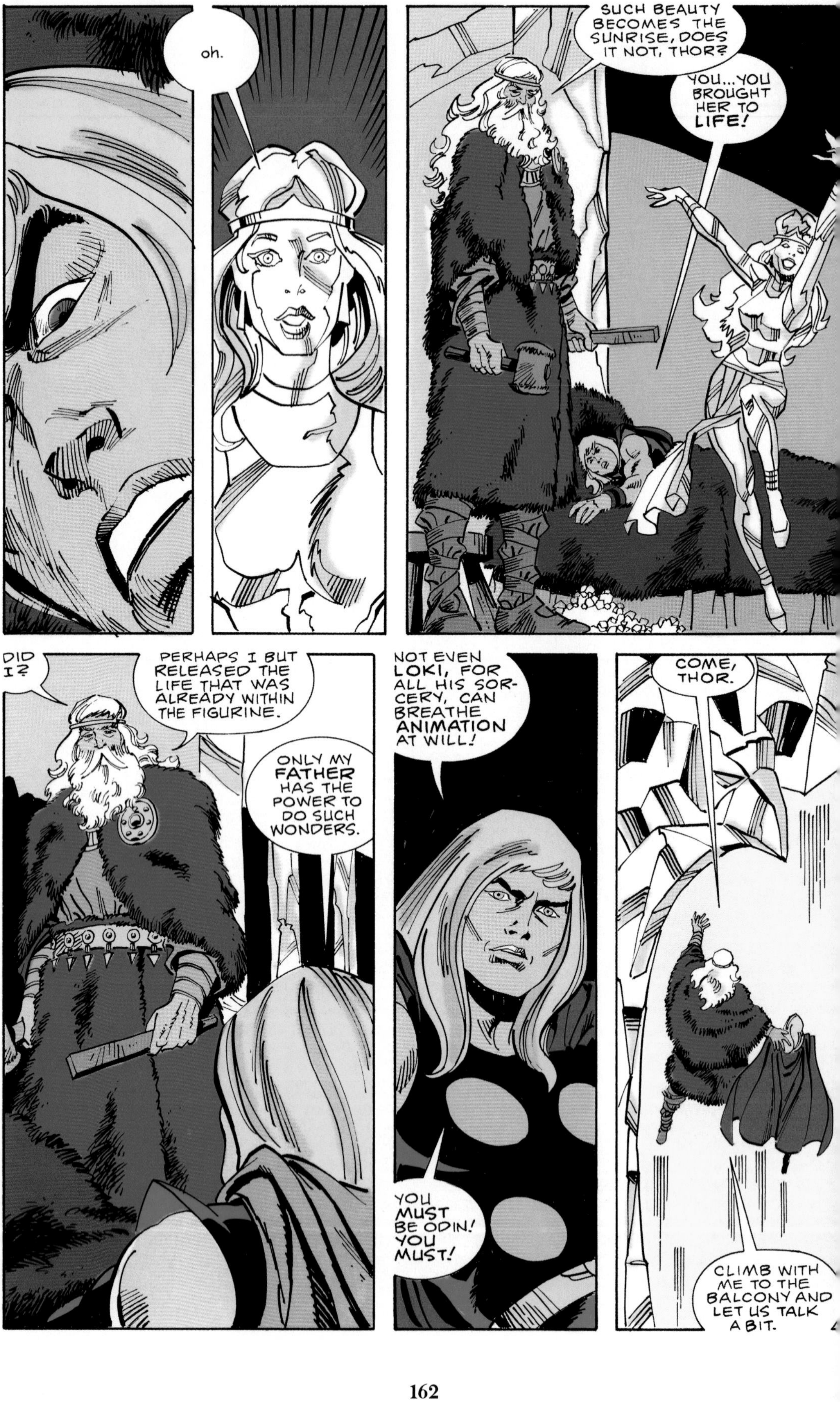
oh.
SUCH BEAUTY BECOMES THE SUNRISE, DOES IT NOT, THOR?
YOU...YOU BROUGHT HER TO LIFE!
DID I?
PERHAPS I BUT RELEASED THE LIFE THAT WAS ALREADY WITHIN THE FIGURINE.
ONLY MY FATHER HAS THE POWER TO DO SUCH WONDERS.
NOT EVEN LOKI, FOR ALL HIS SORCERY, CAN BREATHE ANIMATION AT WILL!
YOU MUST BE ODIN! YOU MUST!
COME, THOR.
CLIMB WITH ME TO THE BALCONY AND LET US TALK A BIT.

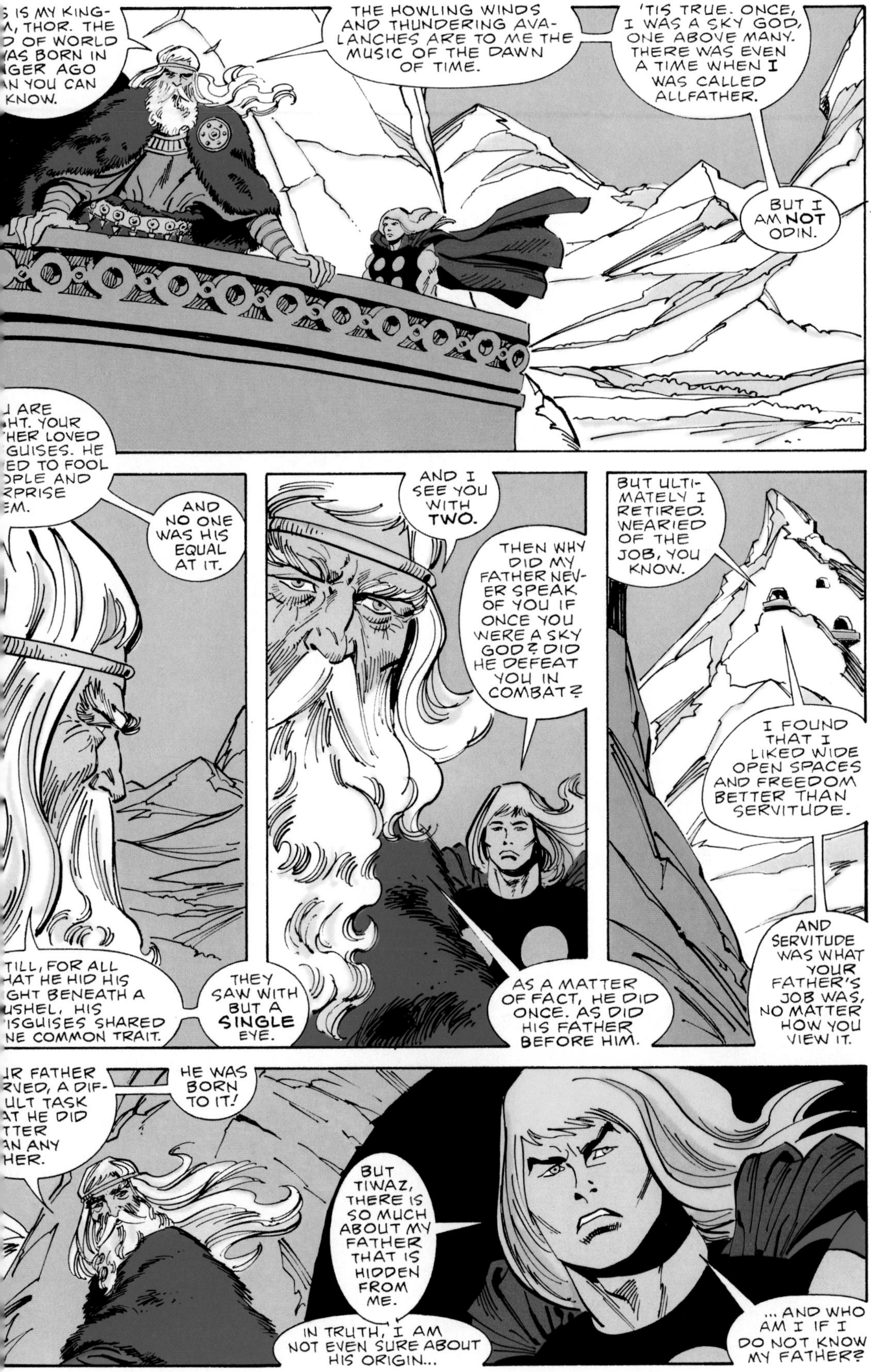
S IS MY KING-
M, THOR. THE
D OF WORLD
VAS BORN IN
IGER AGO
AN YOU CAN
KNOW.
THE HOWLING WINDS AND THUNDERING AVALANCHES ARE TO ME THE MUSIC OF THE DAWN OF TIME.
'TIS TRUE. ONCE, I WAS A SKY GOD, ONE ABOVE MANY. THERE WAS EVEN A TIME WHEN **I** WAS CALLED ALLFATHER.
BUT I AM **NOT** ODIN.
U ARE
HT. YOUR
THER LOVED
GUISES. HE
ED TO FOOL
OPLE AND
RPRISE
EM.
AND NO ONE WAS HIS EQUAL AT IT.
AND I SEE YOU WITH **TWO.**
THEN WHY DID MY FATHER NEVER SPEAK OF YOU IF ONCE YOU WERE A SKY GOD? DID HE DEFEAT YOU IN COMBAT?
BUT ULTIMATELY I RETIRED. WEARIED OF THE JOB, YOU KNOW.
I FOUND THAT I LIKED WIDE OPEN SPACES AND FREEDOM BETTER THAN SERVITUDE.
TILL, FOR ALL
HAT HE HID HIS
GHT BENEATH A
USHEL, HIS
ISGUISES SHARED
NE COMMON TRAIT.
THEY SAW WITH BUT A **SINGLE** EYE.
AS A MATTER OF FACT, HE DID ONCE. AS DID HIS FATHER BEFORE HIM.
AND SERVITUDE WAS WHAT **YOUR** FATHER'S JOB WAS, NO MATTER HOW YOU VIEW IT.
IR FATHER
RVED, A DIF-
ULT TASK
AT HE DID
TTER
AN ANY
HER.
HE WAS BORN TO IT!
BUT TIWAZ, THERE IS SO MUCH ABOUT MY FATHER THAT IS HIDDEN FROM ME.
IN TRUTH, I AM NOT EVEN SURE ABOUT HIS ORIGIN...
...AND WHO AM I IF I DO NOT KNOW MY FATHER?

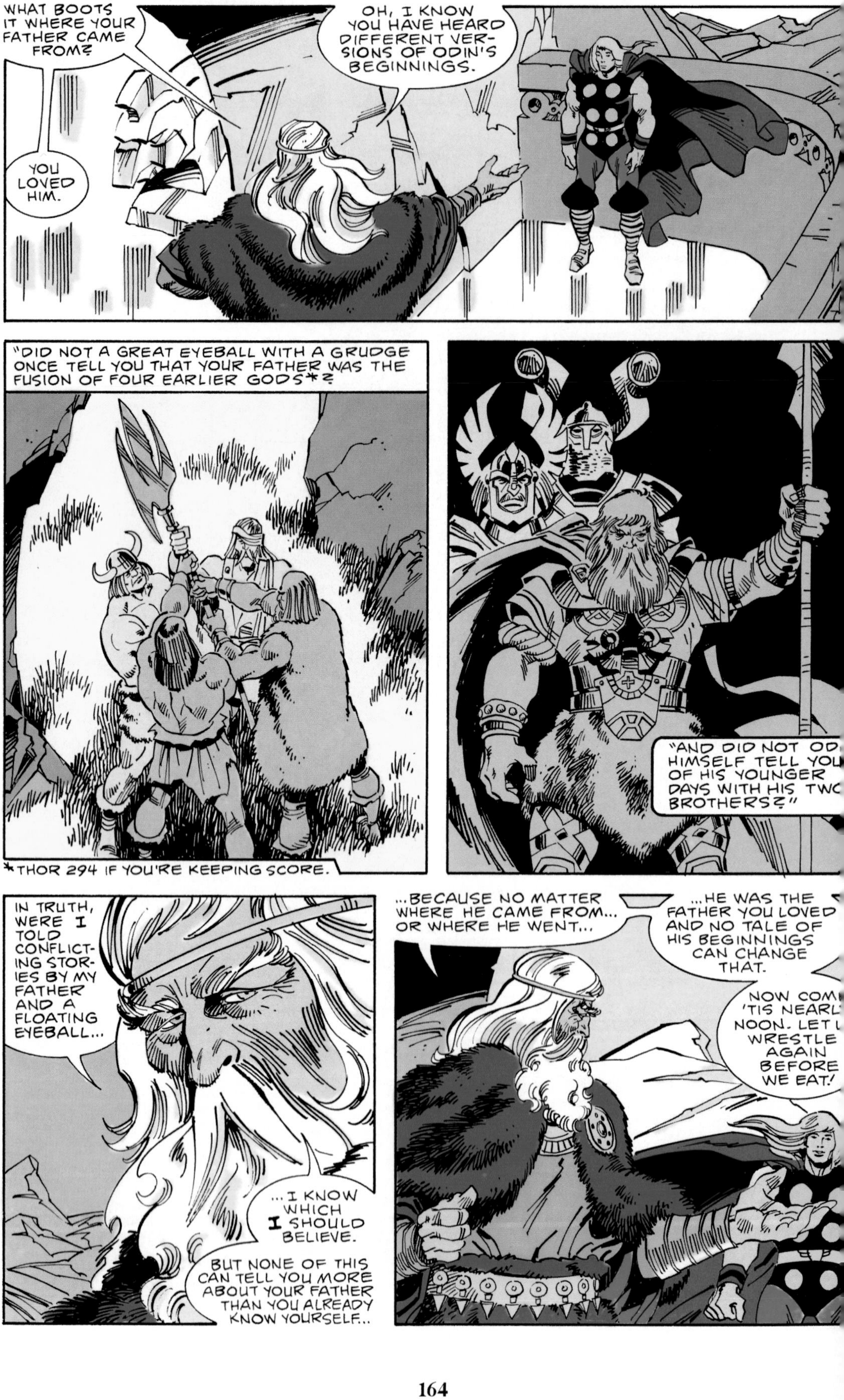
WHAT BOOTS IT WHERE YOUR FATHER CAME FROM?
YOU LOVED HIM.
OH, I KNOW YOU HAVE HEARD DIFFERENT VERSIONS OF ODIN'S BEGINNINGS.
"DID NOT A GREAT EYEBALL WITH A GRUDGE ONCE TELL YOU THAT YOUR FATHER WAS THE FUSION OF FOUR EARLIER GODS*?
*THOR 294 IF YOU'RE KEEPING SCORE.
"AND DID NOT OD HIMSELF TELL YOU OF HIS YOUNGER DAYS WITH HIS TWO BROTHERS?"
IN TRUTH, WERE I TOLD CONFLICTING STORIES BY MY FATHER AND A FLOATING EYEBALL...
...I KNOW WHICH I SHOULD BELIEVE.
BUT NONE OF THIS CAN TELL YOU MORE ABOUT YOUR FATHER THAN YOU ALREADY KNOW YOURSELF...
...BECAUSE NO MATTER WHERE HE CAME FROM... OR WHERE HE WENT...
...HE WAS THE FATHER YOU LOVED AND NO TALE OF HIS BEGINNINGS CAN CHANGE THAT.
NOW COM 'TIS NEARL NOON. LET U WRESTLE AGAIN BEFORE WE EAT!

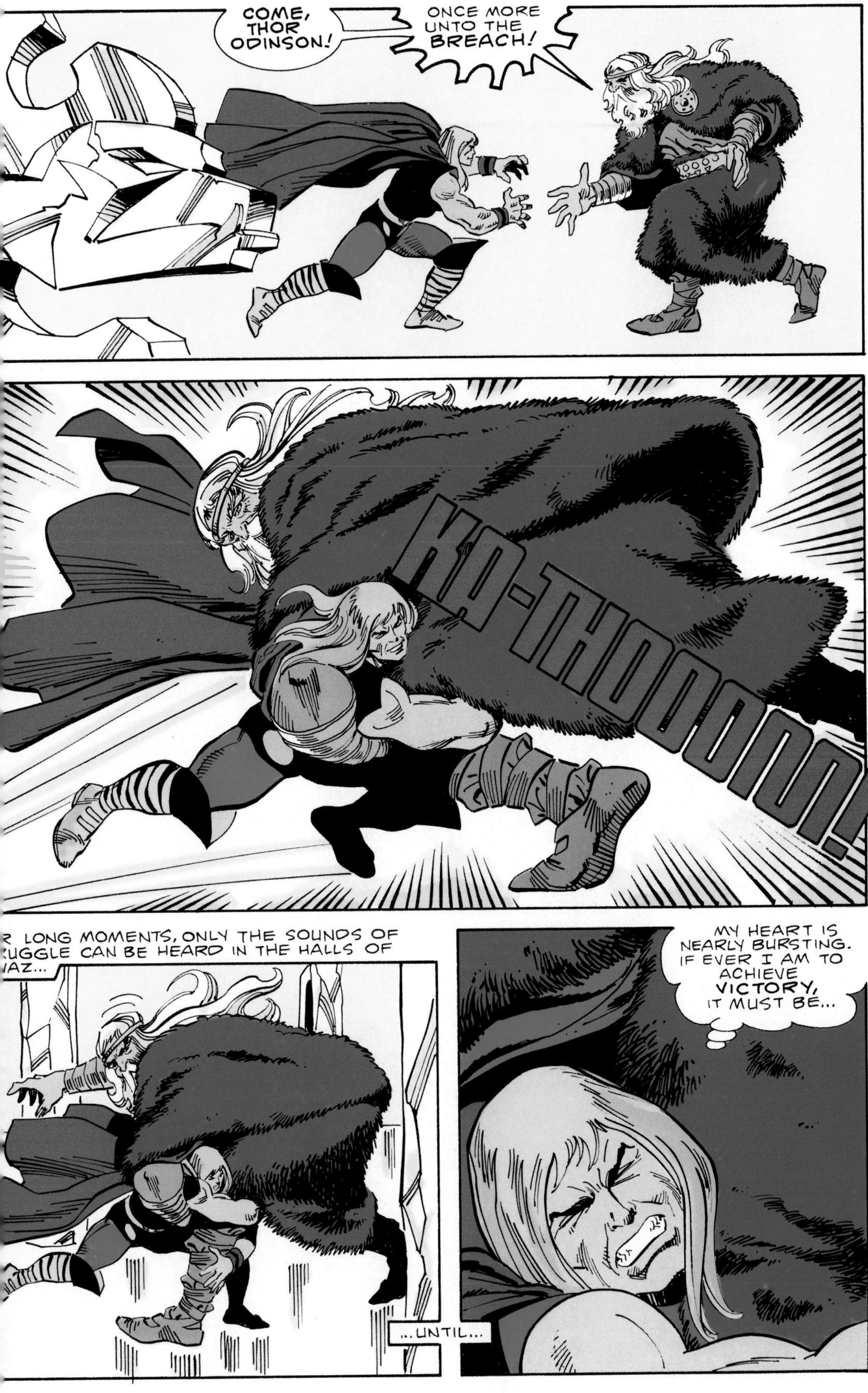
COME, THOR ODINSON!
ONCE MORE UNTO THE BREACH!
KA-THOOOOM!!
R LONG MOMENTS, ONLY THE SOUNDS OF RUGGLE CAN BE HEARD IN THE HALLS OF AZ...
MY HEART IS NEARLY BURSTING. IF EVER I AM TO ACHIEVE VICTORY, IT MUST BE...
...UNTIL...

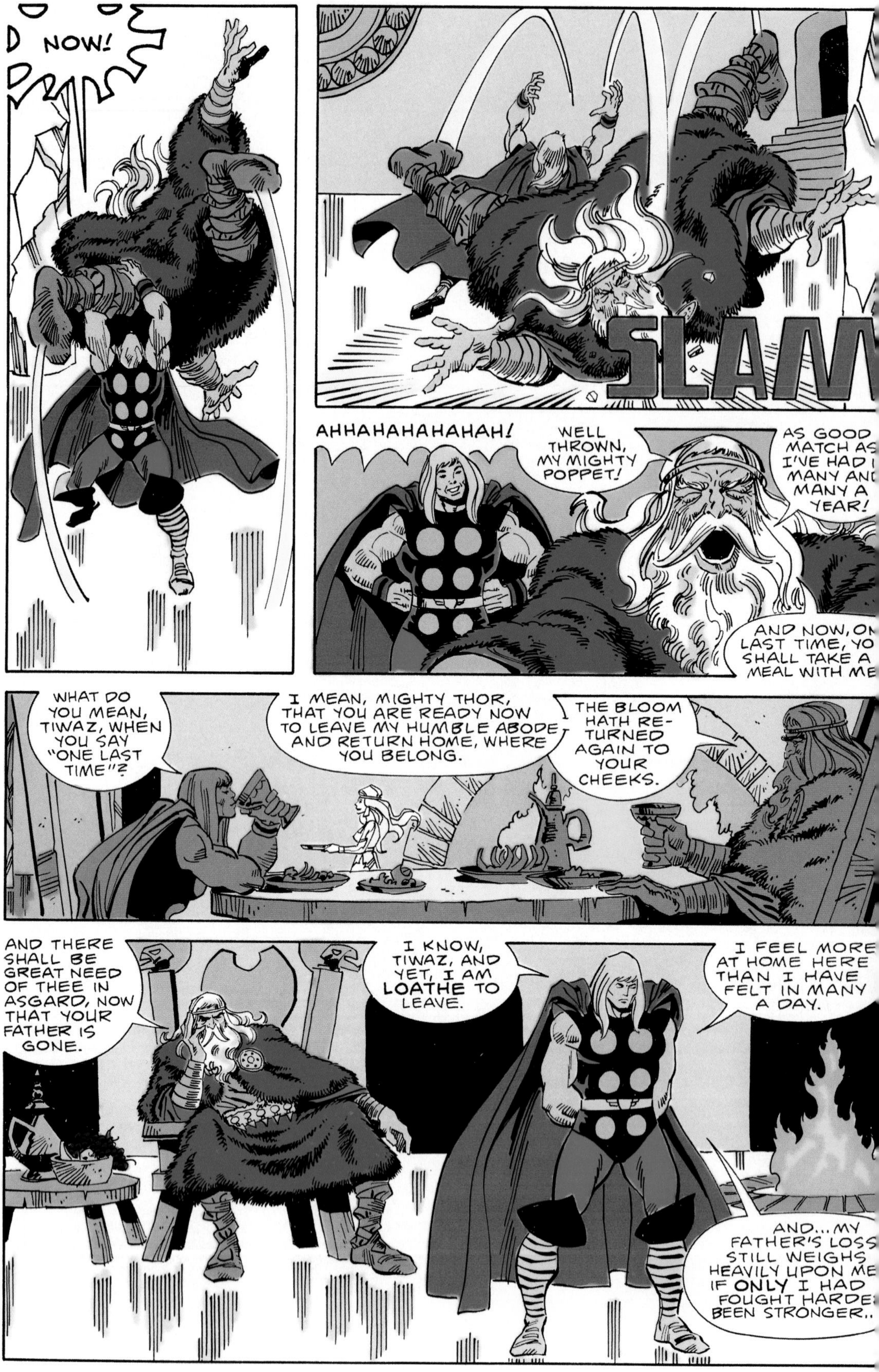

D NOW!
SLAM
AHHAHAHAHAHAH!
WELL THROWN, MY MIGHTY POPPET!
AS GOOD A MATCH AS I'VE HAD IN MANY AND MANY A YEAR!
AND NOW, ONE LAST TIME, YOU SHALL TAKE A MEAL WITH ME!
WHAT DO YOU MEAN, TIWAZ, WHEN YOU SAY "ONE LAST TIME"?
I MEAN, MIGHTY THOR, THAT YOU ARE READY NOW TO LEAVE MY HUMBLE ABODE AND RETURN HOME, WHERE YOU BELONG.
THE BLOOM HATH RE-TURNED AGAIN TO YOUR CHEEKS.
AND THERE SHALL BE GREAT NEED OF THEE IN ASGARD, NOW THAT YOUR FATHER IS GONE.
I KNOW, TIWAZ, AND YET, I AM LOATHE TO LEAVE.
I FEEL MORE AT HOME HERE THAN I HAVE FELT IN MANY A DAY.
AND... MY FATHER'S LOSS STILL WEIGHS HEAVILY UPON ME. IF ONLY I HAD FOUGHT HARDER, BEEN STRONGER...

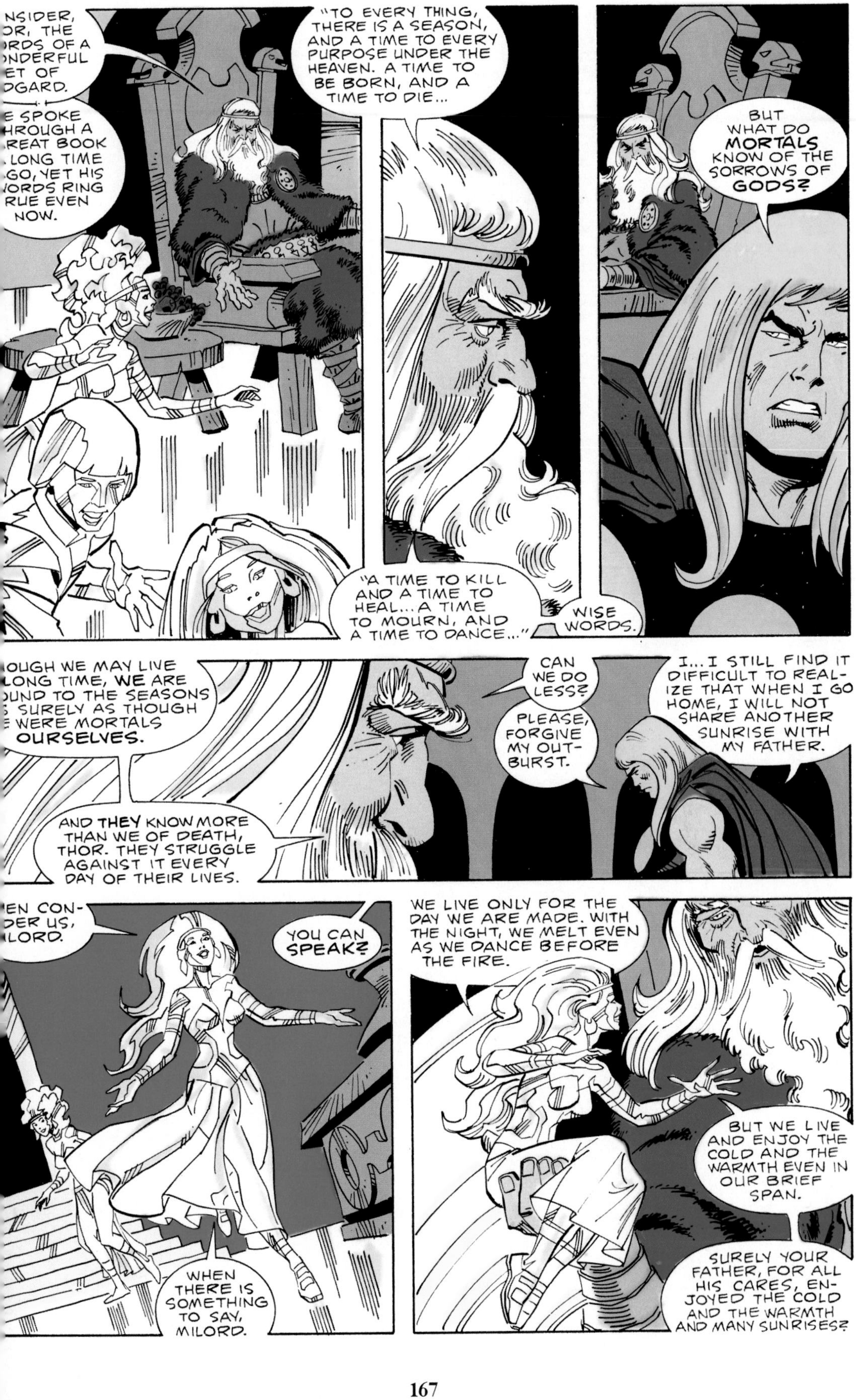
NSIDER, OR, THE ORDS OF A ONDERFUL ET OF DGARD.
E SPOKE HROUGH A REAT BOOK LONG TIME GO, YET HIS WORDS RING RUE EVEN NOW.
"TO EVERY THING, THERE IS A SEASON, AND A TIME TO EVERY PURPOSE UNDER THE HEAVEN. A TIME TO BE BORN, AND A TIME TO DIE...
"A TIME TO KILL AND A TIME TO HEAL... A TIME TO MOURN, AND A TIME TO DANCE..."
WISE WORDS.
BUT WHAT DO MORTALS KNOW OF THE SORROWS OF GODS?
OUGH WE MAY LIVE LONG TIME, WE ARE OUND TO THE SEASONS SURELY AS THOUGH E WERE MORTALS OURSELVES.
AND THEY KNOW MORE THAN WE OF DEATH, THOR. THEY STRUGGLE AGAINST IT EVERY DAY OF THEIR LIVES.
CAN WE DO LESS?
PLEASE, FORGIVE MY OUT-BURST.
I... I STILL FIND IT DIFFICULT TO REAL-IZE THAT WHEN I GO HOME, I WILL NOT SHARE ANOTHER SUNRISE WITH MY FATHER.
EN CON-DER US, LORD.
YOU CAN SPEAK?
WHEN THERE IS SOMETHING TO SAY, MILORD.
WE LIVE ONLY FOR THE DAY WE ARE MADE. WITH THE NIGHT, WE MELT EVEN AS WE DANCE BEFORE THE FIRE.
BUT WE LIVE AND ENJOY THE COLD AND THE WARMTH EVEN IN OUR BRIEF SPAN.
SURELY YOUR FATHER, FOR ALL HIS CARES, EN-JOYED THE COLD AND THE WARMTH AND MANY SUNRISES?

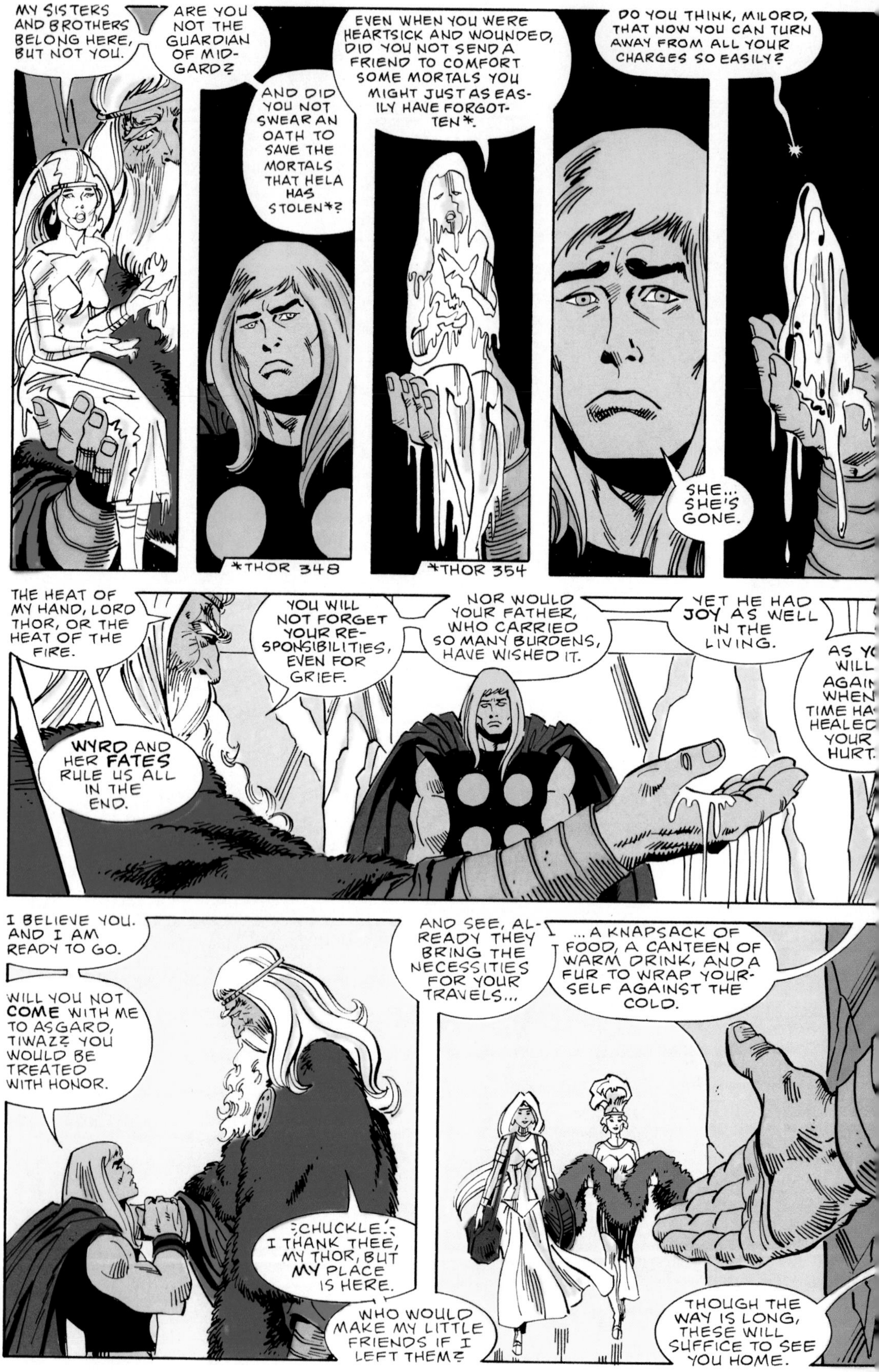
MY SISTERS AND BROTHERS BELONG HERE, BUT NOT YOU.
ARE YOU NOT THE GUARDIAN OF MIDGARD?
AND DID YOU NOT SWEAR AN OATH TO SAVE THE MORTALS THAT HELA HAS STOLEN*?
*THOR 348
EVEN WHEN YOU WERE HEARTSICK AND WOUNDED, DID YOU NOT SEND A FRIEND TO COMFORT SOME MORTALS YOU MIGHT JUST AS EASILY HAVE FORGOTTEN*.
*THOR 354
DO YOU THINK, MILORD, THAT NOW YOU CAN TURN AWAY FROM ALL YOUR CHARGES SO EASILY?
SHE... SHE'S GONE.
THE HEAT OF MY HAND, LORD THOR, OR THE HEAT OF THE FIRE.
WYRD AND HER FATES RULE US ALL IN THE END.
YOU WILL NOT FORGET YOUR RESPONSIBILITIES, EVEN FOR GRIEF.
NOR WOULD YOUR FATHER, WHO CARRIED SO MANY BURDENS, HAVE WISHED IT.
YET HE HAD JOY AS WELL IN THE LIVING.
AS YO WILL AGAIN WHEN TIME HA HEALED YOUR HURT.
I BELIEVE YOU. AND I AM READY TO GO.
WILL YOU NOT COME WITH ME TO ASGARD, TIWAZ? YOU WOULD BE TREATED WITH HONOR.
:CHUCKLE: I THANK THEE, MY THOR, BUT MY PLACE IS HERE.
WHO WOULD MAKE MY LITTLE FRIENDS IF I LEFT THEM?
AND SEE, ALREADY THEY BRING THE NECESSITIES FOR YOUR TRAVELS...
...A KNAPSACK OF FOOD, A CANTEEN OF WARM DRINK, AND A FUR TO WRAP YOURSELF AGAINST THE COLD.
THOUGH THE WAY IS LONG, THESE WILL SUFFICE TO SEE YOU HOME.

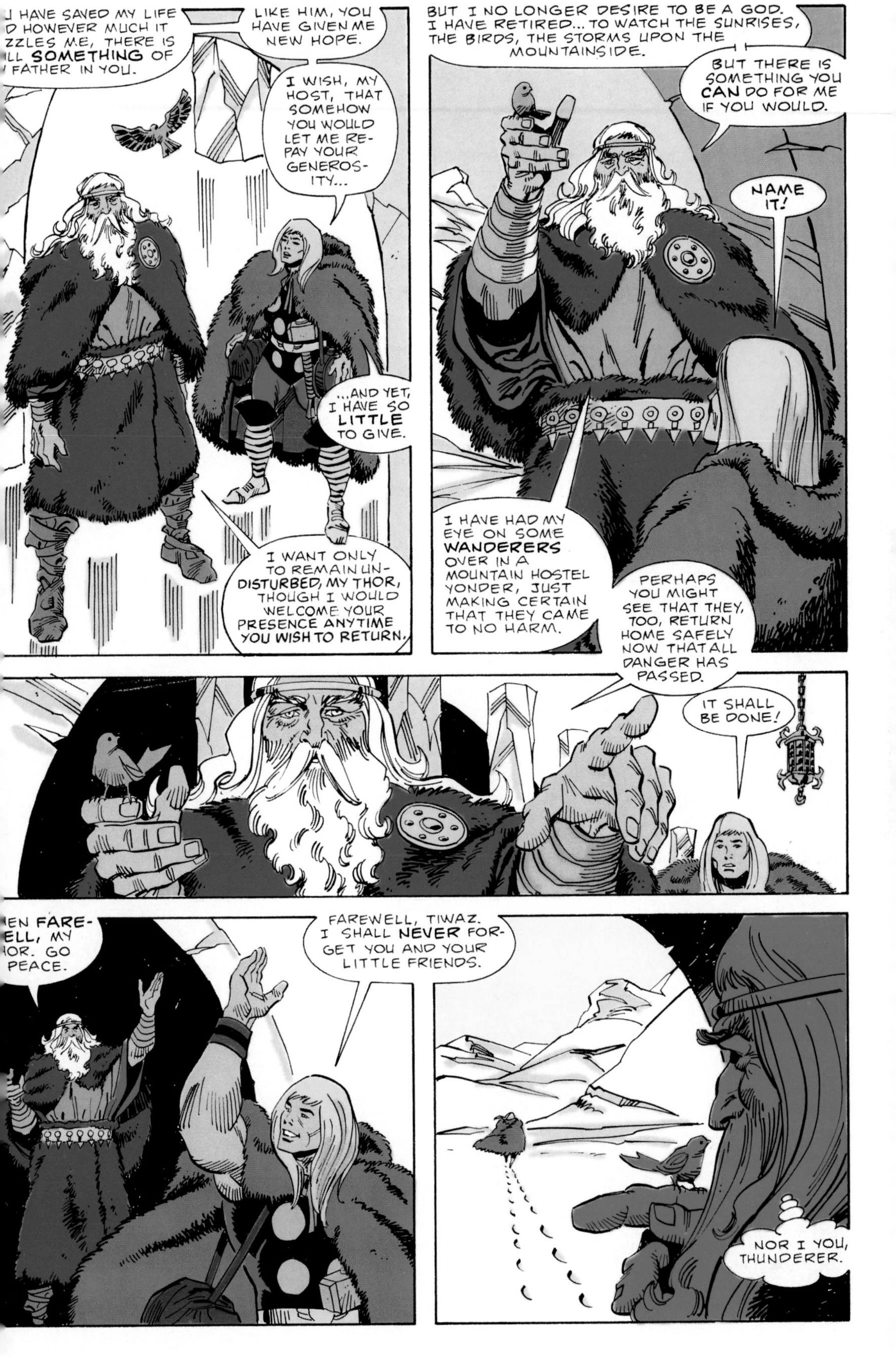
I HAVE SAVED MY LIFE D HOWEVER MUCH IT ZZLES ME, THERE IS LL SOMETHING OF FATHER IN YOU.
LIKE HIM, YOU HAVE GIVEN ME NEW HOPE.
I WISH, MY HOST, THAT SOMEHOW YOU WOULD LET ME RE-PAY YOUR GENEROS-ITY...
...AND YET, I HAVE SO LITTLE TO GIVE.
I WANT ONLY TO REMAIN UN-DISTURBED, MY THOR, THOUGH I WOULD WELCOME YOUR PRESENCE ANYTIME YOU WISH TO RETURN.
BUT I NO LONGER DESIRE TO BE A GOD. I HAVE RETIRED... TO WATCH THE SUNRISES, THE BIRDS, THE STORMS UPON THE MOUNTAINSIDE.
BUT THERE IS SOMETHING YOU CAN DO FOR ME IF YOU WOULD.
NAME IT!
I HAVE HAD MY EYE ON SOME WANDERERS OVER IN A MOUNTAIN HOSTEL YONDER, JUST MAKING CERTAIN THAT THEY CAME TO NO HARM.
PERHAPS YOU MIGHT SEE THAT THEY, TOO, RETURN HOME SAFELY NOW THAT ALL DANGER HAS PASSED.
IT SHALL BE DONE!
EN FARE-ELL, MY OR. GO PEACE.
FAREWELL, TIWAZ. I SHALL NEVER FOR-GET YOU AND YOUR LITTLE FRIENDS.
NOR I YOU, THUNDERER.

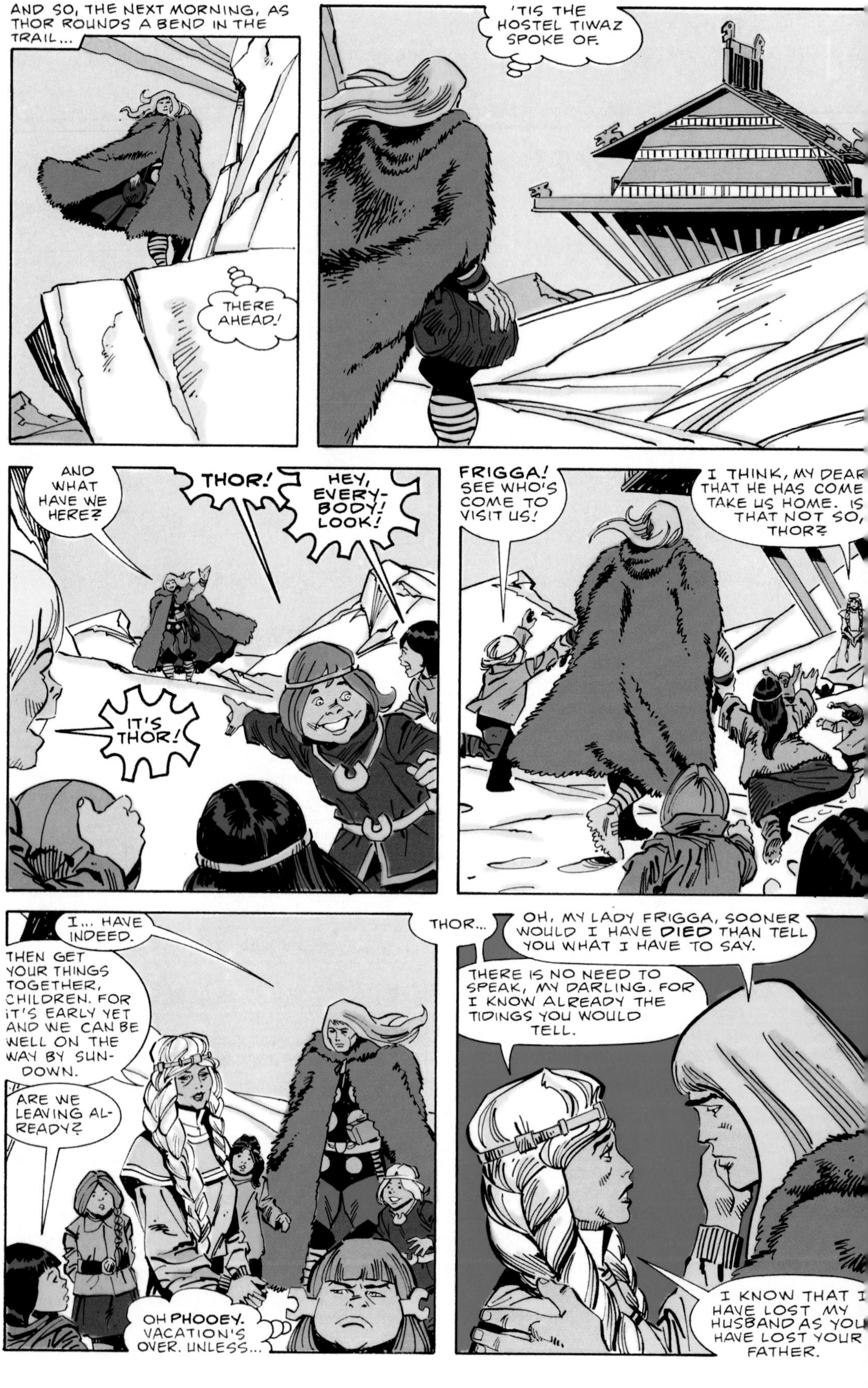
AND SO, THE NEXT MORNING, AS THOR ROUNDS A BEND IN THE TRAIL...
THERE AHEAD!
'TIS THE HOSTEL TIWAZ SPOKE OF.
AND WHAT HAVE WE HERE?
THOR!
HEY, EVERY-BODY! LOOK!
IT'S THOR!
FRIGGA! SEE WHO'S COME TO VISIT US!
I THINK, MY DEAR THAT HE HAS COME TAKE US HOME. IS THAT NOT SO, THOR?
I... HAVE INDEED.
THEN GET YOUR THINGS TOGETHER, CHILDREN. FOR IT'S EARLY YET AND WE CAN BE WELL ON THE WAY BY SUN-DOWN.
ARE WE LEAVING AL-READY?
OH PHOOEY. VACATION'S OVER. UNLESS...
THOR...
OH, MY LADY FRIGGA, SOONER WOULD I HAVE DIED THAN TELL YOU WHAT I HAVE TO SAY.
THERE IS NO NEED TO SPEAK, MY DARLING. FOR I KNOW ALREADY THE TIDINGS YOU WOULD TELL.
I KNOW THAT I HAVE LOST MY HUSBAND AS YOU HAVE LOST YOUR FATHER.

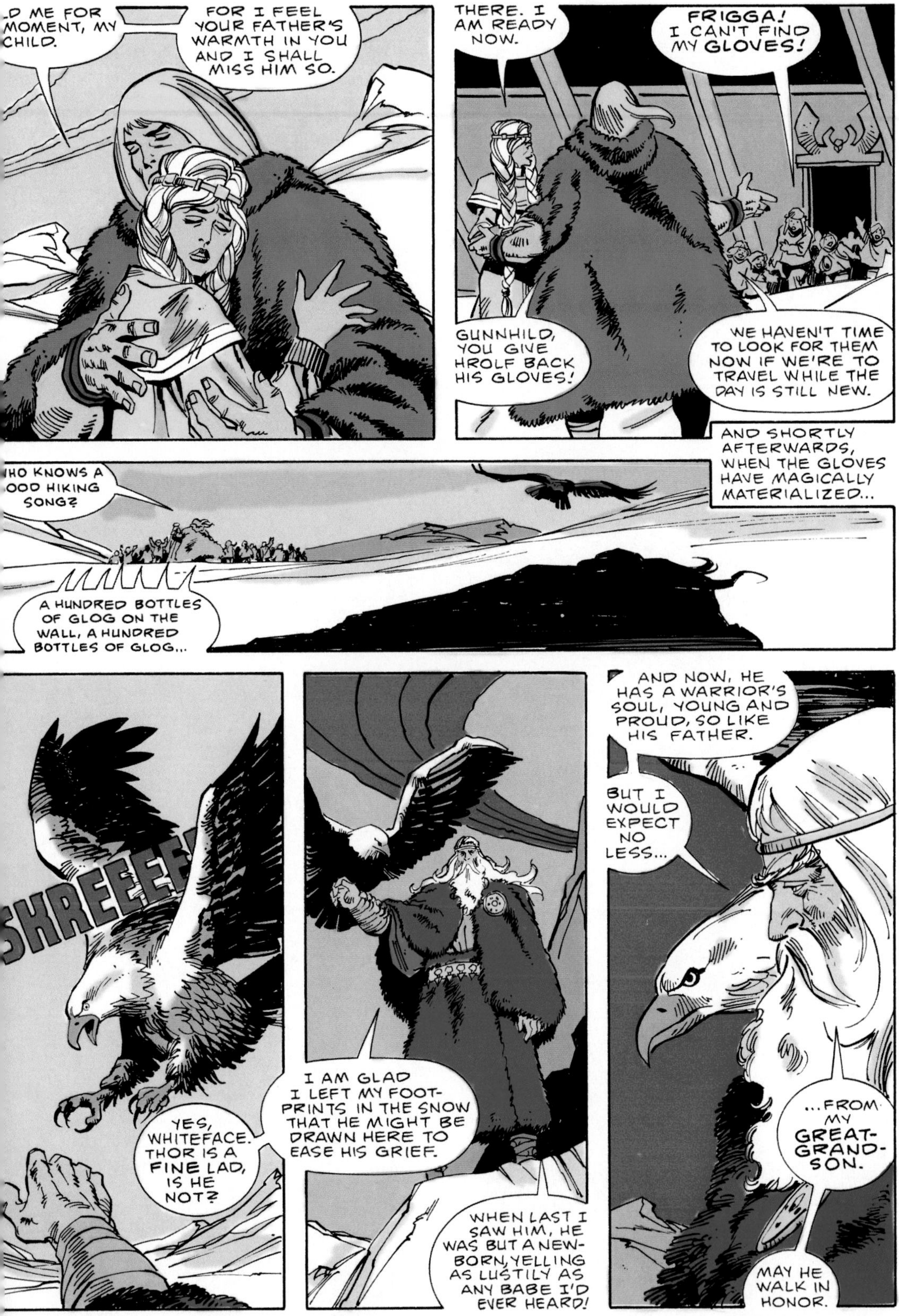

...D ME FOR
MOMENT, MY
CHILD.
FOR I FEEL YOUR FATHER'S WARMTH IN YOU AND I SHALL MISS HIM SO.
THERE. I AM READY NOW.
FRIGGA! I CAN'T FIND MY GLOVES!
GUNNHILD, YOU GIVE HROLF BACK HIS GLOVES!
WE HAVEN'T TIME TO LOOK FOR THEM NOW IF WE'RE TO TRAVEL WHILE THE DAY IS STILL NEW.
AND SHORTLY AFTERWARDS, WHEN THE GLOVES HAVE MAGICALLY MATERIALIZED...
...HO KNOWS A ...OOD HIKING SONG?
A HUNDRED BOTTLES OF GLOG ON THE WALL, A HUNDRED BOTTLES OF GLOG...
SHREEEE
YES, WHITEFACE. THOR IS A FINE LAD, IS HE NOT?
I AM GLAD I LEFT MY FOOT-PRINTS IN THE SNOW THAT HE MIGHT BE DRAWN HERE TO EASE HIS GRIEF.
WHEN LAST I SAW HIM, HE WAS BUT A NEW-BORN, YELLING AS LUSTILY AS ANY BABE I'D EVER HEARD!
AND NOW, HE HAS A WARRIOR'S SOUL, YOUNG AND PROUD, SO LIKE HIS FATHER.
BUT I WOULD EXPECT NO LESS...
...FROM MY GREAT-GRAND-SON.
MAY HE WALK IN HONOR.

WALT SIMONSON SCRIPTER
SAL BUSCEMA GUEST ARTIST
JOHN WORKMAN LETTERER
CHRISTIE SCHEELE COLORIST
RALPH MACCHIO EDITOR
JIM SHOOTER EDITOR IN CHIEF

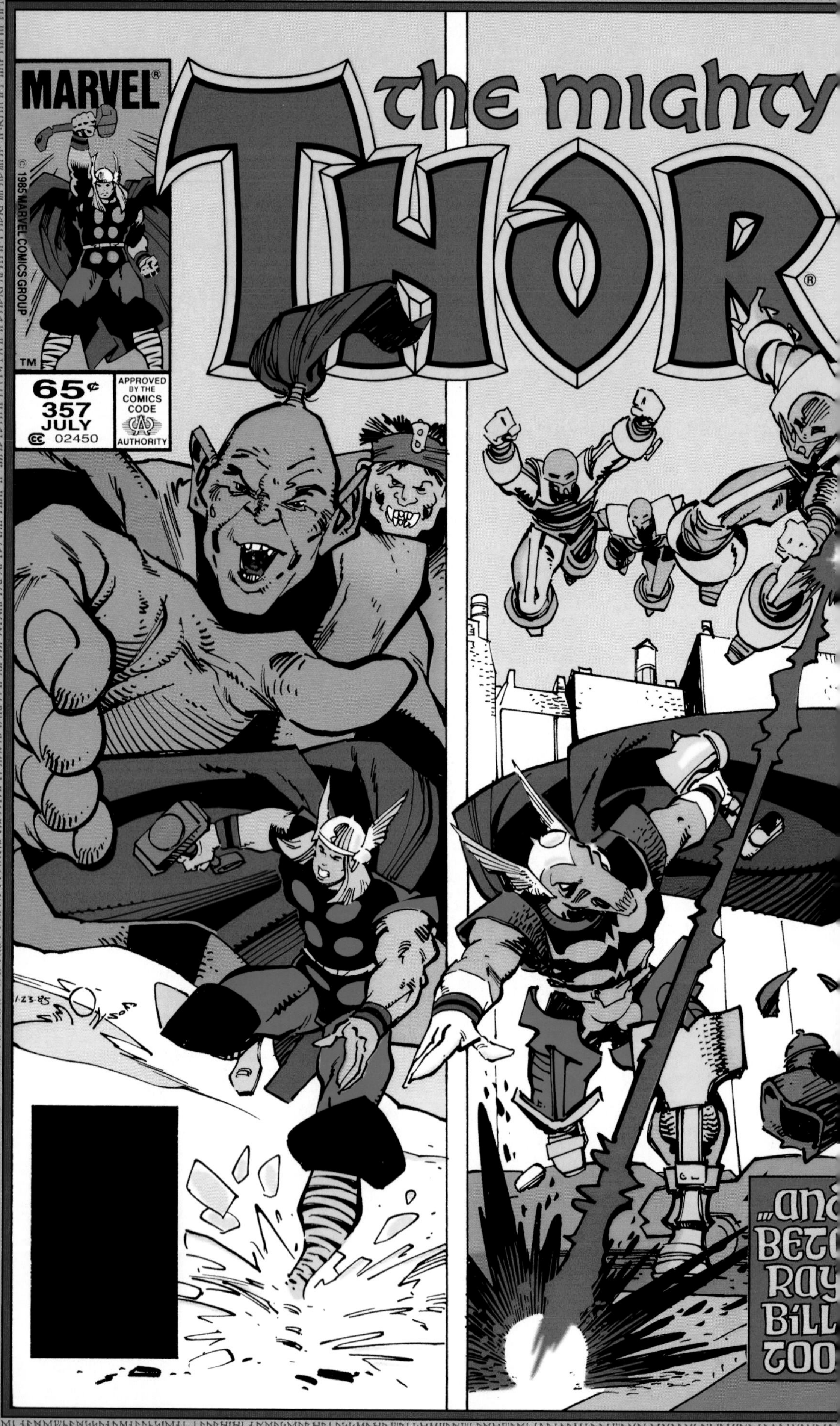
MARVEL
the mighty
THOR
© 1985 MARVEL COMICS GROUP
TM
65¢
357
JULY
02450
APPROVED BY THE COMICS CODE AUTHORITY
...and

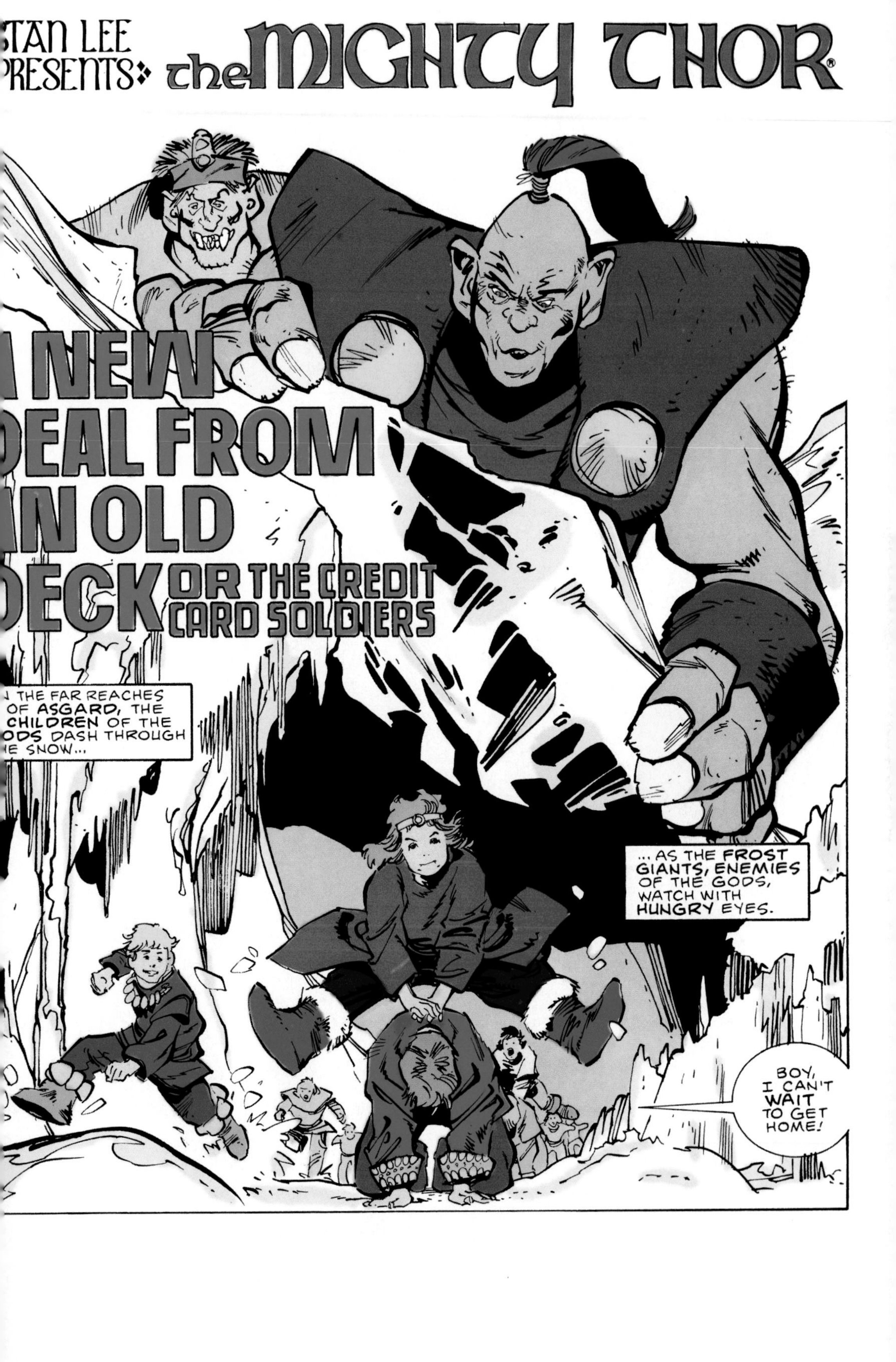

TAN LEE
RESENTS the MIGHTY THOR®
NEW
EAL FROM
N OLD
ECK OR THE CREDIT CARD SOLDIERS
N THE FAR REACHES OF ASGARD, THE CHILDREN OF THE ODS DASH THROUGH E SNOW...
...AS THE FROST GIANTS, ENEMIES OF THE GODS, WATCH WITH HUNGRY EYES.
BOY, I CAN'T WAIT TO GET HOME!

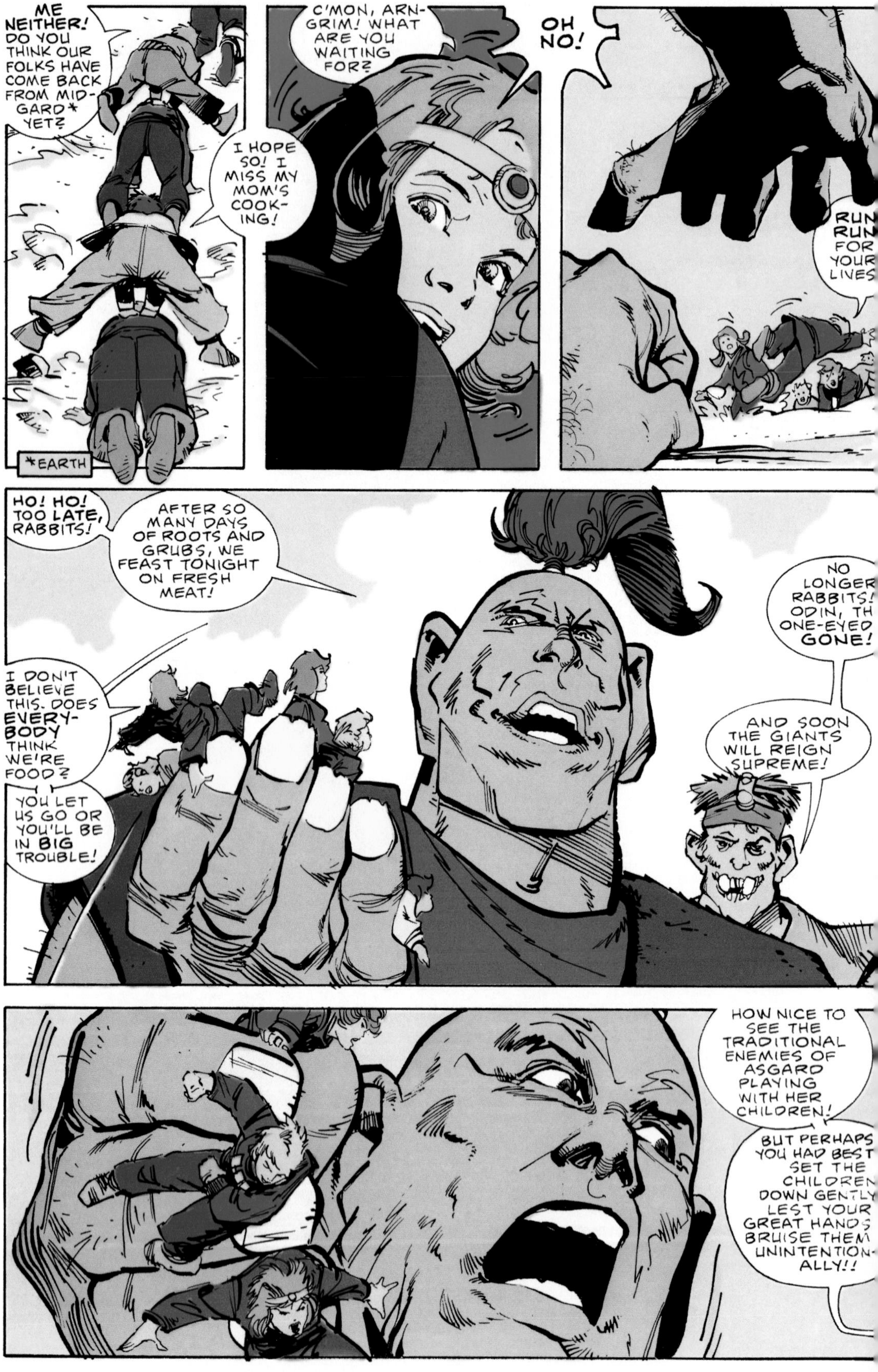

ME NEITHER! DO YOU THINK OUR FOLKS HAVE COME BACK FROM MIDGARD* YET?
I HOPE SO! I MISS MY MOM'S COOKING!
*EARTH
C'MON, ARNGRIM! WHAT ARE YOU WAITING FOR?
OH NO!
RUN RUN FOR YOUR LIVES
HO! HO! TOO LATE, RABBITS!
AFTER SO MANY DAYS OF ROOTS AND GRUBS, WE FEAST TONIGHT ON FRESH MEAT!
NO LONGER RABBITS! ODIN, TH ONE-EYED GONE!
AND SOON THE GIANTS WILL REIGN SUPREME!
I DON'T BELIEVE THIS. DOES EVERYBODY THINK WE'RE FOOD?
YOU LET US GO OR YOU'LL BE IN BIG TROUBLE!
HOW NICE TO SEE THE TRADITIONAL ENEMIES OF ASGARD PLAYING WITH HER CHILDREN!
BUT PERHAPS YOU HAD BEST SET THE CHILDREN DOWN GENTLY LEST YOUR GREAT HANDS BRUISE THEM UNINTENTIONALLY!!

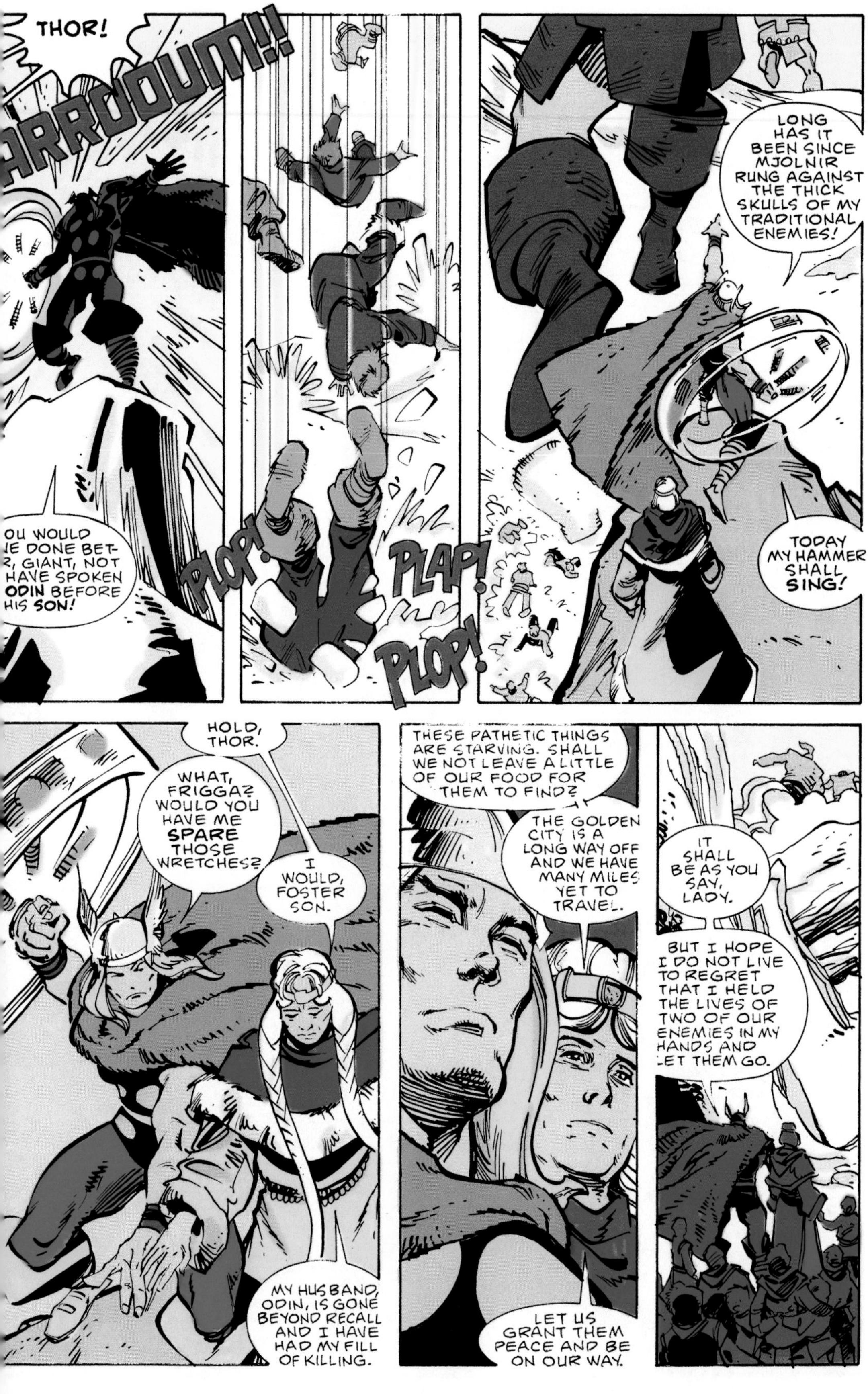
THOR!
ARROOUM!!
OU WOULD
IE DONE BET-
R, GIANT, NOT
HAVE SPOKEN
ODIN BEFORE
HIS SON!
PLOP!
PLAP!
PLOP!
LONG HAS IT BEEN SINCE MJOLNIR RUNG AGAINST THE THICK SKULLS OF MY TRADITIONAL ENEMIES!
TODAY MY HAMMER SHALL SING!
HOLD, THOR.
WHAT, FRIGGA? WOULD YOU HAVE ME SPARE THOSE WRETCHES?
I WOULD, FOSTER SON.
MY HUSBAND, ODIN, IS GONE BEYOND RECALL AND I HAVE HAD MY FILL OF KILLING.
THESE PATHETIC THINGS ARE STARVING. SHALL WE NOT LEAVE A LITTLE OF OUR FOOD FOR THEM TO FIND?
THE GOLDEN CITY IS A LONG WAY OFF AND WE HAVE MANY MILES YET TO TRAVEL.
LET US GRANT THEM PEACE AND BE ON OUR WAY.
IT SHALL BE AS YOU SAY, LADY.
BUT I HOPE I DO NOT LIVE TO REGRET THAT I HELD THE LIVES OF TWO OF OUR ENEMIES IN MY HANDS AND LET THEM GO.

BUT AS THOR WONDERS WHETHER OR NOT HE HAS DONE THE RIGHT THING, WE TURN TO DOW[N] TOWN MANHATTAN WHERE...

...TWO TOURIST[S] WANDER THRO[UGH] THE CITY, TAK[ING] IN THE SIGHTS.

...AND DOING A LITTLE SHOPPING.

BILL, LOOK!

WHAT IS IT, MILADY SIF?

NOW DON'T BE STUFFY MILORD BETA RAY.

JUST BECAUSE YOU'RE AN ALIEN SPENDING A BRIEF SOJOURN ON EARTH DOESN'T MEAN YOU CAN'T ENJOY YOURSELF.

I HAVE BEEN THE WARRIOR-GUARD-IAN OF MY PEOPLE FOR A LONG TIME, SIF.

I HAVE NOT HAD TIME FOR LAUGHTER.

THEN IT'S TIME YOU DID.

AND THESE WOULD BE PERFECT FOR YOU.

I THINK YOU LOOK VERY DIS-TINGUISHED IN GLASSES.

HMMMM.

I'M NOT AT ALL SURE THAT THIS IS HOW AS-GARDIANS OUGHT TO COMPORT THEMSELVES WHEN THEY'RE VISITING A FOREIGN COUNTRY.

YOU'L[L] LEAR[N]

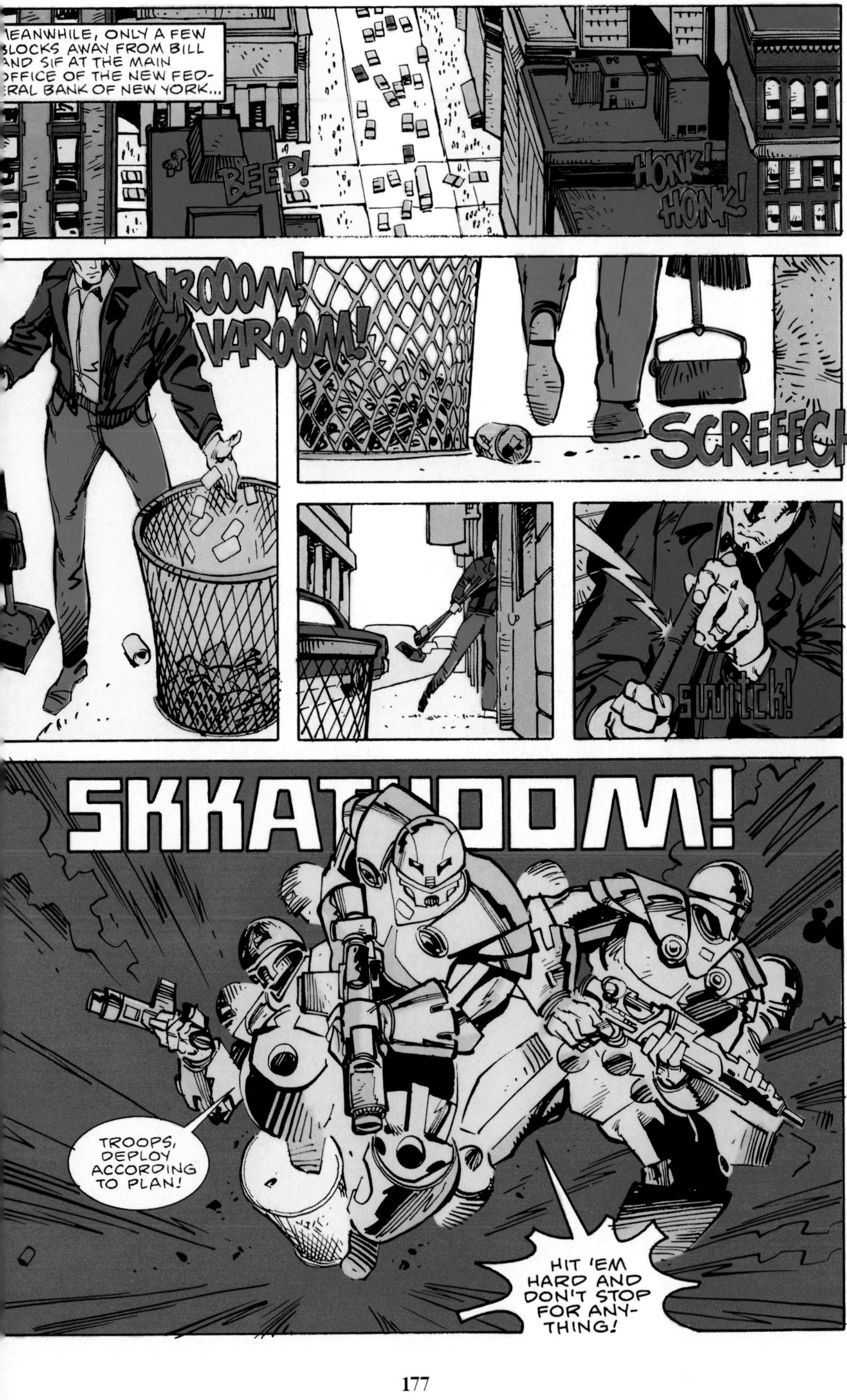
MEANWHILE, ONLY A FEW BLOCKS AWAY FROM BILL AND SIF AT THE MAIN OFFICE OF THE NEW FEDERAL BANK OF NEW YORK...
BEEP!
HONK! HONK!
VROOOM! VAROOM!
SCREEECH!
SWITCH!
SKKATHOOM!
TROOPS, DEPLOY ACCORDING TO PLAN!
HIT 'EM HARD AND DON'T STOP FOR ANYTHING!

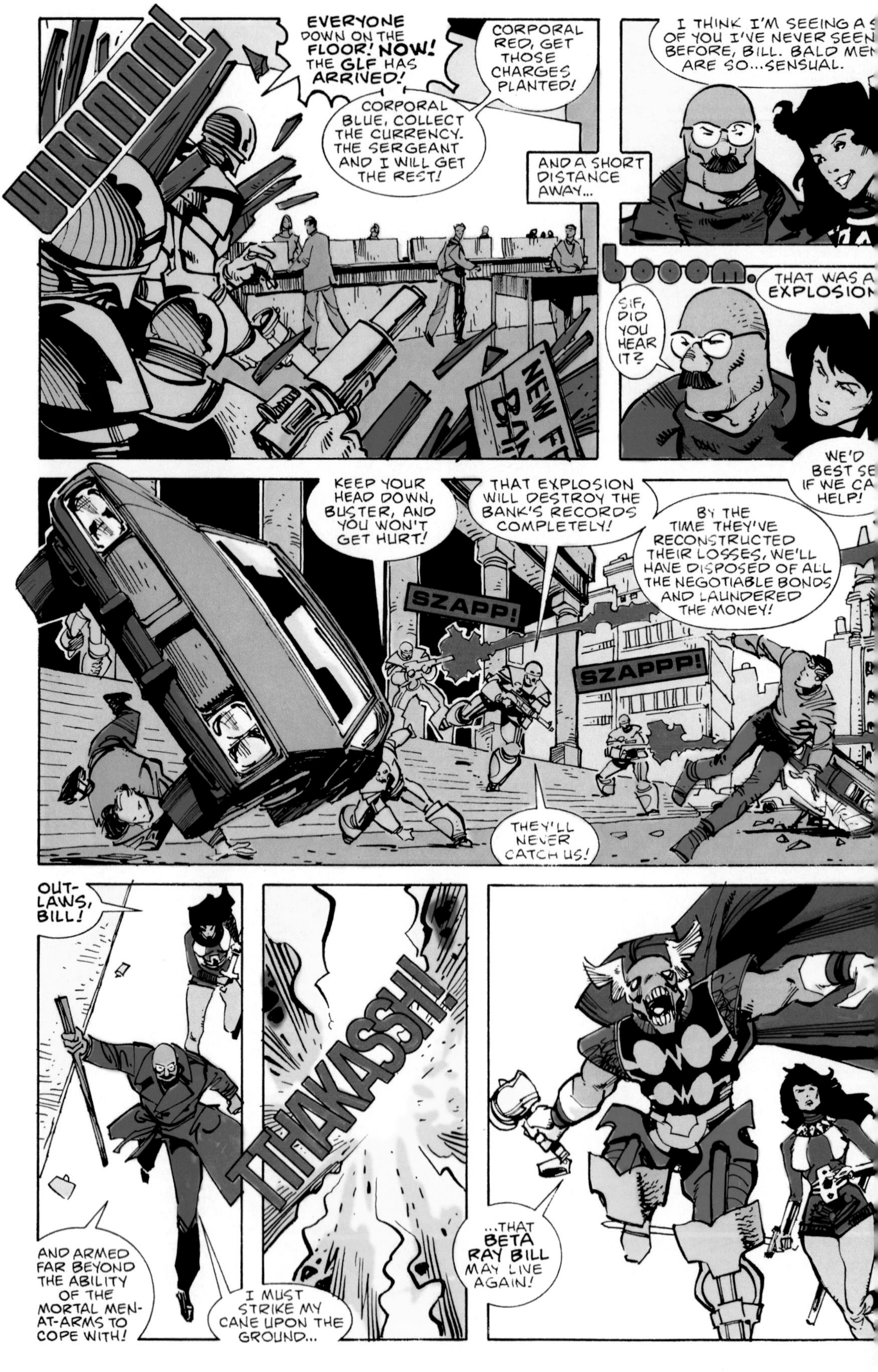

WHOOM!
EVERYONE DOWN ON THE FLOOR! NOW! THE GLF HAS ARRIVED!
CORPORAL RED, GET THOSE CHARGES PLANTED!
CORPORAL BLUE, COLLECT THE CURRENCY. THE SERGEANT AND I WILL GET THE REST!
NEW F
BA
AND A SHORT DISTANCE AWAY...
I THINK I'M SEEING A S
OF YOU I'VE NEVER SEEN
BEFORE, BILL. BALD MEN
ARE SO...SENSUAL.
booom.
THAT WAS A
EXPLOSION
SIF, DID YOU HEAR IT?
KEEP YOUR HEAD DOWN, BUSTER, AND YOU WON'T GET HURT!
THAT EXPLOSION WILL DESTROY THE BANK'S RECORDS COMPLETELY!
BY THE TIME THEY'VE RECONSTRUCTED THEIR LOSSES, WE'LL HAVE DISPOSED OF ALL THE NEGOTIABLE BONDS AND LAUNDERED THE MONEY!
WE'D BEST SE IF WE CA HELP!
SZAPP!
SZAPPP!
THEY'LL NEVER CATCH US!
OUT-LAWS, BILL!
AND ARMED FAR BEYOND THE ABILITY OF THE MORTAL MEN-AT-ARMS TO COPE WITH!
I MUST STRIKE MY CANE UPON THE GROUND...
THAKASSH!
...THAT BETA RAY BILL MAY LIVE AGAIN!

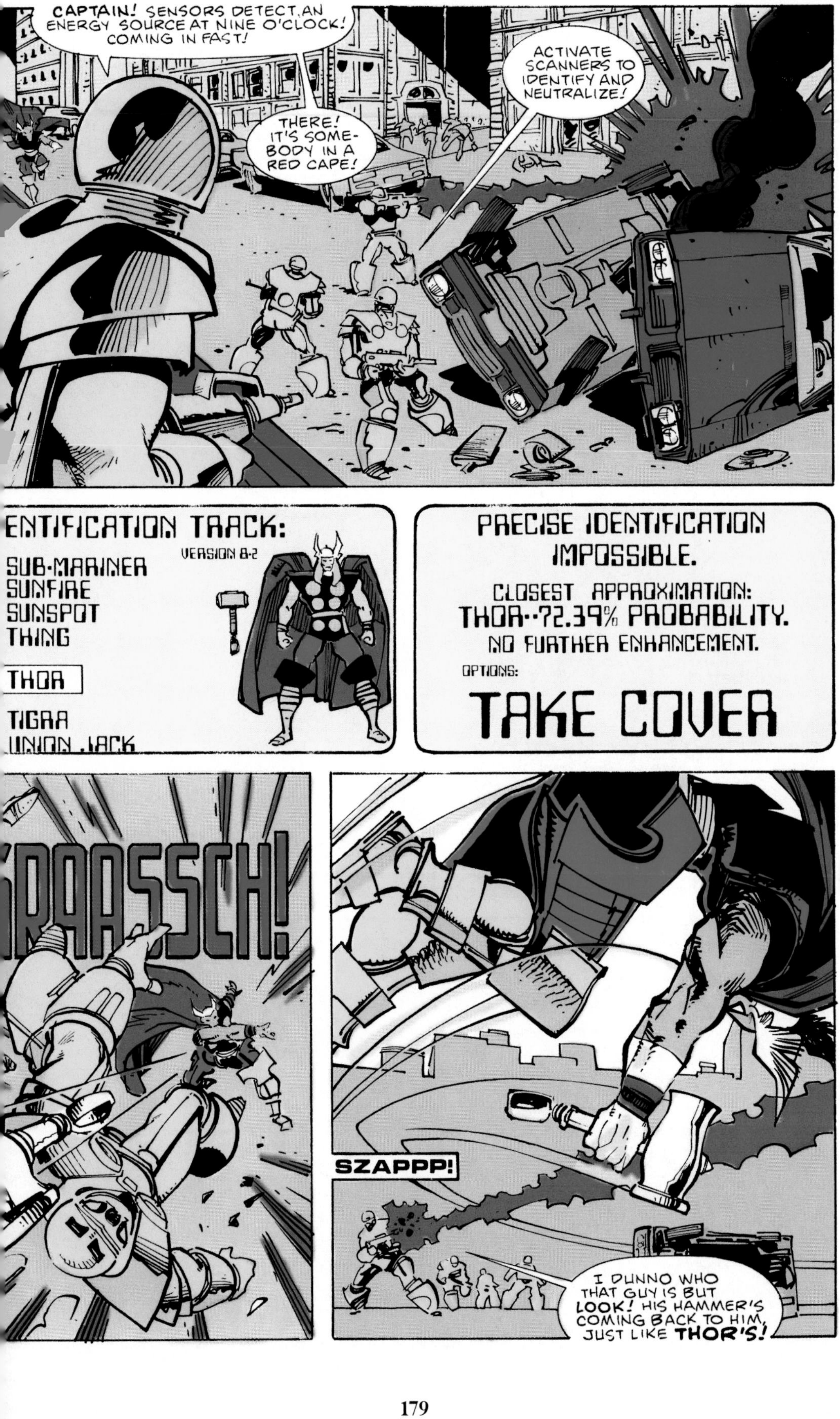

CAPTAIN! SENSORS DETECT AN ENERGY SOURCE AT NINE O'CLOCK! COMING IN FAST!
THERE! IT'S SOMEBODY IN A RED CAPE!
ACTIVATE SCANNERS TO IDENTIFY AND NEUTRALIZE!
ENTIFICATION TRACK:
VERSION 8-2
SUB-MARINER
SUNFIRE
SUNSPOT
THING
THOR
TIGRA
UNION JACK
PRECISE IDENTIFICATION IMPOSSIBLE.
CLOSEST APPROXIMATION:
THOR--72.39% PROBABILITY.
NO FURTHER ENHANCEMENT.
OPTIONS:
TAKE COVER
RAASSCH!
SZAPPP!
I DUNNO WHO THAT GUY IS BUT LOOK! HIS HAMMER'S COMING BACK TO HIM, JUST LIKE THOR'S!

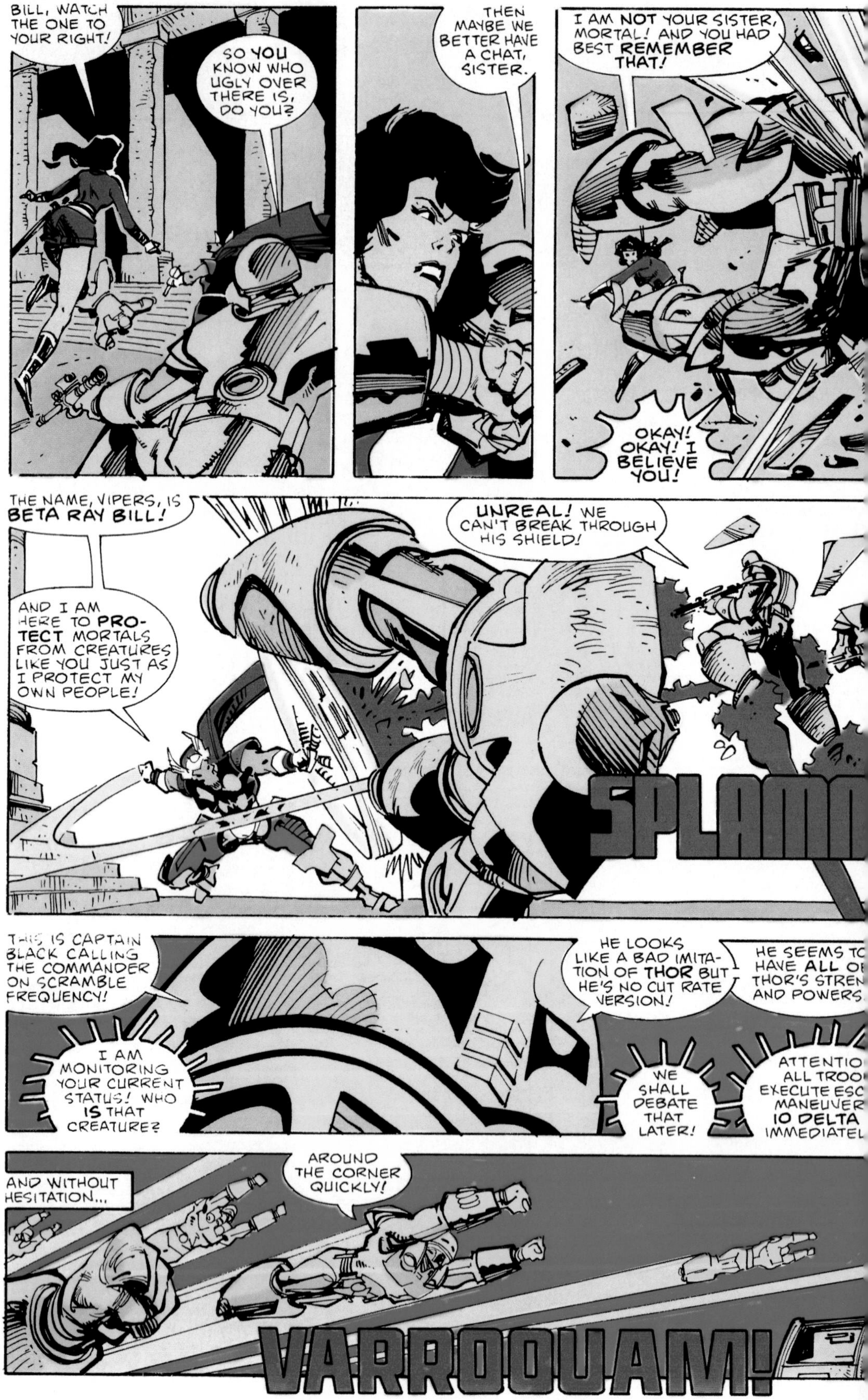

BILL, WATCH THE ONE TO YOUR RIGHT!
SO YOU KNOW WHO UGLY OVER THERE IS, DO YOU?
THEN MAYBE WE BETTER HAVE A CHAT, SISTER.
I AM NOT YOUR SISTER, MORTAL! AND YOU HAD BEST REMEMBER THAT!
OKAY! OKAY! I BELIEVE YOU!
THE NAME, VIPERS, IS BETA RAY BILL!
AND I AM HERE TO PROTECT MORTALS FROM CREATURES LIKE YOU JUST AS I PROTECT MY OWN PEOPLE!
UNREAL! WE CAN'T BREAK THROUGH HIS SHIELD!
SPLAMM
THIS IS CAPTAIN BLACK CALLING THE COMMANDER ON SCRAMBLE FREQUENCY!
I AM MONITORING YOUR CURRENT STATUS! WHO IS THAT CREATURE?
HE LOOKS LIKE A BAD IMITATION OF THOR BUT HE'S NO CUT RATE VERSION!
HE SEEMS TO HAVE ALL OF THOR'S STREN AND POWERS
WE SHALL DEBATE THAT LATER!
ATTENTIO ALL TROO EXECUTE ESC MANEUVER 10 DELTA IMMEDIATEL
AND WITHOUT HESITATION...
AROUND THE CORNER QUICKLY!
VARROOUAM!

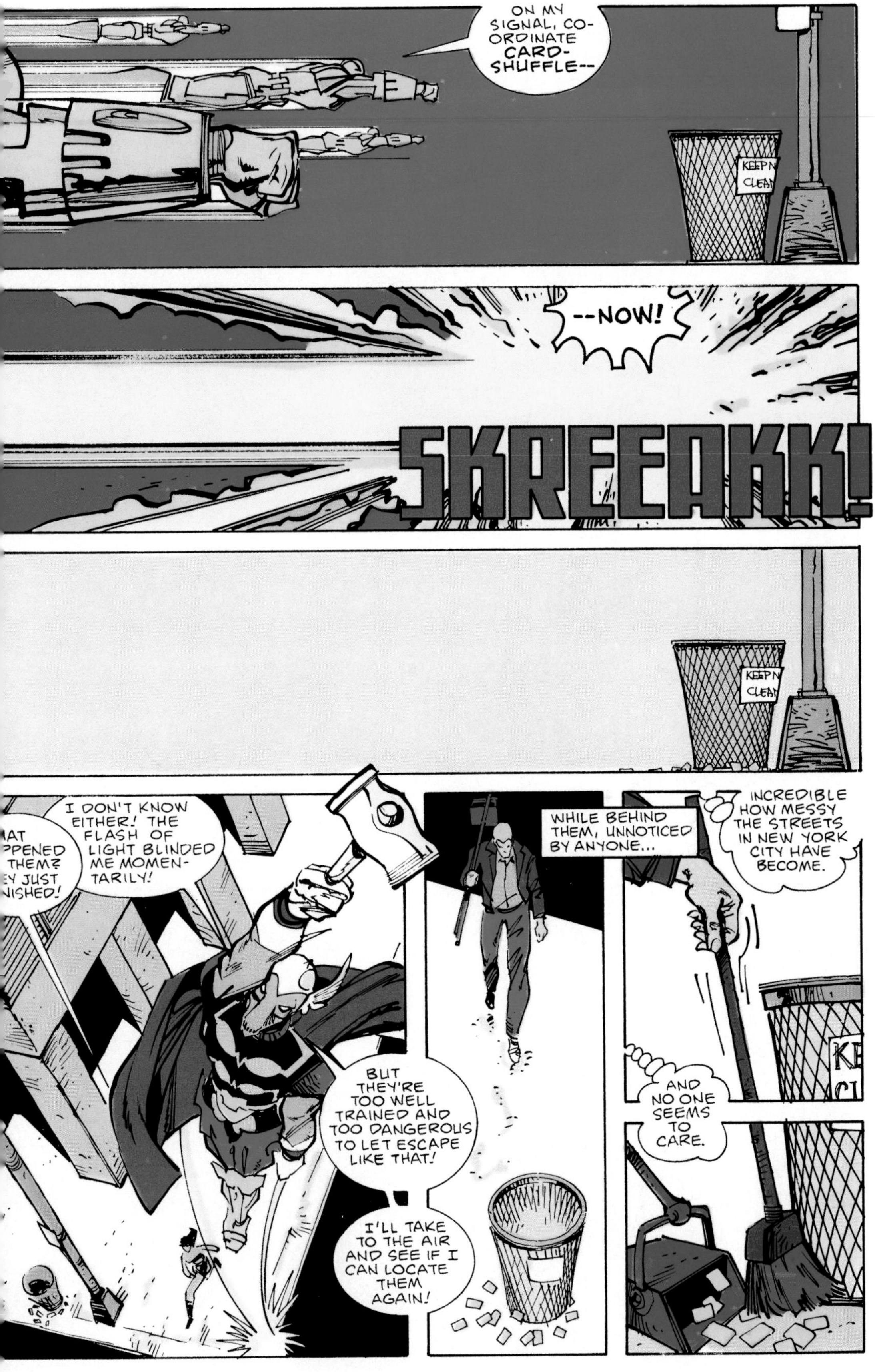
ON MY SIGNAL, CO-ORDINATE CARD-SHUFFLE--
--NOW!
SKREEAKK!
I DON'T KNOW EITHER! THE FLASH OF LIGHT BLINDED ME MOMEN-TARILY!
BUT THEY'RE TOO WELL TRAINED AND TOO DANGEROUS TO LET ESCAPE LIKE THAT!
I'LL TAKE TO THE AIR AND SEE IF I CAN LOCATE THEM AGAIN!
WHILE BEHIND THEM, UNNOTICED BY ANYONE...
INCREDIBLE HOW MESSY THE STREETS IN NEW YORK CITY HAVE BECOME.
AND NO ONE SEEMS TO CARE.

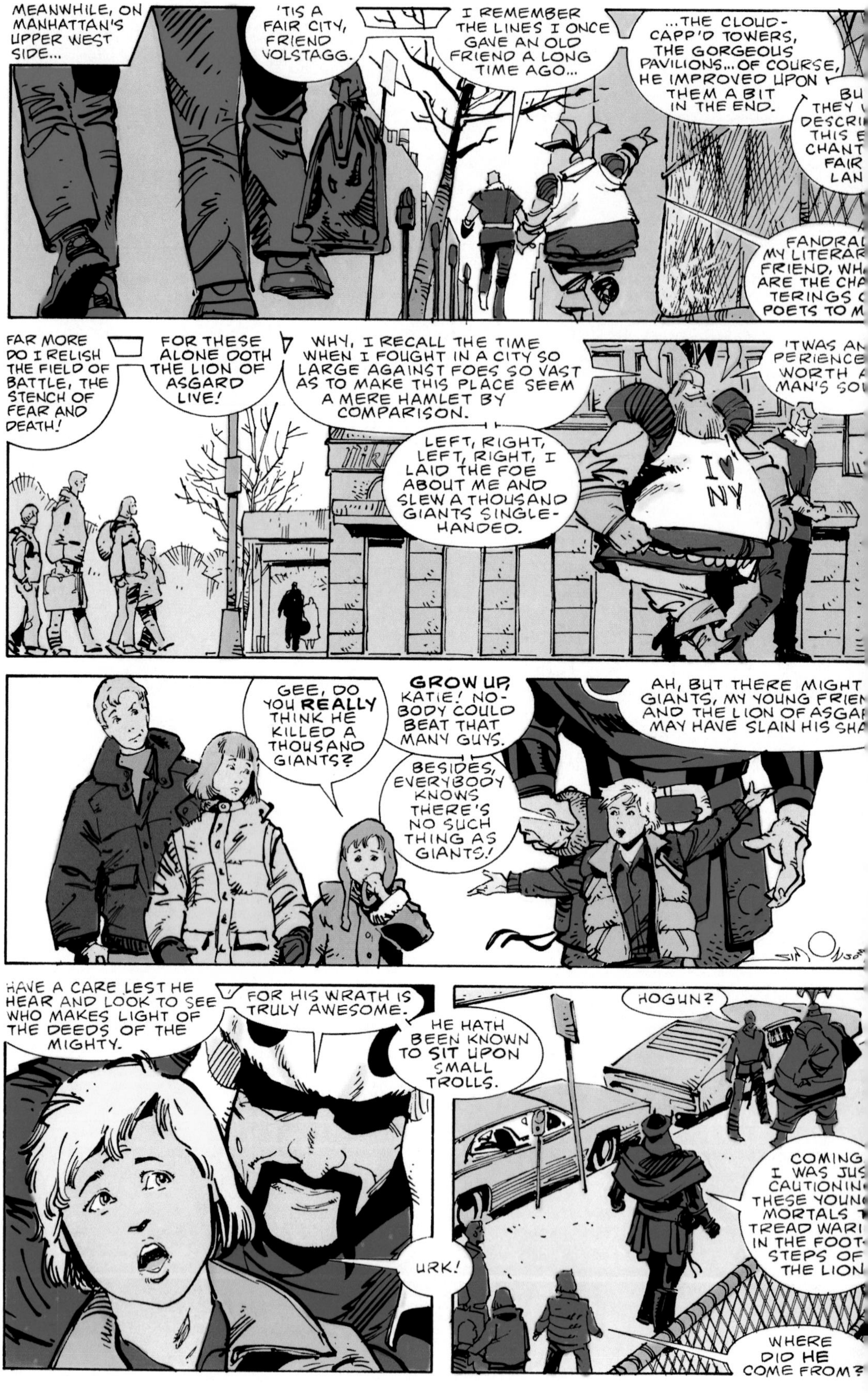
MEANWHILE, ON MANHATTAN'S UPPER WEST SIDE...
'TIS A FAIR CITY, FRIEND VOLSTAGG.
I REMEMBER THE LINES I ONCE GAVE AN OLD FRIEND A LONG TIME AGO...
...THE CLOUD-CAPP'D TOWERS, THE GORGEOUS PAVILIONS... OF COURSE, HE IMPROVED UPON THEM A BIT IN THE END.
BU THEY DESCRI THIS E CHANT FAIR LAN
FANDRAL MY LITERAR FRIEND, WHA ARE THE CHA TERINGS O POETS TO M
FAR MORE DO I RELISH THE FIELD OF BATTLE, THE STENCH OF FEAR AND DEATH!
FOR THESE ALONE DOTH THE LION OF ASGARD LIVE!
WHY, I RECALL THE TIME WHEN I FOUGHT IN A CITY SO LARGE AGAINST FOES SO VAST AS TO MAKE THIS PLACE SEEM A MERE HAMLET BY COMPARISON.
LEFT, RIGHT, LEFT, RIGHT, I LAID THE FOE ABOUT ME AND SLEW A THOUSAND GIANTS SINGLE-HANDED.
'TWAS AN PERIENCE WORTH A MAN'S SOU
I ♥ NY
GEE, DO YOU **REALLY** THINK HE KILLED A THOUSAND GIANTS?
GROW UP, KATIE! NOBODY COULD BEAT THAT MANY GUYS.
BESIDES, EVERYBODY KNOWS THERE'S NO SUCH THING AS GIANTS!
AH, BUT THERE MIGHT GIANTS, MY YOUNG FRIEN AND THE LION OF ASGAR MAY HAVE SLAIN HIS SHA
HAVE A CARE LEST HE HEAR AND LOOK TO SEE WHO MAKES LIGHT OF THE DEEDS OF THE MIGHTY.
FOR HIS WRATH IS TRULY AWESOME.
HE HATH BEEN KNOWN TO **SIT** UPON SMALL TROLLS.
URK!
HOGUN?
COMING I WAS JUS CAUTIONIN THESE YOUN MORTALS T TREAD WARI IN THE FOOT-STEPS OF THE LION
WHERE DID **HE** COME FROM?

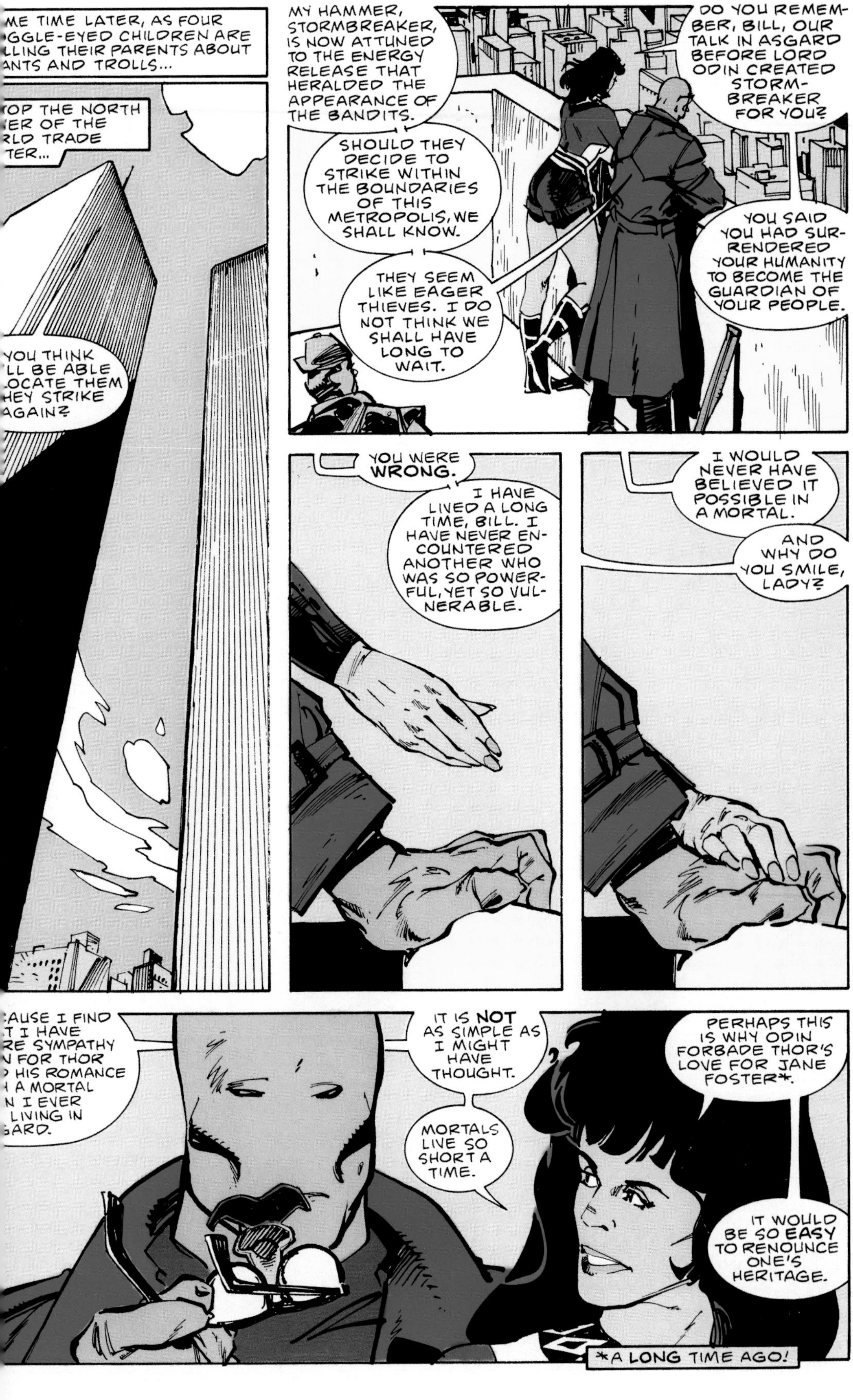
ME TIME LATER, AS FOUR GGLE-EYED CHILDREN ARE LLING THEIR PARENTS ABOUT ANTS AND TROLLS...
TOP THE NORTH ER OF THE RLD TRADE TER...
YOU THINK LL BE ABLE OCATE THEM HEY STRIKE AGAIN?
MY HAMMER, STORMBREAKER, IS NOW ATTUNED TO THE ENERGY RELEASE THAT HERALDED THE APPEARANCE OF THE BANDITS.
SHOULD THEY DECIDE TO STRIKE WITHIN THE BOUNDARIES OF THIS METROPOLIS, WE SHALL KNOW.
THEY SEEM LIKE EAGER THIEVES. I DO NOT THINK WE SHALL HAVE LONG TO WAIT.
DO YOU REMEMBER, BILL, OUR TALK IN ASGARD BEFORE LORD ODIN CREATED STORMBREAKER FOR YOU?
YOU SAID YOU HAD SURRENDERED YOUR HUMANITY TO BECOME THE GUARDIAN OF YOUR PEOPLE.
YOU WERE WRONG.
I HAVE LIVED A LONG TIME, BILL. I HAVE NEVER ENCOUNTERED ANOTHER WHO WAS SO POWERFUL, YET SO VULNERABLE.
I WOULD NEVER HAVE BELIEVED IT POSSIBLE IN A MORTAL.
AND WHY DO YOU SMILE, LADY?
CAUSE I FIND T I HAVE RE SYMPATHY N FOR THOR D HIS ROMANCE H A MORTAL N I EVER LIVING IN GARD.
IT IS NOT AS SIMPLE AS I MIGHT HAVE THOUGHT.
MORTALS LIVE SO SHORT A TIME.
PERHAPS THIS IS WHY ODIN FORBADE THOR'S LOVE FOR JANE FOSTER*.
IT WOULD BE SO EASY TO RENOUNCE ONE'S HERITAGE.
*A LONG TIME AGO!

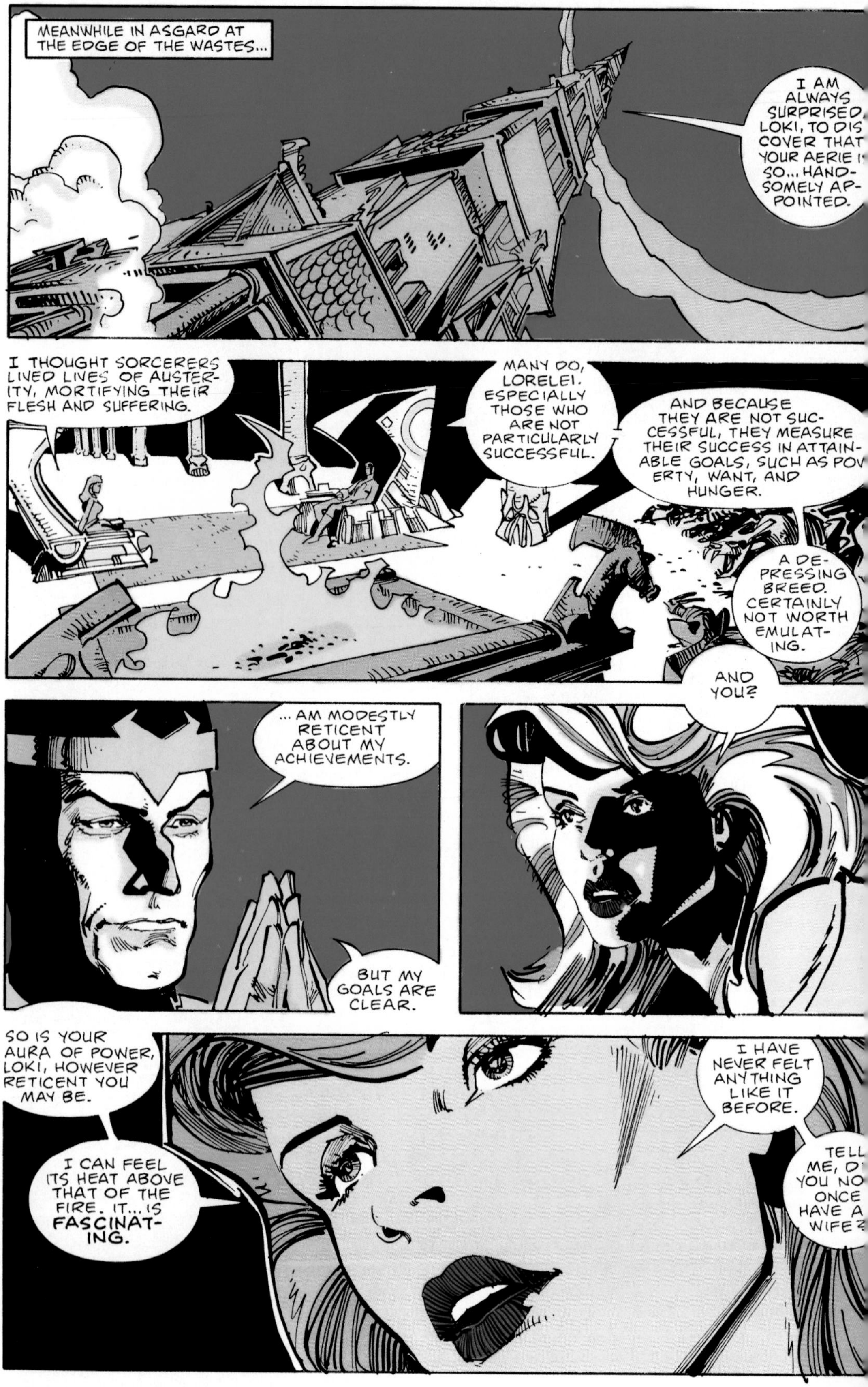
MEANWHILE IN ASGARD AT THE EDGE OF THE WASTES...
I AM ALWAYS SURPRISED, LOKI, TO DISCOVER THAT YOUR AERIE IS SO... HANDSOMELY APPOINTED.
I THOUGHT SORCERERS LIVED LIVES OF AUSTERITY, MORTIFYING THEIR FLESH AND SUFFERING.
MANY DO, LORELEI. ESPECIALLY THOSE WHO ARE NOT PARTICULARLY SUCCESSFUL.
AND BECAUSE THEY ARE NOT SUCCESSFUL, THEY MEASURE THEIR SUCCESS IN ATTAINABLE GOALS, SUCH AS POVERTY, WANT, AND HUNGER.
A DEPRESSING BREED. CERTAINLY NOT WORTH EMULATING.
AND YOU?
... AM MODESTLY RETICENT ABOUT MY ACHIEVEMENTS.
BUT MY GOALS ARE CLEAR.
SO IS YOUR AURA OF POWER, LOKI, HOWEVER RETICENT YOU MAY BE.
I CAN FEEL ITS HEAT ABOVE THAT OF THE FIRE. IT... IS **FASCINATING.**
I HAVE NEVER FELT ANYTHING LIKE IT BEFORE.
TELL ME, DI YOU NO ONCE HAVE A WIFE?

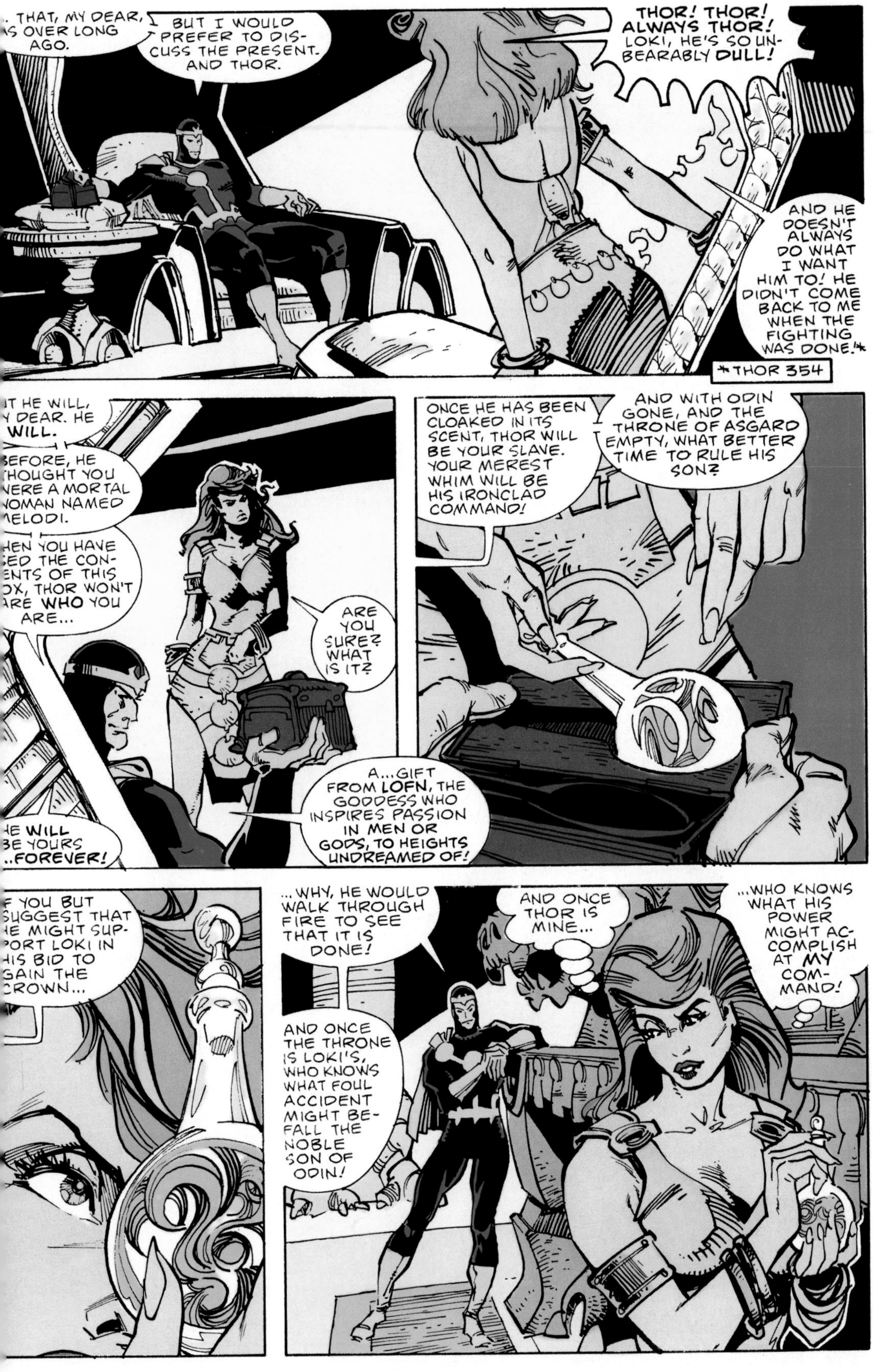

. THAT, MY DEAR, AS OVER LONG AGO.
BUT I WOULD PREFER TO DISCUSS THE PRESENT- AND THOR.
THOR! THOR! ALWAYS THOR! LOKI, HE'S SO UNBEARABLY DULL!
AND HE DOESN'T ALWAYS DO WHAT I WANT HIM TO! HE DIDN'T COME BACK TO ME WHEN THE FIGHTING WAS DONE!*
*THOR 354
IT HE WILL, Y DEAR. HE WILL.
BEFORE, HE THOUGHT YOU WERE A MORTAL WOMAN NAMED MELODI.
WHEN YOU HAVE SED THE CONTENTS OF THIS OX, THOR WON'T ARE WHO YOU ARE...
ARE YOU SURE? WHAT IS IT?
A...GIFT FROM LOFN, THE GODDESS WHO INSPIRES PASSION IN MEN OR GODS, TO HEIGHTS UNDREAMED OF!
HE WILL BE YOURS ..FOREVER!
ONCE HE HAS BEEN CLOAKED IN ITS SCENT, THOR WILL BE YOUR SLAVE. YOUR MEREST WHIM WILL BE HIS IRONCLAD COMMAND!
AND WITH ODIN GONE, AND THE THRONE OF ASGARD EMPTY, WHAT BETTER TIME TO RULE HIS SON?
F YOU BUT SUGGEST THAT HE MIGHT SUPPORT LOKI IN HIS BID TO GAIN THE CROWN...
...WHY, HE WOULD WALK THROUGH FIRE TO SEE THAT IT IS DONE!
AND ONCE THE THRONE IS LOKI'S, WHO KNOWS WHAT FOUL ACCIDENT MIGHT BEFALL THE NOBLE SON OF ODIN!
AND ONCE THOR IS MINE...
...WHO KNOWS WHAT HIS POWER MIGHT ACCOMPLISH AT MY COMMAND!

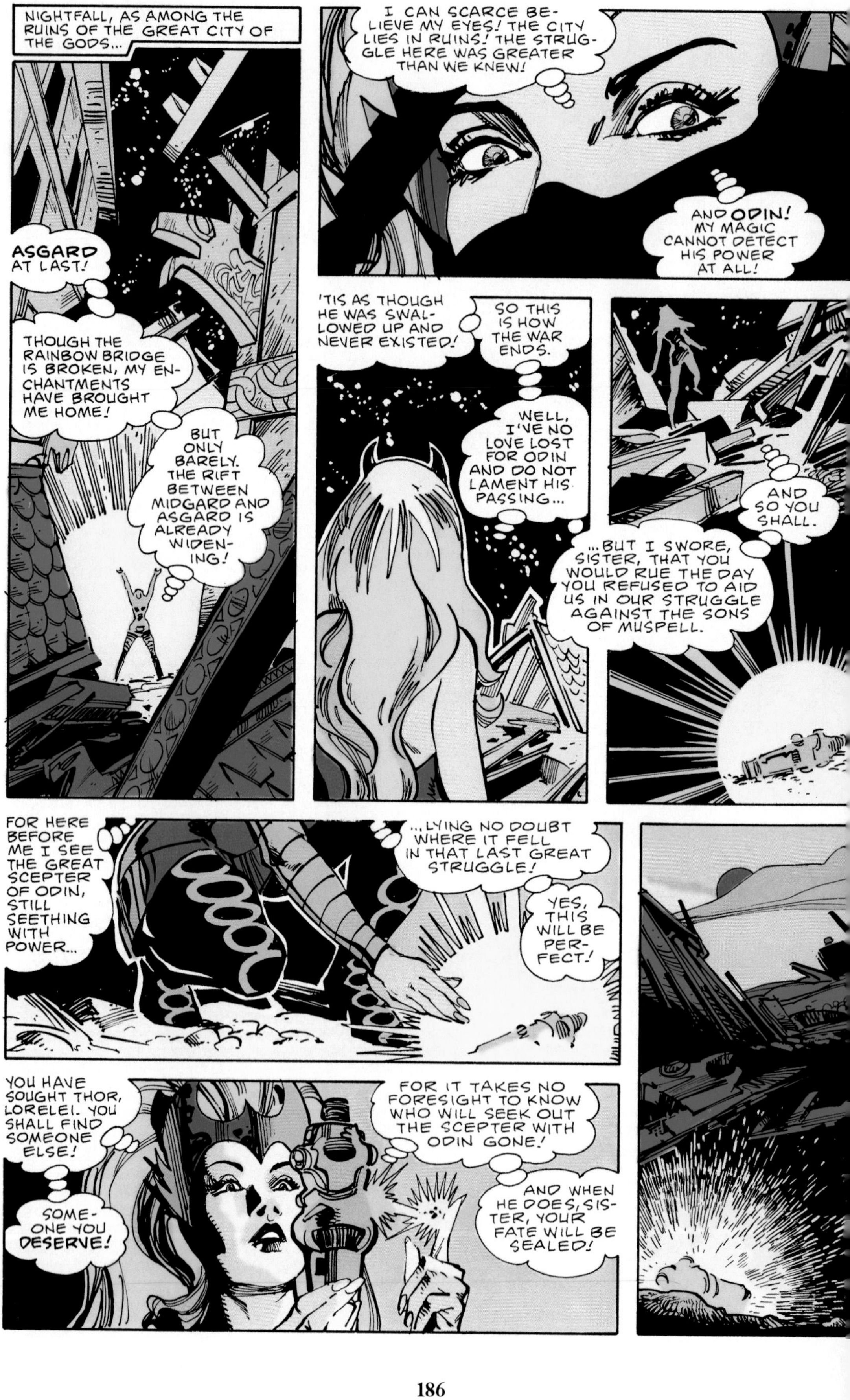

NIGHTFALL, AS AMONG THE RUINS OF THE GREAT CITY OF THE GODS...
ASGARD AT LAST!
THOUGH THE RAINBOW BRIDGE IS BROKEN, MY ENCHANTMENTS HAVE BROUGHT ME HOME!
BUT ONLY BARELY. THE RIFT BETWEEN MIDGARD AND ASGARD IS ALREADY WIDENING!
I CAN SCARCE BELIEVE MY EYES! THE CITY LIES IN RUINS! THE STRUGGLE HERE WAS GREATER THAN WE KNEW!
AND ODIN! MY MAGIC CANNOT DETECT HIS POWER AT ALL!
'TIS AS THOUGH HE WAS SWALLOWED UP AND NEVER EXISTED!
SO THIS IS HOW THE WAR ENDS.
WELL, I'VE NO LOVE LOST FOR ODIN AND DO NOT LAMENT HIS PASSING...
...BUT I SWORE, SISTER, THAT YOU WOULD RUE THE DAY YOU REFUSED TO AID US IN OUR STRUGGLE AGAINST THE SONS OF MUSPELL.
AND SO YOU SHALL.
FOR HERE BEFORE ME I SEE THE GREAT SCEPTER OF ODIN, STILL SEETHING WITH POWER...
...LYING NO DOUBT WHERE IT FELL IN THAT LAST GREAT STRUGGLE!
YES, THIS WILL BE PERFECT!
YOU HAVE SOUGHT THOR, LORELEI. YOU SHALL FIND SOMEONE ELSE!
SOMEONE YOU DESERVE!
FOR IT TAKES NO FORESIGHT TO KNOW WHO WILL SEEK OUT THE SCEPTER WITH ODIN GONE!
AND WHEN HE DOES, SISTER, YOUR FATE WILL BE SEALED!

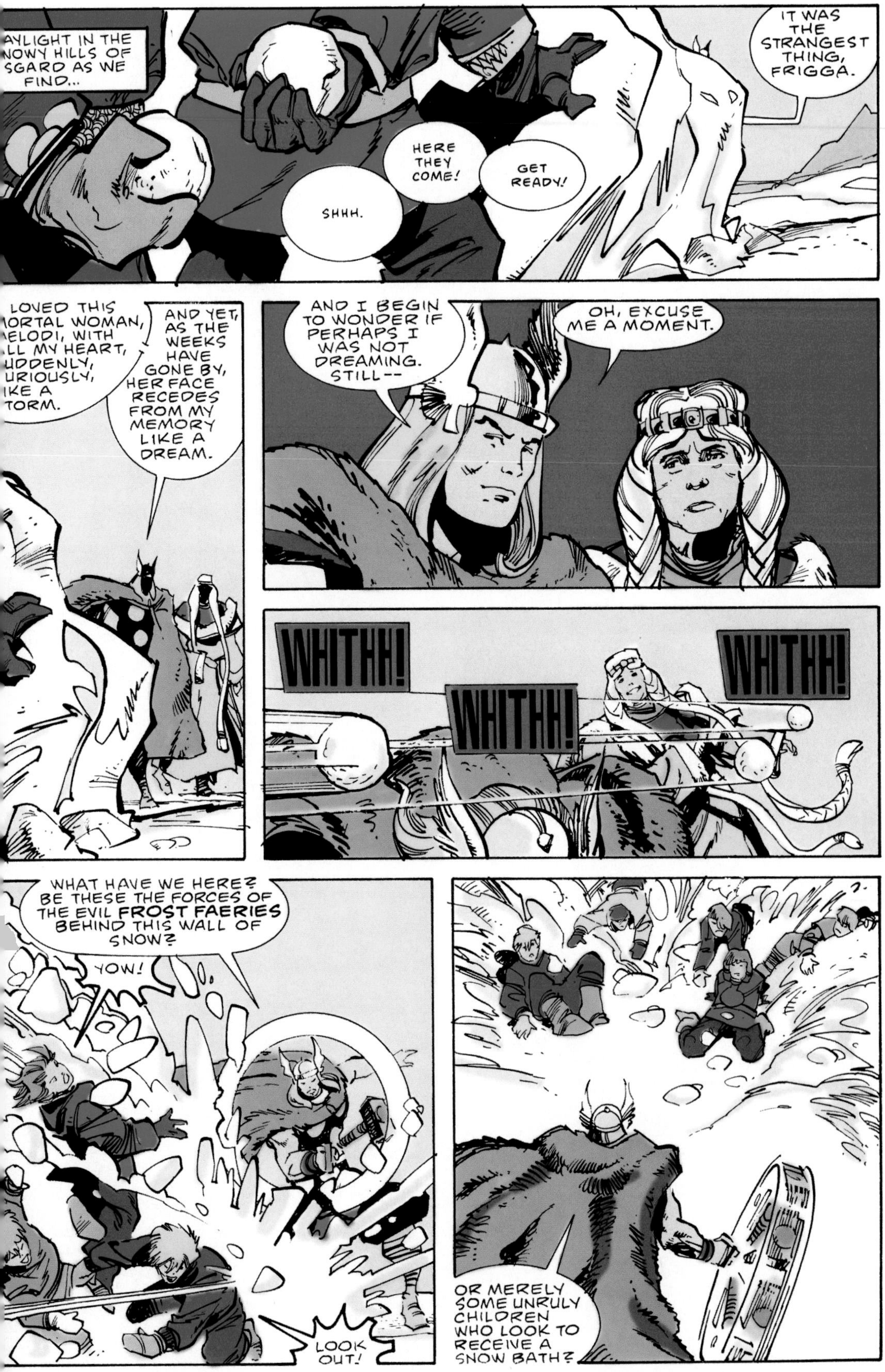
AYLIGHT IN THE NOWY HILLS OF SGARD AS WE FIND...
IT WAS THE STRANGEST THING, FRIGGA.
HERE THEY COME!
GET READY!
SHHH.
LOVED THIS ORTAL WOMAN, ELODI, WITH LL MY HEART, UDDENLY, URIOUSLY, IKE A TORM.
AND YET, AS THE WEEKS HAVE GONE BY, HER FACE RECEDES FROM MY MEMORY LIKE A DREAM.
AND I BEGIN TO WONDER IF PERHAPS I WAS NOT DREAMING. STILL--
OH, EXCUSE ME A MOMENT.
WHITHH!
WHITHH!
WHITHH!
WHAT HAVE WE HERE? BE THESE THE FORCES OF THE EVIL FROST FAERIES BEHIND THIS WALL OF SNOW?
YOW!
LOOK OUT!
OR MERELY SOME UNRULY CHILDREN WHO LOOK TO RECEIVE A SNOW BATH?

AND YET, I DO NOT SEE GUNN-HILD AMONG YOUR NUMBER!

SPLATT!

GOT HIM!

GREAT SHOT!

NICE GOING, HILDY!

LET'S GET OUT OF HERE!

YOU COULD HAVE AVOIDED THAT SNOWBALL, THOR.

I KNOW.

BUT IF THEY WERE NOT ENCOURAGED WITH SOME SMALL DEGREE OF SUCCESS, THE CHILDREN WOULD SOON TIRE OF THE GAME...

...AND THE ROAD HOME WOULD SEEM THAT MUCH LONGER.

AND YOUR ROAD, THOR?

I NO LONGER SEE IT CLEARLY, FRIGGA.

FOR AS THE FACE OF MY ODI RECEDES FROM MY SIGHT, THE VISAGE OF SIF SEEMS SHARPER AND CLEARER.

I DO NOT REGRET THAT SHE WENT WITH BILL. SHE CHOSE WELL.

MIDGARD AND ITS CONFINES ARE NOT FOR HER.

SHE HAD LOST THE SAVOR OF LIVING AND BILL AND HIS NOBLE QUEST PROVIDED IT.

YET MY HEART MISGIVES ME THAT I SHOULD NEVER HAVE LET HER GO, THAT I MAY HAVE LOST HER FOREVER.

AH, EXCUSE ME AGAIN.

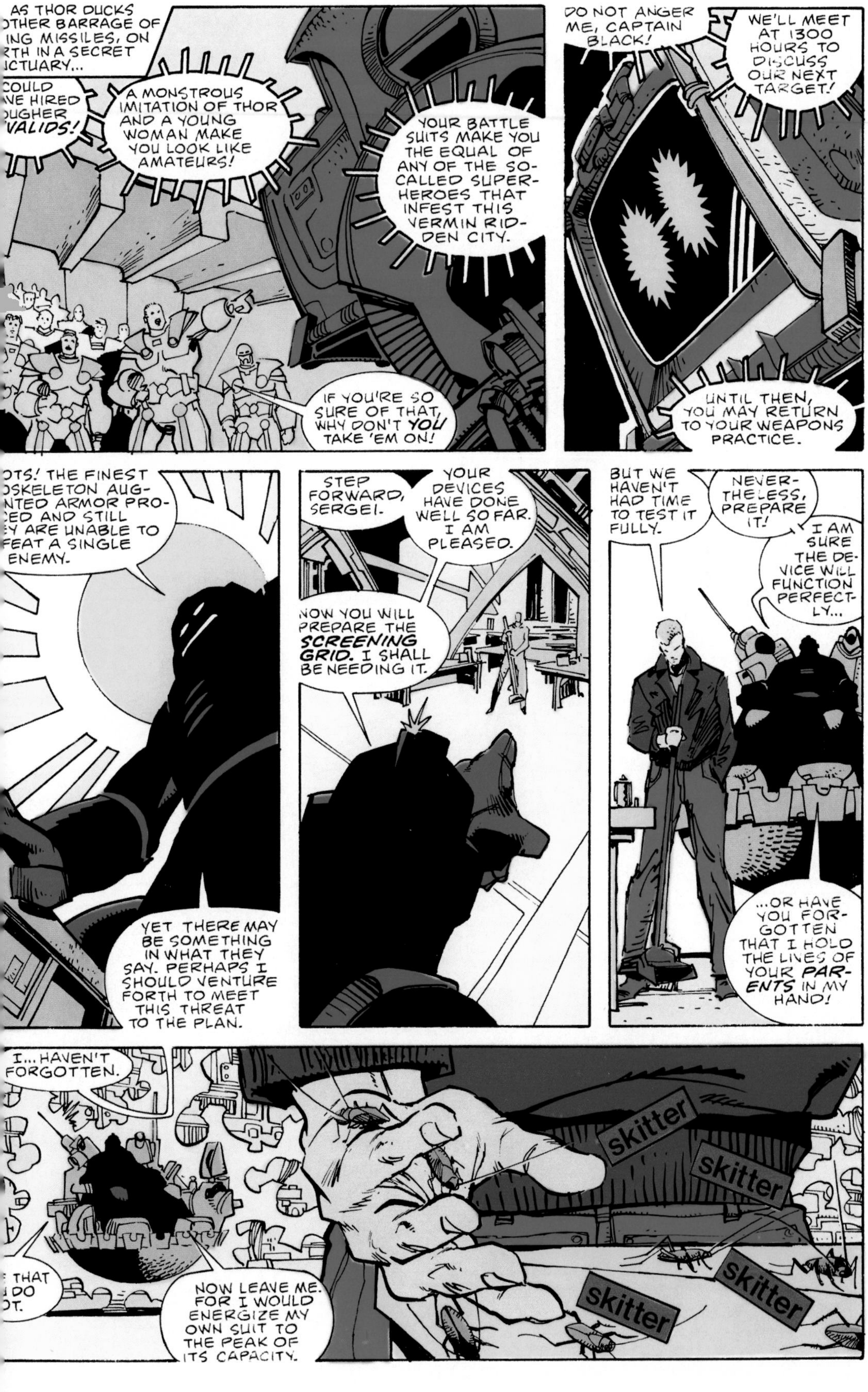
AS THOR DUCKS
OTHER BARRAGE OF
ING MISSILES, ON
RTH IN A SECRET
NCTUARY...
COULD
VE HIRED
OUGHER
VALIDS!
A MONSTROUS IMITATION OF THOR AND A YOUNG WOMAN MAKE YOU LOOK LIKE AMATEURS!
YOUR BATTLE SUITS MAKE YOU THE EQUAL OF ANY OF THE SO-CALLED SUPER-HEROES THAT INFEST THIS VERMIN RID-DEN CITY.
IF YOU'RE SO SURE OF THAT, WHY DON'T YOU TAKE 'EM ON!
DO NOT ANGER ME, CAPTAIN BLACK!
WE'LL MEET AT 1300 HOURS TO DISCUSS OUR NEXT TARGET!
UNTIL THEN, YOU MAY RETURN TO YOUR WEAPONS PRACTICE.
OTS! THE FINEST
OSKELETON AUG-
NTED ARMOR PRO-
CED AND STILL
EY ARE UNABLE TO
FEAT A SINGLE
ENEMY.
YET THERE MAY BE SOMETHING IN WHAT THEY SAY. PERHAPS I SHOULD VENTURE FORTH TO MEET THIS THREAT TO THE PLAN.
STEP FORWARD, SERGEI.
YOUR DEVICES HAVE DONE WELL SO FAR. I AM PLEASED.
NOW YOU WILL PREPARE THE SCREENING GRID. I SHALL BE NEEDING IT.
BUT WE HAVEN'T HAD TIME TO TEST IT FULLY.
NEVER-THELESS, PREPARE IT!
I AM SURE THE DE-VICE WILL FUNCTION PERFECT-LY...
...OR HAVE YOU FOR-GOTTEN THAT I HOLD THE LIVES OF YOUR PAR-ENTS IN MY HAND!
I...HAVEN'T FORGOTTEN.
THAT
DO
OT.
NOW LEAVE ME. FOR I WOULD ENERGIZE MY OWN SUIT TO THE PEAK OF ITS CAPACITY.
skitter
skitter
skitter
skitter

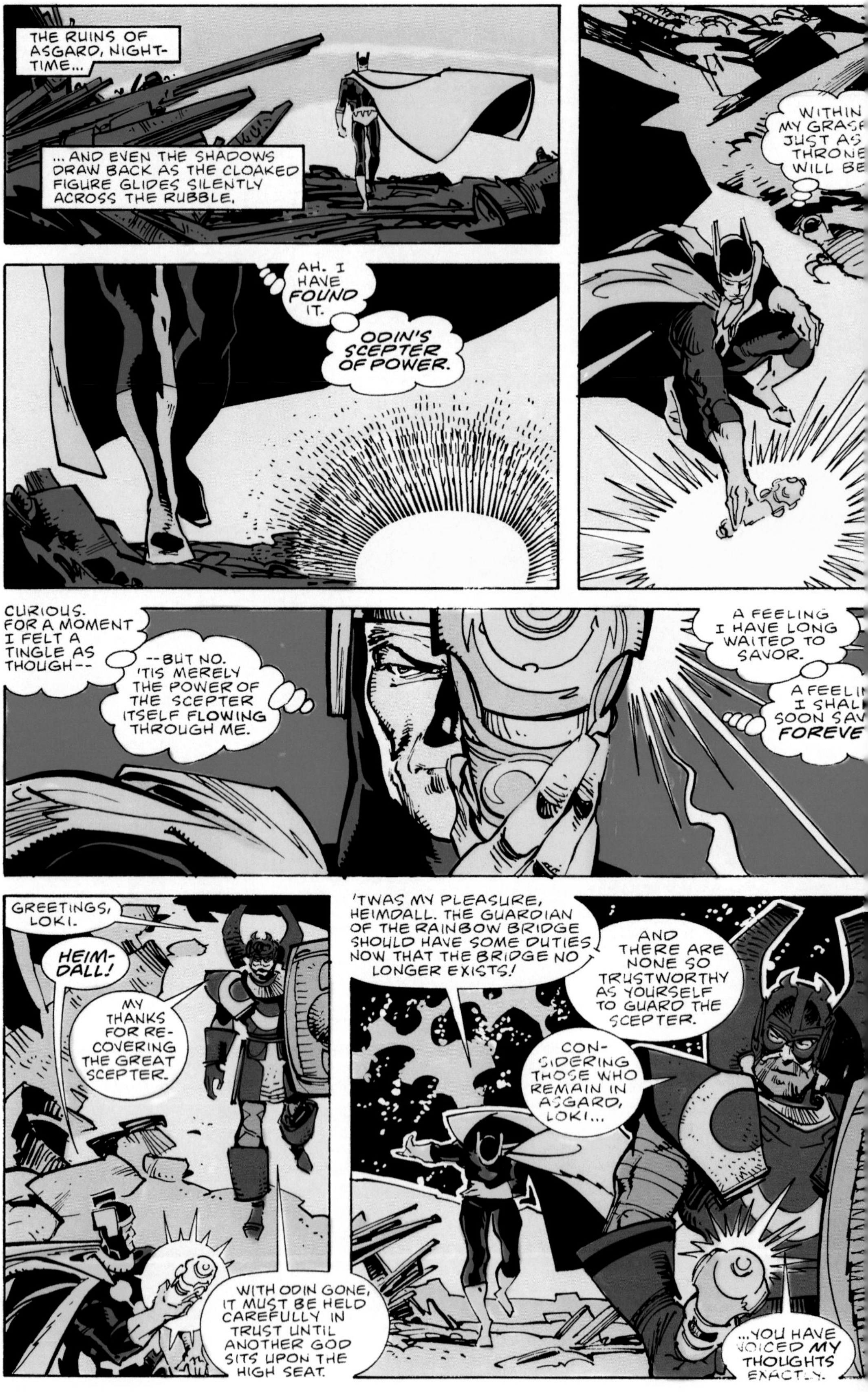
THE RUINS OF ASGARD, NIGHT-TIME...
...AND EVEN THE SHADOWS DRAW BACK AS THE CLOAKED FIGURE GLIDES SILENTLY ACROSS THE RUBBLE.
AH. I HAVE FOUND IT.
ODIN'S SCEPTER OF POWER.
WITHIN MY GRASP JUST AS THRONE WILL BE
CURIOUS. FOR A MOMENT I FELT A TINGLE AS THOUGH--
--BUT NO. 'TIS MERELY THE POWER OF THE SCEPTER ITSELF FLOWING THROUGH ME.
A FEELING I HAVE LONG WAITED TO SAVOR.
A FEELIN I SHALL SOON SAV FOREVE
GREETINGS, LOKI.
HEIM-DALL!
MY THANKS FOR RE-COVERING THE GREAT SCEPTER.
WITH ODIN GONE, IT MUST BE HELD CAREFULLY IN TRUST UNTIL ANOTHER GOD SITS UPON THE HIGH SEAT.
'TWAS MY PLEASURE, HEIMDALL. THE GUARDIAN OF THE RAINBOW BRIDGE SHOULD HAVE SOME DUTIES NOW THAT THE BRIDGE NO LONGER EXISTS!
AND THERE ARE NONE SO TRUSTWORTHY AS YOURSELF TO GUARD THE SCEPTER.
CON-SIDERING THOSE WHO REMAIN IN ASGARD, LOKI...
...YOU HAVE VOICED MY THOUGHTS EXACTLY.

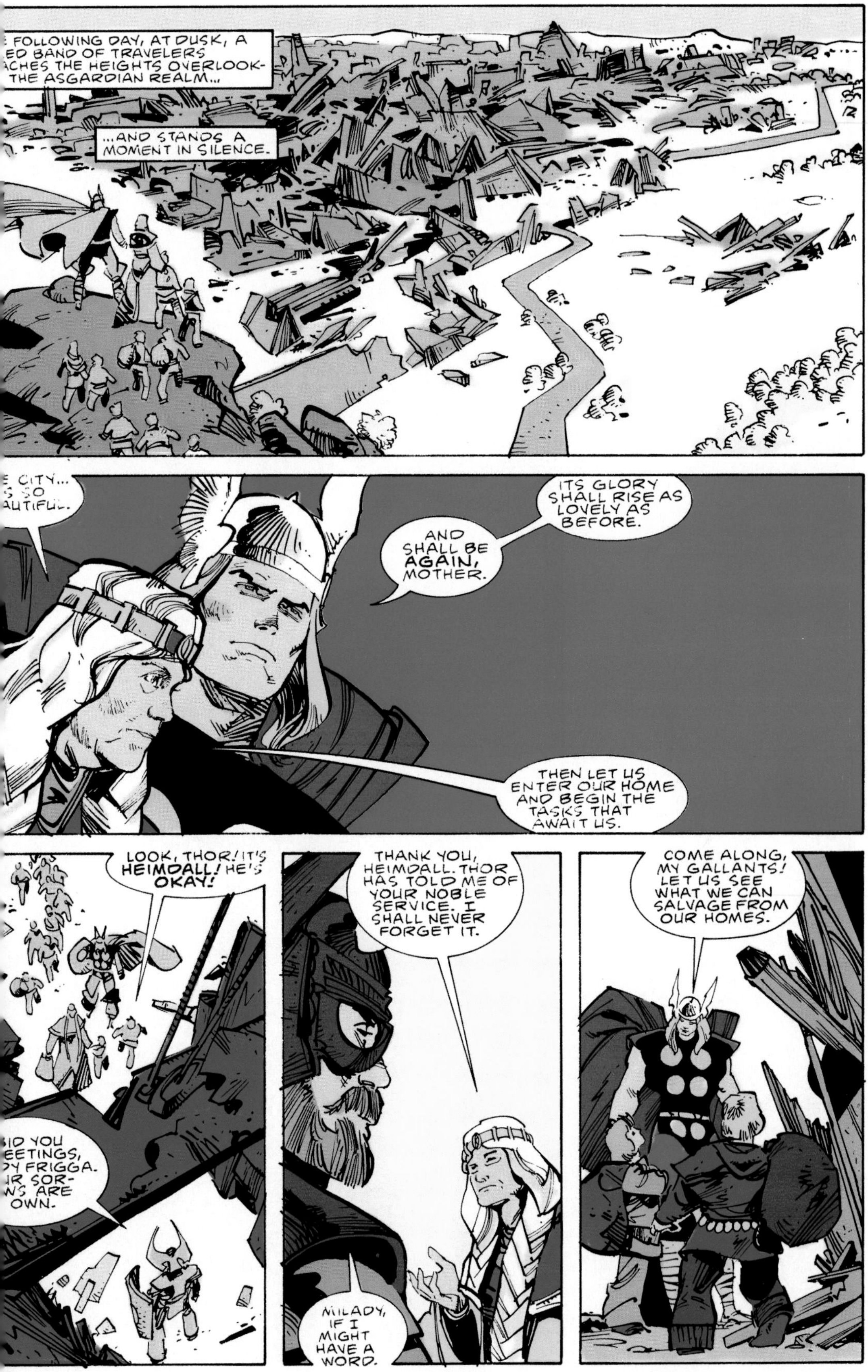
E FOLLOWING DAY, AT DUSK, A
ED BAND OF TRAVELERS
ACHES THE HEIGHTS OVERLOOK-
THE ASGARDIAN REALM...
...AND STANDS A MOMENT IN SILENCE.
E CITY... S SO AUTIFUL.
AND SHALL BE AGAIN, MOTHER.
ITS GLORY SHALL RISE AS LOVELY AS BEFORE.
THEN LET US ENTER OUR HOME AND BEGIN THE TASKS THAT AWAIT US.
LOOK, THOR! IT'S HEIMDALL! HE'S OKAY!
BID YOU EETINGS, DY FRIGGA. UR SOR- WS ARE OWN.
THANK YOU, HEIMDALL. THOR HAS TOLD ME OF YOUR NOBLE SERVICE. I SHALL NEVER FORGET IT.
MILADY, IF I MIGHT HAVE A WORD.
COME ALONG, MY GALLANTS! LET US SEE WHAT WE CAN SALVAGE FROM OUR HOMES.

SOONER WOULD I HAVE CUT OFF MY ARM THAN GIVE THIS GIFT, MILADY.

BUT THERE IS NO HELP FOR IT NOW.

AND NO ONE IS MORE WORTHY TO HOLD THIS SACRED TRUST.

THE GREAT SCEPTER, MILADY. THE SYMBOL OF ALL OUR HOPES...

...A? SOF ROW

FRIGGA! FRIGGA!

MY HOUSE IS GONE! AND I CAN'T FIND MY SKATES ANYWHERE!

WHERE'S MY MOMMY? I WANT MY DADDY!

WHY AREN'T THEY HERE?

SHUSH, MY LITTLE ONE, AND DRY YOUR TEARS.

YOUR PARENTS WILL BE HOME SOON, I PROMISE.

BUT NOW, I WANT YOU ALL TO STAY WITH ME UNTIL EVERYBODY'S PARENTS COME HOME.

WE SHOULD START B TRYING T FIND SOM SUPPER, DON'T YOU THINK?

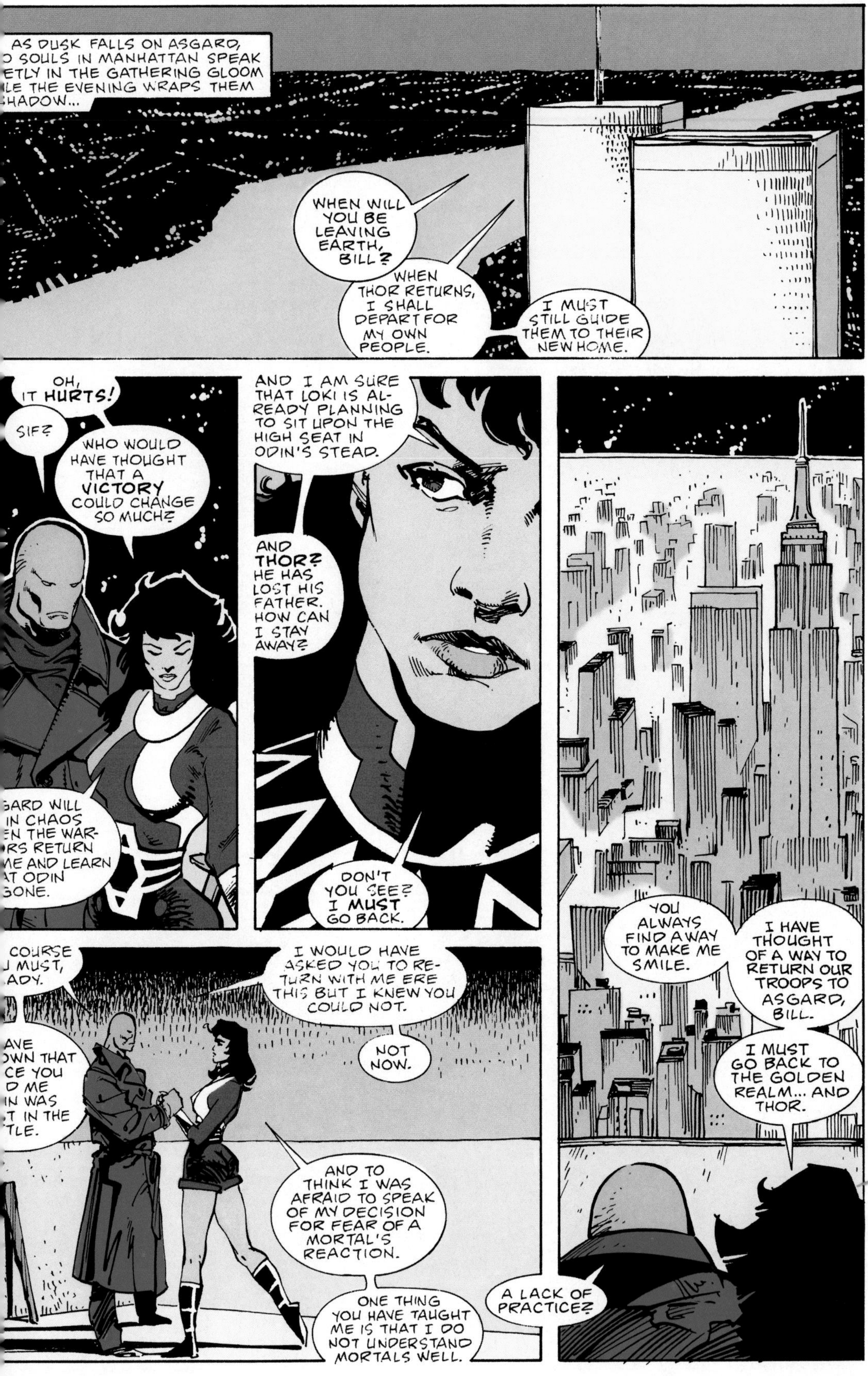
AS DUSK FALLS ON ASGARD, O SOULS IN MANHATTAN SPEAK ETLY IN THE GATHERING GLOOM LE THE EVENING WRAPS THEM SHADOW...
WHEN WILL YOU BE LEAVING EARTH, BILL?
WHEN THOR RETURNS, I SHALL DEPART FOR MY OWN PEOPLE.
I MUST STILL GUIDE THEM TO THEIR NEW HOME.
OH, IT HURTS!
SIF?
WHO WOULD HAVE THOUGHT THAT A VICTORY COULD CHANGE SO MUCH?
GARD WILL IN CHAOS EN THE WAR- RS RETURN ME AND LEARN AT ODIN GONE.
AND I AM SURE THAT LOKI IS AL- READY PLANNING TO SIT UPON THE HIGH SEAT IN ODIN'S STEAD.
AND THOR? HE HAS LOST HIS FATHER. HOW CAN I STAY AWAY?
DON'T YOU SEE? I MUST GO BACK.
COURSE U MUST, ADY.
I WOULD HAVE ASKED YOU TO RE- TURN WITH ME ERE THIS BUT I KNEW YOU COULD NOT.
NOT NOW.
AVE OWN THAT CE YOU D ME IN WAS T IN THE TLE.
AND TO THINK I WAS AFRAID TO SPEAK OF MY DECISION FOR FEAR OF A MORTAL'S REACTION.
ONE THING YOU HAVE TAUGHT ME IS THAT I DO NOT UNDERSTAND MORTALS WELL.
YOU ALWAYS FIND A WAY TO MAKE ME SMILE.
I HAVE THOUGHT OF A WAY TO RETURN OUR TROOPS TO ASGARD, BILL.
I MUST GO BACK TO THE GOLDEN REALM... AND THOR.
A LACK OF PRACTICE?

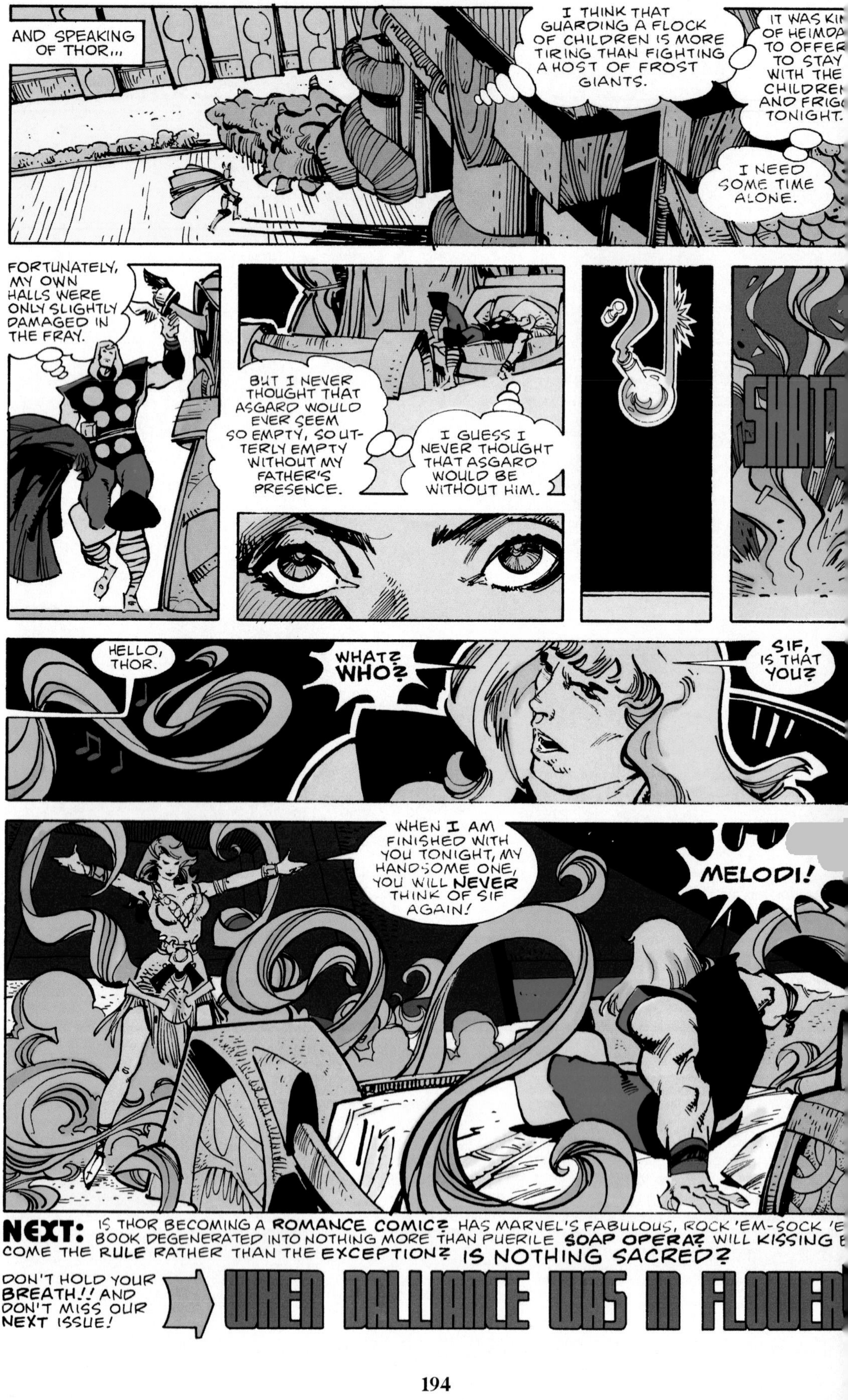
AND SPEAKING OF THOR...
I THINK THAT GUARDING A FLOCK OF CHILDREN IS MORE TIRING THAN FIGHTING A HOST OF FROST GIANTS.
IT WAS KIN OF HEIMDA TO OFFER TO STAY WITH THE CHILDREN AND FRIG TONIGHT.
I NEED SOME TIME ALONE.
FORTUNATELY, MY OWN HALLS WERE ONLY SLIGHTLY DAMAGED IN THE FRAY.
BUT I NEVER THOUGHT THAT ASGARD WOULD EVER SEEM SO EMPTY, SO UTTERLY EMPTY WITHOUT MY FATHER'S PRESENCE.
I GUESS I NEVER THOUGHT THAT ASGARD WOULD BE WITHOUT HIM.
SHATT
HELLO, THOR.
WHAT? WHO?
SIF, IS THAT YOU?
WHEN I AM FINISHED WITH YOU TONIGHT, MY HANDSOME ONE, YOU WILL NEVER THINK OF SIF AGAIN!
MELODI!
NEXT: IS THOR BECOMING A ROMANCE COMIC? HAS MARVEL'S FABULOUS, ROCK 'EM-SOCK 'E BOOK DEGENERATED INTO NOTHING MORE THAN PUERILE SOAP OPERA? WILL KISSING B COME THE RULE RATHER THAN THE EXCEPTION? IS NOTHING SACRED?
DON'T HOLD YOUR BREATH!! AND DON'T MISS OUR NEXT ISSUE!
WHEN DALLIANCE WAS IN FLOWER

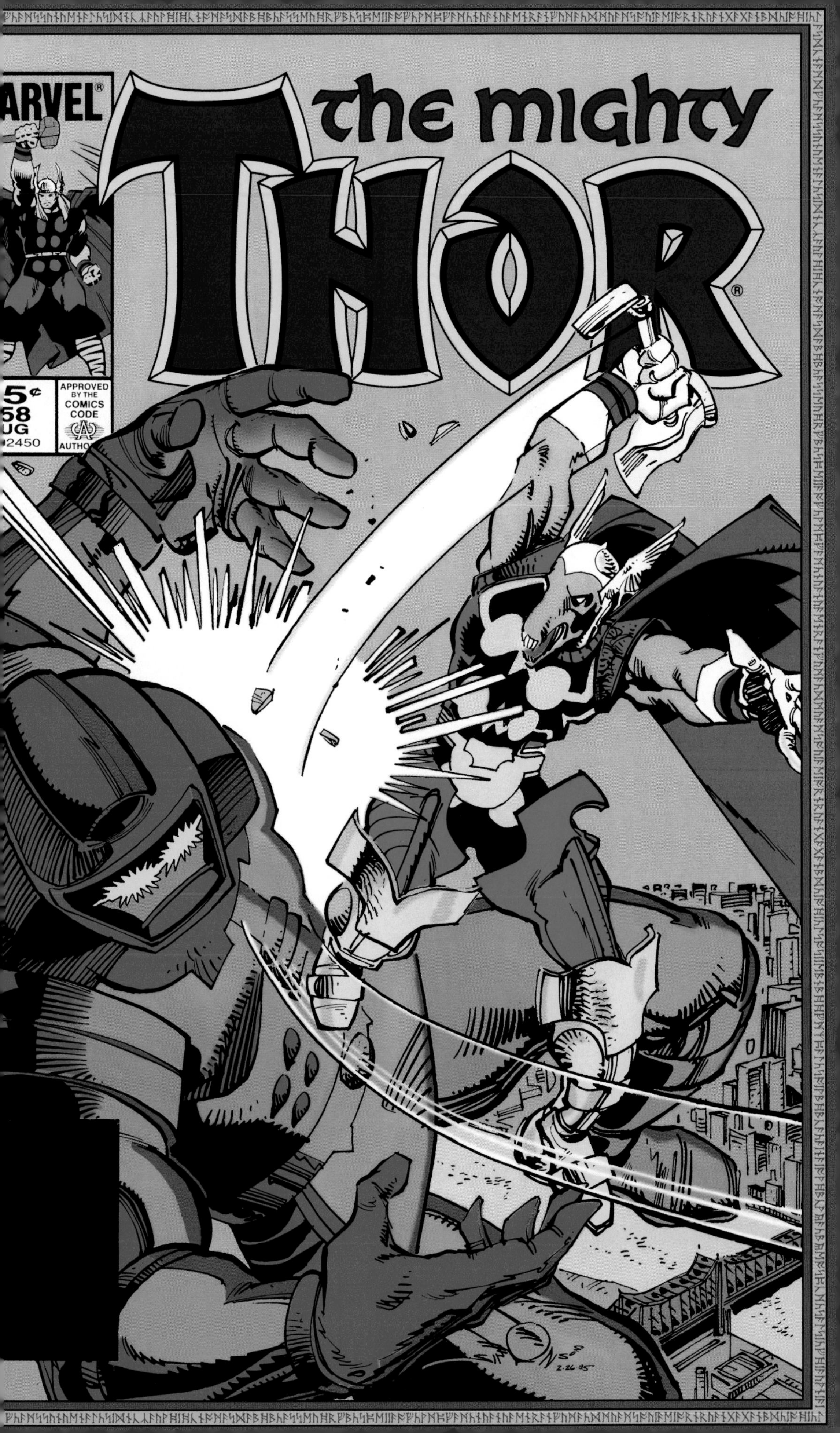
the mighty
THOR
APPROVED BY THE COMICS CODE

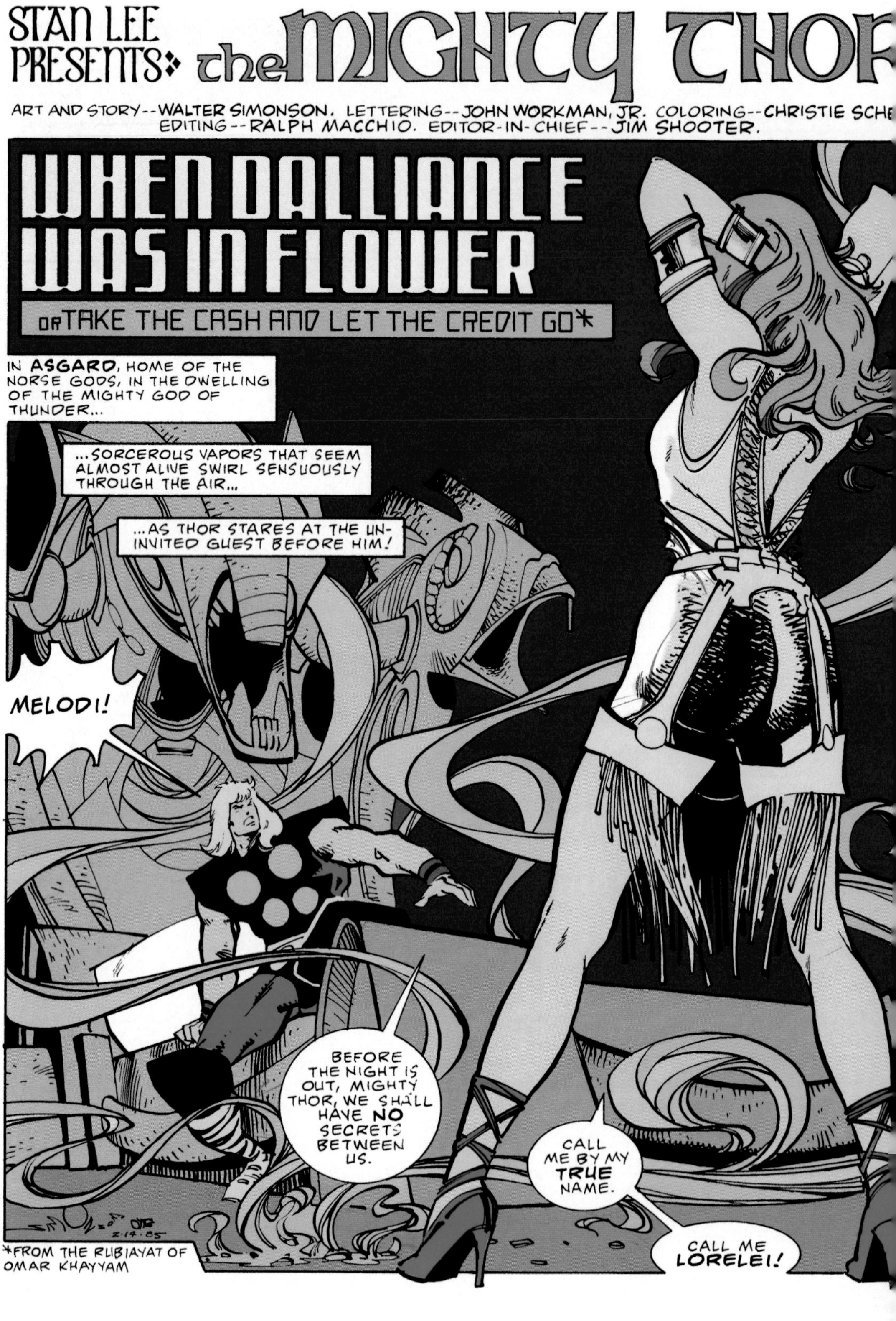

STAN LEE PRESENTS: the MIGHTY THOR
ART AND STORY--WALTER SIMONSON. LETTERING--JOHN WORKMAN, JR. COLORING--CHRISTIE SCHE
EDITING--RALPH MACCHIO. EDITOR-IN-CHIEF--JIM SHOOTER.
WHEN DALLIANCE WAS IN FLOWER
OR TAKE THE CASH AND LET THE CREDIT GO*
IN ASGARD, HOME OF THE NORSE GODS, IN THE DWELLING OF THE MIGHTY GOD OF THUNDER...
...SORCEROUS VAPORS THAT SEEM ALMOST ALIVE SWIRL SENSUOUSLY THROUGH THE AIR...
...AS THOR STARES AT THE UN-INVITED GUEST BEFORE HIM!
MELODI!
BEFORE THE NIGHT IS OUT, MIGHTY THOR, WE SHALL HAVE NO SECRETS BETWEEN US.
CALL ME BY MY TRUE NAME.
CALL ME LORELEI!
*FROM THE RUBIAYAT OF OMAR KHAYYAM

I WAS **RIGHT!** THE MAGICAL VAPORS HAVE ALREADY BEGUN TO **ENTHRALL** HIM.

HE CAN NO LONGER LOOK AWAY FROM ME OF HIS OWN FREE WILL.

LORELEI? BUT THAT WAS THE NAME OF THE ENCHANTRESS' YOUNGER SISTER WHO WAS BUT A CHILD WHEN I LAST SAW HER.

HAVE I NOT **GROWN** SINCE THEN, LORD THOR?

WHY DOES MY HEAD SWIM SO?

I...I CANNOT SEE THE ROOM.

AND IS A ROOM MORE INTEREST-ING THAN I?

GAZE AT ME, THOR. DRINK WITH THINE EYES ALL THAT YOU SEE BEFORE YOU.

WHAT IS HAPPEN-ING TO ME?

AM I NOT **BEAUTI-FUL**, THOR?

YES, YOU ARE.

DO I NOT PLEASE THEE?

YOU ARE DE-SIRABLE BE-YOND WORDS.

THEN I AM **YOURS...**

...AND YOU...

...ARE **MINE!**

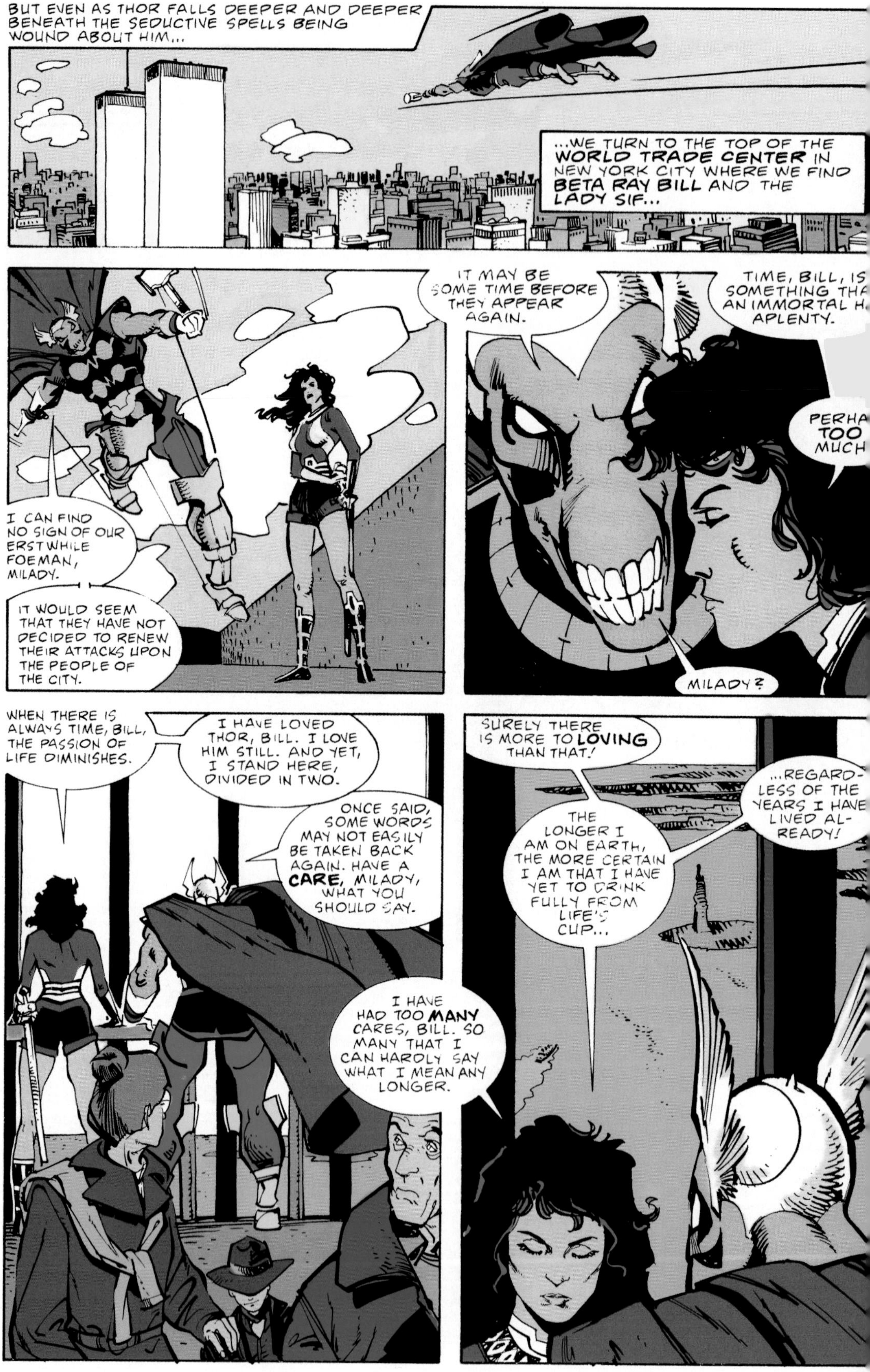

BUT EVEN AS THOR FALLS DEEPER AND DEEPER BENEATH THE SEDUCTIVE SPELLS BEING WOUND ABOUT HIM...
...WE TURN TO THE TOP OF THE WORLD TRADE CENTER IN NEW YORK CITY WHERE WE FIND BETA RAY BILL AND THE LADY SIF...
I CAN FIND NO SIGN OF OUR ERSTWHILE FOEMAN, MILADY.
IT WOULD SEEM THAT THEY HAVE NOT DECIDED TO RENEW THEIR ATTACKS UPON THE PEOPLE OF THE CITY.
IT MAY BE SOME TIME BEFORE THEY APPEAR AGAIN.
TIME, BILL, IS SOMETHING THA AN IMMORTAL HA APLENTY.
PERHA TOO MUCH
MILADY?
WHEN THERE IS ALWAYS TIME, BILL, THE PASSION OF LIFE DIMINISHES.
I HAVE LOVED THOR, BILL. I LOVE HIM STILL. AND YET, I STAND HERE, DIVIDED IN TWO.
ONCE SAID, SOME WORDS MAY NOT EASILY BE TAKEN BACK AGAIN. HAVE A CARE, MILADY, WHAT YOU SHOULD SAY.
I HAVE HAD TOO MANY CARES, BILL. SO MANY THAT I CAN HARDLY SAY WHAT I MEAN ANY LONGER.
SURELY THERE IS MORE TO LOVING THAN THAT!
THE LONGER I AM ON EARTH, THE MORE CERTAIN I AM THAT I HAVE YET TO DRINK FULLY FROM LIFE'S CUP...
...REGARDLESS OF THE YEARS I HAVE LIVED ALREADY!

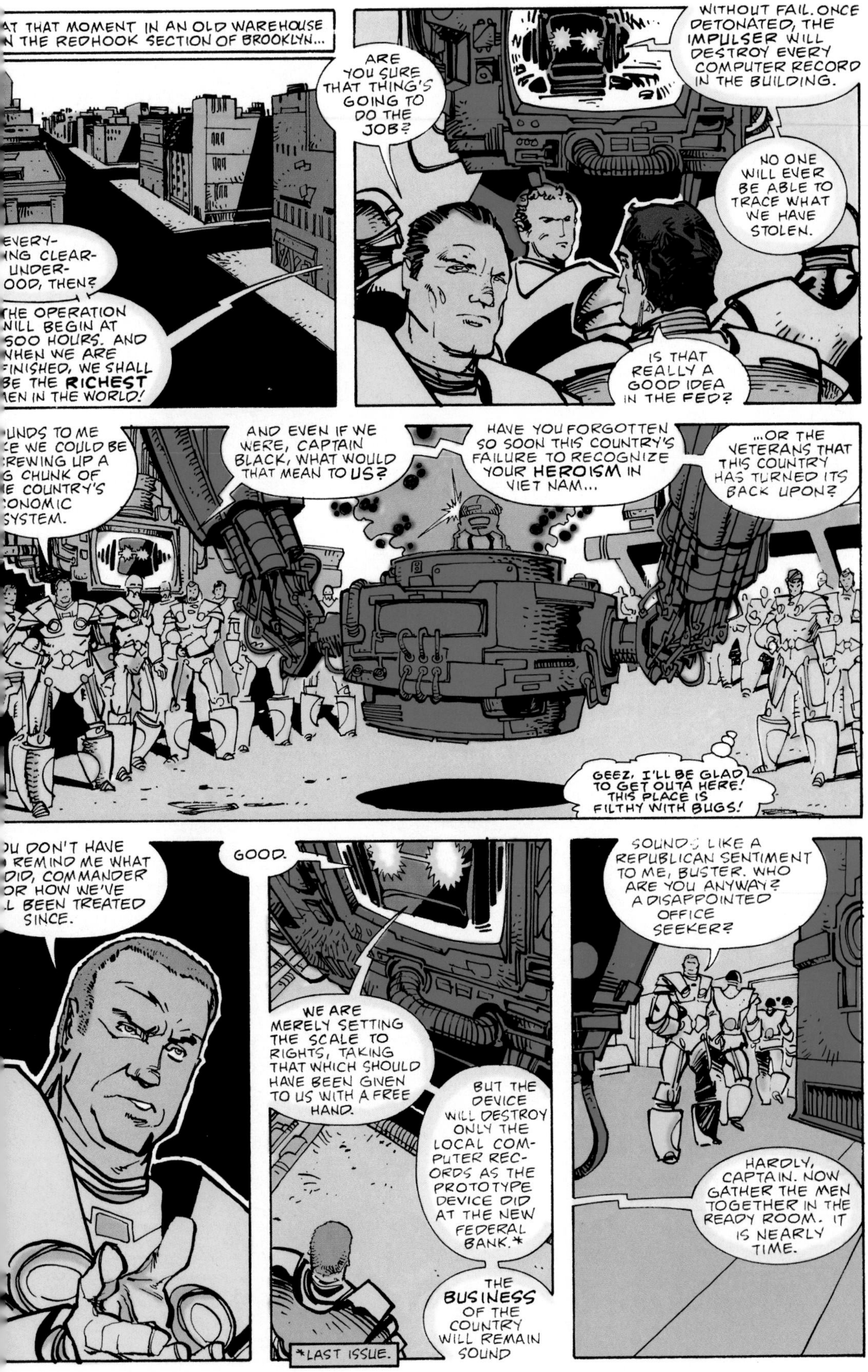
AT THAT MOMENT IN AN OLD WAREHOUSE IN THE REDHOOK SECTION OF BROOKLYN...
EVERYTHING CLEAR-UNDERSTOOD, THEN?
THE OPERATION WILL BEGIN AT 1500 HOURS. AND WHEN WE ARE FINISHED, WE SHALL BE THE RICHEST MEN IN THE WORLD!
ARE YOU SURE THAT THING'S GOING TO DO THE JOB?
WITHOUT FAIL. ONCE DETONATED, THE IMPULSER WILL DESTROY EVERY COMPUTER RECORD IN THE BUILDING.
NO ONE WILL EVER BE ABLE TO TRACE WHAT WE HAVE STOLEN.
IS THAT REALLY A GOOD IDEA IN THE FED?
SOUNDS TO ME LIKE WE COULD BE SCREWING UP A BIG CHUNK OF THE COUNTRY'S ECONOMIC SYSTEM.
AND EVEN IF WE WERE, CAPTAIN BLACK, WHAT WOULD THAT MEAN TO US?
HAVE YOU FORGOTTEN SO SOON THIS COUNTRY'S FAILURE TO RECOGNIZE YOUR HEROISM IN VIET NAM...
...OR THE VETERANS THAT THIS COUNTRY HAS TURNED ITS BACK UPON?
GEEZ, I'LL BE GLAD TO GET OUTA HERE! THIS PLACE IS FILTHY WITH BUGS!
YOU DON'T HAVE TO REMIND ME WHAT I DID, COMMANDER OR HOW WE'VE ALL BEEN TREATED SINCE.
GOOD.
WE ARE MERELY SETTING THE SCALE TO RIGHTS, TAKING THAT WHICH SHOULD HAVE BEEN GIVEN TO US WITH A FREE HAND.
BUT THE DEVICE WILL DESTROY ONLY THE LOCAL COMPUTER RECORDS AS THE PROTOTYPE DEVICE DID AT THE NEW FEDERAL BANK.*
THE BUSINESS OF THE COUNTRY WILL REMAIN SOUND
*LAST ISSUE.
SOUNDS LIKE A REPUBLICAN SENTIMENT TO ME, BUSTER. WHO ARE YOU ANYWAY? A DISAPPOINTED OFFICE SEEKER?
HARDLY, CAPTAIN. NOW GATHER THE MEN TOGETHER IN THE READY ROOM. IT IS NEARLY TIME.

SERGEI, I MAY NEED TO DEAL WITH THAT THOR-LIKE MONSTROSITY MYSELF.

YOU MAY BEGIN FINAL ASSEMBLY OF THE **SCREENING DEVICE.**

WHAT ABOUT MY **PARENTS?**

SAFE, I ASSURE YOU. AND ONLY YOUR CONTINUED COOPERATION ASSURES THAT THEY REMAIN SO.

THE COMMUNICATIONS ALERT! A CODED SIGNAL IS BEING SENT FROM HOME.

GREETINGS, COMRADE. I HAVE GOOD NEWS CONCERNING THE IMPENDING SUCCESS OF OUR PROJECT.

THE TEST AT THE NEW FEDERAL BANK WAS SUCCESSFUL. THE FULL-SCALE COMPUTER FEEDBACK IMPULSER WILL BE ACTIVATED SHORTLY.

AND WITHIN SECONDS, **EVERY** COMPUTER IN THE UNITED STATES CONNECTED TO THE INTERFACE WILL BE OVERLOADED AND **BURNED OUT!**

COMPUTER RECORDS IN BANKS EVERYWHERE WILL BE DESTROYED. AND THE COMPUTERS RENDERED USELESS.

THE UNITED STATES ECONOMY, WITHOUT ACCURATE FINANCIAL RECORDS, WILL BE SHATTERED. AND WE SHALL PICK UP THE PIECES.

AND THE **GLF?**

DISAFFECTED VETERANS OF VIET NAM WHO FEEL THEY HAVE BEEN IGNORED BY THEIR COUNTRY. THEY SUSPECT **NOTHING!**

EXCELLENT, COMRADE BORIS.

BUT THERE IS BAD NEWS CONCERNING SERGEI'S PARENTS. THEY HAVE BOTH **DIED.** WE CAN NO LONGER USE THEM AS A HOLD OVER HIM.

CRCH

WHAT?

AN UNFORTUNATE OCCURRENCE THAT WAS NONE OF OUR DOING, I ASSURE YOU, COMRADE.

WE MUST **KEEP** THE NEWS FROM SERGEI FOR A LITTLE LONGER.

ONCE THIS EPISODE IS FINISHED, IT MAY EVEN WORK TO OUR ADVANTAGE.

IF WE DEMONSTRATE TO THE UNITED STATES GOVERNMENT THAT WE KNEW OF HIS PARENTS' DEATHS BEFORE THE IMPULSER WAS ACTIVATED...

...WE MAY BE ABLE TO PERSUADE THEM THAT SERGEI IS A **TRAITOR** AND DRIVE HIM EVEN DEEPER INTO OUR ARMS!

WE CAN USE HIS GENIUS!

[SOME]WHERE, NEAR CENTRAL PARK, AS SOME OF THE TROOPS [INV]OLVED IN THE RECENT FIGHTING* PREPARE TO DEPART...

...THE ASGARDIAN WARRIORS MINGLE WITH THEIR MORTAL COUNTERPARTS AND DISCUSS TOPICS OF MUTUAL INTEREST.

CAN'T BELIEVE YOU GUYS ARE ACTUALLY USING SWORDS IN A FIRE FIGHT.

* THOR 350-353 IF YOU MISSED IT!

BUT I'LL SAY THIS, HAROKIN. YOU SURE KNOW HOW TO SWING 'EM.

MY DEEPEST THANKS, PETER.

YET I WOULD LEARN MORE OF YOUR OWN DEADLY WEAPON, FOR WE HAVE NONE LIKE IT IN VALHALLA.

[YE]AH, WELL, I'LL [TE]LL YOU, OLD [BU]DDY. IF YOU HAD [A] FEW OF THESE [M-]16'S WITH YOU...

...YOU'D [BE] ABLE TO [CL]EAN UP [VA]LHALLA IN [N]O TIME!

MEANWHILE, IN ASGARD...

LORELEI, MY DARLING, I HAVE NEVER LOVED ANYONE AS I LOVE THEE NOW!

I KNOW, THOR. NOW TELL ME, WHAT ARE THESE THINGS?

A GIFT FROM MY FATHER, ODIN. HE AWARDED ME THE TUSKS OF THE FIRST GREAT BOAR I SLEW.

BREAK THEM.

MY LOVE?

IF YOU TRULY LOVED ME, YOU WOULD NOT HESITATE.

AS YOU COMMAND, MY DEAREST.

GRIND!

NOW THOU ART TRULY MINE! GIVE HEED TO WHAT I SAY, MY THOR!

WHO WILL RULE IN ASGARD NOW THAT YOUR FATHER IS GONE?

201

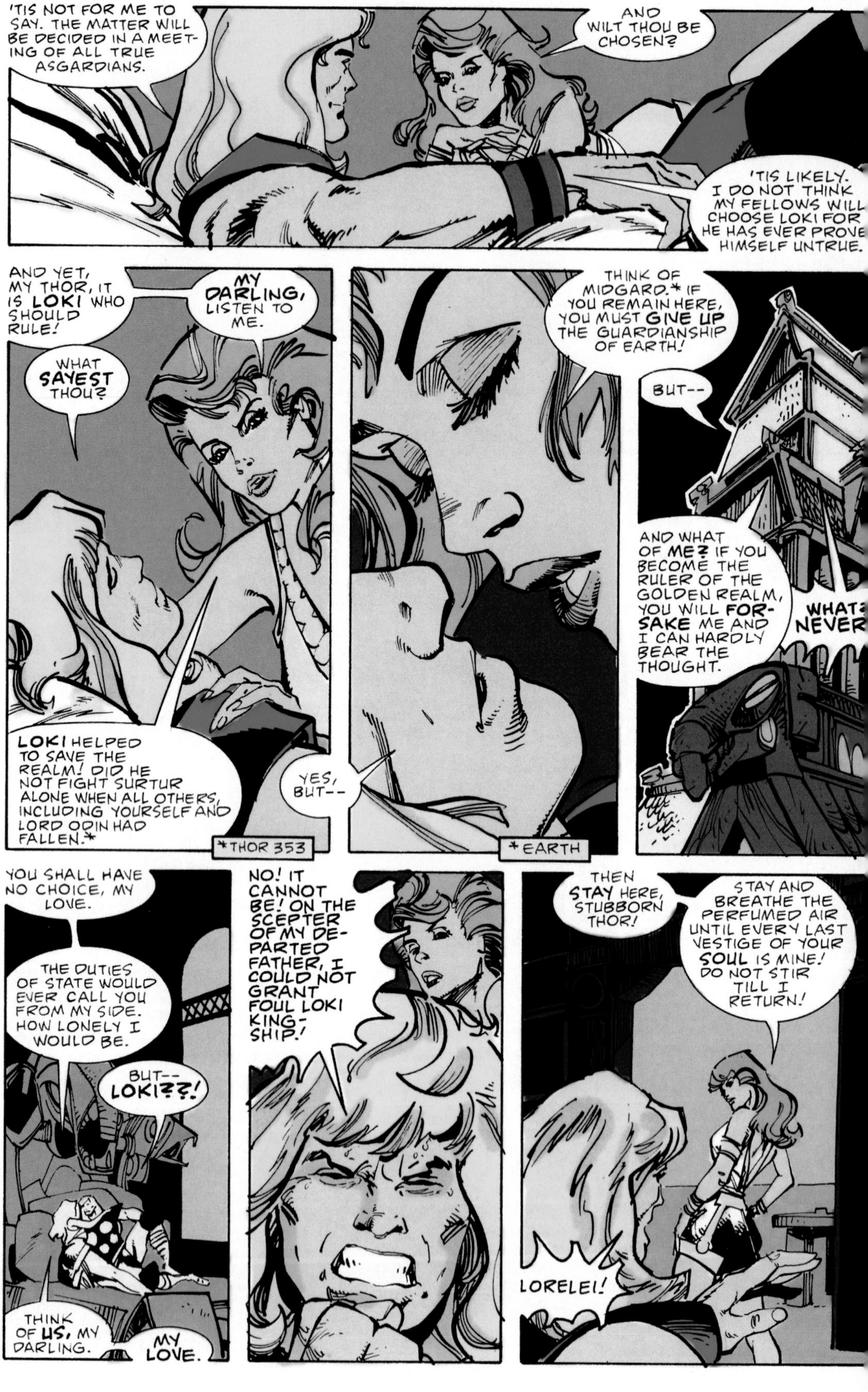
'TIS NOT FOR ME TO SAY. THE MATTER WILL BE DECIDED IN A MEETING OF ALL TRUE ASGARDIANS.
AND WILT THOU BE CHOSEN?
'TIS LIKELY. I DO NOT THINK MY FELLOWS WILL CHOOSE LOKI FOR HE HAS EVER PROVE HIMSELF UNTRUE.
AND YET, MY THOR, IT IS LOKI WHO SHOULD RULE!
MY DARLING, LISTEN TO ME.
WHAT SAYEST THOU?
LOKI HELPED TO SAVE THE REALM! DID HE NOT FIGHT SURTUR ALONE WHEN ALL OTHERS, INCLUDING YOURSELF AND LORD ODIN HAD FALLEN.*
*THOR 353
THINK OF MIDGARD.* IF YOU REMAIN HERE, YOU MUST GIVE UP THE GUARDIANSHIP OF EARTH!
YES, BUT--
*EARTH
BUT--
AND WHAT OF ME? IF YOU BECOME THE RULER OF THE GOLDEN REALM, YOU WILL FORSAKE ME AND I CAN HARDLY BEAR THE THOUGHT.
WHAT? NEVER
YOU SHALL HAVE NO CHOICE, MY LOVE.
THE DUTIES OF STATE WOULD EVER CALL YOU FROM MY SIDE. HOW LONELY I WOULD BE.
BUT-- LOKI??!
THINK OF US, MY DARLING.
MY LOVE.
NO! IT CANNOT BE! ON THE SCEPTER OF MY DEPARTED FATHER, I COULD NOT GRANT FOUL LOKI KINGSHIP!
THEN STAY HERE, STUBBORN THOR!
STAY AND BREATHE THE PERFUMED AIR UNTIL EVERY LAST VESTIGE OF YOUR SOUL IS MINE! DO NOT STIR TILL I RETURN!
LORELEI!

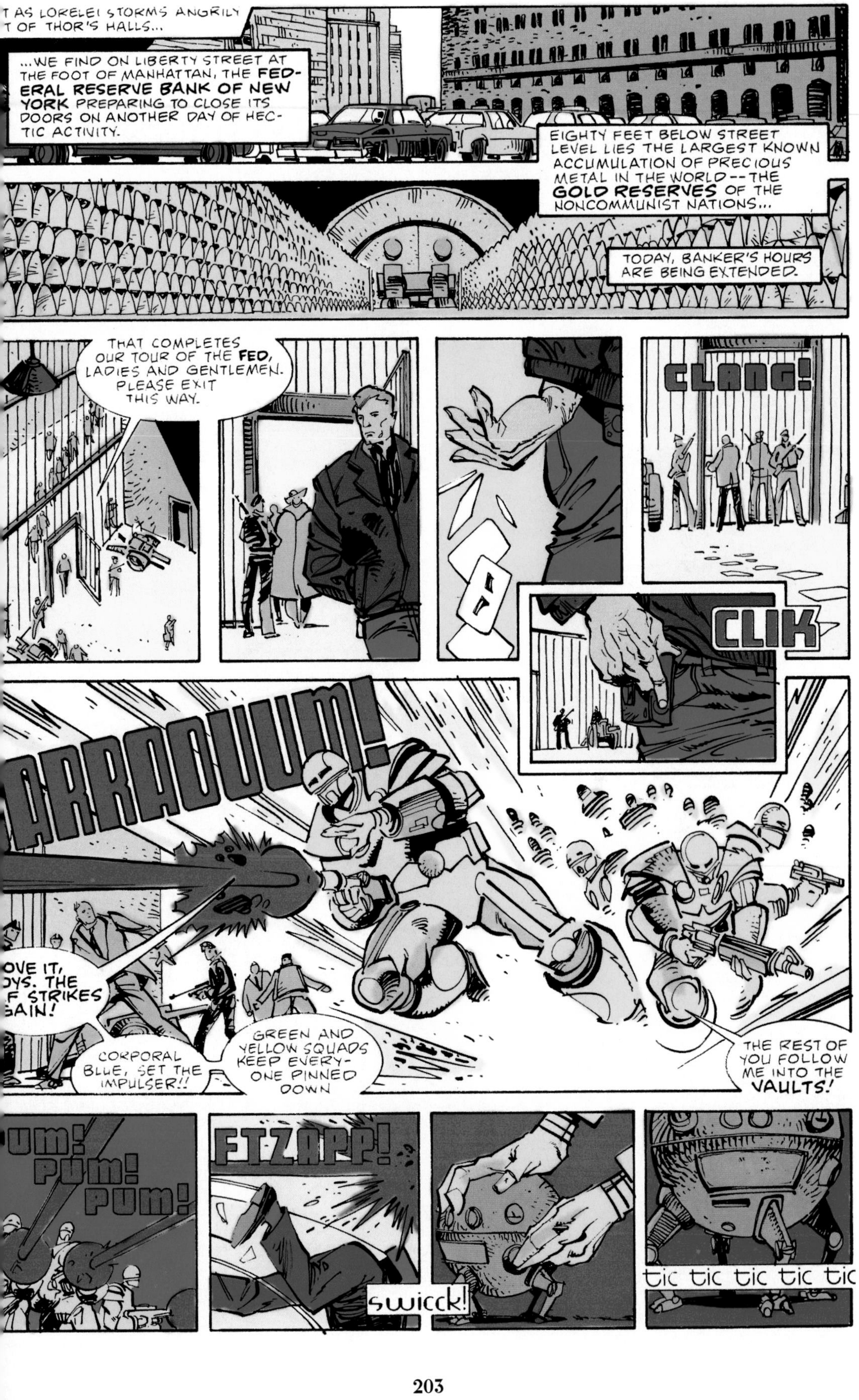

T AS LORELEI STORMS ANGRILY
T OF THOR'S HALLS...
...WE FIND ON LIBERTY STREET AT THE FOOT OF MANHATTAN, THE FEDERAL RESERVE BANK OF NEW YORK PREPARING TO CLOSE ITS DOORS ON ANOTHER DAY OF HECTIC ACTIVITY.
EIGHTY FEET BELOW STREET LEVEL LIES THE LARGEST KNOWN ACCUMULATION OF PRECIOUS METAL IN THE WORLD -- THE GOLD RESERVES OF THE NONCOMMUNIST NATIONS...
TODAY, BANKER'S HOURS ARE BEING EXTENDED.
THAT COMPLETES OUR TOUR OF THE FED, LADIES AND GENTLEMEN. PLEASE EXIT THIS WAY.
CLANG!
CLIK
ARRAOUUM!
OVE IT, OYS. THE F STRIKES GAIN!
CORPORAL BLUE, SET THE IMPULSER!!
GREEN AND YELLOW SQUADS KEEP EVERYONE PINNED DOWN
THE REST OF YOU FOLLOW ME INTO THE VAULTS!
UM! PUM! PUM!
FTZAPP!
swicck!
tic tic tic tic tic

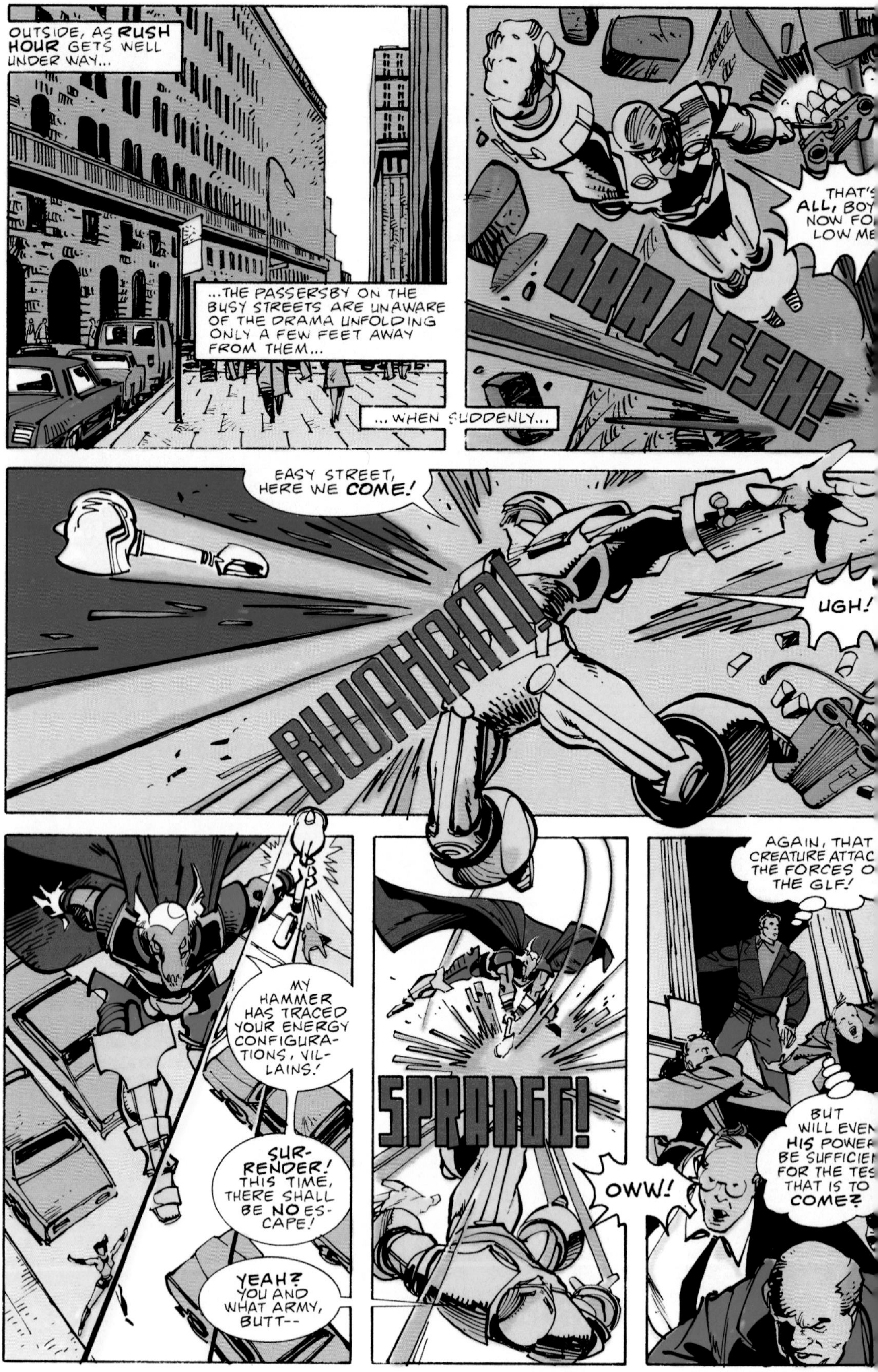

OUTSIDE, AS RUSH HOUR GETS WELL UNDER WAY...
...THE PASSERSBY ON THE BUSY STREETS ARE UNAWARE OF THE DRAMA UNFOLDING ONLY A FEW FEET AWAY FROM THEM...
...WHEN SUDDENLY...
KARASSH!
THAT'S ALL, BOY NOW FO LOW ME
EASY STREET, HERE WE COME!
BWHAM!
UGH!
MY HAMMER HAS TRACED YOUR ENERGY CONFIGURATIONS, VILLAINS!
SURRENDER! THIS TIME, THERE SHALL BE NO ESCAPE!
YEAH? YOU AND WHAT ARMY, BUTT--
SPRANGG!
OWW!
AGAIN, THAT CREATURE ATTAC THE FORCES O THE GLF!
BUT WILL EVEN HIS POWER BE SUFFICIE FOR THE TES THAT IS TO COME?

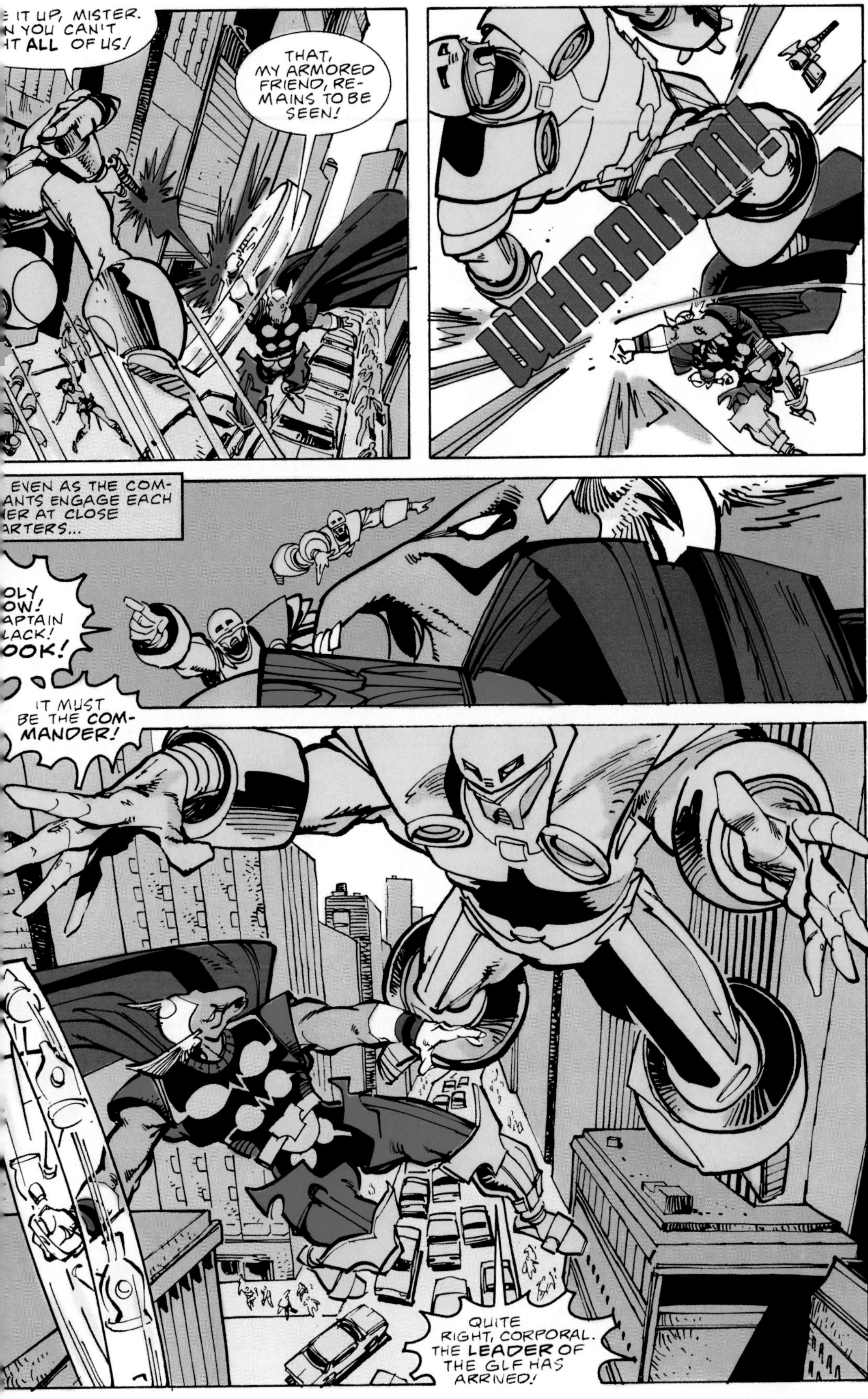
E IT UP, MISTER. N YOU CAN'T IT ALL OF US!
THAT, MY ARMORED FRIEND, RE-MAINS TO BE SEEN!
WHRAMM!
EVEN AS THE COM-ANTS ENGAGE EACH ER AT CLOSE ARTERS...
OLY OW! APTAIN LACK! OOK!
IT MUST BE THE COM-MANDER!
QUITE RIGHT, CORPORAL. THE LEADER OF THE GLF HAS ARRIVED!

MEANWHILE, IN A SLIGHTLY SHABBY SECTION OF MANHATTAN...

METHINKS, FRIEND VOLSTAGG, THAT WE HAVE **LOST** THE PARK WHEREIN OUR FELLOW ASGARDI-ANS ARE BIVOUACKED.

AND OUR MORTAL GUIDE SEEMS SINGULARLY UNWILLING TO DIRECT US FURTHER.

PERHAPS IF YOU HAD NOT **BROKEN** THE REAR **AXLE** OF HIS CONVEYANCE, HE WOULD HAVE PROVEN FRIENDLIER.

FAGH! THESE METAL CHARIOTS ARE NOT **FIT** TO BEAR SO NOBLE A WEIGHT AS MINE!

COME, LET US DROWN OUR SORROWS WITH SOME LIQUID REFRESHMENT IN THIS WORTHY ESTAB-LISHMENT.

HEY GUYS! LOOK WHAT JUST WALKED IN.

DO MY EYES DE-CEIVE ME...

...OR IS THAT THE **GOODYEAR BLIMP?**

THOUGH THY WORDS ARE STRANGE, THE CHALLENGE IS UNMISTAKABLE.

UH, LISTEN, FELLA MAYBE YOU BETTER **LEAVE.**

WE DON'T WANT ANY **TROUBLE.**

NOR SHALL THERE BE ANY, MINE HOST!

TAKE THIS **GOLD** AND FURNISH ME WITH GOOD BREWED ALE.

ALL YOU HAVE!

MOMENTS LATER...

HERE, MY VOLUBLE FRIEND. ALLOW ME TO PUR-CHASE YOU A DRINK!

YER KIDDIN' ME.

AND GATHER YOUR FRIENDS AS WELL.

FOR WE HAVE MUCH TO DIS-CUSS, YOU AND I.

THE TIME HAS COME, T WALRUS SAID, TALK OF MAN THINGS...

...OF SHOES A SHIPS AN SEALING WAX, AN GOODYEA BLIMPS AND THINGS.

KA-THUNK!

I HAVE ALWAYS THOUGHT LEWIS CARROLL WAS AN EXCELLENT POET, HAVEN'T YOU?

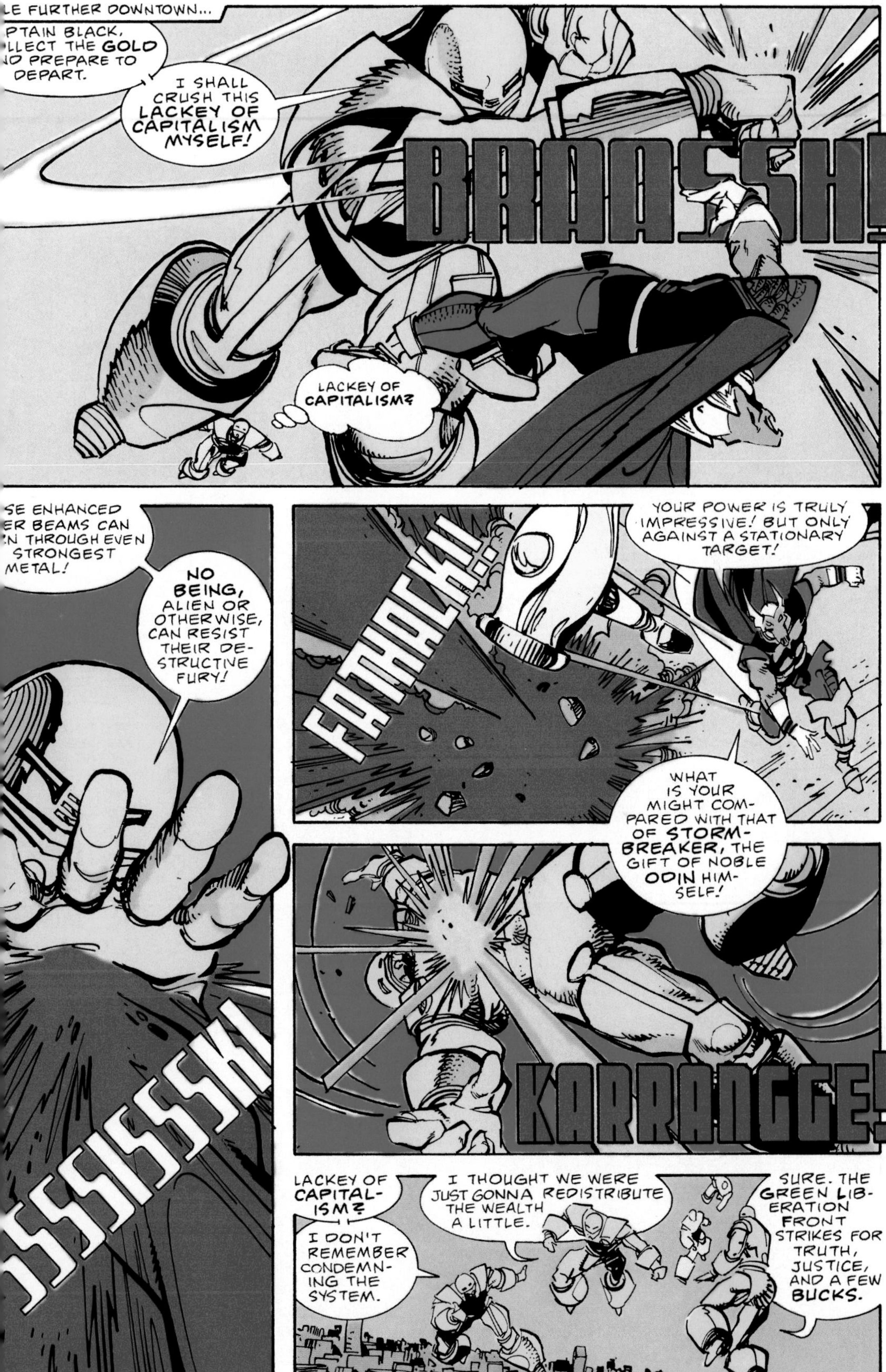

LE FURTHER DOWNTOWN...
PTAIN BLACK, LLECT THE GOLD ND PREPARE TO DEPART.
I SHALL CRUSH THIS LACKEY OF CAPITALISM MYSELF!
BRAASSH!
LACKEY OF CAPITALISM?
SE ENHANCED ER BEAMS CAN N THROUGH EVEN STRONGEST METAL!
NO BEING, ALIEN OR OTHERWISE, CAN RESIST THEIR DESTRUCTIVE FURY!
SSSSSSSK!
YOUR POWER IS TRULY IMPRESSIVE! BUT ONLY AGAINST A STATIONARY TARGET!
FATHACK!!
WHAT IS YOUR MIGHT COMPARED WITH THAT OF STORMBREAKER, THE GIFT OF NOBLE ODIN HIMSELF!
KARRANGGE!
LACKEY OF CAPITALISM?
I DON'T REMEMBER CONDEMNING THE SYSTEM.
I THOUGHT WE WERE JUST GONNA REDISTRIBUTE THE WEALTH A LITTLE.
SURE. THE GREEN LIBERATION FRONT STRIKES FOR TRUTH, JUSTICE, AND A FEW BUCKS.

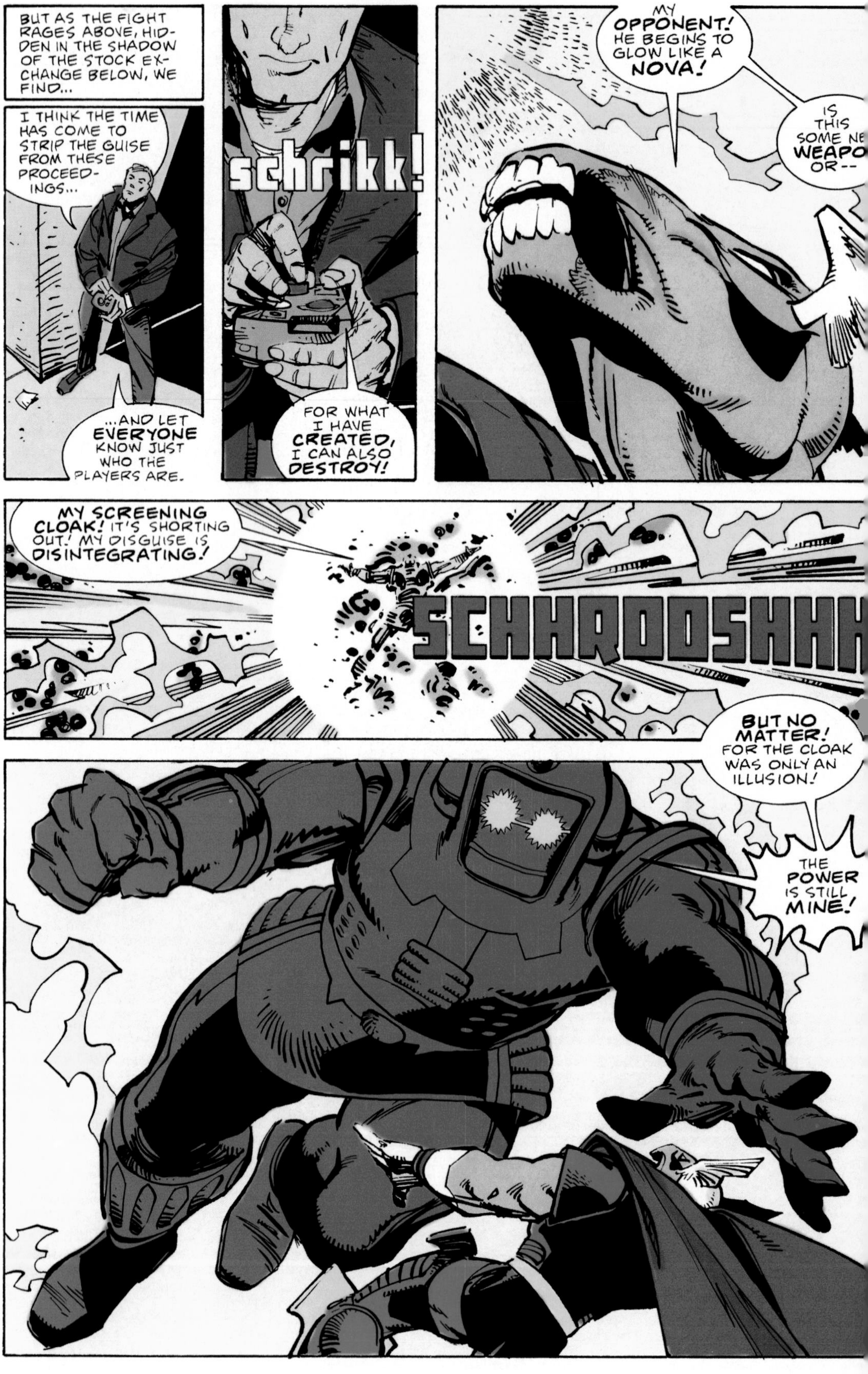

BUT AS THE FIGHT RAGES ABOVE, HIDDEN IN THE SHADOW OF THE STOCK EXCHANGE BELOW, WE FIND...
I THINK THE TIME HAS COME TO STRIP THE GUISE FROM THESE PROCEEDINGS...
...AND LET EVERYONE KNOW JUST WHO THE PLAYERS ARE.
schrikk!
FOR WHAT I HAVE CREATED, I CAN ALSO DESTROY!
MY OPPONENT! HE BEGINS TO GLOW LIKE A NOVA!
IS THIS SOME NE WEAPO OR --
MY SCREENING CLOAK! IT'S SHORTING OUT! MY DISGUISE IS DISINTEGRATING!
SCHHROOSHHH
BUT NO MATTER! FOR THE CLOAK WAS ONLY AN ILLUSION!
THE POWER IS STILL MINE!

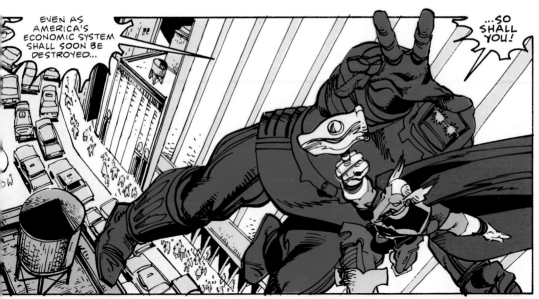

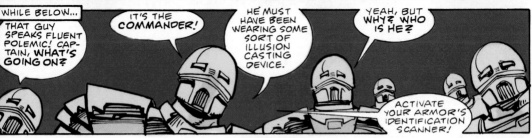

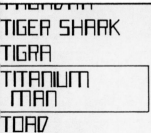

EVEN AS AMERICA'S ECONOMIC SYSTEM SHALL SOON BE DESTROYED...
...SO SHALL YOU!
WHILE BELOW...
THAT GUY SPEAKS FLUENT POLEMIC! CAPTAIN, WHAT'S GOING ON?
IT'S THE COMMANDER!
HE MUST HAVE BEEN WEARING SOME SORT OF ILLUSION CASTING DEVICE.
YEAH, BUT WHY? WHO IS HE?
ACTIVATE YOUR ARMOR'S IDENTIFICATION SCANNER!
TIGER SHARK
TIGRA
TITANIUM MAN
TOAD
TOMORROW MAN
TRAPSTER
NHANCEMENT:
BORIS BULLSKI, SOVIET CITIZEN, COMMUNIST PARTY MEMBER. KNOWN TO HAVE A PERSONAL VENDETTA AGAINST IRON MAN. FOUGHT AND DEFEATED BY IRON MAN SEVERAL TIM
THIS SIDEWINDER IS A RUSSIAN!?!!
CAPTAIN, I DIDN'T FIGHT IN NAM FOR THREE YEARS TO HELP SOME COMMIE SHAFT MY OWN COUNTRY!
NEITHER DID I, CORPORAL BLUE.
WE MAY BE THIEVES, ROBBERS, AND CRIMINALS!
BUT, BY HEAVEN, WE'RE AMERICAN THIEVES, ROBBERS, AND CRIMINALS!
PRIVATE GREEN, WE'VE ONLY SECONDS LEFT.
GET BACK INTO THE FED AND DESTROY THE IMPULSER!
THE REST OF YOU MEN--

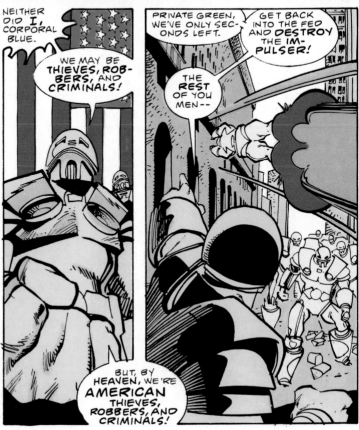

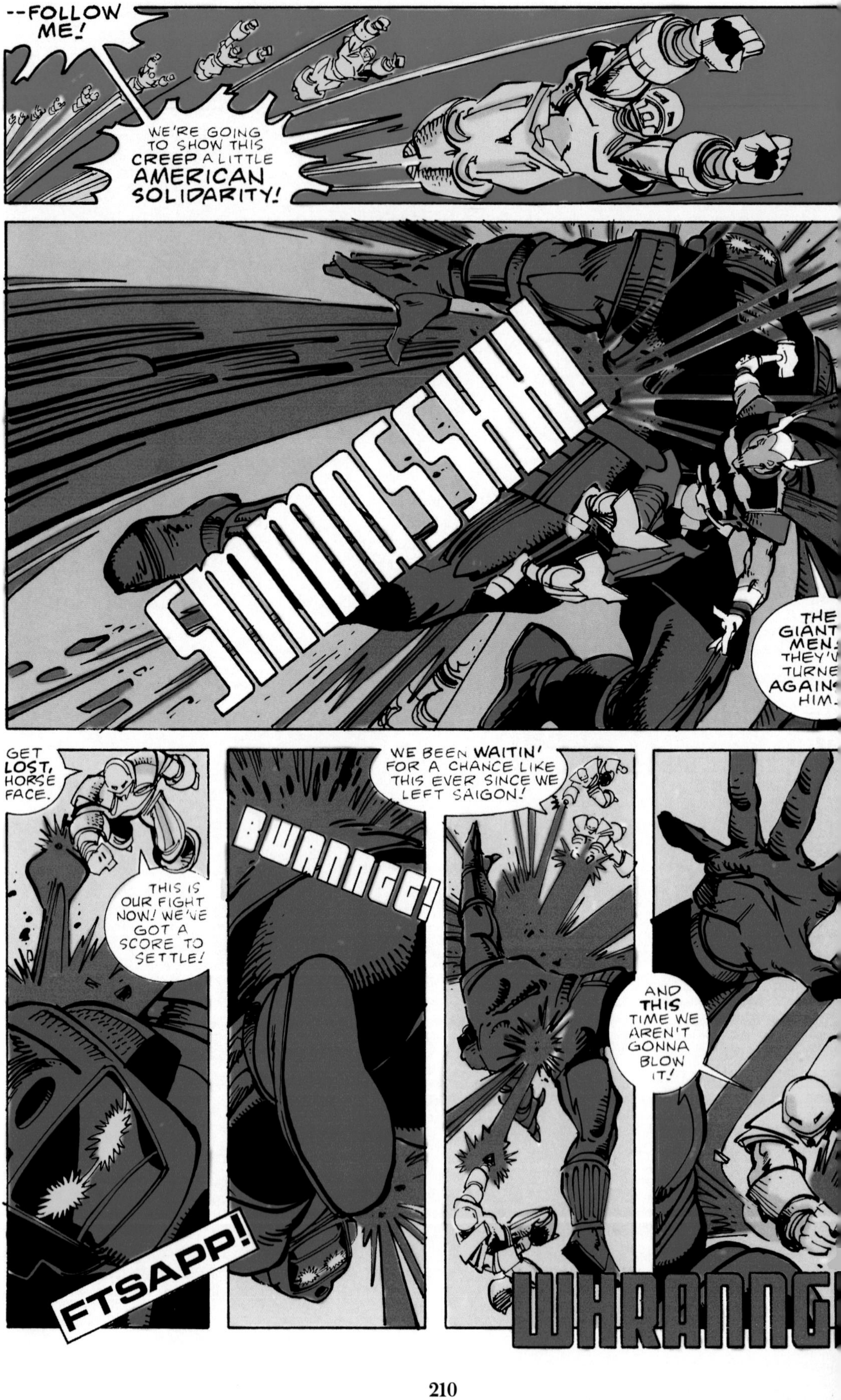
--FOLLOW ME!
WE'RE GOING TO SHOW THIS CREEP A LITTLE AMERICAN SOLIDARITY!
SMMASSHH!
THE GIANT MEN: THEY'V TURNE AGAIN HIM.
GET LOST, HORSE FACE.
THIS IS OUR FIGHT NOW! WE'VE GOT A SCORE TO SETTLE!
FTSAPP!
WE BEEN WAITIN' FOR A CHANCE LIKE THIS EVER SINCE WE LEFT SAIGON!
BWANNGG!
AND THIS TIME WE AREN'T GONNA BLOW IT!
WHRANNG

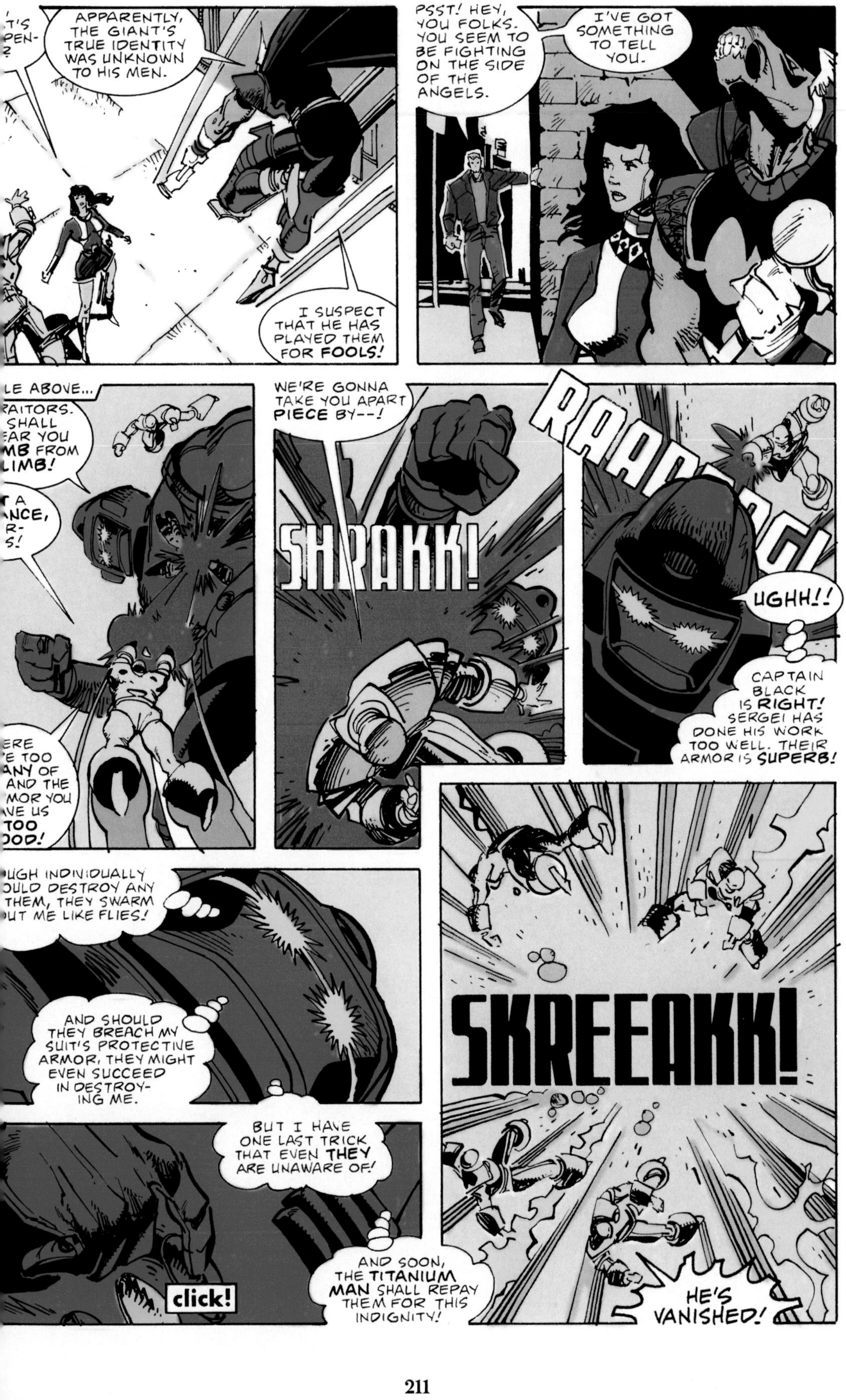

T'S
PEN-
?
APPARENTLY, THE GIANT'S TRUE IDENTITY WAS UNKNOWN TO HIS MEN.
I SUSPECT THAT HE HAS PLAYED THEM FOR **FOOLS!**
PSST! HEY, YOU FOLKS. YOU SEEM TO BE FIGHTING ON THE SIDE OF THE ANGELS.
I'VE GOT SOMETHING TO TELL YOU.
LE ABOVE...
RAITORS. SHALL EAR YOU MB FROM LIMB!
T A NCE, R- S!
ERE E TOO ANY OF AND THE MOR YOU VE US TOO OD!
WE'RE GONNA TAKE YOU APART **PIECE** BY--!
SHRAKK!
UGHH!!
CAPTAIN BLACK IS **RIGHT!** SERGEI HAS DONE HIS WORK TOO WELL. THEIR ARMOR IS **SUPERB!**
UGH INDIVIDUALLY OULD DESTROY ANY THEM, THEY SWARM UT ME LIKE FLIES!
AND SHOULD THEY BREACH MY SUIT'S PROTECTIVE ARMOR, THEY MIGHT EVEN SUCCEED IN DESTROY-ING ME.
BUT I HAVE ONE LAST TRICK THAT EVEN **THEY** ARE UNAWARE OF!
click!
AND SOON, THE **TITANIUM MAN** SHALL REPAY THEM FOR THIS INDIGNITY!
SKREEAKK!
HE'S VANISHED!

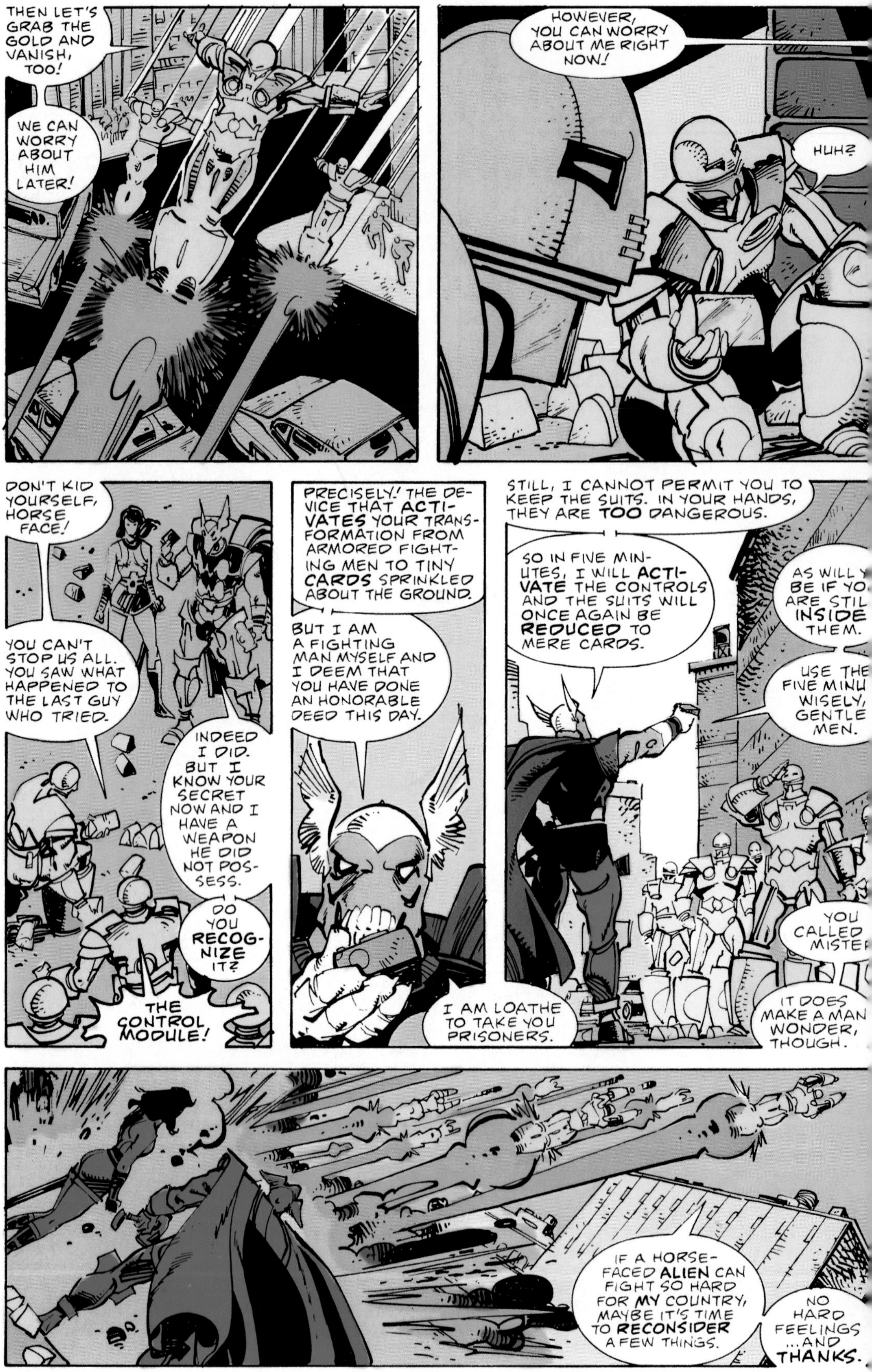
THEN LET'S GRAB THE GOLD AND VANISH, TOO!
WE CAN WORRY ABOUT HIM LATER!
HOWEVER, YOU CAN WORRY ABOUT ME RIGHT NOW!
HUH?
DON'T KID YOURSELF, HORSE FACE!
YOU CAN'T STOP US ALL. YOU SAW WHAT HAPPENED TO THE LAST GUY WHO TRIED.
INDEED I DID. BUT I KNOW YOUR SECRET NOW AND I HAVE A WEAPON HE DID NOT POSSESS.
DO YOU RECOGNIZE IT?
THE CONTROL MODULE!
PRECISELY! THE DEVICE THAT ACTIVATES YOUR TRANSFORMATION FROM ARMORED FIGHTING MEN TO TINY CARDS SPRINKLED ABOUT THE GROUND.
BUT I AM A FIGHTING MAN MYSELF AND I DEEM THAT YOU HAVE DONE AN HONORABLE DEED THIS DAY.
I AM LOATHE TO TAKE YOU PRISONERS.
STILL, I CANNOT PERMIT YOU TO KEEP THE SUITS. IN YOUR HANDS, THEY ARE TOO DANGEROUS.
SO IN FIVE MINUTES, I WILL ACTIVATE THE CONTROLS AND THE SUITS WILL ONCE AGAIN BE REDUCED TO MERE CARDS.
AS WILL Y BE IF YO ARE STIL INSIDE THEM.
USE THE FIVE MINU WISELY, GENTLE MEN.
YOU CALLED MISTE
IT DOES MAKE A MAN WONDER, THOUGH.
IF A HORSE-FACED ALIEN CAN FIGHT SO HARD FOR MY COUNTRY, MAYBE IT'S TIME TO RECONSIDER A FEW THINGS.
NO HARD FEELINGS ...AND THANKS.

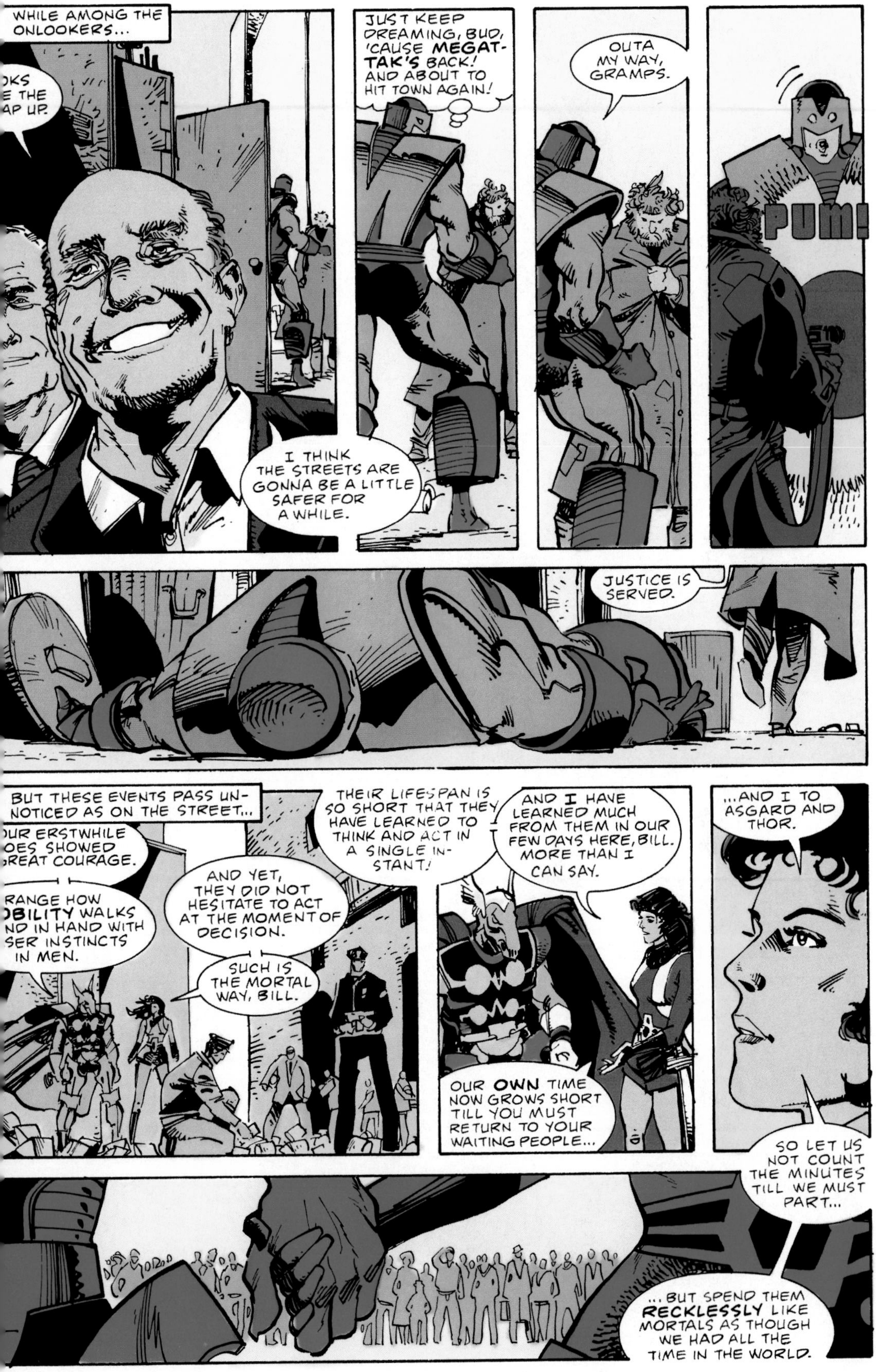
WHILE AMONG THE ONLOOKERS...
OKS E THE AP UP.
I THINK THE STREETS ARE GONNA BE A LITTLE SAFER FOR A WHILE.
JUST KEEP DREAMING, BUD, 'CAUSE MEGATTAK'S BACK! AND ABOUT TO HIT TOWN AGAIN!
OUTA MY WAY, GRAMPS.
PUM!
JUSTICE IS SERVED.
BUT THESE EVENTS PASS UNNOTICED AS ON THE STREET...
OUR ERSTWHILE OES SHOWED GREAT COURAGE.
RANGE HOW OBILITY WALKS ND IN HAND WITH SER INSTINCTS IN MEN.
AND YET, THEY DID NOT HESITATE TO ACT AT THE MOMENT OF DECISION.
SUCH IS THE MORTAL WAY, BILL.
THEIR LIFESPAN IS SO SHORT THAT THEY HAVE LEARNED TO THINK AND ACT IN A SINGLE INSTANT!
AND I HAVE LEARNED MUCH FROM THEM IN OUR FEW DAYS HERE, BILL. MORE THAN I CAN SAY.
OUR OWN TIME NOW GROWS SHORT TILL YOU MUST RETURN TO YOUR WAITING PEOPLE...
...AND I TO ASGARD AND THOR.
SO LET US NOT COUNT THE MINUTES TILL WE MUST PART...
...BUT SPEND THEM RECKLESSLY LIKE MORTALS AS THOUGH WE HAD ALL THE TIME IN THE WORLD.

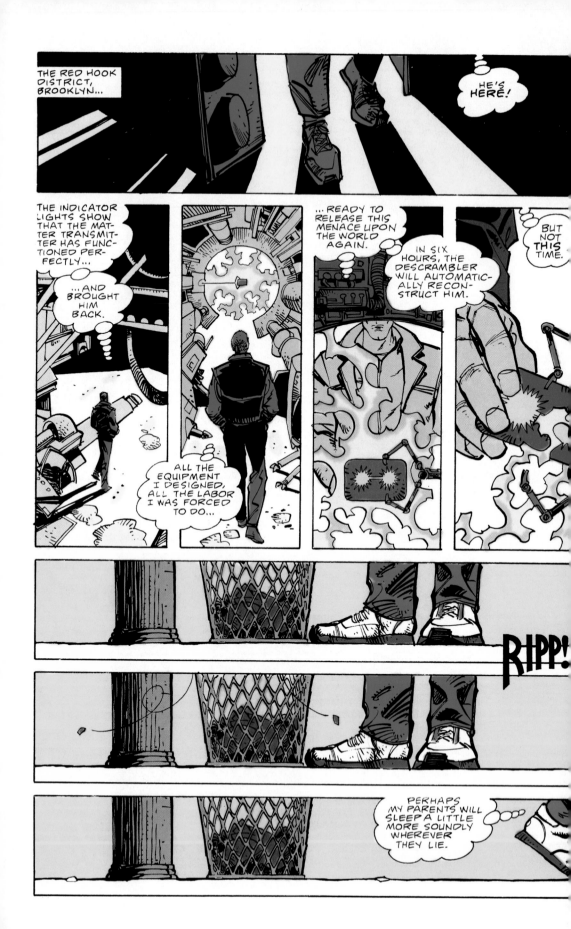

THE RED HOOK DISTRICT, BROOKLYN...

HE'S HERE!

THE INDICATOR LIGHTS SHOW THAT THE MATTER TRANSMITTER HAS FUNCTIONED PERFECTLY...

...AND BROUGHT HIM BACK.

ALL THE EQUIPMENT I DESIGNED, ALL THE LABOR I WAS FORCED TO DO...

...READY TO RELEASE THIS MENACE UPON THE WORLD AGAIN.

IN SIX HOURS, THE DESCRAMBLER WILL AUTOMATICALLY RECONSTRUCT HIM.

BUT NOT THIS TIME.

RIPP!

PERHAPS MY PARENTS WILL SLEEP A LITTLE MORE SOUNDLY WHEREVER THEY LIE.

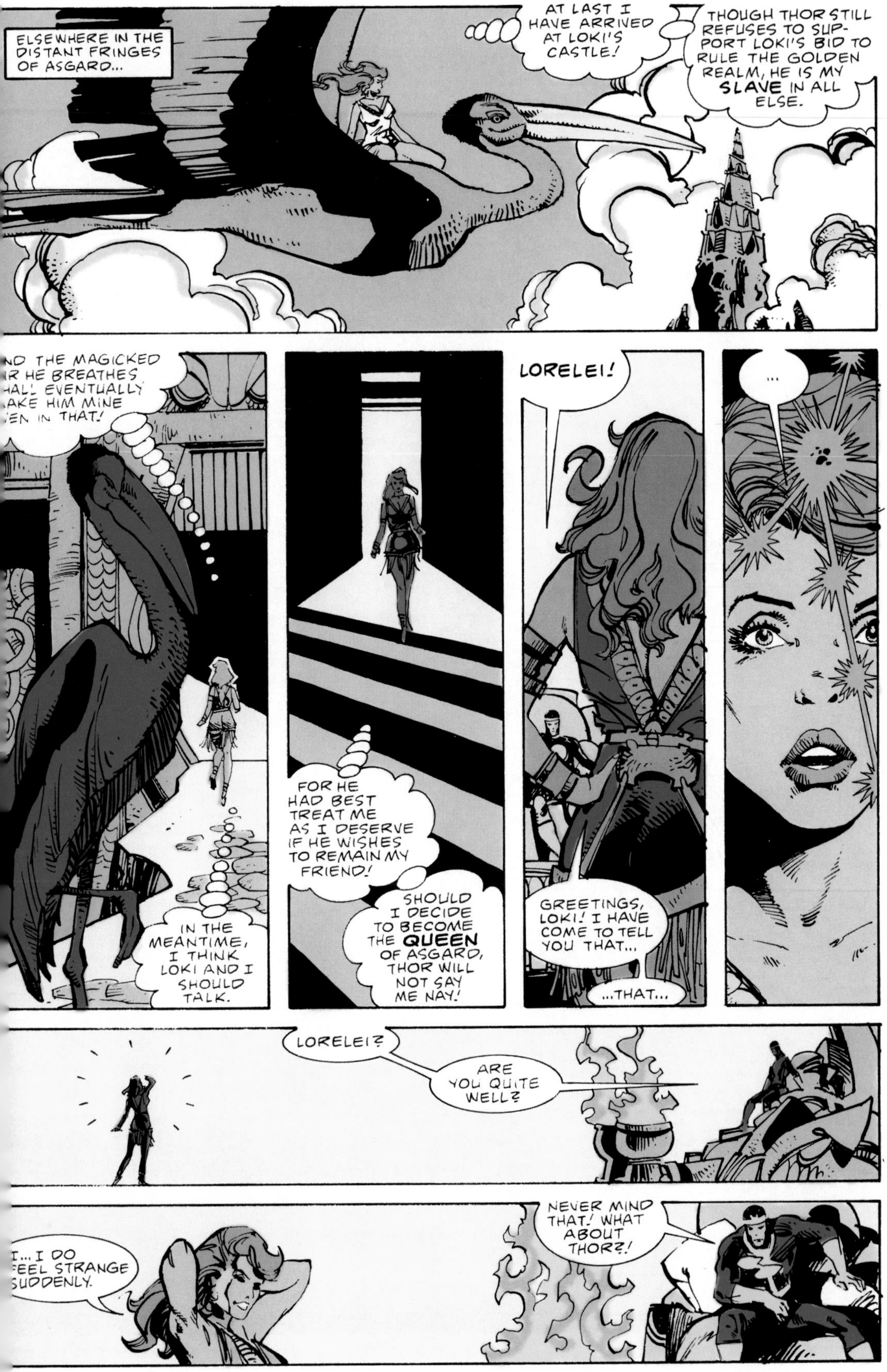
ELSEWHERE IN THE DISTANT FRINGES OF ASGARD...
AT LAST I HAVE ARRIVED AT LOKI'S CASTLE!
THOUGH THOR STILL REFUSES TO SUPPORT LOKI'S BID TO RULE THE GOLDEN REALM, HE IS MY SLAVE IN ALL ELSE.
ND THE MAGICKED IR HE BREATHES HALL EVENTUALLY AKE HIM MINE EN IN THAT!
IN THE MEANTIME, I THINK LOKI AND I SHOULD TALK.
FOR HE HAD BEST TREAT ME AS I DESERVE IF HE WISHES TO REMAIN MY FRIEND!
SHOULD I DECIDE TO BECOME THE QUEEN OF ASGARD, THOR WILL NOT SAY ME NAY!
LORELEI!
GREETINGS, LOKI! I HAVE COME TO TELL YOU THAT...
...THAT...
...
LORELEI?
ARE YOU QUITE WELL?
I... I DO FEEL STRANGE SUDDENLY.
NEVER MIND THAT! WHAT ABOUT THOR?!

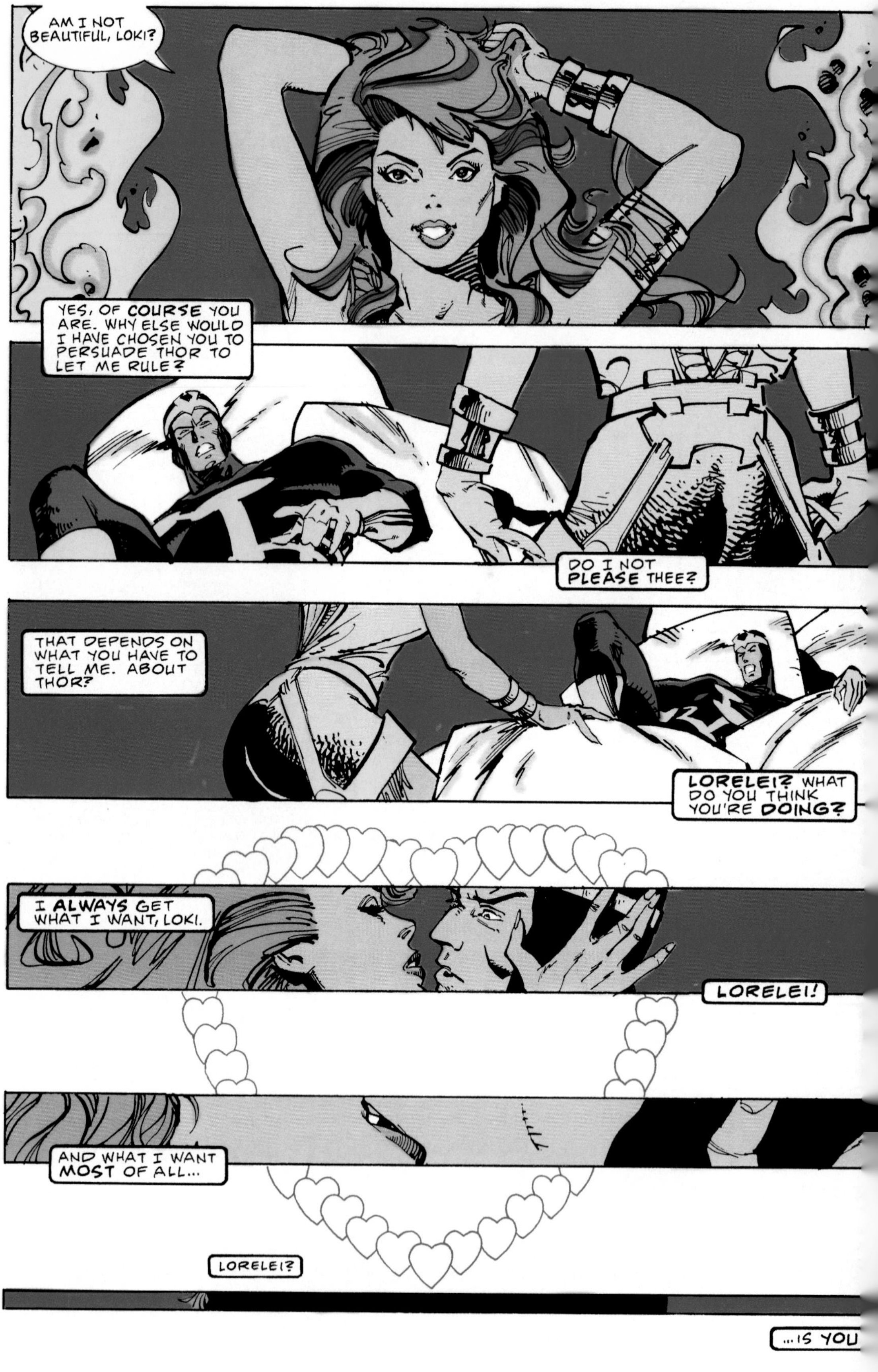

AM I NOT BEAUTIFUL, LOKI?
YES, OF COURSE YOU ARE. WHY ELSE WOULD I HAVE CHOSEN YOU TO PERSUADE THOR TO LET ME RULE?
DO I NOT PLEASE THEE?
THAT DEPENDS ON WHAT YOU HAVE TO TELL ME. ABOUT THOR?
LORELEI? WHAT DO YOU THINK YOU'RE DOING?
I ALWAYS GET WHAT I WANT, LOKI.
LORELEI!
AND WHAT I WANT MOST OF ALL...
LORELEI?
...IS YOU

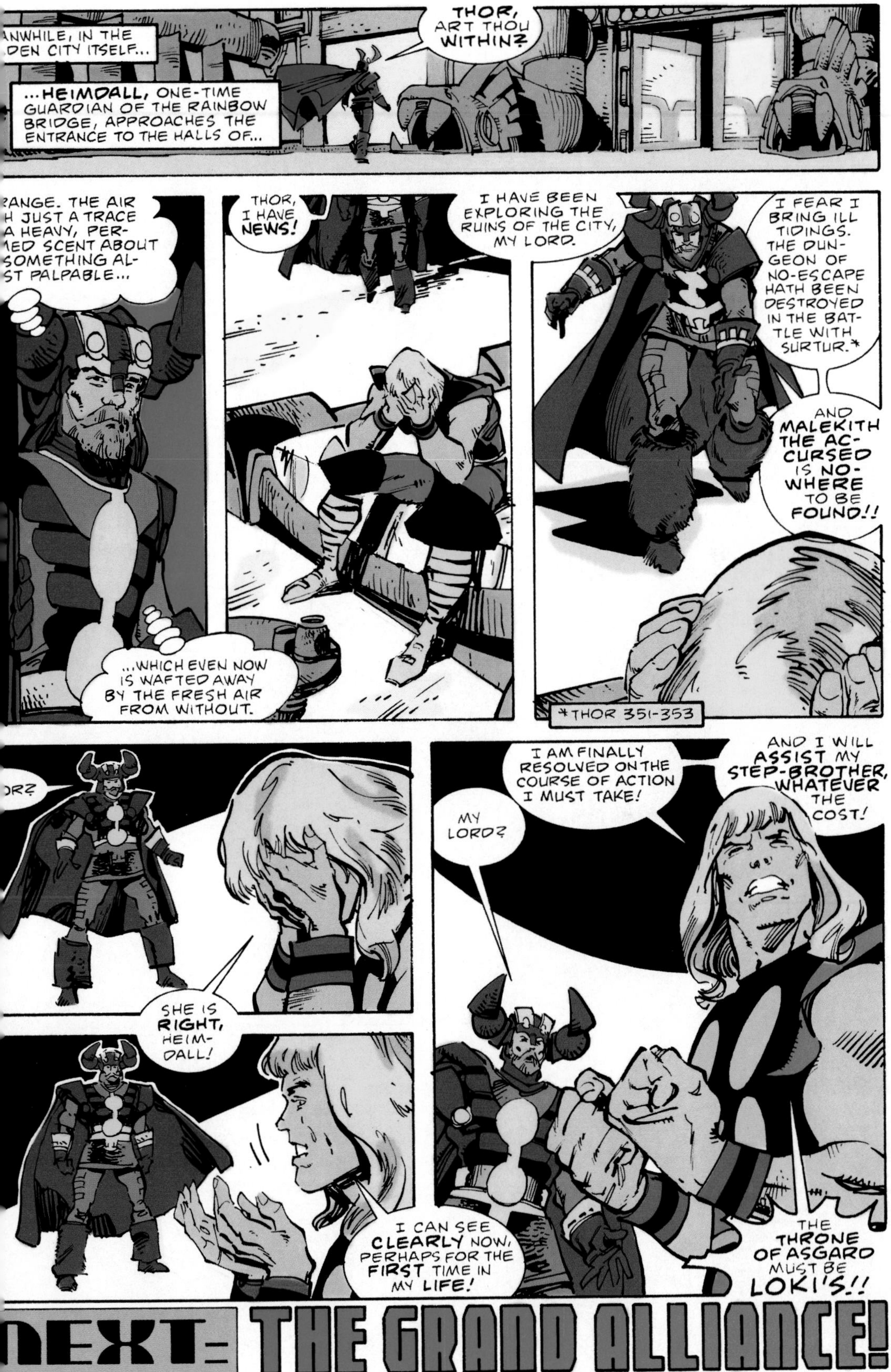

ANWHILE, IN THE
DEN CITY ITSELF...
...HEIMDALL, ONE-TIME GUARDIAN OF THE RAINBOW BRIDGE, APPROACHES THE ENTRANCE TO THE HALLS OF...
THOR, ART THOU WITHIN?
RANGE. THE AIR H JUST A TRACE A HEAVY, PER- MED SCENT ABOUT SOMETHING AL- ST PALPABLE...
...WHICH EVEN NOW IS WAFTED AWAY BY THE FRESH AIR FROM WITHOUT.
THOR, I HAVE NEWS!
I HAVE BEEN EXPLORING THE RUINS OF THE CITY, MY LORD.
I FEAR I BRING ILL TIDINGS. THE DUN- GEON OF NO-ESCAPE HATH BEEN DESTROYED IN THE BAT- TLE WITH SURTUR.*
AND MALEKITH THE AC- CURSED IS NO- WHERE TO BE FOUND!!
*THOR 351-353
OR?
SHE IS RIGHT, HEIM- DALL!
I CAN SEE CLEARLY NOW, PERHAPS FOR THE FIRST TIME IN MY LIFE!
MY LORD?
I AM FINALLY RESOLVED ON THE COURSE OF ACTION I MUST TAKE!
AND I WILL ASSIST MY STEP-BROTHER, WHATEVER THE COST!
THE THRONE OF ASGARD MUST BE LOKI'S!!
NEXT: THE GRAND ALLIANCE!
E STORY YOU NEVER THOUGHT YOU'D SEE--BUT CAN'T WAIT TO READ! (TAKE OUR WORD FOR IT!)

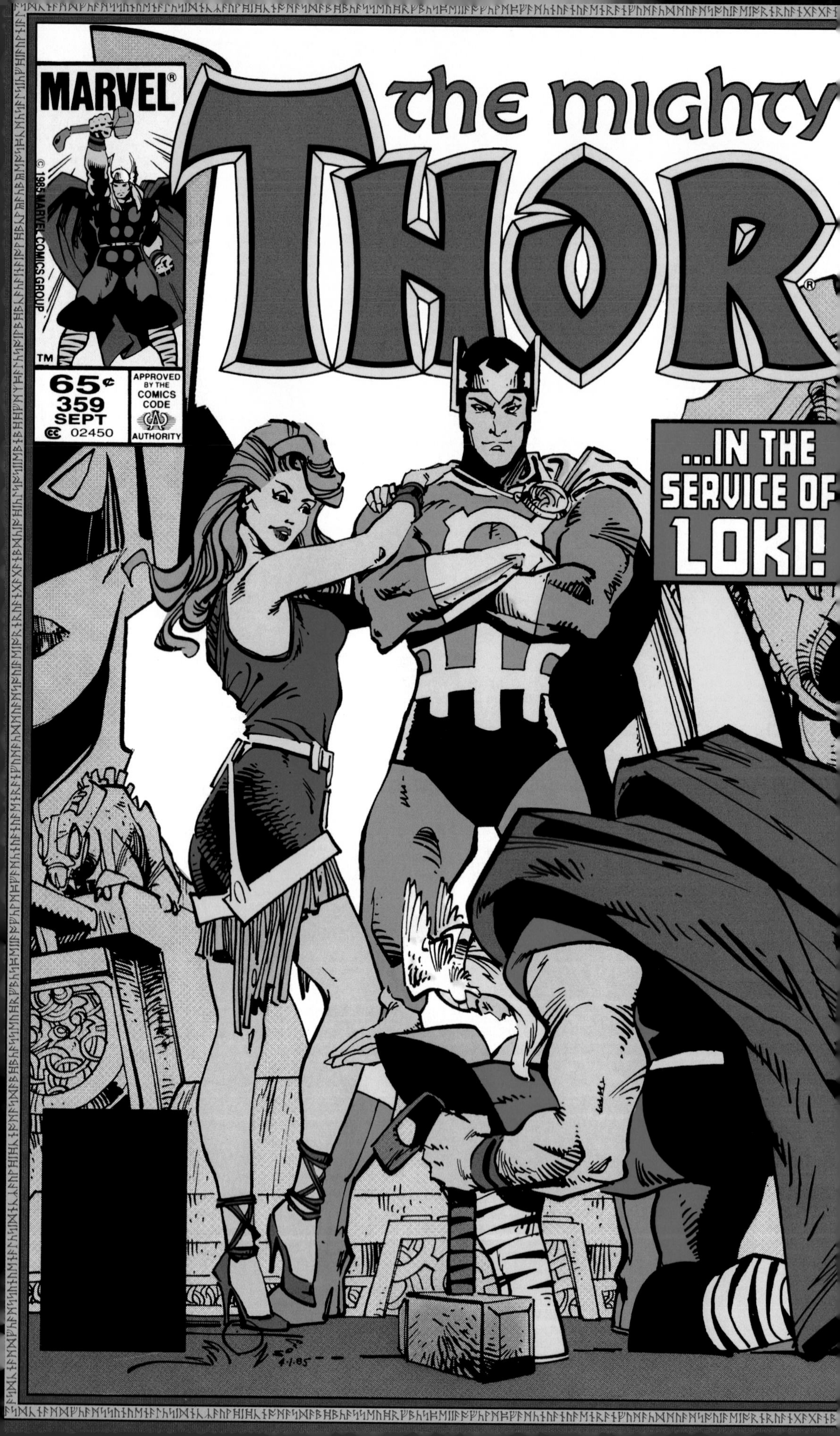
MARVEL®
the mighty
THOR®
TM
© 1985 MARVEL COMICS GROUP
65¢
359
SEPT
02450
APPROVED BY THE COMICS CODE AUTHORITY
...IN THE SERVICE OF LOKI!

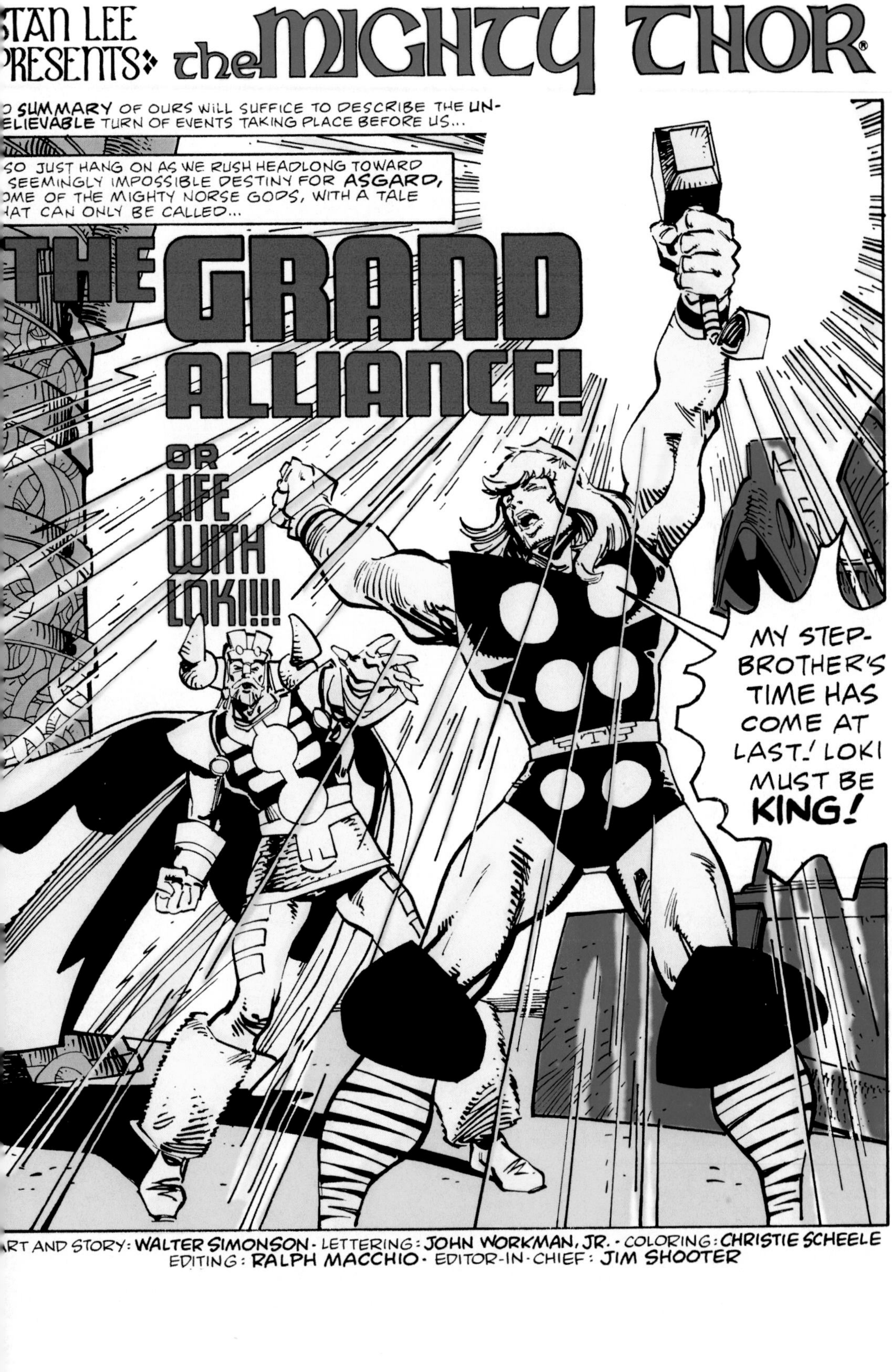
STAN LEE PRESENTS: the MIGHTY THOR
NO SUMMARY OF OURS WILL SUFFICE TO DESCRIBE THE UNBELIEVABLE TURN OF EVENTS TAKING PLACE BEFORE US...
SO JUST HANG ON AS WE RUSH HEADLONG TOWARD A SEEMINGLY IMPOSSIBLE DESTINY FOR ASGARD, HOME OF THE MIGHTY NORSE GODS, WITH A TALE THAT CAN ONLY BE CALLED...
THE GRAND ALLIANCE!
OR LIFE WITH LOKI!!!
MY STEP-BROTHER'S TIME HAS COME AT LAST! LOKI MUST BE KING!
ART AND STORY: WALTER SIMONSON · LETTERING: JOHN WORKMAN, JR. · COLORING: CHRISTIE SCHEELE
EDITING: RALPH MACCHIO · EDITOR-IN-CHIEF: JIM SHOOTER

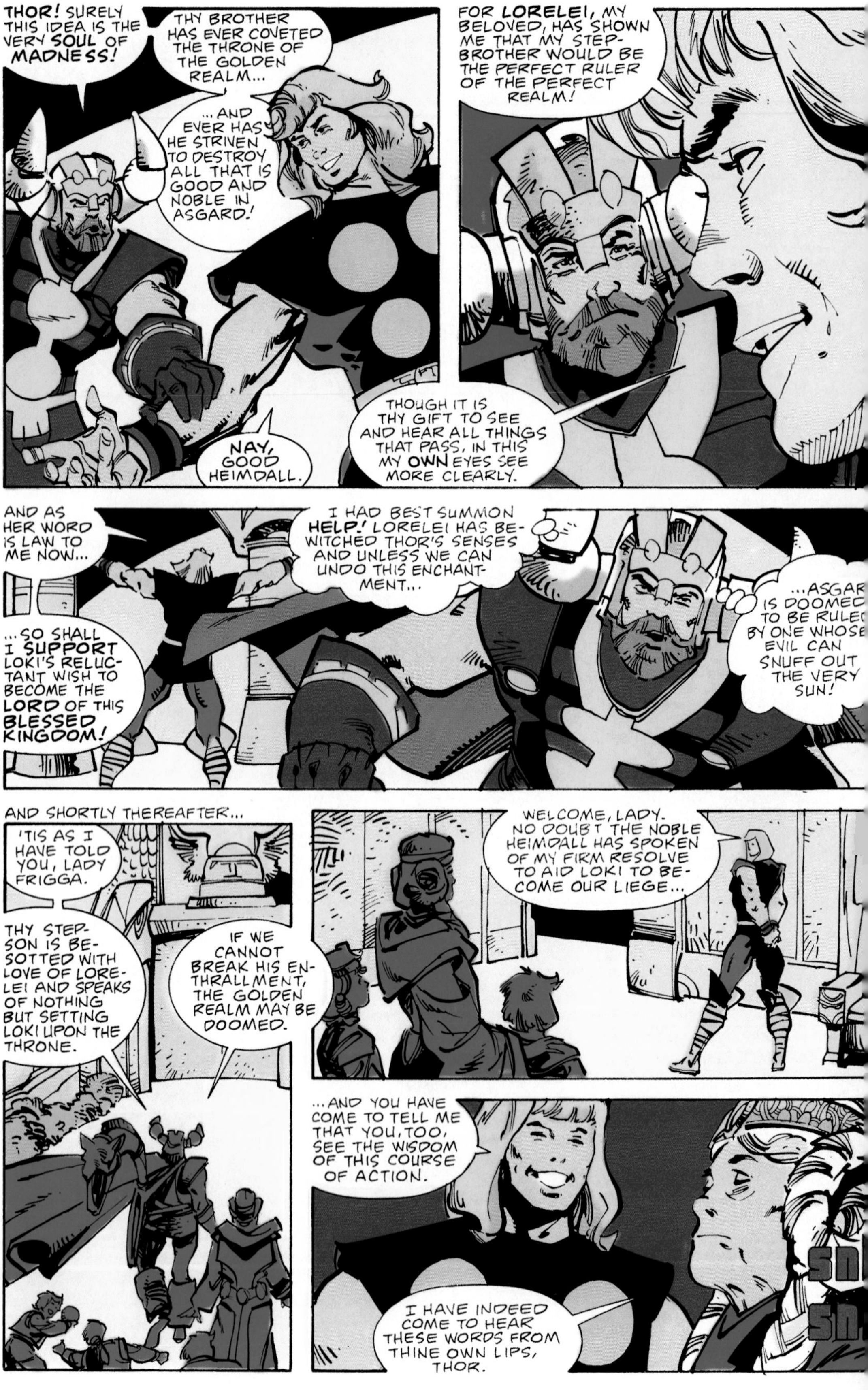
THOR! SURELY THIS IDEA IS THE VERY SOUL OF MADNESS!
THY BROTHER HAS EVER COVETED THE THRONE OF THE GOLDEN REALM...
...AND EVER HAS HE STRIVEN TO DESTROY ALL THAT IS GOOD AND NOBLE IN ASGARD!
NAY, GOOD HEIMDALL.
FOR LORELEI, MY BELOVED, HAS SHOWN ME THAT MY STEP-BROTHER WOULD BE THE PERFECT RULER OF THE PERFECT REALM!
THOUGH IT IS THY GIFT TO SEE AND HEAR ALL THINGS THAT PASS, IN THIS MY OWN EYES SEE MORE CLEARLY.
AND AS HER WORD IS LAW TO ME NOW...
...SO SHALL I SUPPORT LOKI'S RELUCTANT WISH TO BECOME THE LORD OF THIS BLESSED KINGDOM!
I HAD BEST SUMMON HELP! LORELEI HAS BEWITCHED THOR'S SENSES AND UNLESS WE CAN UNDO THIS ENCHANTMENT...
...ASGAR IS DOOMED TO BE RULE BY ONE WHOSE EVIL CAN SNUFF OUT THE VERY SUN!
AND SHORTLY THEREAFTER...
'TIS AS I HAVE TOLD YOU, LADY FRIGGA.
THY STEPSON IS BESOTTED WITH LOVE OF LORELEI AND SPEAKS OF NOTHING BUT SETTING LOKI UPON THE THRONE.
IF WE CANNOT BREAK HIS ENTHRALLMENT, THE GOLDEN REALM MAY BE DOOMED.
WELCOME, LADY. NO DOUBT THE NOBLE HEIMDALL HAS SPOKEN OF MY FIRM RESOLVE TO AID LOKI TO BECOME OUR LIEGE...
...AND YOU HAVE COME TO TELL ME THAT YOU, TOO, SEE THE WISDOM OF THIS COURSE OF ACTION.
I HAVE INDEED COME TO HEAR THESE WORDS FROM THINE OWN LIPS, THOR.

NAY, HILDY. WHY THIS MATTER IS NOW SO OBVIOUS TO ME THAT I WONDER WHY IT HAS TAKEN ME SO LONG TO SEE IT.

IF NOT FOR MY BELOVED LORELEI, I MIGHT STILL BE WANDERING DARKLY THROUGH THE FORESTS OF CONFUSION NOT REALIZING... PATH LAY CLEARLY ...E ONLY I HAD ...EE IT.

LADY, DO YOU NOT CATCH A HINT OF SOME FRAGRANCE THAT LINGERS JUST BEYOND THE SENSES?

I DO, HEIMDALL. IT HAS A SEDUCTIVE SACHET AND ONE THAT MIGHT WELL BEGUILE A GOD.

SUMMON THE ENCHANTRESS...

...FOR MATTERS OF LOVE ARE NOT MATTERS OF THE HEAD...

...AND IN THE SEDUCTIONS OF THE SOUL, AMORA HAS NO EQUAL.

MOMENTS LATER, FROM A PARAPET...

THOUGH MOST OF THE ASGARDIANS ARE STILL ON EARTH, THE ENCHANTRESS RETURNED TO ASGARD THROUGH HER SORCERY.

SO I WILL PLAY A NOTE THAT ONLY SHE MAY HEAR AND KNOW THAT SHE HAS BEEN CALLED.

D FASTER ...N THOUGHT...

FTASSP!

I HAVE COME, HEIMDALL. WHY HAVE YOU TOLLED ME HERE TO THE HALLS OF THOR?

PLEASE STEP INSIDE, AMORA.

...GRAVE ...TTER ...AS ...ISEN...

...ND PER... ...PS ONLY THE ...CHANTRESS, ...LLED IN ALL ...YS OF LOVE, ...N TELL US ...AT HAS ...PPENED.

PERHAPS YOU CAN SMELL THE--

INCREDIBLE! 'TIS THE FRAGRANCE OF THE FABLED ELIXIR OF LOFN, LONG THOUGHT LOST FOREVER!

ONCE INHALED, THE VICTIM FALLS HOPELESSLY IN LOVE.

AND I NEED NOT ASK WHO HAS USED THAT POTENT ELIXIR ON THE MIGHTY THOR.

YOU SEE, ...RELEI WAS ...THAT ONLY ...ULE ASGARD ...S MEANT TO ...BE RULED.

AND ONLY LOKI COULD HAVE OBTAINED THE FORBIDDEN DRUG.

221

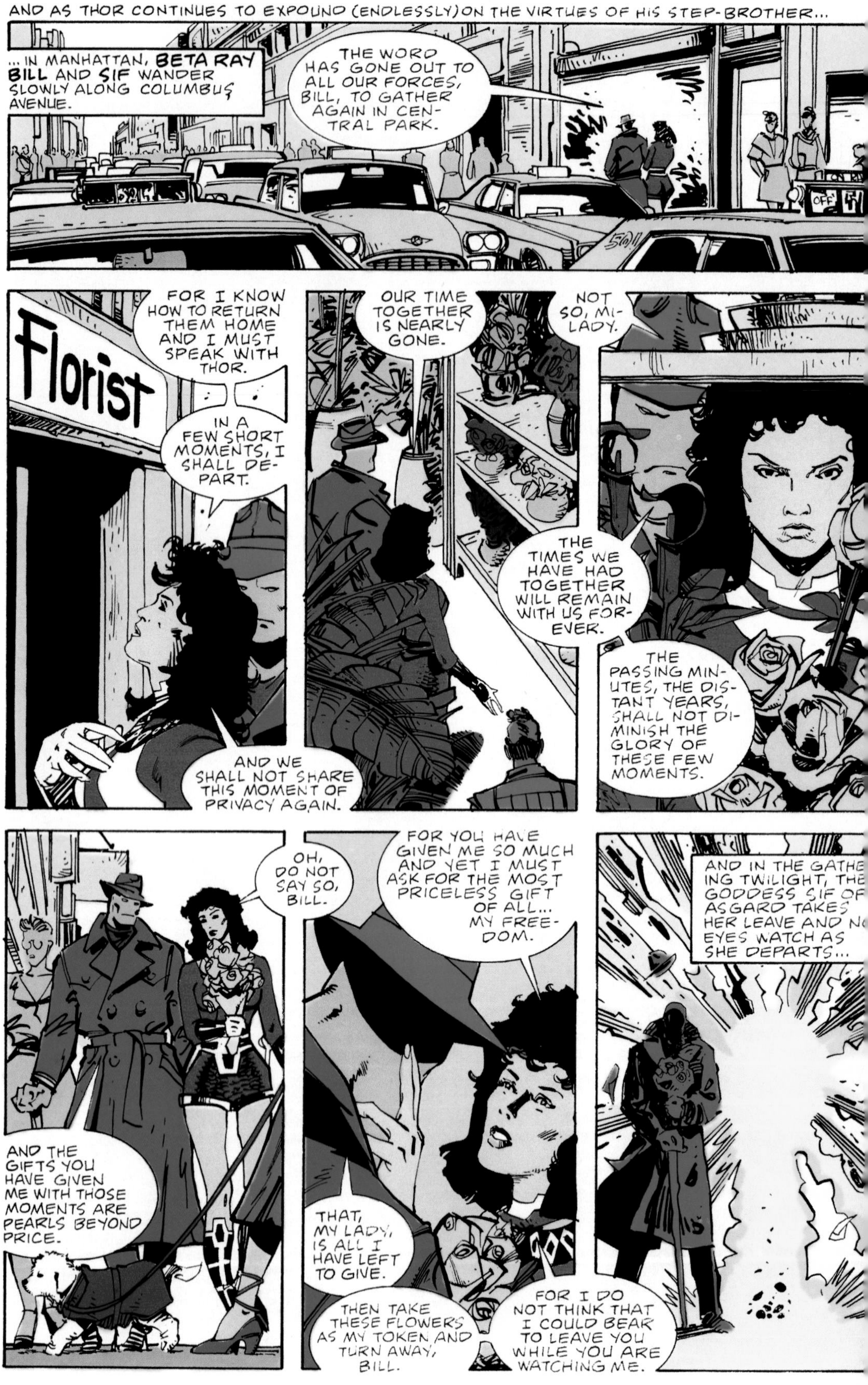
AND AS THOR CONTINUES TO EXPOUND (ENDLESSLY) ON THE VIRTUES OF HIS STEP-BROTHER...
...IN MANHATTAN, BETA RAY BILL AND SIF WANDER SLOWLY ALONG COLUMBUS AVENUE.
THE WORD HAS GONE OUT TO ALL OUR FORCES, BILL, TO GATHER AGAIN IN CENTRAL PARK.
Florist
FOR I KNOW HOW TO RETURN THEM HOME AND I MUST SPEAK WITH THOR.
IN A FEW SHORT MOMENTS, I SHALL DEPART.
AND WE SHALL NOT SHARE THIS MOMENT OF PRIVACY AGAIN.
OUR TIME TOGETHER IS NEARLY GONE.
NOT SO, MILADY.
THE TIMES WE HAVE HAD TOGETHER WILL REMAIN WITH US FOREVER.
THE PASSING MINUTES, THE DISTANT YEARS, SHALL NOT DIMINISH THE GLORY OF THESE FEW MOMENTS.
AND THE GIFTS YOU HAVE GIVEN ME WITH THOSE MOMENTS ARE PEARLS BEYOND PRICE.
OH, DO NOT SAY SO, BILL.
FOR YOU HAVE GIVEN ME SO MUCH AND YET I MUST ASK FOR THE MOST PRICELESS GIFT OF ALL... MY FREEDOM.
THAT, MY LADY, IS ALL I HAVE LEFT TO GIVE.
THEN TAKE THESE FLOWERS AS MY TOKEN AND TURN AWAY, BILL.
FOR I DO NOT THINK THAT I COULD BEAR TO LEAVE YOU WHILE YOU ARE WATCHING ME.
AND IN THE GATHE ING TWILIGHT, THE GODDESS SIF OF ASGARD TAKES HER LEAVE AND N EYES WATCH AS SHE DEPARTS...

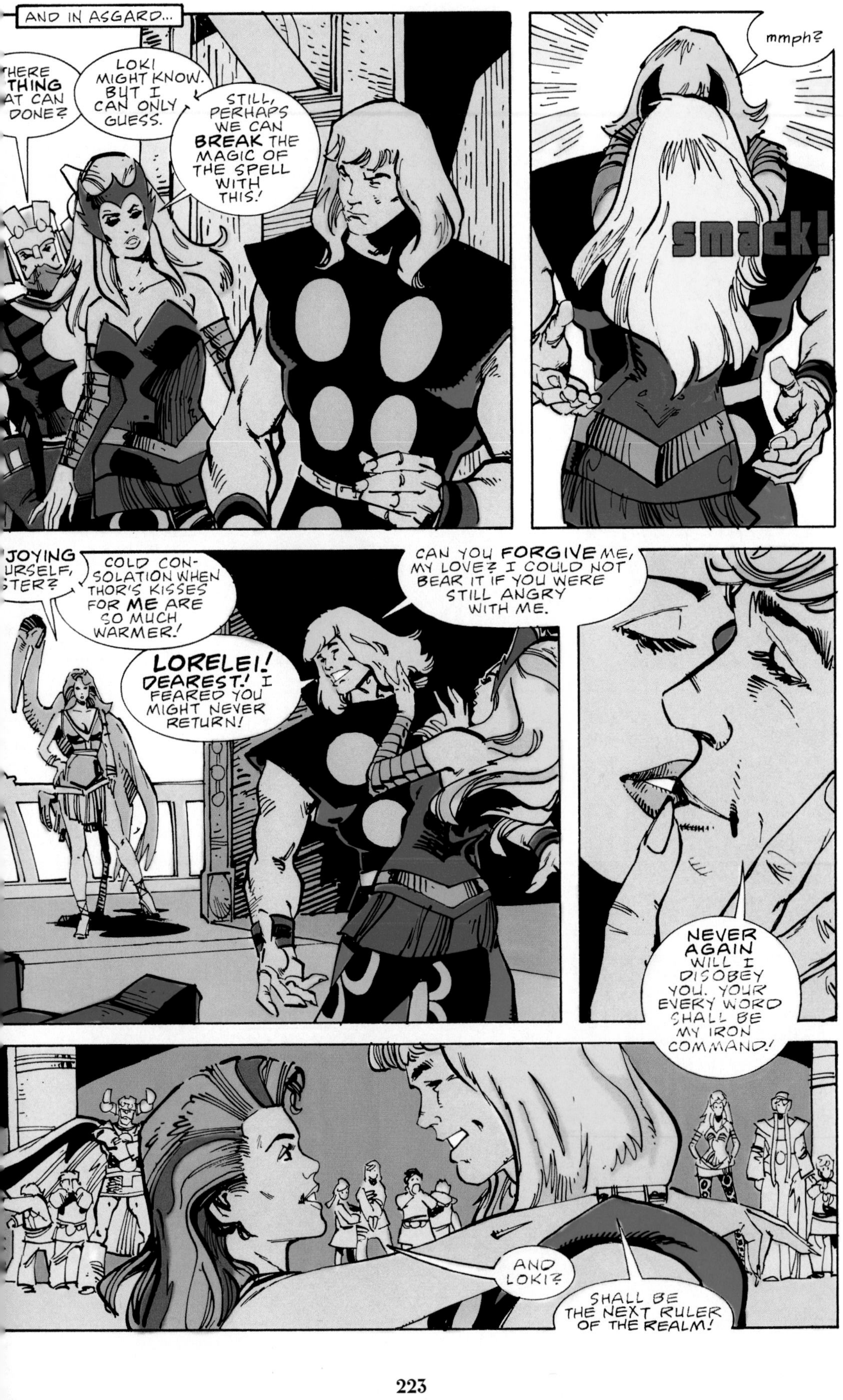

AND IN ASGARD...
THERE THING AT CAN DONE?
LOKI MIGHT KNOW. BUT I CAN ONLY GUESS.
STILL, PERHAPS WE CAN **BREAK** THE MAGIC OF THE SPELL WITH THIS!
mmph?
smack!
JOYING URSELF, STER?
COLD CON-SOLATION WHEN THOR'S KISSES FOR **ME** ARE SO MUCH WARMER!
LORELEI! DEAREST! I FEARED YOU MIGHT NEVER RETURN!
CAN YOU **FORGIVE** ME, MY LOVE? I COULD NOT BEAR IT IF YOU WERE STILL ANGRY WITH ME.
NEVER AGAIN WILL I DISOBEY YOU. YOUR EVERY WORD SHALL BE MY IRON COMMAND!
AND LOKI?
SHALL BE THE **NEXT RULER** OF THE **REALM**!

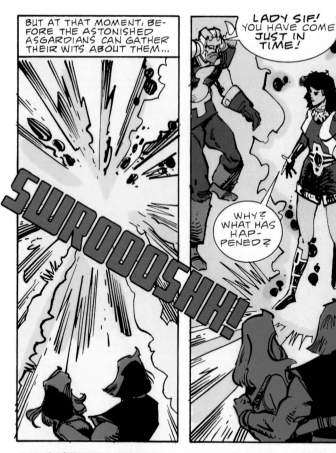

BUT AT THAT MOMENT, BEFORE THE ASTONISHED ASGARDIANS CAN GATHER THEIR WITS ABOUT THEM...

SWROOOSHH!

LADY SIF! YOU HAVE COME JUST IN TIME!

WHY? WHAT HAS HAPPENED?

LORELEI HAS WROUGHT A MAGIC SO POWERFUL THAT THOR IS HER SLAVE, BODY AND SOUL...

...AND AT HER BIDDING, HE WILL STOP AT NOTHING TO PLACE LOKI UPON THE GOLDEN THRONE OF ASGARD!

YOU HAVE DONE THAT?!!

RELEASE HIM, GIRL, OR YOU SHALL HAVE CAUSE TO REGRET IT!!

OWW! YOU'RE HURTING ME!

STAND OFF, LADY SIF.

FOR LORELEI IS UNDER MY PROTECTION AND THOSE WHO WOULD INJURE HER DO SO AT THE RISK OF MY DISPLEASURE.

SHE **HURT** ME, THOR.

THAT WITCH HURT MY **WRIST!**

HURT HER **BACK!**

NEVER AGAIN, LADY, SEEK TO HARM LORELEI! OR IT SHALL BE THE WORSE FOR YOU!

SWAK!

[TH]OR, YOU [D]O LOVE [M]E!

OH, MY **DARLING**, MAY I NOT GO WITH THEE?

[T]WIST [A]IR [A] [M]E!

[L]AY, SEEK NOT TO [AC]COMPANY ME, BUT [ST]AY AND **PERSUADE** [TH]E REST OF THESE [G]ENTLE FOLK THAT [LO]KI SHALL BE THEIR [J]UST MASTER.

[I] SHALL [R]ETURN [SO]ON...

...BUT LET ME TAKE THY **CLOAK,** FOR IT IS CHILLY WHERE I GO.

...AND THE **VERY** THOUGHT OF YOU AS I SIT WRAPPED IN IT WILL WARM ME.

FARE-WELL, MY LOVE!

IS SHE NOT **WONDER-FUL?**

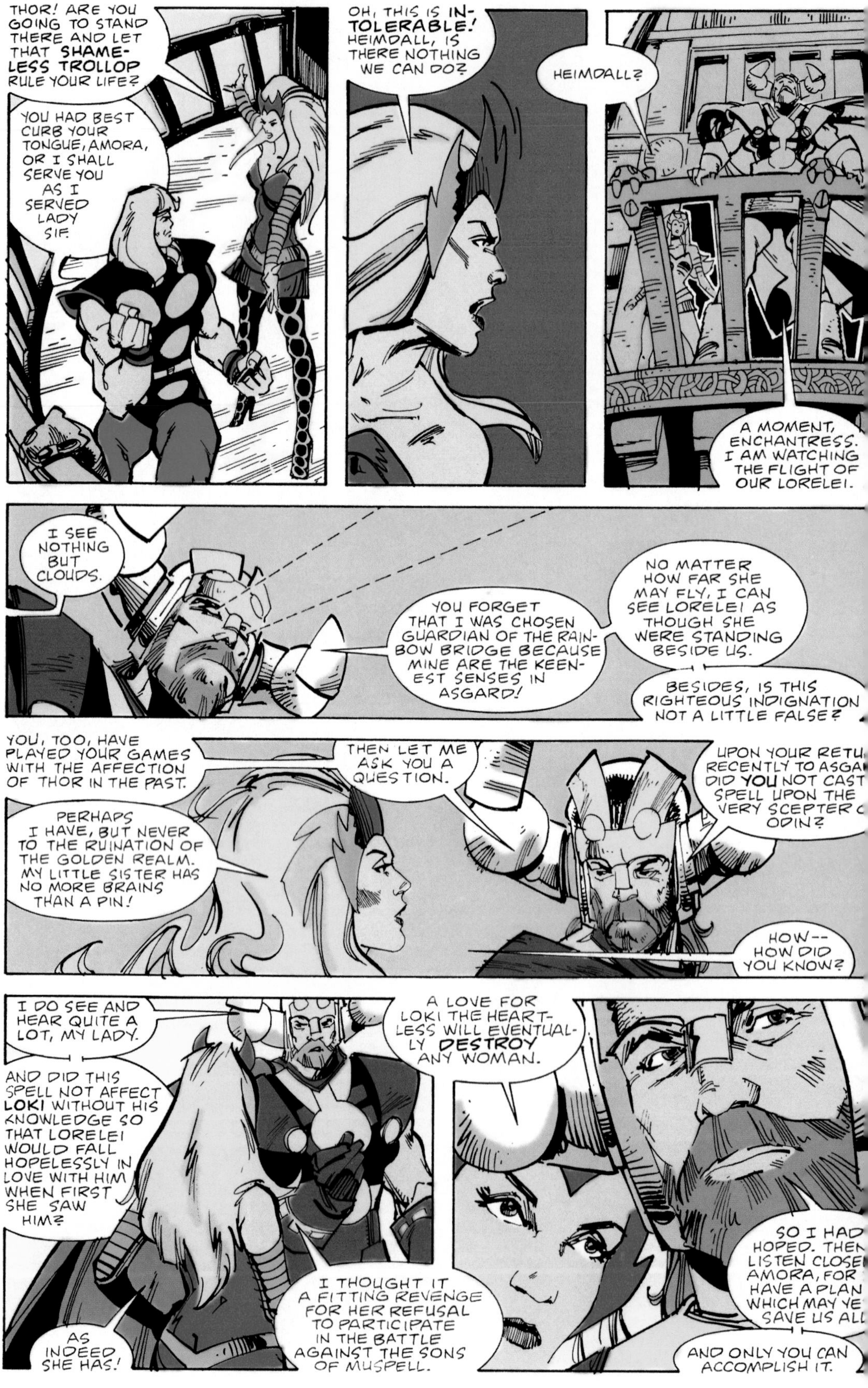
THOR! ARE YOU GOING TO STAND THERE AND LET THAT **SHAMELESS TROLLOP** RULE YOUR LIFE?
YOU HAD BEST CURB YOUR TONGUE, AMORA, OR I SHALL SERVE YOU AS I SERVED LADY SIF.
OH, THIS IS **INTOLERABLE!** HEIMDALL, IS THERE NOTHING WE CAN DO?
HEIMDALL?
A MOMENT, ENCHANTRESS. I AM WATCHING THE FLIGHT OF OUR LORELEI.
I SEE NOTHING BUT CLOUDS.
YOU FORGET THAT I WAS CHOSEN GUARDIAN OF THE RAINBOW BRIDGE BECAUSE MINE ARE THE KEENEST SENSES IN ASGARD!
NO MATTER HOW FAR SHE MAY FLY, I CAN SEE LORELEI AS THOUGH SHE WERE STANDING BESIDE US.
BESIDES, IS THIS RIGHTEOUS INDIGNATION NOT A LITTLE FALSE?
YOU, TOO, HAVE PLAYED YOUR GAMES WITH THE AFFECTION OF THOR IN THE PAST.
PERHAPS I HAVE, BUT NEVER TO THE RUINATION OF THE GOLDEN REALM. MY LITTLE SISTER HAS NO MORE BRAINS THAN A PIN!
THEN LET ME ASK YOU A QUESTION.
UPON YOUR RETU RECENTLY TO ASGA DID **YOU** NOT CAST SPELL UPON THE VERY SCEPTER O ODIN?
HOW-- HOW DID YOU KNOW?
I DO SEE AND HEAR QUITE A LOT, MY LADY.
AND DID THIS SPELL NOT AFFECT **LOKI** WITHOUT HIS KNOWLEDGE SO THAT LORELEI WOULD FALL HOPELESSLY IN LOVE WITH HIM WHEN FIRST SHE SAW HIM?
AS INDEED SHE HAS!
I THOUGHT IT A FITTING REVENGE FOR HER REFUSAL TO PARTICIPATE IN THE BATTLE AGAINST THE SONS OF MUSPELL.
A LOVE FOR LOKI THE HEARTLESS WILL EVENTUALLY **DESTROY** ANY WOMAN.
SO I HAD HOPED. THEN LISTEN CLOSE AMORA, FOR HAVE A PLAN WHICH MAY YE SAVE US AL
AND ONLY YOU CAN ACCOMPLISH IT.

...RTLY...

YOU ARE RIGHT, THOR. HEIMDALL HAS CONVINCED US ALL. LOKI **SHOULD BE** THE NEXT RULER OF ASGARD.

...LL ...D, EN-...ANT-...SS. I ... GLAD ...AT YOU, ...O, HAVE ...EN THE ...HT.

THEN WHY NOT FLY TO LOKI **NOW** AND TELL HIM THAT WE HAVE DECIDED TO SUPPORT HIM.

NO! I DARE NOT! LORELEI SAID I WAS TO STAY HERE.

ONLY THE BET-TER TO PERSUADE US OF THE FITNESS OF LOKI'S RIGHT TO RULE.

AND AS WE ARE ALL NOW **CONVINCED,** SURELY SOME-ONE SHOULD TELL LOKI **SO!**

BESIDES, THINK HOW HAPPY THIS WILL MAKE LORELEI!

THINK HOW PLEASED WITH YOU SHE'LL BE THE NEXT TIME SHE SEES YOU AND TAKES YOU IN HER ARMS.

THINK HOW SHE WILL **LOVE YOU** FOR IT!

SAY NO MORE, AMORA!

I AM **OFF** TO LOKI'S DISTANT FORTRESS TO BRING HIM THE GOOD NEWS!

I CAN HARDLY **WAIT** TO TELL HIM

AND I WOULD GIVE A GOLD CROWN TO SEE THE LOOK ON LOKI'S FACE WHEN YOU ARRIVE!

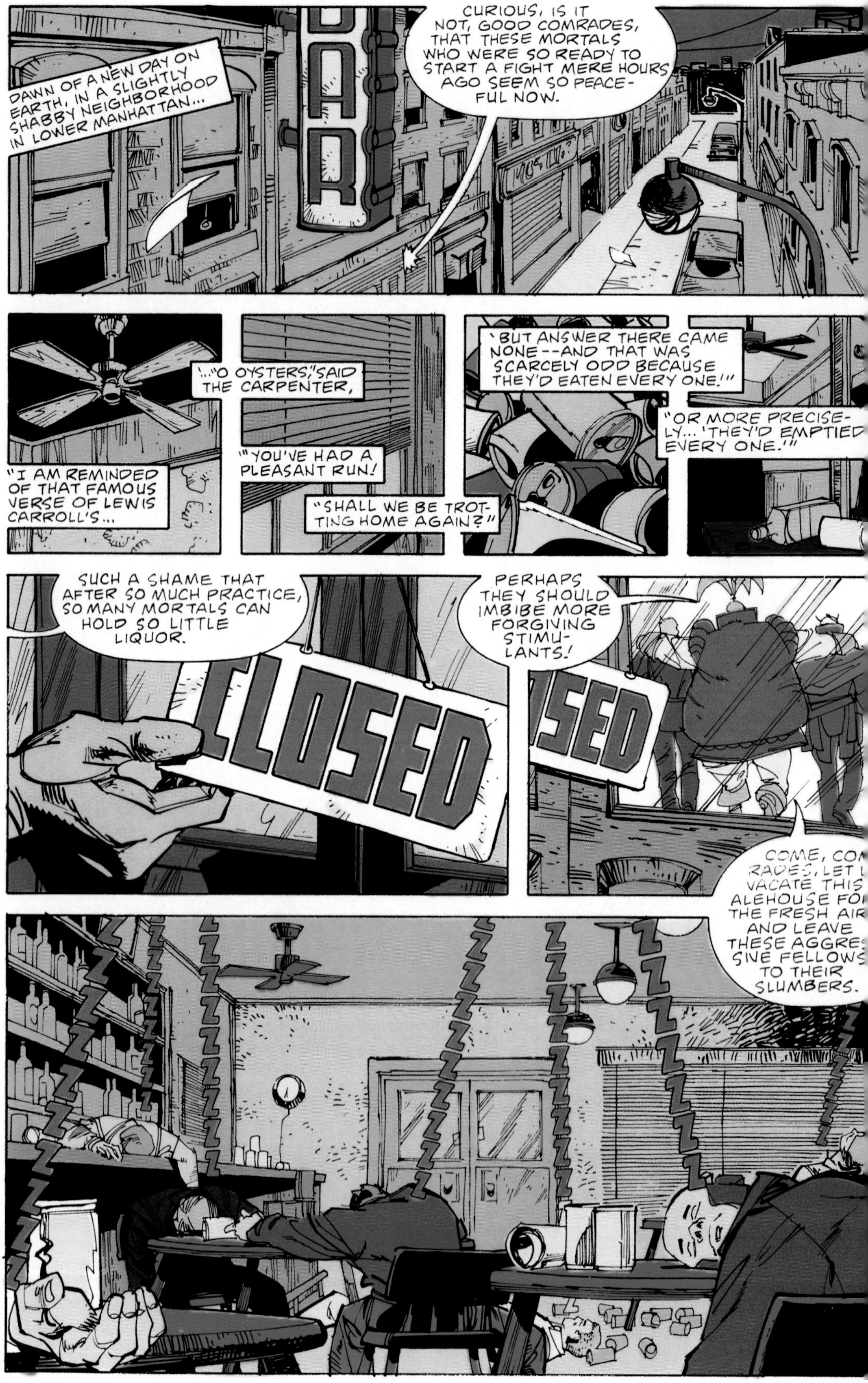
DAWN OF A NEW DAY ON EARTH, IN A SLIGHTLY SHABBY NEIGHBORHOOD IN LOWER MANHATTAN...
CURIOUS, IS IT NOT, GOOD COMRADES, THAT THESE MORTALS WHO WERE SO READY TO START A FIGHT MERE HOURS AGO SEEM SO PEACE-FUL NOW.
"I AM REMINDED OF THAT FAMOUS VERSE OF LEWIS CARROLL'S...
..."O OYSTERS," SAID THE CARPENTER,
"YOU'VE HAD A PLEASANT RUN!
"SHALL WE BE TROTTING HOME AGAIN?"
'BUT ANSWER THERE CAME NONE--AND THAT WAS SCARCELY ODD BECAUSE THEY'D EATEN EVERY ONE.'"
"OR MORE PRECISE-LY... 'THEY'D EMPTIED EVERY ONE.'"
SUCH A SHAME THAT AFTER SO MUCH PRACTICE, SO MANY MORTALS CAN HOLD SO LITTLE LIQUOR.
CLOSED
PERHAPS THEY SHOULD IMBIBE MORE FORGIVING STIMU-LANTS!
SED
COME, COM RADES, LET VACATE THIS ALEHOUSE FO THE FRESH AIR AND LEAVE THESE AGGRES SIVE FELLOWS TO THEIR SLUMBERS.

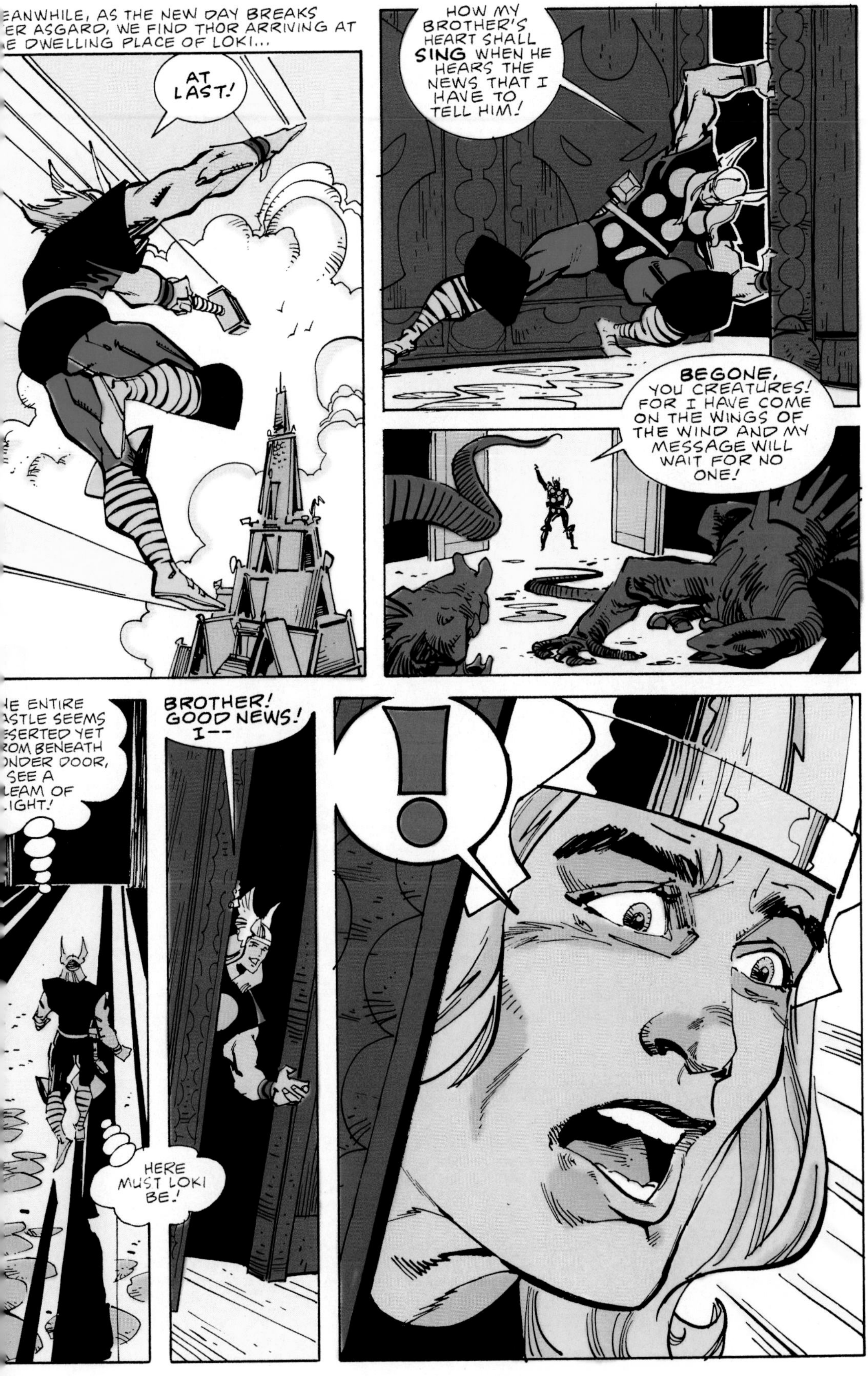
EANWHILE, AS THE NEW DAY BREAKS
ER ASGARD, WE FIND THOR ARRIVING AT
E DWELLING PLACE OF LOKI...
AT LAST!
HOW MY BROTHER'S HEART SHALL SING WHEN HE HEARS THE NEWS THAT I HAVE TO TELL HIM!
BEGONE, YOU CREATURES! FOR I HAVE COME ON THE WINGS OF THE WIND AND MY MESSAGE WILL WAIT FOR NO ONE!
E ENTIRE
ASTLE SEEMS
ESERTED YET
ROM BENEATH
ONDER DOOR,
SEE A
LEAM OF
IGHT!
HERE MUST LOKI BE!
BROTHER! GOOD NEWS! I--
!

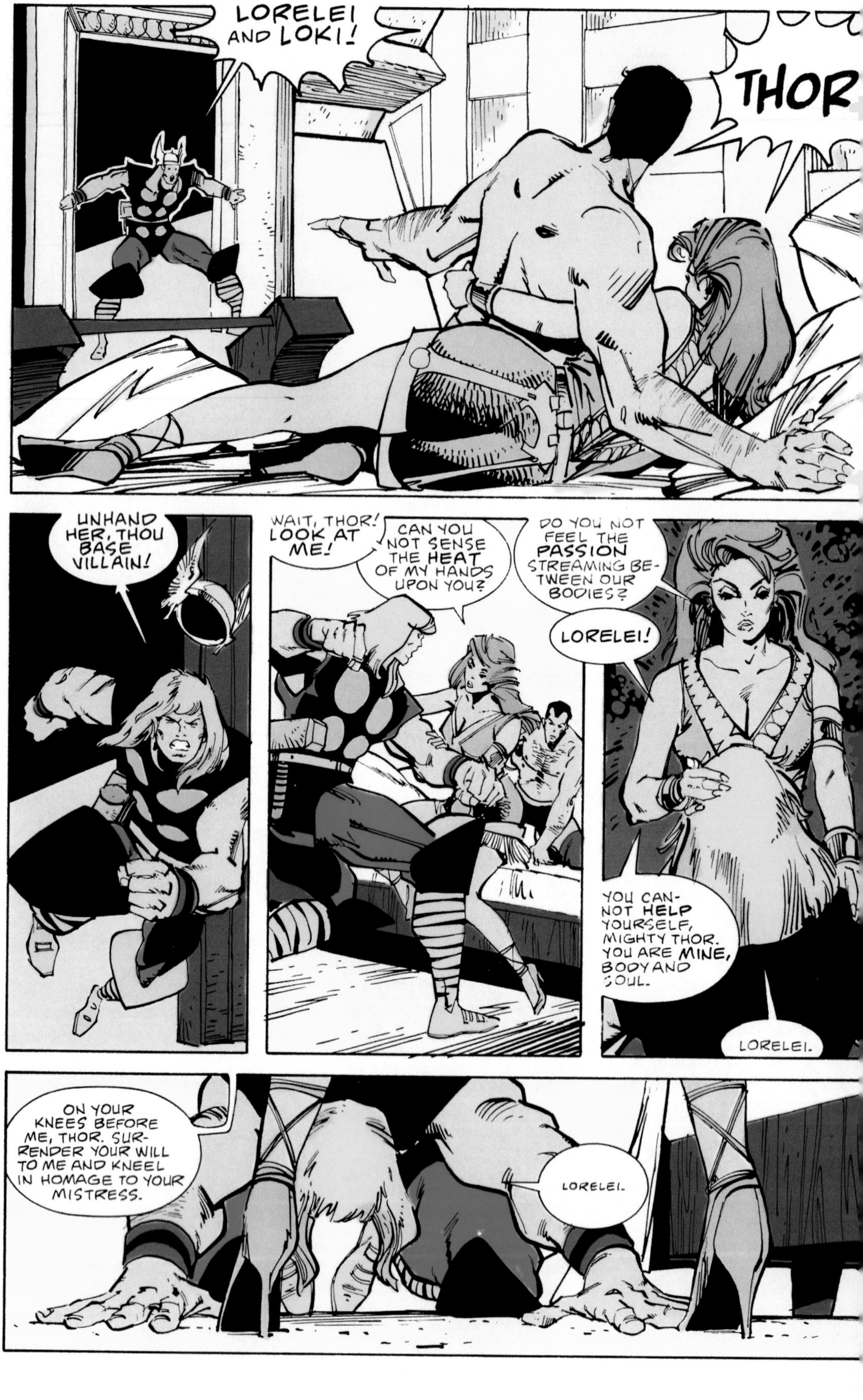

LORELEI AND LOKI!
THOR
UNHAND HER, THOU BASE VILLAIN!
WAIT, THOR! LOOK AT ME!
CAN YOU NOT SENSE THE HEAT OF MY HANDS UPON YOU?
DO YOU NOT FEEL THE PASSION STREAMING BETWEEN OUR BODIES?
LORELEI!
YOU CANNOT HELP YOURSELF, MIGHTY THOR. YOU ARE MINE, BODY AND SOUL.
LORELEI.
ON YOUR KNEES BEFORE ME, THOR. SURRENDER YOUR WILL TO ME AND KNEEL IN HOMAGE TO YOUR MISTRESS.
LORELEI.

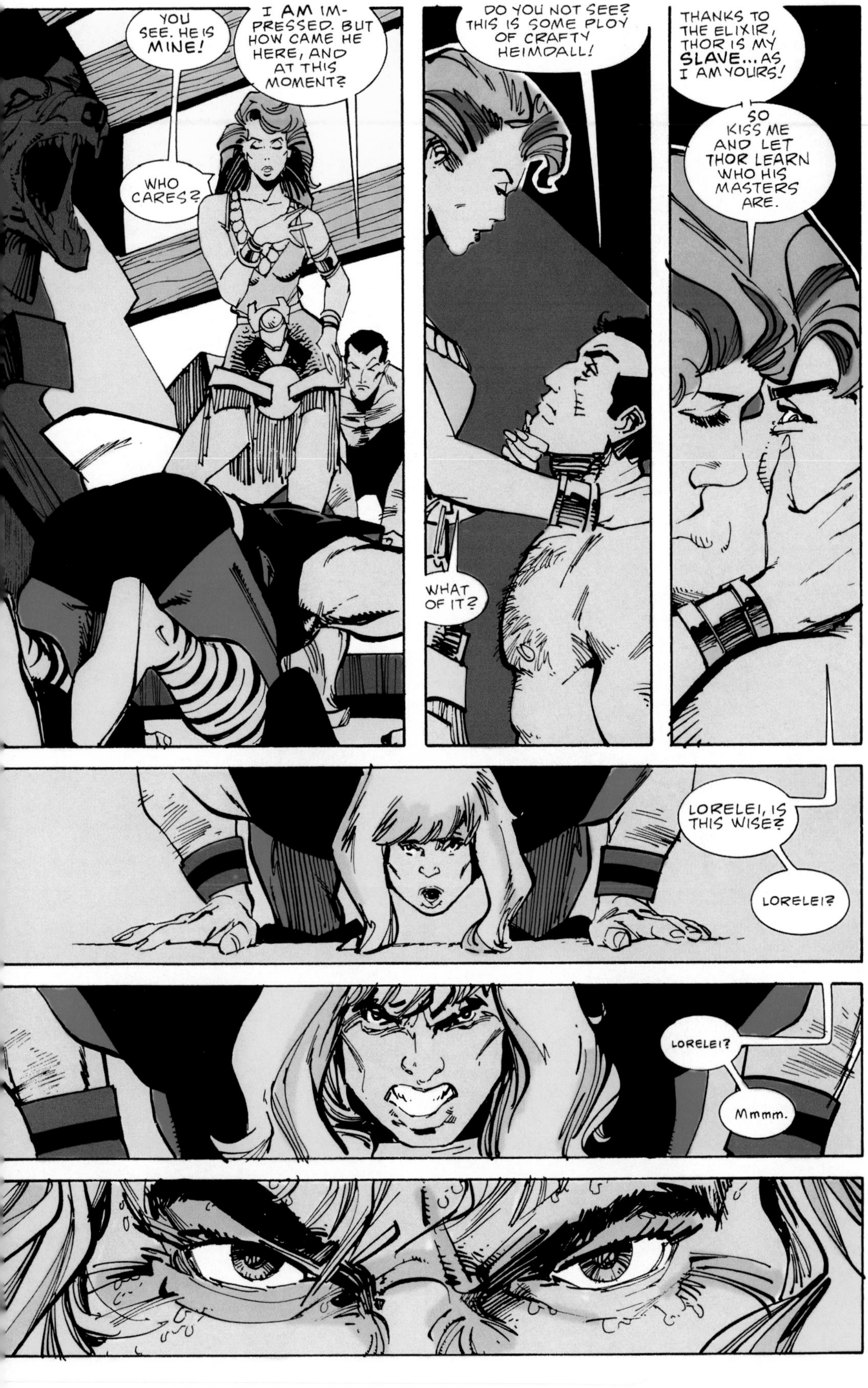
YOU SEE. HE IS MINE!
I AM IM-PRESSED. BUT HOW CAME HE HERE, AND AT THIS MOMENT?
WHO CARES?
DO YOU NOT SEE? THIS IS SOME PLOY OF CRAFTY HEIMDALL!
WHAT OF IT?
THANKS TO THE ELIXIR, THOR IS MY SLAVE... AS I AM YOURS!
SO KISS ME AND LET THOR LEARN WHO HIS MASTERS ARE.
LORELEI, IS THIS WISE?
LORELEI?
LORELEI?
Mmmm.

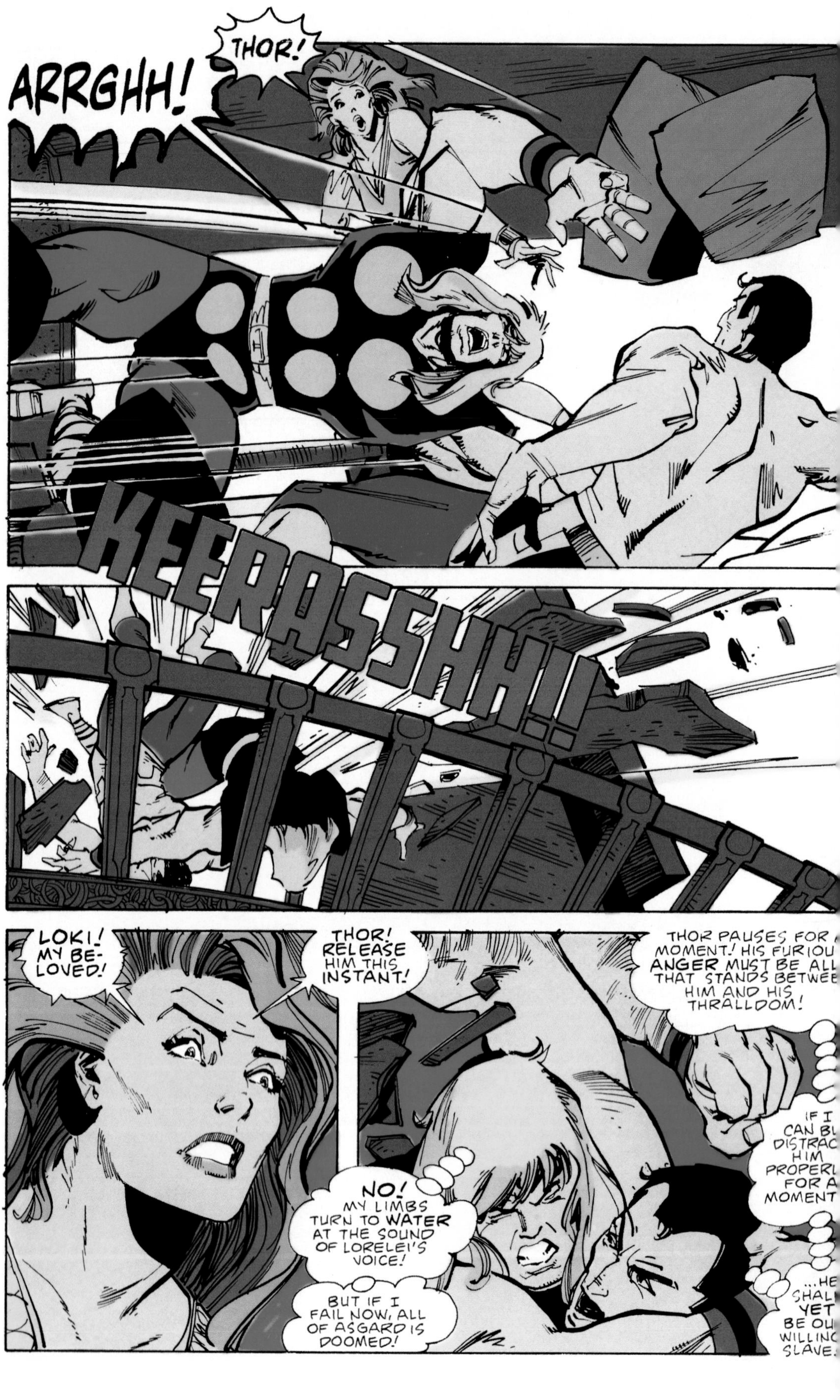
ARRGHH!
THOR!
KEERASSHH!!
LOKI! MY BE-LOVED!
THOR! RELEASE HIM THIS INSTANT!
THOR PAUSES FOR A MOMENT! HIS FURIOU ANGER MUST BE ALL THAT STANDS BETWEE HIM AND HIS THRALLDOM!
NO! MY LIMBS TURN TO WATER AT THE SOUND OF LORELEI'S VOICE!
BUT IF I FAIL NOW, ALL OF ASGARD IS DOOMED!
IF I CAN BU DISTRAC HIM PROPERL FOR A MOMENT
...HE SHAL YET BE OU WILLING SLAVE.

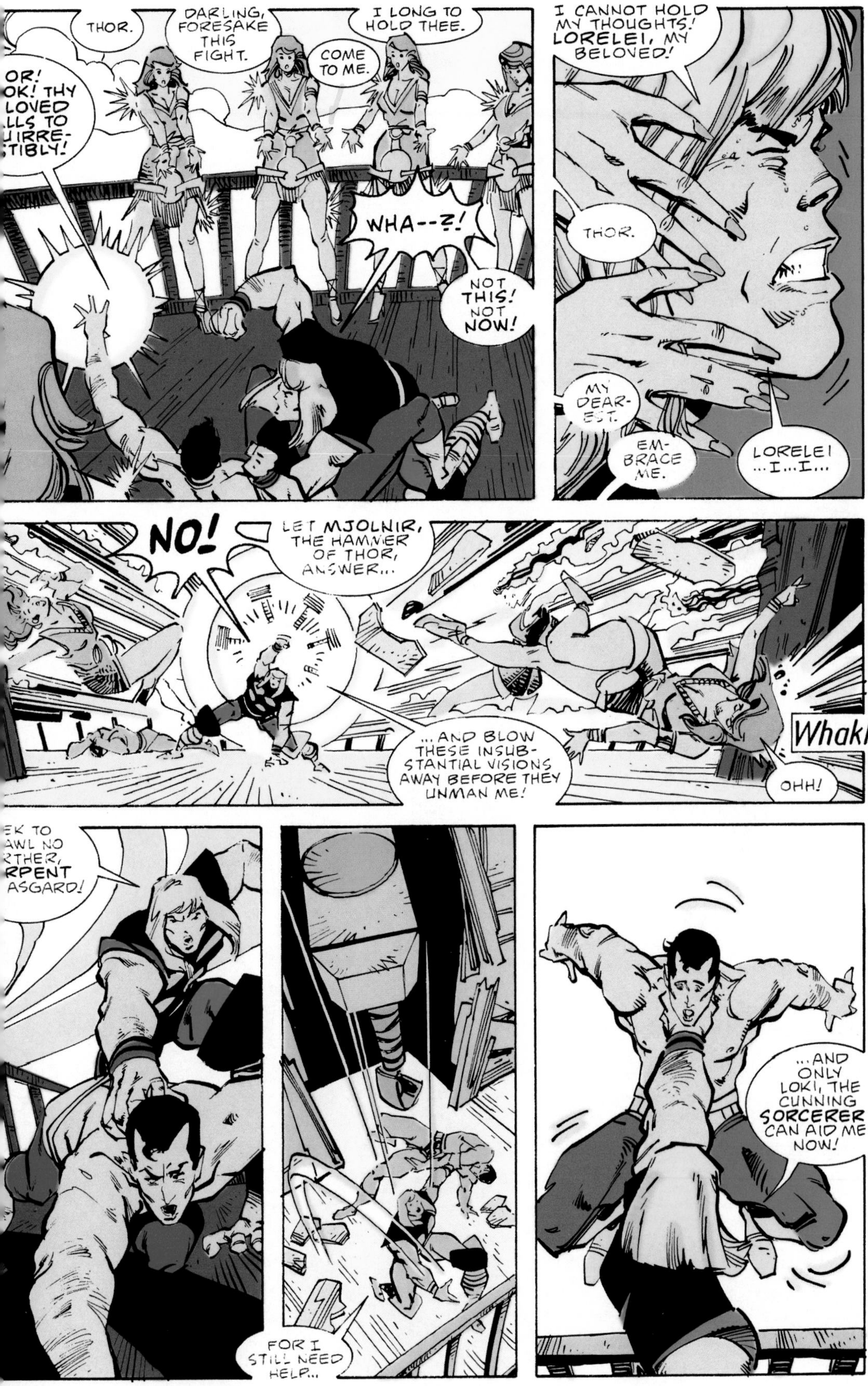
THOR.
DARLING, FORESAKE THIS FIGHT.
I LONG TO HOLD THEE.
COME TO ME.
OR! OK! THY LOVED LLS TO IRRE-STIBLY!
WHA--?!
NOT THIS! NOT NOW!
I CANNOT HOLD MY THOUGHTS! LORELEI, MY BELOVED!
THOR.
MY DEAR-EST.
EM-BRACE ME.
LORELEI ...I...I...
NO!
LET MJOLNIR, THE HAMMER OF THOR, ANSWER...
...AND BLOW THESE INSUB-STANTIAL VISIONS AWAY BEFORE THEY UNMAN ME!
Whakk!
OHH!
EK TO AWL NO RTHER, RPENT ASGARD!
FOR I STILL NEED HELP...
...AND ONLY LOKI, THE CUNNING SORCERER CAN AID ME NOW!

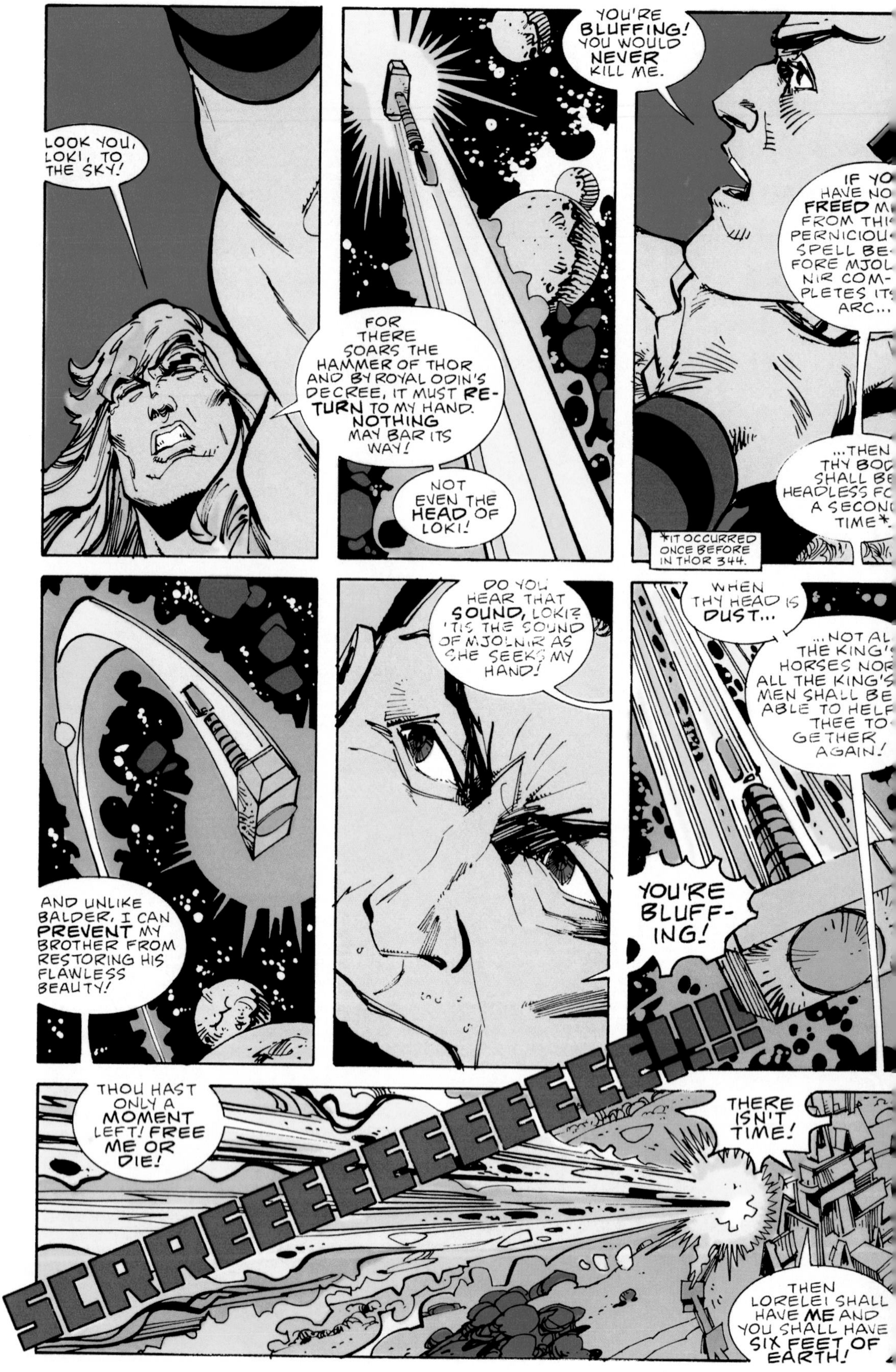
LOOK YOU, LOKI, TO THE SKY!
FOR THERE SOARS THE HAMMER OF THOR AND BY ROYAL ODIN'S DECREE, IT MUST RETURN TO MY HAND. NOTHING MAY BAR ITS WAY!
NOT EVEN THE HEAD OF LOKI!
YOU'RE BLUFFING! YOU WOULD NEVER KILL ME.
IF YO HAVE NO FREED M FROM THI PERNICIOU SPELL BE-FORE MJOLNIR COMPLETES ITS ARC...
...THEN THY BOD SHALL BE HEADLESS FO A SECON TIME*.
*IT OCCURRED ONCE BEFORE IN THOR 344.
AND UNLIKE BALDER, I CAN PREVENT MY BROTHER FROM RESTORING HIS FLAWLESS BEAUTY!
DO YOU HEAR THAT SOUND, LOKI? 'TIS THE SOUND OF MJOLNIR AS SHE SEEKS MY HAND!
WHEN THY HEAD IS DUST...
...NOT AL THE KING'S HORSES NOR ALL THE KING'S MEN SHALL BE ABLE TO HELF THEE TO-GETHER AGAIN!
YOU'RE BLUFF-ING!
THOU HAST ONLY A MOMENT LEFT! FREE ME OR DIE!
SCRREEEEEEEEEEEEEE!!!!!
THERE ISN'T TIME!
THEN LORELEI SHALL HAVE ME AND YOU SHALL HAVE SIX FEET OF EARTH!

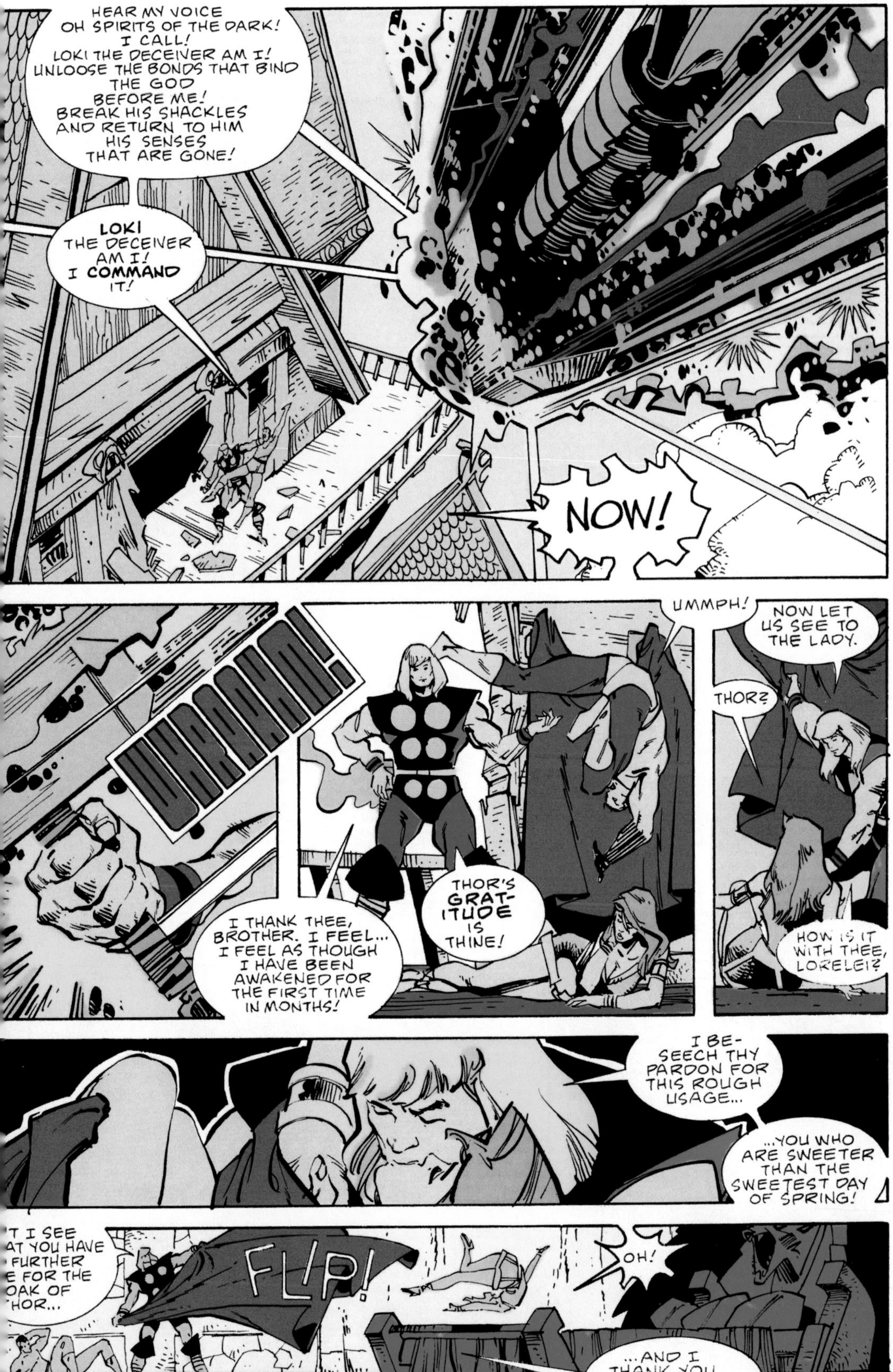
HEAR MY VOICE OH SPIRITS OF THE DARK! I CALL! LOKI THE DECEIVER AM I! UNLOOSE THE BONDS THAT BIND THE GOD BEFORE ME! BREAK HIS SHACKLES AND RETURN TO HIM HIS SENSES THAT ARE GONE!
LOKI THE DECEIVER AM I! I COMMAND IT!
NOW!
I THANK THEE, BROTHER. I FEEL... I FEEL AS THOUGH I HAVE BEEN AWAKENED FOR THE FIRST TIME IN MONTHS!
THOR'S GRAT-ITUDE IS THINE!
UMMPH!
NOW LET US SEE TO THE LADY.
THOR?
HOW IS IT WITH THEE, LORELEI?
I BE-SEECH THY PARDON FOR THIS ROUGH USAGE...
...YOU WHO ARE SWEETER THAN THE SWEETEST DAY OF SPRING!
T I SEE AT YOU HAVE FURTHER E FOR THE OAK OF HOR...
FLIP!
OH!
...AND I THANK YOU MOST HUMBLY FOR ITS RETURN!

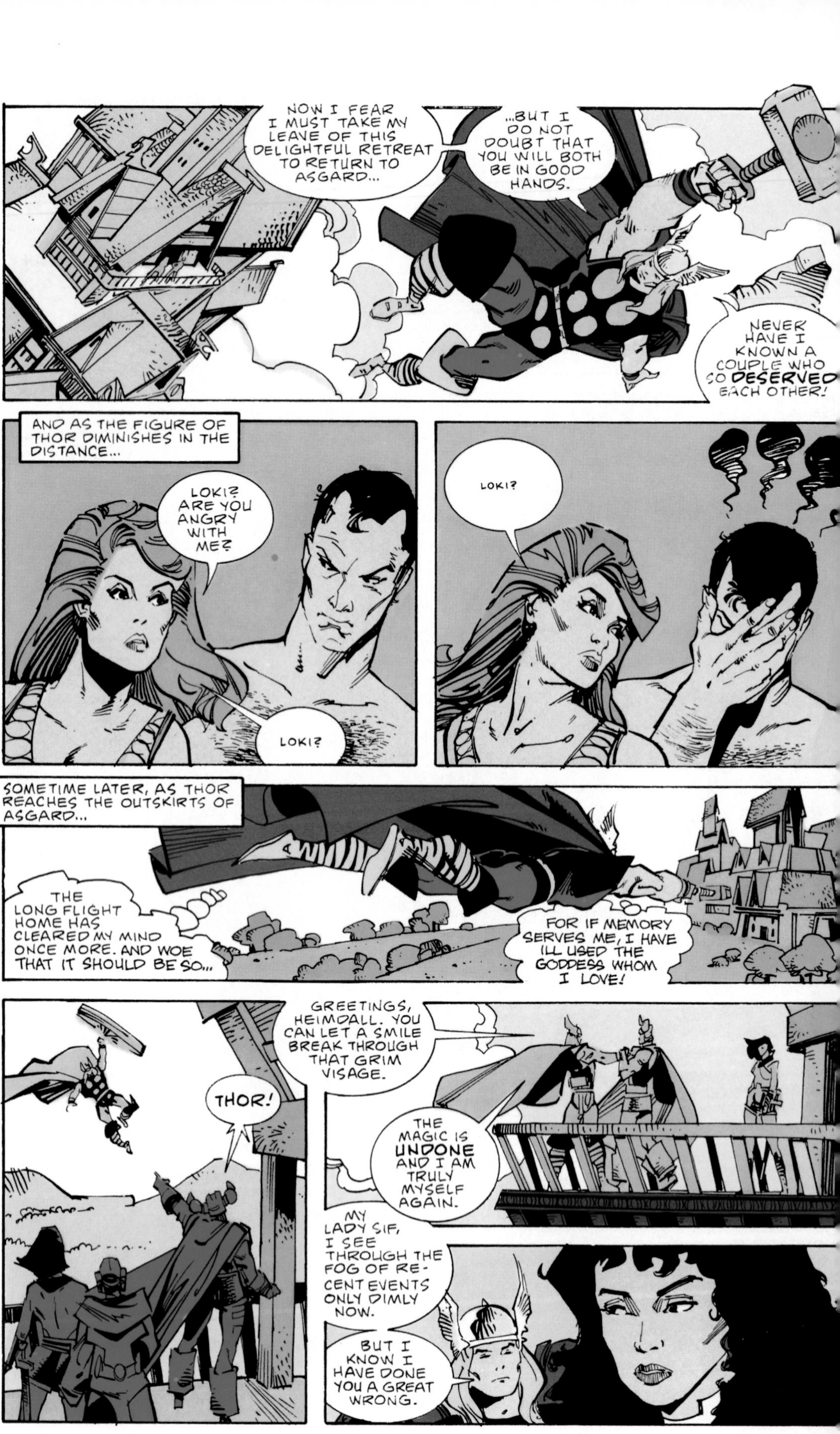
NOW I FEAR I MUST TAKE MY LEAVE OF THIS DELIGHTFUL RETREAT TO RETURN TO ASGARD...
...BUT I DO NOT DOUBT THAT YOU WILL BOTH BE IN GOOD HANDS.
NEVER HAVE I KNOWN A COUPLE WHO SO DESERVED EACH OTHER!
AND AS THE FIGURE OF THOR DIMINISHES IN THE DISTANCE...
LOKI? ARE YOU ANGRY WITH ME?
LOKI?
LOKI?
SOMETIME LATER, AS THOR REACHES THE OUTSKIRTS OF ASGARD...
THE LONG FLIGHT HOME HAS CLEARED MY MIND ONCE MORE. AND WOE THAT IT SHOULD BE SO...
FOR IF MEMORY SERVES ME, I HAVE ILL USED THE GODDESS WHOM I LOVE!
THOR!
GREETINGS, HEIMDALL. YOU CAN LET A SMILE BREAK THROUGH THAT GRIM VISAGE.
THE MAGIC IS UNDONE AND I AM TRULY MYSELF AGAIN.
MY LADY SIF, I SEE THROUGH THE FOG OF RECENT EVENTS ONLY DIMLY NOW.
BUT I KNOW I HAVE DONE YOU A GREAT WRONG.

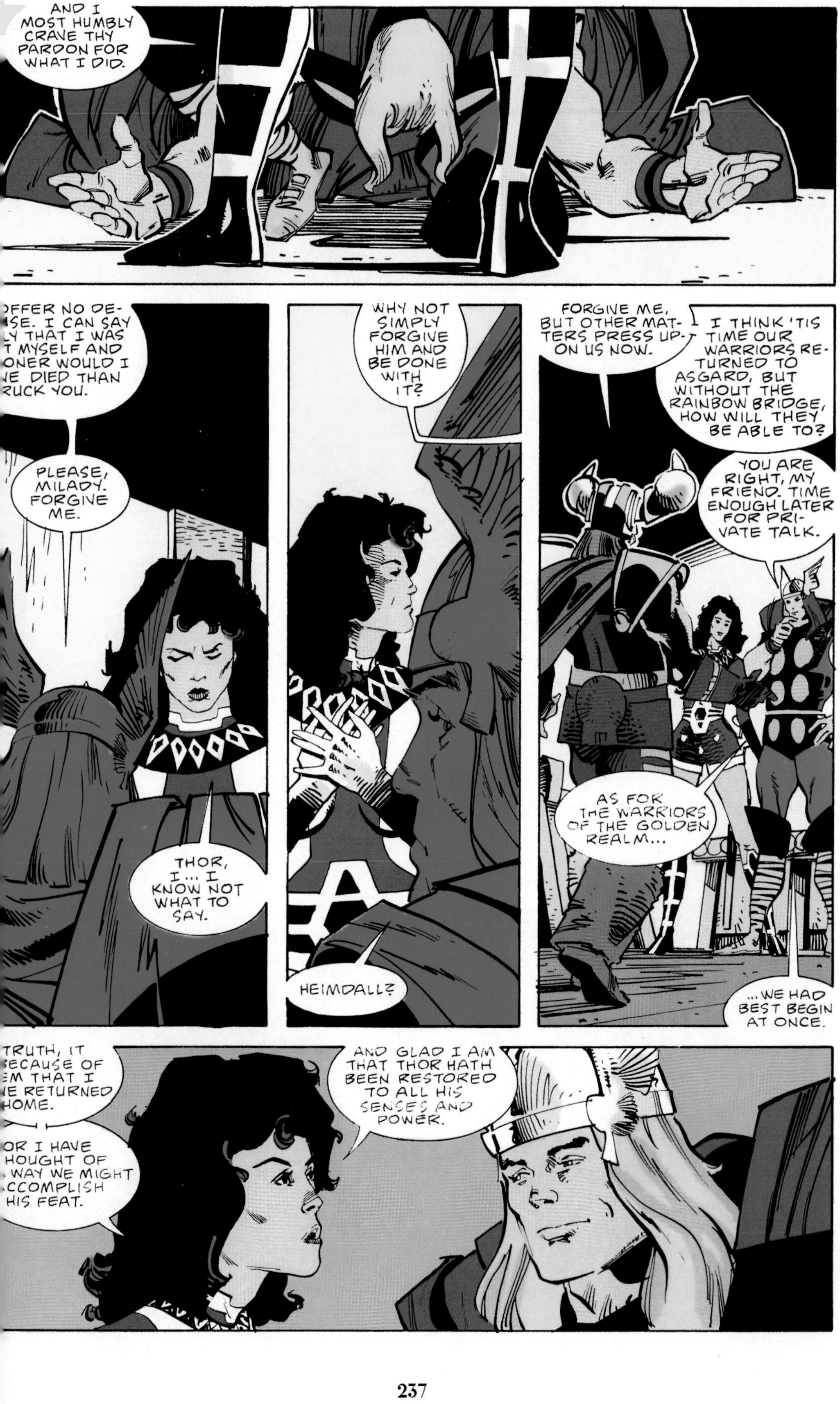
AND I MOST HUMBLY CRAVE THY PARDON FOR WHAT I DID.
)FFER NO DE- ISE. I CAN SAY LY THAT I WAS T MYSELF AND ONER WOULD I VE DIED THAN RUCK YOU.
PLEASE, MILADY. FORGIVE ME.
THOR, I... I KNOW NOT WHAT TO SAY.
WHY NOT SIMPLY FORGIVE HIM AND BE DONE WITH IT?
HEIMDALL?
FORGIVE ME, BUT OTHER MAT- TERS PRESS UP- ON US NOW.
I THINK 'TIS TIME OUR WARRIORS RE- TURNED TO ASGARD, BUT WITHOUT THE RAINBOW BRIDGE, HOW WILL THEY BE ABLE TO?
YOU ARE RIGHT, MY FRIEND. TIME ENOUGH LATER FOR PRI- VATE TALK.
AS FOR THE WARRIORS OF THE GOLDEN REALM...
...WE HAD BEST BEGIN AT ONCE.
TRUTH, IT BECAUSE OF EM THAT I VE RETURNED HOME.
OR I HAVE HOUGHT OF WAY WE MIGHT CCOMPLISH HIS FEAT.
AND GLAD I AM THAT THOR HATH BEEN RESTORED TO ALL HIS SENSES AND POWER.

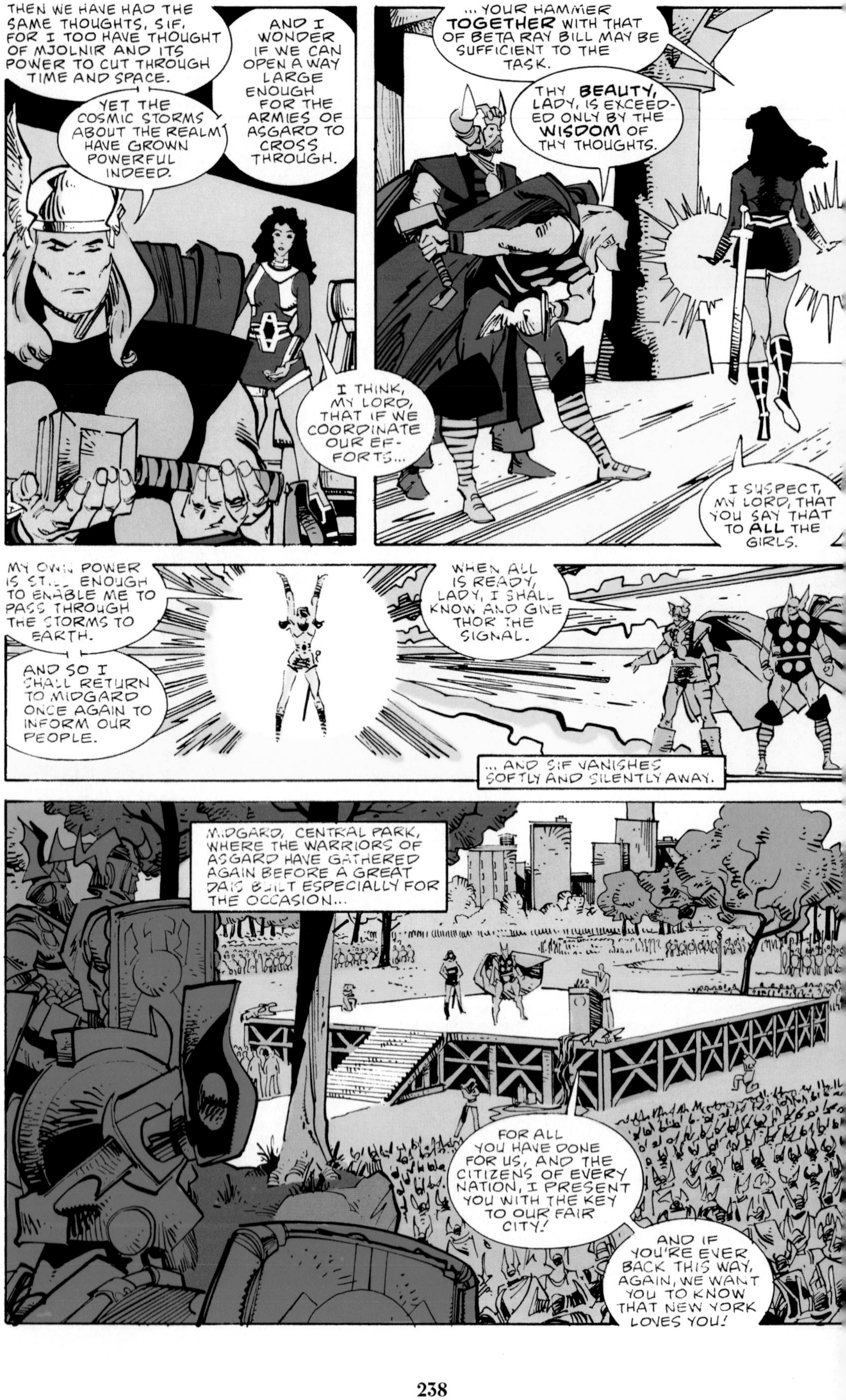

THEN WE HAVE HAD THE SAME THOUGHTS, SIF, FOR I TOO HAVE THOUGHT OF MJOLNIR AND ITS POWER TO CUT THROUGH TIME AND SPACE.
YET THE COSMIC STORMS ABOUT THE REALM HAVE GROWN POWERFUL INDEED.
AND I WONDER IF WE CAN OPEN A WAY LARGE ENOUGH FOR THE ARMIES OF ASGARD TO CROSS THROUGH.
I THINK, MY LORD, THAT IF WE COORDINATE OUR EFFORTS...
...YOUR HAMMER TOGETHER WITH THAT OF BETA RAY BILL MAY BE SUFFICIENT TO THE TASK.
THY BEAUTY, LADY, IS EXCEEDED ONLY BY THE WISDOM OF THY THOUGHTS.
I SUSPECT, MY LORD, THAT YOU SAY THAT TO ALL THE GIRLS.
MY OWN POWER IS STILL ENOUGH TO ENABLE ME TO PASS THROUGH THE STORMS TO EARTH.
AND SO I SHALL RETURN TO MIDGARD ONCE AGAIN TO INFORM OUR PEOPLE.
WHEN ALL IS READY, LADY, I SHALL KNOW AND GIVE THOR THE SIGNAL.
...AND SIF VANISHES SOFTLY AND SILENTLY AWAY.
MIDGARD, CENTRAL PARK, WHERE THE WARRIORS OF ASGARD HAVE GATHERED AGAIN BEFORE A GREAT DAIS BUILT ESPECIALLY FOR THE OCCASION...
FOR ALL YOU HAVE DONE FOR US, AND THE CITIZENS OF EVERY NATION, I PRESENT YOU WITH THE KEY TO OUR FAIR CITY!
AND IF YOU'RE EVER BACK THIS WAY, AGAIN, WE WANT YOU TO KNOW THAT NEW YORK LOVES YOU!

WHAT THE HECK IS GOING ON HERE?

HEY, BOY, YOU'RE BLOCKING MY SHOT.

MOVE IT OR LOSE IT!

IT'S THE AS-GARDIANS, POP! THEY'RE GOING HOME!

UH, SON, MAYBE WE'D BETTER MOVE BACK A BIT.

LOOK! THERE'S HERMOD! AND THERE'S TYR!

AND THAT'S GOTTA BE THE EXECUTIONER!

HE MAY BE AS STRONG AS THOR HIMSELF!

BETTER GIVE THE MAN A LITTLE ROOM, NICO.

AND UP THERE! THAT'S SIF...

...AND THAT HAS TO BE BETA RAY BILL!

WARRIORS, THE TIME HAS COME!

WHOSE TIME HAS COME?

DON'T YOU GET IT, POP?

BILL'S HAMMER IS CREATING A MAGIC DOORWAY! THEY'RE ALL GONNA GO THROUGH IT BACK HOME!

AND IN DISTANT ASGARD...

NOW, THOR!

...AND AS THE WHIRLING HAMMERS MATCH VELOCITIES AND SPIN...

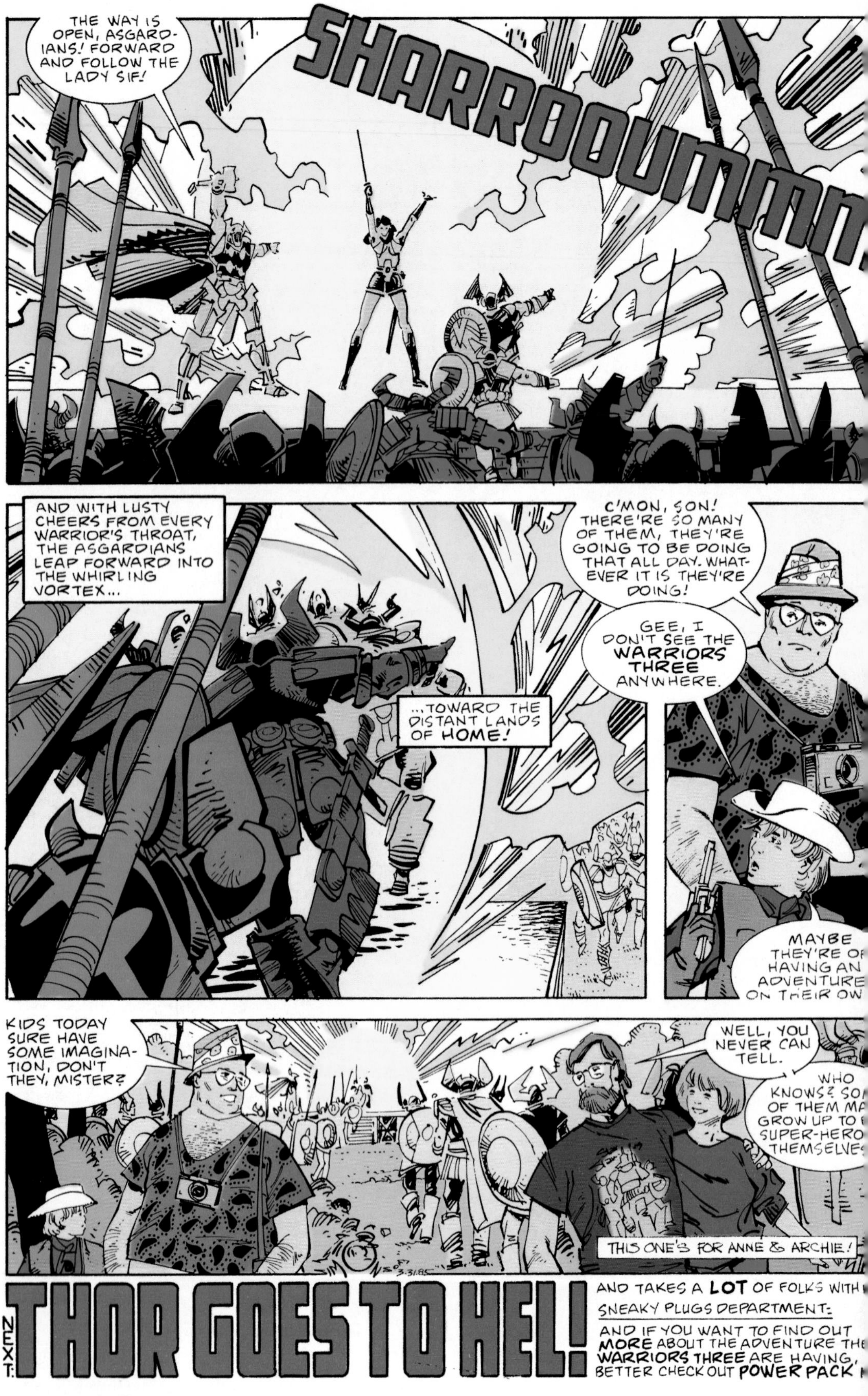
THE WAY IS OPEN, ASGARDIANS! FORWARD AND FOLLOW THE LADY SIF!
SHARROOUMMM
AND WITH LUSTY CHEERS FROM EVERY WARRIOR'S THROAT, THE ASGARDIANS LEAP FORWARD INTO THE WHIRLING VORTEX...
...TOWARD THE DISTANT LANDS OF HOME!
C'MON, SON! THERE'RE SO MANY OF THEM, THEY'RE GOING TO BE DOING THAT ALL DAY. WHATEVER IT IS THEY'RE DOING!
GEE, I DON'T SEE THE WARRIORS THREE ANYWHERE.
MAYBE THEY'RE O HAVING AN ADVENTURE ON THEIR OW
KIDS TODAY SURE HAVE SOME IMAGINATION, DON'T THEY, MISTER?
WELL, YOU NEVER CAN TELL.
WHO KNOWS? SO OF THEM MA GROW UP TO SUPER-HERO THEMSELVES
THIS ONE'S FOR ANNE & ARCHIE!
NEXT: THOR GOES TO HEL!
AND TAKES A LOT OF FOLKS WITH
SNEAKY PLUGS DEPARTMENT:
AND IF YOU WANT TO FIND OUT MORE ABOUT THE ADVENTURE THE WARRIORS THREE ARE HAVING, BETTER CHECK OUT POWER PACK